Advances in Crowdsourcing

Fernando J. Garrigos-Simon
Ignacio Gil-Pechuán · Sofia Estelles-Miguel
Editors

Advances in Crowdsourcing

Springer

Editors
Fernando J. Garrigos-Simon
Departamento de Organización de Empresas
Universidad Politecnica de Valencia
Valencia
Spain

Sofia Estelles-Miguel
Department of Business Administration
Universidad Politecnica de Valencia
Valencia
Spain

Ignacio Gil-Pechuán
Departamento de Organización de Empresas
Universidad Politecnica de Valencia
Valencia
Spain

ISBN 978-3-319-18340-4 ISBN 978-3-319-18341-1 (eBook)
DOI 10.1007/978-3-319-18341-1

Library of Congress Control Number: 2015937378

Springer Cham Heidelberg New York Dordrecht London

Printed on acid-free paper

Springer International Publishing AG Switzerland is part of Springer Science+Business Media (www.springer.com)

Foreword

First and foremost, it is an honour to count on the participation of members of the Universitat Politècnica de València, not only as contributors, but also as editors of "Advances in Crowdsourcing", a valuable and comprehensive resource, containing international research findings on a significant subject for the development of modern society.

So, what exactly is crowdsourcing? Based on the principle that more heads are better than one and taking into account the combination of the words "crowd" and "outsourcing", it is the process of getting tasks done by professionals in massive online communities via a flexible open call.

Used mainly in a business context, but also applicable to many other areas, including research and education, crowdsourcing is an ideal way of stimulating growth and innovation, providing solutions more quickly that are of a better quality and greater in number, whilst lowering costs.

In fact, the very concept of crowdfunding is in itself revolutionary, reinventing the traditional structure of the business and the economy based on hierarchy and control, into a model that is based on the principles of collaboration, acting globally and self-organisation, allowing individuals to participate on a global scale and make an impact on the arts, culture, science, education, government and the economy.

The benefits of crowdsourcing can be seen both globally and locally, and this book examines its application in areas such as tourism and in SMEs (small and medium enterprises), where the potential for development is significant.

From an academic point of view, the possibilities of crowdsourcing are endless and as a dynamic and innovative institution, the *Universitat Politècnica de València* takes pride in its involvement with the creation of "Advances in Crowdsourcing".

Finally, I take this opportunity to thank everyone involved in making the publication of “Advances in Crowdsourcing” possible, and I would especially like to congratulate the researchers who have contributed to the book. I sincerely hope that you find the book informative and I now invite you to discover more about the fascinating concept of crowdsourcing.

Francisco José Mora Más
Universitat Politècnica de València
Valencia, Spain

Contents

Chapter 1
From Crowdsourcing to the Use of Masscapital. The Common Perspective of the Success of Apple, Facebook, Google, Lego, TripAdvisor, and Zara

Fernando J. Garrigos-Simon and Yeamduan Narangajavana

Abstract In the organizational arena, outsourcing processes and the creation of company networks are becoming obsolete in light of the new era of globalization. In the new framework, some mechanisms such as crowdsourcing, defined as outsourcing to the crowd, and essentially the capturing, management, or use of what we call "Masscapital," defined as the capabilities of the mass relevant to the organization, are the answer to new changes. This chapter analyzes the importance of crowdsourcing and its evolution in the so-called management of "Masscapital" and looks at how they are becoming the new business model which is changing the arena of competition. This chapter explains how the most successful companies in the current business environment base their success on the use of what we call "Masscapital" and gives some recommendations about the use of space, time, and volume, in the success of its use as the key competitive factor for organizations.

Keywords Masscapital · Crowdsourcing · Knowledge · Strategy · Technology · Innovation · Entrepreneurship

1.1 Introduction

Advances in new information and communication technologies and the preponderance of social networks are impacting on the new environment of the Web 3.0 era. Technology has expanded horizons (Garrigos-Simon et al. 2012), and in the

F.J. Garrigos-Simon (✉)
Departamento de Organización de Empresas, Universitat Politècnica de València, Valencia, Spain
e-mail: fgarrigos@doe.upv.es

Y. Narangajavana
Departamento de Administración de Empresas y Marketing, Universitat Jaume I, Castellón, Spain
e-mail: ynaranga@uji.es

F.J. Garrigos-Simon et al. (eds.), *Advances in Crowdsourcing*,
DOI 10.1007/978-3-319-18341-1_1

new framework, organizations have to constantly advance and satisfy the needs of the customer [by harvesting information before, during, and after contact with them (ibid)] and to reinvent their business structure to remain competitive. In the new and globalized competitive arena, innovation is growing in all the phases of the value chain, and organizations cannot respond with just their own capabilities or those of their partner firms to face the growing complexity of their environment. While in the past century firstly the vertical integration of multinational firms, and later in recent decades the outsourcing of the diverse phases of the value chain (while maintaining the core resources and capabilities of the organizations) were seen as key elements to remain competitive, mainly due to the advances in new technologies, in the new globalized environment, these perspectives alone are becoming obsolete.

The explanation is that while in the past the key success factor of many companies consisted of the creation of multinational networks of firms that could work together to face the globalization processes, these processes are being overcome. Previously, multinational companies could base their advantage on the economies of scale based mainly on their size and the control of information. In recent decades, new technologies have allowed the new networks to combine the strengths, capabilities, and innovations of the diverse firms in the different phases of the production process and then overcome, with the flexibility of their own networks, the previous advantages of multinational companies. However, in the new socioeconomic arena, this is not enough.

The reason is that nowadays information cannot be controlled and innovation is generally characterized as a process that consists of two broad stages: idea generation and idea implementation (Oldham and Da Silva 2015). Therefore, the only thing that companies can do to remain competitive is to identify and implement the information and new ideas before others and to a broad extent. Here, in the constant innovation in the diverse task, it is essential to compete, but the groups of business networks are not flexible enough to cope with the diverse innovations that continually appear in the globalized world. In addition, companies cannot maintain and promote their core resources and capabilities only by themselves for much time. The explanation is that if previously the innovations of the firms and those of the diverse components of the networks helped them to overcome the other networks' competitiveness, the consolidation of the networks of firms means the consolidation of their own rigidity, and nowadays, individuals, and the crowd, overcome the advantages of the networks of firms.

We have to bear in mind that the development of outsourcing processes for all the secondary task of the firms, and the consolidation of networks of firms, means that the firms that remained as the center or the core of the networks were those that previously searched for efficient partners that allowed them to remain competitive and even to find which resources and capabilities they had to develop first. However, this also means remaining inflexible to new innovations, as these central firms cannot control and have all the information about where the new innovations are, and obviously, all the main innovations cannot be in their partner companies.

The point is that the organizations have to understand that the sources of innovation are not in firms anymore, but in individuals. In addition, it is impossible for firms to continuously be up to date with who has innovated and in what area, as this means a waste of resources. We have to consider that although employees can have an important role, the creative ideas of individuals, not employed by the organization, can also make a substantial contribution to innovation (Bayus 2013; Boudreau and Lakhani 2013; Oldham and Da Silva 2015). As Prahalad and Ramaswamy (2004) point out, the future of competition lies in a new approach to value creation based on an individual-centered co-creation of value between consumers and companies. The co-creation with the virtual participation of the customer is essential nowadays (Fuller 2010), and without the participation of users, we could not understand the new business environment (Garrigos-Simon et al. 2011, 2014). However, customers are not the only ones who can co-create (especially in small and medium organizations or reduced networks). Co-creation should lead to a "value network" in which value must be co-created by a combination of players in the network (Peppard and Rylander 2006), or outside these networks. Diverse and dispersed individuals without a previous relationship with the company can also contribute, and the co-creators can now come from any part of the world.

In order to overcome this situation, organizations have to be creative. If the innovations are in the brains of the individuals from all over the world, and it is impossible for the organizations to constantly find these individuals in the crowd, the perspective needs to change. From our point of view, the way to do it is not by looking anymore, but by creating the conditions that allow them to find us and contribute to our firm. How? By using and improving the crowdsourcing processes? By extending these processes to the use and management of "Masscapital"?

1.2 From Outsourcing to Crowdsourcing, from Crowdsourcing to Masscapital

The analysis of outsourcing is broad in the literature of management (Parmigiani 2007). In particular, the outsourcing process is justified by the classical literature of the resource and capabilities-based view. According to this perspective, organizations must focus on the development of only the activities linked to their strategic resources, capabilities, and core competences (Peteraf 1993) and outsource the other activities (Prahalad and Hamel 1990). In this vein, corporations who outsource non-core aspects of their activities can substantially reduce costs and concentrate in their core activities. Thus, "companies should commit most of their resources to their core competence, while outsourcing the rest of their functions to specialized entities" (Li and Petrick 2008, p. 237).

However, the specialized entities are more and more broadly dispersed, and due to the globalization process, it is difficult for the firm to have information about where the best organizations that can provide the best innovations in the diverse phases of the value chain are, or better, in the "value network" (Peppard and Rylander 2006; Garrigos-Simon et al. 2014) of the firm. In this arena, organizations must concentrate on creating the mechanism to attract these organizations instead of searching for them. Moreover, nowadays, it is not the companies but freelances and individuals dispersed in the mass, who are the ones that can provide the best innovations, in order to improve each and all of the activities of the value chain of the firms. In addition, firms not only need the information from individuals, but also need other kinds of help that the crowd or mass can provide. In this vein, organizations must concentrate on capturing and using the capabilities of the entities or the crowd that are closely related to the company, what we can call "folk capital" or "community capital," or more broadly "global capital" or "Masscapital" from individuals that could have, or not, a previous direct relationship with the organization. Focusing on this aspect, in this work, we conceive "Masscapital" as the capabilities of all the individuals or organizations, related closely or not to the company, which can help it to innovate or improve any of its activities or processes. In our opinion, the core competences are not inside the firm anymore, and the core competences are mainly outside. Organizations can and must create the conditions to capture and manage the continuous core competences needed to compete. These core competences reside in individuals, mainly outside, although in big corporations and networks also inside, although most of them outside the areas where innovation is required, what we call "Masscapital." These will be the successful companies in the new business environment.

Actually, this task is not new. In a broad review of the new business environment, we can find many mechanisms used to reach this goal and to understand them; we only have to take a look at the most successful firms nowadays.

For instance, some authors point to the importance of crowdsourcing processes. Crowdsourcing, also known as "massive outsourcing" or "voluntary outsourcing", is conceived as "the act of taking a specific task and outsourcing it to a large group of people via the Internet, through an open call" (Galdon et al. 2015), or the act of taking a job or a specific task essential for the making or sale of a product, previously performed by an employee of the company, or more widely termed by a "designated agent," such as a contractor (Howe 2006), and outsourcing it through an open call to a large group of people, a community or the general public (crowd or mass) over the Internet (Garrigos-Simon et al. 2014; Kleemann et al. 2008, p. 6). Crowdsourcing can be viewed as a development of the classical "self-service" which emerged with the evolution of department stores and the introduction of the first vending machines at the end of the nineteenth century (Kleemann et al. 2008; Garrigos-Simon et al. 2014) or as a combination of classical outsourcing, with the participation of a wide number of stakeholders or crowd in the process (Galdon et al. 2015).

Authors such as Boudreau et al. (2011), Estellés-Arolas and González-Ladrón-de-Guevara (2012), Garrigos-Simon et al. (2012), Ranade and Varshney (2012), Avolio et al. (2014), and Boudreau and Lakhani (2013) explain the importance of the crowdsourcing process. Hence, Estellés-Arolas and González-Ladrón-de-Guevara (2012) define it as "a participative distributed online process that allows the undertaking of a task for the resolution of a problem," while Boudreau et al. (2011) or Ranade and Varshney (2012) point out that Crowd power has been harnessed to design everything from T-shirts to software to artificial intelligence algorithms by soliciting contributions via open calls. Additionally, managers can use crowdsourcing techniques to collect opinion data on ideas, products, processes, and services that can be used by them to help solve organizational problems and support innovation (Boudreau and Lakhani 2013; Avolio et al. 2014).

Moreover, crowdsourcing can be widely applied not only to the production process, the generation of ideas, or specific problem solving, but as a new source of innovation in almost every step of the value chain (Garrigos-Simon et al. 2014). As Brabham (2008) points out, "the crowd outperforms industry faster and cheaper than even the top minds in the fields" and therefore crowdsourcing techniques are critical because they stand for "a profound paradigm shift in our view of the professional, of the corporation, of the global commons, and of the value of intellectual labor in a transnational world" (ibid, p. 79). Actually, Boudreau and Lakhani (2013) observe that crowdsourcing has been applied by entire industries for years, although it is the development of the technology which has transformed it by allowing the participation and contribution of huge number of people. Hence, and according to its importance, Crowdsourcing is an approach that is receiving substantial attention (Bayus 2013), being currently one of the most discussed key words within the open innovation community (Ebner et al. 2010).

From our point view, the key importance of crowdsourcing, when compared to other networking mechanisms, is that firms do not have to find partners or innovators. The partners are the ones who find the firm, if they think that they can provide the firm with a solution to its problem and if this solution is interesting for them. However, organizations cannot continuously obtain the participation of the crowd by launching open calls. In addition, crowdsourcing is mainly based on the fact that it is the firm that identifies the problem and that asks for the solution to the problem. Crowdsourcing is conceived when it is the firm that focuses on the problem and tries to manage its solution (Benkler 2006). As highlighted by Howe (2006): "It's only crowdsourcing once a company takes the idea, fabricates it in mass quantity and sells it." However, we think that this fact is reduced, especially in an environment where many individuals outside the organization can detect better than the actual organization where the possible problems are, or the tasks that can and must be improved by the firm.

In this vein, some successful companies have found the formula to create mechanisms to continuously capture what we call "Masscapital", the capabilities of the mass, by using more broad crowdsourcing techniques, by rewarding, or not, the individuals in diverse forms (from money to social relevance), without launching open calls and without asking for a solution to concrete problems. For instance, Wikipedia has created a tool to capture "Masscapital," using peer production in order to create their encyclopedia by using the participation of the crowd. In addition, some authors such as Prpic and Shukla (2013, p. 3505) point out the importance of what they call "crowd capital", which means, "heterogeneous organizational knowledge resource, generated by the organization's crowd capability," by focusing on the importance of having an IT mechanism to capture information from the crowd. Actually, these improvements were already pointed by Garrigos-Simon et al. (2012, p. 1881), when they stressed the relevance of Web 3.0 technologies to capture and apply information from the mass and posited that "New networks and the advances in so-called Web 3.0 technologies are changing firm structures and value chains or value networks, and the configuration of decision-making processes for managers."

However, we think that the main capabilities are not essentially inside the organizations, or inside firm networks, but outside, in the mass, so the organizations have to focus on them and formulate a way to capture or take advantage of them. In addition, "Masscapital" cannot be reduced to the management of information or even knowledge from the crowd, because there are capabilities that are not related to simple information and knowledge and because internal machines can also create the possible knowledge required, from the data and information provided by the crowd. For instance, as Garrigos-Simon et al. (2012, p. 1883) stress, Web 3.0 technology "not only allows the use of semantics but also space, images, sounds and feelings in a concept where the traditional static web is transformed into another very interactive one. In the new context, intelligent machines read, understand, interrelate, and can manipulate data from cyberspace, allowing this process to be adapted by different users or firms according to their own needs." Thirdly, the organizations can manage some of the Masscapital, but some of it escapes to the control of the organization. Fourthly, the management of Masscapital cannot be reduced to the use of technological mechanisms. Fifthly, as in the case of crowdsourcing, "Masscapital" cannot be reduced to the participation of the partners of the customers, it must also include the participation of all kinds of stakeholders who are not employees of the organization (Garrigos-Simon et al. 2012), amateurs or even the general public ["students, young graduates, scientists or simply individuals" (Estellés-Arolas and González-Ladrón-de-Guevara 2012, p. 196)], or even the organization's employees, in order to improve the production process, carry out any of the organization's tasks, and undertake the problem solving and the generation of open innovations by the crowd. Finally, we have to consider the importance of space, time, and volume, in the success of using the "Masscapital."

1.3 The Use of Masscapital by Successful Business Firms

Actually, many successful companies are using our "Masscapital" without the use of reduced crowdsourcing processes, "open calls," or asking for the solution to specific problems. In addition, this "Masscapital" is sometimes used with the participation of the mass in processes where the crowd is not conscious of the crucial importance of their diverse contributions to the firms, or simply does not know about their involvement in the process.

In this vein, it has been pointed out in the literature how diverse companies have used the new technologies to appropriate some of the "Masscapital" or capabilities of their customers. For instance, following the approaches of Garrigos-Simon et al. (2012), the new technologies, which help to capture information from customers, combined with their internal information, are used efficiently by firms such as the retail firm Zara, Carrefour, or almost all the main airlines. In this vein, and by using these new technologies, "Zara is able to adapt to rapidly changing markets, and predict the sales of an item in a single store during a replenishment period depending on demand forecasts, the inventory of each size initially available, and the aforementioned store inventory management policy" (Garrigos-Simon et al. 2012, p. 1884). We have to realize that in these processes, "Masscapital" is the one that is continuously revealing the "fashion" to the company, which item they have to produce and in what quantity, through the specific demand for the diverse items of the company.

Similarly, the information systems used by airlines allow them to set prices according to demand and some production factors (Narangajavana et al. 2014). The customers indicate when and how to increase prices and the capacity they have to offer. With a similar perspective, Carrefour and other businesses, by using IT systems, "can also use this information to automatically determine its customers' needs (by knowing the previous products they have consumed and their demographic and family situations) and offer them new promotions according to these needs and the characteristics of the products in stock in its stores" (Garrigos-Simon et al. 2012, p. 1885). With their purchases, individuals indicate which discounts on the next purchase Carrefour has to offer them personally, in order to increase sales of their products.

We can think about the success of companies such as Google and Microsoft, which use their software or search engines, utilized by the mass, based on the cookies and information provided by the people that for instance connect to Internet, visit some Webs, or use and store information in some programs, and which tastes and preferences help these firms for instance to promote and expand their business and products, and to improve the efficiency of their products, such as software, or even efficiency the of the algorithms in the search engines, or the impact of their publicity about their clients (for example with SEO and SEM techniques). When visiting a Web page, when looking at a product or firm, or even when looking at one part of the page, potential customers are indicating their tastes to these companies and hence which similar pages they could search, which publicity must be offered to him/her, how to manage this individual, or the products of their suppliers that can be offered successfully, so that they can take advantage of these individuals personally and individually.

But as we pointed out before, knowledge is not everything. For instance, other firms use some of the "Masscapital" efficiently through innovations in the classical "self-service" or "self-producing." For instance, we could also use the success of firms such as fast food companies, IKEA, low-cost airlines, or even petrol station companies or banks, which use "Masscapital" through the co-work of their customers, with the use or not of Internet and other technological innovations, in their processes of producing and delivering their products. For example, the capabilities of customers are used in diverse ways while serving fast food customers: when reserving, ordering, or in the process of self-delivering the food. These capabilities of customers are also used in self-service processes, when customers are looking for, finding and buying airline tickets, indicating prices and tastes, or in the check-in process of airlines. The self-production of customers of IKEA, when customers indicate their preferences when purchasing or visiting the Web page of the company, and when they are contributing with their capabilities in the transport and assembly the products. The use of self-service in petrol stations, or the use of Internet and other technologies by customers to carry out routine financial services. In this vein, Peppard and Rylander (2006) and Garrigos-Simon et al. (2014) highlight the relevance of the change in the conception of the firms' value chain, especially in cases where both the product and supply chain are digitalized, as in sectors such as banking, insurance, telecommunications, news, entertainment, music, advertising, and certain areas of the public sector.

Nevertheless, we have to highlight that the use of technologies has also allowed the incorporation in the systems of people that are not clients of the organizations. In this point, Garrigos-Simon et al. (2012) posit the importance of the work of community managers, to promote the participation of stakeholders and other possible individuals in the relationship with the firms, and the use of crowdsourcing techniques to enhance crowd participation and so to increase what we call the appropriation of "Masscapital," or individual capabilities of the crowd. Accordingly, many companies are promoting the use of communities, essentially with customers who have specific knowledge about the problems with the products and who are motivated to freely contribute with new ideas (Von Hippel 2005a; Fuller 2010; Bayus 2013). Actually, companies, such as Dell, Starbucks (Sullivan 2010; Bayus 2013), Nike or Lego, are adopting and implementing successful innovations, after the creation and use of what Von Hippel (2005b) calls "Innovation communities" that allow them to create and innovate their products, to reformulate the structures of their firms, and to promote their brands.

Finally, we have to talk also about technological companies such as Apple or Telefonica, which have created platforms to capture the "Masscapital" of individuals and dispersed "developers." These developers are nowadays creating apps for a wide variety of innovations for these companies, acting as suppliers of these companies, or of the systems promoted by these companies, consciously. In addition, some firms are externalizing the service to the clients and customers who are experts in their products. According to Boudreau and Lakhani (2013, p.60), "From Apple to Merck to Wikipedia, more and more organizations are turning to crowds for help in solving their most vexing innovation and research questions." Nevertheless, let us think also, for example, of user-generated content for social media Web sites, such as Facebook (Rieder and Voß 2010), Twitter, YouTube, or even TripAdvisor, which use the advice that customers give to other customers (Buhalis et al. 2011; Sigala 2009). These firms use, and their business models are based on, the information and/or media from the "Masscapital," from individuals that sometimes unconsciously, and without any monetary remuneration, are acting as suppliers of their content.

1.4 Space, Time, and Volume in the Promotion of Masscapital

However, as pointed before, we think that "Masscapital" cannot always be captured or used through a simple mechanism. In addition, sometimes it cannot be managed by the companies; it only can be used by them.

For instance, the promotion of "word of mouth" (both in Internet or outside), the called "viral marketing", some operational marketing activities [i.e., Starbucks Idea (Rieder and Voß 2010; Müller 2011; Sigala 2012a, b)], the fact of publicizing through customers, with the simple carrying of bags from the retail firms in the street, or the use of their labeled products, or the creation of the publicity spots by the mass (e.g., L'Oreal) can also be considered as mechanisms to capture and promote the "Masscapital" that can be important for the organization's competitiveness, as it influences the loyalty of customers and the image of the brands. And these mechanisms are recognized as some of the key factors of success of companies such as Coca Cola, Walmart, or even Apple. Actually, fashion and popularity is a matter of "the mass," and if a firm can capture its essence, or can manage this "Masscapital," of course this can have a determinant influence in the success of this company. However, this "Masscapital," which is also produced with the participation of the crowd, cannot be interiorized inside the organization (although it can be effectively used and promoted by the firm), as in the crowdsourcing processes, a fact that does not make them less important.

Some Masscapital is also in the space or the specific environment where the firms are located and also cannot be captured with technological tools. We have to think for instance about the importance of the theories that emphasize the industrial districts of firms (Pyke and Sengenberger 1992; Becattini 1990), or in the case of popular areas such as Silicon Valley, where of course the "Masscapital" that is interiorized through the employees with their relationships with this environment is in the "ambience" of the specific territory or environment, and although available for the firms, it is not captured with IT techniques. The relevance of "Masscapital" is also when we look at some of the essential conditions of the general or even competitive environment of the firms and its influence on the success of the companies, as was clearly pointed out by Porter (1980, 1985), who stressed how our "Masscapital" (related to the conditions of the society, stakeholders such as suppliers, competitors, and clients), also with other factors in the environment that are not obviously related to this "Masscapital," can have a determinant influence on the success of the firms.

Finally, the use of "Masscapital" also has a temporal dimension, timing, and a dimension of volume. The organizations have to for instance think about the innovations in technology that were not successful at the beginning of our century and that are now successful, just when the mass is prepared for these innovations, or when the "Masscapital" of the capabilities of the mass has been already developed. In this vein, "Masscapital" has to be considered mainly as a source of innovation, but also a receptor and potential element of innovation, as, if the crowd is not prepared, some of its potential cannot be used (i.e., the advances in new technologies cannot be used, or applied to the crowd, or with the use of the mass, if the people do not have the capacity to use them). In addition, innovations from the mass have a caducity, so the important factor is not only to capture them, but the importance is when the organization started to capture them and if they are able to capture them massively before competitors. As we point out, sometimes it is a question of volume. Let us consider for instance the example of Zara, Google, Facebook, or YouTube, models which other companies are trying to replicate, but which is impossible to do in the same way, as they have massively captured the "Masscapital" related to their business, as they innovated first and quicker than their competitors, so no company can now compete with them effectively and efficiently, as they arrived too late to capture the essential and the great volume of the "Masscapital" related to their business.

1.5 Conclusions

In the present environment, from our point of view, the capabilities needed for firms to remain competitive do not reside within the company anymore, but outside, in the mass. In this chapter, we postulate for the importance of what we call "Masscapital," that is, the capabilities of all the individuals or organizations, related closely or not to the company, which can help it to innovate or improve any of its activities or processes.

This chapter explains that our theory of "Masscapital" is an evolution of the theory that includes innovative mechanisms such as crowdsourcing processes, the use of the Web 3.0, or the use of social networks for the improvement of the effectiveness of the organizations. This chapter provides examples of how our "Masscapital" is used and is the basis of the success of the most important firms in the present business environment. This chapter also emphasizes the importance of the time, space, and volume of the "Masscapital" for the success of its use and also stresses that although its use is important, sometimes firms cannot manage it, just use it; and when it is possible manage it, this management is not always related to technology.

This chapter opens new visions to be considered by practitioners and authors, in the search for the key to the competitive advantage of the organizations. This chapter is important for directors of firms and entrepreneurs as it explains some success factors used by firms and opens new ideas to be used to create successful organizations. It also opens new developments and fields in several theoretical perspectives. For instance, the work overcomes the classical strategic theories that focus on the environment or the resources and capabilities of organizations, offering a perspective that includes both, but that extends them highlighting and focusing on the importance of the capabilities of the mass, our "Masscapital." This chapter refers to the importance of the managerial information systems as an important mechanism to capture the essence of the "Masscapital" sometimes and to integrate it with the aims and the information of the organizations, but overcomes its importance, as it focuses on the capabilities of the individual more than on technological capabilities, as the key success factors factor, and because it considers some important factors outside technology that are key to the success of some organizations.

This chapter also postulates for the relevance of factors beyond the management of knowledge and opens new areas of research inside the "Knowledge management" literature, as it considers "Masscapital" as an essential capital to provide knowledge and to be managed and studied. Our postulates also open new themes of research into the analysis of the structure or the design of effective organizations, as our "Masscapital" opens the development of new organizational forms that overcome the classical "networking" structural organizations. This work also opens new spheres of research to the classical human resource management perspectives, as "Masscapital" opens the management of the human capital to individuals that are non-employees of the organizations. Finally, this chapter opens new questions of research in the literature about innovation and entrepreneurship, such as formulating some critical sources of innovation, and on some key success factors for entrepreneurs to be considered in their development.

References

Avolio, B. J., Sosik, J. J., Kahai, S. S., & Baker, B. (2014). E-leadership: Re-examining transformations in leadership source and transmission. *The Leadership Quarterly, 25*(1), 105–131.

Bayus, B. L. (2013). Crowdsourcing new product ideas over time: An analysis of the Dell IdeaStorm community. *Management Science, 59*, 226–244.

Becattini, G. (1990). The Marshallian industrial district as a socio-economic notion. In F. Pyke, G. Becattini, & W. Sengenberger (Eds.), *Industrial districts and local economic regeneration* (pp. 37–51). Geneva: International Institute for Labor Studies.

Benkler, Y. (2006). *The wealth of networks*. New Haven, CT, USA: Yale University Press.

Boudreau, K. J., Lacetera, N., & Lakhani, K. R. (2011). Incentives and problem uncertainty in innovation contests: An empirical analysis. *Management Science, 57*(5), 843–863.

Boudreau, K. J., & Lakhani, K. R. (2013). Using the crowd as an innovation partner. *Harvard Business Review, 91*, 61–69.

Brabham, D. C. (2008). Crowdsourcing as a model for problem solving: An introduction and cases. *Convergence: The International Journal of Research into New Media Technologies, 14* (1), 75–90.

Buhalis, D., Leung, D., & Law, R. (2011). eTourism: Critical information and technologies. In Y. Wang & A. Pizam (Eds.), *Destination marketing and management: Theories and applications* (pp. 205–224). Walling Ford, UK: CAB International.

Ebner, W., Leimeister, J. M., Bretschneider, U., & Krcmar, H. (2010). Leveraging the wisdom of crowds: Designing an IT-supported ideas competition for an ERP Software Company. *Information Systems, 49*(89).

Estellés-Arolas, E., & González-Ladrón-de-Guevara, F. (2012). Towards an integrated crowdsourcing definition. *Journal of Information Science, 38*(2), 189–200.

Fuller, J. (2010). Refining virtual co-creation from a consumer perspective. *California Management Review, 52*(2), 98–122.

Galdon, J. L., Garrigos-Simon, F. J., & Gil, I. (2015). Improving hotel industry processes through crowdsourcing techniques. In R. Egger, I. Gula, & D. Walcher (Eds.), *Open tourism: Open innovation, crowdsourcing and co-creation challenging the tourism industry*. Berlin: Springer.
Garrigos-Simon, FJ. (2010). Interrelationships between professional virtual communities and social networks, and the importance of virtual communities in creating and sharing knowledge. In S. Dasgupta (Ed.), *Social computing: Concepts, methodologies, tools, and applications* (Vol. III). New York: Information Science Publishing.
Garrigos-Simon, F. J., Gil, I., & Narangajavana, Y. (2011). The impact of social networks in the competitiveness of the firms. In A. B. Beckford & J. P. Larsen (Eds.), *Competitiveness: Psychology, production, impact and global trends*. Hauppauge: Nova Science Publishers Inc.
Garrigos-Simon, F. J., Lapiedra, R., & Barberá, T. (2012). Social networks and Web 3.0: Their impact on the management and marketing of organizations. *Management Decision, 50*(10), 1880–1889.
Garrigos-Simon, F. J., Narangajavana, Y., & Galdón-Salvador, J. L. (2014). Crowdsourcing as a competitive advantage for new business models. *Strategies in E-business* (pp. 20–37). US: Springer.
Howe, J. (2006). *Crowdsourcing: A definition*. Available via http://crowdsourcing.typepad.com/cs/2006/06/crowdsourcing_a.html. Accesed January 11, 2011.
Kleemann, F., Voß, G. G., & Rieder, K. (2008). Un(der)paid innovators: The commercial utilization of consumer work through crowdsourcing. *Science, Technology & Innovation Studies, 4*(1), 5–26.
Li, X., & Petrick, J. F. (2008). Tourism marketing in an era of paradigm shift. *Journal of Travel Research, 46*(3), 235–244.
Müller, C. (2011). *Social media marketing. A critical and evaluative account on the emergence and principles of social media marketing and its true potential to enhance the marketing initiatives of hotels and other organisations*. Scholarly Essay, 2011. Available via http://www.grin.com/en/e-book/200590/social-media-marketing. Accesed October 11, 2013.
Narangajavana, Y., Garrigos-Simon, F. J., García, J. S., & Forgas-Coll, S. (2014). Prices, prices and prices: A study in the airline sector. *Tourism Management, 41*, 28–42.
Oldham, G., & Da Silva, D. (2015). The impact of digital technology on the generation and implementation of creative ideas in the workplace. *Computers in Human Behavior, 42*, 5–11.
Parmigiani, A. (2007). Why do firms both make and buy? An investigation of concurrent sourcing. *Strategic Management Journal, 28*(3), 285–311.
Peppard, J., & Rylander, A. (2006). From value chain to value network: Insights for mobile operators. *European Management Journal, 24*(2–3), 128–141.
Peteraf, M. A. (1993). The cornerstone of the competitive advantage: A resource-based view. *Strategic Management Journal, 14*, 179–191.
Porter, M. (1980). *Competitive strategy: Techniques for analyzing industries and competitors*. New York: Free Press.
Porter, M. (1985). *Competitive advantage*. New York: Free Press.
Prahalad, C. K., & Hamel, G. (1990). The core competence of the corporation. *Harvard Business Review, 68*(3), 79–93.
Prahalad, C. K., & Ramaswamy, V. (2004). Co-Creating unique value with customers. *Strategy & Leadership, 32*(3), 4–9.
Prpic, J., & Shukla, P. (2013). *The theory of crowd capital*. In System Sciences (HICSS), 46th Hawaii International Conference, IEEE (pp. 3505–3514).
Pyke, F., & Sengenberger, W. (1992). *Industrial districts and local economic regeneration*. Geneva: International Institute for Labour Studies.
Ranade, G., & Varshney, L. R. (2012). *To crowdsource or not to crowdsource*? In Workshops at the Twenty-Sixth AAAI Conference.
Rieder, K., & Voß, G. G. (2010). The working customer—An emerging new type of consumer. *Psychology of Everyday Activity, 3*(2), 2–10.

Sigala, M. (2009). *WEB 2.0 in the tourism industry: A new tourism generation and new ebusiness models*. Available via http://www.traveldailynews.com/pages/show_page/20554. Accesed October 22, 2011.

Sigala, M. (2012a). Web 2.0 and customer involvement in new service development: A framework, cases and implications in tourism. In M. Sigala, E. Christou, U. Gretzel (Eds.), *Web 2.0 in travel, tourism and hospitality: Theory, practice and cases* (pp. 25–38). Farnham: Ashgate Publishers.

Sigala, M. (2012b). Social networks and customer involvement in new service development (NSD): The case of www.mystarbucksidea.com. *International Journal of Contemporary Hospitality Management, 24*(7), 966–990.

Sullivan, E. (2010). A group effort: More companies are turning to the wisdom of the crowd to find ways to innovate. *Marketing News, 44*(2), 22–28.

Von Hippel, E. (2005a). *Democratizing innovation*. Cambridge, MA: MIT Press.

Von Hippel, E. (2005b). Open source software projects as user innovation networks-no manufacturer required. In J. Feller, B. Fitzgerald, S. Hissam, & K. Lakhani (Eds.), *Perspectives on free and open source software*. Cambridge: MIT Press.

Chapter 2
Recruiting Individuals to a Crowdsourcing Community: Applying Motivational Categories to an Ad Copy Test

Yannig Roth, Daren C. Brabham and Jean-François Lemoine

Abstract This study operationalizes different motivational categories to participate in crowdsourcing and tests them with a series of advertisements in different countries. We found that internalized extrinsic motivations were more appealing to individuals overall and that results differed across countries, which is novel in research about crowdsourcing.

Keywords Crowdsourcing · Online advertising · Click-through rate · Cultural differences

2.1 Introduction

As crowdsourcing becomes an increasingly common way to gather input from an online community for problem solving and product design, businesses have become concerned with how to build and sustain these online communities in the first place. Research into the motivations for participation in crowdsourcing applications has identified a range of extrinsic and intrinsic motivators, but there is, to our knowledge, a lack of empirical evidence that points to which of these many motivators are more effective for recruiting individuals to online communities to participate in crowdsourcing activities. This study aimed to identify which kinds of motivators

Y. Roth
Université Paris 1 Panthéon-Sorbonne, 17 rue de la Sorbonne, 75005 Paris, France
e-mail: yannig.roth@gmail.com

D.C. Brabham (✉)
University of Southern California, 3502 Watt Way, Los Angeles, CA 90089, USA
e-mail: brabham@usc.edu

J.-F. Lemoine
Université Paris 1 Panthéon-Sorbonne/ESSCA Ecole de Management,
17 rue de la Sorbonne, 75005 Paris, France
e-mail: jflemoine30@hotmail.com

F.J. Garrigos-Simon et al. (eds.), *Advances in Crowdsourcing*,
DOI 10.1007/978-3-319-18341-1_2

are most effective for recruiting individuals to crowdsourcing applications. In this study, we crafted a series of Google AdWords advertisements for the crowdsourcing community eYeka, with each ad operationalizing a proven motivational category for participation in crowdsourcing. These 20 different ads ran on Google in late 2011 and gathered a total of 496 click-throughs. We analyzed the click-through rate (CTR) for each ad in order to determine which ads, and, by extension, which kinds of motivators, were most effective for recruiting individuals to a crowdsourcing community. Interestingly, participants from different countries were motivated by different motivational categories. This study contributes to our understanding of motivations in crowdsourcing applications by being among the first to rank motivational categories to join a crowdsourcing community from most effective to least effective. It also contributes to the discussion about the global nature of crowdsourcing ventures and raises additional questions about how best to tailor crowdsourcing experiences for different cultures.

2.2 Literature Review

Crowdsourcing is an online, distributed problem solving and production model that leverages the collective intelligence of online communities for specific purposes (Brabham 2008a). In crowdsourcing applications, an organization broadcasts a challenge to an online community, and the online community supplies ideas and solutions to the organization to address the challenge (Brabham 2008a; Howe 2006, 2008). Crowdsourcing blends the efficiency and control of traditional, top-down managed process with the benefits of bottom-up open innovation and creativity. Furthermore, crowdsourcing takes advantage of the network structure of the Internet by harnessing individual far-flung talent for targeted efforts (Afuah and Tucci 2012; Lévy 1995; Terranova 2004; Wexler 2011). Crowdsourcing has been well documented in such cases as Threadless.com, InnoCentive.com, Amazon's MechanicalTurk.com, TopCoder.com, and TaskCN.com (Barr and Cabrera 2006; Boudreau et al. 2011; Jeppesen and Lakhani 2010; O'Mahony and Lakhani 2011; Zheng et al. 2011). Even though crowdsourcing is a very recent term, we can see that the process has been used in a variety of contexts. Companies can launch crowdsourcing initiatives on their own branded platforms, such as Dell did with IdeaStorm, but they can also commission permanent crowdsourcing platforms which host contests on their Web sites for a fee (Bayus 2013).

One way to engage in crowdsourcing initiatives for a company is indeed to start a private online platform. This is typically suited to traditional companies that want to leverage the power of the crowd but whose core competencies do not lie in setting up, managing, and sustaining a community (Bayus 2013; Feller et al. 2012; Lakhani and Panetta 2007; Penin and Burger-Helmchen 2011). In order to benefit from the creativity of the crowd, they create branded platforms, such as Dell's IdeaStorm, Starbucks' myStarbucksIdea, or Nokia's IdeasProject. These are the examples of participatory Web sites that are being initiated directly by companies.

These companies build Internet platforms on which individuals can contribute ideas and suggestions, allowing them to benefit from the sheer diversity of the crowd to gather innovative and consumer-rooted ideas (Sawhney et al. 2003). The crowd may or may not be asked to select the best ideas, and contributions are open and visible to everyone (Alexy et al. 2012). Here, the initiating company has no experience in crowdsourcing, but it takes the risk to start a platform from scratch, hoping that people will be attracted by the brand's reputation or the topic of the challenge (Fournier and Lee 2009).

Another operative mode to initiate crowdsourcing is to externalize the whole process to a platform whose job is to organize crowdsourcing, often in the form of a contest, on behalf of companies (Penin and Burger-Helmchen 2011; Schenk and Guittard 2011). These platforms are specific in that they leverage a private community of contributors who participate in contests sponsored by client organizations (Lakhani and Panetta 2007; Williams et al. 2011; Zwass 2010). When applied to innovation, these platforms are usually called innomediaries (Sawhney et al. 2003) or idea marketplaces (Morgan and Wang 2010). These platforms count on crowd contributions for the supply and/or selection of ideas and designs (Brabham 2013; Lakhani and Panetta 2007). Typical examples of such crowdsourcing applications can be found in clothing with Web sites such as Threadless.com, Zazzle.com, or LaFraise.com; in multimedia content with platforms such as iStockphoto.com, Fotolia.com, or Jamendo.com; and in industrial design with communities such as Shapeways.com, GrabCAD.com, or Sculpteo.com. Crowdsourcing is not only being used in innovation-related topics; companies also use crowdsourcing to tap external talent in marketing-related tasks. Platforms can also organize crowdsourcing for the creation of print advertising or the production of user-generated video content (Roth and Kimani 2014; Teixeira 2013; Whitla 2009).

Whether platforms use crowdsourcing to generate ideas, designs, or videos, all of these examples describe companies whose business model is based on a crowd of voluntary contributors who regularly add content to the site and participate in contests sponsored by client companies (Zwass 2010). By doing this, participants allow these platforms to receive a constant flow of ideas, which allows the platform to have fresh content from diverse sources while still having a large amount of control over contributors and buyers (Boudreau and Lakhani 2009). These platforms could be described as “pure players” of crowdsourcing since they totally rely on contributions from their own crowds to be sustainable (Feller et al. 2012). They are not producing nor buying the output that they generate, such as creative ideas or videos; they are just acting as intermediaries between client companies and the dispersed problem-solving capability of the crowd (Prpić and Shukla 2013). This is different from traditional companies which use crowdsourcing only on a sporadic basis to get new ideas and content, but have other principal revenue sources (the sale of their products, the fees of their services, etc.) like the ones described above. Because the online community—the crowd—is at the heart of any crowdsourcing application, how to recruit individuals to a crowdsourcing community and sustain their participation are the pressing questions for crowdsourcing practitioners.

Attracting a critical mass of members is the very first milestone to be reached by virtual communities (Hagel and Armstrong 1997). After setting up a functional Web site, companies can attract members with interesting content or useful tools, but also by actively marketing their Web site with online advertisements. In that case, Hagel and Armstrong (1997) highlight that "operating costs in a virtual community have little to do with technology and much more to do with acquisition of members" (p. 63). After the creation of the online environment, there is an initial step of traffic generation, which allows Web site owners to increase awareness and to attract members whose participation will eventually be part of the Web site's value proposition. The advertising budget of community Web sites can be substantial, especially in a phase where organic growth reaches a tipping point. We posit that this is equally true in crowdsourcing communities, which have to rely on active member acquisition to grow the crowd of potential contributors, but also to compensate for churn effects and lurking effects that are present in every virtual community (Fuster Morell 2010; Huberman et al. 2009; Porter et al. 2011).

An emerging body of research has explored motivations for participation in crowdsourcing applications specifically, and these studies have catalogued a wide variety of motivators common across some crowdsourcing cases, but not across all cases. For example, at crowdsourced scientific research company, InnoCentive, Lakhani, Jeppesen, Lohse, and Panetta (Lakhani et al. 2007) found that intrinsic motivators such as "enjoying problem solving," as well as financial reward, were related to success on the site. At crowdsourced stock photography company, iStockphoto, the extrinsic financial motivator was found to be strong, both in a survey of the community (Brabham 2008b) and in anecdotal evidence (Mack 2006). On the other hand, participants in the crowdsourced science fiction film *Star Wreck: In the Pirkinning* were motivated by the sheer enjoyment of creating the film and other altruistic reasons, but not by financial gain (Lietsala and Joutsen 2007). At crowdsourced clothing company Threadless, the love of the community itself—and even addiction to it—was one of the five strong motivators for participation, according to a series of interviews with individuals in the community (Brabham 2010). Also, important for Threadless members, as well as for participants in the crowdsourced bus stop design contest Next Stop Design or the idea contest SAPiens Ideas Competition, is the opportunity to build a portfolio of creative work for future employment (Brabham 2010, 2012b; Leimeister et al. 2009), a concept Kuehn and Corrigan (Kuehn and Corrigan 2013) appropriately term "hope labor." Anecdotally, portfolio-building hope labor is also a driver for some user-generated advertising contest participants (Brabham 2007; Horovitz 2009). In a study conducted among Chinese participants on the crowdsourcing platform, TaskCN.com, Zheng et al. (2011) found that the desire to earn money and to gain recognition were significantly linked to participation intention, even though pure enjoyment of creating was a stronger predictor of participation intention.

Perhaps unsurprisingly, the motivational categories for participation in crowdsourcing activities resonate with motivators for participation in similar online activities, such as open source software production (Bonaccorsi and Rossi 2004; Ge et al. 2006; Hars and Ou 2002; Hertel et al. 2003; Lakhani and Wolf 2005; Oreg and Nov 2008; Shah 2006), editing Wikipedia (Nov 2007; Rafaeli and Ariel 2008; Schroer and Hertel 2009), uploading and tagging photographs on Flickr (Morgan and Wang 2010; Nov et al. 2008), social voting (Smadja 2009), and blogging (Huang et al. 2007; Liu et al. 2007; Nardi et al. 2004). These phenomena have been collectively called "participatory culture" or "Web 2.0," but we find Füller's (2010) label "virtual co-creation" to be more precise and useful for this study. Füller (2010) uses the umbrella term "virtual co-creation" to include "crowdsourcing, co-creation, user innovation, virtual customer integration, and open innovation" which are different forms of the "promising, active role consumers may play in the previously firm-dominated world of product development and production" (p. 98). His work is particularly relevant to the study of motivations in online projects because his work focuses precisely on the link between motivations and online activity.

Summarizing the work of other scholars who have studied motivation for many years, Füller (2010) uses self-determination theory to better understand peoples' participation in online activities. According to Edward L. Deci and Richard M. Ryan, who have been developing this theory since the 1970s, human motivations can be grouped into two broad categories: intrinsic motivations, by which individuals act in a particular way because they enjoy the act in itself, and extrinsic motivations, by which people act in order to receive something else than the mere satisfaction of performing the act (Deci and Ryan 1980; Deci 1972). These two broad motivation categories have recently been refined (Ryan and Deci 2000) to include a third, intermediate category: internalized extrinsic motivations. Internalized extrinsic motivations are extrinsic motivations, meaning that individuals still perform certain behaviors for a specific outcome, but individuals have internalized the reasons to act and assimilated them to the self. In other words, internalized extrinsically motivated individuals force themselves to act, because they have understood the benefit of their actions. "The more one internalizes the reasons for an action and assimilates them to the self, the more one's extrinsically motivated actions become self-determined" (Ryan and Deci 2000). The three aforementioned types of motivations have been used by Füller (2010) in his research about participation about virtual co-creation, but also by Lebraty and Lobre-Lebraty (2013) in their studies of crowdsourcing participation. Building on this solid framework, our study therefore uses the following categories to study individuals' reactions to different ad copy in the context of crowdsourcing:

- *Intrinsic Motivators*, which include tasks that are intrinsically playful;
- *Internalized Extrinsic Motivators*, which include motivators such as self-efficacy, status development and the desire for recognition or visibility, the opportunity to make friends, self-efficacy, information seeking, and skill development; and
- *Extrinsic Motivators*, which include personal need and dissatisfaction as well as the opportunity for monetary compensation.

Many studies mentioned above rely on self-reports through surveys and interviews and are highly valuable in developing our understanding of the variety of motivators for participation in existing crowdsourcing communities. However, it is worth noting that these studies reveal the motivations of the most active and engaged segment of participants, and that these studies' findings are of little use to those who have not yet built an active community of participants. Yet, as explained above, building an active and vibrant community is also one of the most challenging and costly steps to undertake before even thinking about crowdsourcing, and many companies have failed because they could not attract and sustain their crowds of participants (Bishop 2007; Chanal and Caron-Fasan 2010; Feller et al. 2012; Oberoi 2013). To our knowledge, research has not addressed the crucial step of attracting participants to crowdsourcing applications, and the little evidence that suggests what the most important motivators are for individuals in the crowd is not sufficient to help practitioners built a crowdsourcing community ("An Inside Look at Lufthansa's Air Cargo Innovation Challenge," n.d.; Mergel and Desouza 2013). Moving beyond descriptive categories of motivators and into more advanced theory-building is a necessary evolution in motivations and uses and gratifications research (Ruggiero 2000). The several motivational categories for participation listed above are useful, but the question still remains as to what is the most important motivational category for driving initial participation. Given this discussion, then, this exploratory study seeks to answer one broad question:

RQ: What kinds of motivators are most effective for recruiting individuals to a crowdsourcing community?

In light of the discussion of different consumer types, too, it is anticipated that, when operationalized, each of these motivational categories will succeed at least somewhat in getting participants to join a crowdsourcing site. Understanding exactly which motivational categories outperform others in a particular crowdsourcing context may help future crowdsourcing practitioners craft recruitment tactics for growing successful online communities. This is thus the focus of this exploratory study. This study aimed to sort this question out by testing individuals' actual behaviors clicking through online ads that operationalize these motivational categories.

2.3 Method

To field test which motivational categories were most effective at recruiting individuals to a crowdsourcing community, Füller's (2010) three motivational categories for virtual co-creation activities were operationalized in a series of online advertisements using Google AdWords. With AdWords, marketers purchase certain keywords with which they want simple text-only ads to appear alongside in a Google search results page (Kim et al. 2012). For the purposes of this study, for example, the keyword "video contest" was the target keyword for which the test ads would appear. "Video contest" was chosen because the study site, eYeka, is a creative crowdsourcing company that facilitates, among other things, crowdsourced video contests. Presumably, individuals searching for open video contests would have an interest in a site like eYeka and would click on an accompanying ad.

eYeka is a global company based in France which operates a Web site on which brands and organizations can host creative contests (King and Lakhani 2013). These contests are visible to anyone on the Internet, and participation is open to registered members of the platform. In mid-2013, the eYeka community consisted of about 250,000 members from more than 150 countries. In late 2011, when the data for this study were collected, eYeka had about 200,000 members, with a growth rate between 200 and 300 members per day. Discussions with eYeka executives revealed that an estimated 50 % of this growth was fueled by online advertising such as Google AdWords. These members all share a common interest for creative tasks, such as photography, design, or video production. In one of its reports about creative crowdsourcing, Forrester Research claims that "co-creation contest vendors provide a specialized form of crowdsourcing [as they] typically cultivate their own communities" (Williams et al. 2011, para. 9). As one of these vendors, eYeka "develops, manages, and nourishes this community" with incentives such as "cash awards for the top ideas to 'fame'—such as using a winning video in a co-created marketing campaign" (Williams et al. 2011, para. 9). While this description falls in line with previous research about motivations to participate in crowdsourcing, it does not say why people initially chose to enter a crowdsourcing community.

Survey research conducted internally by eYeka shows that 35 % of active users of the site found out about eYeka by clicking on a banner ad or on a link, the most common response. The second most cited answer was that people found out about eYeka through a specific contest, which led them to join and participate (see Table 2.1).

This survey was conducted in March 2011 by eYeka and does not claim to be representative of the whole community, because only active members were surveyed, which may not be representative of the whole community. These results show that external links directing to the eYeka Web site are a major source of traffic, but they do not tell what motivational triggers are most effective in attracting potential members and contributors. This is the objective of this study.

To operationalize the three motivational categories, simple ads were developed to speak to each category. To test the internalized extrinsic motivational category, for instance, this ad appeared in search results for the keyword "video contest":

Table 2.1 How active members of the eYeka community found out about the site

How did you find out about eYeka?	Count	Percentage (%)
A friend/acquaintance of mine	97	21
An article in the press, on the Web or a TV spot	48	11
A specific call for entries that interested me	136	30
A banner on a Web site or a link on a search engine	157	35
Other	15	3
Total	453	100

source internal eYeka community survey, March 2011

"Participate in Video Contests for Free & Improve your Skills!" In this ad, the wording "improve your skills" taps into the "skill development" aspect of the internalized extrinsic motivational category. Examples of wording used in the ad copy to operationalize the motivational categories can be seen in Table 2.2.

Because the Internet is a global medium and participants at eYeka come from all over the world, a diverse selection of countries was chosen for the AdWords campaign. The countries were India, Malaysia, Singapore, the United Kingdom, and the USA. These countries were chosen in collaboration with eYeka because they constituted a strategic priority for the crowdsourcing company at the time of the study and reflected a diversity of countries in terms of user behavior (Chau et al. 2002; Singh and Baack 2004; Singh et al. 2005). The AdWords campaign ran for 14 days in 2011, and all ad copy was tested in English, as represented in Table 2.2.

Ad copy testing is a long-standing method for refining tactics and messaging before or during a campaign and for measuring a campaign's effectiveness. Ad copy testing has been used across several media to determine precisely which words, images, and themes arouse certain feelings in audiences, often with the goal of triggering a specific behavior, such as intent to purchase an advertised product (Cook and Dunn 1996; Dunn 1994; Jones 1998). Early works about virtual communities highlight the importance of online advertising for community member acquisition (Hagel and Armstrong 1997). In her book about community building on the Web, for example, Kim (2000) describes how two different versions of a banner ad were used to attract people to fill out a survey. One version offered monetary compensation, and the other just highlighted the opportunity to contribute; results showed no significant differences between both approaches.

For this study, click-through rate (CTR), defined by the American Marketing Association (American Marketing Association, n.d.) as "the number of click-throughs [the number of users who clicked on a specific Internet advertisement or link] per ad impression, expressed as a percentage," was used to assess the effectiveness of the various motivators as operationalized through the slate of ad copy options.

Table 2.2 Examples of advertising wording used to operationalize motivational categories

Motivational category	Advertisement wording example
Intrinsic	Enjoy yourself by participating in awesome video contests!
	Participate in contests and express your ideas in creative ways!
Internalized extrinsic	Curious to discover and create? Participate in video contests!
	Participate in video contests and challenge yourself on cool briefs!
	Participate in video contests and find new inspiration!
	Participate in video contests for free and improve your skills!
	Participate in video contests on eYeka and be recognized!
Extrinsic	Participate in video contests—show and share your own approach!
	Participate in video contests and win amazing prizes!

2.4 Results

During the campaign, a total of 29,435 impressions resulted in a total of 496 clicks, for an overall CTR of 1.69 % (see Table 2.3). Ads which operationalized the internalized extrinsic motivational category resulted in the highest CTR overall, at 1.76 %, with the lowest CTR, at 1.50 %, tied to the intrinsic motivational category. Parsing the results across the five countries included in the study—India, Malaysia, Singapore, the UK, and the USA—provided more complex picture of overall click-through behavior in the ad campaign (see Table 2.4). The internalized extrinsic motivational category resulted in the highest CTRs for all countries except for Malaysia. The extrinsic motivational category resulted in the highest CTR for Malaysia, with the internalized extrinsic category resulting in the lowest CTR.

There were no consistent patterns among the countries for which motivational categories ranked second or last in terms of CTR, so the researchers recombined the data in various ways to make sense of these results. There are some fault lines between these five countries, as they represent different geographic regions, cultural traditions, and levels of economic development. One comparison was made between countries in Asia (India, Malaysia, and Singapore) and countries in "the West" (UK and the USA). In this comparison of the average CTRs for Asian and Western countries, the extrinsic motivational category resulted in the highest CTR for the Asian countries, while the internalized extrinsic category resulted in the highest CTR for the Western countries (see Table 2.5).

Another comparison was made based on economic development in each country, an especially important analysis given the fact that eYeka functions as a vehicle for participants to potentially earn money for themselves. The International Monetary Fund (IMF) categorizes countries in a three-level hierarchy according to economic development. The least economically developed countries are "developing countries," the most developed are "advanced economies," and countries in between these extremes are "countries in transition." India and Malaysia are considered by the IMF to be developing countries, and Singapore, the UK, and the USA are classified as advanced economies. Comparing these average CTRs for these two groupings shows that the developing countries had a higher CTR for the extrinsic motivational category, while the advanced economy countries had a higher CTR for the internalized extrinsic motivational category (see Table 2.6).

Table 2.3 Total CTRs for the entire campaign, by motivational category

Motivational category	Impressions	Clicks	CTR (%)
Intrinsic	5,943	89	1.50
Internalized extrinsic	15,101	266	1.76
Extrinsic	8,391	141	1.68
TOTAL	29,435	496	1.69

Table 2.4 CTRs for each motivational category, by country

Motivational category	India		Malaysia		Singapore		UK		USA	
	Impress.	CTR (%)	Impress.	CTR (%)	Impress.	CTR (%)	Impress.	CTR (%)	Impress.	CTR (%)
	Clicks		Clicks		Clicks		Clicks		Clicks	
Intrinsic	909	2.86	819	2.56	343	1.46	2,717	0.92	1,155	1.04
	26		21		5		25		12	
Internalized extrinsic	3,287	**3.29**	1,356	2.14	1,267	**1.58**	6,203	**1.05**	2,988	**1.47**
	108		29		20		65		44	
Extrinsic	1,750	3.03	964	**2.90**	641	1.40	3,432	1.02	1,604	1.00
	53		28		9		35		16	
TOTAL	5,946	3.14	3,139	2.48	2,251	1.51	12,352	1.01	5,747	1.25
	187		78		34		125		72	

Top motivational category indicated in bold type

Table 2.5 CTRs for each motivational category, comparing the average of the CTRs of Asian countries (India, Malaysia, and Singapore) and Western countries (UK and the USA)

Motivational category	Asian countries (%)	Western countries (%)
Intrinsic	2.29	0.98
Internalized extrinsic	2.33	**1.26**
Extrinsic	**2.38**	1.13

Top motivational category indicated in bold type

Table 2.6 CTRs for each motivational category, comparing the average of the CTRs of countries considered by the International Monetary Fund to be "developing countries" (India and Malaysia) and "advanced economies" (Singapore, UK, and the USA)

Motivational category	Developing countries (%)	Advanced economy countries (%)
Intrinsic	2.71	1.14
Internalized extrinsic	2.71	**1.37**
Extrinsic	**2.81**	1.26

Top motivational category indicated in bold type

2.5 Discussion

The internalized extrinsic motivational category resulted in the highest CTR overall and for all countries except for Malaysia, for which this category was the worst performing in terms of CTR. These findings suggest that an advertising campaign that tapped into internalized extrinsic motivators—such as self-efficacy, status development and the desire for recognition or visibility, the opportunity to make friends, self-efficacy, information seeking, or skill development—would attract more participants to a crowdsourcing site than an ad campaign driven by wording that connected to intrinsic or extrinsic motivators. In simple terms, then, a crowdsourcing practitioner would do better to build an online community by advertising the opportunity to learn a new skill through participation (internalized extrinsic) than to emphasize the simple enjoyment of playing on the site (intrinsic) or the opportunity to make money (extrinsic). The generally higher CTRs from Indian, Malaysian, and Singaporean participants are perhaps not surprising. In a report from DoubleClick (2010), these countries also had higher CTRs overall for display Internet ads (0.18, 0.30, and 0.19 %, respectively) compared to the USA (0.10 %) and the United Kingdom (0.07 %) (p. 16).

Malaysia's divergent performance in this study, as well as the differing top motivational categories comparing Asian and Western countries and comparing developing countries and advanced economies, raise new and interesting questions about cultural differences and the motivations to participate in crowdsourcing ventures. Because crowdsourcing ventures take place on the global platform of the Internet, even sites targeted to specific national audiences may attract unexpected, international participants, and different management techniques for these communities are required (Brabham 2012a). This means that crowdsourcing sites would be wise to advertise with different ads targeted to different cultures, targeting participants in Asian and developing countries with ads operationalizing extrinsic motivators and targeting participants in Western countries and advanced economies with ads operationalizing internalized extrinsic motivators. This finding is in line with anecdotal findings from research about motivations to participate in Amazon's Mechanical Turk, where a survey found that more Indian workers treat Mechanical Turk as a significant source of income compared to American workers, who see it as a supplementary source of income (Ipeirotis 2010). However, and interestingly, our findings contradict the assumption made by Zheng et al. (2011), who argued that Eastern crowdsourcing participants might be more intrinsically driven to participate than Western participants. Clearly, more rigorous research is needed to explore cultural influences on crowdsourcing participation motivations, which is a surprisingly scant area of interest in academia.

It is unclear, however, how to target participants in countries such as Singapore, which is both an Asian country and an advanced economy. Further still, none of these countries have monolithic cultures. Each country in the study has large numbers of first-generation immigrants and vibrant minority communities that may be driven by different motivators than the majority population. Also, each country has a complex cultural history—and some have colonial pasts with other countries in the study—and is home to at least one large transnational metropolis. Making broad claims about how to target the whole of a country's people in an ad campaign for a crowdsourcing site should be done with caution. Additional research is needed to more fully address this question of culture and motivation in regard to joining crowdsourcing communities (Hsieh 2011; Zheng et al. 2011). The work of Geert Hofstede (De Mooij and Hofstede 2010; Hofstede 1984a, b), Appadurai (1996), Hall (1976), Gelfand et al. (2006, 2011), and other perspectives from a range of disciplines that have examined cultural difference would be useful to further deepen our understanding of crowdsourcing participation across borders.

2.6 Limitations and Conclusions

This study illustrated which motivational category performed best at getting participants to visit a crowdsourcing site by using the CTR as a measure of motivation to participate. While the CTR indeed demonstrates that participants were interested in the advertisement to the point where they chose to click on the link, it does not necessarily indicate that these participants eventually signed up at eYeka and became full participating members of that crowdsourcing community. Surely, many did not. What it does demonstrate, though, is that some ads worked better than others to get participants' attention and get them to explore the eYeka site, and that some motivational categories generated more of these exploratory visits than others. This advances what is known about how crowdsourcing systems work. To date, studies on motivations for participation in crowdsourcing have either simply catalogued which motivators were present among a community or have examined the connection between types of motivation and quality of participation in open innovation contests (Frey et al. 2011), but scant research has been done to sort these motivators by their effectiveness at getting individuals to join a crowdsourcing community.

Another limitation in this study is that broad motivational categories were measured rather than more nuanced levels of analysis. That is, future research could build on this study by tracking the performance of individual motivators even within broad motivational categories, comparing, for instance, whether an ad that taps into the motivator of curiosity performs better than an ad that taps into the motivator of skill development, both of which fall under the umbrella category of internalized extrinsic motivations.

It would be helpful to test an ad campaign in more countries and in different languages as well. The five countries could be clustered into a few groupings—Asian and Western, developing and advanced economies—but the addition of many more countries to a future study could make these groupings more robust and, assuming the inclusion of South American, Middle Eastern, and African countries, could include entirely new groupings for comparison. For crowdsourcing companies who seek global participation, understanding the effect of culture on motivation to participate is an important pursuit.

Acknowledgments The first author acknowledges funding (CIFRE N° 2011/3106) from the Association Nationale Recherche Technologie (ANRT). All three authors sincerely thank Edouard Breine, Traffic and Community Manager at eYeka, for helping in the process of data collection.

References

Afuah, A., & Tucci, C. L. (2012). Crowdsourcing as a solution to distant search. *Academy of Management Review, 37*(3), 355–375.

Alexy, O., Criscuolo, P., & Salter, A. (2012). Managing unsolicited ideas for R&D. *California Management Review, 54*(3), 116–139.

American Marketing Association. (n.d.). AMA dictionary. American Marketing Association.

An Inside Look at Lufthansa's Air Cargo Innovation Challenge. (n.d.). Retrieved from http://www.crowdsourcing.org/editorial/an-inside-look-at-lufthansas-air-cargo-innovation-challenge/20105.

Appadurai, A. (1996). *Modernity at large: Cultural dimensions of globalization*. Minneapolis: University of Minnesota Press.

Barr, J., & Cabrera, L. F. (2006). AI gets a brain: New technology allows software to tap real human intelligence. *ACM Queue, 4*(4), 24–29.

Bayus, B. L. (2013). Crowdsourcing new product ideas over time: An analysis of the Dell IdeaStorm community. *Management Science, 59*(1), 226–244.

Bishop, J. (2007). Increasing participation in online communities: A framework for human-computer interaction. *Computres in Human Behavior, 23*(3), 1881–1893.

Bonaccorsi, A., & Rossi, C. (2004). Altruistic individuals, selfish firms?: The structure of motivation in open source software. *First Monday, 9*(1).

Boudreau, K. J., Lacetera, N., & Lakhani, K. R. (2011). Incentives and problem uncertainty in innovation contests: An empirical analysis. *Management Science, 57*(5), 843–863.

Boudreau, K. J., & Lakhani, K. R. (2009). How to manage outside innovation. *MIT Sloan Management Review, 50*(4), 69–76.

Brabham, D. C. (2007, March 8). Faces in the crowd: Brett Snider. In *Crowdsourcing: Tracking the rise of the amateur*. Retrieved from http://crowdsourcing.typepad.com/cs/2007/03/faces_in_the_cr.html.
Brabham, D. C. (2008a). Crowdsourcing as a model for problem solving: An introduction and cases. *Convergence: The International Journal of Research into New Media Technologies, 14* (1), 75–90.
Brabham, D. C. (2008b). Moving the crowd at iStockphoto: The composition of the crowd and motivations for participation in a crowdsourcing application. *First Monday, 13*(6).
Brabham, D. C. (2010). Moving the crowd at Threadless: Motivations for participation in a crowdsourcing application. *Information, Communication & Society, 13*(8), 1122–1145.
Brabham, D. C. (2012a). Managing unexpected publics online: The challenge of targeting specific groups with the wide-reaching tool of the Internet. *International Journal of Communication, 6*, 1139–1158.
Brabham, D. C. (2012b). Motivations for participation in a crowdsourcing application to improve public engagement in transit planning. *Journal of Applied Communication Research, 40*(3), 307–328.
Brabham, D. C. (2013). *Crowdsourcing*. Cambridge: MIT Press.
Chanal, V., & Caron-Fasan, M.-L. (2010). The difficulties involved in developing business models open to innovation communities: The case of a crowdsourcing platform. *Management, 13*(4), 318–341.
Chau, P. Y. K., Cole, M., Massey, A. P., Montoya-Weiss, M., & O'Keefe, R. M. (2002). Cultural differences in the online behavior of consumers. *Communications of the ACM, 45*(10), 138–143.
Cook, W. A., & Dunn, T. F. (1996). The changing face of advertising research in the information age. *Journal of Advertising Research, 36*(1), 55–71.
De Mooij, M., & Hofstede, G. (2010). The Hofstede model: Applications to global branding and advertising strategy and research. *International Journal of Advertising, 29*(1), 85–110.
Deci, E. L. (1972). Intrinsic motivation, extrinsic reinforcement, and inequity. *Journal of Personality and Social Psychology, 22*(1), 113–120.
Deci, E. L., & Ryan, R. M. (1980). Self-determination theory: When mind mediates behavior. *Journal of Mind and Behavior, 1*(1), 33–43.
DoubleClick. (2010). 2009 year-in-review benchmarks: DoubleClick EMEA report. DoubleClick, by Google.
Dunn, T. F. (1994). *Understanding copy pretesting: An instructional collection of noteworthy papers on the history, role, methods, and validity of copy pretesting research*. New York: Advertising Research Foundation.
Feller, J., Finnegan, P., Hayes, J., & O'Reilly, P. (2012). "Orchestrating" sustainable crowdsourcing: A characterisation of solver brokerages. *Journal of Strategic Information Systems, 21*(3), 216–232.
Fournier, S., & Lee, L. (2009). Getting brand communities right. *Harvard Business Review, 87*(4), 105–111.
Frey, K., Lüthje, C., & Haag, S. (2011). Whom should firms attract to open innovation platforms? The role of knowledge diversity and motivation. *Long Range Planning, 44*, 397–420.
Füller, J. (2010). Refining virtual co-creation from a consumer perspective. *California Management Review, 52*(2), 98–122.
Fuster Morell, M. (2010). Participation in online creation communities: Ecosystemic participation?. In S. S. Shulman & C. M. Schweik (Eds.), *Proceedings of the 2nd annual Journal of Information Technology & Politics thematic conference on The Politics of Open Source* (pp. 270-295). Amherst, MA: University of Massachusetts Amherst.
Ge, X., Dong, Y., & Huang, K. (2006). Shared knowledge construction process in an open-source software development community: An investigation of the Gallery community. In S. A. Barab, K. E. Hay, & D. T. Hickey (Eds.), *Proceedings of the 7th international conference of the learning sciences* (pp. 189–195). Atlanta: International Society of the Learning Sciences.
Gelfand, M. J., Nishii, L. H., & Raver, J. L. (2006). On the nature and importance of cultural tightness-looseness. *Journal of Applied Psychology, 91*(6), 1225–1244.

Gelfand, M. J., Raver, J. L., Nishii, L., Leslie, L. M., Lun, J., Lim, B. C., & Yamaguchi, S. (2011). Differences between tight and loose cultures: A 33-nation study. *Science, 332*(6033), 1100–1104.
Hagel, J., & Armstrong, A. G. (1997). *Net gain: Expanding markets through virtual communities*. Boston: Harvard Business School Press.
Hall, E. T. (1976). *Beyond culture*. New York: Anchor Books.
Hars, A., & Ou, S. (2002). Working for free?: Motivations for participating in open source projects. *International Journal of Electronic Commerce, 6*(3), 25–39.
Hertel, G., Niedner, S., & Hermann, S. (2003). Motivation of software developers in the open source projects: An Internet-based survey of contributors to the Linux kernel. *Research Policy, 32*(7), 1159–1177.
Hofstede, G. (1984a). Cultural dimensions in management and planning. *Asia Pacific Journal of Management, 1*(2), 81–99.
Hofstede, G. (1984b). *Culture's consequences: International differences in work-related values* (2nd ed.). Beverly Hills: Sage.
Horovitz, B. (2009, December). "Two nobodies from nowhere" craft winning Super Bowl ad. *USA Today*.
Howe, J. (2006, June). The rise of crowdsourcing. *Wired Magazine*, *14*(6). Retrieved from http://www.wired.com/wired/archive/14.06/crowds.html.
Howe, J. (2008). *Crowdsourcing: Why the power of the crowd is driving the future of business*. New York: Crown.
Hsieh, G. (2011). *Understanding and designing for cultural differences on crowdsourcing marketplaces*. Presented at the CHI 2011 Workshop on Crowdsourcing and Human Computation, Vancuover, BC. Retrieved from http://crowdresearch.org/chi2011-workshop/papers/hsieh.pdf.
Huang, C. Y., Shen, Y. Z., Lin, H. X., & Chang, S. S. (2007). Bloggers' motivations and behaviors: A model. *Journal of Advertising Research, 47*(4), 472–484.
Huberman, B. A., Romero, D. M., & Wu, F. (2009). Crowdsourcing, attention and productivity. *Journal of Information Science, 35*(6), 758–765.
Ipeirotis, P. G. (2010). Analyzing the Amazon Mechanical Turk marketplace. *XRDS: Crossroads, The ACM Magazine for Students*, *17*(2), 16–21.
Jeppesen, L. B., & Lakhani, K. R. (2010). Marginality and problem-solving effectiveness in broadcast search. *Organization Science, 21*(5), 1016–1033.
Jones, J. P. (1998). Quantitative pretesting for television advertising. In J. P. Jones (Ed.), *How advertising works: The role of research* (pp. 160–169). Thousand Oaks: Sage.
Kim, A. J. (2000). *Community building on the Web*. Berkeley: Peachpit Press.
Kim, C., Park, S., Kwon, K., & Chang, W. (2012). How to select search keywords for online advertising depending on consumer involvement: An empirical investigation. *Expert Systems with Applications, 39*(1), 594–610.
King, A., & Lakhani, K. R. (2013). Using open innovation to identify the best ideas. *MIT Sloan Management Review, 55*(1), 41–48.
Kuehn, K., & Corrigan, T. F. (2013). Hope labor: The role of employment prospects in online social production. *The Political Economy of Communication, 1*(1), 9–25.
Lakhani, K. R., Jeppesen, L. B., Lohse, P. A., & Panetta, J. A. (2007). The value of openness in scientific problem solving (Working paper No. 07-050).
Lakhani, K. R., & Panetta, J. A. (2007). The principles of distributed innovation. *Innovations: Technology, Governance, Globalization*, *2*(3), 97–112.
Lakhani, K. R., & Wolf, R. G. (2005). Why hackers do what they do: Understanding motivation and effort in free/open source software projects. In J. Feller, B. Fitzgerald, S. A. Hissam, & K. R. Lakhani (Eds.), *Perspectives on free and open source software* (pp. 3–22). Cambridge: MIT Press.
Lebraty, J. F., & Lobre-Lebraty, K. (2013). *Crowdsourcing: One step beyond*. London: ISTE/Wiley & Sons.

Leimeister, J. M., Huber, M., Bretschneider, U., & Krcmar, H. (2009). Leveraging crowdsourcing: Activation-supporting components for IT-based ideas competition. *Journal of Management Information Systems, 26*(1), 197–224.
Lévy, P. (1995). *Collective intelligence: Mankind's emerging world in cyberspace* (R. Bononno, Trans.). New York: Plenum.
Lietsala, K., & Joutsen, A. (2007). Hang-a-rounds and true believers: A case analysis of the roles and motivational factors of the Star Wreck fans. In A. Lugmayr, K. Lietsala, & J. Kallenbach (Eds.), *MindTrek 2007 Conference Proceedings* (pp. 25–30). Tampere: Tampere University of Technology.
Liu, S. H., Liao, H. L., & Zeng, Y. T. (2007). Why people blog: An expectancy theory analysis. *Issues in Information Systems, 8*(2), 232–237.
Mack, S. (2006, November 14). Faces in the crowd: Interview series part I. *Crowdsourcing: Tracking the rise of the amateur.* Retrieved from http://crowdsourcing.typepad.com/cs/2006/11/ive_always_said.html.
Mergel, I., & Desouza, K. C. (2013). Implementing open innovation in the public sector: The case of Challenge.gov. *Public Administration Review, 73*(6), 882–890.
Morgan, J., & Wang, R. (2010). Tournaments for ideas. *California Management Review, 52*(2), 77–97.
Nardi, B. A., Schiano, D. J., Gumbrecht, M., & Swartz, L. (2004). Why we blog. *Communications of the ACM, 47*(12), 41–46.
Nov, O. (2007). What motivates Wikipedians? *Communications of the ACM, 50*(11), 60–64.
Nov, O., Naaman, M., & Ye, C. (2008). What drives content tagging: The case of photos on Flickr. In M. Burnett, M. F. Costabile, T. Catarci, B. de Ruyter, D. Tan, M. Czerwinski, & A. Lund (Eds.), *Proceedings of the 26th annual SIGCHI Conference on Human Factors in Computing Systems* (pp. 1097–1100). New York: Association for Computing Machinery.
O'Mahony, S., & Lakhani, K. R. (2011). Organizations in the shadow of communities. In C. Marquis, M. Lounsbury, & R. Greenwood (Eds.), *Communities and Organizations* (Vol. 33, pp. 3–36). Bingley: Emerald.
Oberoi, P. (2013). *The bold new world of open innovations: Sustaining dynamic relationships between online platforms, client firms and virtual communities (Case No. 313-164-1).* Case Centre. Retrieved from http://www.thecasecentre.org/educators/products/view?id=116596.
Oreg, S., & Nov, O. (2008). Exploring motivations for contributing to open source initiatives: The roles of contribution context and personal values. *Computers in Human Behavior, 24*(5), 2055–2073.
Penin, J., & Burger-Helmchen, T. (2011). Crowdsourcing of inventive activities: Definition and limits. *International Journal of Innovation and Sustainable Development, 5*(2/3), 246–263.
Porter, C. E., Donthu, N., MacElroy, W. H., & Wydra, D. (2011). How to foster and sustain engagement in virtual communities. *California Management Review, 53*(4), 80–110.
Prpić, J., & Shukla, P. (2013). The theory of crowd capital. In R. H. Sprague Jr (Ed.), *Proceedings of the 46th Hawaii International Conference on System Sciences* (pp. 3505–3514). Los Alamitos: IEEE Computer Society.
Rafaeli, S., & Ariel, Y. (2008). Online motivational factors: Incentives for participation and contribution to Wikipedia. In A. Barak (Ed.), *Psychological aspects of cyberspace: Theory, research, applications* (pp. 243–267). Cambridge: Cambridge University Press.
Roth, Y., & Kimani, R. (2014). Crowdsourcing in the production of video advertising: The emerging roles of crowdsourcing platforms. In R. J. DeFillippi & P. Wikström (Eds.), *International perspectives on business innovation and disruption in the creative industries: Film, video, photography*. Chamberley: Edward Elgar Publishing.
Ruggiero, T. E. (2000). Uses and gratifications theory in the 21st century. *Mass Communication & Society, 3*(1), 3–37.
Ryan, R. M., & Deci, E. L. (2000). Intrinsic and extrinsic motivations: Classic definition and new directions. *Contemporary Educational Psychology, 25*, 54–67.
Sawhney, M., Prandelli, E., & Verona, G. (2003). The power of innomediation. *MIT Sloan Management Review, 44*(2), 77–82.

Schenk, E., & Guittard, C. (2011). Towards a characterization of crowdsourcing practices. *Journal of Innovation Economics, 7*(1), 93–107.

Schroer, J., & Hertel, G. (2009). Voluntary engagement in an open web-based encyclopedia: Wikipedians and why they do it. *Media Psychology, 12*(1), 96–120.

Shah, S. K. (2006). Motivation, governance, and the viability of hybrid forms in open source software development. *Management Science, 52*(7), 1000–1014.

Singh, N., & Baack, D. W. (2004). Web site adaptation: A cross-cultural comparison of U.S. and Mexican web sites. *Journal of Computer-Mediated Communication*, 9(4).

Singh, N., Zhao, H., & Hu, X. (2005). Analyzing the cultural content of web sites: A cross-national comparison of China, India, Japan, and US. *International Marketing Review, 22*(2), 129–146.

Smadja, F. (2009). *Mixing financial, social and fun incentives for social voting (White paper)*. Wilton: Toluna.

Teixeira, T. (2013). How to profit from "lean advertising". *Harvard Business Review, 91*(6), 23–25.

Terranova, T. (2004). *Network culture: Politics for the information age*. London: Pluto Press.

Wexler, M. N. (2011). Reconfiguring the sociology of the crowd: exploring crowdsourcing. *International Journal of Sociology and Social Policy, 31*(1/2), 6–20.

Whitla, P. (2009). Crowdsourcing and its application in marketing activities. *Contemporary Management Research, 5*(1), 15–28.

Williams, D., Gownder, J. P., Corbett, A. E., & Rose, S. (2011, September 7). *The Forrester Wave: Co-creation contest vendors Q3 2011—A social computing report*. Forrester Research.

Williams, D., Gownder, J. P., & Wiramihardja, L. (2011, January 24). *Market overview: Co-creation vendors 2011*. Forrester Research.

Zheng, H., Li, D., & Hou, W. (2011). Task design, motivation, and participation in crowdsourcing contests. *International Journal of Electronic Commerce, 15*(4), 57–88.

Zwass, V. (2010). Co-creation: Toward a taxonomy and an integrated research perspective. *International Journal of Electronic Commerce, 15*(1), 11–48.

Chapter 3
Crowdsourcing Fundamentals: Definition and Typology

Enrique Estellés-Arolas, Raúl Navarro-Giner and Fernando González-Ladrón-de-Guevara

Abstract Crowdsourcing is a problem-solving and task realization model that is being increasingly used. Thanks to the possibility of harnessing the collective intelligence from the Internet; thanks to the crowdsourcing initiatives people can, for example, find a solution to a complex chemical problem, get images tagged, or get a logo designed. Due to its success and usefulness, more and more researchers have focused their interest on this concept. This fact has shown that the concept of crowdsourcing has no clear boundaries, and although over time the concept has been better explained, some authors describe it differently, propose different types of crowdsourcing initiatives, or even use contradictory crowdsourcing examples. In this paper, an integrated definition and typology, developed in 2012, are analyzed to check whether they are still valid today or whether need a reformulation.

Keywords Crowdsourcing · Typology · Definition · Crowd · Task · Web · Collective intelligence

3.1 Introduction

The development of Web 2.0 has led to the emergence of new models for business, for communication, for personal relationships, for learning, etc. One of these models, related to business and innovation, is known as crowdsourcing.

E. Estellés-Arolas (✉) · R. Navarro-Giner
Catholic University of Valencia, Valencia, Spain
e-mail: enrique.estelles@ucv.es

R. Navarro-Giner
e-mail: raul.navarro@ucv.es

F. González-Ladrón-de-Guevara
Technical University of Valencia, Valencia, Spain
e-mail: fgonzal@omp.upv.es

F.J. Garrigos-Simon et al. (eds.), *Advances in Crowdsourcing*,
DOI 10.1007/978-3-319-18341-1_3

The term "crowdsourcing" was first coined in 2006 by American journalist Jeff Howe. In a first attempt to conceptualize the term, Howe (2006) defined it as "the act of a company or institution taking a function once performed by employees and outsourcing it to an undefined (and general large) network of people in the form of an open call. This can take the form of peer-production (when the job is performed collaborative), but is also often undertaken by sole individual."

Thanks to the collaborative nature of Web 2.0, crowdsourcing allows a person, institution, or company to benefit from the work, ideas, or wisdom of the crowd of Internet. This crowd, usually heterogeneous, can be formed by amateurs, volunteers, experts, companies, etc. (Howe 2008), which may or may not belong to a specific user community (Brabham 2012). The work of this crowd is rewarded in some way: tangible (money, prizes, etc.) or intangible (recognition, entertainment, prestige, etc.).

This model, which was born in the business environment, has evolved and spread. Currently, crowdsourcing is being used for different purposes in fields as diverse as medicine (King et al. 2013a, b) or geography (See et al. 2014).

The problem is that the wide use of crowdsourcing has made many people to use the term referring to any initiative in which a large number of people are recruited through an open call that is usually distributed through Internet (Howe 2008; Brabham 2008; Estellés-Arolas and González-Ladrón-de-Guevara 2012a; Littmann and Suomela 2014).

For this reason, sometimes the boundaries of what is or is not crowdsourcing are not completely clear. An example is the case of Wikipedia: taking it as a crowdsourcing platform raises both defenders (Bazilian et al. 2012; Ghani and Zakaria 2013) and detractors (Brabham 2013; Estellés-Arolas and González-Ladrón-de-Guevara 2012a). The proliferation of different crowdsourcing definitions and typologies neither help too much.

To alleviate this situation, in 2012, Estellés-Arolas and González-Ladrón-de-Guevara carried out a literature review with the objective of stating an integrative crowdsourcing definition (2012a) and crowdsourcing typology (2012b).

Though both the typology and the definition proposed by Estellés-Arolas and González-Ladrón-de-Guevara are correct and useful, the concept of crowdsourcing continues evolving and being applied in different areas. This situation makes necessary the review of both integrative proposals to test its validity.

For that purpose, this chapter contains the results obtained by repeating the literature review realized in Estellés-Arolas and González-Ladrón-de-Guevara (2012a) in order to find new definitions and new typologies since 2012. The aim was to check whether the definition and typology proposal remain valid or need to be reformulated.

It is true that the crowdsourcing definition and typology mentioned above are not the most used within the literature. The most used are the Howe's (2008) and Brabham's (2008). But certainly counts in its favor that both, definition and typology, seek for consensus integrating different proposals.

3.2 Theoretical Background

3.2.1 Toward an Integrated Definition

In 2012, Estellés-Arolas and González-Ladrón-de-Guevara sought through a literature review different crowdsourcing definitions (2012a). The purpose of their research was to extract all the elements which would allow distinguishing between crowdsourcing and any other Internet initiative.

After analyzing more than 200 documents, they found more than 40 different definitions. The authors identified within these definitions eight fundamental elements that any crowdsourcing initiative must contain. These elements are as follows:

1. There is a clearly defined crowd (E1).
2. There exists a task with a clear goal (E2).
3. The recompense received by the crowd is clear (E3).
4. The crowdsourcer is clearly identified (E4).
5. The compensation to be received by the crowdsourcer is clearly defined (E5).
6. It is an online assigned process of participative type (E6).
7. It uses an open call of variable extent (E7).
8. It uses the Internet (E8).

As a result of this research, its authors developed a definition of crowdsourcing, which although being wordy, defines in detail the concept. The definition is as follows: "Crowdsourcing is a type of participative online activity in which an individual, an institution, a nonprofit organization, or company proposes to a group of individuals of varying knowledge, heterogeneity, and number, via a flexible open call, the voluntary undertaking of a task. The undertaking of the task, of variable complexity and modularity, and in which the crowd should participate bringing their work, money, knowledge, and/or experience, always entails mutual benefit. The user will receive the satisfaction of a given type of need, be it economic, social recognition, self-esteem, or the development of individual skills, while the crowdsourcer will obtain and utilize to their advantage that what the user has brought to the venture, whose form will depend on the type of activity undertaken." (Estellés-Arolas and González-Ladrón-de-Guevara 2012a).

3.2.2 Toward an Integrated Typology

Later, Estellés-Arolas and González-Ladrón-de-Guevara (2012b) conducted another literature review searching for different crowdsourcing typologies. They obtained six documents that reported a task-based typology (Reichwald and Piller 2006; Howe 2008; Brabham 2008; Kleemann et al. 2008; Geerts 2009; Burger-Helmchen and Pénin 2010). After comparing all different typologies (Codina 1997; Pinto-Molina et al. 2007), an integrated typology was stated. It comprises 5 main types:

1. Crowdcasting. Contest-like crowdsourcing initiatives, where a problem or a task is proposed to the crowd, being rewarded who solves it first or do it better (i.e., Innocentive).
2. Crowdcollaboration. Crowdsourcing initiatives in which communication between individuals of the crowd occurs, while the initiator of the initiative stays on the sidelines. There can be found two subtypes which differ on the ultimate goal:
   - Crowdstorming. Massive online brainstorming sessions, in which different ideas are raised and the crowd can support those ideas with their comments and votes (e.g., IdeaJam).
   - Crowdsupport. In this case, the customers themselves solve the doubts and problems of other customers, so they do not need to contact the official customer support (i.e., Getsatisfaction).
3. Crowdcontent: In these crowdsourcing tasks, the crowd uses their labor and knowledge to create or find content of various types but not in a competitive way. Three subtypes can be found:
   - Crowdproduction. Initiatives where the crowd should create content, as it is done individually when translating short pieces of text or tagging images (i.e., Amazon Mechanical Turk).
   - Crowdsearching. Crowdsourcing initiatives where the crowd searches for content on the internet for any purpose (i.e., Peer to Patent Review).
   - Crowdanalyzing. Initiatives where the crowd searches but not in the Internet but inside multimedia documents such as videos or images (i.e., Stardust@home).
4. Crowdfunding. In the crowdfunding initiatives, an individual, organization, or company seeks for funding from the crowd in exchange for a reward (i.e., Kickstarter).
5. Crowdopinion. In this case, the objective is to know the user opinions about a particular issue or product through votes, comments, tags, or even sale of shares (i.e., ModCloth, Intrade).

3.3 Methodology

3.3.1 Regarding the Definition

The methodology used to verify whether the integrated crowdsourcing definition is valid is performed in three steps: a systematic review of the literature to find documentation that includes crowdsourcing definitions (as shown in Estellés-Arolas and González-Ladrón-de-Guevara 2012a), the identification of the definition elements following the Tatarkiewicz's approach (1980), and the comparison with the actual integrated definition.

In first place, the systematic review of the literature is done again following the Delgado approach (2010) based on Petitti (2000) and Egger et al. (2008). Five databases have been selected (SAGE, IEEE, ScienceDirect, Emerald, and ACM), and documents with the word "crowdsourcing" in the title, abstract, or keywords have been consulted. Only those documents with an original definition for crowdsourcing, and published from 2012, are selected.

Finally, found definitions will be analyzed. It will be checked whether some of the 8 parameters published in the original article using Tatarkiewicz's approach (1980) appears, or if instead, any new characteristic should be taken into consideration.

3.3.2 Regarding the Typology

Regarding the typology, a similar literature review has been performed. Same databases have been consulted, but search criteria have been modified. In this case, any document containing the term "crowdsourcing" in its title, abstract, or keywords has been selected. Also, in the same fields, the terms "typology" or "taxonomy" (either or both) should appear.

Once obtained the documents, those containing a general typology different to the ones found out previously are selected. These typologies will be compared to Estellés-Arolas and González-Ladrón-de-Guevara typology proposal (2012b), updating it if necessary.

3.4 Results

In this section, the results obtained by performing the reviews of the literature, both in the search for new definitions as in the search for new typologies, are shown.

3.4.1 Results on the Definition

After searching documents in the five databases previously cited, a total of 777 documents were retrieved among journal papers, books reviews, books, and proceedings (Table 3.1). It should be noted that the most numerous documents found

Table 3.1 Summary table of the literature review

	Total	Journal paper	Book review	Book	Proceedings	Use new definition
SAGE	28	24	4	0	0	5
Science Direct	95	86	0	9	0	8
IEEE	248	54	0	0	194	5
ACM	394	1	0	0	393	8
Emerald	12	8	2	2	0	2
Total	777	173	6	11	587	30

are proceedings, fact that coincides with the results of the original review of the literature performed by Estellés-Arolas and González-Ladrón-de-Guevara (2012a).

Among all the documents found, only 28 (the 3.86 %) contains a definition not citing explicitly others such as Howe's (2008) or Brabham's (2008). In Table 3.2, this definitions can be seen.

Table 3.2 New crowdsourcing definitions found through the literature review

No.	Document	Page	Definition: crowdsourcing is …
1.	Folorunso and Mustapha (2014)		"referred to as human computation, a methodology that lets humans process tasks which are difficult to implement in software"
2.	Lee et al., n.d.	60	"the practice of obtaining needed services, ideas, or content by soliciting contributions from a large group of people, particularly from an online community, rather than from traditional employees or suppliers"
3.	Satzger et al. (2013a, b)		"a new paradigm for performing computations in Web-based environments by utilizing the capabilities of human workers. The idea of crowdsourcing is sometimes referred to as human computation, a methodology that lets humans process tasks which are difficult to implement in software. Such tasks include transcription of documents, reviewing of articles or evaluating the quality of ranking algorithms"
4.	Sutherlin (2013)	397	"the technological union of humans and software"
5.	Ambati et al. (2012)	1191	"is the process of farming out tasks to a large user population on the Internet. These tasks broadly belong to the language or vision community, where for a number of tasks it is either impossible or challenging and time-consuming for computers to complete them, whereas only requires a few seconds for a human to complete"
6.	Sprugnoli et al. (2013)	8116	"the process of segmenting a complex task into smaller work units and distributing these among a large pool of non-expert workers, usually via the web"
7.	Pedersen et al. (2013)	579	"a collaboration model enabled by people-centric web technologies to solve individual, organizational, and societal problems using a dynamically formed crowd of people who respond to an open call for participation"
8.	Roopa et al. (2013)	272	"a technique wherein a task is outsourced to a distributed group of people (crowd).Thus crowdsourcing is a collaborative or distributed problem solving model. Problems are broadcast to unknown group of people asking for solutions. Users (crowd) submit the solutions. The solutions are consolidated by the "crowdsourcer". The crowd may be rewarded monetarily, with prizes, with extra talk time or some other form of recognition. In some cases, the reward could be just intellectual satisfaction"

(continued)

Table 3.2 (continued)

No.	Document	Page	Definition: crowdsourcing is …
9.	Wu et al. (2014)	728	"a process that involves outsourcing tasks to a distributed group of people, which is normally much cheaper than hiring experts"
10.	Zeinalipour-Yazti et al. (2013)	1240	"a distributed problem solving model where a population of undefined size, engages in the solution of a complex problem for monetary or ethical (i.e., intellectual satisfaction) benefit through an open call"
11.	Parvanta et al. (2013)	2	"a problem-solving approach that taps the knowledge, energy and creativity of a global, online community"
12.	Brabham et al. (2014a, b)		"an online, distributed, problem-solving, and production model that uses the collective intelligence of networked communities for specific purposes"
13.	Marjanovic et al. (2012)		"under-researched type of open innovation that is often enabled by the web"
14.	Lampe et al. (2014)		"online communities that could help with issues of managing information and users, including the ability to solicit small contributions from a large number of users to help provide important meta-data about people or information"
15.	Britton et al. (2013)	3	"distributed problem-solving technique leveraging the efforts of a group, known as "the crowd." A project is defined and volunteers are invited to contribute to its accomplishment. The volunteers are dispersed and may not even be members of the organization"
16.	Soleymani and Larson (2013)	1111	"human computation techniques that exploit human intelligence and also take advantage of a large population of contributors. Crowdsourcing is frequently facilitated by crowdsourcing platforms where crowd-members can find and carry out microtasks in exchange for a small payment"
17.	Perera and Perera (2014)	93	"a process of outsourcing tasks of an organization to general public, where the term 'crowd' equals to 'general public'"
18.	Gupta and Sharma (2013)	14	"the act of outsourcing tasks, traditionally performed by staff or a contractor, to an undefined large group of people or crowd"
19.	Azzam and Jacobson (2013)	2	"Paid recruitment of an independent global workforce for the objective of working on a specifically defined task or set of tasks"
20.	Demartini et al. (2013a, b)	668	"term used to define those methods to generate or process data asking to a large group of people to complete small tasks. It is possible to categorize different crowdsourcing strategies based on the different types of incentives used to motivate the crowd to perform such tasks"
21.	Schumaker (2013)		"another form of market efficiency where groups of individuals perform forecasts on provided information and results are averaged for use as a predictive tool"

(continued)

Table 3.2 (continued)

No.	Document	Page	Definition: crowdsourcing is …
22.	Raford (2014a, b)		"Large-scale collective intelligence systems"
23.	Geiger and Schader (2014)		"an umbrella term for approaches that harness the diverse potential of large groups of people via an open call for contribution over the Web. Using information technology as a facilitator, crowdsourcing organizations implement socio-technical systems to channel the contribution of human workforce, knowledge, skills, or perspectives into the generation of digital information products and services. Such crowdsourcing information systems have recently gained in popularity for a variety of organizational functions such as problem solving, knowledge aggregation, content generation, and large-scale data processing"
24.	Stanley et al. (2013)	155	"rooted in the process of asking others to help you with a problem that you cannot resolve on your own. This may be due to limited resources, skills, or time constraints"
25.	King et al. (2013a, b)		"Collective effort"
26.	Tong et al. (2014)	861	"a service has a common framework: each employer (a.k.a the task publisher) poses a task, and then this task is responded or finished by many different and unknown crowd employees. Thus, the "task-response pairs" is the unique structure of crowdsourcing data"
27.	Stol and Fitzgerald (2014)	187	"an emerging and promising approach which involves delegating a variety of tasks to an unknown workforce—the crowd"
28.	Chiu et al. (2014)	41	"can be viewed as a method of distributing work to a large number of workers (the crowd) both inside and outside of an organization, for the purpose of improving decision making, completing cumbersome tasks, or co-creation of designs and other projects"

3.4.2 Results on the Typology

The typology literature review results have been much less numerous. In fact, after consulting the same databases, 40 documents have hardly been retrieved, of which only one provides an innovative general typology.

Typologies focused on specific areas were found: Linders (2012a, b) stated a typology of the crowdsourcing initiatives that can be carried out in e-government; and Gomes et al. (2012) stated a crowdsourcing typology focused on musical scene.

The only document that provides a general Typology is the one proposed by Geiger et al. (2012). These authors described an information system-based typology that could sustain the crowdsourcing initiatives. It consists of 4 types:

1. Crowdprocessing, where the crowd produces a large amount of homogenous contributions with equal value. 'Re-captcha' and other microtasks like the ones that can be found in AMT or in many citizen science projects (i.e., Galaxy Zoo), are examples of this type of crowdsourcing.
2. Crowdrating, where the crowd also produces a large amount of contributions, with equal value. In this case, the value that emerges from the total contribution is sought. This is the case of votes, reviews, and opinions (i.e., "eBay reputation system"). It would also include prediction markets (i.e., "Hollywood Stock Exchange").
3. Crowdsolving initiatives seek value from heterogeneous contributions, where each contribution has its own qualitative properties. This crowd solving initiatives look for alternative or complementary solutions to a given task or problem (i.e., Goldcorp Challenge, Netflix prize, or Innocentive).
4. Crowdcreation initiatives, finally, seek the collective value arising from the accumulation and relation of contributions. In this case, also each contribution is important toward the creation of a collective result (i.e., iStockPhoto).

3.5 Discussion

3.5.1 Regarding the Definition

Comparing found definitions with the Estellés-Arolas and González-Ladrón-de-Guevara's (2012a) integrated definition proposal, there cannot be found any relevant difference. All of them meet some of the 8 proposed elements, and those aspects that do not accord with the elements make reference to specific applications or particular visions of crowdsourcing.

Definitions around other concepts or models like to open innovation (Marjanovic et al. 2012), human computation (Demartini et al. 2013a, b; Satzger et al. 2013a, b), or collective intelligence (Raford 2014a, b) can be found. Other definitions are focused in specific crowdsourcing types such as the crowdproduction using microtasking (Sprugnoli et al. 2013; Demartini et al. 2013a, b; Lampe et al. 2014) or the use of crowd contest for complex problem solving (Zeinalipour-Yazti et al. 2013; Stanley et al. 2013).

It is important to highlight that there are two definitions, those of Roopa et al.'s (2013) and Geiger and Schader's (2014), which are highly general, and in fact meet almost all elements of the integrated definition.

About the elements, it is important to notice that almost the totality of the definitions makes reference to a crowd (E1) that undertakes a task (E2). Other elements have been taken much less into account: 9 definitions refer to the use of Internet to carry these initiatives out (E8) and 8 of them refer to a process that involves individual online participation (E6).

The remaining elements are less reflected in the found definitions. This indicates that, although those elements allow crowdsourcing identification, they are not considered fundamental by authors.

3.5.2 Regarding Typology

In this case, the 4 general types Geiger et al. (2012) proposed could be integrated into the types contemplated by Estellés-Arolas and González-Ladrón-De-Guevara (2012b). In fact, there is direct correlation between both typologies. Geiger's Crowdrating, Crowdcreation, and Crowdsolving corresponds with Estellés-Arolas' Crowdopinion, Crowdproduction, and Crowdcontest. In the case of Geiger's Crowdprocessing, this type corresponds with Estellés-Arolas' Crowdsearching and Crowdanalysing.

3.5.3 Regarding the Literature Review Results

Comparing the literature review carried out with the one performed by Estellés-Arolas and González-Ladrón-de-Guevara (2012a) has allowed a limited study of the evolution of crowdsourcing as a research topic.

First of all, it should be highlighted the difference between the number of publications found in 2012 (209) and the number found in 2014 (777). Applying the same criteria and consulting the same databases, 372 % more documents were found. It is also significant the increase in the amount of conference paper (127 in 2012 and 587 in 2014; 462 % more) and also in journal papers (68 in 2012 and 173 in 2014; 254 % more).

These data show that crowdsourcing has gone from being an emerging issue, which in 2012 still did not receive much attention, to an actual issue. Besides, this indicates a consolidation in the scientific research on the subject.

Another fact that supports this statement is that, in the first literature review, the 19.13 % (40 of 209) of the documents found, used original definitions. In this literature review, this percentage has fallen to the 3.86 % (28 of 777). This shows that authors are less interested in defining and conceptualizing crowdsourcing and more interested in researching of concrete applications.

Regarding the definitions found, it is important to highlight some aspects.

1. Firstly, the vast majority of authors use already existing definitions, mainly Howe's (2006) and Brabham's (2008). Estellés-Arolas and González-Ladrón-de-Guevara (2012a) definition, because its integrative nature, is also used although to a lesser extent.
2. Secondly, some documents does not have any definition of the term. Some, like Monahan and Mokos (2013) or Su et al. (2013), for example, obviate the

crowdsourcing definition when mentioning it. It is assumed that the topic already has its own identity or has become popular enough.

3. Occasionally, the verb "crowdsource" is being used naturally (Garrido and Faria 2012; Rana et al. 2014; Kalantari et al. 2014). Although the verb does not exist as such in the dictionary, it is a term frequently used to denote the action of using crowdsourcing. This shows that crowdsourcing use is increasingly widespread.

Concerning definitions which are not based in any other, those typically arise from the need to define crowdsourcing from the point of view of a specific task.

Some authors define crowdsourcing relating it to another concepts or models. King et al. (2013a, b) defined it as a collective effort, referring to tasks where everyone's contribution is necessary. Others focus on the use of crowdsourcing for co-creation activities (Gatautis and Vitkauskaite 2014), open innovation (Feller et al. 2012; Ren et al. 2014), collective intelligence (Garrido and Faria 2012; Filippi et al. 2013; Raford 2014a, b), or human computation (Satzger et al. 2013a, b).

Crowdsourcing is also understood, for example, as a tool for customers' participation in product development (Djelassi and Decoopman 2013), public participation (Hildebrand et al. 2013) and e-government (Linders 2012a, b), citizen science (Harvey et al. 2014), collecting data (Armstrong et al. 2012), search (Ren et al. 2014), or microtasking (Chen et al. 2014).

It is also important to note that in the literature review carried out by Estellés-Arolas and González-Ladrón-de-Guevara (2012a) there were found different papers referred to the theoretical basis of crowdsourcing. Brabham (2008) analyzed and studied the motivations that move the crowd to participate, Geiger et al. (2011) proposed a taxonomy of crowdsourcing activities, Schenk and Guittard (2009) studied what kind of tasks can be performed using crowdsourcing, and so on.

In the literature review carried out in this work, it can be seen that there are practically no such documents. Most items listed study the application of crowdsourcing in some activity or specific area. Schriner and Oerther (2014) study it as way to fight poverty. Brabham et al. (2014a, b) analyze it in the area of public health and medical domain. Related to this field, King et al. (2013a, b) study the use of crowdsourcing in skin self-examination for detecting cancer.

Other applications are establishing the fingerprint of past sea-level changes (Rovere et al. 2012), validate data to generate overall landcover maps (See et al. 2014), urban surveillance (Monahan and Mokos 2013), or animal identification for ecological monitoring and conservation (Duyck et al. 2014).

3.6 Conclusions

Crowdsourcing refers to a problem-solving and completing tasks model which involves the participation of the Internet crowd. It represents just one of the many ways to harness collective intelligence. Its use has spread increasingly, being used in many areas: medicine, biology, astronomy, etc., being business area the one in which it was born and in which has been more used.

The popularity of crowdsourcing has made different authors to define and conceptualize crowdsourcing in different ways, even proposing different typologies and definitions. In 2012, Estellés-Arolas and González-Ladrón-de-Guevara suggested, using a literature review, an integrated definition of crowdsourcing based in 8 elements (2012a) and also an integrated crowdsourcing typology (2012b). It is a wordy definition, but it defines the concept in depth. The same applies to the typology.

In the present work, the same literature review has been carried out. The objective is to see whether the definition and the typology proposed remain valid. Both have been specifically chosen because they share the intention to seek consensus on what is crowdsourcing.

The results of the literature review points that both the definition and the typology remain useful and remain relevant. Firstly, none of the 28 new definitions found identify a new differentiator element. Regarding the typology, only one new general typology has been found. This new typology integrates seamlessly into the 2012b typology.

It is true that there is a limitation resulting from the limited number of databases consulted and from using restrictive search criteria. Despite this fact, the literature review, compared to the one conducted by Estellés-Arolas and González-Ladrón-de-Guevara (2012a, b), has partially revealed the development of crowdsourcing in the scientific field.

Crowdsourcing is clearly a researching field that is burgeoning, that now receives increased attention and that has passed from theoretical approaches to the systematic study of its concrete applications in a wide number of fields.

References

Ambati, V., Vogel, S., & Carbonell, J. (2012). Collaborative workflow for crowdsourcing translation. In *Proceedings of the ACM 2012 Conference on Computer Supported Cooperative Work* (pp. 1191–1194). ACM. doi:10.1145/2145204.2145382.

Armstrong, A. W., Harskamp, C. T., Cheeney, S., Wu, J., & Schupp, C. W. (2012). Power of crowdsourcing: Novel methods of data collection in psoriasis and psoriatic arthritis. *Journal of the American Academy of Dermatology*, *67*(6), 1273–1281.e9. doi:10.1016/j.jaad.2012.05.013.

Azzam, T., & Jacobson, M. R. (2013). Finding a comparison group is online crowdsourcing a viable option? *American Journal of Evaluation, 34*(3), 372–384. doi:10.1177/1098214013490223.

Bazilian, M., Rice, A., Rotich, J., Howells, M., DeCarolis, J., Macmillan, S., et al. (2012). Open source software and crowdsourcing for energy analysis. *Energy Policy, 49*, 149–153. doi:10.1016/j.enpol.2012.06.032.

Brabham, D. C. (2008). Crowdsourcing as a model for problem solving an introduction and cases. *Convergence: The International Journal of Research Into New Media Technologies*, *14*(1), 75–90.

Brabham, D. C. (2012). A model for leveraging online communities. *The participatory cultures handbook, 120*.

Brabham, D. C. (2013). *Crowdsourcing*. MIT Press, Cambridge.

Brabham, D. C., Ribisl, K. M., Kirchner, T. R., & Bernhardt, J. M. (2014a). Crowdsourcing applications for public health. *American Journal of Preventive Medicine, 46*(2), 179–187. doi:10.1016/j.amepre.2013.10.016.

Brabham, D. C., Ribisl, K. M., Kirchner, T. R., & Bernhardt, J. M. (2014b). Crowdsourcing Applications for public health. *American Journal of Preventive Medicine, 46*(2), 179–187. doi:10.1016/j.amepre.2013.10.016.

Britton, C. J., Level, A. V., & Gardner, M. A. (2013). Crowdsourcing: Divide the work and share the success. *Library Hi Tech News, 30*(4), 1–5. doi:10.1108/LHTN-03-2013-0017.

Burger-Helmchen, T., & Pénin, J. (2010). The limits of crowdsourcing inventive activities: What do transaction cost theory and the evolutionary theories of the firm teach us. In *Workshop on Open Source Innovation*, Strasbourg, France (pp. 1–26).

Chen, C., White, L., Kowalewski, T., Aggarwal, R., Lintott, C., Comstock, B., et al. (2014). Crowd-sourced assessment of technical skills: A novel method to evaluate surgical performance. *Journal of Surgical Research, 187*(1), 65–71. doi:10.1016/j.jss.2013.09.024.

Chiu, C.-M., Liang, T.-P., & Turban, E. (2014). What can crowdsourcing do for decision support? *Decision Support Systems, 65*, 40–49. doi:10.1016/j.dss.2014.05.010.

Codina, L. (1997). Una propuesta de metodología para el diseño de bases de datos documentales (parte II). *El profesional de la Información, 6*(12), 20–26.

Delgado, M. (2010). *Revisión sistemática de estudios: Metaanálisis*. Barcelona: Signo.

Demartini, G., Difallah, D. E., & Cudré-Mauroux, P. (2013a). Large-scale linked data integration using probabilistic reasoning and crowdsourcing. *The VLDB Journal, 22*(5), 665–687. doi:10.1007/s00778-013-0324-z.

Demartini, G., Difallah, D. E., & Cudré-Mauroux, P. (2013b). Large-scale linked data integration using probabilistic reasoning and crowdsourcing. *The VLDB Journal, 22*(5), 665–687. doi:10.1007/s00778-013-0324-z.

Djelassi, S., & Decoopman, I. (2013). Customers' participation in product development through crowdsourcing: Issues and implications. *Industrial Marketing Management, 42*(5), 683–692. doi:10.1016/j.indmarman.2013.05.006.

Duyck, J., Finn, C., Hutcheon, A., Vera, P., Salas, J., & Ravela, S. (2014). Sloop: A pattern retrieval engine for individual animal identification. *Pattern Recognition,*. doi:10.1016/j.patcog.2014.07.017.

Egger, M., Smith, G. D., & Altman, D. (Eds.). (2008). *Systematic reviews in health care: meta-analysis in context*. New York: Wiley.

Estellés-Arolas, E., & González-Ladrón-de-Guevara, F. (2012a). Towards an integrated crowdsourcing definition. *Journal of Information science, 38*(2), 189–200.

Estellés-Arolas, E., & González-Ladrón-De-Guevara, F. (2012b). Clasificación de iniciativas de crowdsourcing basada en tareas. *El profesional de la información, 21*(3), 283–291.

Feller, J., Finnegan, P., Hayes, J., & O'Reilly, P. (2012). 'Orchestrating' sustainable crowdsourcing: A characterisation of solver brokerages. *The Journal of Strategic Information Systems, 21*(3), 216–232. doi:10.1016/j.jsis.2012.03.002.

Filippi, F., Fusco, G., & Nanni, U. (2013). User empowerment and advanced public transport solutions. *Procedia—Social and Behavioral Sciences, 87*, 3–17. doi:10.1016/j.sbspro.2013.10.590.

Folorunso, O., & Mustapha, O. A. (2014). A fuzzy expert system to trust-based access control in crowdsourcing environments. *Applied Computing and Informatics,*. doi:10.1016/j.aci.2014.07.001.

Garrido, P., & Faria, N. (2012). MODSSO–A manager-centric global decision support system for organizations. *Procedia Technology, 5*, 616–624. doi:10.1016/j.protcy.2012.09.068.

Gatautis, R., & Vitkauskaite, E. (2014). Crowdsourcing application in marketing activities. *Procedia—Social and Behavioral Sciences, 110*, 1243–1250. doi:10.1016/j.sbspro.2013.12.971.

Geerts, S. (2009). *Discovering crowdsourcing: Theory, classification and directions for use*. Unpublished Master of Science in Innovation Management thesis, Eindhoven University of Technology.

Geiger, D., Rosemann, M., Fielt, E., & Schader, M. (2012). Crowdsourcing Information systems-definition, typology, and design. In *Proceedings of the International Conference on Information Systems (ICIS 2012)*, Atlanta, Ga.

Geiger, D., & Schader, M. (2014). Personalized task recommendation in crowdsourcing information systems—Current state of the art. *Decision Support Systems, 65*, 3–16. doi:10.1016/j.dss.2014.05.007.

Geiger, D., Seedorf, S., Schulze, T., Nickerson, R., & Schader, M. (2011). Managing the crowd: Towards a taxonomy of crowdsourcing processes. In *Proceedings of the Seventeenth Americas Conference on Information Systems.*

Ghani, A. T. A., & Zakaria, M. S. (2013). Business-IT models drive businesses towards better value delivery and profits making. *Procedia Technology, 11*, 602–607. doi:10.1016/j.protcy.2013.12.234.

Gomes, C., Schneider, D., Moraes, K., & de Souza, J. (2012). Crowdsourcing for music: Survey and taxonomy. In *IEEE International Conference on Systems, Man, and Cybernetics (SMC)* (pp. 832–839). IEEE, October 2012.

Gupta, D. K., & Sharma, V. (2013). Exploring crowdsourcing: A viable solution towards achieving rapid and qualitative tasks. *Library Hi Tech News, 30*(2), 14–20. doi:10.1108/LHTN-01-2013-0002.

Harvey, D., Kitching, T. D., Noah-Vanhoucke, J., Hamner, B., Salimans, T., & Pires, A. M. (2014). Observing dark worlds: A crowdsourcing experiment for dark matter mapping. *Astronomy and Computing, 5*, 35–44. doi:10.1016/j.ascom.2014.04.003.

Hildebrand, M., Ahumada, C., & Watson, S. (2013). CrowdOutAIDS: Crowdsourcing youth perspectives for action. *Reproductive Health Matters, 21*(41), 57–68. doi:10.1016/S0968-8080(13)41687-7.

Howe, J. (2006). The rise of crowdsourcing. *Wired Magazine, 14*(6), 1–4.

Howe, J. (2008). *Crowdsourcing: How the power of the crowd is driving the future of business.* New York: Random House.

Kalantari, M., Rajabifard, A., Olfat, H., & Williamson, I. (2014). Geospatial metadata 2.0—An approach for volunteered geographic information. *Computers, Environment and Urban Systems, 48*, 35–48. doi:10.1016/j.compenvurbsys.2014.06.005.

King, A. J., Gehl, R. W., Grossman, D., & Jensen, J. D. (2013a). Skin self-examinations and visual identification of atypical nevi: Comparing individual and crowdsourcing approaches. *Cancer Epidemiology, 37*(6), 979–984. doi:10.1016/j.canep.2013.09.004.

King, A. J., Gehl, R. W., Grossman, D., & Jensen, J. D. (2013b). Skin self-examinations and visual identification of atypical nevi: Comparing individual and crowdsourcing approaches. *Cancer Epidemiology, 37*(6), 979–984. doi:10.1016/j.canep.2013.09.004.

Kleemann, F., Voß, G. G., & Rieder, K. (2008). Un (der) paid innovators: The commercial utilization of consumer work through crowdsourcing. *Science, Technology & Innovation Studies, 4*(1), 5.

Lampe, C., Zube, P., Lee, J., Park, C. H., & Johnston, E. (2014). Crowdsourcing civility: A natural experiment examining the effects of distributed moderation in online forums. *Government Information Quarterly, 31*(2), 317–326. doi:10.1016/j.giq.2013.11.005.

Linders, D. (2012a). From e-government to we-government: Defining a typology for citizen coproduction in the age of social media. *Government Information Quarterly, 29*(4), 446–454. doi:10.1016/j.giq.2012.06.003.

Linders, D. (2012b). From e-government to we-government: Defining a typology for citizen coproduction in the age of social media. *Government Information Quarterly, 29*(4), 446–454.

Littmann, M., & Suomela, T. (2014). Crowdsourcing, the great meteor storm of 1833, and the founding of meteor science. *Endeavour, 38*(2), 130–138. doi:10.1016/j.endeavour.2014.03.002.

Marjanovic, S., Fry, C., & Chataway, J. (2012). Crowdsourcing based business models: In search of evidence for innovation 2.0. *Science and Public Policy, 39*(3), 318–332. doi:10.1093/scipol/scs009.

Monahan, T., & Mokos, J. T. (2013). Crowdsourcing urban surveillance: The development of homeland security markets for environmental sensor networks. *Geoforum, 49*, 279–288. doi:10.1016/j.geoforum.2013.02.001.

Parvanta, C., Roth, Y., & Keller, H. (2013). Crowdsourcing 101 a few basics to make you the leader of the pack. *Health Promotion Practice, 14*(2), 163–167. doi:10.1177/1524839912470654.

Pedersen, J., Kocsis, D., Tripathi, A., Tarrell, A., Weerakoon, A., Tahmasbi, N., et al. (2013). *Conceptual foundations of crowdsourcing: A review of is research* (pp. 579–588). IEEE. doi:10.1109/HICSS.2013.143.

Perera, I., & Perera, P. A. (2014). Developments and leanings of crowdsourcing industry: Implications of China and India. *Industrial and Commercial Training, 46*(2), 92–99. doi:10.1108/ICT-06-2013-0038.

Petitti, D. B. (2000). *Meta-analysis, decision analysis and cost-effectiveness analysis*. New York: Oxford University Press.

Pinto-Molina, M., Alonso-Berrocal, J. L., Doucer, A., et al. (2007). Análisis cualitativo de la visibilidad de la investigación de las universidades españolas a través de sus páginas web. *Revista española de documentación científica, 27*(3), 345–370.

Raford, N. (2014a). Online foresight platforms: Evidence for their impact on scenario planning and strategic foresight. *Technological Forecasting and Social Change,*. doi:10.1016/j.techfore.2014.03.008.

Raford, N. (2014b). Online foresight platforms: Evidence for their impact on scenario planning and strategic foresight. *Technological Forecasting and Social Change,*. doi:10.1016/j.techfore.2014.03.008.

Rana, R., Chou, C. T., Bulusu, N., Kanhere, S., & Hu, W. (2014). Ear-phone: a context-aware noise mapping using smart phones. *Pervasive and Mobile Computing,*. doi:10.1016/j.pmcj.2014.02.001.

Reichwald, R., & Piller, F. (2006). *Interaktive wertschöpfung. Open innovation, individualisierung und neue formen der arbeitsteilung*. Wiesbaden: Gabler Verlag.

Ren, J., Nickerson, J. V., Mason, W., Sakamoto, Y., & Graber, B. (2014). Increasing the crowd's capacity to create: How alternative generation affects the diversity, relevance and effectiveness of generated ads. *Decision Support Systems, 65*, 28–39. doi:10.1016/j.dss.2014.05.009.

Roopa, T., Iyer, A. N., & Rangaswamy, S. (2013). *CroTIS-Crowdsourcing based traffic information system* (pp. 271–277). IEEE. doi:10.1109/BigData.Congress.2013.43.

Rovere, A., Raymo, M. E., O'Leary, M. J., & Hearty, P. J. (2012). Crowdsourcing in the quaternary sea level community: insights from the Pliocene. *Quaternary Science Reviews, 56*, 164–166. doi:10.1016/j.quascirev.2012.09.014.

Satzger, B., Psaier, H., Schall, D., & Dustdar, S. (2013a). Auction-based crowdsourcing supporting skill management. *Information Systems, 38*(4), 547–560. doi:10.1016/j.is.2012.09.003.

Satzger, B., Psaier, H., Schall, D., & Dustdar, S. (2013b). Auction-based crowdsourcing supporting skill management. *Information Systems, 38*(4), 547–560. doi:10.1016/j.is.2012.09.003.

Schenk, E., & Guittard, C. (2009). *Crowdsourcing: What can be crowdsourced to the Crowd and Why?*. Technical Report.

Schriner, A., & Oerther, D. (2014). No really, (crowd) work is the silver bullet. *Procedia Engineering, 78*, 224–228. doi:10.1016/j.proeng.2014.07.060.

Schumaker, R. P. (2013). Machine learning the harness track: Crowdsourcing and varying race history. *Decision Support Systems, 54*(3), 1370–1379. doi:10.1016/j.dss.2012.12.013.

See, L., Schepaschenko, D., Lesiv, M., McCallum, I., Fritz, S., & Comber, A. (2014). Building a hybrid land cover map with crowdsourcing and geographically weighted regression. *ISPRS Journal of Photogrammetry and Remote Sensing,*. doi:10.1016/j.isprsjprs.2014.06.016.

Soleymani, M., & Larson, M. (2013). *Crowdsourcing for multimedia research* (pp. 1111–1112). ACM Press, New York. doi:10.1145/2502081.2502234.

Sprugnoli, R., Moretti, G., Fuoli, M., Giuliani, D., Bentivogli, L., Pianta, E., et al. (2013). Comparing two methods for crowdsourcing speech transcription. In *IEEE International Conference on Acoustics, Speech and Signal Processing (ICASSP)* (pp. 8116–8120), May 2013. IEEE. doi:10.1109/ICASSP.2013.6639246.

Stanley, C., Winschiers-Theophilus, H., Onwordi, M., & Kapuire, G. K. (2013). *Rural communities crowdsource technology development: A Namibian expedition* (pp. 155–158). ACM Press, New York. doi:10.1145/2517899.2517930.

Stol, K.-J., & Fitzgerald, B. (2014). Two's company, three's a crowd: A case study of crowdsourcing software development (pp. 187–198). ACM Press, New York. doi:10.1145/2568225.2568249.

Su, A. I., Good, B. M., & van Wijnen, A. J. (2013). Gene wiki reviews: Marrying crowdsourcing with traditional peer review. *Gene, 531*(2), 125. doi:10.1016/j.gene.2013.08.093.

Sutherlin, G. (2013). A voice in the crowd: Broader implications for crowdsourcing translation during crisis. *Journal of Information Science, 39*(3), 397–409. doi:10.1177/0165551512471593.

Tatarkiewicz, W. (1980). A history of six ideas-an essay in aesthetics. Springer, New York. ISBN:90-247-2233-0.

Tong, Y., Cao, C. C., & Chen, L. (2014). TCS: Efficient topic discovery over crowd-oriented service data (pp. 861–870). ACM Press, New York. doi:10.1145/2623330.2623647.

Wu, B., Zhong, E., Tan, B., Horner, A., & Yang, Q. (2014). Crowdsourced time-sync video tagging using temporal and personalized topic modeling (pp. 721–730). ACM Press, New York. doi:10.1145/2623330.2623625.

Zeinalipour-Yazti, D., Laoudias, C., Costa, C., Vlachos, M., Andreou, M. I., & Gunopulos, D. (2013). Crowdsourced trace similarity with smartphones. *IEEE Transactions on Knowledge and Data Engineering, 25*(6), 1240–1253. doi:10.1109/TKDE.2012.55.

Chapter 4
Crowdsourcing and the Evolution of a Business Ecosystem

Claude Guittard, Eric Schenk and Thierry Burger-Helmchen

Abstract This chapter explores a specific implementation of ideation-oriented crowdsourcing. In the follow-up of previous studies, we consider that ideation crowdsourcing does not necessarily mobilize highly skilled technical competences, but rather the ability of individuals to generate new ideas. Typical applications of ideation or creative crowdsourcing are artistic design activities. One can thus wonder about the role of creative crowdsourcing in the innovation process, upstream from the problem-solving steps. In this paper, we address this issue within a particular context: the evolution of an ecosystem based on an ICT platform. This chapter relies on a case study: Parkeon, a company specialized in the development and manufacture of multi-space parking meters, ran two crowdsourcing competitions in parallel, designed to uncover new ideas for services based on the use of multi-space meters. The case study highlights the convergence between certain conditions for the success of crowdsourcing and the factors contributing to the development of a BE: openness and modularity. Furthermore, it accentuates the role of users, who become the providers of new service concepts, and confirms the central role of the company leader for the development of the BE. Last, we discuss the not-invented-here (NIH) syndrome that can be encountered when crowdsourcing is implemented.

Keywords Crowdsourcing · Knowledge management · Modularization of knowledge · Leadership · Smart city · Creativity

C. Guittard (✉) · T. Burger-Helmchen
BETA-CNRS, University of Strasbourg, Strasbourg, France
e-mail: guittard@unistra.fr

T. Burger-Helmchen
e-mail: burger@unistra.fr

E. Schenk
BETA-CNRS, National Institute of Applied Sciences, Strasbourg, France
e-mail: eric.schenk@insa-strasbourg.fr

F.J. Garrigos-Simon et al. (eds.), *Advances in Crowdsourcing*,
DOI 10.1007/978-3-319-18341-1_4

4.1 Introduction

Crowdsourcing was first described by Jeff Howe in 2006 and in recent years has led to numerous publications. This term is a contraction of the words crowd and outsourcing. Its meaning is thus relatively explicit:

> Simply defined, crowdsourcing represents the act of a company or institution taking a function once performed by employees and outsourcing it to an undefined (and generally large) network of people in the form of an open call. This can take the form of peer-production (when the job is performed collaboratively), but is also often undertaken by sole individuals. The crucial prerequisite is the use of the open call format and the large network of potential laborers. (Howe 2006)

Some crowdsourcing platforms such as InnoCentive are experiencing spectacular results, not only in terms of the number of participants, but also in their success rate in crowdsourcing competitions.[1] The enthusiasm for this approach, in the scope of Web 2.0, calls for clarification of the concept and has led to various proposed taxonomies (Brabham 2012; Burger-Helmchen and Pénin 2011; Estellés-Arolas and González-Ladrón-de-Guevara 2012; Schenk and Guittard 2011, 2012). As pointed out by Estelles-Arolas and González-Ladrón-de Guevara (2012), the highly flexible nature of crowdsourcing allows it to take on various different forms.

Crowdsourcing allows a company to gain access to skills that are far removed from its core business activities. For Afuah and Tucci (2012), crowdsourcing's performance in a context of distant search depends on several factors:

- The characteristics of the problem,
- The characteristics of the knowledge needed to solve it,
- The characteristics of the crowd,
- The evaluation of solutions,
- Access to ICT.

Crowdsourcing is an exploration mode in the sense expressed by March (1991), and one of its natural applications is to deal with the solving of complex problems (Brabham 2008; Lakhani and Jeppesen 2007). This crowdsourcing approach makes use of the outside-in aspects of open innovation (Chesbrough 2003). A second application of this phenomenon, which has been scarcely studied in the literature, is ideation itself (Schenk and Guittard 2011, 2012). This concerns situations in which a business consults the crowd for creative ideas, in the field of design for example. In the follow-up of our previous studies, we consider this type of crowdsourcing to no longer be positioned in the register of problem solving, but rather in that of the emergence of new ideas. Creative crowdsourcing does not necessarily mobilize highly skilled technical competences, but rather the ability of individuals to ideate, and as a consequence is relevant to an extremely broadly defined crowd.

[1] http://www.innocentive.com/about-innocentive/facts-stats.

Typical applications of creative crowdsourcing are artistic design activities. One can thus wonder about the role of creative crowdsourcing in the innovation process, upstream from the problem-solving steps. In this paper, we address this issue within a particular context: the evolution of an ecosystem based on an ICT platform.

The method used in this study is that of a case study: Parkeon, a company specialized in the development and manufacture of multi-space parking meters, ran two crowdsourcing competitions in parallel, designed to uncover new ideas for services based on the use of multi-space meters. The remainder of this paper is organized as follows: Sect. 4.2 provides a theoretical outline of the concepts surrounding a business ecosystem (BE). Section 4.3 presents the methodology used and the studied case. Finally, in Sect. 4.4, we propose our analysis of this case.

4.2 Business Ecosystems

The notion of a BE, introduced by James Moore in the mid 1990s, is based on an analogy with biological ecosystems. This concept makes it possible to account for the development of inter-business relationships, which extend beyond momentary cooperation, to create deeper bonds. Thus, starting from the pioneering work of Moore (1996), Torrès-Blay (2000) defined the BE concept as "a heterogeneous coalition of companies from different industries forming a strategic community of interests or values, structured as a network, around a leader who succeeds in imposing or sharing its business vision or its technological standard."

This BE concept has been widely studied and used in Management Science literature (Attour and Ayerbe 2012; Gueguen and Torrès 2004; Moore 2006; Iansiti and Levien 2004; Loilier and Malherbe 2012; Teece 2007) or, more rarely, has been treated from the theoretical point of view (Koenig 2012). Starting from this set of studies and the definition presented here, we are of the opinion that BE is characterized by two fundamental elements: a technological standard and a network.

The appearance of a technological standard is both the cause and the consequence of the creation of a platform characteristic of BEs. As defined by Koenig (2012), "the design (or layout) is controlled by an actor who, according to rules specified ex ante, makes a key asset available to other actors, so that they can develop their own activity." Moore (2006) also insists on the open and modular nature of this platform. The starting point of a BE is thus a leading business which proposes a platform, although this project can lead to an ecosystem only if it allows others to share this platform. The second fundamental element can then be created: the network.

The notion of business network takes on an entirely new form of importance in the present day, especially in the field of innovation (Nooteboom 2004). This is clearly revealed by Loilier and Malherbe (2012) in their research into the genesis of BEs. They compare this with the more recent concept of open innovation

(Chesbrough 2003) which, although centered on innovation, also reveals the importance of the network's openness. By referring to the pioneering work of Moore (1993), they insist on the diverse phases of the process leading to the development of a BE. Their research is original in that it takes a close look at the genesis of a BE, by mobilizing the dynamic capabilities approach of Teece (2007).

Although the notion of dynamic capability is central to the emergence of a BE, the development of these ecosystems should be associated with the growing importance of digital technology (Gueguen and Torrès 2004). Here, we make the assumption that it is this digital technology that allows BE platforms to become modular and open.

For the leading business, the development of a BE has a strategic dimension and is part of its innovation strategy. In particular, for this company, the identification of partners and activities surrounding the platform depends, at least partially, on exploration in the sense described by March (1991): The stakes are related not only to the selection of partners or complementary activities within an existing base, but also to the need to develop a network of actors and new activities.

In this paper, we investigate a specific aspect of innovation within a BE: the provision of new services. This question was studied by Attour and Ayerbe (2012), through the use of a dual analysis: the theory of BEs and the C/K theory proposed by Le Masson et al. (2010). This theory of innovative design describes innovation as the outcome of the expansion of the concept space (C) and the expansion of the knowledge space (K). When applied to the emergence of a new service, concept space is related to the full set of offered services (Attour and Ayerbe 2012). According to Lenfle (2005), the knowledge space associated with the emergence of a new service is composed of 6 dimensions:

- The types of targeted users;
- The support product;
- The front-office process centered on the management of interactions with the customer;
- The back-office process allowing the service to be delivered;
- A contract defining the reciprocal commitments of the supplier and the beneficiary;
- An economic model for financing of the service.

One of the characteristics of crowdsourcing is indeed that it allows solutions or ideas to be explored through an open call over the Internet. In the remaining sections of this paper, we analyze the role of crowdsourcing in the emergence of new services within an ICT platform ecosystem.

4.3 The Case Study

4.3.1 Methodology

The decision to use a case study (Yin 2009) for our research can be explained in two ways. Firstly, in a constructivist approach, we attempt, via the detailed analysis of a phenomenon, to infer various elements in order to enrich the existing theories. Secondly, we were able to access the particularly rich data corresponding to a specific case: the Parkeon company, member of the "Véhicule du future" competitiveness cluster in France, which implemented two crowdsourcing strategies in parallel. The case study provides us with particularly detailed information concerning the process and its success, as perceived by the company.

Our work began in the autumn of 2013, and data were recorded in several manners. Firstly, interviews with the project leader from the company (2 telephone interviews lasting 1 h each), and with the project leader from the VdF competitiveness cluster (1 telephone interview and a face-to-face interview, each lasting one and a half hours), allowed us to gain detailed insight into the context and the implemented strategies. We were then able to access the qualitative and quantitative elements of analysis produced by the participants, following the crowdsourcing competitions. Finally, we appraised the various documents concerning the Parkeon competition, published on the Internet (Table 4.1).

4.3.2 Presentation of the Case

For 40 years, the Parkeon company has been specialized in the design and manufacture of transportation payment terminals and multi-space meters. The company has more than 1000 employees throughout the world and in 2013 had a turnover of

Table 4.1 Webs pages consulted

List of Web pages
– http://www.clustercrowd.ch/en/
– http://www.clustercrowd.ch/en/projects/Parkeon-Cluster-Contest
– https://clustercrowd.atizo.com/projects/ideas/2237/stellen-sie-sich-einen-parkautomaten-vor-den-sie-m/
– http://cordis.europa.eu/projects/rcn/101331_en.html
– http://www.future-mobility.eu/
– http://www.parkeon.com/
– http://www.parking-net.com/parking-industry-blog/parkeon/parking-meter
– http://www.vehiculedufutur.com/
– http://www.vehiculedufutur.com/lettre/64/

185 M Euros (of which 85 % was from exportation) with more than 200,000 multi-space meters installed in the world, including large cities such as New York, Paris, and Madrid. Parkeon is thus one of the leaders in its industrial sector.

4.3.2.1 Multi-space Meters as BE Platforms

Thanks to their primary function, multi-space meters are positioned at the center of a BE, including the parking management operator (which can be a public or private sector organization) and the payment service provider (banks and other payment intermediaries). There is a need for this ecosystem to evolve, for example, through the emergence of contactless payment solutions. In a context of smart city development (Komninos et al. 2013), the embedded technologies currently used in multi-space meters provide new development opportunities for this BE. Thus, one of Parkeon's strategic orientations is to open its platform, with the aim of allowing it to include new service providers.

The development of a BE around the multi-space meter raises several questions for Parkeon: Which services should be built into the ecosystem? Who are the potential service providers? In 2013, Parkeon introduced two Crowdsourcing competitions designed to tackle these questions.

4.3.2.2 The Parkeon Pulse Your City Project

The Parkeon Pulse Your City project resulted from the convergence of interests expressed by various stakeholders. On the one hand, these included the representatives of the European ELMO project (ELectroMObility solutions for cities and regions[2]): the Vehicle of the future competitiveness cluster, Atizo, Mundi, and the ICT cluster from Berne. On the other hand, the Parkeon company was looking for service concepts that could be implemented through the use of multi-space meters. The aim of the Parkeon Pulse your City project was thus to organize a competition open to the general public, to envision new services associated with the company's multi-space meters. In practice, the technologies embedded into multi-space meters allow new ICT services to be included the following: making a payment, printing a ticket or a coupon, consulting or providing information over the Internet, or even controlling other physical objects.

The Parkeon Pulse your City project was effectively launched in April 2013, through the use of two distinct crowdsourcing competitions.

- The first competition (General public competition) was publicized on the Atizo Crowdsourcing platform, for a total expected duration of 5 months, including the preparation, the competition itself (4 weeks), and selection of the winners.

[2]Project with a total budget of 2.2 M Euros for the period 2011–2014, co-financed by the European Union's 7th FPRD.

The participants' assignment was expressed in very general terms: "Imagine a multi-space meter that you like—if this multi-space meter was converted to an interactive kiosk, which applications and services should it offer?" The total compensation paid to the winners was 2000 Euros. Finally, Atizo's general conditions were applied during this competition.

- A second competition, intended for professionals from the ICT sector only (ICT cluster competition), was publicized via a proprietary crowdsourcing platform from Mundi Consulting, for a total expected duration of 9 months. The competition was designed to take place in three phases: an initial phase open to all ICT service providers, a second concept development phase, and a final phase during which from 3 to 8 finalists would be required to present their ideas to a jury, during the European mobility week. During the first phase, the following was expected of the participants: a short description with an explanation totaling 1000 characters, description of the business model, and presentation of graphical interface. The partners developed the general conditions relevant to all aspects of intellectual property arising from this competition.

A posteriori, the partners' evaluation of the two competitions was irrevocable: With a total of 479 ideas of which 17, proposed by 13 participants, received an award, the general public project was considered to be "totally successful," whereas the project intended for ICT service providers was a failure, since no proposals were received. Following this competitive process, a questionnaire was sent to all potential applicants, to find an explanation for their absence from the competition. Forty-one replies were received, revealing various reasons for their non-participation: The project was not relevant for the service company, the general conditions were too complex, the allocated time was too short, etc.

Table 4.2 summarizes the main elements differentiating the general public and dedicated ICT service provider competitions.

Table 4.2 The *Parkeon pulse your city* project competitions

	General public competition	ICT cluster competition
Public	General public	ICI service providers
Expected outcome	General ideas	Detailed description of the service du service
Participants' rewards	2000 Euros shared among winners	Winner: commercial implementation Finalist: présentation lors de la semaine de la mobilité
Diffusion	Atizo: general platform	Clustercrowd: specific platform
Outcome	479 proposals—17 rewarded ideas	0

4.4 Analysis and Discussion

The two Parkeon competitions are aligned with a methodology for the development of an existing BE, built around the multi-space meter platform, since the aim was to uncover ideas for third-party services, based on the Parkeon multi-space meter.

For Parkeon, crowdsourcing offered two advantages:

- With the general public competition, the aim was to mobilize a large number of potential users, in order to uncover the greatest possible number of ideas for new services.
- In the case of the ICT service providers, the aim was not only to uncover ideas for new services, but also to identify potential partners for the implementation of such services. In fact, this competition was characterized by certain features typical of a call for projects, designed to reveal the skills of potential partners that could be beneficial for the development of the BE.

4.4.1 Mobilized Knowledge: Comparative Analysis of the Competition

The first step of our analysis involves comparing the two competitions, in terms of the nature of the knowledge mobilized by the participants. For the general public competition, the brief expression of new ideas mobilizes the experiential knowledge of the user, associated with the creative aptitude of individuals (Amabile 1988). The generic nature of these skills translates into the existence of a major base of potential respondents. As this has to do with an ideation process, the questions are not asked in terms of the complexity or implicit character of knowledge. The ideation is associated with personal experience and the users' individual needs. One thus encounters one of the principles of innovation by users, defined by von Hippel (1988, 2005). In this context, crowdsourcing takes on its full meaning.

For the ICT service provider competition, the requirements expressed by Parkeon were related to the conditions for the system's future implementation (detailed description of the concept, business model, and graphical interface). Participation in this competition implies both an ideation capacity (to propose a new concept) and the mobilization of professional skills for the design of ICT services (Lenfle 2005). Without necessarily being complex, it is relatively time-consuming to mobilize the skills needed to develop a proposal.

4.4.2 Service Innovation Within a BE

Intrinsically, the multi-space meters lie at the center of a BE, which comprises various actors whose activities are centered on the management of parking. The development of technologies embedded into multi-space meters and their growing connectivity with the Web or even other physical objects offers almost unlimited prospects for the innovation of services within the BE. The literature dealing with BEs emphasizes the importance of openness and modularity as evolutionary factors in these ecosystems. The Parkeon case is in line with this logic, since the company is seeking to make its platform available to digital service providers. As a remote research tool (Afuah and Tucci 2012), crowdsourcing appears to be particularly well adapted to support the expansion of the concept and knowledge spaces, required for the innovation of services (Attour and Ayerbe 2012; Lenfle 2005).

The general public competition is considered to have been a success, since the foreseen awards were granted for ideas related to new services. The implementation of a service proposed by crowdsourcing—that of producing commercial coupons with multi-space meters—is moreover now an ongoing project in Parkeon. This crowdsourcing competition thus contributes to innovation in services and to the evolution of the BE assembled around the Parkeon platform. Paradoxically, although this competition enabled the emergence of new concepts that are useful for the BE's evolution, it did not provide Parkeon with the necessary knowledge for their implementation. Using the terminology of Le Masson et al. (2010) in the context of the C/K theory, this competition generated growth in the concept space. However, the implementation of service ideas requires a knowledge acquisition step (for example, the search for possible partners, evaluation of projects), which is partially disconnected from the crowdsourcing competition. In other words, the crowdsourcing was a success, but the implementation of its results required an increased level of knowledge at Parkeon. The relevance of crowdsourcing is thus placed far upstream in the evolutionary dynamics of the BE: the identification of new concepts.

On the other hand, the ICT service provider competition, which was similar to a call for projects, was designed to mobilize and identify potential service providers. In a certain sense, this competition was intended to generate concepts, but also to reinforce knowledge growth activities. In spirit, the project was intended to bring forward new concepts, but also technico-commercial studies, market research, and of course BE partners. By encouraging the expansion of not only its concept space, but also its knowledge space, for Parkeon, the returns from this competition were potentially greater than those derived from the general public competition.

We interpret the comparative success of the two competitions as the outcome of two different phenomena. On the one hand, due to its nature, crowdsourcing is better adapted to the production of knowledge bricks (modules, tasks) than to the design of knowledge brick systems (Afuah and Tucci 2012; Pénin and Burger-Helmchen 2012; Schenk and Guittard 2011, 2012). On the other hand, the dynamics of a BE are related mainly to the notions of modularity and networks. By inviting a large number of individuals to contribute to the production of ideas and concepts, the general public competition responds both to a fundamental criterion of crowdsourcing and to a factor contributing to the development of the BE. The ideas and concepts indeed correspond to "elementary bricks" of knowledge, which are simply the first elements in a project for the implementation of a new service.

On the other hand, the ICT service provider competition was designed to yield near "turnkey" solutions for Parkeon and to help identify relevant service providers.

The case of Parkeon provides us with input concerning crowdsourcing as a tool for the innovation of BE services around an ICT platform. It turns out that openness and modularity are factors contributing to the success of a crowdsourcing initiative, as well as determinants in the development of a BE.

The case of Parkeon also confirms and complements two results related to the innovation of services in a BE (Attour and Ayerbe 2012). The first of these has to do with the role of the user in the development of a BE. Crowdsourcing is in line with this logic, since it allows potential users to express their needs and desires. The second has to do with the role of the pivot company in the development of the BE. Although Parkeon occupies a leading position within the BE, as a consequence of its expertize in the technologies used for multi-space meters, it is also a driving force in the emergence of new services. Crowdsourcing simplifies this role insofar as interactions with the contributors is externalized to a crowdsourcing platform, using relatively standard procedures.

4.4.3 The Not-Invented-Here Syndrome

Crowdsourcing has been the center of numerous academic studies in recent years. Yet only a few, if any, address the internal management dimensions of crowdsourcing: How to integrate new knowledge or ideas made outside the firm?

Blohm et al. (2013) are interested in the absorptive capacity of firms when they use crowdsourcing to gather ideas and information. The absorptive capacity of the firm allows her to transform the information obtained by crowdsourced knowledge and draw a project. Thus, the absorption capacity of the company depends on the routines that the company has put in place to assess the ideas, diffuse it, and assimilate it (Cohen and Levinthal 1990; Teece 2007).

Besides, the use of crowdsourcing can be interpreted as defiance from the manager toward the internal research ream of the firm or recognition of their inability to find an adequate solution. Management therefore faces the not-invented-here (NIH) syndrome,[3] which is a negative attitude toward knowledge from outside the company boundaries (Lichtenthaler and Ernst 2006; Lichtenthaler et al. 2010; Burcharth et al. 2014). The NIH syndrome leads to the non-utilization or under-utilization of outside knowledge and may have negative consequences on the performance of the company (Katz and Allen 1982; Lichtenthaler and Ernst 2006).

Not only researchers can be exposed to NIH, the managers can also reject solutions coming from outside. The negative attitude of managers toward external

[3]Some authors consider also the opposite situation, a strong attraction toward products and knowledge produce elsewhere, this also can have negative consequences for the firm (Menon and Pfeffer 2003).

knowledge can be explained by the following factors: (a) their belief in their own skills and knowledge, (b) belief in the negative impact of external knowledge on the performance of the company, (c) the fear of a negative impact on their career, (d) adoption of technology produced internally or knowledge that a scientist has developed is a career booster that allows upward mobility in the hierarchy; this method of promotion would disappear, and (e) fear, if type of practice becomes widespread, that a reduction of staff dedicated to the research is establishing or restoring the balance between research and applied research takes place.

The NIH syndrome is a negative attitude toward external knowledge. In a business context, individual attitudes are shaped by the culture, norms, values, and organization-specific routines. Attitude is a major concern for managers because it guides the processing of information and knowledge (Cohendet and Llerena 1999) and influences the behavior of individuals. In general, individuals seek and approve the information and knowledge that are consistent with their past attitudes. They attach more importance and credibility to this type of information. When employees feel threatened by outside ideas, they have a tendency to denigrate them in order to promote internal ideas. Reitzig and Sorenson (2010) speak of "provincialism" of knowledge.

The simplest way to increase the acceptance of a solution that comes from crowdsourcing is to integrate the various individuals who will implement it. More generally, Lichtenthaler and Ernst (2006) list the following tactics that help reducing NIH syndrome:

- All persons involved in the integration of external knowledge should be involved in the process of decision making.
- The presence of a "Gatekeeper" a "leader" is a very important element.
- Conversely, it is conceivable to cut all links between users and producers of knowledge so that no one knows the real origin of the solutions or to blend the external solution with internal knowledge in order to hide the external proposition.
- Find a way to prove the superiority of radical external solution (Menon and Pfeffer 2003).

In the Parkeon case, the crowdsourcing project barely suffered from a NIH syndrome. Internally, the project leader has the characteristics of an intrapreneur (Burgelmann 1983) with large autonomy, legitimacy, and hierarchy support. Several persons form the company were involved in the follow-up of the project, including in the selection of the winning ideas. These ideas did not imply a radical breakthrough for the company. Rather, they converged with ideas already existing within Parkeon, but in a diffused an unrevealed manner.

4.5 Conclusion

Through the use of a case study, we have attempted to understand how creative crowdsourcing can contribute to the development of a BE based on an ICT platform.

In 2013, the Parkeon company launched two crowdsourcing competitions. The knowledge activated through participation in these two competitions was quite different: knowledge through use for the general public competition and professional skills in the case of the ICT service providers' competition. It is revealing to interpret this case in the light of the C/K theory: The general public competition, considered as a success, is associated with the emergence of new concepts. Implementation of the concepts proposed during this competition relies on the acquisition of knowledge, which raises the issue of optimizing the use of knowledge acquired via crowdsourcing. The ICT service providers' competition, which was expected to contribute both concepts and knowledge, was undeniably a failure.

This case study highlights the convergence between certain conditions for the success of crowdsourcing and the factors contributing to the development of a BE: openness and modularity. Furthermore, it accentuates the role of users, who become the providers of new service concepts, and confirms the central role of the company leader for the development of the BE.

The phenomenon described here is part of a strategic vision of knowledge, with the latter being one of the key elements in the innovation process. Complementary aspects which should be further studied in future research include, on the one hand, the absorptive capacities (Cohen and Levinthal 1990) acquired through crowdsourcing and, on the other hand, the relationship between crowdsourcing and dynamic capabilities (Teece et al. 1997).

References

Afuah, A., & Tucci, C. L. (2012). Crowdsourcing as a solution to distant search. *Academy of Management Review, 37*(3), 355–375.

Amabile, T. M. (1988). A model of creativity and innovation in organizations. *Research in Organizational Behaviour, 10*, 123–167.

Attour, A., & Ayerbe, C. (2012). Connaissances et innovation au sein des écosystèmes d'affaires. Le cas des services mobiles. *Revue Française de Gestion, 221*(2), 77–94.

Blohm, I., Leimeister, J. M., & Krcmar, H. (2013). Crowdsourcing: how to benefit from (Too) many great ideas. *MIS Quarterly Executive, 12*(4), 199–211.

Brabham, D. (2008). Crowdsourcing as a model for problem solving: An introduction and cases. *Convergence, The International Journal of Research into New Media Technologies, 14*(1), 75–90.

Brabham, D. (2012). A model for leveraging online communities. In A. Delwiche & J. Henderson (Eds.), *The participatory cultures handbook* (pp. 120–129). New York: Routledge.

Burcharth, A., Knudsen, M., & Søndergaard, H. (2014). Neither invented nor shared here: The impact and management of attitudes for the adoption of open innovation practices. *Technovation, 34*(3), 149–161.

Burgelman, R. A. (1983). Corporate entrepreneurship and strategic management: An insight from a process study. *Management Science, 29*, 1349–1365.
Burger-Helmchen T., & Pénin J. (2011). Crowdsourcing: définition, enjeux, typologie, Management & Avenir, janvier-février, pp 254–269.
Chesbrough, H. (2003). *Open innovation: The new imperative for creating and profiting from technology*. Harvard Business School: Boston, MA.
Cohen, W. M., & Levinthal, D. A. (1990). Absorptive capacity: a new perspective on learning and innovation. *Administrative Science Quarterly, 35*, 128–152.
Cohendet, P., & Llerena, P. (1999). La conception de la firme comme processeur de connaissances. *Revue d'Economie Industrielle, 88*, 211–235.
Estellés-Arolas, E., & González-Ladrón-de-Guevara, F. (2012). Towards an integrated crowdsourcing definition. *Journal of Information Science, 38*, 189–200.
Gueguen, G., & Torrès, O. (2004). La dynamique concurrentielle des écosystèmes d'affaires – Linux contre Microsoft. *Revue Française de Gestion, 148*, 227–248.
Howe, J. (2006). The rise of crowdsourcing. *Wired, 14*(6), 1–4.
Iansiti, M., & Levien, R. (2004). Strategy as ecology. *Harvard Business Review Mars*, 68–78.
Katz, R., & Allen, T. J. (1982). Investigating the not-invented-here (NIH) syndrome: A look at performance, tenure and communication patterns of 50 R&D project groups. *R&D Management, 12*, 7–19.
Koenig, G. (2012). Le concept d'écosystème d'affaires revisité. *M@n@gement, 15*(2), 208–224.
Komninos, N., Pallot, M., & Schaffers, H. (2013). Special issue on smart cities and the future internet in Europe. *Journal of the Knowledge Economy, 4*(2), 119–134.
Lakhani, K. R., & Jeppesen, L. B. (2007). Getting unusual suspects to solve R&D puzzles. *Harvard Business Review, 85*(5), 30–32.
Le Masson, P., Weil, B., & Hatchuel, A. (2010). *Strategic management of innovation and design*. Cambridge: Cambridge University Press.
Lenfle, S. (2005). L'innovation dans les services : les apports de la théorie de la conception. *Économies et Sociétés, 39*, 11–12.
Lichtenthaler, U., & Ernst, H. (2006). Attitudes to externally organising knowledge management tasks: A review, reconsideration and extension of the NIH syndrome. *R&D Management, 36* (4), 367–386.
Lichtenthaler, U., Holger, E., & Martin, H. (2010). Not-sold-here: How attitudes influence external knowledge exploitation. *Organization Science, 21*(5), 1054–1071.
Loilier, T., & Malherbe, M. (2012). Le développement des compétences écosystémiques: Le cas de l'ESA émergent des services mobiles sans contact. *Revue Française de Gestion, 222*, 89–105.
March, J. G. (1991). Exploration and exploitation in organizational learning. *Organization Science, 2*(1), 71–87.
Menon, T., & Pfeffer, J. (2003). Valuing internal vs. external knowledge: Explaining the preference for outsiders. *Management Science, 49*, 497–513.
Moore, J. F. (1993). Predators and prey: A new ecology of competition. *Harvard Business Review, 71*(3), 75–86.
Moore, J. F. (1996). *The death of competition: Leadership and strategy in the age of business ecosystems*. New York: HarperCollins.
Moore, J. F. (2006). Business ecosystems and the view from the firm. *The Antitrust Bulletin, 51*(1), 31–75.
Nooteboom, B. (2004). *Inter-firm collaboration, learning and networks*. London: Routledge.
Pénin, J., & Burger-Helmchen, T. (2012). Crowdsourcing d'activités inventives et frontières des organisations. *Management International, 16*, 101–112.
Reitzig, M., Sorenson, O. (2010). *Intra-organizational provincialism*. Available from SSRN: http://ssrn.com/abstract=1552059.
Schenk, E., & Guittard, C. (2011). Towards a characterization of crowdsourcing practices. *Journal of Innovation Economics, 7*(1), 93–107.

Schenk, E., & Guittard, C. (2012). Une typologie des pratiques de Crowdsourcing: l'externalisation vers la foule, au-delà du processus d'innovation. *Management International, 16*, 89–100.
Teece, D. J. (2007). Explicating dynamic capabilities: The nature and microfoundations of sustainable enterprise formation. *Strategic Management Journal, 28*(13), 1319–1350.
Teece, D. J., Pisano, G., & Shuen, A. (1997). Dynamic capabilities and strategic management. *Strategic Management Journal, 18*(7), 509–533.
Von Hippel, E. (1988). *The sources of innovation*. Oxford: Oxford University Press.
Von Hippel, E. (2005). *Democratizing innovation*. Cambridge, MA: MIT Press.
Yin, R. K. (2009). *Case study research: Design and methods*. Thousand Oakes: Sage publication.

Chapter 5
From Leakage to Crowdsourcing: A Model for Enhancing the Participation of Local Firms

José Luis Galdón Salvador and Ignacio Gil-Pechuán

Abstract Tourism is a critical part of the economy of any country. This is essentially because in addition to being the world's largest industry, tourism also has an important multiplier effect on other industries. However, not all tourism revenue remains in the local region, and for this reason, the concept of leakage becomes critical. Leakage studies the amount of revenue generated by tourists which does not stay in the destination country. This phenomenon occurs especially in developing countries, where lower local industrial development increases dependence on foreign countries. Therefore, the second part of the paper highlights the need to implement new business models in order to minimise leakage. For many authors, the best way to reduce the impact of leakage on the economy of different companies in a region is by enhancing linkages between local companies. The main concept in this case is to achieve the participation of the community. In this vein, one of the most important activities being used by firms is crowdsourcing, an activity defined as taking a specific task and outsourcing it to a large group of people via the Internet through an open call. This study delves into the concept of crowdsourcing presented as a technique for reducing leakage with the aim not only of increasing the satisfaction of employees and customers but also building a new business model that empowers local economies by improving their entrepreneurial environment and helps hotels to improve their profitability.

Keywords Crowdsourcing · Leakage · Participation · Tourism impact · Business models

---

J.L. Galdón Salvador (✉) · I. Gil-Pechuán
Departamento de Organización de Empresas, Universitat Politècnica de València, Valencia, Valencia, Spain
e-mail: jlgaldon12@gmail.com

I. Gil-Pechuán
e-mail: igil@doe.upv.es

F.J. Garrigos-Simon et al. (eds.), *Advances in Crowdsourcing*,
DOI 10.1007/978-3-319-18341-1_5

5.1 Introduction

As has been seen in recent years, tourism has an extremely significant impact on an economy. For decades, numerous authors have emphasised the effects that tourism has on the development of regional economies (Bryant and Wilson 1998; Leiper 1979), whilst the evolution of international tourist arrivals and productivity in the tourism sector evidence the industry's growing share of important ratios, such as production and employment worldwide (Capó et al. 2007).

Given that countries use tourism as an engine for development, such development has to be sustainable. This is the case when the wealth brought by tourists actually leads to an improvement in the local economy. At this point, authors like Mbaiwa (2005) argue that in nations where the tourism industry is dominated by foreign countries, its contribution to the GDP of local economies is greatly diminished. This is because tourism service bookings and payments are made in these foreign countries. Hence, both who really controls the main tourism enterprises (travel agencies, internet channels, tour operators, etc.) and also how many of the products bought by tourists are imported need to be weighed up. In the same vein, Torres (2003) avers that tourism development is usually associated with a growing demand for imported products which results in leakage to the economies of the countries of origin and competition with local producers.

This is where the idea of leakage comes into play, defined as revenue from tourism which does not remain in the country visited (imported products, taxes, foreign suppliers, etc.) (Lejárraga and Walkenhorst 2010). As Sandbrook (2010) puts it, leakage can be seen as "the failure of tourist spending to remain in the destination economy".

Thus, given the potential that tourism has for the development of a particular region on one hand and the problems of leakage on the other, a balance has to be found that enables efficient management of tourism. We are thus faced with a new paradigm which is game changing for tourism businesses which need to adapt to a complex and diverse environment that has to be addressed using new business models (Garrigós-Simón et al. 2014).

In this chapter, the concept of leakage is defined, its problems in the tourist sector are presented, and remedies that make it possible to reduce leakage are proposed. After examining the admittedly sparse literature about leakage, this chapter suggests reducing leakage by encouraging the creation of links that make it possible to build a strong business community in the place that receives the tourists (Chirenje et al. 2013). To achieve this, organisations, local councils, governments, businesses and other stakeholders need to enhance the participation of all local business owners. This will mean that tourism services in a particular region will be delivered by local firms and this directly lessens leakage.

To encourage participation by local business owners, this chapter examines the concept of crowdsourcing and suggests techniques based on it. Since the term is new, this chapter makes an important contribution to the literature as for the first time, it proposes using crowdsourcing techniques as a way of reducing leakage in tourism. Hence, this paper's main contribution is to show that crowdsourcing can increase the participation of local business owners by increasing linkages between firms, thereby reducing leakage and maximising the benefits that tourism brings to the local economy.

5.2 The Importance of Leakage: The Problem and Its Solutions

There are relatively few studies about leakage in spite of its importance for the impact of tourism on the economy of a region. Authors such as Fennel (2003) discuss the importance of studying leakage because of its multiplier effect on the economy of a specific region. Leakage can also impact other industries and sectors, but it is precisely in tourism where leakage is particularly important because tourism is one of the most important sectors for the economic development of any region (Mowforth and Munt 2003).

Although studies of leakage are predominantly qualitative, some authors have quantified approximate leakage rates in certain regions. One of the most interesting conclusions drawn from these studies is the significant gap between developed and developing countries. Thus, developed countries have an average leakage of approximately between 10 and 20 %, whilst in developing countries the average goes up to 40–50 % (Diaz Benavides 2001; Meyer 2007).

The concept of leakage is based on the idea that a major part of tourism expenditure returns to the region of origin. Thus, leakage occurs when income earned from tourist services in the host countries is not available because it does not stay in the local economies (Rahman 2012). Examples are imports from suppliers outside the region (food, beverages, materials, subcontracting, etc.) or even foreign workers (Blake et al. 2008). Another case in which leakage is evident is when tourism spending does not even reach the destination region but stays in the tourists' home country. This happens when, for instance, tourism services are purchased from foreign operators, when commissions are paid to intermediaries and when there are airline taxes.

To better grasp the possible cases of leakage, some authors (Supradist 2004) have differentiated between four types.

Pre-leakage means leakage taking place before tourists arrive in their destination. As mentioned above, the most frequent cases of this type of leakage would be bookings with foreign companies, tour operators, airlines, etc. Internal leakage is the proportion of goods and services which are imported and where direct labour comes from. External leakage is tourism spending that occurs outside the tourist region but is linked to local firms, such as when investors in a company are foreigners. Finally, there is invisible leakage which includes currency payments, currency exchange, taxes, etc. (Supradist 2004).

Some authors maintain that leakage is directly related to the business community of an area. For example, Lejárraga and Walkenhorst (2010) argue that tourism has both direct economic impacts (hotels, transport, etc.) and also indirect impacts which are the ones that directly affect local economies, such as foodstuffs, beverages, furniture and tour operators. In turn, some studies relate job creation in a given area with the level of entrepreneurship of firms in that region (Sexton and Bowman-Upton 1991).

At this point, it is important to note that there are certain localities which are more likely to suffer high levels of leakage than others. Regions whose economies are not able to meet the tourism industry's production and quality requirements for tourism services are much more vulnerable (Meyer 2007). There always has to be a balance between tourism demand in a region and the ability of local companies to meet this demand (Loon and Polakow 2001).

Given the above, it is clear that even though leakage is an as yet little explored term, it is nonetheless a critical factor in tourism development in any community and especially in developing countries (Sandbrook 2010). Hence, a more in-depth quantitative study of leakage is required in lockstep with putting forward solutions to decrease leakage in regions.

Few authors have investigated possible measures to reduce leakage. The study conducted by Supradist (2004) puts forward a series of practical measures to lessen it. These measures are arranged into a number of points that are summarised below:

- Increase online marketing to boost local tourism businesses vis-à-vis foreign ones.
- Try to reduce seasonal workers.
- Encourage setting up local businesses.
- Forge a strong link between local businesses so they become suppliers and meet tourism demand.
- Promote local products in terms of food, beverages, souvenirs and other items.

Furthermore, research by Galdon et al. (2013) suggests an appealing way to reduce leakage by creating an entrepreneurial environment in local businesses. Therefore, we believe that a region will have a greater entrepreneurial spirit when the business community is strongly tied to local economies so that the majority of the benefits associated with tourism stay in the region and consequently lead to economic development. The entrepreneurial framework does not focus on isolated individuals but centres on the ties and links created in order to build a business community that enhances the likelihood of success (Herrera Echeverri 2009).

Chirenje et al. (2013) propose a similar solution which is based on the idea that strong links should be forged between local businesses so that they can cater for all tourist service needs. To accomplish this, the study points out that the active engagement of local communities should be encouraged in order to retain as much tourism revenue in the region as possible (Chirenje et al. 2013).

This leads to the important conclusion that strong links have to be fashioned between local firms generating a powerful business community in order to reduce leakage (Lacher and Sanjay 2010). The resources required to deliver tourism services would thus be provided by local businesses which would mean that the benefits would not leak away from the region.

Therefore, the involvement of entrepreneurs, organisations and workers has to be encouraged to build this local business community. In places where there are high levels of leakage, economic profits dwindle when the participation of local communities in tourism falls (Kokkranikal et al. 2003). Consequently, our major contribution to the literature is to go one step further and propose crowdsourcing techniques as tools for promoting this participation. The next chapter delves into the concept of crowdsourcing and in particular emphasises how it can be used to create ties between local firms and thus directly reduce leakage in any region.

5.3 Crowdsourcing: The Power of Local Participation

Over the past 10 years, there have been significant developments in new information and communication technology (ICT) which, when combined with the rapid expansion of the Internet and social media, have created a new scenario with new business models for entrepreneurs and customers (Egger and Buhalis 2011). This new scenario is based on the active participation of both workers and customers in all business processes. As a result, the importance of participation is crucial to understanding this new business environment (Garrigos et al. 2011).

Many authors have used the term Web 2.0 to describe this new technological environment. In this new scenario, the way we use the Internet changes and, of course, business models based on the Internet also change. The key difference lies in the user's new role as the core of the system. In fact, the main difference from the original Web 1.0 is that in the latter users had a passive role, being merely spectators and consumers of information. By contrast, in Web 2.0 the user becomes an active player and may even become a co-producer and co-creator of information (O'Reilly 2007).

Hence, the transformation of the customer from a passive to a hyperactive one who can participate in all processes (Shiffman 2008), and the development of social media are changing the viewpoint not only of new business models but also production itself. Companies are being forced to adapt to this new paradigm in which they have to work hand in hand with customers and other stakeholders throughout the production process.

Consequently, if we combine the importance of the participation of people with advances in new technology based on Web 2.0, we come directly to the concept of crowdsourcing. The term was coined in 2006 by American journalist Jeffrey Howe, who defined it as "the act of taking a job traditionally performed by a designated agent (usually an employee) and outsourcing it to an undefined, generally large group of people in the form of an open call" (Howe 2006). Even though under this definition proposals are made openly, that is to everyone, it is possible to limit the public who will participate in the proposal. Following Leimister's study (2010), there are two potential audiences to which crowdsourcing proposals can be addressed: the Internet crowd (a large and heterogeneous group) and a smaller group of people who are organised hierarchically. This makes sense because not all Internet users will be able to collaborate and contribute their knowledge to a particular initiative.

This new concept has been gradually clarified and fine-tuned over the years. This is because the concept is very broad and covers a multitude of possibilities, which means the types of crowdsourcing need to be classified in order to examine which one best dovetails with each situation. Howe himself (2008) defined the types of crowdsourcing based on four groups: crowd wisdom, crowd production, crowd voting and crowdfunding. Below is a definition of each one, together with how they can be customised in each case as initiatives to reduce leakage, which is the main purpose of this paper.

Crowd wisdom
This is a type of crowdsourcing based on collective intelligence. In turn, it can be subdivided into other types such as crowdcasting, where a contest is held with a prize for the first person to solve a particular problem, and crowdstorming, where ideas or solutions to tackle a problem are brainstormed.

Customising crowd wisdom as a corrective measure to reduce leakage might, for instance, involve internal competitions held in hotels in which customers suggest improvements. One of the real examples already in place using this approach is the Hesperia Hotels chain "Suite H" project. Under this programme focused on the theme of "putting ideas into practice", customers can share their innovative ideas with hotel managers. After careful examination, the best ideas are implemented and the owners of the ideas get a prize by way of reward. These initiatives improve customer and employee satisfaction and encourage them to take part, which leads to a better environment that decreases leakage. This relationship is anchored in the work of Galdón et al. (2013) in which the connection between leakage and customer and employee satisfaction is empirically demonstrated.

Crowd production
In this case, a specific product is sought rather than a solution to a problem. There are products in any line of business which may require assistance of this kind when it comes to, for example, choosing a design. In the case studied in this paper, we propose using such initiatives for finding local suppliers and companies required to deliver tourist services in a region. More specifically, in the case of the hotel industry, hotel managers could find local suppliers to provide items such as food, consumables, office supplies, furniture and laundry. Thus, these local companies could be invited to "compete" to be subcontracted by the hotels. In this way, and as long as local government policies support such initiatives, a strong local business community could be built that would lead to a significant reduction in leakage in the region (Chirenje et al. 2013).

Crowd voting
This is based on collecting information from users. In the tourism sector in particular, these techniques have been on the rise in recent years. Companies like

Tripadvisor and Booking base their content on information posted by users on their websites. This is extremely significant since having thousands of views for free is invaluable for businesses when getting feedback on the quality of their services and the degree of customer satisfaction. The reviews and ratings given by customers are an important source of information as can be seen in actual cases such as IgoUgo, TripAdvisor and Wayn.com (Buhalis et al. 2011; Sigala 2009), and on the websites of hotel firms such as the Mel Sheraton (Sigala and Marinidis 2009).

Thus, crowd voting can be used to reduce leakage basically by ensuring customer satisfaction is as high as possible so that they choose local businesses (restaurants, entertainment venues, hotels, etc.) because they are the best rated ones.

Crowdfunding

These techniques are used not to solve problems or put forward ideas but rather to obtain direct financing. In this type of initiative, funding is sought for a given project so users participate by making a financial contribution.

In the hotel industry, there are real examples of websites that run crowdfunding projects. Power4projects.com is a crowdfunding platform in the tourism and leisure sector. The platform is aimed at a wide audience who is asked to provide funding for various projects. Another platform with a large number of projects based on crowdfunding is www.lanzanos.com. On this platform, there are entrepreneurs who seek funding, for instance, to open hotels of all types and categories. It also features projects that are underway but need extending or refinancing.

These financing techniques greatly help local enterprises that are starting out or which require funding to undertake business improvements. Again the involvement of people is crucial to foster links between local firms and thus reduce leakage. In addition, this often entails a way to compete with foreign companies that are economically more powerful.

5.4 Conclusions

Considered to be the world's largest industry, tourism is, in turn, crucial as the driving force behind the economies of many countries, especially developing ones. Therefore, companies and agencies alike seek to optimise the benefits that tourism can bring on all levels. Nonetheless, not all revenue from tourism remains in the region since some of it returns to the region of origin or even never reaches the destination. This is called leakage and occurs in all tourist regions, although it is developing regions that suffer from it most. This chapter has defined the concept of leakage and presented possible solutions that researchers have proposed in their studies, even though the newness of the concept means there are very few of them.

One of the first conclusions drawn in this paper is that tourism industry enterprises need to seek out new business models to reduce leakage to the point required to increase their profits and by extension, the benefits for the region. Hence, the measures proposed to remedy leakage consist of those which are geared towards enhancing ties with local businesses in order to build a robust business community able to compete with foreign capital. As has been shown in this chapter, doing this means encouraging local entrepreneurs and customers to get involved in order to join forces and stimulate the local economy.

This active involvement and the expansion of new technology-based applications are the twin pillars on which crowdsourcing rests. This chapter proposes crowdsourcing-based measures to enhance ties between local firms and thus reduce leakage in a given region.

Our study is essential for companies because it sets out measures they can put in place to diminish leakage, and also for tourism planners who can acquire the tools they need to ensure that tourism revenue becomes a bigger driving force for the economic development of their regions by reducing leakage. Therefore, our main contribution to the literature is to have laid the theoretical foundations for reducing leakage using crowdsourcing techniques.

References

Blake, A., Arbache, J. S., Sinclair, M. T., & Teles, V. (2008). Tourism and poverty relief. *Annals of Tourism Research, 35*, 107–126.

Bryant, R., & Wilson G. (1998). Rethinking environmental management. *Progress in Human Geography, 22*, 321–343.

Buhalis, D., Leung, D., & Law, R. (2011). eTourism: Critical information and Technologies. In Y. Wang & A. Pizam (Eds.), *Destination marketing and management: Theories and applications*. Wallingford, UK: CAB International.

Capó, J., Riera, A., & Rosselló, J. (2007). Tourism and long-term growth. A Spanish perspective. *Annals of Tourism Research, 34*(3), 709–726.

Chirenje, L. I., Chitotombe, J., Gukurume, S., Chazovachii, B., & Chitongo, L. (2013). The impact of tourism leakages on local economies: A case study of Nyanga District Zimbabwe. *J Hum Ecol, 42*(1), 9–16.

Diaz Benavides, D., & Perez-Ducy, E. (2001). *Tourism in the least developed countries*. Madrid: WTO and UNCTAD.

Egger, R., & Buhalis, D. (Eds.). (2011). *Etourism case studies*. Routledge.

Fennel, David A. (2003). *Ecotourism: An introduction*. New York: Routledge.

Galdón, J. L., Garrigos, F., & Gil Pechuan, I. (2013). Leakage, entrepreneurship, and satisfaction in hospitality. *The Service Industries Journal, 33*(7–8), 759–773.

Garrigos, F., Gil, I., & Narangajavana, Y. (2011). The impact of social networks in the competitiveness of the firms. In A. B. Beckford & J. P. Larsen (Eds.), *Competitiveness: Psychology, production, impact and global trends*. Hauppauge: NovaScience Publishers, Inc.

Garrigós-Simón, F. J., Galdón-Salvador, J. L., & Gil-Pechuán, I. (2014). The economic sustainability of tourism growth through leakage calculation. *Tourism Economics*.

Herrera Echeverri, H. (2009). Investigación sobre redes sociales y emprendimiento: revisión de la literatura y agenda futura. Innovar. *Revista de Ciencias Administrativas y Sociales, 19*, 19–33.

Howe, J. (2006). The rise of crowdsourcing. *Wired, 14*(6), 1–4.

Howe, J. (2008). *Crowdsourcing: How the power of the crowd is driving the future of business*. Great Britain: Business Books.

Kokkranikal, J., McLellan, R., & Baum, T. (2003). Island tourism and sustainability: A case study of the Lakshadweep Islands. *Journal of Sustainable Tourism, 11*(5), 426–447.

Lacher, G., & Sanjay, K. (2010). From leakages to linkages: Local-level strategies for capturing tourism revenue in northern Thailand. *Tourism Geographies, 12*, 77–99.

Leimeister, J. (2010). Collective Intelligence. *Business & Information Systems Engineering, 2*(4), 245–248.

Leiper, N. (1979). The framework of tourism: Towards a definition of tourism, tourist, and the tourist industry. *Annals of tourism research, 6*(4), 390–407.

Lejárraga, I., & Walkenhorst, P. (2010). On linkages and leakages: Measuring the secondary effects of tourism. *Applied Economics Letters, 17*, 417–421.

Loon, R. L., & Polakow, D. (2001). Ecotourism ventures: Rags or riches? *Annals of Tourism Research, 28*, 892–907.

Mbaiwa, J. E. (2005). The problems and prospects of sustainable tourism development in the Okavango Delta, Botswana. *Journal of Sustainable Tourism, 13*(3), 203–227.

Meyer, D. (2007). Pro-poor tourism: From leakages to linkages. A conceptual framework for creating link- ages between the accommodation sector and 'poor' neighbouring communities. *Current Issues in Tourism, 10*, 558–583.

Mowforth, M., & Munt, I. (2003). *Tourism and sustainability: Development and new tourism in the third world*. London: Routledge.

O'Reilly, T. (2007). What is web 2.0: Design patterns and business models for the next generation of software. *Communications & Strategies, 1*, 17.

Rahman, W. (2012). Cultural tourism and Bangladesh: An overview. *Bangladesh Research Publications Journal, 7*, 6–15.

Sandbrook, C. G. (2010). Putting leakage in its place: The significance of retained tourism revenue in the local context in rural Uganda. *Journal of International Development, 22*(1), 124–136.

Sexton, D. L., & Bowman-Upton, N. B. (1991). *Entrepreneurship: Creativity and growth*. New York: Macmillan.

Shiffman, D. (2008). *The age of engage*. Hunt Street Press.

Sigala, M. (2009). *WEB 2.0 in the tourism industry: A new tourism generation and new ebusiness models*. Retrieved October 22, 2011, from http://www.traveldailynews.com/pages/show_page/20554.

Sigala, M., & Marinidis, D. (2009). *Exploring the transformation of tourism firms' operations and business models through the use of web map services*. Paper presented at the European and Mediterranean Conference on Information Systems 2009 (EMCIS 2009), Founded and Organised by the Information Systems Evaluation and Integration Group, Brunel University, Izmir, July 13–14, 2009.

Supradist, N. (2004). *Economic leakage in tourism sector*. Doctoral Dissertation, Lund University. Retrieved November 2011, from http://www.lub.lu.se/theses.

Torres, R. (2003). Linkages between tourism and agriculture in Mexico. *Annals of Tourism Research, 30*(3), 546–566.

Chapter 6
Crowdsourcing: A New Way to Citizen Empowerment

Diego Álvarez Sánchez, David Pardo Gimilio and Jorge Isnardo Altamirano

Abstract Empowerment has for a long time held a prominent place in the theoretical development of fields as diverse as development studies, community psychology or studies on social movements and organisations, among other areas. In parallel, multilateral agencies and non-profit organisations have launched empowerment processes in different sociocultural and political contexts with an uneven impact. On the other hand, the advance of Web 2.0 technologies has allowed crowdsourcing to establish itself as one of the most successful collaborative approaches through the Internet, particularly in the business world. In this chapter, the authors present a definition of the concept ***empowerment-oriented crowdsourcing*** on the basis of the review of the theoretical and practical developments of both dynamics. The objective is to delineate the framework that facilitates the implementation of processes of citizen empowerment through crowdsourcing projects that seek social benefit.

Keywords Empowerment · Crowdsourcing · Citizenship · Framework · Empowerment-oriented crowdsourcing

---

D. Álvarez Sánchez (✉) · D. Pardo Gimilio
Department of Audiovisual Communication, Documentation and History of Art, Polytechnic University of Valencia, Camino de Vera, s/n, Valencia, Valencia, Spain
e-mail: dalvarez@upv.es

D. Pardo Gimilio
e-mail: dapargi@upv.es

J. Isnardo Altamirano
Master's Degree in Information Management, Polytechnic University of Valencia, Valencia, Valencia, Spain
e-mail: jorisal@ei.upv.es

F.J. Garrigos-Simon et al. (eds.), *Advances in Crowdsourcing*,
DOI 10.1007/978-3-319-18341-1_6

6.1 Introduction

This chapter is concerned with the relationship between empowerment, citizenship and crowdsourcing. The authors believe that the interaction of the three elements can help significantly to facilitate the participation of citizens in processes of social change that pursue the creation of a more just society. Under this approach, our study intends to be a contribution, both from the theoretical reflection and practical application, to the strengthening of citizenship capabilities to achieve this objective.

The notion of empowerment used in this study is built on contributions made in the field of development, and it is complemented with other contributions of disciplines such as education, psychology or social work. On the basis of this review, we establish the elements of the concept of empowerment in the context of a developed country at the present time. From that point, the term crowdsourcing is defined together with its typology, and both a definition and a characterisation are suggested for the empowerment-oriented crowdsourcing.

6.2 Understanding Empowerment

The literature review of the concept of empowerment shows a wide variety of ideas which have in turn resulted in different definitions by different disciplines related to several sociocultural and political contexts. From its origins in popular education approaches, with the development of critical pedagogy described by Freire (1970), empowerment has received theoretical contributions from other disciplines such as the model established by Rappaport (1987) in the theoretical development of community psychology, the study of power from political science by Weber (1977) or Foucault (1999), or the research work on women's empowerment from a gender perspective conducted by Rowlands (1997) and Kabeer (1999), among others. At present, in development studies and practice, the concept of empowerment has transcended the gender perspective and has been widely used in development studies, community and social work or development cooperation, and it is widely used by development agencies, the United Nations or the World Bank, among others (Murguialday et al. 2006).

The remarkable variety of application fields has resulted in an excessive laxity which, although it has helped to spread its use, it has also made it significantly difficult to define a framework for its practical use beyond the approaches aimed at specific groups. An overview of the most significant definitions will establish the elements that will compose the framework for understanding empowerment that can be used to define crowdsourcing empowerment-oriented practice.

Among the works aimed at the development of mechanisms for the empowerment of women, the contributions made by Rowlands (1997) stand out. This author believes that empowerment is bringing people who are outside the decision-making process into it. Therefore, empowerment is related to the different ways in which power operates. Thus, in line with the conventional definition of "power-over", she emphasises the participation in political structures and formal processes of decision-making. On the other hand, on the basis of "generative" forms of power ("power for" and "power with"), empowerment has to do with the processes by which people become aware of their own interests and how these relate to those of others. According to this author, empowerment takes place in three dimensions: personal, developing a sense of self and individual confidence; relational, the ability to influence and negotiate the nature of relations; and collective, working together to achieve a more extensive impact.

Awareness and participation in decision-making is associated with the sense of control over one's own life included in the works of Rappaport et al. (1984) in community psychology. According to this author, empowerment means that people have to acquire new competences in the context of everyday life, rather than such competences come from experts. On this basis, only those people involved in the processes of empowerment can decide the success of them. Thus, he emphasises the rights and abilities rather than the lacks and needs by developing a sense of empowerment from a political conception of the human being as a "citizen" immersed in a political and social context. The idea of the necessity to acquire competences is also found in Kieffer (1984), who suggests a vision of empowerment as a process of learning and long-term development.

At an institutional level, we can find the extensive theoretical and practical work by the World Bank in this field (FRIDE 2006). The World Bank, in a broad sense, considers empowerment as an expansion of the freedom of both choice and action, which means that people acquire control over the resources (assets and capabilities) and the decisions that affect life itself. In order to make this possible, the Bank identifies, along with the suitable institutional condition,[1] four elements that are often present in empowerment projects, namely (Narayan-Parker 2002):

- Access to information: informed citizens are better prepared to seize opportunities, access services, exercise their rights and negotiate effectively.
- Inclusion and participation: it is necessary to create appropriate spaces for people to discuss the issues that affect them, and to participate in the decision-making on such issues (setting priorities, determining budgets, defining services, etc.).
- Accountability: it should be possible to demand that both public and private actors justify and explain their decisions and actions.
- Local organisational ability: it refers to the ability of people to work together, organise themselves and mobilise resources to solve problems of common interest.

[1]This is a concept from political science which is defined as "the set of rules, both formal and informal, to which the different actors try to adjust individually and collectively (…) Institutions define the position of each actor in their mutual relations, how to access these positions, what resources and activities are available and which ones are not, etc." (Vallés 2010: 171, 172).

In this field, it is worth pointing out the work performed by the United Nations (2012) in the context of poverty reduction, social integration and work for everyone. The group of experts convened by this institution to address these issues carried out an extensive review of the literature and the progress made in promoting the empowerment of individuals and groups. On the basis of this work, the group defined empowerment as an iterative process that requires an enabling environment that allows and encourages the participation of any person throughout their life, individually or collectively, in decision-making on issues that affect their lives from the economic, social and political point of view. This includes the necessary access to knowledge and information, for which information and communication technologies play a key role. In this regard, the studies used by the United Nations suggest that the ability to perform problem analysis is a critical factor for people to feel capable of influencing government decisions.

On the basis of the previous contributions, we can set the elements that we think should be integrated in current empowerment dynamics in the context of a developed society, as well as identify the connection with outsourcing projects based on the use of ICTs. In short, we find the following elements of the empowerment framework:

1. Awareness of both individual and collective capacities, as well as of the current situation of the economic, social and political environment.
2. Acquisition and development of competences[2] that allow active participation, either individually or in group, in decision-making processes on issues deemed important.
3. Development of an enabling environment that establishes both formal and informal institutions, ensures access to information, and sets accountability procedures in order to facilitate participation in decision-making processes at a local, national and even international level.

Among the elements identified, a dynamic and mutually influential relationship exists. That is, we believe that a greater awareness of the reality in which people develop their lives allows them to identify the abilities that would enable them to transform them and, in the absence of such abilities, to activate learning processes in order to reverse this situation. From this point on, a more prepared society can contribute significantly to the development of institutions, be more demanding in their requests for information and exercise actively their right to accountability. All this restarts the process and contributes to a greater individual and collective awareness with a better understanding of reality.

In the following section, we address the definition of crowdsourcing, establish the characteristics of this type of projects and analyse how they can promote citizen empowerment according to the framework we have just defined.

[2]We believe that this acquisition of competences is achieved through a process that facilitates the integration of knowledge, skill acquisition and the development of specific capabilities.

6.3 Definition of Crowdsourcing

The term crowdsourcing first appeared in 2006 in Wired magazine, where journalist Jeff Howe described it as the act of a company or institution outsourcing a function normally performed by an employee or undefined group of people (usually a large one) through an open call. This outsourcing may be peer-production when the work is done collaboratively, or it can be performed individually.

Since then, there have been many new definitions that reflect the evolution of the different types of crowdsourcing that have appeared in recent years. For example, Brabham (2009) argues that crowdsourcing is a strategic model to attract an interested, motivated crowd of individuals capable of providing solutions superior in quality and quantity to those that even traditional forms of business can. For her part, Kazai (2011) focuses on the retribution or satisfaction received by participants and defines it as "an open call for contributions from members of the crowd to solve a problem or carry out human intelligent tasks, often in exchange for micro-payments, social recognition or entertainment".

In this sense, it is worth highlighting the definition by Estellés and González (2012b: 9) in the article "Towards an integrated crowdsourcing definition", which accurately integrates most of the numerous definitions of crowdsourcing:

> Crowdsourcing is a type of participative online activity in which an individual, an institution, a non-profit organization, or company proposes to a group of individuals of varying knowledge, heterogeneity, and number, via a flexible open call, the voluntary undertaking of a task. The undertaking of the task, of variable complexity and modularity, and in which the crowd should participate bringing their work, money, knowledge and/or experience, always entails mutual benefit. The user will receive the satisfaction of a given type of need, be it economic, social recognition, self-esteem, or the development of individual skills, while the crowdsourcer will obtain and utilize to their advantage that what the user has brought to the venture, whose form will depend on the type of activity undertaken.

On the other hand, crowdsourcing receives input from other concepts such as open innovation (Chesbrough 2003) and collective intelligence (Schenk and Guittard 2009) developed in the Internet through Web 2.0 tools.[3] The characteristics of this type of tools allow us to extend crowdsourcing to various areas by performing modular tasks executed in parallel by multiple users. This evolution has given rise to many different types of crowdsourcing projects in which countless users perform remotely different sets of tasks.

---

[3]The development of collective outsourcing defined in crowdsourcing would be impossible without the interaction characteristics that define the Web 2.0. The development of tools and contents 2.0 that allow a two-way communication between the users and those responsible for the websites has encouraged the necessary participation and interaction among the users in order to conduct crowdsourcing processes.

6.4 Types of Crowdsourcing Projects

In recent years, various attempts have been made to classify crowdsourcing projects based on different criteria. Among all the proposals, it is worth noting the one made by Geiger et al. (2011) from the perspective of both the organisation and the mechanisms of the process, or that given by Estellés and González (2012a) based on the type of task to be performed and which integrates previous classifications suggested by Howe (2008), Brabham (2008), Geerts (2009), Reichwald and Piller (2006), and Burger-Helmchen and Pénin (2010).

With the aim of bringing the concept of crowdsourcing closer through actual practice, we have compiled the classifications proposed by these authors with illustrative examples of projects that have achieved widespread impact. The categories included are given as follows:

- **Crowdcasting**: it includes those initiatives where the participant who first or better solves the challenge posed receives a reward. An example of this type of project can be found in the challenge issued by the company SunNight Solar in the *Innocentive* platform. The company challenged users to develop a dual-purpose solar light that would function as a lamp and a flashlight to be used in African villages and other areas of the world without electricity. Two months after, the challenge was posted, an electrical engineer from New Zealand solved the challenge and was awarded $20,000 in March 2008.[4]
- **Crowdcollaboration**: it includes projects in which participants bring their knowledge to solve problems or raise ideas collaboratively, usually without reward. The promoting company remains outside the communication between individuals. The following subtypes fall under this category:
  - **Crowdstorming**: it includes initiatives for which online brainstorming sessions are held, solutions are proposed and the crowd participates with their comments and votes. This group includes the session held by Citibank's Global Transaction Services at the IBM platform *Jam Events*.[5] The session was opened to 25,000 people in 88 countries and more than 6000 employees registered for the 55-h event. The purpose was looking to tap into the knowledge of individuals in the field to validate its future strategy and identify growth opportunities (Lesser et al. 2012). Another example is the session held by the toy company LEGO Group, which allowed customers to submit ideas for new products, and even to share the future revenues derived from those ideas (Antorini et al. 2012).
  - **Crowdsupport**: projects that allow customers themselves to solve the questions or problems of others, without resorting to the technical support or customer after-sales service. The company Hootsuite provides an example

[4]Further information on Innocentive website: https://www.innocentive.com/innocentive-solvers-make-difference-rural-africa-and-india. Accessed 6 October 2014.

[5]Website of the platform https://www.collaborationjam.com. Accessed 6 October 2014.

through the *GetSatisfaction* platform[6] with over 2600 community members and 1769 topics posted in the community.

- **Crowdcontent**: it differs from *crowdcasting* in that it is not a competition on a single task to be performed, but a final compilation of the work of all participants (not only the fastest or the best). The following subtypes fall under this category:
  - **Crowdproduction**: they are the projects through which content is created by collaborating with other people or performing tasks of varying difficulty like, for instance, writing articles in *Wikipedia*,[7] or microtasks that humans can perform more efficiently than computers, such as translating short fragments or labelling images of projects published on *Amazon Mechanical Turk*[8] platform.
  - **Crowdsearching**: in this type of projects, the participants seek content available online for a particular purpose. The project *Peer to Patent Peer* by the United States Patent and Trademark Office (USPTO) that opens the patent examination process to public participation is a widely referenced initiative. Peer to Patent is an online system that aims to improve the quality of issued patents by enabling the public to supply the USPTO with information relevant to assessing the claims of pending patent applications.[9]
  - **Crowdanalysing**: similar to the above subtype but in this case the search is performed in text or multimedia documents such as images or videos. A representative example is the American company *BlueServo*, which allows participants to locate illegal immigrants in the United States–Mexico border with by means of the images taken by the cameras placed on the border. The participants can communicate their findings anonymously to the United States Border Patrol so that they can be arrested.[10]
- **Crowdfunding**: it includes projects seeking to be funded by the crowd in return for a reward. There are numerous platforms which can be general or specialised by sectors or cultural areas. The platform *Kikstarter* is a representative example that has room for creative projects seeking collective funding for the development of products or services.[11]
- **Crowdopinion**: it includes projects aimed at getting feedback from users on a particular topic or product, for which the participants contribute their opinion or evaluation. If this is carried out by voting, it is called *crowdvoting*. One of the

[6]Website of the platform http://www.getsatisfaction.com. Accessed 6 October 2014.

[7]Website of the Wikipedia http://www.wikipedia.org. Accessed 6 October 2014.

[8]Website of the Amazon Mechanical Turk platform: https://www.mturk.com. Accessed 6 October 2014.

[9]Website of the Peer to Patent Peer project: http://www.peertopatent.org. Accessed 6 October 2014.

[10]Website of the *BlueServo* initiative: http://www.blueservo.net. Accessed 6 October 2014.

[11]Website of the Kickstarter platform: http://www.kickstarter.com. Accessed 6 October 2014.

most representative international projects is *Tripadvisor*,[12] the world's largest travel site, which contains over 170 million of reviews and opinions[13] of travellers on more than four million lodgings, restaurants, activities and attractions that allow other visitors of the website to plan their trips.

To get a precise approach to the concept of crowdsourcing, it is important to consider the evolution experienced by the sector in recent years. A review of current outlook shows the development of new crowdsourcing projects focused on social interests and away from commercial interests. In this case, their classification requires the introduction of criteria related to the nature of the promoter.

In recent years, several governments around the world have applied crowdsourcing as a way to involve citizens in the political process from the paradigm of Open Government.[14] In line with this approach, Ortiz de Zárate (2012) proposes to use crowdsourcing as a tool for co-creation in the participatory design of policies. For this author, the same way some companies put in value the concept of openness for enriching the design of their services and products, the Administration can enrich the design of public policies thanks to the intelligence of the people. Aitamurto (2012) agrees on how governments use crowdsourcing to achieve a final purpose like producing of a budget, preparing strategies or drafting a law.

One of the characteristics of this type of crowdsourcing projects is that the participation is non-profit. That is, the participants do not receive any compensation for the tasks. Ortiz de Zárate (2012: 15) reminds us that this fact moves the emphasis from the number of participants in these initiatives of political collaboration to the "fact of diversity; that is, we must ensure the participation of agents from all the sectors with an interest in the matter. In other words, we need to engage those who know (epistemological legitimacy), and those with an interest (stakeholders)".

But we cannot talk only about citizens as participants in institutional crowdsourcing projects for Open Government development. Citizens and civil society organisations can create their own platforms or collaborative initiatives intended to improve their environment, contribute ideas, denounce certain situations, or provide further and better transparency and clarity to the information that may be of social interest. Such projects favour the generation of new citizen organisations which, in the words of Gutiérrez-Rubí and Freire (2012), transform lifestyles and the governance of society with proposals.

At another level and more uncommon, there are private initiatives that are developing crowdsourcing projects to encourage critical thinking, solidarity and cooperation in solving common problems. In these cases, the ultimate indirect goal

[12]Tripadvisor website: http://www.tripadvisor.com. Accessed 6 October 2014.

[13]According to its web http://www.tripadvisor.co.uk/PressCenter-c4-Fact_Sheet.html. Accessed 6 October 2014.

[14]New form of governance based on the principles of transparency, collaboration and accountability. Further information http://www.opengovstandards.org. Accessed 7 October 2014.

of the company is usually to improve their brand image or to increase product sales or visits to a particular website.

The above considerations allow us to establish a new classification based on the criterion of the promoter that activates and energises the crowdsourcing projects. According to this criterion, we define the following categories:

- **Crowdsourcing initiatives promoted by public institutions**: These are collaborative projects promoted by the government, administrations or agencies. This group offers different examples at both international and national levels. The first group includes projects such as "*Be A Martian*", conducted by *NASA* in 2009,[15] the constitutional reform in Iceland in 2010 and 2011,[16] the participatory budgeting in Chicago (USA) in 2011,[17] the public consultation on Transparency Act, access to public information and good governance made by the government of Spain in 2012[18] or the process launched by the FBI in 2013 to collect videos and photographs that could help to investigate the Boston Marathon bombing.[19]
- **Crowdsourcing initiatives promoted by citizenship**: they include projects promoted by citizens or NGOs who are ahead of public institutions and generate their own crowdsourcing applications using sometimes open data from the administration and, usually, free open-source software. Some significant examples are: the *Ziudad* project launched in 2009[20] as a website of citizen collaboration, and a way to help solve urban problems, the initiative "*Adopt an MP*" promoted in 2012 by the organisation *What do MPs do*,[21] which asked for the cooperation of the citizens to complete and standardise a spreadsheet with the properties of the MPs, or the collective creation of free geographic databases promoted in recent years by *OpenStreetMap*.[22]
- **Crowdsourcing initiatives promoted by companies**: initiatives undertaken by private entities seeking public participation in solving problems of social interest. This category includes the project carried out by the British newspaper *The Guardian* in 2011[23] for the readers to contribute to the analysis of information about MPs expenses. The information generated was subsequently published openly, which made politicians accountable for their activities, with

[15]Website of the project: http://beamartian.jpl.nasa.gov/welcome. Accessed 24 September 2014.

[16]Website: http://stjornlagarad.is. Accessed 22 September 2014.

[17]Crowdsourcing platform used: http://askchicago.org. Accessed 22 September 2014.

[18]Website: http://www.leydetransparencia.gob.es/index.htm. Accessed 22 September 2014.

[19]Website: https://bostonmarathontips.fbi.gov. The website currently redirects to https://tips.fbi.gov which shows a general form of collaboration with the FBI. Accessed 24 September 2014.

[20]Website: http://ziudad.es. Accessed 24 September 2014.

[21]Website: http://blog.quehacenlosdiputados.net/adopta-a-un-diputado-y-vuelca-su-patrimonio-a-formato-reutilizable. Accessed 22 September 2014.

[22]Website: http://openstreetmap.org. Accessed 24 September 2014.

[23]Website: http://www.theguardian.com/news/datablog/2009/jun/18/mps-expenses-houseofcommons. Accessed 22 September 2014.

some of them even resigning over scandal. A second and more recent example is the initiative *Tomnod* by the company *DigitalGlobe*.[24] Through this platform, people can participate in the analysis of satellite images to locate, for instance, the wreckage of *Malaysia Airlines plane MH370*, disappeared on 8 March 2014 or the search for the *Tunante* sailboat wrecked on the Brazilian coast in September of that year.

6.5 Definition of Empowerment-oriented Crowdsourcing

The analysis of the initiatives set out shows a mixed picture with diffuse boundaries between the different established categories. In fact, the classification of a particular project as a particular type of crowdsourcing can sometimes be obvious; however, some of them can be placed in several categories. Despite this fact, it is possible to identify and define the elements that are integrated into the crowdsourcing projects, namely:

- **Promoter**: it refers to the characteristics of the organisations, both public and private, that implement this type of projects.
- **Objective**: it refers to the type of problems to be solved, whose solution can be addressed by the concurrent performance of individual tasks, and the expected outcomes.
- **People involved**: the selection criteria and the characteristics of the people for whom the participation is open in order to solve the problem.
- **Working method**: it defines the nature of tasks, the rules of the process and the mechanisms that articulate the participation.
- **Tools**: it refers to the set of ICT 2.0 tools that materialise the project and define the working environment.
- **Benefits**: it indicates the results obtained and the satisfaction of the participants during and after the project.

On the basis of these elements, it is possible to establish the relationship between crowdsourcing projects and the empowerment framework described in the previous point. Thus, we see how such projects cover the two dimensions of empowerment: the individual one (related to the awareness that occurs with the decision to participate and with the performance of tasks) and the collective one (related to the collaborative framework that is established in order to address the problem). On the other hand, the benefits obtained by performing tasks include the acquisition of useful skills and abilities for the active participation in the new environment of deliberation and online decision, some of them related to the use of ICT. In addition, the solution reached can also increase the knowledge about the current situation and activate the awareness of the problem addressed.

[24]Website: http://www.tomnod.com. Accessed 24 September 2014.

Furthermore, a closer synergistic relationship between the two dynamics is generated in projects of information analysis. These crowdsourcing projects allow the analysis of complex information, in many cases accessible thanks to the empowerment processes that promote the transformation of the environment. And as a result of these projects, knowledge about reality increases, which facilitates citizen awareness who, in turn, demand more information.

However, despite the potential described, most crowdsourcing projects do not cover the whole process of empowerment. Both dynamics share the need of an environment that, among other things, provides adequate formal and informal institutions or ensure accountability processes that promote the control by citizens.

On the basis of the above reasoning, we propose a definition of what we call empowerment-oriented crowdsourcing, which could set out as follows:

> Online collaborative and non-profit process open to the participation of diverse citizenry in order to perform tasks whose final result brings social benefits to the political, social, economic and/or environmental field, in which the knowledge generated can be accessed, shared and reused freely.

The approaches included in the definition have been implemented by the authors of this chapter through the website analizo.info.[25] It is a crowdsourcing non-profit initiative open to all public, which facilitates the active participation of citizens in the process of analysis of different types of information,[26] which are aimed at the improvement of society in the political, social, economic and/or environmental fields. The initiative maintains a threefold profile: first, it acts as a technology platform[27] for non-profit organisations wishing to set crowdsourcing projects based on the analysis of information[28]; second, it is configured as a community of analysts in order to foster collaboration and a sense of belonging to a group; finally, as a non-profit entity responsible for providing advice and ensuring that the principles set in its code of ethics are respected.[29]

[25]Website of the initiative http://www.analizo.info. Accessed 7 October 2014.

[26]Website of information analysis projects http://proyectos.analizo.info. Accessed 7 October 2014.

[27]The analysis platform is developed using the open-source solution for social data analysis PyBossa. Website: http://pybossa.com. Accessed 7 October 2014.

[28]There are currently published projects of text analysis in election programs, description of media news related to development cooperation and identification of green spaces in the city of Valencia (Spain).

[29]The code of ethics of analizo.info is available at http://proyectos.analizo.info/codigo-ethical. Accessed 7 October 2014.

6.6 Conclusions

Throughout the chapter we have addressed the relationship that can be established between the processes of empowerment and crowdsourcing projects. The contributions support the conclusion that both dynamics share elements that can make crowdsourcing a tool at the disposal of citizen empowerment. However, this conclusion can not be expanded to all the crowdsourcing projects which have been materialised in recent years.

The definition we have specified for the empowerment-oriented crowdsourcing, despite its introductory nature, can serve as a framework for determining which projects can be considered as such. Similarly, not all the projects with established features contribute in equal measure to empowerment. Despite the empowering potential of such projects, it is necessary to consider their limitations. In this sense, mechanisms for evaluating the extent of empowerment must be established, both individually and collectively. Moreover, the participants should take part in it.

Finally, we would like to mention the central element in any empowerment-oriented crowdsourcing process: the participants. Our experience in the different projects published in analizo.info has shown the difficulty of achieving citizen participation. Despite the awakened interest by the media and having become widespread, the number of people involved, with some exceptions, has been considerably low. We believe it is necessary to reflect on the factors that contribute to motivate and mobilise the citizens to participate in such processes. Beyond the dependent relationship that exists between these processes and the characteristics of the environment in which they are developed, it is essential to go more deeply in the elements and characteristics that define this type of processes.

References

Aitamurto, T. (2012). *Crowdsourcing for democracy: A new era in policy-making*. Committee for the Future, Parliament of Finland. http://cddrl.fsi.stanford.edu/sites/default/files/Crowdsourcing_for_DemocracyF_www.pdf. Accessed October 4, 2014.

Antorini, Y. M., Muñiz, A. M., & Askildsen, T. (2012). Collaborating with customer communities: Lessons from the LEGO Group. *MIT Sloan Management Review, 53*(3), 73–79.

Brabham, D. C. (2008). Crowdsourcing as a model for problem solving: an introduction and cases. *Convergence: The International Journal of Research into New Media Technologies, 14*, 75–90. doi:10.1177/1354856507084420.

Brabham, D. C. (2009). Crowdsourcing the public participation process for planning projects. *Planning Theory, 8*, 242–262. doi:10.1177/1473095209104824.

Burger-Helmchen, T., Pénin, J. (2010). *The limits of crowdsourcing inventive activities: What do transaction cost theory and the evolutionary theories of the firm teach us?* In Working Papers of BETA (Bureau d'Economie Théorique et Appliquée), Strasbourg, France.

Chesbrough, H. (2003). *Open innovation: The new imperative for creating and profiting from technology*. Boston: Harvard Business School Press.

Estellés, E., & González, F. (2012a). Clasificación de iniciativas de crowdsourcing basada en tareas. *El Profesional de la Información, 21*(3), 283–291.

Estellés, E., & González, F. (2012b). Towards an integrated crowdsourcing definition. *Journal of Information Science, 38*(2), 189–200.

Foucault, M. (1999). *Estrategias de poder*. Barcelona: Paidós.

Freire, P. (1970). Pedagogía del oprimido. Madrid: Siglo XXI.

FRIDE. (2006). *Empowerment*. In Development Backgrounder, 1. http://www.fride.org/descarga/bgr_empowerment_eng_may06.pdf. Accessed September 14, 2014.

Geerts, S. (2009). *Discovering crowdsourcing: theory, classification and directions for use*. Master's Thesis, Technische Universiteit Eindhoven, Netherlands. http://alexandria.tue.nl/extra2/afstversl/tm/Geerts%202009.pdf. Accessed October 2, 2014.

Geiger, D., Seedorf, S., Schulze, T., Nickerson, R. C., & Schader, M. (2011). Managing the crowd: Towards a taxonomy of crowdsourcing processes. In *AMCIS 011 Proceedings—All Submissions, Paper 430*. http://aisel.aisnet.org/amcis2011_submissions/430. Accessed October 2, 2014.

Gutiérrez-Rubí, A., & Freire, J. (2012). *Manifiesto crowd: La empresa y la inteligencia de las multitudes*. Laboratorio de Tendencias. http://www.gutierrez-rubi.es/wp-content/uploads/2013/03/manifiesto_crowd.pdf. Accessed October 2, 2014.

Howe, J. (2006). The rise of crowdsourcing. *Wired, 14*(6), 1–4. http://www.wired.com/wired/archive/14.06/crowds.html. Accessed October 4, 2014.

Howe, J. (2008). *Crowdsourcing: Why the power of the crowd is driving the future of business*. New York: Crown Business.

Kabeer, N. (1999). Resources, agency, achievements: Reflections on the measurement of women's empowerment. *Development and Change, 30*(3), 435–464.

Kazai, G. (2011). In search of quality in crowdsourcing for search engine evaluation. *Lecture notes in computer science, advances in information retrieval* (pp. 165–176). Berlin, Heidelberg: Springer.

Kieffer, C. H. (1984). Citizen empowerment: A developmental perspective. In J. Rappaport, C. F. Swift, & R. Hess (Eds.), *Studies in empowerment: Steps toward understanding and action* (pp. 9–36). New York: Haworth Press.

Lesser, E., Ransom, D., Shah, R., & Pulver, B. (2012). Collective intelligence: Capitalizing on the crowd. *IBM global business services*. http://www.bic-innovation.com/static/bic/knowledge_base/documents/IBM3.pdf. Accessed April 9, 2015.

Murguialday, C., Pérez-de-Armiño, K., & Eizagirre, M. (2006). Empoderamiento. In Hegoa (Ed.), *Diccionario de Acción Humanitaria y Cooperación al Desarrollo*. http://www.dicc.hegoa.ehu.es/listar/mostrar/86. Accessed September 14, 2014.

Narayan-Parker, D. (2002). *Empowerment and poverty reduction: A sourcebook*. Washington, DC: World Bank Publications.

Ortiz de Zárate, A. (2012). *Modelo LUDO: el gobierno abierto desde la perspectiva del ciclo de las políticas públicas*. GIGAPP- IUIOG. Estudios Working Papers. 2012–2015. http://www.gigapp.org/administrator/components/com_jresearch/files/publications/WP-2012-15.pdf. Accessed October 4, 2014.

Rappaport, J. (1987). Terms of empowernment/exemplars of prevention: Toward a theory for community psychology. *American Journal of Community Pshychology, 15*(2), 121–148.

Rappaport, J., Swift, C. F., & Hess, R. (1984). *Studies in empowerment: Steps toward understanding and action*. New York: Haworth Press.

Reichwald, R., & Piller, F. T. (2006). *Interaktive wertschöpfung. Open innovation, individualisierung und neue formen der arbeitsteilung*. Wiesbaden: Gabler Verlag.

Rowlands, J. (1997). *Questioning empowerment: Working with women in Honduras*. Oxford: Oxfam.

Schenk, E., & Guittard, C. (2009). Crowdsourcing: What can be outsourced to the crowd, and why? *Journal of Innovation Economics, 1*(7), 93–107. http://halshs.archives-ouvertes.fr/halshs-00439256. Accessed October 2, 2014.

United Nations. (2012). *Report of the expert group meeting on "promoting people's empowerment in achieving poverty eradication, social integration and decent work for all"*. http://www.un.org/esa/socdev/csocd/2013/egm-empowerment-final.pdf. Accessed September 14, 2014.

Vallés, J. M. (2010). *Ciencia política. Una introducción*. Barcelona: Editorial Ariel Ciencia Política.

Weber, M. (1977). *Estructuras de poder*. Buenos Aires: Editorial La Pléyade.

Chapter 7
Crowdsourcing in Higher Education

Roberto Llorente and Maria Morant

Abstract Pervasive application of crowdsourcing techniques in Higher Education institutions improves the students' performance by using collaborative projects to enhance each student's skills, optimizes the lecturing process effectively sharing and pooling study materials, and also improves alumni financial situation by supporting tuition crowdfunding. In this chapter, we describe four key areas where the application of crowdsourcing techniques plays an important role in the performance of the alumni in Higher Education institutions. The proposed "crowdteaching" technique optimizes lecturing enabling sharing and exchanging of lecture notes following the different curricula of Higher Education studies. With "crowdlearning," the students learn by execution on collaborative projects where different students share (effectively teaching each other under lecturer supervision), learn the required skills required to carry out the targets of the project and solve the proposed problem. In relation to obtaining funding, with "crowdtuition" the students' tuition fees can be funded via crowdsourcing methods and also "crowdfunding" can be used to obtain laboratory and classroom material or students' learning stays abroad. Using these crowdsourcing methods, the students can find help to pay the university taxes and also interact with other students for a deeper learning process. Applying crowdsourcing to education enables the optimization of the institutions' budget and a more efficient use of time for learning which in the end leads to student's better results.

R. Llorente (✉) · M. Morant
Nanophotonics Technology Center, Universitat Politècnica de València, Camino de Vera, Building 8F, 46022 Valencia, Valencia, Spain
e-mail: rllorent@dcom.upv.es

M. Morant
e-mail: mmorant@ntc.upv.es

F.J. Garrigos-Simon et al. (eds.), *Advances in Crowdsourcing*,
DOI 10.1007/978-3-319-18341-1_7

7.1 Introduction

A single individual cannot hold all available knowledge, not even a small group of people can. Superior knowledge is achieved when a large number minds are connected (i.e., networked), via ad hoc tools and methods. Colleges and universities can use crowdsourcing methods to enable superior knowledge building processes and to optimize lecturing and administrative processes, which ultimately permits an efficient use of time resources for high-quality teaching and a reduction of the alumni expenses, thus enabling more students to attend university (which is of great social benefit).

Crowdsourcing techniques can be a natural framework for learning although by itself it cannot offer the best educational experience. But applying the appropriate methods, it can offer improved education increasing the efficiency of workflows and optimizing the personalized curricula (Weld et al. 2012).

The introduction of crowdsourcing techniques in Higher Education (i.e., university and college), finds application in two key aspects that can dramatically improve alumni performance. On one hand, crowdsourced knowledge building opens up the possibility of collaborative projects where both the professors and the students can interact and exchange information. For instance, professors can share learning resources so a repository of high-quality materials can improve the quality of the lessons and save a lot of time in preparing the lectures. Also students' interaction in crowdlearning proposes to bring different skills to a common project to solve a given problem. And on the other hand, Crowdsourced Grant Schemes (or external crowdfunding) can be applied to student fees. Students with high ranks or excellent performance can take advantage of their skills by crowdfounding their tuition or obtaining funding for stays abroad.

These two applications require university-wide crowdsourcing software tools and platforms (Web-based, by example) which are reviewed in this chapter.

7.2 Crowdsourcing State of the Art

"Crowdsourcing" comes from the combination of words "crowd" and "outsourcing" and defines the distribution of a task among a group of people. Although the concept "crowdsourcing" first appeared in 2006 in Wired Magazine (Howe 2006), several events before that date contributed to the concept of "outsource work to a group of people." One of the most relevant and worldwide-known events was the creation of Wikipedia, a free-access and free-content Internet encyclopedia, launched in 2001 and that at present receive over 500 million visits every month. But several years before, in 1714, the British government offered a monetary prize (know nowadays as the Longitude Prize) to whomever came up with the best solution to measure a ship's longitude (Dawson and Bynghall 2012). This was the starting of crowdsourcing communities working together to solve a given problem.

In the nature of the concept, crowdsourcing does not require online resources, but the truth is that using the Internet makes crowdsourcing much easier and provides access to a wider amount of people around the world in less time and at a reduced cost.

The rise of crowdsourcing was possible thanks to the evolution of the Internet and of the social media technologies which enabled the communities to come together more quickly and to collaborate and exchange information (Isman et al. 2012). The idea of working in the same collaborative project with people located at the other side of the world would be unthinkable and require a huge cost if we could not use the Internet.

In recent years, crowdsourcing have been used in the market to perform a high variety of tasks that are difficult for computers, yet solvable, like in the case of Amazon Mechanical Turk (mturk.com). The ability to attract a crowd enables massive parallel processing which can lead to high throughput on tasks such as image labeling, audio transcription, and product categorization (Zhang et al. 2011). And with the growth of these online parallel solving platforms, crowdsourcing appears as a valid option available to anyone with a task or project in mind. Platforms like Wikipedia provide the clear evidence that coordinating a crowd for complex tasks is possible. Besides Wikipedia, there is a wide range of crowdsourcing community examples, especially in the field of language learning, as we will depict later in this chapter.

The concept of task parallelization based on simple partitioning and distribution of the process evolved to more sophisticated problem-solving procedures. With the correct coordination of the problem-solving crowd, it is possible to complete complex activities, e.g., programming tasks. For example, Little et al. (2009) developed a crowdsourcing platform called Turkit that enables the requesters to write programs executed by human workers on Mechanical Turk. In this case, the crowdsourcing strategy is based on dividing the proposed problem into small pieces that will be programmed by different workers. In fact, one of the main advantages of crowdsourcing is that it enables the possibility of iterative contributions of different people (Zhang et al. 2011).

One of the most common application scenarios of crowdsourcing platforms is gathering ideas about a given topic and vote on the most popular option. Crowdsourcing platforms can be implemented as an open and transparent site where everybody can access to the information and read and exchange opinions, but also the platform can include protection of the ideas where only authorized users can access to the information. In these cases, the proposed challenge is usually sponsored by an organization or industrial company which offers a prize to the best solution of the proposed task (Isman et al. 2012). Using this kind of competition platforms allows, especially for medium and small companies, to access to a wide range of ideas that would not be available in their usual environment or would require a considerable investment with the consulting a single or several external providers (Dawson and Bynghall 2012). For the industry, the main attraction for using a crowdsourcing competition platform is that, in most of the cases, this option is significantly less expensive than contracting a traditional company, e.g., a design agency to prepare a given product logo design or a marketing expert for the proposal of an advertising campaign.

In this chapter, we will overview the advantages of crowdsourcing applied to Higher Education activities.

7.3 Crowdsourcing Methods in Higher Education

Recent studies and first applications at colleges and universities have shown that applying crowdsourcing to education can be fruitful for both students and professors. Students would like to receive personalized education according to their abilities and learning style (Weld et al. 2012) and the recreation of the same lessons over and over is a waste of professors' time. With the proper use of crowdsourcing in Higher Education, professors can prepare high-quality lessons and provide useful instructions in class, and students are able to access to the best learning material and can improve their learning efficiency.

Evaluation techniques oriented to crowdsourcing have been used before in Higher Education at a smaller scale, for example peer-evaluation where the professor asks the students to evaluate each other's work. Early studies have pointed out that crowdsourced peer-grading can lead to more accurate assessments of the student's performance by combining different opinions with diverse perspectives and expertise (Page 2008).

In the last decade, with the emergence of Web technologies, online learning has evolved significantly using adaptive online environments that facilitate social learning (Corneli and Mikroyannidis 2012). For example, in the recent years, online tutoring systems have made considerable progress in Higher Education (Weld et al. 2012). There are four key areas where applied crowdsourcing techniques play an important role in the performance of the alumni in Higher Education institutions:

- Crowdteaching: In this approach, the lecturing staff share and put together lecturing material following the university curricula.
- Crowdlearning: This crowdsourcing technique is based on the "learning by project lecturing scheme." This scheme has been successfully applied in American and European universities. In the crowdlearning approach, the knowledge building process is based on collaborative projects where different students share, effectively teaching each other, and learn jointly the skills that are necessary to carry out the targets of the project.
- Crowdtuition: Crowdsourcing has an important impact for the social benefit. Crowdtuition techniques allow the best performing students' tuition fees to be funded via crowdsourcing methods. Different early experiences have been developed in the last years, including Universitat Politècnica de València (UPV) from Spain.
- Crowdfunding: Lecturing requirements in Higher Education, especially in Engineering Studies, require important investments in laboratory and classroom material. Whether classroom materials are usually funded by Government in the case of public institutions, laboratory inventory material is more difficult to be

obtained. Crowdfunding lecturing laboratories is an interesting technique that permits these laboratories to address specific techniques—to be lectured—for the social benefit, e.g., cancer research.

In this chapter, we describe in detail the different crowdsourcing methods that could be relevant to Higher Education institutions.

7.3.1 *Crowdteaching and Educational Resources*

One of the most common ways of using crowdsourcing in colleges and universities is sharing educational content. Professors seek for educational material with high-quality contents that could teach effectively the topics of a given curricula. But extreme attention should be paid in order to use trusted material, coming from sources with reputation behind it. This is also a problem that the students face when searching information in the Internet, as in some cases they rely in non-trusted sources which leads to misunderstanding and interferes with the learning objectives. In this scenario, UClass application (http://www.uclass.io) can be used as Common Core content repository, where university and college professors can share their resources with other professors in their same district. Using crowdsourcing planning, professors can access to the best curriculum across their district and drive higher student outcomes in their classroom. One of the main objectives of UClass repository is to exchange high-quality learning content with the aim to save professors' time in the preparation of their lessons. Also, UClass offers collaborative features for students to work together in different parts of the world.

In 2011, the Latin American Open Textbook Initiative was created with the main objective of dissemination of cooperative open textbooks aimed for Higher Education (customized per region) in order to avoid the high cost of textbooks in Latin America (Ochoa et al. 2011). This is an example, together with Wikibooks and Connexions platforms, between others, that have been found to reduce significantly (up to an 80 %) the cost of textbooks for the students.

7.3.2 *Crowdlearning and Suitable Platforms*

Crowdlearning appeared with the creation of educational platforms such as Skillshare (http://www.skillshare.com). Skillshare is an online learning community created to master real-world skills through project-based classes. So, "crowdlearning" can be defined as learning through real-case projects with the participation of several students ("crowd"). The advantage of this technique is based on each student to propose skills that already have—that can be useful to reach the final goal of the project—, in order to gather together different aptitudes.

When developing the project, the students share information and skills that automatically are learned when developing the project activities. It is important then to have a platform to effectively propose these skills that should match the competences established in the lecturing curricula. In this way, a categorization of competences should be implemented in the crowdlearning management tool.

After developing the project via crowdlearning, all students have shared their skills and competences, effectively learning other's competences.

Several online platforms are available for the creation of joint projects. Also, the crowdlearning platforms provide online courses that the students can follow at their own pace. Nowadays, it is clear that offering an online course can attract a crowd of hundreds of thousands students or even more. A clear example is Duolingo, a free science-based language education platform with over 38 million users. In only two years, Duolingo has become the most popular way to learn languages online and it was recently selected by TechCrunch as Best Education Startup and application of the year 2013 for iPhone and Android. According to an independent study conducted by the City University of New York and the University of South Carolina, an average of 34 h of Duolingo is equivalent to a full university semester of language education (Vesselinov and Grego 2012). Since one semester university course usually takes more than 34 h of work, this study suggests that Duolingo is more effective than an average university course.

Proper analysis can highlight the student tracking and detect confusion in given topics. For example, Coursera analyzes the student traces to determine which videos are watched again and also in what order, which helps optimizing the curriculum and the question routing. Nowadays, the curriculum design of online courses, e.g., Khan Academy, Coursera and Udacity, is normally centralized, but the great success of Wikipedia indicates that the action of a whole community can create incredible resources. For example, an increasing number of universities are offering nowadays, massive open online courses (MOOCs) dealing with topics requested by their students. Open educational resources (OER) had limited impact and attraction to the students in most of the cases due to the lack of coherence of the curriculum design (Mitros and Sun 2014). In contrast, MOOCs use a centralized approach where the institution (basically colleges and universities) designs a complete and more coherent course. Those courses are used in blended classrooms across many campuses. The main attractive of MOOCs is that typically they are taught by top professors and usually include research-based pedagogies such as active learning, constructive learning, and mastery-learning (Mitros et al. 2013). The centralization of the design and preparation of the MOOCs enables using more and higher quality resources per course than traditional courses. Previous studies suggest that well-designed MOOCs can lead to high-quality students' learning and high satisfaction levels (Lewin 2013).

In addition to these online learning platforms, YouTube's capacity to reach a different audience has made it one of the major media for innovative educational programming. Clear examples of this are the YouTube online channels "Crash

Course" and "SciShow" developed by Green brothers. Crash Course was one of the 100 initial channels of YouTube's $100 million original channel initiative. This initiative was a 100 million dollar program funded by Google to bring original content onto YouTube. The original channel initiative was also meant to kick start Google TV. For example, "Crash courses" is an educational YouTube channel for online teaching world history, biology, literature, ecology, and chemistry. As of December 2014, the "Crash Course" YouTube channel has earned over 2.4 million subscribers and over 160 million video views. The widespread acceptance of online educational videos has attracted the attention of television media contents. As a recent example, in November 2014, a partnership of Crash Courses with PBS Digital Studios was announced to expand the channel.

7.3.3 Crowdtuition

College tuitions increase the financial pressure on the students' families (Mitros and Sun 2014). The global economic turndown in the recent years has limited the number of alumni capable of fulfilling the tuition expenses. For instance in Spain, the university taxes were raised to 60 % in the last two years (Universia 2014) which made even more difficult for the students to access to a Higher Education study degree.

A crowdtuition program can be implemented by the university services, in which a loan is publically offered. The loan is intended to cover tuition expenses of a relevant pupil. This program is similar to the return-grant programs that are dedicated to guarantee that the knowledge and skills acquired at a university or institution are transferred back to that institution by recruiting alumni after finishing their PhD or after their postdoc research. This kind of return-grants is usual in Marie Curie postdoctoral programs and is also available in universities in Europe like by example the international center for genetic engineering and biotechnology of Italy (ICGEB 2014). But in this case what it is proposed in crowdtuition is that the tuition expenses of a given student are supported by an external company.

Crowdtuition proposes a social loan of brilliant students, which will return the loan after graduating when developing his career. These programs can support only brilliant alumni, as the loan was to be paid back after finishing the studies. This implies that a successful career is expected from the student when leaving the university once completed their Higher Education degree.

Early successful implementation of this approach was proposed in 2012 in the Universitat Politècnica de Valencia, Spain, where Comunitae.com offered 12,000 students the possibility of a student loan up to 2,000 euros with an 8 % interest at one year return (ABC 2012).

7.3.4 Crowdfunding Educational Infrastructures

A supplementary application of crowdsourcing can be also applied to raise funding to support a given cause. This concept is also known as "crowdfunding." Educational fund-raising is also possible and currently there are several online crowdsourced funding landscapes that provide educational support. The important investments required to purchase and update the material in laboratories and Higher Education classrooms can also take profit of crowdfunding. Usually, the Government covers the cost of the classroom materials of public institutions, but funding for the technical equipment or laboratory inventory material is more difficult to obtain. Crowdfunding lecturing laboratories is an interesting option that permits improving the research at Higher Education centers.

Crowdfunding can be also applied to support students' stays abroad. As student travel scholarships or educational travel grants are difficult to find, several crowdsourcing Web sites have appeared as a good option to seek for funding. An example of crowdfunding platforms is IndieGoGo where anyone over 13 years old can use the application and where, for instance, an educational summer abroad program is accepted for funding and also small donations that could help the student's travel.

7.4 Conclusion

This chapter provides a comprehensive approach to the advances that the application of crowdsourcing techniques can bring to universities and Higher Education institutions. Four key aspects are identified where crowdsourcing can play a key role: First "crowdteaching" is proposed to optimize lecturing by sharing and exchange of lecturing material. Crowdteaching requires ad hoc platforms supporting share and exchange of lecturing material following the different curricula of the Higher Education studies.

"Crowdlearning" is based on learning by execution principle developed in collaborative projects. Each student provides different skills that are needed to solve the proposed problem as a whole. The students share ideas and teach each other, which improves their preparation for their career.

By "crowdtuition," the students' tuition fees can be publically funded, which is an effective method for high–ranking alumni. Finally, "crowdfunding" is proposed to support laboratory and classroom material or students' expenses.

Applying the appropriate crowdsourcing techniques in Higher Education can increase the efficiency of the learning workflows and optimize the curricula which lead to student's better results.

References

ABC. (2012). Exalumnos de la UPV podrán financiar sus estudios a nuevos estudiantes. Available via ABC Spanish newspaper: http://www.abc.es/local-comunidad-valenciana/20121115/abci-exalumnos-podran-financiar-estudios-201211151410.html. Accessed December 5, 2014.

Corneli, J., & Mikroyannidis, A. (2012). Crowdsourcing education on the Web: A role-based analysis of online learning communities. In: Okada, A., Connolly, T. & Scott, P. (Eds.), *Collaborative learning 2.0: Open educational resources* (pp. 272–286). Hershey, PA: IGI Global.

Dawson, R., & Bynghall, S. (2012). Getting results from crowds. *Advanced Human Technologies*, 9–13.

Howe, J. (2006). The rise of crowdsourcing. WIRED magazine. Issue 14.06. http://archive.wired.com/wired/archive/14.06/crowds.html. Accessed December 5, 2014.

ICGEB. (2014). Education and training. Return grant. Available via http://www.icgeb.org/return-grant.html. Accessed December 5, 2014.

Isman, M., Bennet, J., Judah, J., & Glenzer, A. (2012). *Effectiveness and efficiency. Tapping new sources of innovations and ideas through crowdsourcing*. McLean: Booz Allen Gamilton Inc.

Lewin, T. (2013, April). Colleges adapt online courses to ease burden. *New York Times*.

Little, G., Chilton, L. B, Goldman, M., & Miller, R. C. (2009). Turkit: Tools for iterative tasks on mechanical turk. In *KDD-HCOMP'09*.

Mitros, P., & Sun, F. (2014). Creating educational resources at scale. In *2014 IEEE 14th International Conference on Advanced Learning Technologies* (pp. 16–18).

Mitros, P., Affidi, K., Sussman, G., Terman, C., White, J., Fischer, L., et al. (2013). Teaching electronic circuits online: Lessons from MITx's 6.002x on edX. In *2013 IEEE International Symposium on Circuits and Systems (ISCAS)* (pp 2763–2766).

Ochoa, X., Sprock, A. S., & Silveira, I. F. (2011). Collaborative open textbooks for Latin America—The LATIn project. In *2011 International Conference on Information Society (i-Society)* (pp. 398–403).

Page, S. (2008). The difference: How the power of diversity creates better groups, firms, schools, and societies. Princeton: Princeton University Press.

Universia. (2014). Las tasas universitarias suben un 60 % en dos años. España: emplea. Available via http://emplea.universia.es/detallecontenido/idnoticia/2253/c/candidato/. Accessed December 5, 2014.

Vesselinov, R., & Grego, J. (2012). *Duolingo effectiveness study*. Final Report. Available via http://static.duolingo.com/s3/DuolingoReport_Final.pdf. Accessed December 5, 2014.

Weld, D. S, Adar, E., Chilton, L., Hoffmann, R., Horvitz, E., Koch, M., et al. (2012). Personalized online education—A crowdsourcing challenge. In *Human computation*. AAAI Technical Report WS-12-08 (pp. 159–163).

Zhang, H., Horvitzy, E., Millerz, R. C., & Parkes, D. C. (2011). Crowdsourcing general computation. In: *CHI 2011*, May 7–12, 2011, Vancouver, BC, Canada.

Chapter 8
Crowdsourcing with University Students: Exam Questions

Sofia Estelles-Miguel, Gregorio Rius-Sorolla, Marta Palmer Gato and José Miguel Albarracín Guillem

Abstract Incorporation into the European Higher Education Area (EHEA) has demanded the deployment of major changes in the teaching culture of University academic institutions. The utilization of educational strategies, based on the use of active methodologies that encourage students' active role, the importance of "learning to learn," and the ability to work together as a core competence are essential in change. Thus, active learning has become a priority in the development of curricula, and the center of gravity of the process should move toward methodologies that help students develop their professional skills, interpersonal relationships, and abilities to solve conflicts to apply theory to practice. The authors of the present article decided to do a crowdsourcing experiment with students from course 4 in the Faculty of Business Administration and Management who were studying the Production Management and Logistics (PML) subject. This subject used the PoliformaT platform. The crowdteaching technique optimizes lecturing by enabling the sharing and exchange of lecturing material following subject curricula. With crowdlearning, students learn by execution in collaborative projects. This article intends to demonstrate that students obtained better results when these techniques were applied.

Keywords Collaborative projects · Crowdsourcing · Crowdteaching · Methodologies actives · Generic skills

---

S. Estelles-Miguel (✉) · G. Rius-Sorolla · M. Palmer Gato · J.M. Albarracín Guillem
Departamento de Organización de Empresas, Universitat Politècnica de València, Valencia, Spain
e-mail: soesmi@omp.upv.es

G. Rius-Sorolla
e-mail: greiuso@upv.es

M. Palmer Gato
e-mail: marpalga@doe.upv.es

J.M. Albarracín Guillem
e-mail: jmalbarr@omp.upv.es

F.J. Garrigos-Simon et al. (eds.), *Advances in Crowdsourcing*,
DOI 10.1007/978-3-319-18341-1_8

8.1 Introduction

Crowdsourcing is a problem solving and task performance model that is being increasingly used. The term "crowdsourcing" was first coined in 2006 by Howe (2006), who defined it as "the act of a company or institution taking a function once performed by employees and outsourcing it to an undefined (and general large) network of people in the form of an open call. This can take the form of peer-production (when the job is performed collaborative), but is also often undertaken by sole individual." Crowdsourcing allows a person, institution, or company to benefit from the work, ideas, or wisdom of the Internet crowd.

"Crowdsourcing is a type of participative online activity in which an individual, an institution, a non-profit organization, or a company proposes to a group of individuals of varying knowledge, heterogeneity, and number the voluntary undertaking of a task via a flexible open call. The undertaking of the task, of variable complexity and modularity, in which the crowd should participate by bringing their work, money, knowledge, and/or experience, always entails mutual benefit. The user will receive satisfaction of a given type of need, be it economic, social recognition, self-esteem, or the development of individual skills, while the crowdsourcer will obtain and utilize to what the user has brought to the venture to their advantage, whose form will depend on the type of activity undertaken" (Estellés-Arolas and González-Ladrón-de-Guevara 2012).

The emergence of crowdsourcing has been made possible thanks to the evolution of the Internet and social media technologies that have enabled communities to come together more quickly, and to collaborate and exchange information (Isman et al. 2012). It is the intersection of the "Crowd," "Social Web," and "Outsourcing" elements (Saxton et al. 2013). One of the main advantages of crowdsourcing is that it enables the possibility of iterative contributions of different people (Zhang et al. 2011).

By applying this definition to teaching, crowdsourcing techniques can become a natural framework for learning. However, crowdsourcing itself cannot offer the best educational experience. But by applying appropriate methods, it offers improved education by increasing the efficiency of workflows and optimizing personalized curricula (Weld et al. 2012) without disconnecting the basic "Crowd," "Social Web," and "Outsourcing" elements of the term crowdsourcing.

8.2 Crowdsourcing Techniques in Higher Education

The introduction of crowdsourcing techniques into higher education finds applications in aspects that can improve alumni performance. Crowdsourced knowledge building offers the possibility of collaborative projects where both teachers and students can interact and exchange information. For instance, teachers can share learning resources as a repository of high-quality materials, which can improve the quality of lessons and save time in preparing lectures. Students' interaction in crowdlearning also implies bringing different skills to a common project to help solve a given problem. Students would like to receive personalized education according to their abilities and learning style (Weld et al. 2012). This learning form allows contacts to be made between the teachers and students interested in accurate specialized training. Students acquire practical knowledge that adapts to their demands.

Teachers need to change the dynamics of traditional education based on rote learning to one whereby students play an active role and take responsibility for their own learning (Whitehead 2008). Active learning methodologies emphasize student participation (Braxton et al. 2000 and Huber 2008). Students should play a responsible active role in both learning planning and interacting with teachers and peers to boost intrinsic motivation based on interest and curiosity (Cannon and Newble 2000). Teachers are no longer the main source of knowledge and inquiry, but assume the role of facilitator and guide by accompanying and guiding students through their learning process (Álvarez 2005). With the emergence of web technologies in the last decade, online learning has evolved significantly by using adaptive online environments that facilitate social learning (Corneli and Mikroyannidis 2012). In this chapter, we use these techniques:

CROWDTEACHING: In this approach, the lecturing staff shares and puts together lecturing material following the subject curricula. Crowdteaching as an evolving movement in which thousands upon thousands of educators from all around the world are uploading high-quality educational content online—all free of charge (DeWitt 2012).

CROWDLEARNING: Literally defined as the learning of crowds. This crowdsourcing technique is based on the "learning by project lecturing scheme." Crowdlearning can be defined as learning through real-case projects with the participation of several students ("crowd"). Broadly speaking, the method consists in contacts being made between teachers or experts in specific matters and an alumnus who seeks specialized practical training. The key lies in anyone being able to offer anything to others, and everyone has something to learn.

Finally, it is noteworthy that one of the main reasons for using active teaching methods is to provide students with a deeper understanding of the subject.

8.3 Experiment

It is worth indicating that since teaching is given in a Polytechnic University, the use of new technologies is widespread, and both attitude and teacher training facilitate their implementation to a great extent (Paredes and Estebanell 2005). Therefore, practically since the intranet was set up in the university, the means by which notes, support materials, scientific articles, problems, etc. have been made available to students has been the web. So our situation is enviable when compared to other faculties (Marin et al. 2011). During the 2002/2003 course at the Polytechnic University of Valencia (UPV), an educational platform was set up on the web which facilitates and stimulates the use of new working strategies through forums, chats, as were new evaluation forms. The introduction of this platform and its use, as a result of new technologies, has been a turning point which has led us to consider the present study.

The practical character of this matter is suitable for implementing crowdlearning and crowdteaching.

8.3.1 Context and Sample

Educational innovation forms part of the PML subject taught in course 4 of the Business Administration and Management degree at the UPV. This subject is a core subject that consists in 9 credits. In recent years, 200 and 300 students have registered every year on average. This subject has not been taught since the last course because new study plans have appeared and old ones have terminated. Traditionally, this subject has generated a high percentage of failed exams and, therefore, many students resit exams and take the course again, which meant subsequent failure in incorporating proposed competences. This situation has led the teachers of this subject to often reconsider the approach that is to be applied to teaching it in order to improve the teaching–learning process and to, therefore, increase students' academic results. Finally, 183 students registered for the 2013/2014 course.

8.3.2 Description of the Experiment

As this subject is not being taught in the present course, the following actions have been taken:

All the documents required for the subject (notes, slides, recorded classes, solved problems, questions, etc.) have been uploaded on the intranet platform (PoliformaT).

A teaching guide has informed students about the way the subject is evaluated.

An open platform has been set up on which students can pose problems, solve their own problems or those considered by other students, and can correct problems solved by other students. Students can begin to pose a problem and other students should finish solving it if only the description is published. In this case, a score is given to the group.

Those problems posed by other students will be evaluated on a Likert-type scale from 1 to 5 to evaluate the originality, difficulty, comprehension, and the relation of contents. Based on this evaluation, 10 awards of 2 points can be obtained, which can be awarded to only one person or to the group of people who pose and solve the problem.

Those students who find errors in problems solved by other students will also obtain additional points (from 0.5 to 1.5) depending on the errors found and the number of problems corrected.

8.3.3 Objectives of the Experiment

The following objectives are considered:

Encouraging students' autonomy, reflexive and critical thinking, teamwork, professional skills, and their capacity to evaluate tasks performed by others.
Acquiring and developing the capacity to identify, pose, and solve problems relating to practical subject contents.
Continuous evaluation so that the questions and problems posed by students are corrected while they are worked on and so that students learn from their own mistakes.
Helping students improve their marks and scores.
Arousing interest in the subject so that posing problems involves assimilating knowledge and tools.

8.4 Results

At the end of the experiment, a survey was sent to students and the following results were obtained.

Figure 8.1 shows that of the 183 who registered for the subject, 119 participated in the experiment. In Fig. 8.2 we can seen that 107 of these 119 participants considered that the experiment helped them better learn the subject.

Fig. 8.1 Participation in the experiment. *Source* Own

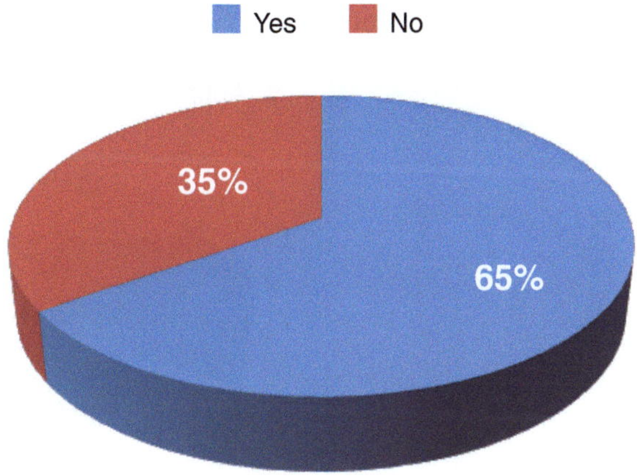

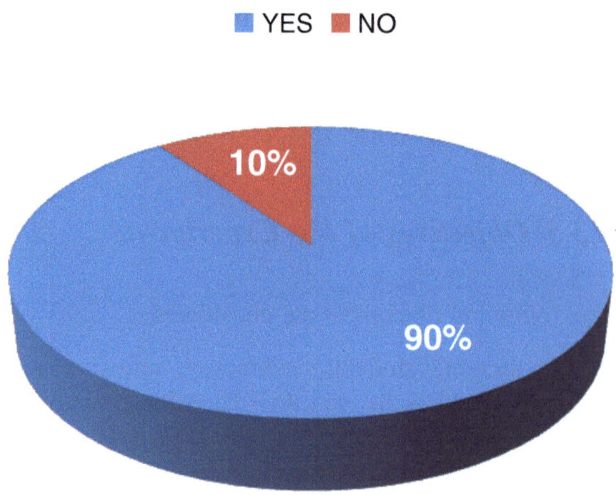

Fig. 8.2 Participants who believe that the experiment was positive for their learning. *Source* Own

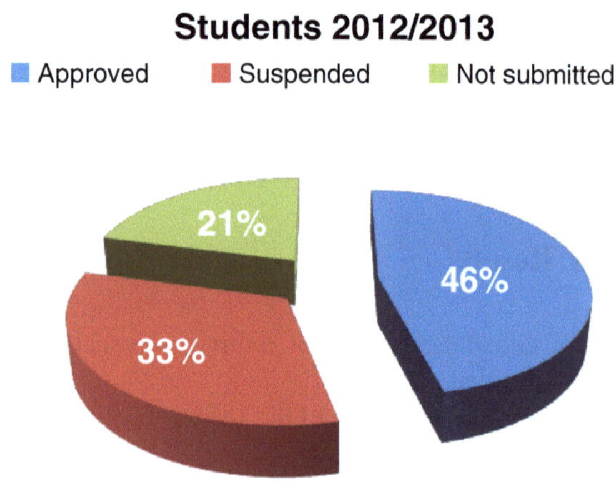

Fig. 8.3 Students 2012/2013. *Source* Own

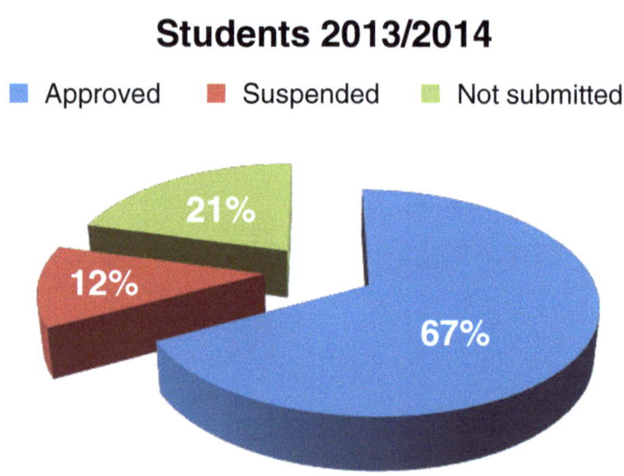

Fig. 8.4 Students 2013/2014. *Source* Own

8.5 Conclusions

This chapter provides a comprehensive approach to the application of crowdsourcing techniques that can be applied to Higher Education institutions. We must highlight the excellent perception that students stated they had about using this tool. This methodology helped clarify the general framework of the work performed and centered students' conversation with their peers.

Each student provides the different skills needed to solve the posed problem as a whole. Students share ideas and teach each other, which improves their preparation (Bloom 1979).

As regards the capacities developed while the subject was underway, in their opinion, students indicated teamwork in particular, along with communication skills (listening, considering other alternatives to solve problems, arguing one's own viewpoints, etc.), as well as organization and coordination skills. Apart from doing much more work than they personally thought they would do at the start of the process, when the experiment was underway, they began to understand that they could do more things than they initially believed they would. Moreover, when they saw other students' examples, they understood that they too were capable of participating and adopting new approaches which, in turn, would encourage other classmates and motivate them to continue on the path that had opened up among them all. All this enabled the collection of solved problems to grow as a repository, and with much more imagination than if considered by one person alone. Students also considered that the concerns of the problems posed by classmates were more like their own.

As demonstrated in Figs. 8.3 and 8.4, the number of pass marks increased since fewer students failed exams. However, the number of students who did not sit exams remained constant. Although data have not been collected, the number of outstanding and excellent marks rose, and the number of passing grades lowered. So we can state that applying crowdsourcing to university teaching is able to improve marks, students become more involved and they perceive a greater sense of belonging.

References

Álvarez, M. B. (2005). Adaptación del método docente al Espacio Europeo de Educación Superior: La motivación de los alumnos como instrumento clave. *Estudios sobre Educación*, 9, 107–126. http://dspace.si.unav.es/dspace/bitstream/10171/8911/1/NB.PDF.

Bloom, B. S. (1979). Taxonomía de los objetivos de la educación. Marfil.

Braxton, J. M., Milen, J. E., & Sullivan, A. S. (2000). The influence of active learning on the college student departure process: Toward a revision of Tinto's theory. *Journal of Higher Education, 71*(5), 569–590.

Cannon, R., & Newble, D. (2000). *A handbook for teachers in universities and colleges*. London: Kogan.

Corneli, J., & Mikroyannidis, A. (2012). Crowdsourcing education on the Web: a rolebased analysis of online learning communities. In: A. Okada, T. Connolly & P. Scott (Eds.), *Collaborative learning 2.0: Open educational resources* (pp. 272–286). Hershey: IGI Global.

DeWitt, T. (2012). Hey science teachers—make it fun TEDxBeaconStreet. Filmed Nov 2012. http://www.ted.com/talks/tyler_dewitt_hey_science_teachers_make_it_fun. Accessed 30 Sept 2014.

Estellés-Arolas, E., & González-Ladrón-de-Guevara, F. (2012). Towards an integrated crowdsourcing definition. *Journal of Information Science, 38*(2), 189–200.

Howe, J. (2006). The rise of crowdsourcing. *WIRED magazine*, 14(06), http://archive.wired.com/wired/archive/14.06/crowds.html. Accessed 5 Sept 2014.

Huber, G. (2008). Aprendizaje activo y metodologías educativas. Revista de Educación, No. Extra, pp. 59–81.

Isman, M., Bennet, J., Judah, J., Glenzer, A. (2012). Effectiveness and efficiency. Tapping new sources of innovations and ideas through crowdsourcing, Booz Allen Gamilton Inc.

Marin, M., Polo, F., & Mateos, A. (2011). Las metodologías activas en la docencia universitaria de contabilidad. In: *En Las metodologías activas de aprendizaje en la Facultad de Administración y Dirección de Empresas* (pp. 15–28). Valencia: Universitat Politècnica de València.

Paredes, J. & Estebanell, M. (2005). Actitudes y necesidades de formación de los profesores antes las TIC y la introducción del crédito europeo: un nuevo desafío para la educación superior, Revista de Educación, núm. 337, mayo-agosto (pp. 125–148).

Saxton, G. D., Oh, O., & Kishore, R. (2013). Rules of crowdsourcing: Models, issues, and systems of control. *Information Systems Management, 30*(1), 2–20.

Weld, D. S., Adar, E., Chilton, L., Hoffmann, R., Horvitz, E., & Koch, M et al. (2012). Personalized online education—A crowdsourcing challenge. In: *Human computation AAAI technical report WS-12-08* (pp 159–163).

Whitehead, D. P. (2008). Thoughts on education and innovation. *Childhood Education, 85*(2), 106–118.

Zhang, H., Horvitzy, E., Millerz, R. C., & Parkes, D. C. (2011). Crowdsourcing general computation. In: *ACM conference on human factors in computing systems*. May 7–12, Vancouver.

Chapter 9
Humanizing Internal Crowdsourcing Best Practices

Alexis J. Bañón-Gomis, Ricardo Martínez-Cañas and Pablo Ruiz-Palomino

Abstract In its short life, the concept of crowdsourcing has been applied in practice to attain various outcomes, such as business goals, innovation processes, social justice, democratic participation and environmental activism. One of its value-adding applications in the business area involves recruiting organizational members to participate in problem-solving activities. However, because this situation could be perceived as a new job parcel involving complex human relationships governed by a values loophole, the need to improve understanding on how to manage this practice optimally remains. By focusing on how value is created through social aspects and how such practice can be optimally managed, this chapter identifies crowdsourcing as a new type of organizational value created through human relationships inside business organizations. More importantly, this chapter uses the case of IBM to explore how this online relationship can be adequately articulated to avoid counterproductive behaviours by internal crowd participants. A proposal of best-practice principles for corporations interested in addressing this business practice in a more humanizing way concludes the chapter.

9.1 Introduction

During the past two decades, the broad generalization of the Internet and the mass adoption of new media technologies have completely redesigned the relationships among employees, suppliers and other stakeholders in corporations (Surowiecki

A.J. Bañón-Gomis (✉)
Universitat Politècnica de València, Valencia, Spain
e-mail: albaogo@upvnet.upv.es

R. Martínez-Cañas · P. Ruiz-Palomino
Universidad de Castilla-La Mancha, Cuenca, Spain
e-mail: Ricardo.Martinez@uclm.es

P. Ruiz-Palomino
e-mail: Pablo.Ruiz@uclm.es

F.J. Garrigos-Simon et al. (eds.), *Advances in Crowdsourcing*,
DOI 10.1007/978-3-319-18341-1_9

2004). The Internet has fostered and cultivated the creation of a participatory culture that provides ways for business managers to leverage the collective intelligence of emerging online communities (Lebraty and Lebraty 2013). That is, top managers are interested in identifying, measuring, using and maintaining the energy of this collective community intelligence to improve key business processes intimately linked to the achievement of business goals. For example, employee participation in governance mechanisms could be fostered, products could be (re)designed, and various and complex organizational and operational problems could be solved (Howe 2008).

Therefore, crowdsourcing can be characterized as a deliberate blend of bottom-up, open, creative processes and top-down organizational goals (Brabham 2013). Organizations are using the Internet to outsource work to individuals. That is, they are taking functions once performed by employees and outsourcing them to (un) defined networks of people in the form of open calls (Howe 2006). This process can take the form of peer production (when the job is performed collaboratively for employees in a workgroup), but it can also be undertaken by isolated individuals working under specific guidelines (Villarroel and Reis 2010).

Research on crowdsourcing has appeared in a variety of academic disciplines, each of which has approached the topic from a different angle. According to Brabham (2013), this concept is dominated by four significant research areas:

1. Computing research, which centres on the design and technical aspects of crowdsourcing systems and is supported by big corporate Internet technology research firms, such as IBM and HP laboratories. These companies are interested in solving problems in a distributed, collective and crowdsourced pattern.
2. Business management, in which researchers are interested in crowdsourcing applications in terms of innovation, profitability and business efficiency, as well as the strategic and managerial dimensions of integrating business operations.
3. Social science research, which focuses on the human dimension of crowdsourcing, which mainly involves finding answers about the motivation to participate in crowdsourcing, as well as other issues such as labour exploitation and ethics.
4. Applied professionally oriented disciplines, which focus on specific industries, such as urban planning, medicine, journalism and national security, among others.

However, the confusing and conflicting results generated by these four large research streams are beginning to disappear. This is because some research questions have merged to provide a more holistic perspective of the important matters in crowdsourcing research. The goal of this chapter is to facilitate the merging of these different lines of research. To do so, the chapter uses IBM as a case study to explain how the firm distributes a problem through small tasks to computer scientists in an open-source culture of sharing a code of values or guidelines. This chapter also analyses the value creation process through a strategic lens that promotes innovation and problem-solving by focusing on open innovation and lead-user innovation. Finally, this chapter takes a social science approach to propose best-practice principles for use in crowdsourcing, so that this practice can be humanized by stimulating ethical behaviours of the crowd.

9.2 Crowdsourcing and Social Networks as Generators of Internal Organizational Value

Crowdsourcing is principally a process for partitioning tedious work and obtaining needed services, ideas or valuable content from an online community (Brabham 2013). Despite the great array of definitions of the concept, Estellés-Arolas and González-Ladrón-de-Guevara (2012: 197) developed a new and integrated definition that synthetizes the core facts included in the concept: "*Crowdsourcing is a type of participative online activity in which an individual, an institution, a non-profit organization, or company proposes to a group of individuals of varying knowledge, heterogeneity, and number, via a flexible open call, the voluntary undertaking of a task. The undertaking of the task, of variable complexity and modularity, and in which the crowd should participate bringing their work, money, knowledge and/or experience, always entails mutual benefit. The user will receive the satisfaction of a given type of need, be it economic, social recognition, self-esteem, or the development of individual skills, while the crowdsourcer will obtain and utilize to their advantage that what the user has brought to the venture, whose form will depend on the type of activity undertaken*".

Thus, the crowd's use of the Internet to pursue a certain prefixed goal is strongly emphasized in crowdsourcing, as is the idea that this goal is attained by realizing a defined small task in which the crowdsourcer engages. In crowdsourcing, strong attention is also paid to the extrinsic or intrinsic rewards that crowd participants usually receive for their participation in the process. Finally, in fulfilling the widespread norm in the business strategy area that business organizations should create value through various activities (Grant 2010), the crowdsourcing practice is conceptualized to achieve such undertaking. For example, business value is achieved when an organization outsources an activity for less cost than what it would have cost to perform internally (Williamson 1985). Value is also created when the organization focuses on exploiting its core, valuable, rare and difficult-to-imitate resources and outsources other (the rest of) activities (Barney 1991). Thus, organizations can clearly benefit from crowdsourcing practices in these two situations (Howe 2008). However, there is a need to identify more clearly what value specifically is created by crowdsourcing (Huberman et al. 2009), especially considering that, in measuring internal value, a wide range of tangible and intangible outputs can be involved (e.g. competitiveness, financial performance, profitability, efficiency, effectiveness, satisfaction, perceived success) and that value creation depends on what participants judge to be important (Moran and Ghoshal 1997).

A review of the literature shows that crowdsourcing activities are oriented to co-create business value through the specificity of electronic connections based on four interconnected value dimensions (Amit and Zott 2001): efficiency, complementarity, community lock-in and novelty. Efficiency value is obtained by controlling costs and outsourcing routine, non-strategic activities and complementary value derives from synergies obtained through more creative crowd opinions and collective knowledge. In contrast, community lock-in value is created by the positive externalities network that is created through usual crowdsourcing operations, which is easily manifested by making the crowdsourcing site more attractive in parallel with the number of Internet users who frequent it. Finally, novelty value comes from the great creative potential of the crowd to propose more and better innovations. Thus, value can be created through the electronic relationships at the heart of every crowdsourcing operation inside an organization (Amit and Zott 2001). As such, a major task for organizations is to implement the crucial instruments to capture the value created by a crowd of virtual relationships (Howe 2008).

Lebraty and Lebraty (2013) identify three probable main sources of value creation: cost reduction, development of innovations and authenticity. Indeed, crowdsourcing is always less costly than a traditional outsourcing operation, though there are some limitations and situations in which crowdsourcing is not applicable. It is clear that crowdsourcers are motivated primarily by benefits gained, including the ability to gather large numbers of solutions and information at a relatively inexpensive cost (Lebraty and Lebraty 2013).

Crowdsourcing also allows for the development of innovations that not only help the organization gain a competitive advantage over competitors but also contribute to value creation, either incrementally or radically, depending on the type of innovation. Finally, this practice favours authenticity, which refers to an organization's improved understanding of its particular environment, market and clients through the adaptation of products and services. However, while cost reduction is a constant in crowdsourcing, it is necessary to choose between innovation and authenticity, because these two objectives cannot coexist in a single crowdsourcing operation (Lebraty and Lebraty 2013). Thus, to be able to choose the objective (innovation vs. authenticity) for the launch of crowdsourcing activities, organizations must be cognizant of the factors that motivate the crowd to participate.

Crowdsourcing may generate solutions coming from a variety of participants, whether amateurs and volunteers working in their spare time (Brabham 2013) or part-time/full-time workers. In large companies, sometimes this process combines the efforts of numerous self-identified volunteers or part-time workers, such that each contributor, by his or her own initiative, adds a small portion to the greater result (Howe 2006). This is why users might be motivated to contribute by obtaining either intrinsic inputs, such as social contacts and intellectual stimulation, or extrinsic inputs, such as financial gains (Howe 2008). Indeed, in some cases, contributors are compensated monetarily, with prizes, promotions or recognition, while in other cases, the only reward received is intellectual satisfaction or just passion for a task well done (Howe 2008).

Lebraty and Lebraty (2013) identify three types of crowd communities that determine the two extremes (intrinsic and extrinsic) of motivation and the centre of a continuum (hybrid or intermediate) for value creation through crowdsourcing.

The first type of community is driven by intrinsic motivation that stems from passion and fervent attention to the brand product or service and to the company. Community members' motivation derives from an individual desire for improvement and self-realization because they are typically not paid for their participation. In this case, it is the task itself (not the task as a means to an end) that motivates this community. Members usually have a clearly defined sense of belonging and might be motivated by the attractiveness of the objectives being pursued for the sake of their community (e.g. sustainable development, ecology, ethics, social welfare, elimination of poverty). In all likelihood, motivation to participate is strengthened by the simple consideration or use of their ideas. The strong sentiment of "*shared paternity*" of the product, along with the feeling of belonging to a community or network, is another important reason for their involvement.

The second type of crowd community is mainly based on extrinsic motivation factors because member satisfaction mainly depends on the financial remuneration received. In this case, it is the external environment of the task that motivates people to participate in this type of activity. The community assembles and then unites around the business model proposed by the organization holding the crowdsourcing operation. This community is attracted by the exploitation of intellectual property rights and discoverer monetary remuneration, which are usually provided to creators. Here, companies must reinforce behaviour and participation by designing credible and trustworthy business models based on rewards.

Finally, the third type of community motivated to participate in crowdsourcing activities—that is the hybrid or intermediate model—includes people who have an average skill level and a limited passion for the task. This includes employees who do not participate in crowdsourcing operations just for the passion and employees who are not solely driven by financial remuneration. This type of crowd can be highly volatile and its contributions extremely variable. Crowd members can be linked initially to financial remuneration, but throughout the course of their participation, motivations could evolve from belonging to a community and the opportunities that come with it. This case is characterized by internalized extrinsic motivations. Members participate with the goal of possibly finding better employment in future or simply of flattering the crowd's ego.

Beyond the different motivations found among crowd participants, distinct interests might also arise. Even when crowdsourcing is planned for internal workers, who are under the umbrella of one business culture, their various and distinct interests may conflict with one another and sometimes also with organizational interests. If so, these situations might give rise to bad ethical and dehumanized behaviours by crowd participants. Internal workers might think of performing these new tasks in a "values loophole", which might lead them to behave in ways that exclusively meet their own interests.

Previous research has deemed this negative (self-interested) use of discretion in crowdsourcing activities as a potential danger to this business practice (Franke et al. 2013). Because such use might induce people to commit behaviours against organizational interests, the positive climate might be hampered and the achievement of the intended objectives of the crowdsourcing activity even undermined.

Thus, organizations must realize that it is likely not enough to simply launch a crowdsourcing activity to solve corporate problems or develop innovative projects. Rather, increasingly often, and given the relatively novelty of this practice in business, organizations must establish a set of behavioural guidelines and provide them to crowd participants in an effort to control operational dysfunction and enhance its humanization. Indeed, under the umbrella of a framework of values consciously established for this unique activity, crowd participants could be guided more effectively in their tasks and persuaded to avoid potential dehumanizing behaviours.

9.3 Internal Crowdsourcing Best Practices

The internal generation of value through crowdsourcing and social networks can be visualized with a real example. In this section, we highlight the existence of "internal crowdsourcing" oriented to current organizational members—that is internal organizational interactions based not on mass communications but on masses of communicators—and we review their best-practice methodology. With this in mind, we selected the case of IBM and the IBM Social Computing Guidelines (hereinafter ISCG).[1] We chose IBM because it has a systematized code of conduct around crowdsourcing and social networks and also because IBM interprets this as an opportunity to build trust between the different crowd participants and the organization. We begin by analysing IBM's evolution.

In 1997, when many companies were looking for ways to restrict their employees' Internet access, IBM was actively recommending that they use the Internet. Later on, in 2003, IBM made a strategic decision to embrace the blogosphere and encouraged IBMers to participate. Instead of treating all these changes as threats, the firm considered them facilitators of the interaction among IBM's members and, more importantly, as a chance to build trust between them and IBM as an organization.

In the spring of 2005, IBM created guidelines for the use of wikis. At that time, IBMers used wikis to create a set of guidelines for all IBMers who wanted to blog. The firm repeated this call in 2008 and again in 2010 when it asked organizational members to re-examine the guidelines in light of ever-evolving technologies and online social tools.

In other words, IBM aroused an "internal crowdsourcing" conception by encouraging organizational members—its "internal crowds"—to regulate the way all IBMers should blog. By doing so, the same users provided helpful and practical advice to protect both IBM bloggers and IBM. Whether they knew it or not, they created an auto-regulation structure based on an "internal crowdsourcing" conception capable of generating value in two ways. First, IBM's own organizational

[1] See http://www.ibm.com/blogs/zz/en/guidelines.html.

members could internally contribute to the generation of their own guidelines, contributing to reinforce their sense of belonging. Second, this was a way to ensure that IBM's senior personnel remained current to the needs of lower level employees.

This internal crowdsourcing approach is a new relationship model founded on individual interactions based on masses of communicators and not on mass communications. As with any crowdsourcing approach, it has external and visual consequences but also internal consequences, which are singular.

With regard to the external consequences, this model of interactions allows IBM to share with clients, shareholders and the communities in which it operates its greatest asset—that is the expertise of its employees—thus accomplishing four main objectives: describing, learning, contributing and applying. In terms of describing, the ISCG state the following: "To empower IBMers as global professionals, innovators and citizens through online social computing". The firm promotes learning because "[s]social computing is an important arena for organizational and individual development opening an exchange for learning between IBM and its clients, and among the many constituents of the emerging business and societal ecosystem" (ISCG). IBM also contributes by sharing "with the world the exciting things IBM is learning and doing" (ISCG). Finally, IBM applies forms of online publishing and discussion, such as blogs, wikis, file-sharing, user-generated videos and audio, virtual worlds, social networks and so on.

The innovative part of the "internal crowdsourcing" conception is IBM's capacity to generate internal value through the detached effort of its members, and its conception is based on trust and personal responsibility as the two core values underlying all relationships. Because of these values, IBM can manage freedom among IBMers and support an open dialogue and exchange of ideas in different scenarios: between IBMers and their partner clients, among members of the many communities in which they participate and among the general public.

IBM regulates its internal crowdsourcing relationships, which are voluntary relationships, through its official ISCG, which are based on 12 guidelines (see Annex I). It is important to understand that as voluntary relationships, internal crowdsourcing cannot be imposed. Rather, because these are voluntary relationships, ethics, as the discipline that conceptualizes actions in terms of its goodness or badness for human beings (Hoffman et al. 2014), must be present in the relationships. The ISCG aid us in elucidating a series of ethical values and principles for internal crowdsourcing practice, providing a humanizing framework to prevent and solve conflicts and to inspire an ordered free will.

9.4 Humanizing the Crowdsourcing Best Practices

By reviewing and analysing the current official 12 guidelines of the ISCG (see Annex I), we can extract an underlying internal logic. The type of guidance these guidelines aim to provide to relate to a common subject can be easily discerned—

that is, the ISCG are geared towards building a strong battery of principles around the concept of responsibility. But responsibility with regard to what?

Again, a review of the ISCG enables us to extract the core elements of guidance IBM aims to provide. The ISCG are about responsibility with regard to the following: G.1: respect of general rules; G.2: own generated content; G.3: personal brand; G.4: corporate brand; G.5: mandatory elements (copyright and legal and financial aspects); G.6: confidentiality, or loyalty to corporate confidentiality; G.7: confidentiality, or loyalty to client confidentiality; G.8: general audience; G.9: other organizational members; G.10: others and their opinions; G.11: crowdsourcing purposes (value addition); and G.12: corporate image.

These 12 topics around responsibility can be further aggregated into four groups focused on responsibility: responsibility in general—in the generation of added value (G.11); responsibility with regard to consequences on the corporation—dealing with the corporate brand (G.4) and the corporate image (G.12); responsibility to its organizational members—to own content (G.2), the personal brand (G.3), corporate confidentiality (G.6), clients' confidentiality (G.7), the general audience (G.8), organizational members (G.9), and other agents and their opinions (G.10); and mandatory responsibility—to respect guidelines (G.1) and the law (G.5).

This analysis helps us outline two functionalities of the ISCG instrument regarding the actions of crowd participants: (1) the ISCG instrument restricts crowd participants' actions and (2) the ISCG instrument provides the conditions for crowd participants' actions. On the one hand, the negative approach used to restrict participant actions is intended to avoid the arbitrariness in the interactions of the crowd in the internal crowdsourcing. On the other hand, establishment of the conditions aims to provide a solid framework to create a concrete discretionary space of interaction. In other words, the generation of guidelines is an instrument to delimit the discretionary behavioural framework of the crowd (hereinafter DBFC).

DBFC is a useful and necessary tool for internal crowdsourcing behaviours, but according to its nature, it is also insufficient. As we noted previously, internal crowdsourcing is a relationship rooted in volunteerism and, as such, cannot be based on regulation and control. These limitations lead to serious problems when the crowd interacts in areas not accounted for by the DBFC. In these cases, what must the crowd do? If the DBFC is considered insufficient, how can firms guide the crowd?

Certainly, the answer is complex because, on the one hand, there is a need to regulate this (voluntary) relationship and, on the other hand, there is a strong limitation established by its own nature (volunteerism) that requires the respect of the individual freedoms of crowd participants. Thus, it is necessary to extract a series of ethical values (or goods to be pursued; McGhee and Grant 2008), to guide the decisions and actions of crowd participants in an unrestricted and open manner. According to Argandoña (2003: 16), values are "central desires or beliefs regarding final states or desirable conducts that transcend specific situations, guide the choice and evaluation of our decisions and, therefore, of our conducts, becoming an integral part of our way of being and acting to the point of shaping our character". Furthermore, when these values are ethically based, they are worth having because they contribute to the perfection of the individual as a human being and resemble the objective moral goods of the person (McGhee and Grant 2008). Therefore, with the enumeration of a series of ethical values (goods) to commit and pursue, human relationships that form from the crowdsourcing practice can be humanized. In addition, crowd participants' respective individual freedoms can be simultaneously preserved.

Table 9.1 'Internal crowdsourcing' values and principle proposition

	Value	Principle
	Trust	Promote an open dialogue and the exchange of ideas based on trust
General	Justice	Add value to others
		Add value without forgetting your day job
		Add value recognizing your own mistakes
		Add value with rigour
	Prudence	Add value using your best judgement
Knowledge	Justice	(*Intra*-organizational) know the organization (business conduct guidelines)
	Prudence	(*Extra*-organizational) respect copyright and fair use laws
Corporation	Responsibility	Speak in the first person
		Use a disclaimer
	Temperance and prudence	Understand the potential dangers of publishing personal thoughts (especially if you are a manager or an executive)
	Prudence	Be cautions in the use of the corporate brand
Organizational members	Coherence	Be thoughtful about how you present yourself in online social networks
	Consistency	Be consistent about how you present yourself and your professional activity
	Dignity	Respect others' dignity
	Honesty	Be clear on who you are
		Be the first to point it out
		Be who you are
	Prudence	Be careful and judicious in disclosing personal details
		Protect confidential and proprietary information
		Organizational business performance and other sensitive "inside information"
	Respect	Protect the organization's clients, business partners and suppliers
		Respect your audience
		Respect your co-workers
	Transparency	Use your real name

Source Own elaboration

Based on the four groups of responsibilities extracted previously from the IBM DBFC, a series of ethical values and principles can be proposed as "best-practice" guidelines for other corporations interested in launching internal crowdsourcing activities in their strategic plans. The major value to attain is trust because trust promotes an open dialogue and the exchange of ideas. Other values, such as coherence, consistency, dignity, honesty, justice, prudence, respect, responsibility, temperance and transparency (see Table 9.1), are also applicable according to the scope of the action affected. For example, with regard to responsibility in general, actions involved in this business practice should serve to reach justice and prudence goods (e.g. adding value without forgetting the daily job or using the best judgment). These same values, justice and prudence, should be applicable to the knowledge about the mandatory responsibilities that any party should have (e.g. respecting copyright and fair use laws). Responsibility, temperance and prudence are also values to be committed, so as not to damage the corporation (e.g. speaking in first person, being cautious in the use of the corporate brand, using a disclaimer). Finally, with regard to organizational members, ethical values such as coherence, consistency, dignity, honesty, prudence and respect all help crowd participants take humanizing actions (e.g. being thoughtful about how they present themselves in online social networks, respecting others' dignity, being careful in disclosing personal details). In summary, the application of these values in action, together with their corresponding principles, can serve as a proposal for internal crowdsourcing activities, one that contributes to building a humanizing framework of guidance for this type of crowd participant.

9.5 Conclusions

This chapter provides valuable contributions to the literature by specifying a series of operational and ethical values and principles in response to the need to humanize the internal crowdsourcing practice. In particular, we addressed the issue of value addition that goes along with the launching of this business practice to better understand how to manage the human relationships involved, with regard to one major firm's stakeholders: organizational members.

Although a great deal of attention has been paid to this emerging crowdsourcing concept in the recent past (Zhao and Zhu 2014), scant research has provided cues for practitioners on how to manage and guide actions of those who want to participate in new tasks. This is an aspect that merits consideration by managers. Otherwise, the positive and innovative results expected from the launching of a collaborative project might fall by the wayside, if the crowdsourcing work climate becomes permeated with dehumanizing acts and decisions.

The crowdsourcing practice constitutes new working situations in which connection and collaboration with others are the norm in achieving the newest and greatest products. As a result, the temptation might arise to act in this scenario outside the umbrella of current values established by the corporation. Crowd participants might be motivated to participate in the crowdsourcing activities because of reasons that both differ and are opposite to those of the corporation. As we described in this chapter, each internal crowd participant might become involved in new tasks for myriad motives (i.e. intrinsic, extrinsic and intermediate) and, as a result, act in ways that might conflict with one another.

With this in mind, and with the need to avoid dehumanized behaviours by giving exclusive importance to the production of newer and greater things, in this chapter, we drew on the case of IBM and, specifically, its ISCG (see Annex I) to design a series of best-practice principles to address internal crowdsourcing on a humanizing basis. While the design of a series of sanctioning regulations might be useful in many different contexts, it is not wholly compatible with the crowdsourcing practice. By its very nature, internal corporate crowdsourcing involves people, societies and organizations' desire to collaborate in projects in a voluntary manner. It is clear that considering the freedom of crowds in the logic of human relationships is a risky challenge. In doing so, management would be basing the proper functioning of these relationships on the goodwill of each party. Thus, management needs to rethink ways to interrelate with others beyond paradigms based on regulation and control; in turn, these ways must be in accord with the voluntary nature of crowdsourcing.

This proposal should merit management consideration to build a humanizing framework to guide internal crowd participants in their firms. However, the successful implementation of this code for internal crowdsourcing participants will be useless if employees fail to recognize that the values underlying these guidelines should become a reality in aspects that directly affect their working lives. Indeed, several limitations that could interfere with the proper influence of these guidelines on internal crowd participants must be taken into account around crowdsourcing. For example, because large companies may conceive of crowdsourcing as an easy path to fast, cheap, high-quality labour, they could try to benefit from the work of crowds without offering the kinds of monetary rewards that are the norm in traditional work arrangements (Brabham 2013). This lack of rewards could be perceived as unfair and dishonest and thus infringe on the ethical values underlying the best-practice guidelines in crowdsourcing. This perception is not uncommon, and crowdsourcing is sometimes called "digital slavery" and "crowdsploitation" (Brabham 2013), meaning that management's self-interests permeate the real purposes for launching certain business activities. However, the perception of a dishonest or unfair situation would strongly influence the likelihood of future participation beyond considerations of self-interest (Franke et al. 2013).

The IBM case has greatly helped us in elucidating a series of practical and ethical values and principles to guide participants in internal corporate crowdsourcing, but more efforts should be undertaken to collect information from other companies that also issue open calls for people to get involved in temporary problem-solving activities—that is crowdsourcing activities. In addition, the focus in this chapter was on one specific type of crowdsourcing activity—involving internal personnel. However, many other stakeholders (e.g. consumers, local communities, Internet users, suppliers, non-governmental organization activists) could be involved in these activities to help the firm. By adopting the methodology used here (i.e. case study), research could analyse the different modalities of crowdsourcing according to the stakeholders involved to extract the best-practice principles to operate optimally in such cases. Finally, further work on our proposal is necessary to clarify how managers can humanize their internal corporate crowdsourcing operations from an ethical standpoint. For example, perhaps virtues would be a logical next step to consider.

Annex I: Current and Official IBM's Social Computing Guidelines

1. Know and follow IBM's Business Conduct Guidelines.
2. IBMers are personally responsible for the content they publish on-line, whether in a blog, social computing site or any other form of user-generated media. Be mindful that what you publish will be public for a long time-protect your privacy and take care to understand a site's terms of service.
3. Identify yourself-name and, when relevant, role at IBM—when you discuss IBM-related matters such as IBM products or services. You must make it clear that you are speaking for yourself and not on behalf of IBM.
4. If you publish content online relevant to IBM in your personal capacity it is best to use a disclaimer such as this: "The postings on this site are my own and don't necessarily represent IBM's positions, strategies or opinions."
5. Respect copyright, fair use and financial disclosure laws.
6. Don't provide IBM's or a client's, partner's or supplier's confidential or other proprietary information and never discuss IBM business performance or other sensitive matters about business results or plans publicly.
7. Don't cite or reference clients, partners or suppliers on business-related matters without their approval. When you do make a reference, link back to the source and do not publish content that might allow inferences to be drawn which could damage a client relationship with IBM.
8. Respect your audience. Don't use ethnic slurs, discriminatory remarks, personal insults, obscenity, or engage in any similar conduct that would not be appropriate or acceptable in IBM's workplace. You should also show proper consideration for others' privacy.
9. Be aware of your association with IBM in online social networks. If you identify yourself as an IBMer, ensure your profile and related content is consistent with how you wish to present yourself with colleagues and clients.
10. Spirited and passionate discussions and debates are fine, but you should be respectful of others and their opinions. Be the first to correct your own mistakes.

11. Try to add value. Provide worthwhile information and perspective. IBM's brand is best represented by its people and what you publish may reflect on IBM's brand.
12. Don't misuse IBM logos or trademarks and only use them if you have the authority to do so. For example, you shouldn't use IBM in your screen name or other social media ID.

References

Amit, R., & Zott, C. (2001). Value creation in e-business. *Strategic Management Journal, 22*, 493–520.

Argandoña, A. (2003). Fostering values in organizations. *Journal of Business Ethics, 45*, 15–28.

Barney, J. (1991). Firm resources and sustained competitive advantage. *The Journal of Management, 17*(1), 99–120.

Brabham, D. C. (2013). *Crowdsourcing*. The MIT press essential knowledge series. Cambridge, MA: MIT Press.

Estellés-Arolas, E., & González-Ladrón-de-Guevara, F. (2012). Towards an integrated crowdsourcing definition. *Journal of Information Science, 38*(2), 189–200.

Franke, N., Keinz, P., & Klausberger, K. (2013). Does this sound like a fair deal?: Antecedents and consequences of fairness expectations in the individual's decision to participate in firm innovation. *Organization Science, 24*(5), 1495–1516.

Grant, R. M. (2010). *Contemporary strategy analysis* (7th ed.). New York: Wiley.

Hoffman, W. M., Frederick, R. E., & Schwartz, M. S. (2014). General introduction: The nature of business ethics. In *Business ethics: Readings and cases in corporate morality*. Malden, MA: Wiley.

Howe, J. (2006). Pure, unadulterated (and scalable) crowdsourcing. *Crowdsourcing: Tracking the Rise of the Amateur* (blog). http://crowdsourcing.typepad.com/cs/2006/06/pure_unadultera.html.

Howe, J. (2008). *Crowdsourcing: Why the power of the crowd is driving the future of business*. New York: Crown.

Huberman, B. A., Romero, D. M., & Wu, F. (2009). Crowdsourcing, attention and productivity. *Journal of Information Science, 35*(6), 758–765.

Lebraty, J. F., & Lebraty, K. L. (2013). *Crowdsourcing: One step beyond* (1st ed.). London: ISTE.

McGhee, P., & Grant, P. (2008). Spirituality and ethical behaviour in the workplace: Wishful thinking or authentic reality. *Electronic Journal of Business Ethics and Organization Studies, 13*(2), 61–69.

Moran, P., & Ghoshal, S. (1997). Value creation by firms. Insead working paper series. https://flora.insead.edu/fichiersti_wp/inseadwp1997/97-19.pdf.

Surowiecki, J. (2004). *The wisdom of crowds: Why the many are smarter than the few and how collective wisdom shapes business, economies, societies, and nations*. New York: Doubleday.

Villarroel, J. A., & Reis, F. (2010). *Intra-corporate crowdsourcing (ICC): Leveraging upon rank and site marginality for innovation*. Paper presented at Crowd Conference 2010: The World's First Conference on the Future of Distributed Work, San Francisco. http://www.crowdconf2010.com/images/finalpapers/villarroel.pdf.

Williamson, O. E. (1985). *The economic institutions of capitalism: Firms, markets, relational contracting*. New York: The Free Press.

Zhao, Y., & Zhu, Q. (2014). Evaluation on crowdsourcing research: Current status and future direction. *Information Systems Frontiers, 16*, 417–434.

Chapter 10
Using Crowdsourcing to Overcome Barriers to Women Entrepreneurship

Norat Roig-Tierno, Cristina Blasco-Carreras, Alicia Mas-Tur and Belén Ribeiro-Navarrete

Abstract This chapter presents crowdsourcing as a novel way of overcoming barriers facing women entrepreneurs, offering alternatives to conventional solutions. The study analyzes three barriers to women entrepreneurship: access to financing, access to specific management knowledge, and access to information and communication technologies (ICTs). For each barrier, a different form of crowdsourcing is proposed: crowdfunding, crowd wisdom, and crowdfunded media, respectively. Using these crowdsourcing tools, women entrepreneurs can overcome major difficulties when starting businesses.

Keywords Business angels · Crowfunding · Crowdsourcing · Crowd wisdom · Entrepreneurship · Women entrepreneurs

10.1 Introduction

Crowdsourcing means using the "crowd" to obtain ideas, information, and solutions to succeed in business. Crowdsourcing covers both intellectual and financial resources. The term "crowdfunding" applies to financial resources, whereas crowd wisdom refers to intellectual resources (Fig. 10.1).

Crowdsourcing is a mechanism that can improve organizations. It can also be used to solve problems and perform simple and complex tasks (Brabham 2008a, b). According to Schuurman et al. (2012), crowdsourcing can be used in two ways: first, as "integrative sourcing without remuneration," which includes free user-generated content (YouTube, Wikipedia comments, tags, etc.), and second, as

N. Roig-Tierno
Universitat Politècnica de València, Valencia, Spain

C. Blasco-Carreras · A. Mas-Tur (✉) · B. Ribeiro-Navarrete
Universitat de València, Valencia, Spain
e-mail: alicia.mas@uv.es

F.J. Garrigos-Simon et al. (eds.), *Advances in Crowdsourcing*,
DOI 10.1007/978-3-319-18341-1_10

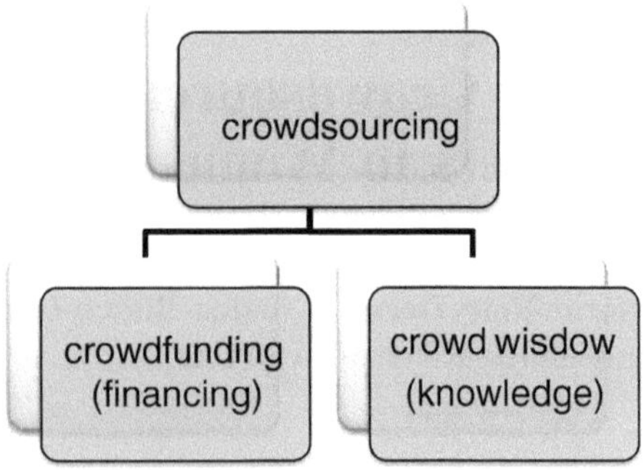

Fig. 10.1 Crowdsourcing's components

"selective crowdsourcing without evaluation," which refers to crowdsourcing whereby people with knowledge in a given subject evaluate information on that subject. In crowdsourcing, businesses and the crowd cooperate via information and communication technologies (ICTs) to pursue the common good (Howe 2008).

Crowdfunding, on the other hand, refers to the practice whereby diverse groups collaborate to raise money (Ordanini et al. 2011), creatively solving financial problems through social networks. Crowdfunding's mission consists of using the "crowd" to solve small challenges or raise capital for projects unable to secure financing by traditional means. Crowdfunding uses online platforms to allow initiators and contributors to exchange resources and thereby make their ideas a reality (Gerber et al. 2012), and is often associated with community experiences whereby participants create "benefits for the community" (Belleflamme et al. 2014). Sport, music, video games, and education are some of the main areas where crowdfunding offers solutions. Participants make crowdfunding transactions on online platforms where several crowdfunding actions occur concurrently (Lawton and Marom 2010). Crowdfunding initiatives provide great support to entrepreneurs who lack financial resources—the principal crowdfunding users.

Finally, crowd wisdom arises from the need to spread knowledge through Web sites that allow groups of people with outstanding intelligence to solve problems. Diversity of opinion, participants' geographic decentralization, and the power of the crowd mean that crowd wisdom is becoming more widely used to solve business problems (Surowiecki 2004).

Building on this foundation, this chapter presents three difficulties women entrepreneurs must overcome to succeed in business. We first examine women entrepreneurs' difficulties in accessing financing. We then discuss how crowdfunding can provide women entrepreneurs with the necessary resources to start businesses. Next, we investigate how women entrepreneurs can access greater specific business knowledge through crowd wisdom. Finally, we analyze technological sectors, discussing how these sectors can foster business creation through crowdsourcing.

10.2 Using Crowdsourcing to Overcome Barriers to Women Entrepreneurship

When starting a business, women entrepreneurs may encounter financial, management, and administrative difficulties (Akehurst et al. 2012). Crowdsourcing represents an attractive solution to overcome all three barriers.

10.2.1 Access to Financing

The scarcity of early-stage capital creates a significant barrier to entrepreneurship (Cosh et al. 2009). Numerous studies have addressed women entrepreneurs' disadvantage with respect to men regarding access to financial resources. Coleman (2000) reported that women encounter greater difficulties in accessing financing and pay higher interest rates than men. Relations between women entrepreneurs and financial institutions are subject to widespread stereotypes and discrimination (Carter and Storey 1994).

The scarcer resources invested by women when starting a business may indicate greater problems and obstacles in obtaining financial resources necessary to undertake a business venture. Thus, numerous studies (Orhan and Scott 2001; Verheul and Thurik 2001) have concluded that women encounter greater difficulties in accessing the necessary early-stage capital and that financial institutions may doubt women entrepreneurs' credibility. After analyzing findings from numerous empirical studies, authors have concluded that women perceive that banks discriminate against them and that barriers to accessing early-stage capital are greater for women than for men (Stoner et al. 1990; Brush 1992; Akehurst et al. 2012).

Entrepreneurs must identify which resources they lack and which they already possess. A shortage of early-stage capital can negatively affect a business in the long term. Similarly, less early-stage capital affects entrepreneurs' chances of securing bank financing (Storey 1994). Gundry and Welsch (2001) showed that women often start and run their businesses with less capital and scarcer financial resources. This lack of financial resources affects women entrepreneurs' future performance.

Without bank financing, women business owners must seek more costly forms of raising capital (Hayes 2000), which is perhaps why women perceive that traditional financing instruments fail to suit women-led businesses. This need to seek more costly forms of raising capital could also explain why some authors have claimed women entrepreneurs prefer to finance businesses with their own personal savings or family loans (Petersen and Rajan 1994). This preference leads to lower initial investment by women. Women business owners seem to lack awareness of available financing options, which may prevent women from seeking alternative financing sources such as crowdfunding.

10.2.1.1 Alternative: Crowdfunding

Crowdfunding helps women entrepreneurs raise capital to crystallize new ideas, especially when resources are scarce (Greenberg and Gerber 2012; Lambert and Schwienbacher 2010). Crowdfunding projects vary greatly, from small artistic projects to large entrepreneurial projects hoping to raise millions of dollars in seed capital as an alternative to traditional financing (Schwienbacher and Larralde 2010).

Crowdfunding platforms can be open source, whereby resources belong to the community and can be exploited individually (with no restriction on who may use them), or generically, whereby the entity seeking crowdfunding owns and exploits the resources. Crowdfunding begins with an open call, normally on an online platform, requesting donations in exchange for future products or some reward for supporting the initiative (Belleflamme et al. 2014). These platforms are currently having enormous effects (Greenberget al. 2013).

Through crowdfunding, project initiators aim to raise capital via online social networks. Instead of raising capital from a small group of sophisticated investors, crowdfunding projects obtain money from large audiences (the "crowd"), where many individuals contribute a small sum (Kuppuswamy and Bayus 2013; Mollick 2014). Therefore, when raising financial resources to start a business, crowdfunding may offer an attractive alternative for women who, as previously discussed, encounter serious problems in accessing traditional financing. If the crowdfunding project meets its goals, the money passes to the entrepreneur. Although the entrepreneur has no legal obligation to carry out the project, in practice, all projects are carried out (Mollick 2013).

Thus, given the difficulties faced by new businesses in attracting financing from "business angels," banks, and venture capitalists, entrepreneurs in general, and women entrepreneurs particularly, can take advantage of these large online communities of consumers/investors (Cumming 2012). Furthermore, because it is often anonymous, crowdfunding benefits women entrepreneurs, who need not reveal their sex when presenting a project.

Women entrepreneurs' family economy is important because women entrepreneurs often rely on seed capital from family and friends to start new business projects (Cumming and Johan 2009). Since entrepreneurial projects often rely on family and friends for funding, crowdfunding can favor women especially (Parker 2009). The motives that drive women to start businesses are primarily empathy, sympathy, happiness, and identification with the entrepreneurial project. All these factors directly affect the quantity donated (Gerber et al. 2012).

Crowdfunding has been successful because it eliminates economic and geographic barriers, and because virtual platforms facilitate donations from contributors (Schwienbacher and Larralde 2010). Furthermore, the current financial crisis has forced entrepreneurs to seek alternatives to finance their projects. Currently, policymakers are working toward a regulatory framework that will mitigate serious fraud risk and alleviate restrictions.

To conclude, although women entrepreneurs have increased their access to financial resources, accessing financing remains a barrier to women entrepreneurship. Crowdfunding may thereby help women create and develop businesses.

10.2.2 Knowledge Transfer

Knowledge transfer has undergone considerable changes in two areas. Once conceived as a one-way (offer/demand) relationship, knowledge transfer is now understood as an interactive two-way relationship in which the transfer agent and recipient both actively participate. The "long tail" thesis posits that users can select an increasing amount of information, contents, knowledge, products, and services in numerous ways besides traditional communication media. This range of options encourages consumer choice (Anderson 2006). Furthermore, knowledge transfer is no longer limited to engineering or medicine, but now also includes other knowledge areas such as social sciences and humanities (D'Este et al. 2014).

On average, women entrepreneurs boast fewer years' work experience than men, and the kind of experience differs. Less work experience and specific training in business-related areas prevents women from developing their own skills to drive business growth or obtain financial resources to start a business. Hence, differences in work experience affect business size.

According to the "long tail" theory, knowledge transfer lets society access information more easily. Nevertheless, women entrepreneurs still struggle to access the training they need to acquire skills to create and develop businesses. Crowd wisdom, a new crowdsourcing form, offers a plausible alternative to reduce these problems.

10.2.2.1 Alternative: Crowd Wisdom

In recent years, women have enjoyed greater training in the management skills necessary to start a business and participate more in a historically male-dominated activity. Nevertheless, opportunities are unequal because the culture in many countries impedes women's professional development. We therefore propose crowd wisdom as an alternative for women to access the necessary knowledge to create businesses and develop the skills required for entrepreneurship. Outsourcing innovation combined with "the knowledge of the crowd" creates crowd wisdom, a term coined by Howe (2008).

Similarly, the concept of collective intelligence (i.e., intelligent decisions by individuals who combine their knowledge) has arisen. Through social interaction, the crowd shares, corrects, opens, processes, enriches, and evaluates intellectual knowledge (Lévy 1994).

Crowd wisdom arises from the need for groups of people with outstanding knowledge to spread their knowledge through virtual platforms and solve problems

(Surowiecki 2004). Therefore, this specific business knowledge transfer could prove useful for women entrepreneurs who lack the necessary intellectual resources. Thus, these relations could contribute to two-way knowledge flows between actors with complementary competencies. Specific contributions from each user could help women entrepreneurs achieve innovative results. In addition, crowd wisdom could help form stable social networks and generate relationships of trust between actors. Such trust would create favorable conditions so that people with complementary knowledge could share sensitive information and learn to solve complex problems.

Knowledge transfer through media such as the Internet contributes to resolving business problems on an international level. Web sites increase diversity of opinion and, consequently, diverse solutions to the same problem, thanks to independence and decentralization of opinions (Goldfarb and Tucker 2010). Thus, in crowd wisdom, open innovation with users transcends merely identifying user needs—an approach associated with classic research—and implies developing solutions to generic market needs.

Web sites encourage innovation through new technologies (Terranova 2004), while creators of interactive platforms and projects learn new ways of addressing new knowledge forms (Gerber et al. 2012). Crowd wisdom lets participants learn through responses to calls for financing, Web analysis, qualitative feedback, and tutorials about how to seek financing, fill orders, and so forth (Terranova 2004). People thus learn through participation and obtain information through regular, public interaction (Kolonder et al. 1998). Thanks to the Internet, people with outstanding knowledge (e.g., university researchers) can help businesses in general, and women-led businesses in particular, by providing advice on optimally managing resources and maximizing present and future financial profits.

In many cases, although women entrepreneurs obtain the financing they need, without the necessary knowledge, their businesses may fail. Therefore, crowd wisdom offers an alternative to provide women with the knowledge they need to succeed in business.

10.2.3 Access to Technological Sectors

Women enjoy greater managerial presence in certain economic sectors (Blum et al. 1994; Huarng et al. 2012). Nevertheless, numerous authors (Brush 1990; Romero 1990; ENSR 1996; Akehurst et al. 2012) have concluded that women-led businesses tend to proliferate in the services sector, especially in activities where women have traditionally played a prominent role: retail, hospitality, personal assistance services, and education. Scholars have proposed several reasons to explain women's business orientation toward services. For instance, service and retail businesses require low up-front investment and less technical training. These requirements help women entrepreneurs nullify their disadvantage with respect to men regarding obtaining financial resources and specific business skills (Blake 2006).

In contrast, women entrepreneurs are underrepresented in sectors such as manufacturing and ICTs (Du Rietz and Henrekson 2000). Accordingly, some research (Loscocco and Robinson 1991; Anna et al. 1999) has shown that women are less likely to own businesses in technology-intensive sectors. Yet, ICTs supply knowledge to innovative societies and enhance people's knowledge and creativity. Therefore, women entrepreneurs' access to the ICT sector should be fostered, not only so that women can work in all sectors, but also because access to ICTs can help businesses in other sectors develop.

Digital platforms can help reduce grazes stemming from geographic distances between markets. In addition, ICTs have increased access to the global market, accelerated information transmission, and reduced costs. Therefore, as previously mentioned, ICTs facilitate women entrepreneurship not only in the ICT sector, but also in other sectors (Haliburton et al. 1998).

10.2.3.1 Alternative: Crowdfunded Media

Through crowdfunding, particularly crowdfunded media, women entrepreneurs can build a basis to access the ICT sector and use this technology to develop their businesses.

Crowdfunded media link resources in a novel way (Sanfiel 2008) so that users can access technological knowledge. Therefore, these media give women entrepreneurs access to the ICT knowledge necessary to develop their businesses.

Through global digital platforms, ICTs drive entrepreneurs' knowledge and creativity. By lowering the costs of access to services, knowledge, and information, ICTs have contributed to reducing transaction costs in developed countries. Women entrepreneurs can develop capabilities and skills by using ICTs (Huyer and Sikoska 2003). The potential of crowdsourcing, driven by ICTs, encourages businesses to create interdependencies and synergies and thereby operate with greater ease in global markets.

The idea of combining traditional business skills with business activity in innovation, technology, and information constitutes a relatively new concept (Sahlfeld 2007). ICT use is important for business competitiveness. Thanks to the Internet and its applications, new and quicker ways of communicating and transmitting information have partially substituted more conventional communication methods (Sahlfeld 2007). Nevertheless, as already shown, women lack access to this new technology. They lack both the necessary resources for external access and the necessary technical training.

New platforms with highly diverse contents (e.g., blogs and social networks) have gradually been emerging. These contents often give individuals the knowledge they need to correctly implement ICTs in entrepreneurship. In short, ICTs help women develop their potential and realize their business projects. With a global reach, ICTs can increase the chances that women access the help they need. In addition, ICTs can help women learn to manage and develop their businesses.

10.3 Conclusions

This chapter shows the importance of the "crowd" for women to achieve not only financing but also the necessary knowledge to start and develop businesses. Each section begins by presenting a different barrier to women entrepreneurship and then introduces an alternative solution: crowdsourcing.

Thus, by offering women equal access to financing, knowledge, and ICTs, global virtual platforms, the basis of crowdsourcing, can help create gender equality in business creation.

By giving women entrepreneurs greater access to the resources necessary to create businesses, these online platforms mean that initiatives can have global repercussions. First, women entrepreneurs can use crowdfunding to access basic financial resources for entrepreneurial projects. Second, crowd wisdom grants women entrepreneurs access to specific entrepreneurial knowledge to create and develop their businesses. Third, through crowd funded media, women entrepreneurs can access ICTs, so that, in addition to operating in this historically male-dominated sector, women can also use ICTs to develop their businesses.

Empirically analyzing crowdsourcing's effect in Spain would enhance this study. In addition, further research should explore different branches of crowdsourcing such as crowsdvertising, which allows entrepreneurs to market their ideas through advertising financed by public participation.

References

Akehurst, G., Simarro, E., & Mas-Tur, A. (2012). Women entrepreneurship in small service firms: Motivations, barriers and performance. *The Service Industries Journal, 32*(15), 2489–2505.

Anderson, B. (2006). *Imagined communities: Reflections on the origin and spread of nationalism*. Verso Books. London

Anna, A.L., Chandler, G.N., Jansen, E., & Mero, N.P. (2000). Women business owners in traditional and non-traditional industries. *Journal of Business Venturing*, *15*, 279–303.

Belleflamme, P., Lambert, T., & Schwienbacher, A. (2014). Crowdfunding: Tapping the right crowd. *Journal of Business Venturing, 29*(5), 585–609.

Blake, M.K. (2006). Gendered lending: Gender, context and the rules of business lending. *Venture Capital*, *8*, 183–201.

Blum, T.C., Fields, D.L., & Goodman, J.S. (1994). Organization level determinants of women in management. *Academy of Management Journal*, *37*, 241–269.

Brabham, D. C. (2008a). Moving the crowd at iStockphoto: The composition of the crowd and motivations for participation in a crowdsourcing application. *First Monday*, 13(6).

Brabham, D. C. (2008b). Crowdsourcing as a model for problem solving an introduction and cases. *Convergence: The International Journal of Research into New Media Technologies*, *14* (1), 75–90.

Brush, C.G. (1992). Research on women business owners: Past trends, a new perspective and future directions. *Entrepreneurship Theory and Practice*, *16*(4), 5–30.

Coleman, M. (2000). The female secondary headteacher in England and Wales: Leadership and management styles. *Educational Research, 4*(1), 13–27.

Cosh, A., Cumming, D., & Hughes, A. (2009). Outside enterpreneurial capital. *The Economic Journal, 119*(540), 1494–1533.

Cumming, D., & Johan, S. (2009). Pre-seed government venture capital funds. *Journal of International Entrepreneurship, 7*(1), 26–56.

Du Rietz, A., & Henrekson, M. (2000). Testing the female under-performance hypothesis. *Small Business Economics, 14*(1), 1–10.

D'Este, P., García Quevedo, J., & Mas-Verdú, F. (2014). Transferencia del conocimiento: del modelo transaccional al relacional. *Mediterráneo Económico., 25*, 279–296.

Gerber, E. M., Hui, J. S., & Kuo, P. Y. (2012). Crowdfunding: Why people are motivated to post and fund projects on crowdfunding platforms. In *CSCW Workshop*.

Goldfarb, A., & Tucker, C. (2010). Advertising bans and the substitutability of online and offline advertising. *Journal of Marketing Research, 48*(2), 207–227.

Greenberg, M., & Gerber, E. (2012). Crowdfunding: A survey and taxonomy. Northwestern University Segal Design Institute (Technical Report 12–03).

Greenberg, M. D., Pardo, B., Hariharan, K., & Gerber, E. (2013). Crowdfunding support tools: predicting success & failure. In *CHI'13 Extended Abstracts on Human Factors in Computing Systems* (pp. 1815–1820). ACM.

Gundry, L. K., &. Welch, H. P. (2001). The ambitious entrepreneur: high growth strategies of women-owned enterprises. *Journal of Business Venturing*, 16(5), 453–470.

Haliburton, W., Thweatt, M., & Wahl, N. J. (1998). Gender differences in personality components of computer science students: A test of Holland's congruence hypothesis (Vol. 30, No. 1, pp. 77–81). ACM.

Hayes, N. (2000). *Doing psychological research*. London: Taylor & Francis Group.

Howe, J. (2008). *Crowd sourcing: Why the power of the crow is driving the future of business*. New York: Crown Publishing.

Huarng, K. H., Mas-Tur, A., & Yu, T. H. K. (2012). Factors affecting the success of women entrepreneurs. *International Entrepreneurship and Management Journal*, *8*(4), 487–497.

Huyer, S., & Sikoska, T. (2003). *Overcoming the gender digital divide: Understanding ICTs and their potential for the empowerment of women*. INSTRAW.

Kolodner, J. L., Crismond, D., Gray, J., Holbrook, J., & Puntambekar, S. (1998). Learning by design from theory to practice. In *Proceedings of the International Conference of the Learning Sciences* (Vol. 98, pp. 16-22).

Kuppuswamy, V., & Bayus, B. L. (2013). Crowdfunding creative ideas: The dynamics of project backers in Kickstarter. *UNC Kenan-Flagler Research Paper*, 2013–2015.

Cumming, D. (Ed.) (2012). *The oxford handbook of entrepreneurial finance*, Oxford: Oxford University Press.

Lawton, K., & Marom, D. (2010). The Crowdfunding Revolution: Social Networking Meets Venture Finance.

Lévy, P. (1994). *L'intelligence collective: Pour une anthropologie du cyberspace,11*. Paris: La Découverte.

Loscocco, K. A., & Robinson, J. (1991). Barriers to women's small-business success in the United States. *Gender and Society, 5*(4), 511–532.

Mollick, E. R. (2013). Swept away by the crowd? crowdfunding, venture capital, and the selection of entrepreneurs. *Venture Capital, and the Selection of Entrepreneurs, 25*.

Mollick, E. (2014). The dynamics of crowdfunding: An exploratory study. *Journal of Business Venturing, 29*(1), 1–16.

Ordanini, A., Miceli, L., Pizzetti, M., & Parasuraman, A. (2011). Crowd-funding: Transforming customers into investors through innovative service platforms. *Journal of Service Management, 22*(4), 443–470.

Orhan, M., & Scott, D. (2001). Why women enter into entrepreneurship: An explanatory model. *Women in management review, 16*(5), 232–247.

Parker, S. C. (2009). *The economics of entrepreneurship*. Cambridge: Cambridge University Press.

Petersen, M. A., & Rajan, R. G. (1994). The benefits of lending relationships: Evidence from small business data. *The journal of Finance, 49*(1), 3–37.

Romero, M. (1990). *La actividad empresarial femenina en España. Instituto de la mujer*. Madrid: Ministerio de asuntos sociales.
Sahlfeld, M. (2007). How does ICT work for development? A review of the challenges and opportunities. *ATDF Journal, 4*(1), 22–36.
Schuurman, D., Baccarne, B., De Marez, L., & Mechant, P. (2012). Smart ideas for smart cities: investigating crowdsourcing for generating and selecting ideas for ICT innovation in a city context. *Journal of theoretical and applied electronic commerce research, 7*(3), 49–62.
Schwienbacher, A., & Larralde, B. (2010). Crowdfunding of small entrepreneurial ventures. *SSRN Electronic Journal*.
Sanfiel, M. T. S. (2008). Cross media training (para crear en tiempos de convergencia). *Anàlisi: quaderns de comunicació i cultura*, 36, 139–158.
Stoner, C., Hartman, R., & Arora, R. (1990). Work-home role conflict in female owners of small business: An exploratory study. *Journal of Small Business Management*, *28*(1), 30–38.
Storey, D. J. (1994). Understanding the small business sector. *University of Illinois at Urbana-Champaign's Academy for Entrepreneurial Leadership Historical Research Reference in Entrepreneurship*.
Surowiecki, J. (2004). *The wisdom of crowds: Why the many are smarter than the few and how collective wisdom shapes business*. Societies and Nations: Economies.
Terranova, T. (2004). *Network culture: Politics for the information age* (Vol. 23, p. 25). London: Pluto Press.
Verheul, I., & Thurik, R. (2001). Start-up capital: Does gender matter?. *Small Business Management*, *16*, 329–345.

Chapter 11
Gamification for Crowdsourcing Marketing Practices: Applications and Benefits in Tourism

Marianna Sigala

Abstract The use of gamification for directing and motivating customers' behaviour and supporting crowdsourcing practices in marketing is increasingly spreading. This chapter reviews the literature for identifying the game principles and elements that can lead to effective gamification, and it then demonstrates the applicability and implications of this theory by discussing various gamification applications developed for supporting crowdsourcing marketing practices in tourism. The examples demonstrate that gamification can be used for crowdsourcing any marketing practice and influencing customer behaviour at any stage of the consumer behaviour process. Implications for future research are also provided.

Keywords Gamification · Game mechanics · Funware · Motivation · Tourism · Marketing · Applications · Benefits · Crowdsourcing

11.1 Introduction

Crowdsourcing (defined as the process of obtaining needed services, ideas, or content by soliciting contributions from a large group of people, and especially from online communities, rather than from traditional employees or suppliers) is increasingly being used in marketing. Specifically in the tourism sector, firms heavily use crowdsourcing for exploiting travellers as marketers and actively involving them into their marketing strategies, because the user-generated content and communications amongst travellers are perceived as more effective, authentic and reliable content for promoting the intangible tourism experiences (Sigala et al. 2012). However, as with all crowdsourcing practices, the success of crowdsourced marketing heavily depends on the motivation and willingness of people to engage and contribute in activities (Brabham 2012).

M. Sigala (✉)
School of Business, Department of Business Administration,
University of the Aegean, Michalon 8, 82100 Chios, Greece
e-mail: m.sigala@aegean.gr

F.J. Garrigos-Simon et al. (eds.), *Advances in Crowdsourcing*,
DOI 10.1007/978-3-319-18341-1_11

In this vein, gamification is increasingly integrated within marketing strategies (Zichermann and Cunningham 2011; Witt et al. 2011) in order to increase the customers' engagement, participation, learning and motivation by directing their behaviour (i.e. increased activity, social interaction, consumption and purchasing actions) through the design and affordances of positive and intrinsically motivating gameful experiences (Hamari 2013; Conejo 2014; Sigala 2015). Moreover, well-implemented gamification does not only motivate consumers to show desired behaviours (Zichermann and Linder 2010; Conejo 2014), but it can also make the marketing practices more interesting by adding motivational incentives that enhance the enjoyment of consumers (Sigala 2015).

However, although firm's spending in gamification is increasing (i.e. more than 50 % of the organisations will gamify aspects of their business by 2015, Gartner 2012), many of the gamified applications for marketing will also fail to meet business objectives due to weak gamification designs (Gartner 2012). Furthermore, despite the great potential of gamification in tourism marketing (e.g. Cramer et al. 2011), studies examining the gamification's effectiveness in tourism are also scant (Sigala 2015; Xu et al. 2013). Consequently, it is urgent to examine how firms can design effective gamification applications that can increase the business results and provide added value to their customers.

Thus, the aim of this chapter is twofold: (a) to review the literature in order to identify and summarise the principles and issues that need to be considered for designing effective gamification applications in marketing that can enhance the customers' participation and outcomes and (b) to analyse various examples of gamified marketing applications in tourism. To that end, the book chapter first discusses the concept and implementation of gamification in marketing, and then, it shows the applicability and the implications of the gamification theory by discussing the funware design and the aims of various gamification examples from the tourism industry. Finally, as there is limited knowledge about the effectiveness of gamification on influencing consumer behaviour in a marketing context (Hamari et al. 2014), the chapter concludes by discussing directions for future research that can advance our insight into this topic.

11.2 Gamification in Marketing: Concept, Aims, Applications and Benefits

Gamification is widely known as the use of game-play mechanics for non-game applications (Deterding et al. 2011a, b). Thus, "gamified" applications only need to incorporate some (and not all) of the game design elements, and this differentiates them from "serious games" (the design of full-fledged games for educational purposes). Although there are various definitions of gamification, all of them highlight its aim to create a gameful experience by including two elements (Sigala 2015): a systemic component defining how the game is constructed/designed and an experiential component describing the human involvement within the game. Overall, the major aim of gamification is to effectively motivate and direct the users' behaviour and to increase the users' engagement with the "play" tasks (Lee and Hammer 2011; Shneiderman 2004) by using game-like techniques (e.g. scoreboards, points and personalised fast feedback) that make people feel more ownership, flow and purpose when engaging with the "play" tasks (Pavlus 2010).

Two types of gamification applications are found in the marketing literature (Terlutter and Capella 2013): 1) advergames, which are full computer games specifically designed and created to promote goods or ideas, where the entertainment content mimics traditional game forms; and 2) marketing practices with gameful designs that are only partially based on elements of digital games. Advergames and gamified marketing practices are usually less complex than a "real" game (e.g. no complex rules, short playing time), and so, they can be easily distributed on different platforms (e.g. websites and smart phones) and so, easily played quite repeatedly, (e.g. during short breaks in the day, such as waiting times or travelling). Moreover, their interactive context increases the users' "situational" involvement (i.e. user active control and two-way communication), which in turn enables users to experience flow (Csikszentmihalyi 1990). Flow is characterised as an enjoyable experience that leads to feelings of immersion in a task, accompanied by a sense of control over the situation, and it also leads to increased learning and exploratory and participatory behaviour. In the state of flow, the individual is focused on the flow-eliciting interaction, with irrelevant thoughts and stimuli being screened out, and sense of time being distorted.

Thus, gamified marketing applications create pleasurable experiences that can lead to numerous marketing benefits, because they attract the attention of their users to the interactive content and engage users into cognitively learning (Sigala 2015). Indeed, gamification can lead to positive users' behavioural (i.e. task involvement and task performance) and psychological (e.g. flow, enjoyment) outcomes (Sigala 2015; Hamari et al. 2014), which in turn can significantly increase the performance outcomes of marketing practices, such as enhanced customers' brand recall and awareness as well as positive attitudes, purchase intentions and actual sales (Cauberghe and De Pelsmacker 2010; Terutter and Capella 2013).

11.3 Implementing Gamification: Elements and Principles of Funware Design

Implementing gamification requires the design of funwares, which is the use of game mechanics to encourage desired user actions and to generate customer loyalty (Zichermann and Linder 2010). Game mechanics are rule-based systems/simulations that facilitate and encourage a user to explore and learn the properties of their space by generating intrinsic (i.e. motivation that comes from within) and extrinsic (when one is motivated to do something for its expected outcome) motivational affordances (Hamari et al. 2014; Deci and Ryan 1985). There are numerous game mechanics that are usually grouped into three categories (Yee 2006): behavioural (e.g. discovery/exploration, ownership, community collaboration, lottery, virality, status, story/theme); feedback (e.g. bonuses, countdown, reward schedules); and progress (e.g. achievements/badges, levels, (redeemable or social) points, progress bar, challenge).

Different types of game mechanics can afford the generation of different types of motivation. Intrinsic motivation in games results when one is motivated to do something for its own satisfaction (e.g. for fun/joy, interest, self-expression, curiosity, challenge, altruism, competition, cooperation, sense of belonging, love or aggression) and it can be triggered by the following game mechanics (Wood et al. 2004): avatar (virtual alter ego), role-playing, content (storyline), interaction (feedback/motivation), level of control (freedom of choices), possibility of losing points, amount of choices and feeling connected. In sum, role-playing in games can trigger the following five primary intrinsic motivations (Companion and Sambrook 2008; Crawford 1982): choice, control, collaboration, challenge and achievement. Extrinsic motivation in games happens when users are encouraged to engage in play tasks for achieving performance and obtaining rewards, and it is generated by game mechanics such as, pressure, classifications, levels, points, badges, awards, missions (Deterding et al. 2011a, b)

Points, badges and leaderboards (PBL) are clearly the most commonly used mechanics for triggering the users' motivation and raising their engagement with play tasks by giving them information about their achievements, progress and high scores. (Hamari and Eranti 2011). However, PBLs are not enough to make gamification successful (Chorney 2012), while their exclusive use is also found to diminish the users' intrinsic motivation (Benabou and Tirole 2005), creativity (Toubia 2006) and behavioural involvement (Deci et al. 1999). This is because when the games offer the player extrinsic incentives for something the player already intrinsically enjoys, there is the danger that extrinsic incentives may diminish the intrinsic motivation of consumers (Benabou and Tirole 2005). Moreover, once gamification is used to provide external motivation, the user's internal motivation decreases: e.g. if the organisation starts using gamification based upon the provision of external rewards and then it decides to stop these rewards, the organisation will be worse off than when it started, as the users will be less likely to return to the behaviour without the external reward (Deci et al. 1999). Funware designs should also avoid the superficial "pointsification", as they miss the elements of playfulness and experiences (triggers of intrinsic motivation), which are central to what makes a game effective (Robertson 2010).

Hence, some researchers (e.g. Deterding et al. 2011a, b; Kim 2010) emphasise the need to design an effective player's experience with intrinsic rewards preferred over extrinsic rewards, because extrinsic rewards may lead to short-term activity increase, but reduction in long-range interest and use of a product/service (Lazzaro 2011); and intrinsic motivation more significantly leads users to experience flow, a state of energised focus that can generate greater user involvement and enjoyment (Deci and Ryan 1985; Csíkszentmihályi 1990). On the other hand, others (Sigala 2015; Hamari et al. 2014) stress the need to combine extrinsic and intrinsic motivation by using a mixture of game mechanics, because the use of extrinsic incentives can further enhance the users' intrinsic motivation, specifically when the aim is to develop a sense of competence and mastery in the user/consumer. This sense of competence can be supported by the presence of extrinsic game elements, such as bonuses or rewards that may help establish intrinsic motivation.

However, instead of considering the two motivations as independently, research recognises the systematic interactions between intrinsic and extrinsic motivations referred to as the crowding theory (Frey 1997) or motivational synergy (Amabile 1993) suggesting that the externally imposed rewards (e.g. extrinsic motivation) may undermine (crowd-out/non-synergetic effects) or in other cases, magnify (crowd-in/synergetic effects) intrinsic motivation (e.g. Frey and Jegen 2001). Crowd-out effects are observed where the provision of monetary rewards and fines indicates a shift in the locus of control, and so, they lessen the autonomy and the possibility of the user to act in a personally driven and meaningful way, or when the users perceive the quantification of contribution as changing a task from relational (internally driven) to transactional (reward driven). Crowd-in effects happen when a user perceive external rewards as supportive and congruent with their motivational preference such as, when the external interventions (game mechanics) provide feedback, recognise and confirm quality of performance, and help the users improve their competences. Hence, the psychological conditions under which the crowding effects occur are the following: game mechanics crowd-out intrinsic motivation if they are perceived as controlling; and game mechanics crowd-in intrinsic motivation if they are perceived as supportive.

The crowding theory and its implications for funware design are also explained and justified by the following theories. Self-determination theory (SDT) advocates that when external motivations are integrated with the underlying activity into someone's own sense-of-self, then he better understands the importance of the activity to himself and internalises its regulation, which in turn self-motivates him to also perform the activity (Zichermann and Cunningham 2011). Situational relevance also argues that when someone else creates goals for a user, the user perceives an external judge deciding what is relevant to him, and this in turn creates a negative feeling demotivating the user to engage with the activity (Nicholson 2012). So, external rewards unrelated to the user's needs (e.g. badges, points) are the least likely to be integrated by the user, as the perception is that someone else is controlling his behaviour. This is because, rewards based upon gaining or losing status that tap into the user's ego create an introjected regulation of behaviour, and while this can be intrinsically accepted, the controlling aspect of these rewards causes the loss of internal motivation. On the contrary, allowing the user to self-identify with goals or groups that are meaningful to him is much more likely to produce autonomous, internalised behaviours, because in this way, the user is able to connect these goals to other values that he already holds. Finally, games using role-playing in their funware can generate significant motivational affordances, because they provide users with control upon the selection of game mechanics. Specifically, role-playing allows the users to affirm their self-identity (Bartle 2007) and to interact with the gaming world and the other players by using and controlling the behaviour of avatars, which are user customisable agents (Chan and Vorderer 2006).

Overall, the literature recognises that in order for the game mechanics to generate motivational affordances, they should (Yee 2006; Deterding et al. 2011a, b) work towards personally meaningful goals and match the user's profile (i.e. his/her needs, values and interests). The latter is also very important, because several studies (Hamari et al. 2014; Yee 2006; Bartle 1996; Kim 2010) have found that there are various types of gamification users, whose motivation to get engaged in gamified tasks is driven and influenced by different needs and goals, e.g. socialising, enhancing personal ego, interacting with the game environment. Thus, in summarising the literature on effective funware design, Sigala (2015) identified the following major principles when selecting game mechanics for designing effective gamification applications:

- The use of a variety of game mechanics for generating the mix of extrinsic and intrinsic motivation and appealing and meeting the various objectives, motivational needs and personality types of the various gamification users. Table 11.1 provides more details about the match of game mechanics, gamers' motivation and types.
- The empowerment of the users to select (i.e. choice and control) and customise the game mechanics to their own motivational needs so that they can self-identify the game goals with their own values, create meaningful game elements and goals, and internalise the game activities.
- The integration of game mechanics with social network and media features, because by incorporating network friends into the game play, the funwares can magnify intrinsic motivation (due to the increased interactions amongst friends and the empowerment of the user to customise/control game mechanics to his/her goals and context) and escalate the promotion and wider adoption of the gamified application due to the viral marketing and intensified exchanges taking place within the network.

Finally, recent research provides the additional suggestions for designing effective gamification marketing applications. According to marketing theory, consumers' responses to marketing stimuli follow two stages (Cauberghe and De Pelsmacker 2010). The first stage is a "wear-in", or learning, phase, whereby the consumer gets familiar with the advertising message, leading to an increase in recall rates: after a first level of message repetition, the initial hostility and uncertainty towards the message declines and positive habituation increases, and more positive brand responses also develop. The second stage is "wear-out", or tedium, phase, advertising effectiveness declines with continuing repetition due to boredom, irritation and/or consumer reactance towards the message. Moreover, according to the persuasion knowledge model (PKM), the more knowledge people possess about the persuasion intentions of marketing stimuli, the more negative brand attitudes they generate. Because of these (Tertutter and Capella 2013), in situations of intensive processing, consumers are more likely to rely on negative thoughts about the marketing goals, while repetitive exposure to simple stimuli speeds up and accelerates the wear-in and wear-out phases of marketing campaigns.

Table 11.1 Matching game mechanics with gamers' types and their motivations

Motivation of users of online games and gamification applications (e.g. Yee 2006; Kim 2010; Hamari et al. 2014)	Gamers' types in game contexts (Bartle 1996)	Game mechanics (e.g. Xu 2011; Hamari et al. 2014)
Autonomy: Autonomy refers to the sense of will when performing a task	Achievers	Profiles, avatars, macros, configurable interface, alternative activities, privacy control, notification control
Competence *Advancement*—The desire to gain power, progress rapidly and accumulate in game symbols of wealth or status *Mechanics*—Having an interest in analysing the underlying rules and system in order to optimise character performance *Competition*—The desire to challenge and compete with others	Status seekers, achievers, killers	Positive feedback, optimal challenge, progressive information, intuitive controls, points, levels, leader boards, status, badges, levels
Relatedness/social component: Relatedness is experienced when a person feels connected to others *Socialising*—Having an interest in helping and chatting with other players *Relationship*—The desire to form long-term meaningful relationships with others *Teamwork*—Deriving satisfaction from being part of a group effort	Socialisers, Harmonisers	Groups, messages, blogs, connection to social networks, chat, gifting items to other users
Immersion Component *Discovery*—Finding and knowing things that most other players do not know about *Role-playing*—Creating a persona with a background story and interacting with other players to create an improvised story *Customisation*—an interest in customising the appearance of their character *Escapism*—Using online environment to avoid thinking about real-life problems	Explorers, lurkers	Avatars Gifting items for discovery for use of the gamified application Areas/levels unlock only when inviting others to play

In this vein, the characteristics of (adver) gaming environments (simple design, repeat usage, interactive nature, flow experience) increases the users' focused attention and the likability of the experience, leading to a high motivation and ability to process the interactive content. In turn, the intensive processing of gamified marketing campaigns can significantly accelerate their wear-in and wear-out phases (Conejo 2014). Moreover, the repetition of the gamified tasks not only increases users' knowledge and understanding, but it also frees up cognitive resources, which based on PKM can also make the users to more likely rely on negative thoughts about the persuasive goals of advertisers (Tertutter and Capella 2013). Therefore, it can be expected that the wear-out phase of gamified marketing practices is achieved relatively quickly, leading to no further increase in brand recall and to the development of negative brand attitudes even after low levels of exposure. Thus, playing the game several times may have no positive influence on brand recall as well as negative impacts on brand attitudes. Consequently, advertisers should avoid situations where the consumer repeatedly plays the same game (i.e. use games only for short periods), while they also need to build in variations in the gamified applications (specifically those that are played for longer periods) by changing the game scenario, challenge, context or other design elements.

11.4 Gamification Application in Marketing

As marketing has always been about persuasion, motivation and manipulation, the affordances and the potential of gamification in marketing are enormous (Zichermann and Linder 2010). Indeed, following the success of Foursquare in using points and badges to motivate users' activity and retention, the interest of firms on using gamification for revolutionalising the human–computer interaction and the user experience has mushroomed. For example, in consumer-oriented websites and mobile applications, firms use gamification for encouraging people to use the e-commerce applications, for driving and enhancing customer loyalty, brand awareness and effective marketing engagement (Deterding et al. 2011a, b; Daniels 2010). Theoretically, any marketing practice can be gamified for influencing consumer behaviour and motivating the customers' engagement into the marketing tasks. The latter is critically important specifically when firms aim to crowdsource marketing activities to customers. In this vein, this section analyses various gamified marketing applications in tourism (including advergames and gamified practices) in order to show how the previously discussed theory on gamification design is applied for developing and exploiting gamification in order to motivate travellers to participate and support the marketing activities and goals of the firms. Although the gamification examples influence all the stages of consumer behaviour, they are grouped into three categories based on which is the major stage of consumer behaviour that they aim to influence, before, during and after the purchase/consumption tourism experience.

11.4.1 Before the Purchase/Consumption of the Tourism Experience

This is the stage whereby the travellers' interest and willingness to take a trip are triggered and formulated, and so, travel information provision is essential for helping travellers: specifying their travel needs; considering, evaluating and selecting various travel suppliers/products. Hence, at this stage, the tourism firms aim to provide information to the travellers in order to influence and trigger their travel needs, curiosity and preferences, and make them aware of their products/services so that they are included into the customers' search/consideration set.

Lufthansa created an interactive edutainment online game (www.snapshot-traveller.gr) enabling its users to virtually experience three destinations (Canada, Thailand and Brazil). While navigating the virtual words and interacting with their content and objects, users are asked to search for and photograph any animals they find. By interacting with the virtual words, the users explore and learn about the destinations' tourist resources and attractions as well as of the available travel experiences and options. The following game mechanics are incorporated into the funware for engaging users' engagement with the play tasks: rewards for performance achievement (i.e. points for photographing animals, and badges of "destination expert") and the opportunity of "destination experts" to enter a competition for winning several Lufthansa's travel awards. Apart from extrinsic motivation, other game elements are also incorporated for generating users' motivation and flow experiences. The advergames is played individually, but its funware is linked with social media (Facebook and Twitter) so that its users can share their game activity and performance with their network friends. In this way, the funware:

- enhances the users' intrinsic motivation and game involvement by providing social–relatedness motivational affordances (i.e. one does not feel that he plays the game alone, as his performance is visible to others); this virtual presence can in turn enhance the user's self-image, ego and social profile, while by sharing and commenting play task content/performance with others, the users can more effectively enter and experience a flow and fun state;
- exploits the users' social networks to diffuse and promote the game and its content to all their friends and connections. These viral marketing effects enable Lufthansa to exploit the social networks for crowdsourcing: the online game promotion for attracting more users; the generation and online diffusion of game related content for booming consumers' awareness of Lufthansa's destinations/travel products and triggering their travel interest; and the creation of intrinsic users' motivation (social–relatedness, competition) by incorporating game mechanics that enable the users to relate and control their play tasks to their known personal network and goals (i.e. interact with known friends and compete with them for achieving knowledge, points and social recognition). The use of social networks for empowering the users to create such personal meaningful game experience can lead to crowd-in synergetic motivation effects.

This advergames is part of the Lufthansa's campaign to launch these three flight destinations in the Greek market by making the game users' aware of the travel experiences and products of these destinations and triggering theirs and their friends' interest to undertake a trip. The Lufthansa brand and products do not get a prominent promotion place within the advergames (i.e. placed only on the background information of the game content), but the game scenario is directly linked to the Lufthansa's product. The game was available online for six months, and the users had the opportunity to "play" it and try to enter the award competition as many times as they wished. The six-month period of the advergames was considered as a good period to exploit its marketing impacts before its marketing effects wear-out.

Advergames are also used for creating destination awareness and promotion. The destination management organisation of Melbourne (Australia) used the following game elements for stimulating the interest and travel motivation of potential travellers to its destination: (real) avatars, social networks, a real destination as the game context and a scenario similar to reality shows as a game story. The advergames is called Remote Control Tourist (http://remotecontroltourist.com and http://www.visitvictoria.com/rct) and represents a real-life gaming application, because four real people wore helmet-mounted cameras and received information and guidelines on what to explore in Melbourne by others via Twitter and Facebook. The game allowed people from around the world to experience Melbourne in real time via live video feeds—their eyes and ears—as the virtual tourists visited the city and chatted with locals. The ability of the online users to control the play tasks and experiences (i.e. how to explore Victoria and what to learn/interact with) via a real person triggered the users' interests, game involvement and flow experience, as well as their willingness to create and spread electronic word of mouth. Over the five days of the game, the remote control tourists received 8,700 requests, visited 321 firms and attractions, travelled over 109 km by bike or foot, while people from over 158 countries and 3888 cities checked out the website, attracting more than 103,000 hits and over 150,000 views of YouTube videos. Thus, the advergames was proved as a good example on how destinations can exploit gamification for supporting their crowdsourcing practices for instilling destination awareness and promotion, creating users' interest to visit the destination and generating and diffusing destination content online.

The European Travel Commission (ETC) has launched "Roll the Dice" (https://rollthedicegame.com/auth, https://www.youtube.com/watch?v=NFNitZA8cdY), an interactive online advergames campaign aimed to educate, motivate and engage users to discover Europe as the most diverse travel destinations worldwide. "Roll the Dice" is an online board game developed as a multiplatform application with strong focus on social media. Game players can create the perfect itinerary by answering quiz questions about European destinations in a very entertaining way and share their travel experience with friends by sending funny postcards via different social media channels. The quiz questions (game scenario) support the edutainment element of the game, while a competition (a board game developed for the EuroShorts Film Competition) is also provided for increasing the users' participation. Moreover, the integration of the funware with the social media aims to exploit crowdsourcing by motivating players to create and share pan-European routes for inspiring others players and viewers of the game and so driving them to real action in Europe.

11.4.2 During the Purchase/Consumption of the Tourism Experience

At the stage of the service consumption/purchase, the aim of the firms is to motivate the customers to increase the level of their consumption and the use of the firm/product, while also generate enjoyable and memorable nice experiences. Gamification can also be applied at this stage for instilling and motivating crowdsourcing effects in such marketing practices.

Gamification is used for motivating the increased use of travel websites and generating greater user awareness and interaction with the website content and tasks.

iXiGO.com created a destination gaming app (Yo! India, http://www.ixigo.com/yoindia) that tests a player's knowledge of Indian destinations by asking them to keep guessing places in India from their pictures and giving players points for answering correctly in a short period of time. By browsing through hundreds of destination photographs, the players learn and explore the destination, win badges and share their scores and achievements on Facebook, with the ultimate objective of becoming the "Travel God" of Yo! India by topping the scoreboard. Seven levels of achievements (starting as a "Beginner", moving up to the level of "Scout" and the final destination of becoming a "Travel God") are build into the game, in order to balance challenge with users' skills and enable the creation of flow (i.e. avoidance of boredom but also anxiety and stress). Hence, the funware design aims to create and trigger edutainment experiences and flow (i.e. allow the users to sharpen their knowledge of destinations and discover new interesting places) by combining fun, intellectual curiosity and performance achievement. The game can be played also through smart phones, enabling repeated/continuous use, so that the players can be updated about their score and the performance of others, while also fill in time periods with edutainment activities. To avoid fast wear-out, the company frequently updates its curating and challenges by creating new content. Game content and players' performance/scores are shared on Facebook. This integration aims to exploit social networks for generating greater intrinsic user motivation (i.e. competition and self-esteem/ego affordances), while also supporting and fuelling crowdsourcing effects for increasing website content, popularity, traffic/visitation, user engagement with website tasks as well as triggering the users travel interest for designing and purchasing travel itineraries and services. For example, the photograph puzzles of the game became so popular over time that the iXiGO fan page's popularity sky-rocketed from 20,000 fans to a whopping 235,000+ fans within two years, with over 36,000 fans liking, sharing and commenting daily, which boomed users' engagement.

MountVacation.com (an online holidays shopping website) has also gamified its website design for instilling the users' interest and use of the website tasks as well as exploiting crowdsourcing for enriching its website with user-generated content (travel reviews and ideas for travelling), for attracting website traffic and supporting users to conduct online purchases by reducing their risk (i.e. which resort is best to buy). To achieve that an application called *SkiBook* (and available only to Facebook users) allows its users to rate ski resorts/firms (e.g. criteria include ski, Snow Park, hiking trails, cross-country tracks, free style, family-friendly, apres-ski entertainment), review their skiing experience (complete with appraisals, scores and stats) about the European ski resorts that they have visited, relate it with and share it amongst their Facebook friends and connections. Users can compete against their friends and other connected skiers as to how many European ski resorts or skiing areas they have already visited and they are able to compare their rankings. All the reviews and stats are aggregated, thus allowing all users to find and preview the ski resorts other Facebook users have been to. With all that data at hand, MountVacation.com actively interacted with the targeted audience from whom all the data are extracted in order to help skiers and snowboarders make an educated choice when selecting their holidays in the mountain. Thus, the SkiBook is a gamified application that enables the website to generate and motivate crowdsourcing marketing practices for providing value to both types of their clients: helping tourists to select holidays and ski firms by providing reviews and stats; and assisting firms to improve their performance and services by comparing them against their competitors.

Sigala (2015) analysed how TripAdvisor has also applied gamification for supporting crowdsourcing and motivating its users to generate website content (i.e. travel reviews), interact with others, that in turn make the TripAdvisor website more appealing, useful and popular amongst travellers but also tourism suppliers alike. TripAdvisor is a website whose success depends on the provision of travel reviews. To motivate travellers to upload many and good quality reviews, game mechanics are used for gamifying various website tasks. For example, users get points when uploading reviews and interacting with others on forums for providing suggestions; get social points and achieve badges (i.e. travel experts) when others evaluate the travellers' reviews of good quality. To avoid crowd-out effects and further support the crowdsourcing effects of gamification, the TripAdvisor has also created a gamified application (by integrating its website design with the Facebook social graph) that allows its users to control and personalise the game mechanics and play tasks to their own interests, goals and other co-players/context so that the users can create more meaningful and engaging gameful experiences for themselves. The application allows the users to log into the TripAdvisor website in order to add travel content to their profile and receive points to enhance their scorecard performance; filter website content to reviews provided by their known friends; identify friends that have been to destinations/firms and interact with them online for getting personal advise; share and compare their travel performance (i.e. destinations visited, reviews and points) with their known Facebook friends. Specifically, the Facebook enabled gamified application allows the users to self-identify with the goals of the "play" tasks, because:

- The users are motivated to add content on the TripAdvisor website, because by doing so, they can create their own personalised travel map, their personalised wish travel list and/or their travel profile and expertise that enhances their ego and prestige; and
- The TripAdvisor users can customise the TripAdvisor's website to filter and show content contributed only by their Facebook friends; by doing so, the TripAdvisor users have access to travel content that they find more reliable, authentic and trustful (since it is contributed by people they know and belong to their Facebook network), and can identify themselves with their Facebook friends for sharing and discussing content as well as comparing their travel profile and scorecard performance with that of their friends (i.e. the gamification app incorporates and supports a type of a multi-player online game and competition that can drive and motivate user engagement).

Thus, the Facebook-gamified app aims to boom the crowdsourcing effects by enabling the users to easier and better internalise the play tasks to their activity.

Gamification is also used for motivating the travellers to explore destinations and increase their visitation and experience on destination places and geographies. For example, the city of Pafos has created a gamified destination application (Pafos Treasure Hunt) for informing and motivating visitors to explore and learn the destination in an edutainment way. Visitors download the application on their smart phone, and they can use a map for identifying their location and creating itineraries; identifying nearby attractions and tourism firms and reading content about them (e.g. interpretation, guides); and writing and sharing their reviews; getting points for checking in places and firms and receiving special prices, points and competition awards. The application allows treasure hunters to also share their progress and scorecard with friends and family via social networking sites—Facebook and Twitter, and so, by sharing their "hunt" and its "treasures", crowdsourcing is used for promoting the destination, creating wider awareness as well as help others to select itineraries and suppliers by reading others' reviews. Thus, the funware generate and reinforce both extrinsic and intrinsic motivational affordances that provide both functional value (travel content and services) as well as emotional/ social value by enabling travellers to connect with others and experience and learn destinations in a more edutainment way. The application has enabled destinations to attract greater visitation, persuade visitors to spend more time and money at places, while it helps suppliers generate useful travel demand content (e.g. tourists' preferences, feedback and visitation paths and spending behaviour).

A similar application is created by Stockholm in order to educate the visitors and motivate them to experience and promote the city in an entertainment and educational way. The application uses the story theme of sounds as a challenging/game scenario for triggering users' interest and involvement with play tasks. Stockholm Sounds (http://www.swedavia.com/about-swedavia/news/discover-stockholm-with-the-stockholm-sounds-app/) challenge tourists to discover Stockholm through game missions, interactive experiences and visits to exciting places based on the sounds and music of the city. The application is available on smart phones and features a city map, so visitors can use it; while they explore the city, users have to answer questions related to music elements they find in various location throughout the city in order to learn about the destination, gain points and receive awards. Visitors can also share their experiences from different game activities with social network friends, which creates opportunities for viral marketing and crowdsourcing effects.

11.4.3 After the Purchase/Consumption of the Tourism Experience

At this stage, firms aim to create positive post-purchase intentions to their customers, increase their loyalty and develop/enrich customer relations. Gamified applications aiming to help the firms to exploit the crowdsourcing effects for building a customer database and enhancing customers' loyalty include the following.

JetBlue uses gamification for converting its loyalty programme (TrueBlue) to a social loyalty programme by exploiting crowdsourcing in order to enhance customers' loyalty and engagement with the company as well as exploit their word of mouth for building its customer database. Its funware include the following game elements and motivational affordances: Trueblue members register on the JetBlue's Facebook page and when they check in at a JetBlue airport location with their mobile device, they earn 25 TrueBlue points; Travellers earn JetBlue badges when they tag a travelling companion; a location-based social media application (called Go Places) also allows users to gain loyalty points that can be exchanged for free services/upgrades and status privileges by checking into JetBlue places as well as by contributing content on the JetBlue Facebook page. In this vein, the gamified social loyalty programme generates and exploits crowdsourcing amongst the loyalty members for collecting website content (user-generated content), increasing customer loyalty and generating traffic and usage of its Facebook page (i.e. increase the online promotion and readership of its content).

Lufthansa has also created a gamified location-based social media application for rewarding customers for their repeat usage and purchase of Lufthansa flights as well as for exploiting them and generating crowdsourcing effects in promoting its firm and services to the online audience. The app (Blue Legends) connects frequent flyers by inviting them to virtually check in (to airports, lounges and Lufthansa flights through Foursquare flights) for getting points and badges. For example, passengers are rewarded with ranks and badges for regularly checking in virtually to Lufthansa sites. For example, users can become "Expert Pilots" on the routes they fly most frequently. Early risers who check in before 6 a.m. are awarded the "Early Bird" badge. Anyone who racks up more than 388,000 km with Lufthansa receives the "To the Moon" badge, travellers who check in most frequently to Lufthansa sites can become true "legends of the skies". Users can also share their journey/flight information and travel performance/scorecard with others via social networks. The combination of extrinsic rewards with social networks (that generate intrinsic motivation affordances) supports positive crowd-in effects and provides the crowdsourcing of a great marketing exposure, brand awareness and repeat purchases.

11.5 Conclusion

The use of gamification for directing and motivating customers' behaviour and supporting crowdsourcing practices in marketing is increasingly spreading. This chapter reviewed the literature about gamification design for identifying the principles and elements that can lead to effective gamification and it then applied these principles by discussing various gamification applications developed for supporting tourism crowdsourcing marketing practices. It was shown that gamification can be used for crowdsourcing any marketing practice and influencing customer behaviour at any stage of the consumer behaviour process. However, as the literature does not provide any conclusive results regarding the impact of the various gamification design elements on marketing outcomes (e.g. brand recall, awareness and consumer attitudes and purchase intentions) (Terlutter and Capella 2013), further research is required in order to answer numerous questions such as What type of gamification design is most appropriate for which type of marketing practice and goal? What is the impact of the various gamification elements (such as playing frequency, congruity between brand and game design social interaction with peers, the rhetoric of the game) on the users' (conative, affective and cognitive) outcomes towards the brand and the game? What variable mediate the relation between game design elements and users' outcomes (e.g. users' cognitive capabilities, personality, game familiarity/ experience, persuasion knowledge and susceptibility to advertising). Overall, to maximise the marketing effectiveness of gamification applications, more research is required in order to get more understanding on how to better match gamification design with the users' characteristics, marketing goals and gaming context.

References

Amabile, T. M. (1993). Motivational synergy: Toward new conceptualization of intrinsic and extrinsic motivation in the workplace. *HRM Review, 3*(3), 185–201.

Bartle, R. (1996). Hearts, clubs, diamonds, spades: players who suit muds. *Journal of MUD research, 1*(1), 19.

Bartle, R. (2007). Virtual worlds: Why people play. *Massively Multiplayer Game Development, 2*, 1–16.

Benabou, R., & Tirole, J. (2005). Incentives and prosocial behavior. *American Economic Review, 96*(5), 1652–1678.

Brabham, D. C. (2012). Motivations for participation in a crowdsourcing application to improve public engagement in transit planning. *Journal of Applied Communication Research, 40*(3), 307–328.

Cauberghe, V., & De Pelsmacker, P. (2010). Advergames. *Journal of Advertising, 39*(1), 5–18.

Chan, E., & Vorderer, P. (2006). Massively multiplayer online games. In P. Vorderer & J. Bryant (Eds.), *Playing video games: Motives, responses, and consequences* (pp. 77–88). Hillsdale, NJ: Erlbaum.
Chorney, A. (2012). Taking the game out of gamification. *Dalhousie Journal of Interdisciplinary Management, 8*(1), 23–39.
Companion, M., & Sambrook, R. (2008). The influence of sex on character attribute preferences. *CyberPsychology & Behavior, 11*(6), 673–674.
Conejo, F. (2014). Loyalty 3.0: how to revolutionize customer and employee engagement with big data and gamification. *Journal of Consumer Marketing*, 31(1): 86–87.
Cramer, H., Ahmet, Z., Rost, M., & Holmquist, L. (2011). Gamification and location-sharing: Some emerging social conflicts. In *proceedings of the international conference of the ACM on Computer-Human Interaction*, May 7–12, 2012, Vancouver, Canada.
Crawford, C. (1982). *Art of computer game design*. Berkeley, CA: Osborne/McGraw Hill.
Csíkszentmihályi, M. (1990). *Flow: The psychology of optimal experience*. NY: Harper Collins.
Daniels, M. (2010). Businesses need to get in the game. Marketing week. http://www.marketingweek.co.uk/disciplines/market-research/opinion/businesses-need-to-get-in-the-game/3018554.article. Assessed 13 Nov 2014.
Deci, E., & Ryan, R. (1985). *Intrinsic motivation and self-determination in human behavior*. New York, NY: Plenum.
Deci, E. L., Koestner, R., & Ryan, R. M. (1999). A meta-analytic review of experiments examining the effects of extrinsic rewards on intrinsic motivation. *Psychological Bulletin, 125*(6), 68–627.
Deterding, S., Dixon, D., Khaled, R., & Nacke, L., (2011a). From game design elements to gamefulness: defining gamification. In *Proceedings of the 15th International Academic MindTrek Conference: Envisioning Future Media Environments* (pp. 9–15). Tampere, Finland, ACM. 28–30 Sept, 2011.
Deterding, S., Sicart, M., Nacke, L., O'Hara, K., & Dixon, D. (2011b). Gamification: Using game-design elements in non-gaming contexts. In *Proceedings of CHI Abstracts* (pp. 2425–2428).
Frey, B. S., & Jegen, R. (2001). Motivation crowding theory. *Journal of Economic Surveys, 15*(5), 589–611.
Frey, B. S. (1997). A constitution for knaves crowds out civic virtues. *Economic Journal, 107* (433), 1043–1053.
Gartner. (2012). Gartner says by 2014, 80 percent of current gamified applications will fail to meet business objectives primarily due to poor design. Available at: www.gartner.com/newsroom/id/2251015. Accessed 5 Apr 2014.
Hamari, J., & Eranti, V. (2011). Framework for designing and evaluating game achievements. *Proceedings of DiGRA 2011: Think Design Play, September 14–17, 2011* (pp. 122–134). The Netherlands: Hilversum.
Hamari, J. (2013). Transforming homo economicus into homo ludens: A field experiment on gamification in a utilitarian Peer-To-Peer trading service. *Electronic Commerce Research and Applications, 12*(4), 236–245.
Hamari, J., Koivisto, J., Sarsa, H. (2014). Does gamification work?—A literature review of empirical studies on gamification. In *Proceedings of the 47th Hawaii International Conference on System Sciences*, Hawaii, USA, 6–9 Jan, 2014.
Kim, A. J. (2010). Designing the player journey. http://www.slideshare.net/amyjokim/gami_cation-101-design-the-player-journey. Accessed 15 Mar 2014.
Lazzaro, N. (2011). Chasing wonder and the future of engagement. www.slideshare.net/NicoleLazzaro/chasing-wonder-and-the-future-of-engagement. Accessed 12 Apr 2014.
Lee, J., & Hammer, J. (2011). Gamification in education: What, how, why bother? *Academic Exchange Quarterly, 15*(2), 34–48.
Nicholson, S. (2012). A User-Centered theoretical framework for meaningful gamification. In *Paper Presented at Games + Learning + Society 8.0*. Madison, WI.
Pavlus, J. (2010). The game of life. *Scientific American, 303*, 43–44.

Robertson, M. (2010). Can't play, won't play. http://www.hideandseek.net/2010/10/06/cant-play-wont-play/. Accessed 21 Aug 2013.

Shneiderman, B. (2004). Designing for fun: How can we design user interfaces to be more fun? *Interactions, 11*(5), 48–50.

Sigala, M. (2015). The application and impact of gamification funware on trip planning and experiences: The case of TripAdvisor's funware. *Electronic Markets: The International Journal of Networked Markets.*

Sigala, M., Christou, E., Gretzel, U. (2012). Web 2.0 in Travel, Tourism and Hospitality: theory, practice and cases. Farnham: Ashgate Publishers.

Terlutter, R., & Capella, M. L. (2013). The Gamification of advertising: Analysis and research directions of in-game advertising, advergames, and advertising in social network games. *Journal of Advertising, 42*(2/3), 95–112.

Toubia, O. (2006). Idea generation, creativity, incentives. *Marketing Science, 25*(5), 411–425.

Witt, M., Scheiner, C., Robra-Bissantz, S. (2011). Gamification of online idea competitions: Insights from an explorative case. In *Proceedings of the INFORMATIK 2011 Jahrestagung der Gesellschaft für Informatik*, 4–7 Oct 2011, Berlin.

Wood, R. T., Griffiths, M. D., Chappell, D., & Davies, M. N. (2004). The structural characteristics of video games: A psycho-structural analysis. *Cyber Psychology and Behavior, 7*(1), 1–10.

Xu, Y. (2011). Literature review on web application gamification and analytics. CSDL Technical report, 11-05

Xu F, Weber J, Buhalis D (2013) Gamification in Tourism. In Information and Communication Technologies in Tourism 2014 (pp. 525-537). Springer International Publishing, Vienna.

Yee, N. (2006). Motivations for play in online games. *Cyberpsychology & Behavior, 9*(6), 772–775.

Zichermann, G., Cunningham, C. (2011). *Gamification by design: Implementing game mechanics in web and mobile apps*. Sebastopol, CA: O'Reilly Media.

Zichermann, G., & Linder, J. (2010). *Game-Based marketing: Inspire customer loyalty through rewards, challenges, and contests*. Hoboken, NJ: Wiley.

Chapter 12
Crowdsourcing: An Application of Promotional Marketing

Silvia Sanz-Blas, Sandra Tena-Monferrer and Javier Sánchez-García

Abstract Groups are more creative than individuals; therefore, they also contain more knowledge, and this assumption represents the central principle of crowdsourcing. The term "crowdsourcing" is a contraction of the words crowd (a large number of people) and outsourcing (the use of external assistance or help). The crowdsourcing concept was popularized and clearly defined in a Wired Magazine article published by the American journalist Jeff Howe in 2006, and since then, it has been implemented in a wide range of industries. Nowadays, with the proliferation of the crowdsourcing practices, it has become necessary to clearly define what crowdsourcing really is and what its specific limits are. So, while there is not one unique way to categorize the crowdsourcing landscape, the most popular classifications done by experts and researchers on the subject classify crowdsourcing performances according to the task or labour performed, the features of the crowd or even the problem or task being solved. All in all, before launching any crowdsourcing initiative, it is important to determine what your ultimate goal is, and the answer to that question will help you decide which crowdsourcing model can maximize strengths and minimize weaknesses. Any crowdsourcing project turns into a promotion and marketing campaign, since the diffusion performed for the campaign, in order to be successful, should be managed in the same way as any marketing action would be.

Keywords Crowd · Knowledge · Marketing · Open innovation · Community · Market research · Problem-solving

S. Sanz-Blas (✉)
Marketing and Market Research, Universitat de València, Valencia, Spain
e-mail: silvia.sanz@uv.es

S. Tena-Monferrer · J. Sánchez-García
Business Administration and Marketing, Universitat Jaume I, Castellón, Spain

F.J. Garrigos-Simon et al. (eds.), *Advances in Crowdsourcing*,
DOI 10.1007/978-3-319-18341-1_12

12.1 Crowdsourcing, the Power of the Crowd

The term "crowdsourcing" is a contraction of the words crowd (a large number of people) and outsourcing (the use of external assistance or help). Crowdsourcing (the process of using the help of a large number of people to get something done) is a word that was popularized and clearly defined in a Wired Magazine article published by the American journalist Jeff Howe in 2006, but the first crowdsourcing practices were applied as early as in the eighteenth century.

At that time, it was referred to as "the longitude problem". In 1714, the British Government was trying to find a solution for the difficulties in sailing that seamen were experiencing, with more than one thousand deaths per year. In the search for a solution, the British Government offered £20,000 as a prize for the person who could solve the problem. The contest was won by the son of a carpenter, who invented the marine chronometer, a striking fact for the aristocracy, but it represented a great example on how innovation and creativity can arise anywhere around us.

12.1.1 Definition

The official crowdsourcing definition was introduced by Jeff Howe and Mark Robinson in their article published in Wired Magazine in 2006. Howe proposed the following definition: "Simply defined, crowdsourcing represents the act of a company or institution taking a function once performed by employees and outsourcing it to an undefined (and generally large) network of people in the form of an open call. This can take the form of peer-production (when the job is performed collaboratively), but it is also often undertaken by sole individuals. The crucial prerequisite is the use of the open call format and the wide network of potential labourers" (Howe 2006b). From the definition given above, it is clear that crowdsourcing activities are strongly linked to the development of the new technologies, especially to explore the opportunities offered by Web 2.0 technologies, which simplifies the communication and connection between large groups of dispersed individuals.

Three years later, Howe offered an updated definition in his new book "Why the power of the crowd is driving the future of business" (2009): "Crowdsourcing is the act of taking a job traditionally performed by a designated agent (usually an employee) and outsourcing it to an undefined, generally large group of people in the form of an open call".

Several other authors have also tried so far to develop a complete crowdsourcing definition; Brabham (2013) asserts that crowdsourcing is an online, distributed problem-solving and production model that leverages the collective intelligence of online communities to serve specific organizational goals. Taking other point of views, some authors focus on the use of it as a way to outsource tasks (Oliveira et al. 2009) and others as a problem-solving process (Vukovic 2009) or even as a specific manifestation of open innovation (Sloane 2011). But the conclusion emanating from this type of actions always involves two parts: the person or company organizing the challenge and the crowd or group of people trying to solve it (see Appendix 1—Crowdsourcing concept definitions).

Let us consider how the theoretical crowdsourcing framework can be put into practice. A random company selects a task that it is currently being carried out by its own employees. Rather than continuously being performed by the employees, the company decides to outsource it to a crowd. This crowd is invited to perform this activity on behalf of the firm for a previously established reward or prize. An open call is launched, and anyone who is interested in developing the task is invited to complete it. However, some limitations can be established by the company regarding the characteristics or knowledge of the participants, depending on the objectives of requirements of the task. Then, the members of the crowd accept to undertake the task in a specific time allowance also previously given by the company. When the task is completed, it should be submitted to the firm through the platform established for that purpose. Many variations in the following steps exist. Sometimes, a group of experts evaluate the quality of the work done by the participants or it can also be only checked by the company and then released to the social networks where the participants themselves will evaluate its quality. Finally, the prize or reward will be given to the member or members who come up with the best solution to the task.

Therefore, crowdsourcing is a way of outsourcing not directed to other companies but to the crowd through an open call, commonly by the use of an Internet platform. As Whitla (2010) asserts, crowdsourcing defines a process of organizing labour, where firms parcel out work to some form of (generally online) community, offering payment for anyone within the "crowd" who completes the task the firm has set. Through outsourcing to a crowd rather than performing operations in-house, firms can gain access to a very large community of potential workers who have a diverse range of skills and expertise and who are willing and able to complete activities within a short time frame and often at a much reduced cost as compared to performing the task in-house (Howe 2006a).

12.2 Crowdsourcing Types

With the proliferation of the crowdsourcing practices, it has become necessary to clearly define what crowdsourcing really is and which its specific limits are. So, while there probably is no unique way to categorize the crowdsourcing scenery, the most popular classifications done by experts and researchers on the subject classify crowdsourcing performances according to the following four aspects.

12.2.1 Based on the Type of Task that Is Crowdsourced

The most popular classification categorizes crowdsourcing based on the type of task that is crowdsourced. Howe (2009) presented this approach in his book in order to classify crowdsourcing in the following four categories:

Crowdwisdom: The first type assumes that the crowd contains more knowledge than the individual. This type of practices uses people's knowledge in order to solve problems or predict future changes and help directly the company's development. Howe states that "Given the right set of conditions the crowd will almost always outperform any number of employees—a fact that many companies are increasingly attempting to exploit. The key lies in creating the conditions in which they will express their knowledge". Three subtypes of crowdwisdom practices can be distinguished:

- Crowdcasting: A complex challenge is raised and those who solve it are rewarded, such as those raised at the Innocentive platform.
- Crowdstorming: Online brainstorming sessions: the crowd is involved with reviews and votes as in the case of the Idea Jam platform by IBM.
- Market predictions: a community of private investors vote for several different alternatives according to the descriptive information provided, as in the case of Iowa Electronic Markets.

Crowdproduction: The second type and, perhaps, the best-known forms of crowdsourcing are "production" activities such as asking individuals to film TV advertisements or even performing language translation. In this case, the promoter of the initiative (crowdsourcer) outsources activities that require creativity effort from the employees in order to develop new products or services (a database or any user-generated content). Wikipedia or iStock is the most remarkable example of this type of practices.

Crowdvoting: The third type represents basically a free market research. Through the public's votes and feedback on any product or idea, companies can take advantage of the comments and improve their business. A typical example of this type of practices is Threadless.com, a T-shirt manufacturer that uses crowd-voting to decide which designs are finally sold on their Website. The key of this specific crowdsourcing practice relies on being able to organize vast quantities of information and transform it into useful data for strategic decisions.

Crowdfunding: This fourth type refers to the public's disposition to finance projects they believe in: funding independent films, microfinancing projects, etc. A certain amount of money is requested in exchange for a reward; MyFootballClub is a football club which, in return for an annual fee, investors decide on the selection of the players or the price of tickets. Being transparent about where money is really going is one of the most important tasks in this type of crowdsourcing activities.

12.2.2 Based on the Type of Labour Performed

The economic analyst Nicholas Carr (2010) categorized the crowdsourcing practices based on the type of labour performed by the crowd and how the members of the crowd collaborate between them. This categorization provides a better understanding of the different aptitudes possessed by the crowds and how they can be managed in order to perform a certain task. The following four types of crowds represent four alternatives on how the communities can work together.

- **Averaging crowds**: It basically works as a survey group, providing an average judgment about some complex questions that, in many cases, is more precise than the judgment of an individual. Some examples are the crowds behind prediction markets such as the Iowa Electronic Markets.
- **Datamine crowds**: A large group of people (usually without any knowledge about its members) produce a set of behavioural data that can be collected and analysed in order to gain insight into behavioural or market patterns. A good example is the crowd that feeds Google's search algorithm or Amazon's recommendation system.
- **Networking crowds**: A community that shares information through a communication system such as the phone network or Facebook.
- **Social production crowds**: A large group of individuals offer their individual talents to the development of some type of product or platform. Wikipedia or Linux is feed by social production crowds.
- **Transactional crowds**: A group of people coordinated mainly around point-to-point transactions. A representative example is eBay.

12.2.3 Based on the Problems that Crowdsourcing Is Trying to Solve

According to Brabham (2013), a precise segmentation of crowdsourcing practices should be focused on the kind of problem an organization wants to solve when it turns to a crowd. His segmentation is in fact based on the type of problems that crowdsourcing is best suitable to solve:

- **Knowledge detection and management**: A crowd is asked to gather information, organizing it in a standard format and reporting problems, for example Peer-to-Patent or SeeClickFix.
- **Distributed human intelligence tasking**: Suitable for data processing, large data packages are decomposed into small tasks requiring human intelligence, and individuals in the crowd are compensated for processing pieces of data. It requires monetary compensation as a motivator; Amazon Mechanical Turk is the perfect example.

- **Broadcast search**: A crowd is asked to solve experiential problems. It is suitable for scientific challenges such as the Innocentive platform.
- **Peer-vetted creative production**: The organization asks the crowd to create and develop creative ideas. The Doritos contest represents a great example of peer-vetted productions.

12.2.4 Based on the Motivation to Participate

Finally, Martineau (2012) proposes a crowdsourcing categorization based on the motivations that drive the crowds to participate in crowdsourcing initiatives. According to his proposal, four types of crowd members can be established:

- **Communals**: Members of this first group incorporate the crowdsourcing community's group-based identity into their social self. Furthermore, they develop cultural and social capital through presumption.
- **Utilizers**: Members of the second group, utilizers, improve their skills through participation and, consequently, creating cultural capital.
- **Aspirers**: Members of the third group, aspirers, do not create content, but rather participate in the selection of the content. They aspire to be perceived as a "stereotypical" member of the first two groups.
- **Lurkers**: The ones who simply observe. This group is composed of individuals who participate in crowdsourcing solely by browsing.

According to the above different classifications, it is important to remark that when it comes to select the most suitable crowdsourcing solution, a holistic approach should be adopted in order to take into consideration all the key factors.

12.3 Basic Crowdsourcing Principles

Before launching any crowdsourcing initiative, it is important to determine what your ultimate goal is. The answer to that question will help you decide which crowdsourcing model can maximize strengths and minimize weaknesses. Crowdsourcing provides opportunities for emerging talents that otherwise would be impossible to access. Any crowdsourcing project turns into a promotion and marketing campaign, since the diffusion performed for the campaign, in order to be successful, should be managed in the same way as any marketing action would be. Therefore, some of the key issues when implementing any crowdsourcing initiative are as follows:

- **Choosing the right crowd**:
  Choosing the appropriate crowd size is a decisive step when designing a crowdsourcing initiative. On the one hand, if the size of crowd is too big, the

amount of obtained data could also be disproportionate, making it too difficult to organize and process it with the available resources. Spending too much time reviewing the proposals would affect the daily organization routine. On the other hand, if the crowd is too small, the results could be poor and unsatisfactory, so that the essence of crowdsourcing would be lost.

But it also needs to be the right people; this task is also related to choosing the right crowdsourcing model. If you are creating a service in which sports teams can tap the best performance for their aggregated wisdom, a crowd of ten thousand scientist will not be much good (Howe 2009).

- **Offering the correct incentives**:
  The project participants (crowdworkers) can get a zero reward when a single individual of the crowd gets the reward or a much reduced reward if all individuals get a reward (Amazon Mechanical Turk). However, getting people involved requires understanding what motivates them to contribute. People might freely donate their knowledge and labour to a NGO, but feel far more hesitated about spending that energy or money to benefit a start-up. The crowd is really smart, and if it thinks you are trying to take advantage of its effort, it will never come back.
- **Keeping it simple**:
  The need to keep procedures simple is not because people are senseless, but because they are quite busy. Keeping the nature of tasks simple ensures meeting the basic standard of quality for a diverse crowd. Through clearness and simplicity, the probability of getting the crowd involved in your initiative increases considerably.
- **Thinking about the crowd**:
  Crowdsourcing works best when an individual or company gives the crowd something it wants (Howe 2009). People participate in this kind of initiative because some psychological, social or emotional need is being met. And when the need is not met, they stop participating. If iStockphoto had approached community by trying to create a low-paid workforce of amateur photographers, it would have failed. Instead, they created a place where photography enthusiasts could share and critique one another's work.

  Finally, there is no real guarantee that the resulting creation meets the expected quality. In 2010, a BP oil crowdsourcing initiative launched immediately after the dramatic episode in the Gulf of Mexico in order to find possible solutions to eliminate the effects of the oil spill on the environment, never reached any effective solution. More than 120,000 contributions were received through the online platform. At first, it seemed good news to get as many ideas as possible, but only 30 of them were finally implemented and unfortunately no one succeeded in achieving their goal. A successful crowdsourcing project requires time, effort and extensive planning in order to obtain the maximum benefit from the information provided by the crowd.

12.4 Crowdsourcing Success Stories: An Implementation of Promotional Marketing

12.4.1 Lay's

Lay's is a snack food brand founded in 1938 in Nashville (Tennessee), owned by PepsiCo Inc., the world's second largest food and beverage company. In Spain, the brand operates through PepsiCo Iberia and more specifically through PepsiCo Spain Foods business division, selling chips, potato and cereal snacks, gazpacho, juice and nuts under such iconic brands as Lay's, Matutano, Cheetos, Ruffles, Doritos, Sunbites, Alvalle or Tropicana Pure Premium.

In 2011, Lay's launched in Spain its successful campaign "Casting of Flavours" ("Do us a flavor" in USA), an innovative campaign that represented a turning point for the fast-moving consumer goods (FMCG) market and its relationship with consumers. The purpose of the brand was to create the foundations for a revolution in the snack food market, making a significant change in the media, on the supermarket shelves and through the network and sales in order to enhance and strengthen the relationship with consumers (PepsiCo 2011).

The campaign was based on a contest in which the person who proposed the most original flavour could win 20,000 euros and 1 % of the sales of that snack flavour for a year in Spain. It was a new flavour created by and for the Spanish public. The promotion was accessed through the following links: www.facebook.com/CastingdeSaboresLays and www.lays.es (Fig. 12.1).

The "Casting of Flavours" campaign started in April 2011 and concluded in December of that year. The contest consisted of three phases: the first phase was the call for flavour proposals from the Spanish public; the second one involved the

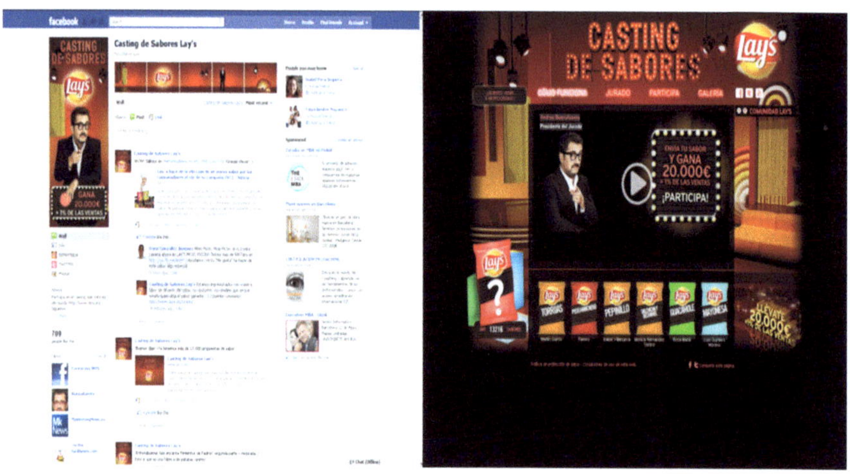

Fig. 12.1 Lay's promotion. *Source* lays.es

Fig. 12.2 Casting of Flavours. *Source* PepsiCo (2012)

selection of the three finalist flavours by a multidisciplinary jury; and finally, the third one included the vote on the winning flavour by the general public. It is worth noting that in just 10 days, 14,600 flavour proposals were uploaded on the Website of the company, achieving over 1000 new fans on Twitter. In addition, there were over 30,000 views of the uploaded videos on the YouTube channel (PepsiCo 2011).

The successful "Casting of Flavours" campaign concluded with the announcement of the winning flavour: Garlic Prawn Lay's, the new and innovative Lay's flavour in Spain during 2012. Garlic Prawn Lay's were chosen from over 350,000 proposals received by the company and they were sold in limited edition along with Bravas and Kebab Lay's, the other two finalist flavours (PepsiCo 2012) (Fig. 12.2).

As a result of the "Casting of Flavours" campaign, Lay's gave voice to the consumers through an innovative participation format, an exceptionally talented demonstration where it was the public who proposed and decided the new Lay's flavour in Spain. Lay's moved all the attention to its consumers, and at the same time, an innovative communication channel was created.

12.4.2 Doritos

The Doritos brand, also owned by PepsiCo Inc., employs crowdsourcing techniques through inviting their fans to design the brand's advertisements. Each year, the participants, each in its own distinctive style, are asked to create a 30 s advertisement as original and attractive as possible showing their love for Doritos.

For the ninth consecutive year, Doritos has launched the contest that captures the attention of half of the world before and during the Super Bowl. After selecting the ten finalist ads, two of them are released during the Super Bowl: one is chosen by consumers worldwide who vote via the Doritos' Website (www.doritos.com) and the other is chosen by the Doritos brand. The creator of the final advertisement with

Fig. 12.3 Crash the Super Bowl. *Source* Doritos.com

the highest number of total votes receives the impressive prize of one million dollars and he or she also has the "opportunity of a lifetime" of working at Universal Pictures, where he or she could be working first hand with writers, directors and producers of the actual entertainment industry that forms Hollywood's core. Working at Universal Pictures, the winner could experience the daily working routine of this remarkable film studio and also having the significant the opportunity of learning sharing creative talents for a wide variety of projects (Fig. 12.3).

In 2013, Doritos broke down all barriers with the campaign "Crash the Super Bowl" allowing not only US citizens to participate in the contest but also participants from Canada, Australia, Denmark, Israel, South Africa, Mexico or China, among many other countries. Therefore, the annual competition was opened to participants from the 46 countries in which these snacks are sold, allowing the brand to obtain higher-quality and more diverse proposals. A total of 5400 new entrants from 30 countries participated in 2013 after opening the competition to fans from the participating worldwide countries.

Viewers and followers can participate not only in creating advertisements but also in voting for their favourite spots, allowing the best ones to reach the top of the list of the most popular ads (Marketingdirecto 2011a, b).

Since the "Crash the Super Bowl" campaign was first introduced, the Doritos brand has received over 27,000 advertisements created by its consumers, and the winning ads are constantly ranked among the most memorable and notorious Super Bowl advertisements. Through "Crash the Super Bowl", Doritos is offering an unprecedented opportunity to his fans from all over the world to share their talent and creativity in one of the largest and most important advertising platforms in the world (PepsiCo 2013).

12.4.3 LEGO CUUSOO

LEGO is an emotional brand, a "lovemark" for many people; consumers are emotionally engaged to LEGO as it is related and reminds them of their childhood (ICEMD 2012). The brand has created so strong intergenerational links that influence purchasing behaviour: people want their children to experience the most pleasurable play experiences they remember from their own childhoods.

In 2003, faced with the prospect of closing due to the excessive loss of money, LEGO decided to start developing its digital transformation: they redesigned their future prospects, they simplified their plastic bricks production tasks, and they also focused their strategies on people. For a number of years now, LEGO is considering consumers as the fundamental pillar for innovation in their brand (Vila 2013).

Until January 2012, LEGO maintained the Lego Design ByMe initiative, a program where users were able to design their model on the computer and then buy it with its own LEGO box. That initiative allowed the reinvention of a traditional offline brand into a virtual brand, as the product was computer-designed and it was also now adapted to the digital stage (ICEMD 2012).

From 2008 until 2011 in Japan exclusively, and from April 2011 worldwide, LEGO launched the campaign LEGO CUUSOO (in Japanese means "desire") (the union of CUUSOO Systems and LEGO Group), a crowdsourcing platform that enables users to propose their ideas and to develop potential products (Fig. 12.4).

On the platform, users create their own page to highlight their ideas and share them with the aim of achieving the maximum possible support. A form should be filled attaching the images of the idea proposed and it can be a photograph of a building that has been made with plastic blocks, a design made with LEGO software, or a descriptive sketch of the idea. The description and the labels should also be included. During the voting process, fans also set the price they are willing to pay for the product.

Fig. 12.4 LEGO CUUSOO. *Source* Gustafsson (2014)

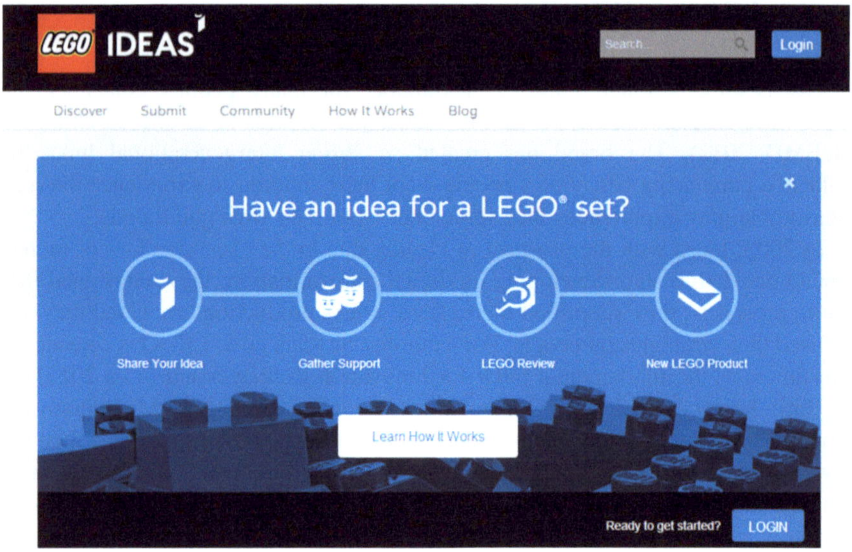

Fig. 12.5 LEGO Ideas: *Source* Lego Ideas (2014)

Every project must have the support and vote of 10,000 followers (pass mark) in order to be considered by LEGO in its quarterly review to examine whether it becomes an official LEGO product. If the project is selected, the design goes into production as part of the countless family of LEGO products. The creator of the design gets 1 % of net sales of the product (ICEMD 2012).

Lego is a pioneer company in developing open innovation techniques. In late 2013, the company already had about 5500 proposals in LEGO CUUSOO, from which many varied and successful projects have been developed (Vila 2013). As a consequence of the success, the company decided to integrate more closely the concept CUUSOO in the LEGO experience, and they created what is now known as LEGO Ideas (Lego 2014). LEGO therefore concentrated its efforts on its consumers, with an initiative that goes beyond collaboration and empowerment of users (Fig. 12.5).

12.5 Conclusions

Nowadays, it is fundamental for companies to be open to methodologies or techniques based on open innovation, as through consumer collaboration initiatives, a positive effect on businesses' evolution and success is ensured.

This relevant change involves moving from a traditional model where ideas come from within the company, to another one in which crowdsourcing represents the central pillar providing countless advantages. Among them, we should point out brand update, improving the performance of innovation processes, increasing creativity in the organization, offering a more personalized offer, more satisfied and loyal customers or easier identification of new talents, among many others.

Therefore, crowdsourcing represents how the knowledge of a community can be decisive to achieve feats that were before the responsibility of a few specialized ones. The crowd is talented and creative, and this emerging phenomenon can be used for the completion of marketing-related tasks, concentrating the efforts on product development, advertising, promotion and market research.

When planning any crowdsourcing initiative, it is essential to clearly define its main objective. A precise description of its context and the expected results will allow the company to select the most suitable crowdsourcing model according to its needs, ensuring at the same time meeting the basic expected standard.

Crowdworkers are now decisive agents for brand development, having great impact on companies worldwide. Therefore, businesses must reverse the thinking that normally goes into employee relationships. Keeping always in mind that if they think you are trying to take advantage of their effort, they will never come back.

Appendix 1 Crowdsourcing Concept Definitions

Author	Definition
Howe (2006a, b)	"Simply defined, crowdsourcing represents the act of a company or institution taking a function once performed by employees and outsourcing it to an undefined (and generally large) network of people in the form of an open call"
Howe (2009)	"Crowdsourcing is the act of taking a job traditionally performed by a designated agent (usually an employee) and outsourcing it to an undefined, generally large group of people in the form of an open call"
Brabham (2013)	"Crowdsourcing is an online, distributed problem-solving and production model that leverages the collective intelligence of online communities to serve specific organizational goals"
Oliveira et al. (2009)	"A way of outsourcing to the crowd tasks of intellectual assets creation, often collaboratively, with the aim of having easier access to a wide variety of skills and experience"
Vukovic (2009)	"A new on-line distributed problem solving and production model in which networked people collaborate to complete a task"
Sloane (2011)	"One particular manifestation of open innovation. It is the act of outsourcing a task to a large group of people outside your organization, often by making a public call for response. It is based on the open source philosophy, which used a large 'crowd' of developers to build the Linux operating system"
Whitla (2010)	"Crowdsourcing defines a process of organising labour, where firms parcel out work to some form of (normally online) community, offering payment for anyone within the 'crowd' who completes the task the firm has set"

References

Brabham, C. (2013). *Crowdsourcing*. Massachusetts: Mit Press.

Carr, N. G. (2010). The ignorance of crowds, strategy + business. *Magazine 47*, 1–5.

Gustafsson, K. (2014). Lego crowdsources its way to new toys. Business week. Available at http://www.businessweek.com/articles/2014–04-03/lego-crowdsources-its-way-to-new-toys. Accessed April 03, 2014.

Hempel, J. (2006). Crowdsourcing: Milk the masses for inspiration. *Business Week 25*, 38–39.

Howe, J. (2006a, June 14) The rise of crowdsourcing, wired. Available at http://www.wired.com/wired/archive/14.06/crowds.html.

Howe, J. (2006b, June 2). Crowdsourcing: a definition. Wired Blog Network: Crowdsourcing. Available at http://crowdsourcing.typepad.com/cs/2006/06/crowdsourcing_a.html.

Howe, J. (2009). *Crowdsourcing: Why the power of the crowd is driving the future of business*. New York: Three Rivers Press.

ICEMD. (2012). LEGO y su innovación gracias al crowdsourcing. Available at http://blogs.icemd.com/blog-colaboracion-y-co-creacion-de-usuarios-y-consumidores-crowdsourcing/lego-y-su-innovacion-gracias-al-crowdsourcing/. Accessed July 07, 2012.

LEGO. (2014). The LEGO® CUUSOO beta has ended and is now replaced by LEGO® Ideas. The Official LEGO® CUUSOO Blog. Available at http://blog.lego.cuusoo.com/about/.

LEGO Ideas. (2014). Web Lego, Available at https://ideas.lego.com/.

Marketingdirecto. (2011a). La campaña de Doritos para la Super Bowl se convierte en el viral más visto. Available at http://www.marketingdirecto.com/actualidad/publicidad/la-campana-de-doritos-para-la-super-bowl-se-convierte-en-el-viral-mas-visto/. Accessed Jan 09, 2011.

Marketingdirecto. (2011b). El "Crash the Super Bowl" de Doritos se vuelve internacional. Available at http://www.marketingdirecto.com/actualidad/anunciantes/el-crash-the-super-bowl-de-doritos-se-vuelve-internacional/. Accessed Sept 13, 2013.

Martineau, E. (2012). A typology of crowdsourcing participation styles. Masters thesis, Concordia University.

Oliveira, F., Ramos, I., & Santos, L. (2009). Definition of a crowdsourcing innovation service for the European SMEs. *Current Trends in Web Engineering, 6385*, 412–416.

Pepsico. (2011). Casting de Sabores Lay's La innovadora campaña de PepsiCo marca un antes y un después en gran consumo y en su relación con el consumidor. Available at http://www.pepsico.es/media/releases/view/casting-de-sabores-lays-la-innovadora-campana-de-pepsico-marca-un-antes-y-un-despues-en-gran-consumo-y-en-su-relacion-con-el-consumidor-.html. Accessed May 6, 2011. Press Release.

Pepsico. (2012). Lay's Gambas al Ajillo, nuevo sabor de las patatas Lay's en España. Available at http://www.pepsico.es/media/releases/view/lay-s-gambas-al-ajillo-sabor-ganador.html. Accessed Jan 9, 2012. Press Release.

Pepsico. (2013). La marca de snacks Doritos pone en marcha un concurso dirigido a sus consumidores de todo el mundo con un premio de un millón de dólares. Available at http://www.pepsico.es/media/releases/view/la-marca-de-snacks-doritos-pone-en-marcha-un-concurso-dirigido-a-sus-consumidores-de-todo-el-mundo-con-un-premio-de-un-mill-n-de-d-lares-.html. Accessed Oct 29, 2013.

Sloane, P. (2011). The brave new world of open innovation. *Strategic Direction, 27*(5), 3–4.

Vila, M. (2013). LEGO Cuusoo, construyendo la innovación con el cliente, TCBlog. Available at http://www.territoriocreativo.es/etc/2013/11/lego-cuusoo-construyendo-la-innovacion-con-el-cliente.html. Accessed Nov 26, 2013.

Vukovic, M. (2009). Crowdsourcing for enterprises. In: *Proceedings of the 2009 Congress on Services—I* (pp. 686–692). Washington, DC: IEEE Computer Society.

Whitla, P. (2010). Crowdsourcing and its application in marketing activities. *Contemporary Management Research, 5*(1), 15–28.

Chapter 13
Advances in Crowdsourcing: Surveys, Social Media and Geospatial Analysis: Towards a Big Data Toolkit

Steven Gray, Richard Milton and Andrew Hudson-Smith

Abstract The collection, mining and analysis of social media are arguably one of the core examples of "big data" sets for the social sciences. The dynamic nature of the media makes it a new and emerging base for the analysis of human behaviour and brings new opportunities to understand groups, movements and society. Analysing the results of billions of conversations has already revolutionised marketing and advertising. However, these datasets, by their very nature, are complex, time-consuming and computationally difficult to analyse. We put in place a series of examples to utilise such datasets with a view of exploring non-complex workflows via the use of new toolkits, linking into data collection via the crowd and opening up systems for analysis.

Keywords Crowdsourcing · Geospatial · Toolkit · MYSQL · Mapping · Geographic · SurveyMapper · MapTube · Tweet-o-Meter

13.1 Introduction

A key method to process large datasets is to outsource basic analysis to human volunteers and, in some cases, large groups, to help process this data by manually identifying patterns, features or interesting events within the datasets. This process has been called "Crowdsourcing", first coined in the article "The Rise of Crowdsourcing" (Howe 2006b).

S. Gray (✉) · R. Milton · A. Hudson-Smith
The Bartlett Centre for Advanced Spatial Analysis,
University College London, London, UK
e-mail: steven.gray@ucl.ac.uk

R. Milton
e-mail: richard.milton@ucl.ac.uk

A. Hudson-Smith
e-mail: a.hudson-smith@ucl.ac.uk

F.J. Garrigos-Simon et al. (eds.), *Advances in Crowdsourcing*,
DOI 10.1007/978-3-319-18341-1_13

"Simply defined, crowdsourcing represents the act of a company or institution taking a function once performed by employees and outsourcing it to an undefined (and generally large) network of people in the form of an open call. This can take the form of peer-production (when the job is performed collaboratively), but is also often undertaken by sole individuals. The crucial prerequisite is the use of the open call format and the large network of potential laborers" (Howe 2006a).

Crowdsourcing in the realm of a read/write Web (known as Web 2.0) is the process of collecting individual actions that can be aggregated together to create a collective result (Hudson-Smith et al. 2009). Projects such as Galaxy Zoo (Sloan Digital Sky Survey 2010) have had notable success with this process for astronomical datasets from sensors collecting data from sunspots to radar images from distant galaxies. Members of the public have successfully identified candidate galaxies in different solar systems through these highly specialised, custom-built systems by splitting up huge datasets into small pieces, a process that would take traditional forms of research a number of years to analyse. These crowdsourced systems have proven to be extremely important as the amount of data collected has increased due to the rise of real-time sensors and live streams of situational data that make up the deluge of data available today (Demarest 2011).

However, many crowdsourced projects suffer from a lack of users or simply not enough members of the public willing to help through other means, such as lack of exposure or a poorly designed interface. Good exposure of a project is vital to getting users to contribute data and, more importantly, getting users to join the community. Crowdsourced projects need a crowd—so that new data are being generated, processed and outcomes obtained.

Services such as Amazon's Mechanical Turk (Amazon 2011) and those such as Solar Stormwatch (Zooniverse 2009) use volunteers who are either interested in the subject matter or offer some sort of financial reward to entice users to use these services. Users in the Mechanical Turk ecosystem offer a price per action, a Human Intelligence Task or HIT, for a worker, to carry out an action such as categorising an image or translating a passage from one language to another (Ross et al. 2011). If the worker is qualified to carry out the HIT, then after completion, their associated Amazon account will be credited by an amount from $0.02 for a simple task up to $20 for a more complicated task. This is one way to get users to carry out tasks, but puts up barriers to research, as many projects cannot afford to provide monetary compensation to users.

Researchers have explored these rich datasets of social information available through the open APIs as a by-product of the rise in popularity of social media services. Twitter officially released an interface to the data for the service 6 months after their initial launch due to the number of third-party developers creating applications from Twitter data by automatically "scraping" pages of data rather than using a machine readable API (Stone 2006).

In this chapter, we will document the various experiments and toolkits created at the Centre for Advanced Spatial Analysis (CASA) for crowdsourcing data and look to the future of crowdsourcing using modern computing techniques to automate collection. The first such example we explore is SurveyMapper.

13.2 SurveyMapper

Collecting data on a global scale require outreach beyond the traditional methods. Traditionally, services are built from the ground up to support the collection of data for specific needs rather than a general need for many users. In late 2009, CASA was approached by the BBC to carry out a real-time survey for broadcast exploring the anti-social behaviour around the BBC Look East region (Norfolk, Suffolk, Essex, Cambridgeshire, Northamptonshire, Bedfordshire, Hertfordshire and Northern Buckinghamshire, UK) using the popular MapTube platform, allowing the visualisation of both survey and geographical data. At that time, few, if any, technologies existed for collecting real-time crowdsourced data in this fashion and so a bespoke application built on top of MapTube was created that allowed a single survey to be carried out with the results updated every 30 min. This survey resulted in 6902 responses overall with an average of 1340 results generated after broadcast over 3 evenings. MapTube was developed as part of the Generative e-Social Science project (GeNESIS). It provides a dynamic API (called MapTubeD) to render data into raster tiles and the ability to create and clear tiles on request. As a user provides a response to a survey, the system updates a database of responses and alerts the MapTubeD system to fetch a new datafile. When the map is next requested on the page load, the new raster files are downloaded from MapTubeD and placed on top of the survey map. These requests appear transparent, and the complexity is abstracted away from the user who only sees an updated map of responses in real time. It became apparent after the BBC survey that there was a need for this type of generalised platform and this bespoke project became the genesis of SurveyMapper.

The application, defined as "SurveyMapper", is a platform, which allows users to set up their own surveys and collect geographical locations from participants along with their views on the survey (Fig. 13.1). It was specifically created to tap into the crowd and visualise the results not only geographically but also in near real time. To set up a survey, users are asked to provide some metadata about the survey such as a title, description, keywords for searching, and start and end date along with the questions they want to ask participants. What makes SurveyMapper different to other platforms, such as Survey Monkey, is that a survey is tied to geographical boundary areas and visualised as a choropleth map of responses to a particular question. There are seven possible geographical types a user can select to visualise data: countries, US zip codes, UK postcodes, EU countries, US states, UK counties, London boroughs or London electoral wards. In addition to these geographical areas, there are 2 point-based visualisations that users can select to provide locations to responses: a latitude/longitude marker that is placed on the map and a heat map visualisation. Tens of thousands of inputs can be collected quickly, providing a near real-time view of research questions, instead of the 30-min delay of the original MapTube system. The data and subsequent visualisation are updated immediately. Data can be exported later for more rigorous analysis or integration with existing datasets.

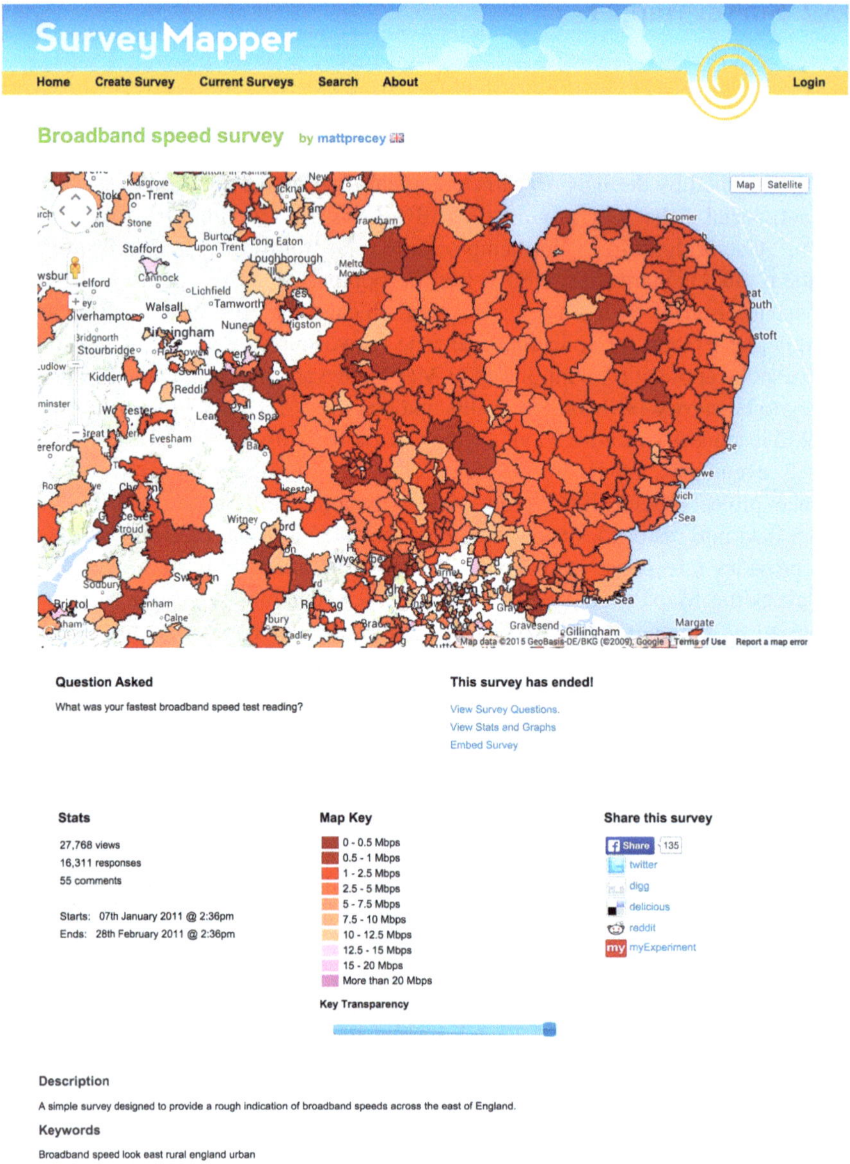

Fig. 13.1 SurveyMapper Survey-Broadband Speed Test January 2011. *Source* own

SurveyMapper can also be extended to provide custom visualisations for surveys that need specific and specialised information capture. The Greater London Authority approached the SurveyMapper team to help carry out a safety survey of parks around London. They wanted to ask users of the park, "How satisfied or dissatisfied are you with the quality of your local parks and green spaces?" through

12 questions that probed citizens' views on their local park. The issue with this type of survey is that citizens do not necessarily know the name of the local park, which is held by the GLA. By adding a London park dataset, sourced from green spaces data on OpenStreetMap to the MapTube rendering system, we were able to customise the experience of SurveyMapper to allow users to select their local park by dragging a pin around the Greater London area and dropping the pin on a parkland area. When the pin was dropped on the map, the name of the park was populated automatically and submitted to the database with the remainder of responses. At the end of the survey, the GLA downloaded the individual and aggregated data of responses and were able to integrate the data with their own internal datasets.

SurveyMapper was built with 2 specific purposes: to provide social scientists with a series of online tools to collect and visualise data in near real time allowing the creation of "mood maps" linked to a backend geographic information system, and to remove the traditional academic look to scientific software services. SurveyMapper achieves the latter by "skinning" the application and focuses on usability by removing the complexity and the science of the software from the user. Throughout the Web application, users are presented with a fun and bright design (Fig. 13.2), which incorporates the mascot "Roger the Giraffe", named after Roger

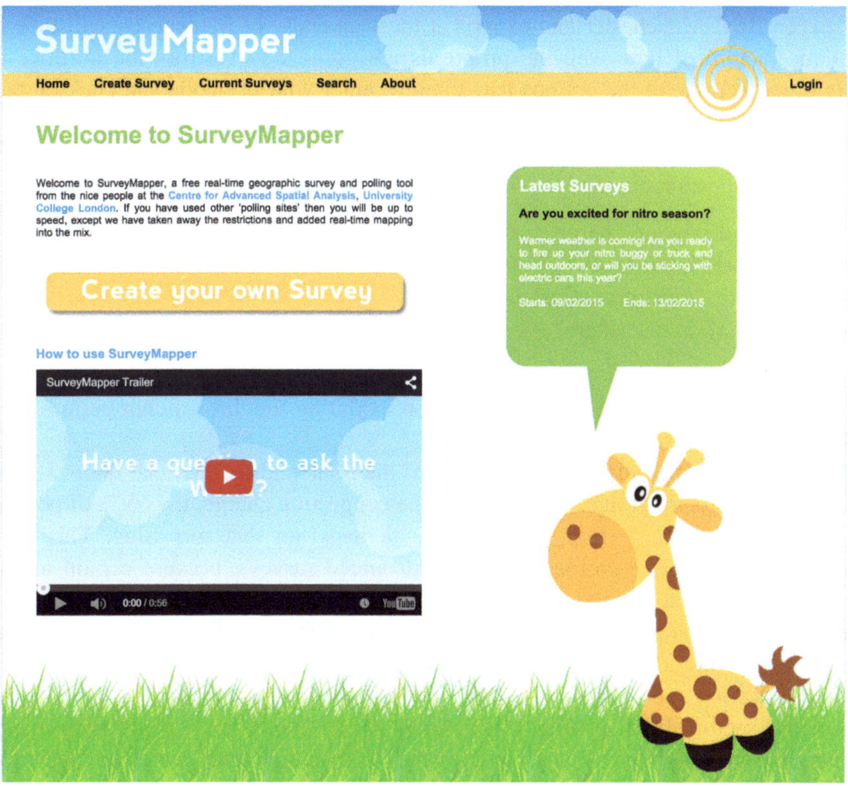

Fig. 13.2 SurveyMapper home page—non-academic branding, Roger the Giraffe mascot. *Source* own

Tomlinson who is commonly acknowledged as the "father of GIS" (Greiner 2007). This design decision was taken early on in the process of creating SurveyMapper to give the system a look and feel more akin of a Web 2.0 project rather than a scientific academic project.

As users set up a survey, they are encouraged to share the survey on social media platforms as we have found the most successful surveys on the platform use social media to reach participants. The system provides short URLs and custom links too as well as links that allow users to embed surveys on personal Websites and share with social networks such as Facebook and Twitter. The system also allows users to comment about individual surveys and to promote discussion on the platform about results of surveys. Collecting this data allows research into and users of the application to flag up interesting results within the dataset. To date, more than 500 surveys have been created with a combined total of 152,310 responses and 210,000 views in the first 5 years of SurveyMapper being available to the public.

During October to December 2008, CASA ran a survey to gauge the public response to the proposed congestion charge in Greater Manchester. This asked the question:

If you have an interest in how the £2.7 billion plan to reshape Manchester's transport system will affect your neighbourhood then here's your chance to add what you think to an interactive map of the region. This online collaboration between BBC Manchester and experts at the University of Manchester will give a unique picture of how well the proposals are going down across the northwest. Simply select one of the options listed below, enter your postcode and click on the submit button.

MapTube will include your answer in the next new map.

"If a congestion charge was brought in would you:

Drive and pay the charge?
Drive at different times?
Use public transport/motorbike/bicycle?
Work or shop elsewhere?
Not Affected?"

This resulted in a total of 15,902 responses during the three-month period with the final data are represented in Fig. 13.3.

Due to the politically sensitive nature of the issue and the fact that there were a number of pressure groups who opposed the congestion charge, the 45 % of people responding "Work or shop elsewhere" is perhaps not that surprising. This also highlighted the major problem with crowdsourced surveys, because certain members of the general public were deliberately submitting large numbers of responses in an attempt to manipulate the survey. This was something that was expected and is relatively simple to filter out the data.

By selecting and counting duplicate IP addresses and then mapping the data by postcode sector, the map (Fig. 13.4) clearly shows "OL8" and "M31" with many more responses for "Drive and pay the charge" than any other postcode. Our only explanation for this is that somebody was trying to make the predominantly blue

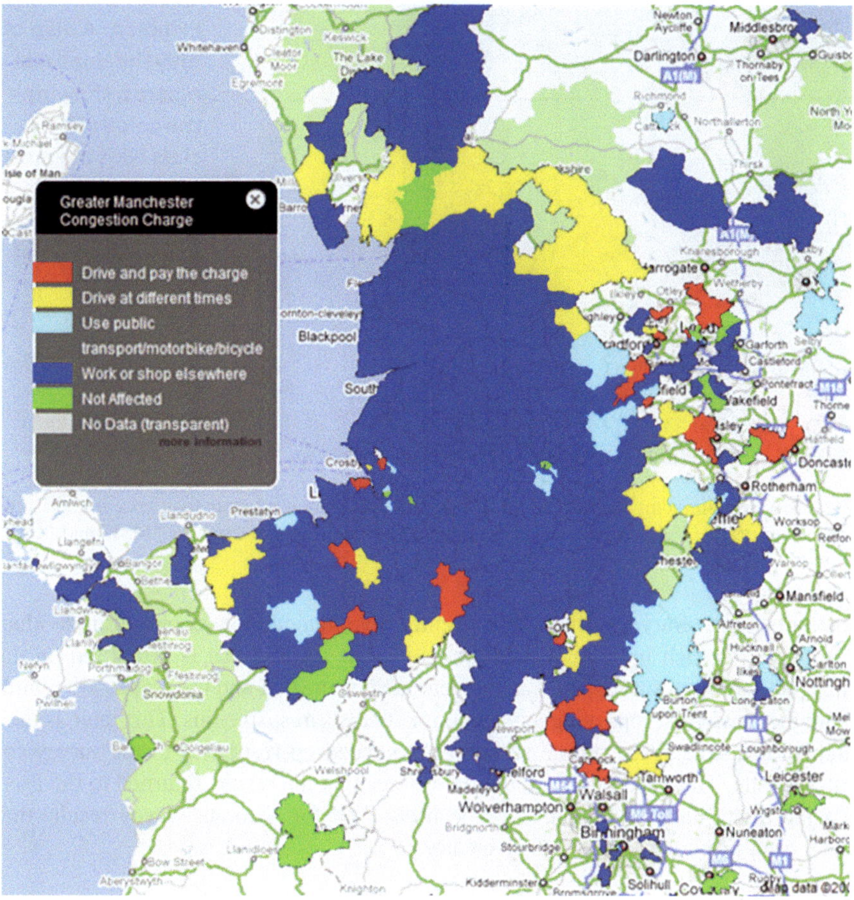

Fig. 13.3 Greater Manchester Congestion Charge Survey—live map can be viewed at the following link: http://www.maptube.org/map.aspx?mapid=239. *Source* own

map turn red for his or her own postcode. Geographic density of responses is an important issue with georeferenced surveys, as the non-uniform nature of the responses needs to be taken into account when analysing the data.

SurveyMapper has preventions built into the core of the system to prevent users, as well as identifying, from gaming the system and adding extra responses to a survey. By default, each survey only allows a single IP address to vote on a survey. If a user is logged into the system, their response is logged and the interface will prevent the user from viewing the "Enter Response" page. As SurveyMapper also allows users to vote from embed surveys, third-party apps that implement the SurveyMapper API as well as users who are not logged in, extra precautions have been implemented to detect irregularities in patterns of response. A database table of all responses, which serves as a time series master list, is checked nightly for patterns of burst activity in the remote chance that a user has defeated the response

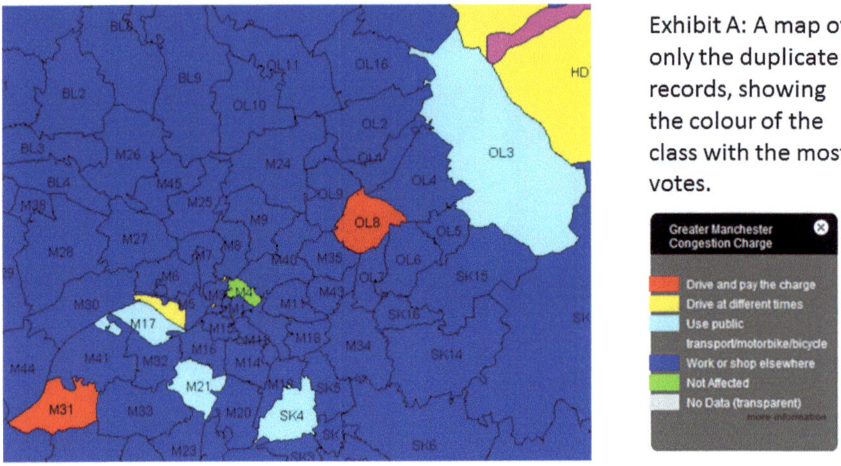

Fig. 13.4 Selecting only the data for IP addresses which were used more than once reveals some interesting results. Further analysis shows hundreds of responses entered for "M31" and "OL8" from two addresses. *Source* own

lockout event. Surveys that are currently live maintain a count of individual responses for each individual question as well as a value that is visualised on the map. As soon as a survey ends, a transient table is created and the results are rebuilt from the master list removing any responses that seem suspicious. This table is then archived to save space on the server and to speed up responses to the survey for future visits. This method of validation ensures that the results returned to the user, via the direct data download, have been checked for accurate survey results that have been provided to the survey creator.

13.3 Tweet-o-Meter

While exploring use cases of the SurveyMapper system, the team identified that to promote usage of the platform outside the Website, an API would be needed to submit responses to surveys from third-party applications and that allowing users to quickly submit responses without visiting the main SurveyMapper Web application. Twitter, a social media platform, that enables users to send messages of 140 characters or less proved to be the best solution to allow users to quickly respond to a survey. It was envisioned that a user would learn of a survey from posts within their social network and be able to submit a response by either retweeting a post, the process of sharing a tweet with your own network, or creating a post with the survey id and the response value.

This method of posting real time using tweets was popularised during the winter of 2010 when the UK experienced an unusually prolonged spell of severe cold weather that resulted in heavy snowfall (Met Office 2011). Twitter users started to organically share regional snow reports throughout the UK in real time by rating the current snowfall on a scale from 0 to 10 and including the first half of their postcode within the tweet. As this trend started to spread, various Websites appeared mapping the real-time results on top of online maps. One such Website was UK Snow Map (Marsh 2014) created by Ben Marsh, a freelance Web developer. At the same time, the team at UCL CASA started to experiment with collecting the UK Snow tweets from Twitter and mapping them using the choropleth mapping technique used for SurveyMapper.

Figure 13.5 shows the total number of tweets collected during January 2010 when some of the heaviest snowfall was taking place. Of all the tweets collected, 36.4 % included a postcode ("Steady heavy snow in Chesham HP5 #uksnow"), while 28.8 % included a postcode and an amount ("#uksnow SG10 3/10"). This exposes a basic problem with this type of crowdsourcing, because not everybody has the same opinion about the amount of snow. One person's 5/10 might be another person's 8/10, depending on where they live in the country and how much snow they are used to. Using the synoptic data from the Meteorological Office, the reported depth of snow in centimetres was compared with tweets in the same postcode, leading to the conclusion that there was no measurable correlation between the two (Fig. 13.6). However, when looking at the general question of whether there was any snow in the area, the crowdsourced data compared more favourably with the official Met Office snow amounts.

Twitter exposes the data stored within the system via two authenticated APIs: the Streaming and the Search API. The Streaming API allows developers to make a connection with the API and receive updates automatically as they happen. A persistent connection is made to the API endpoint, and data are fed to the third-party program when a user sends a publically available tweet. The Search API requires a third-party program to request the data from the API endpoint repeatedly over a period

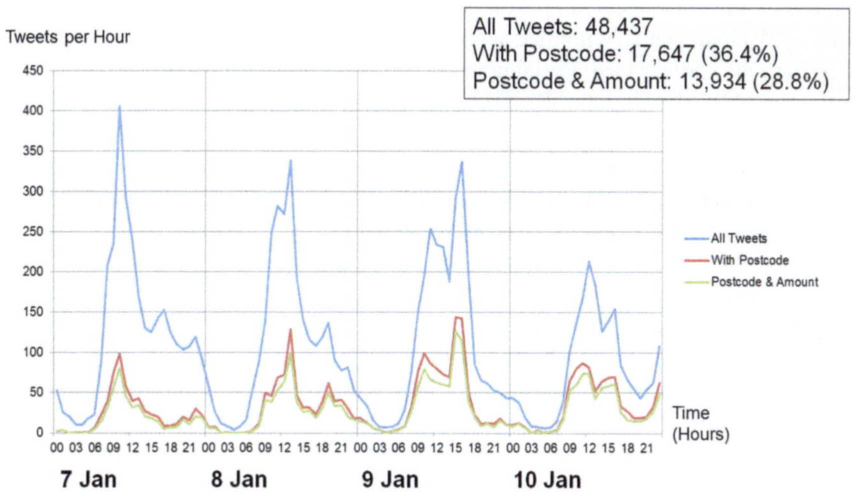

Fig. 13.5 Tweets collected from UK geoboundary during 2010 snowfall. *Source* own

Fig. 13.6 Data for 6 January 2010 12Z, the map on the *left* shows postcode sectors where there is snow on the ground using the Meteorological Office data. The map on the *right* shows the #uksnow counts from Twitter. *Source* own

of time. As the data are requested, the API returns the last available tweets (up to a maximum of 100 tweets) depending on the search query passed to the API. By making multiple requests over a period of time and tracking the last message collected, the third-party application can build a subset of tweets over time. The API serves tweet data in 3 different capacities: the Firehose, the Garden Hose and the Spritzer. The FireHose represents an unfiltered, raw feed of all tweets globally for the search query provided. The Garden Hose is a 10 % sample of all tweets queried, and the spritzer represents a 2 % statistical sample of data. Both the Firehose and Garden Hose require prior agreements with Twitter for access, which is assessed on a case-by-case basis; therefore, the spritzer feed is commonly used by third-party applications. Unlike the Streaming API, the Search API is rate limited by the number of requests within a period of time. At the time of development (2010 version 1 of the API), this limit was undocumented, but through experimentation was calculated at around 350 requests per hour. As per version 1.1 of the Twitter API, this rate limit has been extended to 180 requests per 15-min period—720 requests an hour.

During the experimentation phase with SurveyMapper and the Twitter API, we started archiving and storing the tweet and relevant metadata returned from the API using several machines inside the laboratory. Each machine ran several processes to collect data from the Search API asynchronously and aggregated the data within a central data repository for analysis at a later date. Automating the data collection between multiple distributed machines in this fashion, we were able to collect more than the 2 % sample provided by the Streaming API. A central visualisation was created to monitor and control the individual machines' collection, as each machine was located in different physical locations around the laboratory.

Tweet-o-Meter is a visualisation of 16 real-time gauges monitoring the rate of activity of individual tweets geolocated 30 km from the administrative centre of 16 cities around the world, focusing on New York, London, Paris, Munich, Tokyo, Moscow, Sydney, Toronto, San Francisco, Barcelona and Oslo (Fig. 13.7). The first candidate cities were chosen based on the first line of chorus to the song "Pop Musik" by band M ("New York, London, Paris, Munich, Everybody talk about pop musik.") This served to ground the project into popular culture to attract users to view and use the site. The visualisation also serves a secondary purpose as a visual indicator of multiple processes on a given machine's output over time. Each gauge monitors the aggregated rate of tweets, or tweets per minute (TPM), in a given city, and the value is updated in real time.

Having multiple processes, mining data on separate physical hardware yielded approximately 12 million tweets over 3 days of collection (Weekend Friday–Monday) for a 30 km radius around London. Two separate categories of geocoded data were returned from the API: public tweets that were geolocated from a device capable of determining location (e.g. smartphone with GPS sensor) and tweets that have been positioned by reverse geocoding the location from a user's profile location. It is important to note that these tweets were flagged as publically available tweets by the creator which allowed the geolocation of a tweet to be shared with third-party applications. Through experimentation and various collections at differing times, it was found that that approximately 2 % of all tweets in a 30 km radius had detailed latitude/longitude coordinates associated with a tweet.

Using this, collection method allowed the system to successfully experiment by collecting responses for surveys created within SurveyMapper. By mining tweets for the hashtag #5Acts4wildlife, the 5Acts4wildlife campaign aimed to

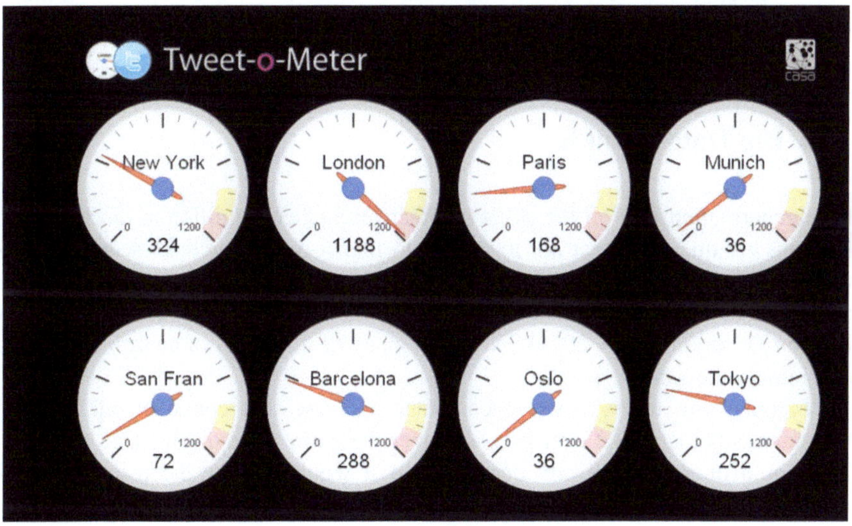

Fig. 13.7 Tweet-o-Meter real-time gauges for 8 cities. *Source* own

crowdsourced opinion on 5 campaigns that affect wildlife during a single week in January 2011. Due to the resource-intensive nature of setting up collectors to mine data for a specific survey, this process was set up manually to feed data to SurveyMapper, but recent advances in cloud computing now allow clusters of virtualised hardware to be set up automatically to mine data from Twitter and collect response data.

Tweet-o-Meter has featured on and been used by various media outlets across the world, namely CNN and Discovery Channel, Canada, during the Fukushima Earthquake in 2011 and has been used by various companies to collect social media data for visualisation and analysis. Storing the data in a central repository allowed social scientists within the laboratory to create new visualisations based on the archived city data. One such project set out to create a set of "New Cities Landscapes" which highlighted the landscape of the peaks and troughs of these hidden cities using the geolocated Twitter data. The team also collected and analysed data for the mobile phone network, EE, for analysis of the 4G mobile connectivity roll-out. The data for 10 major cities across the UK and the top 250 trending words in each city were extracted and passed on to a digital artist who created an infographic and set of visualisations for art galleries in each city.

Collecting and archiving approximately 5 million tweets a day to power the Tweet-o-Meter dials and subsequent research uses significant hardware resources. The collection of Twitter data, including relevant metadata for each tweet, for the 2 weeks of the London 2012 Olympics Games for the 22 separate venues, utilises approximately 1.5 TB of hard drive space. Therefore, to provide an archive of 4 years' worth of data for each of the 16 cities became unsustainable. At present, the system discards data 48 h after collection by the Tweet-o-Meter collectors. This ensures that space on the physical machines is not overloaded, but at the same time allows researchers to recall data within the 16 cities in the eventuality of a major incident happening within the collection boundary.

13.4 Big Data Toolkit

Researchers often rely on the skills of other researchers in different disciplines to help answer questions that are important to their own research. Researchers normally contact data suppliers and are given access to interesting datasets or discover a set of data that have been released on an Open Data store, such as the GLA London DataStore (GLA 2011). However, many of the issues of analysing the data still remain the same.

"Imagine you had a massive computer database that contained all possible measurements that could ever be made over the entire span of all space and time. You could query it with any question and it would deliver the result instantaneously. All big data is merely a subset of this the biggest data that could ever exist. What would your project ask it?" (Ramalingam 2013).

Providing a generalised toolkit for social scientists, not only to collect the data but also to analyse the data from the different services, will empower them to ask questions of the social media output without the need to learn complex APIs or build bespoke tools to gather data.

Many of the social media services provide different APIs to access the data each with differing server technologies. For example, some APIs rely on simple authentication, username and password or API keys, to access data while others require complex handshakes to be performed, oAuth2, for example. Technically proficient researchers are able to write custom applications to collect the data from these services, but lack the skill in analysing and visualising the data. Conversely, spatial, geographical and social scientists are able to analyse and visualise the data to draw conclusions about use of our cities, but sometimes lack the technical expertise to acquire the data from the source. The Big Data Toolkit seeks to help researchers by providing a toolkit with a simple interface to break down these barriers to the data and allow researchers to analyse the data in varying ways (Fig. 13.8).

Cloud Computing allows users to pool vast numbers of computing resources together to build complex and dynamic systems. The emergence of cloud computing providers has increased in modern-day computing, allowing developers to leverage the vast amount of computing power available using idle computing cycles of large companies' infrastructure. In recent years, the decrease in cost of CPU time, storage and the competitive nature of these platforms have made burst cloud computing affordable. For example, a standard virtualized machine consisting of a modest CPU (2.8 Gb Quad Core) and 50 Gb of storage, networking, bandwidth and power, situated in one of the American Amazon data centres, costs approximately $0.80 per hour, whereas the same physical machine running in a local cluster would

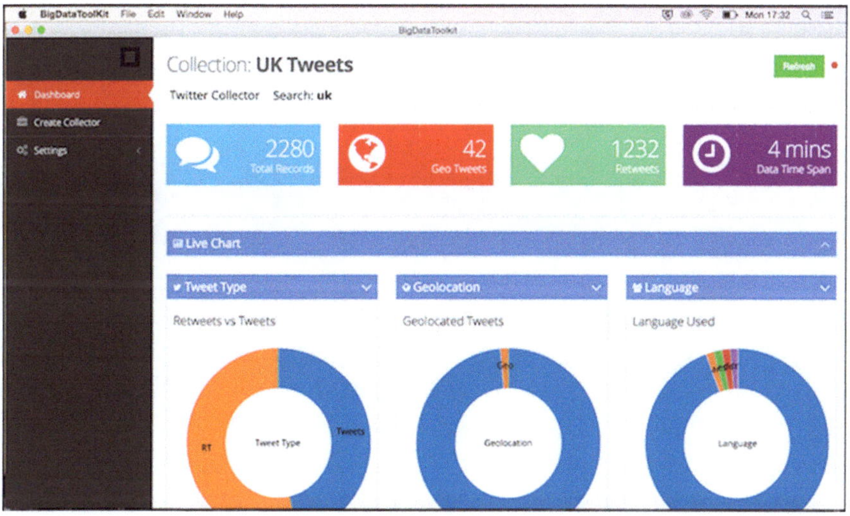

Fig. 13.8 Big Data Toolkit collection page showing real-time collection statistics. *Source* own

cost a few thousand pounds at the outset, which does not including ongoing running costs such as machine (electric, cooling systems, etc.).

The toolkit utilises these cloud platforms to outsource computing capacity for data collection, for a nominal cost to the end-user. By creating virtualised machines in the cloud, the user can create multiple collectors, gathering data from various locations.

To test this new method of data collection, we distributed multiple collectors on Amazon's Web Service infrastructure (AWS) during the 2011 presidential debates between Barack Obama and Mitt Romney. We decided to experiment by collecting Twitter data for an entire nation, for a single specific event, capturing the maximum amount of data possible and to test the architecture of the system. A single virtual machine image of the Big Data Toolkit was created and replicated on 87 virtual machines (each running 4 regional collectors) for a period of 4 h (Fig. 13.9). A master database served as single repository of data, and each machine over time correlated its own records and merged them into the master MySQL database. A master server acted as an intermediary between the cluster on AWS and the Big Data Toolkit desktop application, providing jobs to each machine after initial installation and configuration. Each machine connected to the master server and retrieved a latitude/longitude coordinate pair, radius and a unique collector identifier to set up the collectors, which was logged by the master server for tracking purposes. This control server relayed collection statistics, current collection totals and snapshots of data collected back to the application, providing a real-time dashboard of collection statistics. A total of 692,986 geolocated tweets (approximately 8 % of all tweets sourced) were collected in the master database (Fig. 13.10), which allowed social scientists to analyse the differences in sentiment between the East and West Coast voter opinions over a 10 min rolling average throughout the 4-h period.

Fig. 13.9 Distributed collection experiment showing collector radius for virtual machines. *Source* own

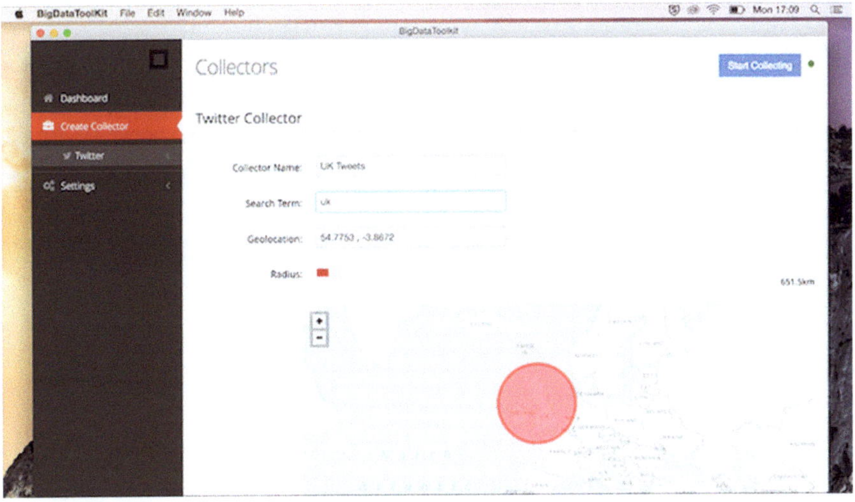

Fig. 13.10 Big Data Toolkit application—setting geographical radius for collection. *Source* own

The toolkit allows users, by combining the tools documented within the chapter, to mine and analyse various social media data in one application without having previous knowledge of the underpinning APIs. The toolkit is modular by design, and modules are added to allow users to collect data from various API (Fig. 13.8). As new services and APIs are identified, modules can then be added to the toolkit without making significant changes to base system. This data can be fed into different analytical packages, included within the toolkit, giving real-time feedback on the collection to the user. The feedback is provided via charts, data feeds, maps and dynamic interactive word clouds (Fig. 13.11) which allows the user to define new search terms, change locational regions where the data are collected or edit the data while the collection is being carried out.

The Big Data Toolkit currently provides data for a number of services that are central to UCL CASA research. The toolkit provides social media data collection for City Dashboard, a real-time dashboard of open data for various cities in the UK, and various visualisations including the London Data Table, PigeonSim, iPad Video Wall, as well as Tweet-o-Meter and SurveyMapper. The system also provides data collection services for Internet of schools, a partnership of schools that are equipped with real-time sensors and QRator, a collaboration with UCL Digital Humanities and the UCL Grant museum providing visitor engagement through digital tablets.

The toolkit stores all data within a MySQL database, which is installed locally on a user's system. All data that are collected are visualised from this central location so that the various processes and applications can share datasets. Due to the terms and conditions stipulated by some of the APIs, the sharing of data outside of the application is forbidden; therefore, by using the users' own login credentials and datastore, they can legitimately use the API while keeping within the application's terms and conditions.

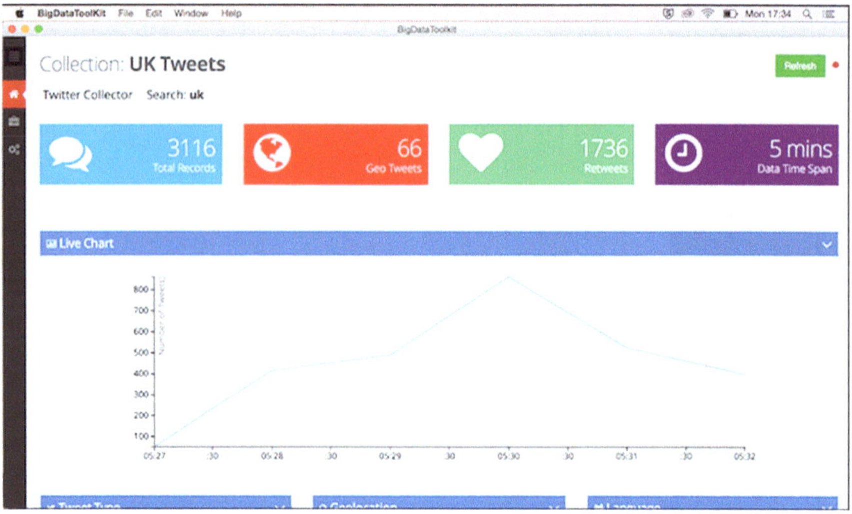

Fig. 13.11 Big Data Toolkit application—live chart of data collected within first 5 min of collection. *Source* own

Due to the modular design of the toolkit and the ability to use cloud computing to create multiple collectors to watch geographical areas, we can build a workflow to mine data continuously from different services and compare and analyse the data in real time. This provides social scientists with a complete view of all social media output for multiple locations and allows them access to the raw textual data for research purposes.

13.5 Conclusion

Crowdsourcing data for scientific projects has yielded interesting results for various applications. Projects such as Galaxy Zoo and Zooniverse have brought citizen science to the forefront of research and reduced the time taken to analyse large datasets, which would have not been possible using standard, algorithmic and processing techniques. Systems and techniques for social scientists are emerging, but there is a key need, while simplifying the collection and analysis and ensuring access to the raw data, to provide toolkits that do not require specialist tools. The crowdsourcing of geographically tagged social media has notable potential for the humanities, not to replace any current techniques but to add to the availability of data, "big data", that can be collected on demand, regardless of location and at short notice. It is moving towards an era of "as required" data collection with analysis in real time and removing the current need for knowledge about APIs or complex data collection systems. The backend to social science data collection is a complex computer science problem, the front end, now thanks to systems such as the Big Data Toolkit, which is simply a new workflow in the research method database and the ability to tap into the crowd.

References

Amazon. (2011). Amazon mechanical turk—artificial, artificial intelligence. https://www.mturk.com/mturk/welcome. Retrieved Nov 2013.

Demarest, M. (2011). Data overload threatens with rise of smart tech and real-time sensors FCW. http://fcw.com/articles/2011/02/28/comment-marc-demarest-sensor-data.aspx. Retrieved Mar 2011.

GLA. (2011). London datastore. http://data.london.gov.uk. Retrieved Aug 2011.

Greiner, (2007). Putting Canada on the map. http://www.theglobeandmail.com/technology/putting-canada-on-the-map/article1092101, Retrieved Dec 2014.

Howe, J. (2006a). Crowdsourcing: A definition. http://crowdsourcing.typepad.com/cs/2006/06/crowdsourcing_a.html. Retrieved Sept 2011.

Howe, J. (2006b). The rise of crowdsourcing. http://www.wired.com/wired/archive/14.06/crowds.html. Retrieved Dec 2013.

Hudson-Smith, A., Batty, M., Crooks, A., & Milton, R. (2009). Mapping for the masses: Accessing web 2.0 through crowdsourcing. *Social Science Computer Review, 27*, 524.

Marsh, (2014). #UKsnow Map. http://uksnowmap.com. Retrieved Jan 2015.

Met Office. (2011). The big freeze—Nov-Dec 2010. http://www.metoffice.gov.uk/about-us/who/how/case-studies/big-freeze. Retrieved July 2015.

Ramalingam, B. (2013). Lies, damned lies and big data | aid on the edge of chaos. http://aidontheedge.info/2013/02/01/lies-damned-lies-and-big-data. Retrieved Nov 2013.

Ross, C., Terras, M., Warwick, C., & Welsh, A. (2011). Enabled backchannel: Conference Twitter use by digital humanists. *Journal of Documentation, 67*(2), 214–237. doi: 10.1108/00220411111109449.

Sloan Digital Sky Survey. (2010). Galaxy Zoo. http://www.galaxyzoo.org. Retrieved July 2011.

Stone, B. (2006). Introducing the Twitter API. https://blog.twitter.com/2006/introducing-twitter-api. Retrieved Jan 2014.

Zooniverse. (2009). Zooniverse—real science online. https://www.zooniverse.org/. Retrieved Jan 2015.

Index

F.J. Garrigos-Simon et al. (eds.), *Advances in Crowdsourcing*,
DOI 10.1007/978-3-319-18341-1

MIX
Papier aus verantwortungsvollen Quellen
Paper from responsible sources
FSC® C105338

If you have any concerns about our products,
you can contact us on
ProductSafety@springernature.com

In case Publisher is established outside the EU,
the EU authorized representative is:
Springer Nature Customer Service Center GmbH
Europaplatz 3, 69115 Heidelberg, Germany

Printed by Libri Plureos GmbH
in Hamburg, Germany

Mean-Field Magnetohydrodynamics and Dynamo Theory

F. KRAUSE K.-H. RÄDLER

Mean-Field Magnetohydrodynamics and Dynamo Theory

With 46 Figures and 5 Tables

AKADEMIE-VERLAG · BERLIN 1980

Authors:

Prof. Dr. rer. nat. habil. Fritz Krause

Dr. rer. nat. Karl-Heinz Rädler

Zentralinstitut für Astrophysik
der Akademie der Wissenschaften der DDR

Erschienen im Akademie-Verlag, DDR-108 Berlin, Leipziger Str. 3—4

Lizenznummer: 202 · 100/544/80
Gesamtherstellung: VEB Druckhaus Köthen, 437 Köthen,
Straße der Thälmannpioniere 11/12
Bestellnummer: 7616267 (5948) · LSV 1195
Printed in GDR
DDR 48,— M

PREFACE

This book is intended to give a systematic introduction to mean-field magnetohydrodynamics and the dynamo theory which is based on it, and to provide a survey of the results achieved. Our first attempt in this direction, which at the same time constitutes the basis for this book, was an extensive contribution in the hand-book "Ergebnisse der Plasmaphysik und der Gaselektronik" (Krause and Rädler [2]). Since that article first appeared, mean-field magnetohydrodynamics as well as the theory of the turbulent dynamo have been considerably advanced by contributions from scientists in various parts of the world. We have endeavoured to incorporate the essential contents of the latest papers. The fairly comprehensive bibliography also includes works not mentioned in the text.

Chapters 1 to 10 deal with mean-field magnetohydrodynamics. We consider mean-field electrodynamics as the central core of this theory which only comprises the kinematic aspects. This fills the largest portion of the book and it is only after a systematic discussion of it that the back-reaction of the magnetic field on motion is then taken into consideration. The systematic elaboration of the theory requires demanding mathematical formalisms. Therefore, we thought it advisable first to demonstrate in Chapters 1 to 3 a simple approach to the essential results, and to employ the more ambitious means only in later chapters.

Chapters 11 to 17 first give a general introduction to the dynamo problem of magnetohydrodynamics, and then explain the dynamo theory which is based on mean-field magnetohydrodynamics, known as the theory of the turbulent dynamo, and discuss its application to cosmical objects.

We wish to express our sincere gratitude and appreciation to our teacher, Professor M. Steenbeck, with whom we have had the honour to work over many years in establishing the fundamentals of the theories presented here. We are also pleased to thank our colleagues Dr. O. A. Lielausis (Riga), Professor K. H. Moffatt (Bristol) and Professor P. H. Roberts (Newcastle upon Tyne) with whom we have maintained a fruitful exchange of ideas for a long time. We also thank our co-workers Dr. H. Bräuer, Dr. L. Oetken and Dr. G. Rüdiger (Potsdam), with whom we are constantly working.

Finally, we ought to mention that since we did not write this book in our native language we needed the advice of Herr Ch. Uhl (Potsdam), whom we thank very much.

CONTENTS

CHAPTER 1

INTRODUCTION

1.1. Turbulence and large-scale structures

Stimulated by astrophysics and geophysics an increasing interest has developed in the behaviour of electromagnetic fields in electrically conducting fluids carrying out irregular, especially turbulent motions. Above all two prominent phenomena were the foci of investigations: the Earth's magnetic field and the solar activity cycle. Their origin has been shown to be closely connected with turbulent motions in the core of the Earth and in the convection zone of the Sun.

From elementary experience the general conviction has developed that turbulent motions destroy structures of all kinds. The magnetic fields in sunspots, for instance, decay within weeks. According to estimations without considering turbulence they should be able to exist for more than a thousand years. The rapid decay is ascribed to the influence of the turbulent motion of matter in the solar convection zone.

It is a remarkable new finding that turbulence need not always be a cause of destruction, but it can give rise to large-scale structures under certain conditions. As L. Biermann [1] (1951) has shown, it is an anisotropic turbulence which is responsible for the non-uniform rotation of the convection zone of the Sun and of other stellar objects. Similarly, turbulent motions may also lead to the generation of large-scale magnetic fields. Ya. H. Frenkel [1] (1945) and L. E. Gurevich and A. H. Lebedinskij [1] (1945) had the idea that convective motions were responsible for the existence of the magnetic fields of the Earth and in the sunspots. E. N. Parker [2] (1955) was the first to discover a generating mechanism. The crucial point is the induction effect of a "cyclonic turbulence" occurring in convective layers of rotating bodies. If this effect occurs in combination with a non-uniform rotation, it allows for self-excitation of large-scale magnetic fields.

The processes described by Biermann and Parker are two examples of how large-scale structures are brought about by small-scale turbulent motions. The feature they have in common is the so-called "inverse cascade", i.e. the flow of energy from the small scales to the large scales, and this is just the opposite of what is normally expected to happen in a turbulent motion.

Recently, further examples of this kind have been found in hydrodynamics, which are known as "negative viscosity phenomena".

Based on a concept suggested by M. STEENBECK [1] (1961) a rather general theory has been developed which describes the behaviour of mean electromagnetic fields, i.e. of the large-scale parts of the electromagnetic fields, in electrically conducting matter carrying out turbulent motions. This theory is generally called "mean-field electroydnamics". Within this frame the conditions for the generation of large-scale magnetic fields from small-scale turbulent motions are most clearly revealed. A completely disordered, i.e. homogeneous isotropic mirrorsymmetric turbulence only influences the decay rate of the mean magnetic fields, which is enhanced in almost all cases of physical interest. A turbulence with the weakest possible deviation from complete disorder is one which is still homogeneous and isotropic but lacks mirrorsymmetry. In this case, right-handed and left-handed helical motions do not occur with the same probability. A homogeneous isotropic non-mirrorsymmetric turbulence

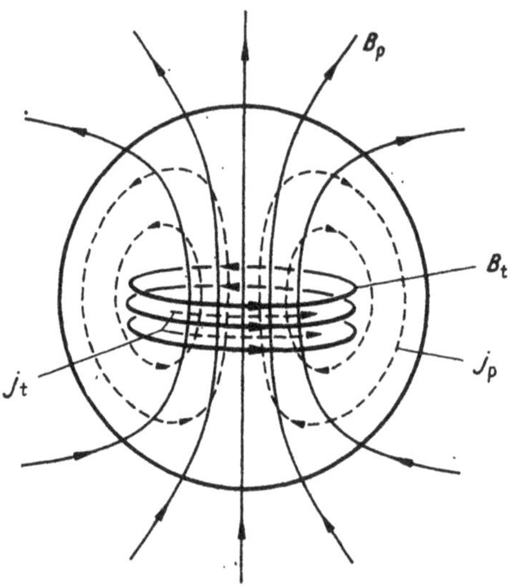

Fig. 1.1. A possible self-maintaining magnetic field configuration in an electrically conducting sphere with α-effect, i.e. Ohm's law reads $\boldsymbol{j} = \sigma(\boldsymbol{E} + \alpha\boldsymbol{B})$. The conducting sphere is embedded in the empty, insulating space. The magnetic field, $\boldsymbol{B}$, is axisymmetric. It is composed of a poloidal part, $\boldsymbol{B}_p$, with the field lines in the meridional planes with respect to the axis of symmetry, and a toroidal part, $\boldsymbol{B}_t$, with the field lines encircling the axis of symmetry. Because of the α-effect $\boldsymbol{B}_t$ drives a toroidal current, $\boldsymbol{j}_t$ (dashed lines). This current $\boldsymbol{j}_t$ is accompanied by the poloidal magnetic field $\boldsymbol{B}_p$ which, in turn, drives a poloidal current, $\boldsymbol{j}_p$ (dashed lines), accompanied by the toroidal magnetic field $\boldsymbol{B}_t$

provides for the quite unusual effect of the appearance of a mean electromotive force parallel to the magnetic field, the so-called α-effect. It is easy to understand that, for sufficiently strong α-effect, a magnetic field as depicted in figure 1.1 can be maintained against Ohmic decay.

In convective layers of rotating bodies, the Coriolis forces provide for a helical structure of the motions. There are regions in which one kind of helical motions dominate, thus causing the α-effect. This opens a direct approach to the explanation of the origin of cosmical magnetic fields.

Another theory of magnetic field generation due to more or less irregular motions has been initiated and elaborated by S. I. Braginskij [1, 2, 3] (1964). Since the large-scale fields are assumed to deviate only weakly from symmetry with respect to the rotational axis of the conducting body this theory has become known as the theory of the "nearly symmetric dynamo". This theory has been widely discussed with respect to the magnetic field of the Earth.

1.2. On the general concept of mean-field magnetohydrodynamics

In this book we shall deal with mean-field magnetohydrodynamics and its applications to the dynamo problem, known as the theory of the turbulent dynamo.

Mean-field magnetohydrodynamics is concerned with the behaviour of mean electromagnetic and hydrodynamic fields in turbulently moving electrically conducting media. It covers the mean-field electrodynamics which is restricted to the investigation of the mean electromagnetic fields in the case of prescribed hydrodynamic fields, i.e. without considering the influence of the electromagnetic fields on the motions.

This theory shall be developed on the basis of usual magnetohydrodynamics and all suppositions apply which are necessary for its justification. In all the following considerations a Euclidian space is supposed. The matter is considered to be a continuous fluid medium with sufficiently high electrical conductivity. Its velocity shall be small compared with the velocity of light in vacuum.

Let us give a short outline of the general concept and some special features of mean-field magnetohydrodynamics. We start from the basic equations of magnetohydrodynamics, which mainly consist of Maxwell's and the corresponding constitutive equations and the Navier-Stokes equation. From these equations corresponding equations for the mean fields shall be derived by an appropriate averaging operation, in the course of which non-linear terms give rise to new terms describing the mean effects of the fluctuating fields on the mean fields. With this we follow Reynolds's treatment of the Navier-

Stokes equation by which Reynolds's stresses were introduced. The corresponding quantity in mean-field electrodynamics is the average of the electromotive force due to the fluctuations of the velocity and the magnetic field, in the following called turbulent electromotive force. One of the major problems is to find representations of the turbulent electromotive force as a functional of the mean magnetic field in order to obtain a closed system of equations.

With this procedure detailed results can only be gained if restricting assumptions are introduced. In almost all deductions a two-scale turbulence shall be considered, i.e. the characteristic time and length scales of the fluctuations are small compared with those of the mean fields. The two-scale property does not only provide a simplified functional dependence of the turbulent electromotive force on the mean magnetic field, it guarantees that the basic rules of averaging operations hold for averages over space and time coordinates too.

In addition, the second order correlation approximation is often applied, in which the turbulent electromotive force, and other quantities of that kind, are calculated by taking into account only the statistical moments up to the second order, and the statistical moments of the third and higher orders are neglected. It has, however, to be noted that the second order correlation approximation is not a primary constituent of mean-field magnetohydrodynamics, it is rather a first step in a convergent approximation procedure. Even this first step provides for a fairly comprehensive insight into the physical processes under consideration. Higher order approximations require far more mathematical effort.

1.3. Technical remarks

The international system of units shall be used throughout. In addition to the unit T (tesla) for the magnetic flux density also the unit G (gauss) is used, where $1\,\mathrm{T} \doteq 10^4\,\mathrm{G}$.

As far as the representation of mathematical relations is concerned some stipulations shall apply.

Vector equations will not only be written in the usual symbolic notation but also in component representations. Unless defined otherwise these representations are related to a Cartesian coordinate system and the summation convention is used.

Integrals without indication of limits are to extend over all space and time.

As usual the complex conjugate of a quantity shall be denoted by an asterisk.

Averages shall be denoted by an overbar. In some of the later chapters the overbar will again be omitted since only averaged quantities are considered.

CHAPTER 2

BASIC IDEAS OF MEAN-FIELD ELECTRODYNAMICS

2.1. Basic equations

Our considerations are based on non-relativistic magnetohydrodynamics. Let $\boldsymbol{B}$ be the magnetic flux density, $\boldsymbol{H}$ the magnetic field, $\boldsymbol{E}$ the electric field, $\boldsymbol{j}$ the electric current density, μ the permeability, σ the electrical conductivity, and $\boldsymbol{u}$ the fluid velocity; μ and σ shall be supposed to be constant.

We shall adopt the magnetohydrodynamic approximation, i.e. suppose that these fields are related by the equations

$$\operatorname{curl} \boldsymbol{E} = -\frac{\partial \boldsymbol{B}}{\partial t}, \quad \operatorname{curl} \boldsymbol{H} = \boldsymbol{j}, \quad \operatorname{div} \boldsymbol{B} = 0, \tag{2.1}$$

$$\boldsymbol{B} = \mu \boldsymbol{H}, \quad \boldsymbol{j} = \sigma(\boldsymbol{E} + \boldsymbol{u} \times \boldsymbol{B}). \tag{2.2}$$

These equations determine $\boldsymbol{B}$, $\boldsymbol{H}$, $\boldsymbol{E}$ and $\boldsymbol{j}$ from an assigned $\boldsymbol{u}$. They show that

$$\frac{\partial \boldsymbol{B}}{\partial t} = \operatorname{curl} (\boldsymbol{u} \times \boldsymbol{B}) + \frac{1}{\mu\sigma} \Delta \boldsymbol{B}, \quad \operatorname{div} \boldsymbol{B} = 0. \tag{2.3}$$

Once $\boldsymbol{B}$ has been determined from this equation, $\boldsymbol{H}$, $\boldsymbol{E}$ and $\boldsymbol{j}$ may be obtained from (2.1) and (2.2).

Here, and in most of the following chapters, we shall consider $\boldsymbol{u}$ to be given. In this way we shall avoid the problems raised by the reaction of the magnetic field on the motion, but occasionally discuss this effect qualitatively. Finally, in chapter 10, we shall give a survey of the results obtained in mean-field magnetohydrodynamics up to now.

2.2. Averaging operations

In a turbulent medium, all the fields so far introduced vary irregularly in space and time. Let F be such a fluctuating field, considered as a random function. The corresponding mean field, $\overline{F}$, is then defined to be the expectation value of F in an ensemble of identical systems, and F' shall be used to denote the difference, $F - \overline{F}$, between F and $\overline{F}$. The following relations, the Reynolds relations, hold:

$$F = \overline{F} + F', \quad \overline{\overline{F}} = \overline{F}, \quad \overline{F'} = 0, \tag{2.4}$$
$$\overline{F + G} = \overline{F} + \overline{G}, \quad \overline{\overline{F}G} = \overline{F}\,\overline{G}, \quad \overline{\overline{F}G'} = 0,$$

where G is another fluctuating field. The averaging operator commutes with the differentiation and integration operators in both space and time.

Instead of averaging over an ensemble, we may also define mean values by integration over space or time. Some of the relations (2.4) are then only approximate, although they will be the more accurate the less the means vary over the integration range concerned. We shall not need to refer to the nature of the averaging operation in our work, but only to the properties (2.4) and to the commutation rules mentioned.

Observations of the solar surface, for example, give evidence for both velocity field and magnetic field, showing fluctuations of different kind with different scales. There are: (i) the granules with diameters of about 1,000 km and a life time of some minutes, (ii) the supergranules with diameters of about 30,000 km and life times of about one day, (iii) the giant cells with diameters of the order of the solar radius and life times of some months, (iv) the sunspots with diameters ranging from some hundreds to some ten thousands of kilometers and life times from some hours to some months. However, the mean magnetic field of the Sun is responsible for the solar cycle, consequently it has a time scale of 22 years. Naturally, the length scale is of the order of the solar radius only. From these data we can infer that it is possible to find a proper time scale for the averaging operation with respect to the time, e.g. one year, but the same does not hold for averaging with respect to the space coordinate.

It is worth remarking that the Sun offers the possibility of constructing an ensemble by taking the Sun during one cycle as one member of the ensemble. Then one can take the average over a number of cycles.

2.3. The equations for the mean fields

The problem of mean-field electrodynamics is that of determining $\overline{\boldsymbol{B}}$, $\overline{\boldsymbol{H}}$, $\overline{\boldsymbol{E}}$ and $\overline{\boldsymbol{j}}$ when $\overline{\boldsymbol{u}}$ and some of the properties of $\boldsymbol{u}'$ are known.

On averaging (2.1) and (2.2) we obtain

$$\operatorname{curl} \overline{\boldsymbol{E}} = -\frac{\partial \overline{\boldsymbol{B}}}{\partial t}, \quad \operatorname{curl} \overline{\boldsymbol{H}} = \overline{\boldsymbol{j}}, \quad \operatorname{div} \overline{\boldsymbol{B}} = 0, \tag{2.5}$$

$$\overline{\boldsymbol{B}} = \mu \overline{\boldsymbol{H}}, \quad \overline{\boldsymbol{j}} = \sigma(\overline{\boldsymbol{E}} + \overline{\boldsymbol{u}} \times \overline{\boldsymbol{B}} + \overline{\boldsymbol{u}' \times \boldsymbol{B}'}). \tag{2.6}$$

These equations would be identical with (2.1) and (2.2), were it not for the single new term $\overline{\boldsymbol{u}'\times\boldsymbol{B}'}$ arising from a non-linearity, which gives rise to an additional electromotive force in Ohm's law for the mean fields. We shall speak of the "turbulent electromotive force" and, following P. H. ROBERTS [3], introduce the notation

$$\mathfrak{E} = \overline{\boldsymbol{u}'\times\boldsymbol{B}'}. \tag{2.7}$$

In order to determine $\overline{\boldsymbol{B}}$, $\overline{\boldsymbol{H}}$, $\overline{\boldsymbol{E}}$ and $\overline{\boldsymbol{j}}$, we must know not only $\overline{\boldsymbol{u}}$ but also this electromotive force $\mathfrak{E}$.

Let us now consider the electromotive force $\mathfrak{E}$ in more detail. Substituting $\boldsymbol{B} = \overline{\boldsymbol{B}} + \boldsymbol{B}'$ and $\boldsymbol{u} = \overline{\boldsymbol{u}} + \boldsymbol{u}'$ in (2.3), we obtain

$$\begin{aligned}&\frac{\partial \boldsymbol{B}'}{\partial t} - \operatorname{curl}(\overline{\boldsymbol{u}}\times\boldsymbol{B}') - \operatorname{curl}(\boldsymbol{u}'\times\boldsymbol{B}') - \frac{1}{\mu\sigma}\Delta\boldsymbol{B}' \\ &= -\frac{\partial\overline{\boldsymbol{B}}}{\partial t} + \operatorname{curl}(\overline{\boldsymbol{u}}\times\overline{\boldsymbol{B}}) + \operatorname{curl}(\boldsymbol{u}'\times\overline{\boldsymbol{B}}) + \frac{1}{\mu\sigma}\Delta\overline{\boldsymbol{B}}, \quad \operatorname{div}(\overline{\boldsymbol{B}} + \boldsymbol{B}') = 0.\end{aligned} \tag{2.8}$$

These equations determine $\boldsymbol{B}'$, if $\overline{\boldsymbol{B}}$, $\overline{\boldsymbol{u}}$ and $\boldsymbol{u}'$ are known. We may therefore consider $\mathfrak{E}$ as a functional of $\overline{\boldsymbol{B}}$, $\overline{\boldsymbol{u}}$ and (since $\mathfrak{E}$ is a mean field) the average statistical properties of $\boldsymbol{u}'$. The solution of (2.8) depends, of course, on initial and boundary conditions on $\boldsymbol{B}'$, but we shall postpone a discussion of these until later.

Let us return to equations (2.5) and (2.6). Insofar that the turbulent electromotive force $\mathfrak{E}$ as a functional of $\overline{\boldsymbol{B}}$, $\overline{\boldsymbol{u}}$ and $\boldsymbol{u}'$ is known, it becomes possible to determine $\overline{\boldsymbol{B}}$, $\overline{\boldsymbol{H}}$, $\overline{\boldsymbol{E}}$ and $\overline{\boldsymbol{j}}$ from a knowledge of $\overline{\boldsymbol{u}}$ and $\boldsymbol{u}'$. Consequently, the determination of that functional is the crucial point in the development of mean-field electrodynamics.

2.4. General properties of the turbulent electromotive force

It is a characteristic of turbulence that quantities like $\boldsymbol{u}'$ and $\boldsymbol{B}'$ at a certain space-time point have a correlation with some other quantity at another space-time point only if the separation with respect to space as well as to time is not too large. Accordingly, for a determination of $\mathfrak{E}$ at a certain space-time point the quantities $\overline{\boldsymbol{B}}$, $\overline{\boldsymbol{u}}$ and $\boldsymbol{u}'$ only need to be known in a certain neighbourhood of the point considered. As a consequence initial and boundary conditions on $\boldsymbol{B}'$ will not influence $\mathfrak{E}$ if we assume the initial time point and the boundaries to lie outside this neighbourhood. The following investigations are based on this assumption.

As already mentioned, $\boldsymbol{B}'$ may be determined from equations (2.8), and an inspection of these shows that $\boldsymbol{B}'$ is a linear functional of the mean magnetic field $\overline{\boldsymbol{B}}$. Obviously the same statement holds for the turbulent electromotive force $\mathfrak{E}$ defined by (2.7). We cannot completely exclude the possibility that there may be non-trivial solutions $\boldsymbol{B}'$ of equations (2.8) when $\overline{\boldsymbol{B}} = 0$. Such a possibility is indicated by results deduced by Kazantsev [1], Gailitis [4] and Kraichnan [4]. In this case we have to expect that $\mathfrak{E}$ may be an inhomogeneous linear functional of $\overline{\boldsymbol{B}}$ (Rädler [15]). Initial and boundary conditions may also provide for an inhomogeneity but, due to our assumption in the previous paragraph, they are of no influence.

However, in most of the following we adopt the viewpoint that $\boldsymbol{B}'$, and with that the turbulent electromotive force $\mathfrak{E}$, owes its existence to the interaction of the fluctuating velocity field $\boldsymbol{u}'$ with the mean magnetic field $\overline{\boldsymbol{B}}$ and, consequently, that $\mathfrak{E}$ can be assumed to be a linear homogeneous functional of $\overline{\boldsymbol{B}}$.

CHAPTER 3

ELEMENTARY TREATMENT OF A SIMPLE EXAMPLE

3.1. Assumptions

By way of introduction, we now investigate a rather simple case, but one which allows the clarification of fundamental questions and the deduction of certain far-reaching results.

As already mentioned, for the determination of $\mathfrak{E}$ at a special space-time point it is necessary to know the mean field $\overline{\boldsymbol{B}}$ in a proper neighbourhood only. In this region we suppose $\overline{\boldsymbol{B}}$ is so weakly dependent on time and position that a sufficient representation is provided by the components of $\overline{\boldsymbol{B}}$ itself and its first spatial derivatives.

We assume, furthermore, the medium to have no mean motion, i.e. $\overline{\boldsymbol{u}} = 0$, and the turbulence, $\boldsymbol{u}'$, to be homogeneous, isotropic and steady in the statistical sense. Sometimes we shall also consider the turbulence to be mirror-symmetric.

3.2. Homogeneity, isotropy and mirrorsymmetry of turbulent fields

A homogeneous turbulent field is defined by the property that every average derived from it is independent of position, or—in other words—every such quantity is invariant if the field undergoes a translation. For a steady turbulent field the same will hold with respect to the time.

We speak of an isotropic turbulent field if no direction exists which is preferred over any other. We define such a field by the property that every mean quantity derived from it does not vary if the field undergoes an arbitrary rotation about an arbitrary axis.

Finally, we shall speak of a mirrorsymmetric turbulent field if the mean quantities derived from it are invariant if the field is reflected in an arbitrary plane.

It is less restrictive to demand the latter properties in special circumstances only, e.g. a turbulent field can be isotropic at one point only, or it can show mirrorsymmetry with respect to a special plane or a set of planes only. An illustration of the latter is the turbulent motion in the solar convection zone:

The mean properties of this field remain unchanged only it is reflected in the Sun's equatorial plane or any meridional plane.

In a turbulent motion it may happen that left-handed helical motions are more probable than right-handed ones, or vice-versa. We shall speak of a turbulence with a preferred "Schraubensinn" (Steenbeck, Krause and Rädler [2]) or—to use the English equivalent introduced by Moffatt [2]—we say that the turbulence has helicity. A reflection transforms a left-handed screw into a right-handed one, and vice versa. Consequently, if a turbulent field is mirrorsymmetric to at least one plane, it cannot have helicity, i.e. motions associated with a left-handed screw are as probable as motions associated with a right-handed screw.

It is worth noting some relations between homogeneity, isotropy and mirror symmetry. A homogeneous turbulent field need not be isotropic, and an isotropic field need not be mirrorsymmetric. However, if a homogeneous field is isotropic at least at one point, then it is isotropic in all points. Furthermore, if a field which is isotropic at one point is mirrorsymmetric with respect to at least one plane through this point, then it has this property with respect to every plane through this point. Conversely, a turbulent field is homogeneous, if it is isotropic at every point, and it is isotropic at one point if it is mirrorsymmetric with respect to every plane through this point. The latter statements are due to the facts that any translation can be represented by two rotations about two parallel axes, and any rotation can be represented by two reflections in planes containing the axis of rotation.

Insofar as homogeneous isotropic turbulence exists in nature it is difficult to find convincing reasons for such turbulence to be non-mirrorsymmetric. For this reason, in the literature of hydrodynamic turbulence the word "isotropy" is often used to describe the isotropic mirrorsymmetric case. However, by assuming homogeneity and isotropy without demanding mirrorsymmetry, an aspect important for dynamo theory is most clearly identified.

3.3. Symmetry laws

Mirror symmetry is a fundamental property of the basic equations of classical physics. The background of this is the idea that from any real system another real system can be derived by reflecting the former in an arbitrary plane or at an arbitrary point. However, in the definition of some quantities, right-handedness is involved; such quantities are the cross-product, or those defined by the curl-operation and the volume (triple scalar product). Since right-handedness is not invariant with respect to reflections, these quantities show different transformation properties if compared with those which do not need the right-handedness for their definition. We have the relations for a reflection at a certain point

$$\boldsymbol{a}^{\text{ref}} = -\boldsymbol{a}, \quad \boldsymbol{a}^{\text{ref}} \times \boldsymbol{b}^{\text{ref}} = \boldsymbol{a} \times \boldsymbol{b}, \quad \text{curl } \boldsymbol{a}^{\text{ref}} = \text{curl } \boldsymbol{a}. \tag{3.1}$$

$$v^{\text{ref}} = (\boldsymbol{a}^{\text{ref}} \times \boldsymbol{b}^{\text{ref}})\, \boldsymbol{c}^{\text{ref}} = -(\boldsymbol{a} \times \boldsymbol{b}) \cdot \boldsymbol{c} = -v;$$

$\boldsymbol{a}$, $\boldsymbol{b}$, $\boldsymbol{c}$ are arbitrary vectors and v denotes the volume of the parallelepiped defined by the vectors $\boldsymbol{a}$, $\boldsymbol{b}$, $\boldsymbol{c}$. The superscript"ref" denotes the reflected quantity.

Our basic equations (2.1), (2.2) relate quantities which have different transformation properties if the system under consideration is reflected. Let $\boldsymbol{E}, \boldsymbol{j}, \boldsymbol{H}, \boldsymbol{B}$ be a solution of (2.1), (2.2) for a given $\boldsymbol{u}$. If we carry out a reflection at a point, obviously $\boldsymbol{u}$ as a motion of particles has to change sign and with it $\boldsymbol{j}$ and $\boldsymbol{E}$, whereas $\boldsymbol{H}$ and $\boldsymbol{B}$ according to (3.1) and (2.1), remain unchanged. We have, if reflecting at the point $\boldsymbol{x} = 0$,

$$\boldsymbol{u}^{\text{ref}}(\boldsymbol{x}, t) = -\boldsymbol{u}(-\boldsymbol{x}, t), \quad \boldsymbol{E}^{\text{ref}}(\boldsymbol{x}, t) = -\boldsymbol{E}(-\boldsymbol{x}, t),$$
$$\boldsymbol{j}^{\text{ref}}(\boldsymbol{x}, t) = -\boldsymbol{j}(-\boldsymbol{x}, t), \tag{3.2}$$

but

$$\boldsymbol{H}^{\text{ref}}(\boldsymbol{x}, t) = \boldsymbol{H}(-\boldsymbol{x}, t), \quad \boldsymbol{B}^{\text{ref}}(\boldsymbol{x}, t) = \boldsymbol{B}(-\boldsymbol{x}, t). \tag{3.3}$$

Vectors which behave like the quantities (3.2) are usually called polar vectors, those like $\boldsymbol{H}$ and $\boldsymbol{B}$ axial vectors. Other synonyms are "pseudo" and "skew" for quantities which are dependent on using right-handedness, e.g. a scalar like the volume v is called a pseudo-scalar.

For turbulence a pseudo-scalar of interest is defined by the average

$$h = \overline{\boldsymbol{u}' \cdot \text{curl } \boldsymbol{u}'}. \tag{3.4}$$

Obviously, $h \neq 0$ is an indicator that the turbulence has helicity. In the mirrorsymmetric case h has on the one hand to be unchanged since all statistical properties of $\boldsymbol{u}'$ are unchanged under a reflection, on the other hand h has to change the sign since it is skew. Hence, $h = 0$ for mirror-symmetric turbulence.

The symmetry laws often prove to be a useful tool for simplifying a general ansatz for a solution of the basic equations. If we know that $F + G = 0$ is an integral of the basic equations and G is skew but F not, then $F - G = 0$ is a solution of the basic equations too. Consequently, $F = 0$ and $G = 0$ must be valid.

It is possible that we are concerned with products of different quantities. As we can see from (3.1), (3.2), (3.3) the scalar product of a polar and an axial vector is a pseudoscalar, whereas the cross-product of these quantities is a polar vector; in particular, the turbulent electromotive force $\mathfrak{E}$ is, of course, a polar vector.

3.4. The structure of the turbulent electromotive force

As already mentioned, $\mathfrak{E}$ is a functional of $\overline{\boldsymbol{B}}$, $\overline{\boldsymbol{u}}$ and $\boldsymbol{u}'$. We consider this quantity at a certain space-time point. On the assumptions introduced in 3.1. it may depend on $\overline{\boldsymbol{B}}$ and its first spatial derivatives at this point and on $\boldsymbol{u}'$ at the neighbourhood of this point only. Naturally, only mean quantities derived from $\boldsymbol{u}'$ are relevant.

We notice that $\mathfrak{E}$ varies with position only as far as $\overline{\boldsymbol{B}}$ and its first spatial derivatives do. This is simply a consequence of the homogeneity assumed for $\boldsymbol{u}'$.

Now we have to take into account the fact that $\mathfrak{E}$ is a vector quantity. The only vectors available to construct it are $\overline{\boldsymbol{B}}$, curl $\overline{\boldsymbol{B}}$, $\overline{\boldsymbol{B}} \times \text{curl}\, \overline{\boldsymbol{B}}$, $(\overline{\boldsymbol{B}} \cdot \nabla)\, \overline{\boldsymbol{B}}, \ldots,$ where the dots stand for vector products of higher order in $\overline{\boldsymbol{B}}$. No contribution can be furnished by $\boldsymbol{u}'$, as is easily seen: Since $\boldsymbol{u}'$ is isotropic any mean quantity derived from it must be invariant under an arbitrary rotation. The only vector with this property is the zero-vector.

Noting finally that $\mathfrak{E}$ is a linear functional of $\overline{\boldsymbol{B}}$ we find as the only possible representation

$$\mathfrak{E} = \overline{\boldsymbol{u}' \times \boldsymbol{B}'} = \alpha \overline{\boldsymbol{B}} - \beta\, \text{curl}\, \overline{\boldsymbol{B}}. \tag{3.5}$$

α and β are constant mean quantities determined by the turbulent velocity field $\boldsymbol{u}'$.

Relation (3.5) is deduced from our basic equations (2.1), (2.2) and consequently the symmetry laws discussed in the foregoing paragraph will apply. In this way we find that β is scalar whereas α is pseudo-scalar.

We now assume, in addition, that $\boldsymbol{u}'$ is mirrorsymmetric, i.e. in the ensemble of fields one realisation $\boldsymbol{u}'$ and every other derived from it by a reflection have the same probability. Then, on the one hand, the quantities α and β do not change if a reflection is carried out, since the ensemble is not altered. On the other hand, however, α must change its sign since it is skew. Consequently $\alpha = 0$ for homogeneous isotropic mirrorsymmetric turbulence. A connection with the helicity h defined by (3.4) is thus indicated.

3.5. Ohm's law

Returning now to the equations for the mean fields (2.5) and (2.6) and substituting (3.5) we find the relation

$$\overline{\boldsymbol{j}} = \sigma_T(\overline{\boldsymbol{E}} + \alpha \overline{\boldsymbol{B}}) \tag{3.6}$$

as Ohm's law for the mean fields, where σ_T, the turbulent conductivity, is given by

$$\sigma_T = \frac{\sigma}{1 + \mu\sigma\beta}. \tag{3.7}$$

Using (3.6) instead of Ohm's law in (2.6) the equations (2.5) and (3.6) form a complete set of equations to determine $\overline{\boldsymbol{B}}, \overline{\boldsymbol{H}}, \overline{\boldsymbol{E}}$ and $\overline{\boldsymbol{j}}$ when α and β are known.

In the mirrorsymmetric case, $\alpha = 0$, our equations for the mean fields, i.e. (2.5) and (2.6) with Ohm's law from (3.6), are in formal conformity with the equations for the unaveraged fields, i.e. (2.1) and (2.2) with $\boldsymbol{u} = 0$. The replacement of the molecular conductivity, σ, by the turbulent conductivity, σ_T, is the only difference. The ratio σ_T/σ can be determined if β is known.

In the non-mirrorsymmetric case an electromotive force $\alpha\overline{\boldsymbol{B}}$ appears in Ohm's law for the mean fields, which is parallel ($\alpha > 0$) or antiparallel ($\alpha < 0$) to the mean magnetic field $\overline{\boldsymbol{B}}$. This new effect due to the turbulent motion, called α-effect, is of great importance in dynamo theory as we shall see later on.

3.6. Preliminary steps for a determination of α and β on special assumptions

We start from equations (2.8) assuming $\overline{\boldsymbol{u}} = 0$. If we subtract the equations obtained from (2.3) by taking the average we find

$$\frac{\partial \boldsymbol{B}'}{\partial t} - \frac{1}{\mu\sigma}\Delta\boldsymbol{B}' - \text{curl}\,(\boldsymbol{u}'\times\boldsymbol{B}' - \overline{\boldsymbol{u}'\times\boldsymbol{B}'}) = \text{curl}\,(\boldsymbol{u}'\times\overline{\boldsymbol{B}}),$$

$$\text{div}\,\boldsymbol{B}' = 0. \tag{3.8}$$

It is our intention to determine $\boldsymbol{B}'$ from these equations. However, in order to do so, further assumptions are needed to exclude the non-linear terms. In a certain sense, which is specified later, we demand the turbulent velocity field to be small, and omit all terms of higher order in $\boldsymbol{u}'$ and $\boldsymbol{B}'$. Thus, we replace (3.8) by

$$\frac{\partial \boldsymbol{B}'}{\partial t} - \frac{1}{\mu\sigma}\Delta\boldsymbol{B}' = \text{curl}\,(\boldsymbol{u}'\times\overline{\boldsymbol{B}}), \quad \text{div}\,\boldsymbol{B}' = 0. \tag{3.9}$$

Furthermore, we restrict our investigations to two limiting cases which allow additional mathematical simplification, although they are of high physical importance. Dissipative effects are neglected in the first case, i.e. we replace (3.9) by

$$\frac{\partial \boldsymbol{B}'}{\partial t} = \text{curl}\,(\boldsymbol{u}'\times\overline{\boldsymbol{B}}), \quad \text{div}\,\boldsymbol{B}' = 0. \tag{3.10}$$

In the second case dissipative effects are assumed to be so strong that $\boldsymbol{B}'$ is stationary at any time. Hence we can omit the derivative with respect to time in (3.9) and arrive at the equations

$$\Delta \boldsymbol{B}' = -\mu\sigma \operatorname{curl} (\boldsymbol{u}' \times \overline{\boldsymbol{B}}), \quad \operatorname{div} \boldsymbol{B}' = 0. \tag{3.11}$$

Before the conditions are formulated under which the simplifications just introduced are warranted, it is worth remarking that they are not a fundamental ingredient of mean-field magnetohydrodynamics. The remarkable relation (3.5), for example, is not based on them. However, these simplifications enable us to calculate certain models in a rather simple manner.

We now introduce two scales characterizing the variation of $\boldsymbol{u}'$ with time and position, i.e. the correlation time, τ_{cor}, and the correlation length, λ_{cor}. Since $\boldsymbol{B}'$ is assumed to be caused by the interaction of $\boldsymbol{u}'$ with $\overline{\boldsymbol{B}}$, we conclude that τ_{cor} and λ_{cor} are the scales of $\boldsymbol{B}'$ too, since $\overline{\boldsymbol{B}}$ is assumed to depend weakly on time and position.

Our first simplification—the discard of the terms of second order in the fluctuations—is justified if at least one of the terms, $\dfrac{\partial \boldsymbol{B}'}{\partial t}$, $\dfrac{1}{\mu\sigma} \Delta \boldsymbol{B}'$, is large compared with the term $\operatorname{curl} (\boldsymbol{u}' \times \boldsymbol{B}' - \overline{\boldsymbol{u}' \times \boldsymbol{B}'})$. This is the case if

$$\min (\text{Rm}, \text{S}) \ll 1, \tag{3.12}$$

where Rm is the magnetic Reynolds number

$$\text{Rm} = \mu\sigma u' \lambda_{\text{cor}}, \tag{3.13}$$

and S the Strouhal number

$$\text{S} = u' \frac{\tau_{\text{cor}}}{\lambda_{\text{cor}}}. \tag{3.14}$$

When defining Rm and S we have already used the notation u' for the r.m.s. velocity fluctuation, i.e.

$$u' = \sqrt{\overline{\boldsymbol{u}'^2}}. \tag{3.15}$$

The theory which is based on equation (3.9) and is justified if the inequality (3.12) holds, shall be referred to here as the "second order correlation approximation", other descriptions are "first order smoothing theory" or "the discard of third order cumulants". The first and the last terminologies become clearer if one realizes that $\overline{\boldsymbol{u}' \times \boldsymbol{B}'}$ (rather than $\boldsymbol{B}'$) is the quantity of interest.

Equation (3.9) was further simplified by directing our interest to two limiting cases, by assuming that one of the terms of the left-hand side will dominate. Obviously, the first case is characterized by the inequality

$$\tau_{\text{cor}} \ll \mu\sigma\lambda_{\text{cor}}^2, \tag{3.16}$$

—we shall speak of the high-conductivity limit—and the second one by

$$\tau_{\mathrm{cor}} \gg \mu\sigma\lambda_{\mathrm{cor}}^2, \tag{3.17}$$

the low-conductivity limit.

From (3.13) and (3.14) we find the relation

$$\mathrm{Rm} = \frac{\mu\sigma\lambda_{\mathrm{cor}}^2}{\tau_{\mathrm{cor}}}\,\mathrm{S}. \tag{3.18}$$

Taking into account (3.12) it becomes obvious that the applicability of the second order correlation approximation implies $\mathrm{S} \ll 1$ in the high-conductivity limit, but $\mathrm{Rm} \ll 1$ in the low-conductivity limit. In the former case there is no restriction on Rm, especially, Rm can be very large as is often the case for cosmical objects. Since one generally expects $\mathrm{S} \approx 1$ the application of results deduced on the basis of the second order correlation approximation in the high-conductivity limit is an extrapolation from $\mathrm{S} \ll 1$ to $\mathrm{S} \approx 1$ only. That may, perhaps, explain the sometimes convincing quantitative agreement with the observations as we shall see later.

3.7. The high-conductivity limit

The governing equation for this case, (3.10), can be solved by the expression

$$\boldsymbol{B}'(\boldsymbol{x}, t) = \boldsymbol{B}'(\boldsymbol{x}, t_0) + \int_{t_0}^{t} \operatorname{curl}\,(\boldsymbol{u}'(\boldsymbol{x}, t') \times \overline{\boldsymbol{B}}(\boldsymbol{x}, t'))\,\mathrm{d}t', \quad \operatorname{div} \boldsymbol{B}'(\boldsymbol{x}, t_0) = 0. \tag{3.19}$$

t_0 is arbitrary. According to earlier assumptions $t - t_0$, however, is to be chosen so large that no correlation between $\boldsymbol{u}'(\boldsymbol{x}, t)$ and $\boldsymbol{B}'(\boldsymbol{x}, t_0)$ exists. It is, moreover, convenient to assume the initial time point so distant that any initial fluctuating magnetic field has disappeared. Thus we assume

$$t - t_0 \gg \mu\sigma\lambda_{\mathrm{cor}}^2 \gg \tau_{\mathrm{cor}}, \tag{3.20}$$

and the appropriate solution of (3.10) takes the form

$$\boldsymbol{B}'(\boldsymbol{x}, t) = \int_{t_0}^{t} \operatorname{curl}\,(\boldsymbol{u}'(\boldsymbol{x}, t') \times \overline{\boldsymbol{B}}(\boldsymbol{x}, t'))\,\mathrm{d}t'. \tag{3.21}$$

We shall now derive the turbulent electromotive force $\mathfrak{E}$ by multiplying (3.21) with $\boldsymbol{u}'(\boldsymbol{x}, t)$ and taking the average. The resulting expression does not depend on t_0 as far as (3.20) holds. Hence we can put $t_0 = -\infty$ and obtain

$$\mathfrak{E}(\boldsymbol{x}, t) = \int_{-\infty}^{t} \overline{\boldsymbol{u}'(\boldsymbol{x}, t) \times \operatorname{curl}\,(\boldsymbol{u}'(\boldsymbol{x}, t') \times \overline{\boldsymbol{B}}(\boldsymbol{x}, t'))}\,\mathrm{d}t'. \tag{3.22}$$

The integrand is significantly different from zero only if $t - t' < \tau_{\text{cor}}$. According to the assumptions introduced in 3.1. $\overline{\boldsymbol{B}}$ does not vary in this time interval and, consequently, $\overline{\boldsymbol{B}}(\boldsymbol{x}, t)$ can be substituted for $\overline{\boldsymbol{B}}(\boldsymbol{x}, t')$. If we finally replace t' by $t - \tau$ we derive

$$\mathfrak{E}(\boldsymbol{x}, t) = \int_0^\infty \overline{\boldsymbol{u}'(\boldsymbol{x}, t) \times \operatorname{curl}\left(\boldsymbol{u}'(\boldsymbol{x}, t - \tau) \times \overline{\boldsymbol{B}}(\boldsymbol{x}, t)\right)}\, \mathrm{d}\tau. \tag{3.23}$$

We will now write (3.23) in a representation by vector components with respect to a right-handed cartesian coordinate system x_1, x_2, x_3. Considering homogeneous isotropic turbulence we already know that (3.23) is of the form (3.5). Thus for $\mathfrak{E}_1$, we have only to write down the terms with $\overline{B}_1$, $\frac{\partial \overline{B}_3}{\partial x_2}$ and $\frac{\partial \overline{B}_2}{\partial x_3}$; the others $\overline{B}_2$, $\overline{B}_3$, $\frac{\partial \overline{B}_1}{\partial x_1}$, ..., can be dropped from the beginning. In this way we obtain

$$\begin{aligned}
\mathfrak{E}_1 &= -(w_{312} - w_{213})\, \overline{B}_1 - w_{22} \frac{\partial \overline{B}_3}{\partial x_2} + w_{33} \frac{\partial \overline{B}_2}{\partial x_3}, \\
\mathfrak{E}_2 &= -(w_{123} - w_{321})\, \overline{B}_2 - w_{33} \frac{\partial \overline{B}_1}{\partial x_3} + w_{11} \frac{\partial \overline{B}_3}{\partial x_1}, \\
\mathfrak{E}_3 &= -(w_{231} - w_{132})\, \overline{B}_3 - w_{11} \frac{\partial \overline{B}_2}{\partial x_1} + w_{22} \frac{\partial \overline{B}_1}{\partial x_2},
\end{aligned} \tag{3.24}$$

where the notations

$$w_{ijk} = \int_0^\infty \overline{u_i'(\boldsymbol{x}, t) \frac{\partial u_k'(\boldsymbol{x}, t - \tau)}{\partial x_j}}\, \mathrm{d}\tau, \tag{3.25}$$

$$w_{ij} = \int_0^\infty \overline{u_i'(\boldsymbol{x}, t)\, u_j'(\boldsymbol{x}, t - \tau)}\, \mathrm{d}\tau, \tag{3.26}$$

have been used. Comparing (3.24) with (3.5) we immediately find that

$$\begin{aligned}
\alpha &= -(w_{312} - w_{213}) = -(w_{123} - w_{321}) = -(w_{231} - w_{132}) \\
&= -\frac{1}{3}(w_{123} + w_{231} + w_{312} - w_{132} - w_{321} - w_{213}),
\end{aligned} \tag{3.27}$$

and

$$\beta = w_{11} = w_{22} = w_{33} = \frac{1}{3}(w_{11} + w_{22} + w_{33}). \tag{3.28}$$

Inserting (3.25) and (3.26) into (3.27) and (3.28) we find finally

$$\alpha = -\frac{1}{3} \int_0^\infty \overline{\boldsymbol{u}'(\boldsymbol{x}, t) \cdot \operatorname{curl} \boldsymbol{u}'(\boldsymbol{x}, t - \tau)}\, \mathrm{d}\tau, \tag{3.29}$$

and

$$\beta = \frac{1}{3} \int_0^\infty \overline{\boldsymbol{u}'(\boldsymbol{x}, t) \cdot \boldsymbol{u}'(\boldsymbol{x}, t - \tau)} \, \mathrm{d}\tau. \tag{3.30}$$

Deducing these formulae we used the knowledge of (3.5). However, without this knowledge, (3.24) has only at first a more complicated form because for reasons of isotropy, relations between the coefficients w_{ijk}, w_{ij} are easily established. These coefficients have to be unchanged if undergoing an arbitrary rotation. If, for example, a 90°-rotation about the x_3-axis is carried out, x_1 is transformed into x_2, u_1' into u_2'; but x_2 is transformed into $-x_1$ and u_2' into $-u_1'$; x_3 and u_3' remain unchanged. Inspecting (3.25) and (3.26) we find that $w_{123} = -w_{213}$, and $w_{222} = -w_{111}$ but also $w_{111} = w_{222}$ which leads to $w_{111} = w_{222} = 0$. Similarly we conclude $w_{11} = w_{22}$; or $w_{13} = w_{23}$ but $w_{23} = -w_{13}$, thus $w_{12} = w_{13} = 0$. In this way a direct derivation of (3.24), (3.29) and (3.30) is provided.

An interesting property of α, which is a pseudo-scalar, becomes obvious from (3.29). The integrand is related to the quantity h defined by (3.4). In the case of a turbulence where motions corresponding to a right-handed screw are more probable than those corresponding to a left-handed screw, α takes negative values, in the opposite case positive values.

For an estimate of the order of magnitude we evaluate the integrals in (3.29) and (3.30) such that

$$\alpha = -\frac{1}{3} \overline{\boldsymbol{u}' \cdot \operatorname{curl} \boldsymbol{u}'} \, \tau_{\mathrm{cor}} = -\frac{1}{3} h \, \tau_{\mathrm{cor}}, \tag{3.31}$$

and (Rädler (1966) [2], Kazantsev (1967) [1])

$$\beta = \frac{1}{3} u'^2 \tau_{\mathrm{cor}}. \tag{3.32}$$

Inserting (3.32) into (3.7) we find for the turbulent conductivity

$$\sigma_T = \frac{\sigma}{1 + \frac{1}{3} \mu \sigma u'^2 \tau_{\mathrm{cor}}}, \tag{3.33}$$

which shows that this quantity is smaller than the molecular conductivity.

3.8. Applications to the solar convection zone

The solar convection zone is an interesting example. Considering the granules we can take as characteristic scales, according to the observations,

$$\lambda_{\mathrm{cor}} = 10^6 \mathrm{~m}, \tau_{\mathrm{cor}} = 3 \cdot 10^2 \mathrm{~s}; u' = 3 \cdot 10^2 \frac{\mathrm{m}}{\mathrm{s}}; \tag{3.34}$$

furthermore, the conductivity is generally assumed to be $\sigma = 3 \cdot 10^3\, \Omega^{-1}\,\mathrm{m}^{-1}$ and for the permeability we take the vacuum value, i.e. $\mu = \mu_0 = 4\pi \cdot 10^{-7}$ $\mathrm{Vs\,A^{-1}\,m^{-1}}$. The decay time of a magnetic field having the length scale λ_{cor} is thus of the order $3 \cdot 10^9\,\mathrm{s} = 100$ years, hence the condition (3.16) for the high-conductivity limit is well satisfied. From the data given in (3.34) and below, we find furthermore

$$\mathrm{Rm} = 10^6, \quad \mathrm{S} = 10^{-1}, \tag{3.35}$$

so that (3.12) is at least reasonably well satisfied.

If we apply (3.33) despite the fact that S is smaller than 1 but not very small compared with it, we find

$$\frac{1}{3}\,\mu\sigma u'^2 \tau_{\mathrm{cor}} \approx 10^4, \tag{3.36}$$

and thus

$$\sigma_T = 10^{-4}\,\sigma, \tag{3.37}$$

for the solar convection zone.

This result must be seen in relation to processes in the Sun connected with magnetic fields. The large scale magnetic field of the Sun is an alternating field with a period of about 22 years, twice the period of the solar activity cycle for which it is responsible. The characteristic length scale, $\bar{\lambda}$, of this field is the skin depth, which must be at least of the order of the diameters of the largest sunspots, i.e. some ten thousands of kilometers. Taking $\bar{\lambda} \approx 50 \cdot 10^3$ km we obtain for the time scale, $\bar{\tau}$, if using the turbulent conductivity, $\tau = \mu\sigma_T\bar{\lambda}^2 \approx 30$ years, which is just the correct order of magnitude. Using the molecular conductivity this time scale will be, obviously, too large by a factor 10^4. Thus we find a good quantitative agreement.

One is tempted to apply (3.37) to the decay of sunspots and will find again a good quantitative agreement. In sunspots the convective motion must, however, be expected to be strongly influenced by the magnetic field, otherwise their darkness can hardly be understood. This influence was neglected in the derivation of (3.37) so that we have to discuss the decay of sunspots later.

3.9. The low-conductivity limit

Now we are concerned with equation (3.11). We consider the whole space, but assume at first that $\boldsymbol{u}'$ is different from zero in a bounded region only, for this reason $\boldsymbol{B}'$ tends to zero if the argument tends to infinity. The solution of (3.11) is then given by

$$\boldsymbol{B}'(\boldsymbol{x}, t) = \frac{\mu\sigma}{4\pi} \int \frac{\operatorname{curl}' \left(\boldsymbol{u}'(\boldsymbol{x}', t) \times \overline{\boldsymbol{B}}(\boldsymbol{x}', t)\right)}{|\boldsymbol{x}' - \boldsymbol{x}|} \, \mathrm{d}\boldsymbol{x}'. \tag{3.38}$$

We multiply this expression by $\boldsymbol{u}'(\boldsymbol{x}, t)$ and average. After inserting $\boldsymbol{\xi} = \boldsymbol{x}' - \boldsymbol{x}$ one finds for the turbulent electromotive force

$$\mathfrak{E} = \frac{\mu\sigma}{4\pi} \int \overline{\boldsymbol{u}'(\boldsymbol{x}, t) \times \operatorname{curl} \left(\boldsymbol{u}'(\boldsymbol{x} + \boldsymbol{\xi}, t) \times \overline{\boldsymbol{B}}(\boldsymbol{x} + \boldsymbol{\xi}, t)\right)} \, \frac{\mathrm{d}\boldsymbol{\xi}}{\xi}. \tag{3.39}$$

Now we can withdraw the assumption made above that $\boldsymbol{u}'$ has to be different from zero in a bounded region only, since $\overline{\boldsymbol{u}'(\boldsymbol{x}, t) \cdot \boldsymbol{u}'(\boldsymbol{x} + \boldsymbol{\xi}, t)} \to 0$ if $\xi \to \infty$.

Noting that $\overline{\boldsymbol{B}}$ varies weakly over distances of the order of λ_{cor} we insert

$$\overline{\boldsymbol{B}}(\boldsymbol{x} + \boldsymbol{\xi}, t) = \overline{\boldsymbol{B}}(\boldsymbol{x}, t) + (\boldsymbol{\xi} \cdot \operatorname{grad}_x) \, \overline{\boldsymbol{B}}(\boldsymbol{x}, t) \tag{3.40}$$

into (3.39) and, by carrying out the vector operations as in the previous section, we find

$$\begin{aligned}
\mathfrak{E}_1 &= -(w_{312} - w_{213}) \, \overline{B}_1 \\
&\quad - (w_{22} + w_{3223} + w_{2211} + w_{2222}) \frac{\partial \overline{B}_3}{\partial x_2} + (w_{33} + w_{2332} + w_{3311} + w_{3333}) \frac{\partial \overline{B}_2}{\partial x_3}, \\
\mathfrak{E}_2 &= -(w_{123} - w_{321}) \, \overline{B}_2 \\
&\quad - (w_{33} + w_{1331} + w_{3322} + w_{3333}) \frac{\partial \overline{B}_1}{\partial x_3} + (w_{11} + w_{3113} + w_{1122} + w_{1111}) \frac{\partial \overline{B}_1}{\partial x_1}, \\
\mathfrak{E}_3 &= -(w_{231} - w_{132}) \, \overline{B}_3 \\
&\quad - (w_{11} + w_{2112} + w_{1133} + w_{1111}) \frac{\partial \overline{B}_2}{\partial x_1} + (w_{22} + w_{1221} + w_{2233} + w_{2222}) \frac{\partial \overline{B}_1}{\partial x_2},
\end{aligned} \tag{3.41}$$

where the quantities w_{ij}, w_{ijk}, w_{ijkl} are defined by

$$w_{ij} = \frac{\mu\sigma}{4\pi} \int \overline{u_i'(\boldsymbol{x}, t) \, u_j'(\boldsymbol{x} + \boldsymbol{\xi}, t)} \, \frac{\mathrm{d}\boldsymbol{\xi}}{\xi}, \tag{3.42}$$

$$w_{ijk} = \frac{\mu\sigma}{4\pi} \int \overline{u_i'(\boldsymbol{x}, t) \, \frac{\partial u_k'(\boldsymbol{x} + \boldsymbol{\xi}, t)}{\partial \xi_j}} \, \frac{\mathrm{d}\boldsymbol{\xi}}{\xi}, \tag{3.43}$$

$$w_{ijkl} = \frac{\mu\sigma}{4\pi} \int \overline{u_i'(\boldsymbol{x}, t) \, \xi_j \frac{\partial u_k'(\boldsymbol{x} + \boldsymbol{\xi}, t)}{\partial \xi_l}} \, \frac{\mathrm{d}\boldsymbol{\xi}}{\xi}. \tag{3.44}$$

A similarity between (3.41) and the analogous relation in the high-conductivity limit, (3.24), only exists for the terms proportional to $\overline{\boldsymbol{B}}$; for those with partial derivatives the more complicated additional quantities w_{ijkl} appear.

By comparing (3.41) with (3.5) we obtain

$$\begin{aligned}\alpha &= -(w_{312} - w_{213}) = -(w_{123} - w_{321}) = -(w_{231} - w_{132}) \\ &= -\frac{1}{3}(w_{123} - w_{132} + w_{231} - w_{213} + w_{312} - w_{321}),\end{aligned} \tag{3.45}$$

and, furthermore,

$$\begin{aligned}\beta &= (w_{22} + w_{3223} + w_{2211} + w_{2222}) = (w_{33} + w_{2332} + w_{3311} + w_{3333}) \\ &= (w_{33} + w_{1331} + w_{3322} + w_{3333}) = (w_{11} + w_{3113} + w_{1122} + w_{1111}) \\ &= (w_{11} + w_{2112} + w_{1133} + w_{1111}) = (w_{33} + w_{1221} + w_{2211} + w_{2222}) \\ &= \frac{1}{3}(w_{11} + w_{22} + w_{33} + w_{1111} + w_{1133} + w_{2211} + w_{2222} \\ &\quad + w_{1331} + w_{2112} + w_{3322} + w_{3223} + w_{3333}).\end{aligned} \tag{3.46}$$

Hence we find

$$\alpha = -\frac{\mu\sigma}{12\pi}\int \overline{\boldsymbol{u}'(\boldsymbol{x}, t) \cdot \operatorname{curl} \boldsymbol{u}'(\boldsymbol{x} + \boldsymbol{\xi}, t)}\,\frac{\mathrm{d}\boldsymbol{\xi}}{\xi}, \tag{3.47}$$

and

$$\beta = \frac{\mu\sigma}{12\pi}\int \overline{(\boldsymbol{\xi} \cdot \boldsymbol{u}'(\boldsymbol{x}, t))\,(\boldsymbol{\xi} \cdot \boldsymbol{u}'(\boldsymbol{x} + \boldsymbol{\xi}, t)}\,\frac{\mathrm{d}\boldsymbol{\xi}}{\xi^3}. \tag{3.48}$$

An alternative derivation of relations (3.47) and (3.48) for α and β can be given with the help of a representation of the turbulent velocity field by vector potentials. If we define the fields $\boldsymbol{a}_1$, $\boldsymbol{a}_2$, φ by

$$\boldsymbol{u}' = \operatorname{curl} \boldsymbol{a}_1 - \nabla\varphi, \quad \operatorname{div} \boldsymbol{a}_1 = 0, \tag{3.49}$$

and

$$\boldsymbol{a}_1 = \operatorname{curl} \boldsymbol{a}_2, \quad \varphi = \operatorname{div} \boldsymbol{a}_2, \tag{3.50}$$

we have

$$\boldsymbol{u}' = -\Delta \boldsymbol{a}_2. \tag{3.51}$$

Restricting our attention firstly to a derivation of the quantity α we regard $\overline{\boldsymbol{B}}$ as constant, thus having

$$\operatorname{curl}(\Delta \boldsymbol{a}_2 \times \overline{\boldsymbol{B}}) = \operatorname{curl} \Delta(\boldsymbol{a}_2 \times \overline{\boldsymbol{B}}) = \Delta \operatorname{curl}(\boldsymbol{a}_2 \times \overline{\boldsymbol{B}}). \tag{4.52}$$

For equations (3.11) we can now write

$$\Delta \boldsymbol{B}' = \mu\sigma \Delta \operatorname{curl}(\boldsymbol{a}_2 \times \overline{\boldsymbol{B}}), \quad \operatorname{div} \boldsymbol{B}' = 0 \tag{3.53}$$

and solve them by the relation

$$\boldsymbol{B}' = \mu\sigma \operatorname{curl} (\boldsymbol{a}_2 \times \overline{\boldsymbol{B}}) + \boldsymbol{c}, \tag{3.54}$$

where $\boldsymbol{c}$ is constant with zero mean, if the same is true for the potential $\boldsymbol{a}_2$. Hence, we can put $\boldsymbol{c} = 0$. Multiplying (3.54) by the turbulent velocity field $\boldsymbol{u}'$ we obtain

$$\mathfrak{E} = \mu\sigma \overline{\boldsymbol{u}' \times \operatorname{curl} (\boldsymbol{a}_2 \times \overline{\boldsymbol{B}})}, \tag{3.55}$$

and with the arguments leading to (3.29) we find

$$\alpha = -\frac{\mu\sigma}{3} \overline{\boldsymbol{u}' \cdot \operatorname{curl} \boldsymbol{a}_2}, \tag{3.56}$$

or, taking (3.49) and (3.50) into account,

$$\alpha = -\frac{\mu\sigma}{3} (\overline{\boldsymbol{a}_1 \cdot \operatorname{curl} \boldsymbol{a}_1} - \overline{\boldsymbol{a}_1 \cdot \nabla\varphi}). \tag{3.57}$$

The latter summand vanishes, since it is equal to div $\overline{(\boldsymbol{a}_1\varphi)}$ because of (3.49), and the quantity $\overline{\boldsymbol{a}_1\varphi}$ is constant since $\boldsymbol{u}'$ is assumed to be homogeneous. Thus we finally find

$$\alpha = -\frac{\mu\sigma}{3} \overline{\boldsymbol{a}_1 \cdot \operatorname{curl} \boldsymbol{a}_1}. \tag{3.58}$$

The equivalence of the formulae just derived with (3.47) is easily seen if $\boldsymbol{a}_2$ as the solution of the Poisson equation (3.51) is represented by the well-known integral expression and then inserted in (3.56).

A determination of β in the same way is possible if $\overline{\boldsymbol{B}}$ is assumed to depend on position. One will find then

$$\beta = \frac{\mu\sigma}{3} (\overline{\boldsymbol{a}_1^2} - \overline{\varphi^2}). \tag{3.59}$$

It is notable that

$$\beta = -\frac{\mu\sigma}{3} \overline{\varphi^2} < 0, \tag{3.60}$$

if

$$\boldsymbol{u}' = -\operatorname{grad} \varphi, \tag{3.61}$$

i.e. if $\boldsymbol{u}'$ is a potential random field (Krause and Roberts [13]). It can easily be deduced from (3.48). If we substitute (3.61) we have

$$\beta = \frac{\mu\sigma}{12\pi} \int \overline{\xi_i \frac{\partial\varphi(\boldsymbol{x}, t)}{\partial x_i} \xi_j \frac{\partial\varphi(\boldsymbol{x}+\boldsymbol{\xi}, t)}{\partial \xi_j}} \frac{\mathrm{d}\boldsymbol{\xi}}{\xi^3}$$

$$= \frac{\mu\sigma}{12\pi} \int \xi_i\xi_j \left[\frac{\partial}{\partial x_i}\left(\overline{\varphi(\boldsymbol{x}, t)\frac{\partial\varphi(\boldsymbol{x}+\boldsymbol{\xi}, t)}{\partial\xi_j}}\right) - \overline{\frac{\partial^2\varphi(\boldsymbol{x}, t)\,\varphi(\boldsymbol{x}+\boldsymbol{\xi}, t)}{\partial\xi_i\,\partial\xi_j}}\right] \frac{\mathrm{d}\boldsymbol{\xi}}{\xi^3}.$$

Here, and in the following, the summation convention is adopted. The first summand in the brackets vanishes since $\boldsymbol{u}'$, and thus φ too, is homogeneous. Introducing the correlation function,

$$\Phi(\xi, \tau) = \overline{\varphi(\boldsymbol{x}, t)\,\varphi(\boldsymbol{x}+\boldsymbol{\xi}, t+\tau)}, \tag{3.62}$$

which is a function of $\xi = \sqrt{\boldsymbol{\xi}^2}$ only, we obtain

$$\beta = -\frac{\mu\sigma}{12\pi} \int \frac{\xi_i\xi_j}{\xi^3} \frac{\partial^2\Phi(\xi, 0)}{\partial\xi_i\,\partial\xi_j} \mathrm{d}\boldsymbol{\xi} = -\frac{\mu\sigma}{12\pi} \int \frac{1}{\xi} \frac{\partial^2\Phi}{\partial\xi^2} \mathrm{d}\boldsymbol{\xi}$$

$$= -\frac{\mu\sigma}{3} \int_0^\infty \xi \frac{\partial^2\Phi}{\partial\xi^2} \mathrm{d}\xi = -\frac{\mu\sigma}{3} \Phi(0, 0) = -\frac{\mu\sigma}{3} \overline{\varphi'^2}. \tag{3.63}$$

From (3.7) we find with (3.60) in this case

$$\sigma_{\mathrm{T}} = \frac{\sigma}{1 - \frac{1}{3}\overline{(\mu\sigma\varphi)^2}}, \tag{3.64}$$

i.e. the conductivity with respect to the mean fields is larger than the molecular conductivity. A realization of such a turbulence is provided by a random superposition of sound waves.

It is worth noting that

$$\overline{(\mu\sigma\varphi)^2} \approx (\mu\sigma u'\lambda_{\mathrm{cor}})^2 = \mathrm{Rm}^2 \ll 1 \tag{3.65}$$

according to (3.12), (3.17) and (3.18). For this reason no singularity of σ_T is indicated by the result (3.64).

For reasons of the results just deduced we restrict our attention to incompressible turbulence in estimating the order of magnitude of β from (3.48). Since $\overline{(\boldsymbol{\xi u}')\,(\boldsymbol{\xi u}')} \approx \frac{1}{3}\xi^2 u'^2$ we find

$$\beta = \frac{1}{9}\mu\sigma u'^2\lambda_{\mathrm{cor}}^2, \tag{3.66}$$

and

$$\sigma_T = \frac{\sigma}{1 + \frac{1}{9}(\mu\sigma u'\lambda_{cor})^2}, \tag{3.67}$$

a result which was first published by Steenbeck [2] in 1963.

3.10. Illustration of the α-effect and the α-experiment

The turbulent electromotive force $\alpha\overline{\boldsymbol{B}}$ which is proportional to the mean magnetic field clearly represents an effect of quite a new quality. For this reason it is advisable to illuminate the physical background by illustrating examples. Moreover, there is an experimental verification which inspires reliable confidence in this effect.

For a first illustration we introduce a cartesian coordinate system (fig. 3.1) where the x-axis and the z-axis are lying in the plane of the drawing, and the y-direction perpendicular to it. Let $\overline{\boldsymbol{B}}$ be a mean magnetic field parallel to the

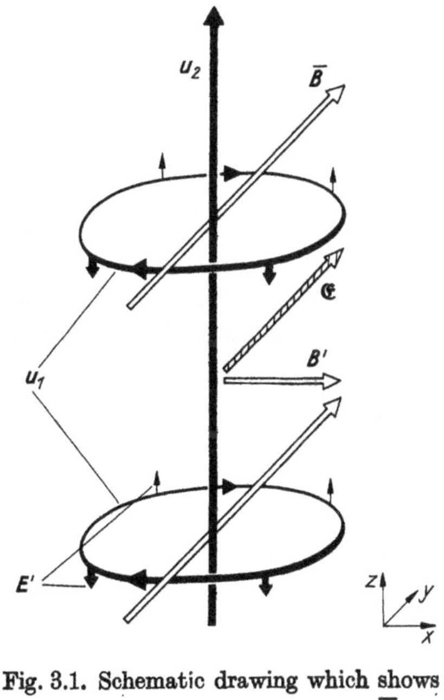

Fig. 3.1. Schematic drawing which shows that a helical motion, $\boldsymbol{u} = \boldsymbol{u}_1 + \boldsymbol{u}_2$, in a homogeneous magnetic field, $\overline{\boldsymbol{B}}$, provides for an electromotive force, $\mathfrak{E}$, parallel to the magnetic field (α-effect)

y-direction and $\boldsymbol{u}'$ a velocity corresponding to a left-handed helical motion. We represent $\boldsymbol{u}'$ by the sum $\boldsymbol{u}' = \boldsymbol{u}_1 + \boldsymbol{u}_2$, where $\boldsymbol{u}_1$ is a rotational motion about the z-axis and $\boldsymbol{u}_2$ is the motion parallel to the z-direction. The interaction of the rotational motion $\boldsymbol{u}_1$ with the mean magnetic field provides for an electrical field $\boldsymbol{E}' = \boldsymbol{u}_1 \times \overline{\boldsymbol{B}}$, which is directed parallel to the z-direction, downwards in front of the plane of the drawing and upwards behind it. $\boldsymbol{E}'$ drives a current $\boldsymbol{j}'$, in the same manner directed downwards in front of the plane of the drawing and upwards behind it. This current is combined with a magnetic field $\boldsymbol{B}'$ in the positive x-direction. The crossproduct of $\boldsymbol{u}_2$ with this magnetic field $\boldsymbol{B}'$ is directed in the positive y-direction, i.e. parallel to the applied mean magnetic field $\overline{\boldsymbol{B}}$.

This statement can also be established if the interaction of $\boldsymbol{u}_2$ with the mean magnetic field is considered first. It is also true if the axis of the helical motion is turned within the (x, z)-plane. A helical motion with arbitrary direction of its axis can be considered as the sum of two helical motions, one with its axis within the (x, z)-plane and one with its axis parallel to the mean magnetic field. All helical motions of the first type provide for an electromotive force $\boldsymbol{u}' \times \boldsymbol{B}'$ parallel to the mean magnetic field. In this way we clearly see that randomly distributed left-handed helical motions produce a mean electromotive force which is directed parallel to the mean magnetic field. This electromotive force will be antiparallel to the mean magnetic field for randomly distributed right-handed helical motions.

Having just illustrated the α-effect in the low-conductivity limit we can also do so in the high-conductivity limit. Under this condition a flux rope of the mean magnetic field is deformed to a twisted Ω by a local helical motion (fig. 3.2). The current $\boldsymbol{j}'$ flowing through the loop of the Ω has, because of the twist, a component which is antiparallel to the original magnetic field for a right-handed helical motion as depicted here. A left-handed helical motion gives rise to a current parallel to the mean magnetic field. So we again find

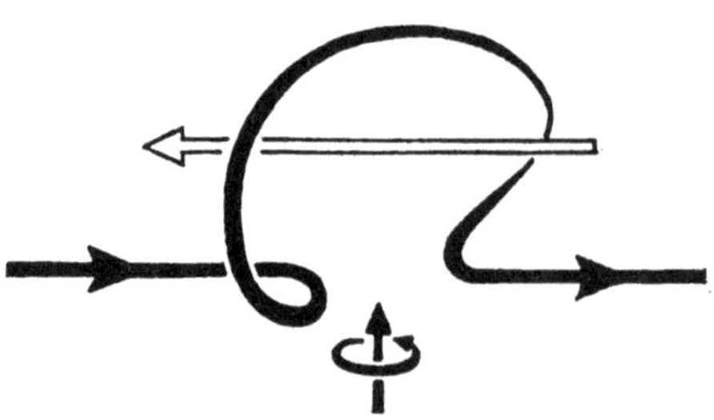

Fig. 3.2. A magnetic flux rope undergoing the influence of a helical motion is shaped into a twisted Ω. The loop is accompanied by a current which, in case of right-handed helical motions, has a component anti-parallel to the magnetic field

that such local helical motions randomly appearing in a conducting fluid have a common property, i.e. to drive a current parallel or antiparallel to an applied mean magnetic field.

This illustration very much resembles that given by PARKER [2] for the effect of the so-called cyclonic turbulence. We shall see later that Parker's effect can be, indeed, interpreted as a special case of the α-effect.

Let us now consider (fig. 3.3) a box in which we assume an electrically conducting fluid carrying out turbulent motions. The turbulence should be homogeneous and isotropic but have helicity, i.e. one kind of helical motions shall be more probable than the other one. Let us assume we have a higher probability of left-handed helical motions. Let a magnetic field $\overline{\boldsymbol{B}}$ be directed from the

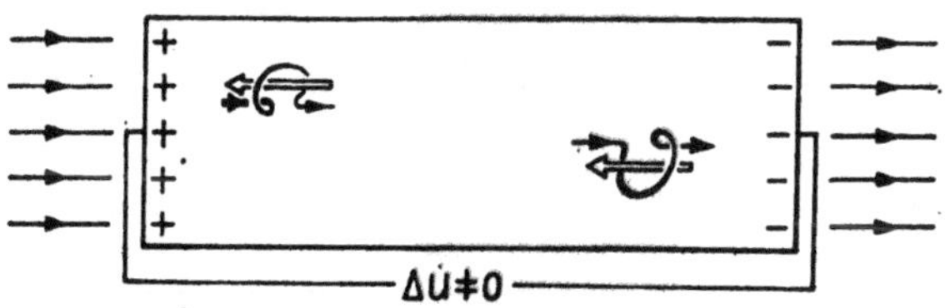

Fig. 3.3. Small-scale helical motions in a box provide a voltage along a magnetic field

left to the right. With these conditions the α-effect must be expected and, consequently, an electrical field parallel to the magnetic field. It provides for positive electrical charges at the right wall of the box and for negative at the left. From the outside we can measure a voltage parallel to the applied magnetic field.

Experimental evidence for the existence of the α-effect was given by an experiment (STEENBECK, KIRKO, GAILITIS, KLAWINA, KRAUSE, LAUMANIS and LIELAUSIS [1, 2]) which is depicted in fig. 3.4. Liquid sodium was used as the working fluid, its flow was compelled to be non-mirrorsymmetric. A system of copper plates created two channels which wound about each other orthogonally (cf. fig. 3.4a). In this way, the direction of flow was twisted in steps about the direction of the magnetic field, $\overline{\boldsymbol{B}}$; this type of motion is clearly not mirrorsymmetric. The conditions drafted in fig. 3.4 give rise to right-handed helical motions. The liquid sodium flowed through a non-corroding steel box. Figure 3.5 is a photograph of this box. A section of the outer wall being removed we are able to see the copper walls inside the box, which force the motion to take the desired helical structure.

An estimation of the electromotive force $\mathfrak{E}$ caused by this motion shall be provided by considering a simplified model. Let $u(x)$, $0 \leq x \leq l$, be the velocity

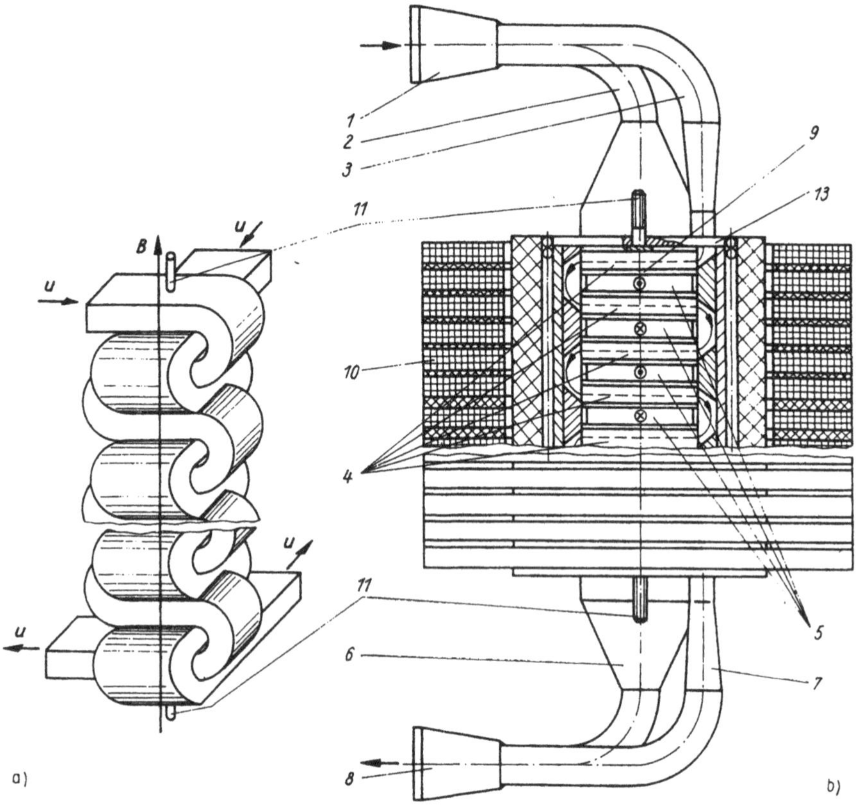

Fig. 3.4. The α-experiment

a) The flow pattern
b) Diagram of the apparatus:
 1. Main entrance of the liquid sodium
 2., 3. Entrances to the flow channels
 4. Flow, in the plane of the paper
 5. Flow, perpendicular to the plane of the paper ($\odot$ out and $\otimes$ in)
 6., 7. Exits from the two flow channels
 8. Main exit of the liquid sodium
 9. Copper plates separating the channels
 10. The coil generating the applied magnetic field
 11., 12. Electrodes between which the voltage created by the α-effect was measured
 13. Walls of non-corroding steel

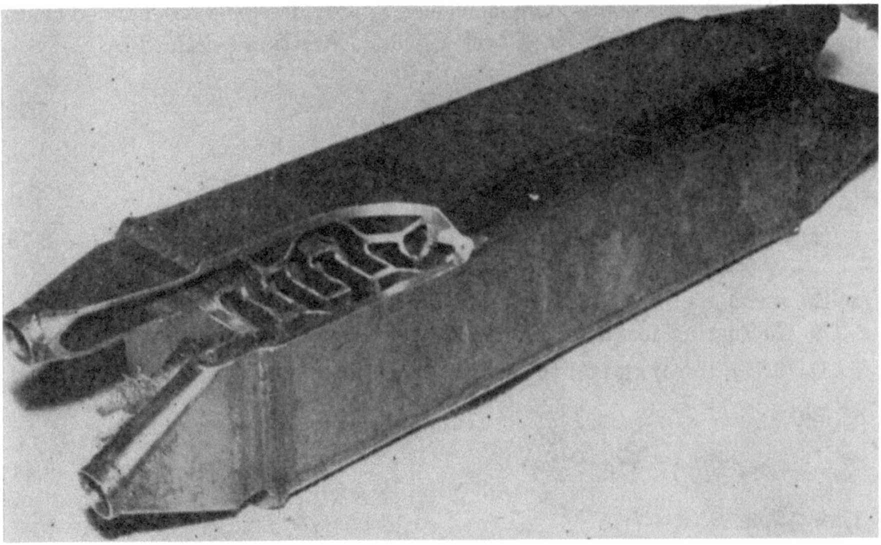

Fig. 3.5. Photograph of the "α-yashchik", i.e., of the box which is the essential piece of the α-experiment. A section of the outer wall is removed and we can see the copper walls inside the box, which force the motion of liquid sodium to take the helical structure

profile in one channel, and

$$u' = \frac{1}{l} \int_0^l u(x)\, \mathrm{d}x . \tag{3.68}$$

We define the function $\varphi(x)$ to be periodic with the period $4l$ and

$$\varphi(x) = \begin{cases} \dfrac{u(x)}{u'}, & \text{if } 0 \leqq x \leqq l, \\ 0, & \text{if } l \leqq x \leqq 2l, \\ -\dfrac{u(x-2l)}{u'}, & \text{if } 2l \leqq x \leqq 3l, \\ 0, & \text{if } 3l \leqq x \leqq 4l. \end{cases} \tag{3.69}$$

By definition we have

$$\int_0^l \varphi(x)\, \mathrm{d}x = 1 . \tag{3.70}$$

The velocity field of the experiment we represent by

$$\boldsymbol{u}' = u'(0, \varphi(x), \pm\varphi(x-l)) . \tag{3.71}$$

The positive sign of the z-component clearly provides for a left-handed helical motion if $\varphi(x) \geqq 0$ for $0 \leqq x \leqq l$ (cf. fig. 3.6). Function f defined by

$$f(x) = \int_0^x \varphi(\xi)\, d\xi - \frac{1}{2}, \tag{3.72}$$

we have

$$\int_0^{4l} f(x)\, dx = 0, \tag{3.73}$$

i.e. the average of f taken over the interval $0 \leqq x \leqq 4l$ is zero.

The fluctuating magnetic field shall be derived from equation (3.11). With (3.71), (3.72), (3.73) and on the assumption $\overline{\boldsymbol{B}} = (\overline{B}, 0, 0)$, $\overline{B} = \text{const}$ we find

$$\begin{aligned} B'_x &= 0, \\ B'_y &= -\mu\sigma u'\overline{B} f(x), \\ B'_z &= \mp\mu\sigma u'\overline{B} f(x-l). \end{aligned} \tag{3.74}$$

Hence we obtain for the cross product

$$(\boldsymbol{u}' \times \boldsymbol{B}')_x = \pm\mu\sigma u'^2 \overline{B}\{f(x)\,\varphi(x-l) - \varphi(x)\,f(x-l)\}. \tag{3.75}$$

In figure 3.6 this electromotive force is depicted where the positive sign is taken for the z-component in (3.71). It has a unique direction, parallel to $\overline{\boldsymbol{B}}$ for the positive sign in (3.71) and antiparallel to $\overline{\boldsymbol{B}}$ for the negative one. From (3.75) we obtain for the voltage over one channel

$$\Delta U = \int_0^l (\boldsymbol{u}' \times \boldsymbol{B}')_x\, dx = \pm\frac{1}{2}\mu\sigma u'^2 l^2 \overline{B}, \tag{3.76}$$

and for the voltage over the whole box with n channels

$$U = \pm\frac{1}{2}\mu\sigma u'^2 l^2 \overline{B} n. \tag{3.77}$$

The two signs reflect that we can have either left-handed or right-handed helical motions.

The result of the experiment is best seen in figure 3.7, where the ratio of the measured voltage U_m and the theoretical value U given in (3.77) is plotted as a function of the Stuart number

$$N = \frac{\overline{B}^2 \sigma l}{\varrho u'}, \tag{3.78}$$

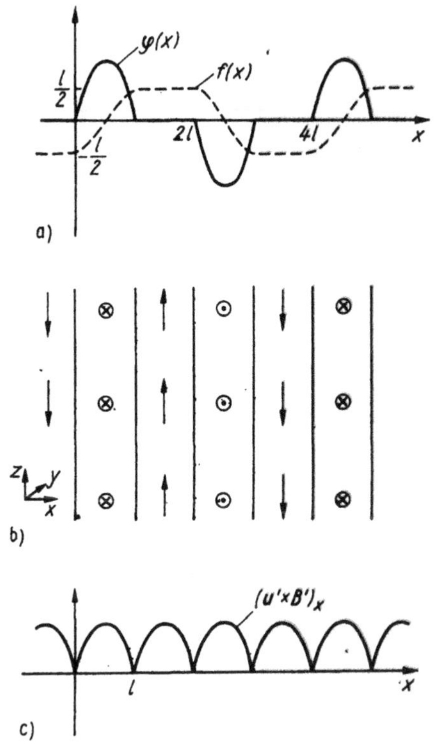

Fig. 3.6. Simplified model of the α-experiment
a) Representation of the profile of the y-component of the velocity field in dependence on x
b) The flow pattern
c) Profile of the x-component of the induced electromotive force

ϱ denoting the mass density. We observe that the two are related in a unique way. For small N, when the fluid velocity is large and the magnetic field is not, the measured voltage U_m was about 20% of that given in (3.77). This is the result of boundary effects, because we assumed the model to have infinite extension in the y- and z-directions. It was also found that, if the Stuart number is increased, the voltage decreases. This is clearly due to the influence of the magnetic field on the velocity field. It is of interest that the ratio U_m/U was found to be independent of the magnetic Reynolds number $\mathrm{Rm} = \mu\sigma l u'$.
Two predictions of (3.77), crucial to the validity of the theory, were verified by the experiment; (i) the sign of the voltage difference U_m between the electrodes is independent of the sense of the flow; (ii) it reverses if the applied magnetic field is reversed. Figure 3.8 shows that, for several values of the magnetic

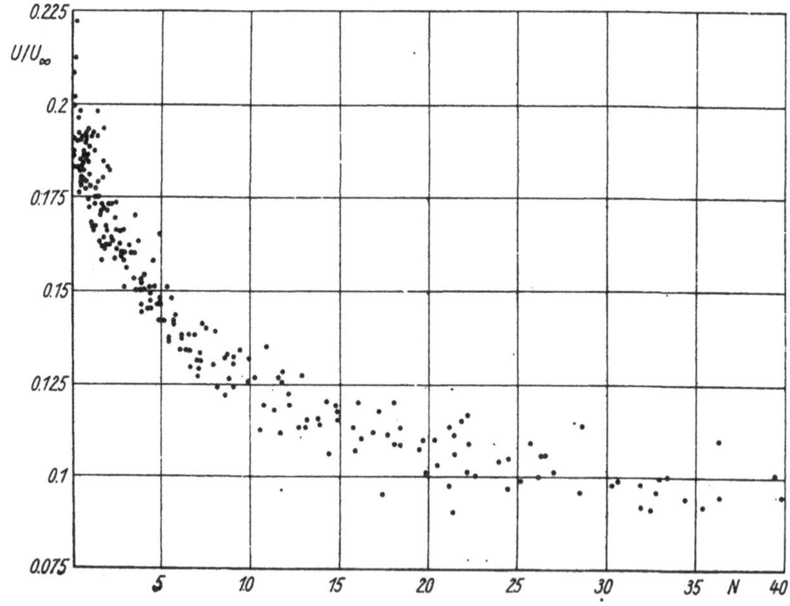

Fig. 3.7. Representation of the voltage measured along the magnetic field in dependence on the Stuart number

field, U_m is indeed proportional to u'^2. Figure 3.9 demonstrates that, when the magnetic field is small, U_m is proportional to it. For large fields, however, the effect is nonlinear in the $\overline{\boldsymbol{B}}$ applied.

It is also easy to illustrate that the α-effect is closely connected with dynamo excitation, as was mentioned above. Let us connect the two ends of the box in figure 3.3 by a wire which is wound around the box in such a way, that it produces the applied $\overline{\boldsymbol{B}}$. Then, for a sufficiently strong α-effect, this device will act as a self-excited dynamo. Another illustration is depicted in figure 3.10. The two rings shall contain an electrically conducting medium with α-effect. Let us assume a magnetic field $\boldsymbol{B}_0$ in ring (I). It drives a current $\boldsymbol{j}_1$, because of the α-effect. This current $\boldsymbol{j}_1$ is combined with a magnetic field $\boldsymbol{B}_1$, in ring (II). $\boldsymbol{B}_1$ drives a current $\boldsymbol{j}_2$ which is combined with a magnetic field $\boldsymbol{B}_2$ in ring (I). $\boldsymbol{B}_2$ clearly supports $\boldsymbol{B}_0$. Consequently, we can expect that the fields are maintained for sufficiently strong α-effect in spite of Ohmic losses. The energy of the Joule heat produced by the currents comes from the energy of the turbulent motion which has helicity.

We finally mention that a more realistic model of that kind was described in section 1.2.

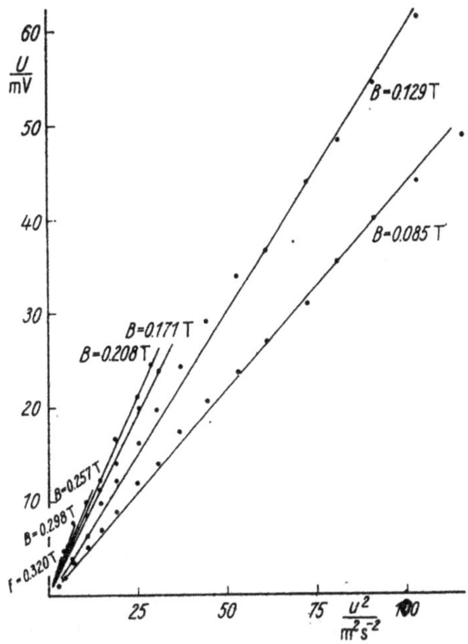

Fig. 3.8. The voltage created by the α-effect as a function of the square of the velocity, for a number of different applied fields

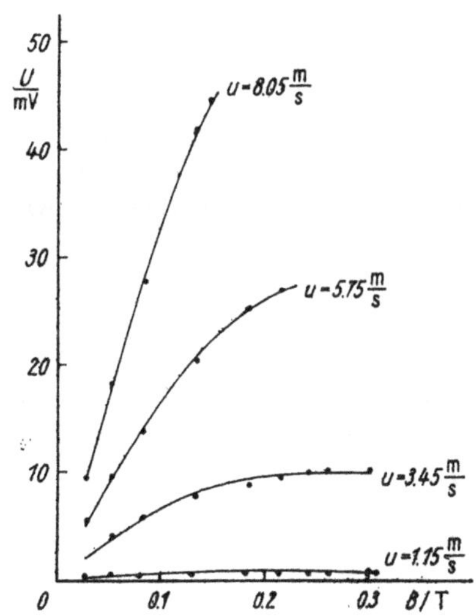

Fig. 3.9. The voltage created by the α-effect as a function of the applied magnetic field strength, for a number of different flow velocities

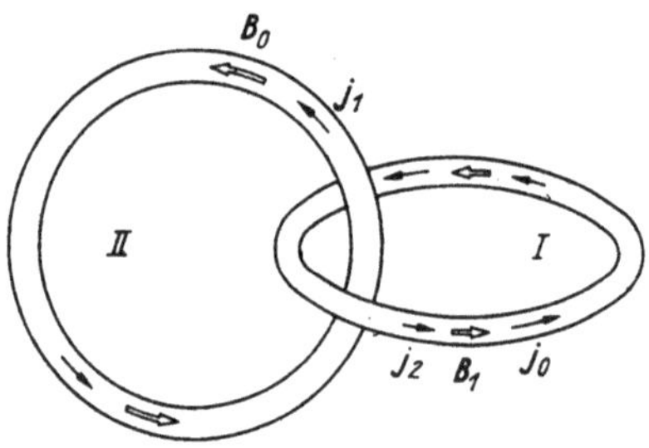

Fig. 3.10. Model illustrating the self-excited generation of a magnetic field in a medium with Ohm's law $\boldsymbol{j} = \sigma(\boldsymbol{E} + \alpha\boldsymbol{B})$

3.11. The mean square of the fluctuations

For a treatment of the high-conductivity limit it is necessary to describe the physical background in more detail. We adopt the standpoint that $\boldsymbol{B}'$ is produced by the interaction of the velocity field $\boldsymbol{u}'$ with the mean magnetic field $\overline{\boldsymbol{B}}$. Within the framework of the second order correlation approximation this production works over a time of order τ_{cor}, producing a field element $\boldsymbol{B}'_{el}$ of order

$$B'_{el} \approx \frac{u'\tau_{cor}}{\lambda_{cor}} \overline{B} \tag{3.79}$$

according to equation (3.10). After that the velocity field $\boldsymbol{u}'$ changes nearly completely and by interaction with $\overline{\boldsymbol{B}}$ a new field element $\boldsymbol{B}'_{el}$ is produced, being uncorrelated to the former, and so on. However, such a field element, once produced, will exist over the time $\mu\sigma\lambda_{cor}^2$, which is large compared with τ_{cor} according to (3.16). Hence the really existing field $\boldsymbol{B}'$ is the superposition of such uncorrelated field elements $\boldsymbol{B}'_{el}$, the number of them, n, will approximately be given by

$$n \approx \frac{\mu\sigma\lambda_{cor}^2}{\tau_{cor}}. \tag{3.80}$$

Since $\boldsymbol{B}'$ is the statistical sum of the uncorrelated field elements $\boldsymbol{B}'_{el}$, its order of magnitude is given by the square root of n times the order of one element, hence according to (3.79) and (3.80)

$$B' \approx \sqrt{n}\, B'_{el} \approx \sqrt{\mu\sigma u'^2\tau_{cor}}\, \overline{B} \tag{3.81}$$

or

$$\overline{\boldsymbol{B}'^2} \approx \mu\sigma u'^2\tau_{cor}\overline{\boldsymbol{B}}^2. \tag{3.82}$$

This derivation is due to STEENBECK and KRAUSE [6]. A similar result was derived by PARKER [14],

$$\overline{B'^2} \approx \mathrm{Rm}\,\overline{B}^2, \tag{3.83}$$

which is in agreement with (3.82) if $S \approx 1$ as assumed by PARKER. Finally, a result due to MOSS [1] may be added. Carrying out numerical experiments with two-dimensional turbulence MOSS found

$$\overline{B'^2} \approx \mathrm{Rm}^{0.7}\,\overline{B}^2. \tag{3.84}$$

A direct comparison with (3.82) is not possible since the range of the parameter S considered by MOSS is different.

We can derive the estimate (3.82) directly from (3.21) if $t - t_0$ is taken as the lifetime of one field element, i.e. $t = t_0 - \mu\sigma\lambda_{\mathrm{cor}}^2$. We obtain

$$\overline{B'^2} = \int\limits_{t-\mu\sigma\lambda_{\mathrm{cor}}^2}^{t} \int\limits_{t-\mu\sigma\lambda_{\mathrm{cor}}^2}^{t} \overline{\mathrm{curl}\,(\boldsymbol{u}'(\boldsymbol{x}, t') \times \overline{\boldsymbol{B}}) \cdot \mathrm{curl}\,(\boldsymbol{u}'(\boldsymbol{x}, t'') \times \overline{\boldsymbol{B}})}\, \mathrm{d}t'\, \mathrm{d}t''. \tag{3.85}$$

The integrand is significantly different from zero only in a strip of width τ_{cor} along the line $t' = t''$ in the (t', t'')-plane. Thus we find in the isotropic case

$$\overline{B'^2} \approx (\mu\sigma\lambda_{\mathrm{cor}}^2\tau_{\mathrm{cor}}) \left(\frac{\overline{u'^2}}{\lambda_{\mathrm{cor}}^2}\, \overline{B}^2\right)$$

in agreement with (3.82).

In our derivation of the latter results we have used rather qualitative considerations. It is, therefore, important to note that the results (3.82), and the analogous one for the low-conductivity case are confirmed by a rigorous deduction in chapter 7.

In the low-conductivity limit the estimate of $\overline{B'^2}$ analogue to (3.82) is immediately derived from (3.54) if we are confined to the incompressible case. We obtain from (3.54)

$$\overline{B'^2} = \mu^2\sigma^2 \overline{(\overline{\boldsymbol{B}} \cdot \mathrm{grad})\, \boldsymbol{a}_2 \cdot (\overline{\boldsymbol{B}} \cdot \mathrm{grad})\, \boldsymbol{a}_2}$$

$$= \mu^2\sigma^2 \left\{ \overline{B}_1^2 \left[\overline{\left(\frac{\partial a_{21}}{\partial x_1}\right)^2} + \overline{\left(\frac{\partial a_{22}}{\partial x_1}\right)^2} + \overline{\left(\frac{\partial a_{23}}{\partial x_1}\right)^2} \right] + \overline{B}_2^2 \left[\overline{\left(\frac{\partial a_{21}}{\partial x_2}\right)^2} + \cdots \right] + \cdots \right\},$$

which simplifies in the isotropic case to

$$\overline{B'^2} = q\overline{B}^2, \tag{3.86}$$

where

$$\frac{q}{\mu^2\sigma^2} = \overline{\left(\frac{\partial a_{21}}{\partial x_1}\right)^2} + \overline{\left(\frac{\partial a_{22}}{\partial x_1}\right)^2} + \overline{\left(\frac{\partial a_{23}}{\partial x_1}\right)^2} = \overline{\left(\frac{\partial a_{21}}{\partial x_2}\right)^2} + \overline{\left(\frac{\partial a_{22}}{\partial x_2}\right)^2} + \overline{\left(\frac{\partial a_{23}}{\partial x_2}\right)^2}$$
$$= \overline{\left(\frac{\partial a_{21}}{\partial x_3}\right)^2} + \overline{\left(\frac{\partial a_{22}}{\partial x_3}\right)^2} + \overline{\left(\frac{\partial a_{23}}{\partial x_3}\right)^2}$$
$$= \frac{1}{3}\left\{\overline{\left(\frac{\partial a_{21}}{\partial x_1}\right)^2} + \overline{\left(\frac{\partial a_{22}}{\partial x_1}\right)^2} + \overline{\left(\frac{\partial a_{23}}{\partial x_1}\right)^2} + \overline{\left(\frac{\partial a_{21}}{\partial x_2}\right)^2} + \overline{\left(\frac{\partial a_{22}}{\partial x_2}\right)^2}\right.$$
$$\left. + \overline{\left(\frac{\partial a_{23}}{\partial x_2}\right)^2} + \overline{\left(\frac{\partial a_{21}}{\partial x_3}\right)^2} + \overline{\left(\frac{\partial a_{22}}{\partial x_3}\right)^2} + \overline{\left(\frac{\partial a_{23}}{\partial x_3}\right)^2}\right\}. \quad (3.87)$$

Hence we find as an estimate of the order of magnitude

$$\frac{q}{\mu^2\sigma^2} = \frac{1}{3}\, 3\, \frac{\overline{a_2^2}}{\lambda_{\mathrm{cor}}^2} = \frac{\overline{a_2^2}}{\lambda_{\mathrm{cor}}^2} \approx u'^2 \lambda_{\mathrm{cor}}^2, \quad (3.88)$$

and obtain finally in the low-conductivity limit

$$\overline{\boldsymbol{B}'^2} \approx \mathrm{Rm}^2 \overline{\boldsymbol{B}}^2. \quad (3.89)$$

CHAPTER 4

GENERAL METHODS FOR A CALCULATION OF THE TURBULENT ELECTROMOTIVE FORCE

4.1. Introductory remarks. Definitions

The treatment of the two limiting cases in the foregoing chapter makes it clear that for a general investigation more efficient mathematical methods are needed. We now make wide use of tensor calculus. Often the isotropic tensors of the Euclidean space will appear, i.e. the Kronecker-tensor,

$$\delta_{ij} = \begin{cases} 1 \text{ if } i = j \\ 0 \text{ if } i \neq j \end{cases}, \tag{4.1}$$

and the Levi-Civita skew-symmetric tensor,

$$\varepsilon_{ijk} = \begin{cases} 1 & \text{if } \; i, j, k = 1, 2, 3, \text{ or } 3, 1, 2, \text{ or } 2, 3, 1 \\ 0 & \text{if } \; i = j \text{ or } i = k \text{ or } j = k \\ -1 & \text{if } \; i, j, k = 2, 1, 3, \text{ or } 3, 2, 1 \text{ or } 1, 3, 2. \end{cases} \tag{4.2}$$

The averages of products of vector quantities lead to the introduction of correlation tensors. We have the two-point-two-time correlation tensor of the velocity field,

$$Q_{ik}(\boldsymbol{x}, \boldsymbol{\xi}, t, \tau) = \overline{u_i'(\boldsymbol{x}, t)\, u_k'(\boldsymbol{x} + \boldsymbol{\xi}, t + \tau)}, \tag{4.3}$$

the mixed two-point-two-time correlation tensor of the velocity field and the magnetic field,

$$P_{ik}(\boldsymbol{x}, \boldsymbol{\xi}, t, \tau) = \overline{u_i'(\boldsymbol{x}, t)\, B_k'(\boldsymbol{x} + \boldsymbol{\xi}, t + \tau)}, \tag{4.4}$$

and the two-point-two-time correlation tensor of the magnetic field,

$$B_{ik}(\boldsymbol{x}, \boldsymbol{\xi}, t, \tau) = \overline{B_i'(\boldsymbol{x}, t)\, B_k'(\boldsymbol{x} + \boldsymbol{\xi}, t + \tau)}. \tag{4.5}$$

If we again look at the deduction in the previous chapter we see that the quantities just introduced have been used before. For the quantity h, for example, defined by (3.4) we have

$$h = \varepsilon_{ijk} \frac{\partial Q_{ik}}{\partial \xi_j}\bigg|_{\xi=0,\tau=0}, \tag{4.6}$$

if (4.2) and (4.3) are taken into account. Furthermore, the quantities w_{ik}, w_{ijk}, defined by (3.25) and (3.26) are closely connected with the tensor Q_{ik} too. We find

$$w_{ij} = \int_0^\infty Q_{ij}(\boldsymbol{x}, 0, t, -\tau)\,\mathrm{d}\tau\,, \tag{4.7}$$

$$w_{ijk} = \int_0^\infty \frac{\partial Q_{ik}(\boldsymbol{x}, 0, t, -\tau)}{\partial x_j}\,\mathrm{d}\tau\,. \tag{4.8}$$

Analogous relations exist for the similar quantities defined by (3.42), (3.43) and (3.44).

Moreover, relations (3.27) and (3.28) between the components of the tensors w_{ij} and w_{ijk} reflect a relation between these tensors and the isotropic tensors. One easily confirms the relations

$$w_{ijk} = -\frac{\alpha}{2}\,\varepsilon_{ijk}\,, \quad w_{ij} = \beta\,\delta_{ij}\,. \tag{4.9}$$

Finally, we remark in this connection that the turbulent electromotive force $\mathfrak{E}$ can be represented by

$$\mathfrak{E}_i = \varepsilon_{ijk} P_{jk}(\boldsymbol{x}, 0, t, 0)\,, \tag{4.10}$$

and the mean square of the magnetic field fluctuations by

$$\overline{\boldsymbol{B}'^2} = B_{ii}(\boldsymbol{x}, 0, t, 0)\,. \tag{4.11}$$

There are good reasons for introducing correlation tensors of higher rank, i.e. the velocity correlation tensor of third rank

$$Q_{ijk}(\boldsymbol{x}, \boldsymbol{\xi}, \boldsymbol{\eta}, t, \tau, \sigma) = \overline{u_i'(\boldsymbol{x}, t)\, u_j'(\boldsymbol{x} + \boldsymbol{\xi}, t + \tau)\, u_k'(\boldsymbol{x} + \boldsymbol{\xi} + \boldsymbol{\eta}, t + \tau + \sigma)}\,, \tag{4.12}$$

the mixed tensor of third rank

$$P_{ijk}(\boldsymbol{x}, \boldsymbol{\xi}, \boldsymbol{\eta}, t, \tau, \sigma) = \overline{u_i'(\boldsymbol{x}, t)\, u_j'(\boldsymbol{x} + \boldsymbol{\xi}, t + \tau)\, B_k'(\boldsymbol{x} + \boldsymbol{\xi} + \boldsymbol{\eta}, t + \tau + \sigma)}\,, \tag{4.13}$$

and the corresponding quantities of fourth rank

$$\begin{aligned} &Q_{ijkl}(\boldsymbol{x}, \boldsymbol{\xi}, \boldsymbol{\eta}, \boldsymbol{\zeta}, t, \tau, \sigma, \varrho) \\ &= \overline{u_i'(\boldsymbol{x}, t)\, u_j'(\boldsymbol{x} + \boldsymbol{\xi}, t + \tau)\, u_k'(\boldsymbol{x} + \boldsymbol{\xi} + \boldsymbol{\eta}, t + \tau + \sigma)} \\ &\quad \overline{u_l'(\boldsymbol{x} + \boldsymbol{\xi} + \boldsymbol{\eta} + \boldsymbol{\zeta}, t + \tau + \sigma + \varrho)}\,, \end{aligned} \tag{4.14}$$

$$\begin{aligned} &P_{ijkl}(\boldsymbol{x}, \boldsymbol{\xi}, \boldsymbol{\eta}, \boldsymbol{\zeta}, t, \tau, \sigma, \varrho) \\ &= \overline{u_i'(\boldsymbol{x}, t)\, u_j'(\boldsymbol{x} + \boldsymbol{\xi}, t + \tau)\, u_k'(\boldsymbol{x} + \boldsymbol{\xi} + \boldsymbol{\eta}, t + \tau + \sigma)} \\ &\quad \overline{B_l'(\boldsymbol{x} + \boldsymbol{\xi} + \boldsymbol{\eta} + \boldsymbol{\zeta}, t + \tau + \sigma + \varrho)}\,. \end{aligned} \tag{4.15}$$

In the following the correlation tensors P_{ij}, P_{ijk}, P_{ijkl} shall appear where the last set of coordinates is equal to zero. Therefore we shall introduce, in addition, the tensors p_{ij}, p_{ijk}, p_{ijkl} defined by

$$p_{ij}(\boldsymbol{x}, t) = P_{ij}(\boldsymbol{x}, 0, t, 0), \quad p_{ijk}(\boldsymbol{x}, \boldsymbol{\xi}, t, \tau) = P_{ijk}(\boldsymbol{x}, \boldsymbol{\xi}, 0, t, \tau, 0),$$
$$p_{ijkl}(\boldsymbol{x}, \boldsymbol{\xi}, \boldsymbol{\eta}, t, \tau, \sigma) = P_{ijkl}(\boldsymbol{x}, \boldsymbol{\xi}, \boldsymbol{\eta}, 0, t, \tau, \sigma, 0). \tag{4.16}$$

According to these definitions the turbulent electromotive force shall be given by

$$\mathfrak{E}_i = \varepsilon_{ijk} p_{jk}. \tag{4.17}$$

For reasons of convenience we introduce the operators

$$\mathfrak{D}_{jn} = \left(\frac{\partial}{\partial t} - \eta \Delta\right) \delta_{jn} - \varepsilon_{jkl}\varepsilon_{lmn} \frac{\partial}{\partial x_k} \bar{u}_m \tag{4.18}$$

and

$$\mathfrak{D}_{jmn} = \varepsilon_{jkl}\varepsilon_{lmn} \frac{\partial}{\partial x_k}, \tag{4.19}$$

which are derived from the induction equation (2.3).

In the formulae (4.18) and (4.19) defining the operators $\mathfrak{D}_{jn}$ and $\mathfrak{D}_{jmn}$, $\boldsymbol{x}$ and t are written as the coordinates with respect to which the differentiation is to be carried out. However, applying these operators to one of the correlation tensors our understanding will always be that the differentiation is to be carried out with respect to the last set of space or time coordinates, i.e., for example, if written explicitly

$$\mathfrak{D}_{jn} P_{in} = \left[\left(\frac{\partial}{\partial \tau} - \eta \frac{\partial^2}{\partial \xi_p\, \partial \xi_p}\right) \delta_{jn} - \varepsilon_{jkl}\varepsilon_{lmn} \frac{\partial}{\partial \xi_k} \bar{u}_m(\boldsymbol{x} + \boldsymbol{\xi}, t + \tau)\right] P_{in}(\boldsymbol{x}, \boldsymbol{\xi}, t, \tau)$$

and

$$\mathfrak{D}_{jn} P_{ipn} = \left[\left(\frac{\partial}{\partial \sigma} - \eta \frac{\partial^2}{\partial \eta_r\, \partial \eta_r}\right) \delta_{jn} - \varepsilon_{jkl}\varepsilon_{lmn} \frac{\partial}{\partial \eta_k} \bar{u}_m(\boldsymbol{x} + \boldsymbol{\xi} + \boldsymbol{\eta}, t + \tau + \sigma)\right]$$
$$P_{ipn}(\boldsymbol{x}, \boldsymbol{\xi}, \boldsymbol{\eta}, t, \tau, \sigma),$$

but

$$\mathfrak{D}_{jn} p_{ipn} = \left[\left(\frac{\partial}{\partial \tau} - \eta \frac{\partial^2}{\partial \xi_r\, \partial \xi_r}\right) \delta_{jn} - \varepsilon_{jkl}\varepsilon_{lmn} \frac{\partial}{\partial \xi_k} \bar{u}_m(\boldsymbol{x} + \boldsymbol{\xi}, t + \tau)\right] p_{ipn}(\boldsymbol{x}, \boldsymbol{\xi}, t, \tau).$$

The argument of the mean velocity field is always the sum of all the coordinate sets, as indicated here.

4.2. The hierarchy of equations for the correlation tensors

We start from the induction equation (2.3), which we now write in the form

$$\mathfrak{D}_{jn} B_n = \mathfrak{D}_{jmn} u_m' B_n. \tag{4.20}$$

Taking the average we arrive at the equation

$$\mathfrak{D}_{jn}\overline{B}_n = \mathfrak{D}_{jmn}p_{mn}, \tag{4.21}$$

where the correlation tensor p_{mn} appears on the right.

We now exchange in the equation (4.20) the arguments $\boldsymbol{x}$, t for $\boldsymbol{x} + \boldsymbol{\xi}$, $t + \tau$ and take the derivatives with respect to $\boldsymbol{\xi}$ and τ. In addition we replace the subscripts m and n on the right by n and p. Multiplying the resulting equation by $u'_m(\boldsymbol{x}, t)$ and taking the average we find

$$\mathfrak{D}_{jn}P_{mn} = \mathfrak{D}_{jnp}(Q_{mn}\overline{B}_p) + \mathfrak{D}_{jnp}p_{mn}. \tag{4.22}$$

In equation (4.21) for the mean field—a first order statistical moment—a correlation tensor of second rank appears, i.e. a second order statistical moment. In equation (4.22) for the correlation tensor P_{mn} a correlation tensor of third rank appears, i.e. a third order statistical moment. This behaviour continues. Thus we find a hierarchy of equations for the unknown quantities $\overline{B}_n$, P_{mn}, P_{mnp}, ..., where the first equations are given by

$$\begin{aligned}
\mathfrak{D}_{jn}\overline{B}_n &= \mathfrak{D}_{jmn}p_{mn}, \\
\mathfrak{D}_{jn}P_{mn} &= \mathfrak{D}_{jnp}(Q_{mn}\overline{B}_p) + \mathfrak{D}_{jnp}p_{mnp}, \\
\mathfrak{D}_{jp}P_{mnp} &= \mathfrak{D}_{jpq}(Q_{mnp}\overline{B}_q) - \mathfrak{D}_{jp}(Q_{mn}\overline{B}_p) + \mathfrak{D}_{jpq}p_{mnpq},
\end{aligned} \tag{4.23}$$

The system (4.23) represents an infinite set of equations. For deriving a finite one some closure technique is needed. This is a well known general problem of turbulence theory, which is not yet satisfactorily solved. It is not our intention to discuss this sort of problem.

We derive a finite system of equations out of (4.23) by taking into account the perturbing turbulent velocity field $\boldsymbol{u}'$ up to a certain order. Thus we deal—in a certain sense—with weak turbulence only. However, effects deduced in the frame of our theory can, indeed, be very large without breaking up the scales, as already indicated in the foregoing chapter.

4.3. Second order correlation approximation

In this case we develop a theory which takes into account the perturbing turbulent velocity field $\boldsymbol{u}'$ up to the second order only. Since the second term on the right-hand side of the second equation of the system (4.23) is of third order, we find

$$\mathfrak{D}_{jn}\overline{B}_n(\boldsymbol{x}, t) = \mathfrak{D}_{jmn}p_{mn}(\boldsymbol{x}, t), \tag{4.24}$$

$$\mathfrak{D}_{jn}P_{mn}(\boldsymbol{x}, \boldsymbol{\xi}, t, \tau) = \mathfrak{D}_{jnp}(Q_{mn}(\boldsymbol{x}, \boldsymbol{\xi}, t, \tau)\,\overline{B}_p(\boldsymbol{x} + \boldsymbol{\xi}, t + \tau)),$$

In addition, we have equations which express the fact that the magnetic field is source-free, i.e.

$$\frac{\partial B_n(\boldsymbol{x}, t)}{\partial x_n} = 0, \quad \frac{\partial P_{mn}(\boldsymbol{x}, \boldsymbol{\xi}, t, \tau)}{\partial \xi_n} = 0, \tag{4.25}$$

and, finally, the initial condition

$$P_{mn}(\boldsymbol{x}, \boldsymbol{\xi}, t, \tau) \to 0 \quad \text{if} \quad \tau \to -\infty. \tag{4.26}$$

The latter is obvious from the definition (4.4) of P_{mn}: There is no correlation between the velocity field at time t and the magnetic field at a much earlier time.

(4.24), (4.25) and (4.26) are the basic equations of mean-field electrodynamics within the framework of second order correlation approximation. For a justification (Krause and Roberts [4]) of the neglect of the third order cumulant in the second equation of (4.23) we remark that

$$p_3 \leqq u' p_2, \tag{4.27}$$

if p_2 is a measure of the order of magnitude of P_{mn} and p_3 the same for P_{mnp}. Equality holds in the completely correlated case only. Accordingly, the order of magnitude of the third order term $\mathfrak{D}_{jnp} p_{mnp}$ can be estimated by

$$|\mathfrak{D}_{jnp} p_{mnp}| \approx \frac{p_3}{\lambda_{\text{cor}}} \leqq \frac{u' p_2}{\lambda_{\text{cor}}}. \tag{4.28}$$

On the other hand the order of magnitude of the second order term $\mathfrak{D}_{jn} P_{mn}$ can be estimated by

$$|\mathfrak{D}_{jn} P_{mn}| \gtrapprox \max\left\{\frac{p_2}{\tau_{\text{cor}}}, \frac{p_2}{\mu\sigma\lambda_{\text{cor}}^2}\right\}, \tag{4.29}$$

where the ">" sign is included only to avoid discussion of the term connected with the mean velocity field in the operator $\mathfrak{D}_{jn}$.

Comparing now (4.28) and (4.29) we find that the second order correlation approximation is applicable if either $u' p_2/\lambda_{\text{cor}} \ll p_2/\tau_{\text{cor}}$, or $u' p_2/\lambda_{\text{cor}} \ll p_2/\mu\sigma\lambda_{\text{cor}}^2$ or both. Hence, we have the condition

$$\min(\text{Rm}, \text{S}) \ll 1 \tag{4.30}$$

already mentioned in the foregoing chapter, which is a guarantee for the applicability of second order correlation approximation. The Strouhal number, S, and the magnetic Reynolds number, Rm, are defined by (3.13) and (3.14).

4.4. Higher order correlation approximation

As in the second order case similar developments of higher order theories are possible. If we neglect the fourth order terms in the third equation of (4.23) we arrive at the system

$$\mathfrak{D}_{jn}\overline{B}_n(\boldsymbol{x}, t) = \mathfrak{D}_{jmn}p_{mn}(\boldsymbol{x}, t), \tag{4.31}$$

$$\mathfrak{D}_{jn}P_{mn}(\boldsymbol{x}, \xi, t, \tau) = \mathfrak{D}_{jnp}(Q_{mn}(\boldsymbol{x}, \xi, t, \tau)\, \overline{B}_p(\boldsymbol{x} + \xi, t + \tau)) + \mathfrak{D}_{jnp}p_{mnp}(\boldsymbol{x}, \xi, t, \tau),$$

$$\mathfrak{D}_{jp}P_{mnp}(\boldsymbol{x}, \xi, \boldsymbol{\eta}, t, \tau, \sigma) = \mathfrak{D}_{jpq}(Q_{mnp}(\boldsymbol{x}, \xi, \boldsymbol{\eta}, t, \tau, \sigma)\, \overline{B}_q(\boldsymbol{x} + \xi + \boldsymbol{\eta}, t + \tau + \sigma)).$$

In addition, we have the conditions

$$\frac{\partial \overline{B}_n(\boldsymbol{x}, t)}{\partial x_n} = 0, \quad \frac{\partial P_{mn}(\boldsymbol{x}, \xi, t, \tau)}{\partial \xi_n} = 0, \quad \frac{\partial P_{mnp}(\boldsymbol{x}, \xi, \boldsymbol{\eta}, t, \tau, \sigma)}{\partial \eta_p} = 0, \tag{4.32}$$

and the initial conditions

$$P_{mn}(\boldsymbol{x}, \xi, t, \tau) \to 0 \text{ if } \tau \to -\infty, \tag{4.33}$$

$$P_{mnp}(\boldsymbol{x}, \xi, \boldsymbol{\eta}, t, \tau, \sigma) \to 0 \text{ if } \sigma \to -\infty.$$

(4.31), (4.32) and (4.33) form the system of basic equations of mean-field electrodynamics in the frame of third order correlation approximation.

Finally, we give the analogous set of equations and conditions for the fourth order correlation approximation:

$$\mathfrak{D}_{jn}\overline{B}_n(\boldsymbol{x}, t) = \mathfrak{D}_{jmn}p_{mn}(\boldsymbol{x}, t), \tag{4.34}$$

$$\mathfrak{D}_{jn}P_{mn}(\boldsymbol{x}, \xi, t, \tau) = \mathfrak{D}_{jnp}(Q_{mn}(\boldsymbol{x}, \xi, t, \tau)\, \overline{B}_p(\boldsymbol{x} + \xi, t + \tau)) + \mathfrak{D}_{jnp}p_{mnp}(\boldsymbol{x}, \xi, t, \tau),$$

$$\begin{aligned}\mathfrak{D}_{jp}P_{mnp}(\boldsymbol{x}, \xi, \boldsymbol{\eta}, t, \tau, \sigma) &= \mathfrak{D}_{jpq}(Q_{mnp}(\boldsymbol{x}, \xi, \boldsymbol{\eta}, t, \tau, \sigma)\, \overline{B}_q(\boldsymbol{x} + \xi + \boldsymbol{\eta}, t + \tau + \sigma)) \\ &\quad - Q_{mn}(\boldsymbol{x}, \xi, t, \tau)\, \mathfrak{D}_{jp}\overline{B}_p(\boldsymbol{x} + \xi + \boldsymbol{\eta}, t + \tau + \sigma) + \mathfrak{D}_{jpq}p_{mnpq}(\boldsymbol{x}, \xi, \boldsymbol{\eta}, t, \tau, \sigma),\end{aligned}$$

$$\begin{aligned}\mathfrak{D}_{jq}P_{mnpq}(\boldsymbol{x}, \xi, \boldsymbol{\eta}, \zeta, t, \tau, \sigma, \varrho) &= \mathfrak{D}_{jqr}(Q_{mnpq}(\boldsymbol{x}, \xi, \boldsymbol{\eta}, \zeta, t, \tau, \sigma, \varrho) \\ &\qquad \overline{B}_r(\boldsymbol{x} + \xi + \boldsymbol{\eta} + \zeta, t + \tau + \sigma + \varrho));\end{aligned}$$

$$\frac{\partial \overline{B}_n(\boldsymbol{x}, t)}{\partial x_n} = 0, \quad \frac{\partial P_{mn}(\boldsymbol{x}, \xi, t, \tau)}{\partial \xi_n} = 0, \tag{4.35}$$

$$\frac{\partial P_{mnp}(\boldsymbol{x}, \xi, \boldsymbol{\eta}, t, \tau, \sigma)}{\partial \eta_p} = 0, \quad \frac{\partial P_{mnpq}(\boldsymbol{x}, \xi, \boldsymbol{\eta}, \zeta, t, \tau, \sigma, \varrho)}{\partial \zeta_q} = 0;$$

$$P_{mn}(\boldsymbol{x}, \xi, t, \tau) \to 0 \quad \text{if} \quad \tau \to -\infty;$$

$$P_{mnp}(\boldsymbol{x}, \xi, \boldsymbol{\eta}, t, \tau, \sigma) \to 0 \quad \text{if} \quad \sigma \to -\infty; \tag{4.36}$$

$$P_{mnpq}(\boldsymbol{x}, \xi, \boldsymbol{\eta}, \zeta, t, \tau, \sigma, \varrho) \to 0 \quad \text{if} \quad \varrho \to -\infty.$$

4.5. Green's function tensor of the induction equation

Looking for general solutions of the equations deduced in the foregoing paragraphs we now introduce the Green's function tensor $G_{jp}(\boldsymbol{x}, \boldsymbol{\xi}, t, \tau)$ of the induction equation which is defined by the following conditions:

(i) $G_{jp}(\boldsymbol{x}, \boldsymbol{\xi}, t, \tau) = 0$ if $t < \tau$;

(ii) $G_{jp}(\boldsymbol{x}, \boldsymbol{\xi}, t, \tau) \to 0$ if $|\boldsymbol{x} - \boldsymbol{\xi}| \to \infty$;

(iii) $$\mathfrak{D}_{jk} G_{kp}(\boldsymbol{x}, \boldsymbol{\xi}, t, \tau) = \left\{\left(\frac{\partial}{\partial t} - \eta \Delta\right) \delta_{jk} - \varepsilon_{jlm} \varepsilon_{mnk} \frac{\partial}{\partial x_l} \bar{u}_n(\boldsymbol{x}, t)\right\} G_{kp}(\boldsymbol{x}, \boldsymbol{\xi}, t, \tau)$$
$$= \delta_{jp}\, \delta(\boldsymbol{x} - \boldsymbol{\xi}, t - \tau) \quad \text{if} \quad t > \tau .$$

$\delta(\boldsymbol{x} - \boldsymbol{\xi}, t - \tau)$ denotes the Dirac δ-function.

It is easily shown that the field

$$B_k(\boldsymbol{x}, t) = \int_0^\infty \int G_{kp}(\boldsymbol{x}, \boldsymbol{\xi}, t, \tau)\, q_p(\boldsymbol{\xi}, \tau)\, \mathrm{d}\boldsymbol{\xi}\, \mathrm{d}\tau \tag{4.37}$$

is the solution of the equation

$$\mathfrak{D}_{jk} B_k = q_j \tag{4.38}$$

for $t > t_0$ with the initial condition $B_k(\boldsymbol{x}, t_0) = 0$, since we will find by applying the operator $\mathfrak{D}_{jk}$ to the field (4.37) and taking into account condition (iii)

$$\begin{aligned} \mathfrak{D}_{jk} B_k &= \int_{t_0}^\infty \int \mathfrak{D}_{jk} G_{kp}(\boldsymbol{x}, \boldsymbol{\xi}, t, \tau)\, q_p(\boldsymbol{\xi}, \tau)\, \mathrm{d}\boldsymbol{\xi}\, \mathrm{d}\tau \\ &= \int_{t_0}^\infty \int \delta_{jp} \delta(\boldsymbol{x} - \boldsymbol{\xi}, t - \tau)\, q_p(\boldsymbol{\xi}, \tau)\, \mathrm{d}\boldsymbol{\xi}\, \mathrm{d}\tau = q_j(\boldsymbol{x}, t) . \end{aligned} \tag{4.39}$$

Furthermore, we will show that the initial value problem

$$\mathfrak{D}_{jk} B_k = 0 \quad \text{if} \quad t > \tau, \quad B_k(\boldsymbol{x}, \tau) = B_k^{(0)}(\boldsymbol{x}) \tag{4.40}$$

is solved by the expression

$$B_k(\boldsymbol{x}, t) = \int G_{kp}(\boldsymbol{x}, \boldsymbol{\xi}, t, \tau)\, B_p^{(0)}(\boldsymbol{\xi})\, \mathrm{d}\boldsymbol{\xi} . \tag{4.41}$$

In order to prove this we remark first that

$$\begin{aligned} \mathfrak{D}_{jk} B_k &= \int \mathfrak{D}_{jk} G_{kp}(\boldsymbol{x}, \boldsymbol{\xi}, t, \tau)\, B_p^{(0)}(\boldsymbol{\xi})\, \mathrm{d}\boldsymbol{\xi} \\ &= \int \delta_{jp} \delta(\boldsymbol{x} - \boldsymbol{\xi}, t - \tau)\, B_p^{(0)}(\boldsymbol{\xi})\, \mathrm{d}\boldsymbol{\xi} = B_j^{(0)}(\boldsymbol{x})\, \delta(t - \tau) , \end{aligned} \tag{4.42}$$

and hence the differential equation (4.40) is satisfied for $t > \tau$. Secondly, we find that

$$\int_{\tau-\varepsilon}^{\tau+\varepsilon} \mathfrak{D}_{jk} B_k\, \mathrm{d}t = B_j^{(0)}(\boldsymbol{x}) \tag{4.43}$$

for any positive number ε. In the limit $\varepsilon \to 0$ and with the explicit definition of the operator $\mathfrak{D}_{jk}$ it follows that

$$B_j(\boldsymbol{x}, \tau + \varepsilon) - B_j(\boldsymbol{x}, \tau - \varepsilon) + O(\varepsilon) = B_j^{(0)}(\boldsymbol{x}).$$

Since, by definition, $B_j(\boldsymbol{x}, \tau - \varepsilon) = 0$, we have

$$\lim_{\varepsilon \to 0} B_j(\boldsymbol{x}, \tau + \varepsilon) = B_j^{(0)}(\boldsymbol{x}),$$

thus showing that (4.41), indeed, solves the initial value problem of the induction equation.

A general discussion of the existence of the tensor G_{jp} and related problems will not be our concern. In cases of interest in connection with the following deductions we shall restrict ourselves to special mean velocity fields where we can represent G_{jp} by explicit expressions. However, one point of interest has to be mentioned: The tensor G_{jp} can have the property

$$G_{jp} \to 0 \quad \text{if} \quad t - \tau \to \infty, \tag{4.44}$$

but need not. If not, the initial value problem (4.40) of the induction equation has non-decaying solutions. In physical terms, this means that the initial magnetic field does not decay by Ohmic dissipation. The induction action of the mean velocity field overcomes the losses of magnetic energy by Ohmic dissipation and, consequently, the magnetic field either remains stationary or grows indefinitely. In both these cases the model under discussion is referred to as a self-excited dynamo.

By assumption we exclude the possibility that a self-excited dynamo is provided by the mean velocity field. We confine ourselves to those mean velocity fields for which condition (4.44) holds. We can now, under this restriction, solve the inhomogeneous problem (4.38) where $\boldsymbol{q}(\boldsymbol{x}, t)$ is given and bounded for $-\infty < t < +\infty$ by the expression

$$B_k(\boldsymbol{x}, t) = \iint G_{kp}(\boldsymbol{x}, \boldsymbol{\xi}, t, \tau)\, q_p(\boldsymbol{\xi}, \tau)\, \mathrm{d}\boldsymbol{\xi}\, \mathrm{d}\tau. \tag{4.45}$$

If $\boldsymbol{B}$, as defined by (4.37) or (4.45), represents a magnetic field it has to be source-free. We shall now prove for both representations that $\operatorname{div} \boldsymbol{B} = 0$ if $\operatorname{div} \boldsymbol{q} = 0$.

From the property (iii) of the Green's tensor and the definition (4.18) of the operator $\mathfrak{D}_{jk}$ we obtain

$$\frac{\partial}{\partial x_j} \mathfrak{D}_{jk} G_{kp} = \left(\frac{\partial}{\partial t} - \eta \Delta\right) \frac{\partial G_{kp}}{\partial x_k} = - \frac{\partial \delta(\boldsymbol{x} - \boldsymbol{\xi}, t - \tau)}{\partial \xi_p}, \tag{4.46}$$

and subsequently from (4.37)

$$\left(\frac{\partial}{\partial t} - \eta\Delta\right) \operatorname{div} \boldsymbol{B} = \int_{t_0}^{\infty}\int \left(\frac{\partial}{\partial t} - \eta\Delta\right) \frac{\partial G_{kp}}{\partial x_k} q_p(\xi, \tau)\, d\xi\, d\tau$$

$$= -\int_{t_0}^{\infty}\int \frac{\partial \delta(\boldsymbol{x} - \xi, t - \tau)}{\partial \xi_p} q_p(\xi, \tau)\, d\xi\, d\tau = \int_{t_0}^{\infty}\int \delta(\boldsymbol{x} - \xi, t - \tau) \frac{\partial q_p(\xi, \tau)}{\partial \xi_p}\, d\xi\, d\tau$$

$$= \operatorname{div} \boldsymbol{q}\,.$$

Thus we find $\left(\frac{\partial}{\partial t} - \eta\Delta\right) \operatorname{div} \boldsymbol{B} = 0$ if $\operatorname{div} \boldsymbol{q} = 0$.

It is well known that a solution $U(\boldsymbol{x}, t)$ of the equation

$$\left(\frac{\partial}{\partial t} - \eta\Delta\right) U(\boldsymbol{x}, t) = 0 \tag{4.47}$$

identically vanishes for $t > t_0$ if it is zero for $t = t_0$.

The field $\boldsymbol{B}$ defined by (4.37) vanishes for $t = t_0$, hence $\operatorname{div} \boldsymbol{B} = 0$ for $t = t_0$. Consequently, we have $\operatorname{div} \boldsymbol{B} = 0$ for all $t \geqq t_0$ if $\operatorname{div} \boldsymbol{q} = 0$. The same holds for the representation (4.45) if the integral is sufficiently converging in the limit $t_0 \to -\infty$.

4.6. Application of the Green's function tensor to the equations of mean-field electrodynamics

With the aid of the Green's function tensor we are able to transform the equations deduced from the hierarchy (4.23) into integro-differential equations. In the case of second order correlation approximation, e.g., we find from the second equation of (4.24)

$$P_{mn}(\boldsymbol{x}, \xi, t, \tau) = \iint G_{np}(\boldsymbol{x} + \xi, \boldsymbol{x} + \xi', t + \tau, t + \tau') \tag{4.48}$$
$$\mathfrak{D}_{pqr}(Q_{mq}(\boldsymbol{x}, \xi', t, \tau')\, \overline{B}_r(\boldsymbol{x} + \xi', t + \tau'))\, d\xi'\, d\tau'\,.$$

Noting that $\boldsymbol{x} + \xi$ and $t + \tau$ are the arguments of the operator $\mathfrak{D}_{jp}$ in the second equation of (4.24), one understands the same arguments appearing in the Green's tensor on the right-hand side of (4.48). According to the statements at the end of the foregoing paragraph the quantity P_{mn} given by (4.48) satisfies the second condition (4.25). Moreover, since $Q_{mq} \to 0$ if $\tau' \to -\infty$, the condition (4.26) is likewise satisfied. Hence we can replace the basic equations of the second order correlation approximation (4.24), (4.25) and (4.26) by the equivalent set

$$\mathfrak{D}_{jn}\overline{B}_n(\boldsymbol{x}, t) = \mathfrak{D}_{jmn}p_{mn}(\boldsymbol{x}, t),$$

$$p_{mn}(\boldsymbol{x}, t) = \iint G_{np}(\boldsymbol{x}, \boldsymbol{x} + \boldsymbol{\xi}, t, t + \tau)\, \mathfrak{D}_{pqr}(Q_{mq}(\boldsymbol{x}, \boldsymbol{\xi}, t, \tau)\, \overline{B}_r(\boldsymbol{x} + \boldsymbol{\xi}, t + \tau))\, \mathrm{d}\boldsymbol{\xi}\, \mathrm{d}\tau,$$

$$\frac{\partial \overline{B}_k(\boldsymbol{x}, t)}{\partial x_k} = 0. \tag{4.49}$$

One advantage of (4.49) over (4.25) and the related equations is obvious. The second equation of (4.49) is one that directly yields the quantity, p_{mn}, whereas the second equation of (4.25) governs P_{mn}, a quantity not directly relevant to our problem, the determination of the mean magnetic field. Therefore, we are able to cast the basic equations of the second order correlation approximation in the form of a system of integro-differential equations, i.e.

$$\left\{\left(\frac{\partial}{\partial t} - \eta \Delta\right)\delta_{jn} - \varepsilon_{jkl}\varepsilon_{lmn}\frac{\partial}{\partial x_k}\bar{u}_m(\boldsymbol{x}, t)\right\}\overline{B}_n(\boldsymbol{x}, t)$$

$$= -\varepsilon_{jkl}\varepsilon_{lmn}\varepsilon_{pqr}\varepsilon_{rst}\frac{\partial}{\partial x_k}\iint \frac{\partial G_{np}(\boldsymbol{x}, \boldsymbol{x} + \boldsymbol{\xi}, t, t + \tau)}{\partial \xi_q} \tag{4.50}$$

$$Q_{ms}(\boldsymbol{x}, \boldsymbol{\xi}, t, \tau)\, \overline{B}_t(\boldsymbol{x} + \boldsymbol{\xi}, t + \tau)\, \mathrm{d}\boldsymbol{\xi}\, \mathrm{d}\tau,$$

$$\frac{\partial \overline{B}_k(\boldsymbol{x}, t)}{\partial x_k} = 0.$$

A similar procedure can be applied in the higher order approximations. We thus find in the third order case

$$\left\{\left(\frac{\partial}{\partial t} - \eta \Delta\right)\delta_{jn} - \varepsilon_{jkl}\varepsilon_{lmn}\frac{\partial}{\partial x_k}\bar{u}_m(\boldsymbol{x}, t)\right\}\overline{B}_n(\boldsymbol{x}, t)$$

$$= -\varepsilon_{jkl}\varepsilon_{lmn}\varepsilon_{j'k'l'}\varepsilon_{l'm'n}\frac{\partial}{\partial x_k}\iint \frac{\partial G_{nj'}(\boldsymbol{x}, \boldsymbol{x} + \boldsymbol{\xi}, t, t + \tau)}{\partial \xi_{k'}} \tag{4.51}$$

$$\Bigg\{Q_{mm'}(\boldsymbol{x}, \boldsymbol{\xi}, t, \tau)\, \overline{B}_{n'}(\boldsymbol{x} + \boldsymbol{\xi}, t + \tau)$$

$$- \varepsilon_{j''k''l''}\varepsilon_{l''m''n''}\iint \frac{\partial G_{n'j''}(\boldsymbol{x} + \boldsymbol{\xi}, \boldsymbol{x} + \boldsymbol{\xi} + \boldsymbol{\eta}, t + \tau, t + \tau + \sigma)}{\partial \eta_{k''}}$$

$$Q_{mm'm''}(\boldsymbol{x}, \boldsymbol{\xi}, \boldsymbol{\eta}; t, \tau, \sigma)\, \overline{B}_{n''}(\boldsymbol{x} + \boldsymbol{\xi} + \boldsymbol{\eta}, t + \tau + \sigma)\, \mathrm{d}\boldsymbol{\eta}\, \mathrm{d}\sigma\Bigg\}\, \mathrm{d}\boldsymbol{\xi}\, \mathrm{d}\tau,$$

$$\frac{\partial \overline{B}_k(\boldsymbol{x}, t)}{\partial x_k} = 0;$$

and in the case of fourth order correlation approximation

$$\left\{\left(\frac{\partial}{\partial t} - \eta\Delta\right)\delta_{jn} - \varepsilon_{jkl}\varepsilon_{lmn}\frac{\partial}{\partial x_k}\bar{u}_m(\boldsymbol{x}, t)\right\}\overline{B}_n(\boldsymbol{x}, t)$$

$$= -\varepsilon_{jkl}\varepsilon_{lmn}\varepsilon_{j'k'l'}\varepsilon_{l'm'n'}\frac{\partial}{\partial x_k}\iint\frac{\partial G_{nj'}(\boldsymbol{x}, \boldsymbol{x}+\boldsymbol{\xi}, t, t+\tau)}{\partial \xi_{k'}} \tag{4.52}$$

$$\Big\{Q_{mm'}(\boldsymbol{x}, \boldsymbol{\xi}, t, \tau)\,\overline{B}_{n'}(\boldsymbol{x}+\boldsymbol{\xi}, t+\tau)$$

$$-\varepsilon_{j''k''l''}\varepsilon_{l''m''n''}\iint\frac{G_{n'j''}(\boldsymbol{x}+\boldsymbol{\xi}, \boldsymbol{x}+\boldsymbol{\xi}+\boldsymbol{\eta}, t+\tau, t+\tau+\sigma)}{\partial \eta_{k''}}$$

$$[Q_{mm'm''}(\boldsymbol{x}, \boldsymbol{\xi}, \boldsymbol{\eta}, t, \tau, \sigma)\,\overline{B}_{n''}(\boldsymbol{x}+\boldsymbol{\xi}+\boldsymbol{\eta}, t+\tau+\sigma)$$

$$-\varepsilon_{j'''k'''l'''}\varepsilon_{l'''m'''n'''}\iint\frac{\partial G_{n''j'''}(\boldsymbol{x}+\boldsymbol{\xi}+\boldsymbol{\eta}, \boldsymbol{x}+\boldsymbol{\xi}+\boldsymbol{\eta}+\boldsymbol{\zeta}, t+\tau+\sigma, t+\tau+\sigma+\varrho)}{\partial \zeta_{k'''}}$$

$$(Q_{mm'm''m'''}(\boldsymbol{x}, \boldsymbol{\xi}, \boldsymbol{\eta}, \boldsymbol{\zeta}, t, \tau, \sigma, \varrho)$$

$$-\,Q_{mm'}(\boldsymbol{x}, \boldsymbol{\xi}, t, \tau)$$

$$Q_{m''m'''}(\boldsymbol{x}+\boldsymbol{\xi}+\boldsymbol{\eta}, \boldsymbol{x}+\boldsymbol{\xi}+\boldsymbol{\eta}+\boldsymbol{\zeta}, t+\tau+\sigma, t+\tau+\sigma+\varrho))$$

$$\overline{B}_{n'''}(\boldsymbol{x}+\boldsymbol{\xi}+\boldsymbol{\eta}+\boldsymbol{\zeta}, t+\tau+\sigma+\varrho)\,\mathrm{d}\boldsymbol{\zeta}\,\mathrm{d}\varrho]\,\mathrm{d}\boldsymbol{\eta}\,\mathrm{d}\sigma\Big\}\,\mathrm{d}\boldsymbol{\xi}\,\mathrm{d}\tau,$$

$$\frac{\partial \overline{B}_k(\boldsymbol{x}, t)}{\partial x_k} = 0\,.$$

When we now recall that $\overline{\boldsymbol{B}}$ is governed by the induction equation

$$\frac{\partial \overline{\boldsymbol{B}}}{\partial t} - \operatorname{curl}\,(\overline{\boldsymbol{u}}\times\overline{\boldsymbol{B}}) - \frac{1}{\mu\sigma}\Delta\overline{\boldsymbol{B}} = \operatorname{curl}\,\mathfrak{E}, \tag{4.53}$$

it becomes obvious that the turbulent electromotive force $\mathfrak{E}$ can be represented by the expression

$$\mathfrak{E}_l = \iint K_{lt}(\boldsymbol{x}, \boldsymbol{\xi}, t, \tau)\,\overline{B}_t(\boldsymbol{x}-\boldsymbol{\xi}, t-\tau)\,\mathrm{d}\boldsymbol{\xi}\,\mathrm{d}\tau. \tag{4.54}$$

The tensor K_{lt} may be obtained by the methods discussed in this chapter where a restriction to a low level of approximation is necessary for technica reasons only: The mathematical effort grows rapidly with the degree of approximation.

From (4.50) we derive in the case of the second order correlation approximation

$$K_{lt}(\boldsymbol{x}, \boldsymbol{\xi}, t, \tau) = \varepsilon_{lmn}\varepsilon_{pqr}\varepsilon_{rst}\frac{\partial G_{np}(\boldsymbol{x}, \boldsymbol{x}-\boldsymbol{\xi}, t, t-\tau)}{\partial \xi_q}Q_{ms}(\boldsymbol{x}, -\boldsymbol{\xi}, t, -\tau), \tag{4.55}$$

and for the third order approximation from (4.51)

$$K_{lt}(\boldsymbol{x}, \boldsymbol{\xi}, t, \tau) = \varepsilon_{lmn}\varepsilon_{j'k'l'}\varepsilon_{l'm'n'} \left[\frac{\partial G_{nj'}(\boldsymbol{x}, \boldsymbol{x}-\boldsymbol{\xi}, t, t-\tau)}{\partial \xi_{k'}} Q_{mm'}(\boldsymbol{x}, -\boldsymbol{\xi}, t, -\tau)\, \delta_{n't}\right.$$
$$+ \varepsilon_{j''k''l''}\varepsilon_{l''m''t} \iint \frac{\partial G_{nj'}(\boldsymbol{x}, \boldsymbol{x}-\boldsymbol{\xi}', t, t-\tau')}{\partial \xi'_{k'}} \frac{\partial G_{n'j''}(\boldsymbol{x}-\boldsymbol{\xi}', \boldsymbol{x}-\boldsymbol{\xi}, t-\tau', t-\tau)}{\partial \xi_{k''}}$$
$$\left. Q_{mm'm''}(\boldsymbol{x}, -\boldsymbol{\xi}', \boldsymbol{\xi}'-\boldsymbol{\xi}, t, -\tau', \tau'-\tau)\, \mathrm{d}\boldsymbol{\xi}'\, \mathrm{d}\tau'\right]. \tag{4.56}$$

We shall not give here the expression of the tensor K_{lt} in the fourth order approximation, which may easily be derived from (4.52).

In section 2.4. we stated already that $\mathfrak{E}$ is a linear functional of $\overline{\boldsymbol{B}}$. Relation (4.54) in combination with (4.55) or (4.56) defining the tensor K_{lt} furnishes now a rather explicit representation of this functional for different approximation levels.

4.7. On the convergence of the correlation approximation

For a mathematical justification of the correlation approximation we first discuss the convergence of a field sequence derived from the induction equation.

In the case of a vanishing velocity field the tensor G_{jp} introduced in section 4.5. is given by

$$G_{jp}(\boldsymbol{x}, \boldsymbol{\xi}, t, \tau) = \delta_{jp} G(\boldsymbol{x}-\boldsymbol{\xi}, t-\tau), \tag{4.57}$$

where

$$G(\boldsymbol{x}, t) = \begin{cases} 0, & \text{if} \quad t < 0, \\ \left(\dfrac{\mu\sigma}{4\pi t}\right)^{3/2} \exp\left(-\dfrac{\mu\sigma x^2}{4t}\right), & \text{if} \quad t \geqq 0. \end{cases} \tag{4.58}$$

Let us consider the induction equation (2.3) in the form

$$\frac{\partial B_j}{\partial t} - \frac{1}{\mu\sigma} \Delta B_j = \varepsilon_{jkl}\varepsilon_{lmn} \frac{\partial u_m B_n}{\partial x_k}, \tag{4.59}$$

which can be replaced by the integral equation

$$B_j(\boldsymbol{x}, t) = \int G(\boldsymbol{x}-\boldsymbol{x}', t-t_0)\, B_j(\boldsymbol{x}', t_0)\, \mathrm{d}\boldsymbol{x}'$$
$$- \varepsilon_{jkl}\varepsilon_{lmn} \int_{t_0}^{t}\int \frac{\partial G(\boldsymbol{x}-\boldsymbol{x}', t-t')}{\partial x'_k} u_m(\boldsymbol{x}', t')\, B_n(\boldsymbol{x}', t')\, \mathrm{d}\boldsymbol{x}'\, \mathrm{d}t'. \tag{4.60}$$

We define a sequence of fields $\boldsymbol{B}^{(\nu)}(\boldsymbol{x}, t)$, $\nu = 0, 1, 2, \ldots$ by

$$\boldsymbol{B}^{(0)}(\boldsymbol{x}, t) \ \text{arbitrary}, \quad B_j^{(\nu)}(\boldsymbol{x}, t) = \int G(\boldsymbol{x} - \boldsymbol{x}', t - t_0)\, B_j(\boldsymbol{x}', t_0)\, \mathrm{d}\boldsymbol{x}' \tag{4.61}$$

$$- \varepsilon_{jkl}\varepsilon_{lmn} \int_{t_0}^{t}\int \frac{\partial G(\boldsymbol{x} - \boldsymbol{x}', t - t')}{\partial x_k'} u_m(\boldsymbol{x}', t')\, B_n^{(\nu-1)}(\boldsymbol{x}', t')\, \mathrm{d}\boldsymbol{x}'\, \mathrm{d}t', \quad \nu = 1, 2, \ldots$$

It is obvious that $B_j^{(\nu)}(\boldsymbol{x}, t_0) = B_j(\boldsymbol{x}, t_0)$ for any $\nu \geqq 1$ and that, in the case of convergence, the field

$$\boldsymbol{B}^{(\infty)}(\boldsymbol{x}, t) = \lim_{\nu \to \infty} \boldsymbol{B}^{(\nu)}(\boldsymbol{x}, t)$$

solves the integral equation (4.60) and with it the induction equation (4.59). Consequently, the field $\boldsymbol{B}^{(\infty)}(\boldsymbol{x}, t)$ is a solution of the initial value problem of the induction equation.

We shall not give a detailed proof of convergence here but restrict ourselves to some remarks: We can obtain from sequence (4.61) another one by

$$\boldsymbol{b}^{(0)}(\boldsymbol{x}, t) = \boldsymbol{B}^{(0)}(\boldsymbol{x}, t), \tag{4.62}$$

$$\boldsymbol{b}^{(\nu)}(\boldsymbol{x}, t) = \boldsymbol{B}^{(\nu)}(\boldsymbol{x}, t) - \boldsymbol{B}^{(\nu-1)}(\boldsymbol{x}, t), \quad \nu \geqq 1,$$

and represent $\boldsymbol{B}^{(\infty)}$ by the series

$$\boldsymbol{B}^{(\infty)}(\boldsymbol{x}, t) = \sum_{\nu=0}^{\infty} \boldsymbol{b}^{(\nu)}(\boldsymbol{x}, t). \tag{4.63}$$

It has been proved that the series (4.63) is absolutely convergent for arbitrary finite values of t and t_0 and any bounded velocity field $\boldsymbol{u}$ (Krause [1, 2]). It is also necessary to impose certain conditions concerning the continuity and the differentiability of the functions involved in our problem, which we shall not specify here.

If we now construct a sequence $\boldsymbol{B}^{(\nu)}(\boldsymbol{x}, t)$ by choosing

$$B_j^{(0)}(\boldsymbol{x}, t) = \int G(\boldsymbol{x} - \boldsymbol{x}', t - t_0)\, B_j(\boldsymbol{x}', t_0)\, \mathrm{d}\boldsymbol{x}', \tag{4.64}$$

we can obtain from (4.61) the representation

$$B_j^{(\nu)}(\boldsymbol{x}, t) = \int G_{jp}^{(\nu)}(\boldsymbol{x}, \boldsymbol{x}', t, t_0)\, B_p(\boldsymbol{x}', t_0)\, \mathrm{d}\boldsymbol{x}', \tag{4.65}$$

where the tensors $G_{jp}^{(\nu)}(\boldsymbol{x}, \boldsymbol{x}', t, t_0)$ are defined by

$$G_{jp}^{(0)}(\boldsymbol{x}, \boldsymbol{x}', t, t_0) = \delta_{jp} G(\boldsymbol{x} - \boldsymbol{x}', t - t_0),$$

$$G_{jp}^{(\nu)}(\boldsymbol{x}, \boldsymbol{x}', t, t_0) = \delta_{jp} G(\boldsymbol{x} - \boldsymbol{x}', t - t_0) \tag{4.66}$$

$$+ \varepsilon_{jkl}\varepsilon_{lmn} \int_{t_0}^{t}\int \frac{\partial G(\boldsymbol{x} - \boldsymbol{x}'', t - t'')}{\partial x_k} u_m(\boldsymbol{x}'', t'')\, G_{np}^{(\nu-1)}(\boldsymbol{x}'', \boldsymbol{x}', t'', t_0)\, \mathrm{d}\boldsymbol{x}''\, \mathrm{d}t''.$$

The convergence of the sequence of tensors $G_{jp}^{(\nu)}$ is guaranteed by that of the sequence $\boldsymbol{B}^{(\nu)}$. Consequently, the recurrence relation (4.66) provides the possibility of representing the tensor G_{jp} introduced in section 4.5. by

$$G_{jp}(\boldsymbol{x}, \boldsymbol{x}', t, t_0) = \lim_{\nu\to\infty} G_{jp}^{(\nu)}(\boldsymbol{x}, \boldsymbol{x}', t, t_0). \tag{4.67}$$

With this representation the existence of the tensor G_{jp} is guaranteed for any bounded velocity field.

Let us now consider the equation

$$\frac{\partial B_j}{\partial t} - \varepsilon_{jkl}\varepsilon_{lmn}\frac{\partial \bar{u}_m B_n}{\partial x_k} - \frac{1}{\mu\sigma}\Delta B_j = \varepsilon_{jkl}\varepsilon_{lmn}\frac{\partial u'_m B_n}{\partial x_k}, \tag{4.68}$$

and let $G_{jp}(\boldsymbol{x}, \boldsymbol{x}', t, t')$ be the Green's tensor of the left-hand side of this equation. We can replace equation (4.68) by the integral equation

$$B_j(\boldsymbol{x}, t) = \int G_{jp}(\boldsymbol{x}, \boldsymbol{x}', t, t_0)\, B_p(\boldsymbol{x}', t_0)\, \mathrm{d}\boldsymbol{x}' \tag{4.69}$$

$$- \varepsilon_{pkl}\varepsilon_{lmn}\iint \frac{\partial G_{jp}(\boldsymbol{x}, \boldsymbol{x}', t, t')}{\partial x'_k} u'_m(\boldsymbol{x}', t')\, B_n(\boldsymbol{x}', t')\, \mathrm{d}\boldsymbol{x}'\, \mathrm{d}t',$$

and define a sequence of fields $\tilde{\boldsymbol{B}}^{(\nu)}(\boldsymbol{x}, t)$ similar to (6.41) by
$\tilde{\boldsymbol{B}}^{(0)}(\boldsymbol{x}, t)$ arbitrary,

$$\tilde{B}_j^{(\nu)}(\boldsymbol{x}, t) = \int G_{jp}(\boldsymbol{x}, \boldsymbol{x}', t, t_0)\, B_p(\boldsymbol{x}', t_0)\, \mathrm{d}\boldsymbol{x}' \tag{4.70}$$

$$- \varepsilon_{pkl}\varepsilon_{lmn}\int_{t_0}^{t}\int \frac{\partial G_{jp}(\boldsymbol{x}, \boldsymbol{x}', t, t')}{\partial x'_k} u'_m(\boldsymbol{x}', t')\, \tilde{B}_n^{(\nu-1)}(\boldsymbol{x}', t')\, \mathrm{d}\boldsymbol{x}'\, \mathrm{d}t'.$$

It is not necessary to prove convergence again. We can define the sequence

$$\tilde{\boldsymbol{b}}^{(0)}(\boldsymbol{x}, t) = \tilde{\boldsymbol{B}}^{(0)}(\boldsymbol{x}, t), \quad \tilde{\boldsymbol{b}}^{(\nu)}(\boldsymbol{x}, t) = \tilde{\boldsymbol{B}}^{(\nu)}(\boldsymbol{x}, t) - \tilde{\boldsymbol{B}}^{(\nu-1)}(\boldsymbol{x}, t), \tag{4.71}$$

and represent the field $\boldsymbol{B}^{(\infty)}$ by the series

$$\boldsymbol{B}^{(\infty)}(\boldsymbol{x}, t) = \sum_{\nu=0}^{\infty} \boldsymbol{b}^{(\nu)}(\boldsymbol{x}, t) \tag{4.72}$$

as was done subsequently to (4.61). We can, however, also arrive at the series (4.72) by substituting $\boldsymbol{u} = \bar{\boldsymbol{u}} + \boldsymbol{u}'$ into (4.61) and carrying out some rearrangement. Since the series (4.63) has been proved to be absolutely convergent, the same will hold for the series (4.72).

It is now obvious that the correlation approximation is based on a convergent procedure: We construct a sequence $\tilde{\boldsymbol{B}}^{(\nu)}(\boldsymbol{x}, t)$, $\nu = 0, 1, 2, \ldots$ by choosing in the formula (4.70) $\tilde{\boldsymbol{B}}^{(0)} = \bar{\boldsymbol{B}}$ and determine the fields

$$\mathfrak{E}^{(n)} = \overline{\boldsymbol{u}' \times \tilde{\boldsymbol{B}}^{(n)}}. \tag{4.73}$$

Assuming that the order of the operations of taking the limit and the average can be exchanged, we find that this field sequence will converge as well, and we can represent the turbulent electromotive force by the limit

$$\mathfrak{E}(\boldsymbol{x}, t) = \lim_{n\to\infty} \mathfrak{E}^{(n)}(\boldsymbol{x}, t) = \lim_{n\to\infty} \overline{\boldsymbol{u}'(\boldsymbol{x}, t) \times \tilde{\boldsymbol{B}}^{(n)}(\boldsymbol{x}, t)}. \tag{4.74}$$

CHAPTER 5

TWO-SCALE TURBULENCE

5.1. Introductory remarks

We mentioned in section 2.2. that we shall not have to refer to the nature of the averaging operation, but only to the properties (2.4) and to the commutation rules. If, however, the theory is applied to a certain observation or measurement, in most cases averages with respect to space or time coordinates must be taken. Then in particular the rules

$$\overline{\overline{F}} = \overline{F}, \quad \overline{F'} = 0 \tag{5.1}$$

are only approximately valid. The validity will be better the smaller the characteristic scales of the fluctuations compared with those of the mean fields.

Therefore, having in mind applications of the theory it is appropriate to require that either

$$\lambda_{\text{cor}} \ll \bar{\lambda}, \tag{5.2}$$

or

$$\tau_{\text{cor}} \ll \bar{\tau}, \tag{5.3}$$

or both the relations are fulfilled. Here and in the following, $\bar{\lambda}$ and $\bar{\tau}$ denote the characteristic length and time scales of the mean fields. If one of the relations (5.2), (5.3), or both, are fulfilled we speak of two-scale turbulence.

Already in section 2.4. the turbulent electromotive force was shown to be a functional of $\overline{\boldsymbol{B}}, \overline{\boldsymbol{u}}, \boldsymbol{u}'$, and we also found that only those of their values contribute to the value of $\mathfrak{E}$, which are taken from a certain neighbourhood of the space-time point under consideration. In the case of two-scale turbulence, i.e. (5.2) and (5.3) being fulfilled, $\overline{\boldsymbol{B}}$ can be represented by Taylor's formula, and, consequently, $\mathfrak{E}$ as a linear functional of $\overline{\boldsymbol{B}}$ by

$$\begin{aligned}\mathfrak{E}_i = \overline{(\boldsymbol{u}'\times\boldsymbol{B}')}_i = g_{ij}^{(00)}\overline{B}_j + g_{ijk}^{(10)}\frac{\partial\overline{B}_j}{\partial x_k} + g_{ijkl}^{(20)}\frac{\partial^2\overline{B}_j}{\partial x_k\,\partial x_l} + \cdots \\ + g_{ij}^{(01)}\frac{\partial\overline{B}_j}{\partial t} + g_{ijk}^{(11)}\frac{\partial^2\overline{B}_j}{\partial x_k\,\partial t} + g_{ijkl\ldots n}^{(\varkappa\nu)}\frac{\partial^{(\varkappa+\nu)}\overline{B}_j}{\partial x_k\,\partial x_l\ldots\partial x_n\,\partial t}.\end{aligned} \tag{5.4}$$

Now the tensor quantities $g^{(\varkappa\nu)}_{i\ldots n}$ appear, which are functionals of $\overline{\boldsymbol{u}}$, $\boldsymbol{u}'$. If in (5.4) space derivatives are taken into account up to the order $\varkappa$ and time derivatives up to the order ν, an error has to be expected of the order

$$O\left\{\left(\frac{\lambda_{\rm cor}}{\bar\lambda}\right)^{\varkappa}, \left(\frac{\tau_{\rm cor}}{\bar\tau}\right)^{\nu}\right\}.$$

If the back-reaction of the magnetic field is taken into account, the velocity fields $\overline{\boldsymbol{u}}$ and $\boldsymbol{u}'$ depend on $\overline{\boldsymbol{B}}$. It is worth noting that in this case the validity of (5.4) is not affected, whereas the tensors $g^{(\varkappa\nu)}_{ij\ldots n}$ are now functionals of $\overline{\boldsymbol{u}}$, $\boldsymbol{u}'$ and $\overline{\boldsymbol{B}}$.

5.2. Isotropic tensors

A property of the turbulence, e.g. isotropy, has to be reflected in the structure of the tensors $g_{i\ldots n}$. For an isotropic turbulence all mean quantities derived from it remain unchanged if undergoing a rotation. Tensors with this property are called isotropic tensors.

We already know isotropic tensors, e.g. the Kronecker tensor δ_{ij}. This tensor has the same components in all coordinate systems, this is clearly equivalent to the property of having unchanged components if undergoing an arbitrary rotation. The ε-tensor is a further example of an isotropic tensor of third rank and the product $\delta_{ij}\,\delta_{kl}$ is an isotropic tensor of fourth rank.

We shall now prove the following statements which are important in our deductions:

(i) If the tensor a_{ij} of second rank is isotropic, then

$$a_{ij} = \alpha\,\delta_{ij}\,. \tag{5.5}$$

(ii) If the tensor a_{ijk} of third rank is isotropic, then

$$a_{ijk} = \beta\varepsilon_{ijk}\,. \tag{5.6}$$

(iii) If the tensor a_{ijkl} of fourth rank is isotropic, then

$$a_{ijkl} = a\,\delta_{ij}\delta_{kl} + b\,\delta_{ik}\delta_{jl} + c\,\delta_{il}\delta_{jk}\,. \tag{5.7}$$

We denote the matrix of a rotation by D_{ij} where

$$D_{ij}D_{kj} = \delta_{ik}, \quad D_{ij}D_{il} = \delta_{jl}\,. \tag{5.8}$$

Hence a tensor undergoing this rotation is transformed by

$$a^{(\rm rot)}_{ij} = D_{ik}D_{jl}a_{kl}\,, \tag{5.9}$$

and the relation

$$a_{ij} = D_{ik}D_{jl}a_{kl} \tag{5.10}$$

holds for an isotropic tensor of rank two, where D_{ij} is an arbitrary rotation.

Let us first consider the 180°-rotation about the 3-axis given by

$$(D_{ij}^{(3)}) = \begin{pmatrix} -1 & 0 & 0 \\ 0 & -1 & 0 \\ 0 & 0 & 1 \end{pmatrix}. \tag{5.11}$$

Inserting (5.11) into (5.10) we find

$$a_{13} = -a_{13},\, a_{31} = -a_{31},\, a_{23} = -a_{23},\, a_{32} = -a_{32}, \tag{5.12}$$

and other relations which are fulfilled identically. From (5.12) we conclude

$$a_{13} = a_{31} = a_{23} = a_{32} = 0. \tag{5.31}$$

If we now consider the 180°-rotation about the 2-axis given by

$$(D_{ij}^{(2)}) = \begin{pmatrix} -1 & 0 & 0 \\ 0 & 1 & 0 \\ 0 & 0 & -1 \end{pmatrix}, \tag{5.14}$$

we find in addition

$$a_{12} = a_{21} = 0. \tag{5.15}$$

Let us now consider the 90°-rotation about the 3-axis given by

$$(\tilde{D}_{ij}^{(3)}) = \begin{pmatrix} 0 & -1 & 0 \\ 1 & 0 & 0 \\ 0 & 0 & 1 \end{pmatrix}. \tag{5.16}$$

Inserting it into (5.10) we obtain

$$a_{11} = a_{22}, \tag{5.17}$$

and in the same way we shall find

$$a_{11} = a_{33}, \tag{5.18}$$

if the 90°-rotation about the 2-axis is considered.

(5.12), (5.13), (5.15) and (5.17), (5.18) show that an isotropic tensor of second rank is indeed given by (5.5).

Statement (ii) may be proved analogously. For an isotropic tensor of third rank the relation

$$a_{ijk} = D_{il}D_{jm}D_{kn}a_{lmn} \tag{5.19}$$

must hold. Let us first consider those components with two or three equal indices. By inserting $D_{ij}^{(3)}$ or $D_{ij}^{(2)}$ into (5.19) relations are found which show that these components are equal to their opposite values and therefore vanish. Accordingly, only components with three different indices can be non-zero. Applying now $\tilde{D}_{ij}^{(3)}$ given by (5.16) to a_{123} we find

$$a_{123} = -a_{213}. \tag{5.20}$$

Also considering the 90°-rotation about the 1-axis and the 2-axis we see that by an exchange of any pair of indices the sign of the component will change. Thus, an isotropic tensor of third rank results which is given by (5.6).

For an isotropic tensor of fourth rank a_{ijkl} the relation

$$a_{ijkl} = D_{im}D_{jn}D_{kp}D_{lq}a_{mnpq} \tag{5.21}$$

must hold for any rotation D_{ij}. Considering the 180°-rotations about the coordinate axes we easily find that all components vanish apart from those which have an even number of equal indices. From an application of the 90°-rotations about the coördinate axes to (5.21) we conclude that any pair of indices can be exchanged without altering the value of the component. Thus we find four groups of equal components:

$$\begin{aligned}
&a_{1111} = a_{2222} = a_{3333} = A\,,\\
&a_{1122} = a_{2211} = a_{1133} = a_{3311} = a_{2233} = a_{3322} = B\,,\\
&a_{1212} = a_{2121} = a_{1313} = a_{3131} = a_{2323} = a_{3232} = C\,,\\
&a_{1221} = a_{2112} = a_{1331} = a_{3113} = a_{2332} = a_{3223} = D\,.
\end{aligned} \tag{5.22}$$

It is remarkable at this point that we have four free parameters in (5.22) whereas in (5.7) there are three free parameters only. For a final decision we shall now consider an arbitrary rotation about the 3-axis given by

$$D_{ij} = \begin{pmatrix} \cos\varphi & -\sin\varphi & 0 \\ \sin\varphi & \cos\varphi & 0 \\ 0 & 0 & 1 \end{pmatrix}, \tag{5.23}$$

where φ denotes the angle of rotation. For the component a_{1111} we obtain by inserting (5.23) into (5.20)

$$\begin{aligned} a_{1111} = {} & a_{1111}\cos^4\varphi + a_{2222}\sin^4\varphi + \cos^2\varphi\sin^2\varphi(a_{1122} \\ & + a_{2211} + a_{1212} + a_{2121} + a_{1221} + a_{2112}). \end{aligned} \tag{5.24}$$

With the notation (5.22) and the identity $\cos^4\varphi + \sin^4\varphi = 1 - 2\cos^2\varphi\sin^2\varphi$ we have the relation

$$A = A + 2\cos^2\varphi\sin^2\varphi\,(-A + B + C + D), \tag{5.25}$$

which is fulfilled for any φ if

$$A = B + C + D. \tag{5.26}$$

In agreement with (5.7) the number of free parameters is reduced to three, and it is easily confirmed that (5.22) and (5.26) are identical with (5.7) if $B = a$, $C = b$, $D = c$.

As far as isotropic tensors of arbitrary rank are concerned we shall only mention that such tensors of even rank can be represented by a sum of products of δ-tensors, and those of odd rank by a sum of tensors, where any summand is a product of one ε-tensor with δ-tensors.

Finally, an application of statements (i) and (iii) may be presented. We intend to evaluate the integrals

$$\int f(\xi)\, \xi_i \xi_j\, d\xi \quad \text{and} \quad \int f(\xi)\, \xi_i \xi_j \xi_k \xi_l\, d\xi$$

where $f(\xi)$ is a function of $\xi = \sqrt{\xi^2}$, which vanishes sufficiently strongly if $\xi \to \infty$, thus providing for convergence. Both integrals are clearly isotropic tensors, therefore from (i) and (iii) follows

$$\int f(\xi)\, \xi_i \xi_j\, d\xi = A\, \delta_{ij}, \tag{5.27}$$

$$\int f(\xi)\, \xi_i \xi_j \xi_k \xi_l\, d\xi = B(\delta_{ij}\delta_{kl} + \delta_{ik}\delta_{jl} + \delta_{il}\delta_{jk}).$$

For the ansatz of the second integral we have already used its symmetry with respect to all four indices. Contracting (5.27) we find

$$\int f(\xi)\, \xi^2\, d\xi = 3A, \quad \int f(\xi)\, \xi^4\, d\xi = 15B, \tag{5.28}$$

and finally

$$\int f(\xi)\, \xi_i \xi_j\, \mathrm{d}\xi = \delta_{ij} \frac{1}{3} \int f(\xi)\, \xi^2\, \mathrm{d}\xi, \tag{5.29}$$

$$\int f(\xi)\, \xi_i \xi_j \xi_k \xi_l\, \mathrm{d}\xi = (\delta_{ij}\delta_{kl} + \delta_{ik}\delta_{jl} + \delta_{il}\delta_{jk}) \frac{1}{15} \int f(\xi)\, \xi^4\, \mathrm{d}\xi. \tag{5.30}$$

5.3. Structures of the tensors $g_{ij\ldots n}$

Let us consider a physical system and the processes within it, and another system derived from this first one by rotating it. According to our fundamental knowledge of nature the processes in the rotated system are just those which are obtained by rotating the corresponding processes of the original system. Tensors decribing physical quantities in one system are, therefore, to be derived from the corresponding tensors in the other system by the same rotation. Fundamental relations between physical quantities are independent of whether the one system or the other is considered. Consequently, relations between tensors can only be provided by tensors which are invariant with respect to rotation, hence those relations are provided by the isotropic tensors. In our special case we can conclude that the tensors $g_{ij\ldots n}$ introduced in (5.4) are to be related by isotropic tensors to the tensor quantities characterizing the turbulent motion under consideration.

It is fundamental knowledge too that we can derive a real physical system by reflecting a given one, e.g. as described in section 3.3. A fundamental relation connecting physical quantities has, therefore, to remain unchanged if a reflection is carried out. We have mentioned before that there are vector quantities of different behaviour with respect to reflections, the polar vectors and the axial vectors. In order to generalize this definition we consider a tensor of rank n, $a_{i_1 i_2 \ldots i_n}$, being constructed as a product of n vectors, where k of these vectors are axial and $n-k$ polar. If a reflection is carried out, according to (3.2), (3.3), this tensor will transform like

$$a^{(\mathrm{ref})}_{i_1\ldots i_n}(\boldsymbol{x}, t) = (-1)^{n-k}\, a_{i_1\ldots i_n}(-\boldsymbol{x}, t). \tag{5.31}$$

If k is odd we have, by definition, a pseudo-tensor, for even k a tensor. Hence a tensor of arbitrary rank will behave like

$$a^{(\mathrm{ref})}_{i_1\ldots i_n}(\boldsymbol{x}, t) = (-1)^{n}\, a_{i_1\ldots i_n}(-\boldsymbol{x}, t), \tag{5.32}$$

if reflected, and a pseudo-tensor like

$$a^{(\mathrm{ref})}_{i_1\ldots i_n}(\boldsymbol{x}, t) = (-1)^{n+1}\, a_{i_1\ldots i_n}(-\boldsymbol{x}, t). \tag{5.33}$$

Since δ_{ik} and ε_{ikl} are constant by definition, according to (5.32) and (5.33), δ_{ik} is a tensor but ε_{ikl} a pseudo-tensor.

An equality of two tensor quantities can only exist if both are either tensors or pseudo-tensors, because of the symmetry with respect to the reflections just mentioned. Therefore, since the turbulent electromotive force $\mathfrak{E}$ is a polar vector but the mean magnetic field an axial one, all the quantities $g_{ij\ldots n}$ introduced in (5.4) must be pseudo-tensors.

5.4. Examples for the turbulent electromotive force

With the considerations carried out in the foregoing section a rather definite structure of the functional becomes visible which describes the connection between $\mathfrak{E}$ and $\overline{\boldsymbol{B}}$. In the following we shall restrict ourselves to the case where a sufficiently accurate description is possible if in (5.4) only the spatial derivatives up to the first order are taken into account. Then an error of the order $O\left\{\left(\frac{\lambda_{\text{cor}}}{\bar{\lambda}}\right)^2, \frac{\tau_{\text{cor}}}{\bar{\tau}}\right\}$ must be expected. Simplifying the notation by writing

$$a_{ik} = g_{ik}^{(00)}, \quad b_{ikl} = g_{ikl}^{(10)}, \tag{5.34}$$

from (5.4) we arrive at the relation

$$\mathfrak{E}_i = a_{ik}\overline{B}_k + b_{ikl}\frac{\partial \overline{B}_k}{\partial x_l}, \tag{5.35}$$

where a_{ik} and b_{ikl} are pseudo-tensors depending on $\overline{\boldsymbol{u}}$ and $\boldsymbol{u}'$.

As a first example we choose a vanishing mean velocity field, $\overline{\boldsymbol{u}} = 0$, and a homogeneous isotropic steady turbulent velocity field $\boldsymbol{u}'$. The only tensors available for the construction of a_{ik} and b_{ikl} are the isotropic tensors, and therefore we have, according to section 5.2.

$$a_{ik} = \alpha\, \delta_{ik}, \quad b_{ikl} = \beta\varepsilon_{ikl}, \tag{5.36}$$

where α is a pseudo-scalar. Hence we find for the turbulent electromotive force

$$\mathfrak{E} = \alpha\overline{\boldsymbol{B}} - \beta \operatorname{curl} \overline{\boldsymbol{B}}, \tag{5.37}$$

thus confirming relation (3.5). If the turbulent field $\boldsymbol{u}'$ is also assumed to be mirrorsymmetric, α must vanish, since it has to change its sign if $\boldsymbol{u}'$ is reflected, whereas $\boldsymbol{u}'$ does not change.

It is worth mentioning that a real turbulence undergoing no external influence is in good approximation a homogeneous isotropic mirrorsymmetric turbulence if it has grown old. For example, a turbulence excited in a homogeneous flow by a grid has these properties at a certain distance from the grid. There are no conditions known, where such a turbulence is non-mirrorsymmetric. Thus our foregoing example is rather academic. None the less we shall discuss it, since it is of great interest in dynamo theory. As we shall see in one of our following examples there are, indeed, real turbulences with non-vanishing α, but they are not isotropic.

As a second example we take again $\overline{\boldsymbol{u}} = 0$, with the turbulent motion being anisotropic now. Responsible for the anisotropy shall be a vector field $\boldsymbol{g}$, which can be the gradient of the turbulence intensity or the gradient of the density. Constructing the pseudo-tensors a_{ik}, b_{ikl} we shall restrict ourselves to linear expressions in the quantity $\boldsymbol{g}$ thus finding

$$a_{ik} = \gamma\varepsilon_{ikl}g_l, \quad b_{ikl} = \beta\varepsilon_{ikl}. \tag{5.38}$$

For the turbulent electromotive force we obtain

$$\mathfrak{E} = -\beta \operatorname{curl} \overline{\boldsymbol{B}} - \gamma\boldsymbol{g}\times\overline{\boldsymbol{B}}. \tag{5.39}$$

The electromotive force perpendicular to g and $\overline{B}$ shall later on be interpreted as a pumping effect.

In our third example the mean motion may be a rigid rotation and the turbulence u' shall be influenced by the motion $\overline{u}$ and the angular velocity Ω. Again, with the restriction to linear expressions in $\overline{u}$ and Ω we find

$$a_{ik} = \gamma' \varepsilon_{ikl} \overline{u}_l, \quad b_{ikl} = \beta \varepsilon_{ikl} - \beta_1 \Omega_i \delta_{kl} - \beta_2 \Omega_k \delta_{il} - \beta_3 \Omega_l \delta_{ik}. \tag{5.40}$$

From this we obtain for the turbulent electromotive force

$$\mathfrak{E} = -\beta \operatorname{curl} \overline{B} - \gamma' \overline{u} \times \overline{B} - \beta_3 (\Omega \cdot \operatorname{grad}) \overline{B} - \beta_2 \operatorname{grad} (\Omega \cdot \overline{B}); \tag{5.41}$$

the term with β_1 does not contribute since $\overline{B}$ is source-free. Suppose we neglect the influence of the mean motion, i.e. $\gamma' = 0$. Then both examples deal with turbulences under an influence described by one vector quantity. However, since in the one case g is a polar vector whereas in the other case Ω is an axial one, we get quite different results.

(5.41) describes the turbulent electromotive force $\mathfrak{E}$ for a turbulence undergoing the influence of Coriolis forces. It can be rewritten in the form

$$\mathfrak{E} = -\beta \operatorname{curl} \overline{B} - \gamma' \overline{u} \times \overline{B} + \mu \beta_3 \Omega \times \overline{j} - (\beta_3 + \beta_2) \operatorname{grad} (\Omega \cdot \overline{B}). \tag{5.42}$$

As we shall see later, the electromotive force proportional to $\Omega \times \overline{j}$ can lead to dynamo action.

Our fourth example is closely related to the turbulent motions in a convective layer on a rotating body. There, apart from the angular velocity, we have to take into account that the radial direction is preferred. This is already the case for geometrical reasons, moreover, the gradient of density or the gradient of turbulence intensity or both will be parallel to this direction. Thus we have a turbulence under influences described by the polar vector quantities $\overline{u}$ and g and the axial vector Ω. Assuming again linearity we find

$$a_{ik} = -\alpha_1'(g \cdot \Omega)\, \delta_{ik} - \alpha_2' g_i \Omega_k - \alpha_3' g_k \Omega_i + \gamma \varepsilon_{ikl} g_l + \gamma'' \varepsilon_{ikl} \overline{u}_l, \tag{5.43}$$

$$b_{ikl} = \beta \varepsilon_{ikl} - \beta_1 \Omega_i \delta_{kl} - \beta_2 \Omega_k \delta_{il} - \beta_3 \Omega_l \delta_{ik}. \tag{5.44}$$

Hence, for the turbulent electromotive force in a convective layer on a rotating body we obtain

$$\begin{aligned} \mathfrak{E} = &-\beta \operatorname{curl} \overline{B} - \gamma g \times \overline{B} - \gamma'' \overline{u} \times \overline{B} - \beta_3 (\Omega \cdot \operatorname{grad}) \overline{B} - \beta_2 \operatorname{grad} (\Omega \cdot \overline{u}) \\ &- \alpha_1'(g \cdot \Omega)\, \overline{B} - \alpha_2'(g \cdot \overline{B})\, \Omega - \alpha_3'(\Omega \cdot \overline{B})\, g. \end{aligned} \tag{5.45}$$

We emphasize the appearance of the electromotive force $-\alpha_1'(g \cdot \Omega)\, \overline{B}$, which is parallel to the mean magnetic field. In contrast to the first example it is clearly to be seen here that this electromotive force may be a quite natural phenomenon in a convective layer on a rotating body.

Up to this point of our considerations on the structure of $\mathfrak{E}$ we have not gained any information whether the coefficients α, β, γ, ... are non-zero. This requires additional investigations.

5.5. Representation of the tensors $g_{ij\ldots n}$

Before arriving at first results by combining the derivations of this and the foregoing chapter we want to assess what we have achieved with our deductions so far.

The relations (5.37), (5.39), (5.41), (5.42), (5.45) give rather explicit expressions for the turbulent electromotive force $\mathfrak{E}$. Only the scalars α_1', α_2', α_3', β, β_1, β_2, β_3, γ, γ'' appear as unknown quantities. It is essential that these expressions for $\mathfrak{E}$ are deduced with a rather weak restriction: the two-scale property of the turbulence.

A final determination of $\mathfrak{E}$ would, of course, require a general solution of the turbulence problem, which does not exist. However, since in our case uncertainty exists for a few scalars only, the insufficiency of the theory of turbulence is of minor importance here.

We shall now use the results of the foregoing chapter for the derivation of more explicit expressions for the pseudo-tensors $g_{ij\ldots n}$. Representing $\overline{\boldsymbol{B}}$ in (4.54) by Taylor's formula and comparing the results with (5.4) we easily find

$$a_{ij} = g_{ij}^{(00)} = \iint K_{ij}(\boldsymbol{x}, \boldsymbol{\xi}, t, \tau)\, \mathrm{d}\boldsymbol{\xi}\, \mathrm{d}\tau, \tag{5.46}$$

$$b_{ijk} = g_{ijk}^{(10)} = -\iint K_{ij}(\boldsymbol{x}, \boldsymbol{\xi}, t, \tau)\, \xi_k\, \mathrm{d}\boldsymbol{\xi}\, \mathrm{d}\tau, \tag{5.47}$$

and, generally,

$$g_{ij}^{(0\nu)} = \frac{(-1)^\nu}{\nu!} \iint K_{ij}(\boldsymbol{x}, \boldsymbol{\xi}, t, \tau)\, \tau^\nu\, \mathrm{d}\boldsymbol{\xi}\, \mathrm{d}\tau, \tag{5.48}$$

$$g_{ijk}^{(1\nu)} = \frac{(-1)^{\nu+1}}{\nu!} \iint K_{ij}(\boldsymbol{x}, \boldsymbol{\xi}, t, \tau)\, \xi_k \tau^\nu\, \mathrm{d}\boldsymbol{\xi}\, \mathrm{d}\tau, \tag{5.49}$$

$$g_{ijk\ldots n}^{(\varkappa\nu)} = \frac{(-1)^{\varkappa+\nu}}{\varkappa!\,\nu!} \iint K_{ij}(\boldsymbol{x}, \boldsymbol{\xi}, t, \tau)\, \xi_k \ldots \xi_n \tau^\nu\, \mathrm{d}\boldsymbol{\xi}\, \mathrm{d}\tau. \tag{5.50}$$

The tensor K_{ij} can be used as in (4.55) or in another form for a higher approximation level.

In order to give an impression of some of the following deductions we now deduce α and β for a homogeneous isotropic and steady turbulence and a vanishing mean velocity field. Using the second order correlation approximation we obtain from (5.46), (5.47) with (4.55) and (4.57)

$$a_{ij} = \varepsilon_{ilm}\varepsilon_{mnp}\varepsilon_{pqj} \iint \frac{\partial G(\xi, \tau)}{\partial \xi_n} Q_{lq}(-\xi, -\tau)\, d\xi\, d\tau, \tag{5.51}$$

$$b_{ijk} = -\varepsilon_{ilm}\varepsilon_{mnp}\varepsilon_{pqj} \iint \frac{\partial G(\xi, \tau)}{\partial \xi_n} \xi_k Q_{lq}(-\xi, -\tau)\, d\xi\, d\tau. \tag{5.52}$$

Since for homogeneous turbulence the correlation tensor Q_{lq} as defined by (4.3) does not depend on $\boldsymbol{x}, t$ we simply write

$$Q_{lq}(\xi, \tau) = \overline{u_l'(\boldsymbol{x}, t)\, u_q'(\boldsymbol{x} + \xi, t + \tau)}, \tag{5.53}$$

and by exchanging $\boldsymbol{x}, t$ for $\boldsymbol{x} - \xi, t - \tau$ we find the symmetry relation

$$Q_{lq}(-\xi, -\tau) = Q_{ql}(\xi, \tau). \tag{5.54}$$

We already know that $a_{ij} = \alpha\, \delta_{ij}$. Hence we get by contracting (5.51)

$$\alpha = \frac{1}{3} \varepsilon_{ilm}\varepsilon_{mnp}\varepsilon_{pqi} \iint \frac{\partial G(\xi, \tau)}{\partial \xi_n} Q_{ql}(\xi, \tau)\, d\xi\, d\tau$$

$$= \frac{1}{3} \varepsilon_{nlq} \iint \frac{\partial G(\xi, \tau)}{\partial \xi_n} Q_{ql}(\xi, \tau)\, d\xi\, d\tau = -\frac{1}{3} \iint G(\xi, \tau)\, \varepsilon_{nlq} \frac{\partial Q_{ql}(\xi, \tau)}{\partial \xi_n}\, d\xi\, d\tau.$$

Inserting now the definition of the correlation tensor (5.53) we finally obtain (Krause [1])

$$\alpha = -\frac{1}{3} \iint G(\xi, \tau)\, \overline{\boldsymbol{u}'(\boldsymbol{x}, t) \cdot \operatorname{curl} \boldsymbol{u}'(\boldsymbol{x} + \xi, t + \tau)}\, d\xi\, d\tau. \tag{5.55}$$

This formula is a generalization of both the formulae (3.29) and (3.47). We find these earlier results as limiting cases of (5.55). Let us first consider the high-conductivity limit characterized by $\tau_{cor} \ll \mu\sigma\lambda_{cor}^2$. Concerning the spatial integration we note that $G(\xi, \tau)$ is significantly different from zero only if $\xi \lesseqgtr \sqrt{\tau/\mu\sigma}$. Since the scalar product vanishes if $\tau > \tau_{cor}$ we have $\xi \lesseqgtr \sqrt{\tau_{cor}/\mu\sigma} \ll \lambda_{cor}$ for the region where the integrand is significantly different from zero in the high-conductivity limit. On these conditions the scalar product does not vary and we obtain (3.29), since

$$\int G(\xi, \tau)\, d\xi = 1. \tag{5.56}$$

Alternatively, $\mu\sigma\lambda_{cor}^2 \ll \tau_{cor}$, we can carry out the τ-integration by assuming the scalar product $\overline{\boldsymbol{u}' \operatorname{curl} \boldsymbol{u}'}$ to be constant. Since

$$\int G(\xi, \tau)\, d\tau = \frac{\mu\sigma}{4\pi\xi}, \tag{5.57}$$

we obtain (3.47).

As for a_{ij} we know that the tensor b_{ijk} has the form $\beta\varepsilon_{ijk}$. Hence, by multiplying (5.52) by ε_{ijk} we find

$$\beta = \frac{1}{6}\,\varepsilon_{ijk}b_{ijk} = -\varepsilon_{ijk}\varepsilon_{ilm}\varepsilon_{mnp}\varepsilon_{pqj}\iint \frac{\partial G(\xi,\tau)}{\partial \xi_n}\,\xi_k Q_{ql}(\xi,\tau)\,\mathrm{d}\xi\,\mathrm{d}\tau$$

$$= -\,(\delta_{kl}\delta_{nq} + \delta_{kq}\delta_{nl})\,\frac{1}{6}\iint \frac{\partial G(\xi,\tau)}{\partial \xi_n}\,\xi_k Q_{ql}(\xi,\tau)\,\mathrm{d}\xi\,\mathrm{d}\tau. \tag{5.58}$$

We now take into account that G depends on the magnitude ξ only, hence we have

$$\frac{\partial G(\xi,\tau)}{\partial \xi_n} = \frac{\xi_n}{\xi}\,\frac{\partial G(\xi,\tau)}{\partial \xi}, \tag{5.59}$$

and find

$$\beta = -\,\frac{1}{3}\iint \frac{1}{\xi}\,\frac{\partial G(\xi,\tau)}{\partial \xi}\,\overline{(\boldsymbol{\xi}\cdot\boldsymbol{u}'(\boldsymbol{x},t))\,(\boldsymbol{\xi}\cdot\boldsymbol{u}'(\boldsymbol{x}+\boldsymbol{\xi},t+\tau)}\,\mathrm{d}\xi\,\mathrm{d}\tau. \tag{5.60}$$

This formula confirms both the formulae (3.30) and (3.48), and generalizes them.

We can arrive at an alternative expression by introducing the longitudinal correlation function f defined by

$$\xi_k Q_{kl}(\xi,\tau) = f(\xi,\tau)\,\xi_l. \tag{5.61}$$

Inserting (5.59) and (5.61) into (5.58) we obtain

$$\beta = -\,\frac{1}{3}\iint \xi\,\frac{\partial G(\xi,\tau)}{\partial \xi}\,f(\xi,\tau)\,\mathrm{d}\xi\,\mathrm{d}\tau, \tag{5.62}$$

a relation which is due to Rädler [2].

CHAPTER 6

HOMOGENEOUS TURBULENCE

6.1. Introductory remarks

We start our more detailed discussion with the treatment of homogeneous and steady turbulence. For this kind of turbulence all mean quantities are constant with respect to variations in space and time, and thus, in particular, the pseudo-tensors $g_{ij\ldots h}$ introduced in the foregoing chapter are constant.

Moreover, since there is a close connection between the turbulent velocity field and the mean velocity field, we assume the mean velocity field to be constant, i.e. that we have $\overline{\boldsymbol{u}} = 0$ in a proper system of reference. Hence the Green's tensor G_{jp} is well known, given by (4.57) and (4.58).

We have already mentioned that the two-point two-time correlation tensor Q_{ij} is a function only of the relative coordinates ξ, τ and that it fulfils the symmetry condition (5.54). There is still another condition: Let x_ν, t_ν, $\nu = 1, \ldots, N$, be space-time points. Then for any set of complex numbers $c_{i\nu}$, $i = 1, 2, 3$; $\nu = 1, \ldots, N$ we have

$$\overline{\left\{\sum_{\nu=1}^{N} c_{i\nu} u_i'(\boldsymbol{x}_\nu, t_\nu)\right\} \left\{\sum_{\mu=1}^{N} c_{k\mu}^* u_k'(\boldsymbol{x}_\mu, t_\mu)\right\}} \geqq 0. \tag{6.1}$$

Carrying out the multiplications and taking the average we obtain

$$\sum_{\nu,\mu=1}^{N} c_{i\nu} c_{k\mu} Q_{ik}(\boldsymbol{x}_\nu - \boldsymbol{x}_\mu, t_\nu - t_\mu) \geqq 0. \tag{6.2}$$

This inequality demonstrates Bochner's theorem (BOCHNER [1], cf. also CRAMER [1]), which states that Q_{ik} can be the correlation tensor of a homogeneous stationary random field, $\boldsymbol{u}'$, if and only if it is positive semi-definite in the sense of (6.2).

If, in addition, the turbulence is isotropic, then for the construction of Q_{ik} there are only available the isotropic tensors δ_{ik} and ε_{ikl} and the vector ξ. Therefore the general expression reads

$$Q_{ik}(\xi, \tau) = A(\xi, \tau)\, \delta_{ik} + B(\xi, \tau)\, \xi_i \xi_k + C(\xi, \tau)\, \varepsilon_{ikl} \xi_l. \tag{6.3}$$

A, B, C depend only on the magnitude of ξ, i.e. $\xi = \sqrt{\xi^2}$, and therefore constitute even functions of ξ. Then (5.54) implies that they are even also with respect to τ. Bochner's theorem (6.2) provides for additional restrictions on these functions. But we shall not record them here, since a more convenient form will be available by considering the Fourier transformed quantities.

6.2. Fourier transformation of homogeneous steady random fields

Let $F(\boldsymbol{x}, t)$ be a function of space and time. By $\hat{F}(\boldsymbol{k}, \omega)$ we denote its Fourier transform defined by

$$\hat{F}(\boldsymbol{k}, \omega) = \frac{1}{(2\pi)^4} \int\int F(\boldsymbol{x}, t)\, \mathrm{e}^{-\mathrm{i}(\boldsymbol{kx}-\omega t)}\, \mathrm{d}\boldsymbol{x}\, \mathrm{d}t; \tag{6.4}$$

or the inversion formula

$$F(\boldsymbol{x}, t) = \int\int \hat{F}(\boldsymbol{k}, \omega)\, \mathrm{e}^{\mathrm{i}(\boldsymbol{kx}-\omega t)}\, \mathrm{d}\boldsymbol{k}\, \mathrm{d}\omega. \tag{6.5}$$

Some basic relations may be noted:

(i) If $F(\boldsymbol{x}, t)$ is real it follows that

$$\hat{F}(-\boldsymbol{k}, -\omega) = \hat{F}^*(\boldsymbol{k}, \omega). \tag{6.6}$$

(ii) The Fourier transform of the product of the two functions $F(\boldsymbol{x}, t)$ and $G(\boldsymbol{x}, t)$ is given by the convolution integral

$$(\widehat{F \cdot G})\,(\boldsymbol{k}, \omega) = (\hat{F} * \hat{G})\,(\boldsymbol{k}, \omega) = \int\int \hat{F}(\boldsymbol{k}', \omega')\, \hat{G}(\boldsymbol{k} - \boldsymbol{k}', \omega - \omega')\, \mathrm{d}\boldsymbol{k}'\, \mathrm{d}\omega'. \tag{6.7}$$

(iii) For $\boldsymbol{k} = 0$, $\omega = 0$ in (ii) we obtain Parseval's theorem:

$$\int\int F(\boldsymbol{x}, t)\, G(\boldsymbol{x}, t)\, \mathrm{d}\boldsymbol{x}\, \mathrm{d}t = (2\pi)^4 \int\int \hat{F}(\boldsymbol{k}, \omega)\, \hat{G}^*(\boldsymbol{k}, \omega)\, \mathrm{d}\boldsymbol{k}\, \mathrm{d}\omega, \tag{6.8}$$

or, in scalar product notation,

$$(F, G) = (2\pi)^4\, (\hat{F}, \hat{G}). \tag{6.9}$$

For a homogeneous and steady random field like $\boldsymbol{u}'(\boldsymbol{x}, t)$ the Fourier transform in the classical sense is not defined, since $\boldsymbol{u}'$ generally does not vanish if $\boldsymbol{x}$ and t tend to infinity. They can, however, be defined as functionals. That is, we understand the symbol (F, φ) not as a scalar product of functions F and φ but as a functional $(F, \cdot)$ operating on the finite function φ, and we take Parseval's theorem as a definition of the Fourier transform $(\hat{F}, \cdot)$ of the functional $(F, \cdot)$:

$$(\hat{F}, \hat{\varphi}) = \left(\frac{1}{2\pi}\right)^4 (F, \varphi). \tag{6.10}$$

$\hat{\varphi}$ exists in the classical sense because φ is a finite function, i.e. a function which is zero outside a finite region. For the sake of convenience we shall write again F, $\hat{F}$ instead of $(F, \cdot)$, $(\hat{F}, \cdot)$.

We are now in a position to work with Fourier transforms of homogeneous steady random fields. It will be useful to know that in the definition of $\hat{F}$ the functions φ need not be finite but may be functions which are exponentially decreasing as $\boldsymbol{x}$, t tend to infinity. Thus if F is a homogeneous steady random field (taken as a functional) and G a function of that kind, then $\hat{F}$ is given by

$$(\hat{F}, \hat{G}) = \frac{1}{(2\pi)^4} \int\int F(\boldsymbol{x}, t)\, G(\boldsymbol{x}, t)\, \mathrm{d}\boldsymbol{x}\, \mathrm{d}t, \tag{6.11}$$

As a useful example we choose $F(\boldsymbol{x}, t) \equiv 1$. From (6.11) and (6.4) we obtain

$$(\hat{F}, \hat{G}) = \frac{1}{(2\pi)^4} \int\int G(\boldsymbol{x}, t)\, \mathrm{d}\boldsymbol{x}\, \mathrm{d}t = \hat{G}(0, 0), \tag{6.12}$$

and $\hat{F}$ turns out to be the Dirac δ-functional centered at $\boldsymbol{k} = 0$, $t = 0$.

As a second example we take $F(\boldsymbol{x}, t) = x_i$. We find

$$(\hat{F}, \hat{G}) = \frac{1}{(2\pi)^4} \int\int x_i G(\boldsymbol{x}, t)\, \mathrm{d}\boldsymbol{x}\, \mathrm{d}t = \left(i\, \frac{\partial \hat{G}(\boldsymbol{k}, \omega)}{\partial k_i}\right)_{\boldsymbol{k}=0, \omega=0}.$$

i.e., that $\hat{F}$ is proportional to a derivative of the Dirac δ-functional.

Thus we have the pairs

$$F(\boldsymbol{x}, t) = 1, \quad \hat{F}(\boldsymbol{k}, \omega) = \delta(\boldsymbol{k}, \omega); \tag{6.13}$$

and

$$F(\boldsymbol{x}, t) = x_i, \quad \hat{F}(\boldsymbol{k}, \omega) = \mathrm{i}\, \frac{\partial \delta(\boldsymbol{k}, \omega)}{\partial k_i}. \tag{6.14}$$

As a third example we note the pair

$$F(\boldsymbol{x}, t) = x_i x_j, \quad \hat{F}(\boldsymbol{k}, \omega) = -\frac{\partial^2 \delta(\boldsymbol{k}, \omega)}{\partial k_i\, \partial k_j}. \tag{6.15}$$

6.3. A basic relation connecting the means of the Fourier transforms with the Fourier transform of the correlation tensor

For the functionals $\hat{u}_i$, $\hat{u}_j$ we have in the above sense

$$\begin{aligned}\overline{(\hat{u}_i, \hat{F})\, (\hat{u}_j, \hat{G})} &= \frac{1}{(2\pi)^8} \int\int\int\int \overline{u_i'(\boldsymbol{x}, t)\, F(\boldsymbol{x}, t)\, u_j'(\boldsymbol{x}', t')\, G(\boldsymbol{x}', t')}\, \mathrm{d}\boldsymbol{x}'\, \mathrm{d}t'\, \mathrm{d}\boldsymbol{x}\, \mathrm{d}t \\ &= \frac{1}{(2\pi)^8} \int\int\int\int Q_{ij}(\boldsymbol{x}' - \boldsymbol{x}, t' - t)\, F(\boldsymbol{x}, t)\, G(\boldsymbol{x}', t')\, \mathrm{d}\boldsymbol{x}\, \mathrm{d}t\, \mathrm{d}\boldsymbol{x}'\, \mathrm{d}t'.\end{aligned} \tag{6.16}$$

Taking into account that the Fourier transform of $Q_{ij}(\boldsymbol{x}' - \boldsymbol{x}, t' - t)$ with respect to $\boldsymbol{x}'$, t' is given by $\hat{Q}_{ij}(\boldsymbol{k}', \omega') \exp[-i(\boldsymbol{k}'\boldsymbol{x} - \omega' t)]$ we obtain by the definition of the Fourier transforms for real functions F and G

$$\overline{(\hat{u}_i, \hat{F})\,(\hat{u}_j, \hat{G})} = \iint \hat{Q}_{ij}(\boldsymbol{k}', \omega')\,\hat{F}(\boldsymbol{k}', \omega')\,\hat{G}^*(\boldsymbol{k}', \omega')\,\mathrm{d}\boldsymbol{k}'\,\mathrm{d}\omega' \tag{6.17}$$
$$= \iiiint \hat{Q}_{ij}(\boldsymbol{k}', \omega')\,\delta(\boldsymbol{k} + \boldsymbol{k}', \omega + \omega')\,\hat{F}^*(\boldsymbol{k}, \omega)\,\hat{G}^*(\boldsymbol{k}', \omega')\,\mathrm{d}\boldsymbol{k}'\,\mathrm{d}\omega'\,\mathrm{d}\boldsymbol{k}\,\mathrm{d}\omega\,.$$

Let S be the space of all real-valued admitted functions. Then (6.16) and (6.17) define functionals on the product space $S \times S$:

$$\left(\frac{1}{2\pi}\right)^8 (\overline{u_i' \times u_j'}, F \times G) = (\overline{\hat{u}_i \times \hat{u}_j}, \hat{F} \times \hat{G})$$

(with obvious symbolic notation), where $\overline{\hat{u}_i \times \hat{u}_j}$ is the Fourier transform of the functional $\overline{u_i' \times u_j'}$. These functionals are integral transformations with the kernels

$$\overline{u_i'(\boldsymbol{x}, t)\,u_j'(\boldsymbol{x}', t')} = Q_{ij}(\boldsymbol{x}' - \boldsymbol{x}, t' - t)$$

and

$$\overline{\hat{u}_i(\boldsymbol{k}, \omega)\,\hat{u}_j(\boldsymbol{k}', \omega')} = \hat{Q}_{ij}(\boldsymbol{k}', \omega')\,\delta(\boldsymbol{k} + \boldsymbol{k}', \omega + \omega') \tag{6.18}$$

respectively.

6.4. Bochner's theorem

$Q_{ij}(\boldsymbol{\xi}, \tau)$ is a real quantity, therefore we have from (6.6)

$$\hat{Q}_{ij}(-\boldsymbol{k}, -\omega) = \hat{Q}_{ij}^*(\boldsymbol{k}, \omega)\,. \tag{6.19}$$

Moreover, from the symmetry relation (5.54) we obtain

$$\hat{Q}_{ij}(\boldsymbol{k}, \omega) = \hat{Q}_{ji}(-\boldsymbol{k}, -\omega)\,. \tag{6.20}$$

Combining the relations (6.19) and (6.20) we find

$$\hat{Q}_{ji}(\boldsymbol{k}, \omega) = \hat{Q}_{ij}^*(\boldsymbol{k}, \omega)\,, \tag{6.21}$$

i.e. the Fourier transform of the correlation tensor is Hermitian.

The inequality (6.2) can be cast in the form

$$\iint \hat{Q}_{ij}(\boldsymbol{k}, \omega) \sum_{\nu,\mu=1}^{N} c_{i\nu} \mathrm{e}^{\mathrm{i}(\boldsymbol{k}\boldsymbol{x}_\nu - \omega t_\nu)}\, c_{j\mu}^* \mathrm{e}^{-\mathrm{i}(\boldsymbol{k}\boldsymbol{x}_\mu - \omega t_\mu)}\,\mathrm{d}\boldsymbol{k}\,\mathrm{d}\omega \geqq 0\,. \tag{6.22}$$

If we introduce the quantities

$$X_i = \sum_{\nu=1}^{N} c_{i\nu} e^{i(\boldsymbol{k}\boldsymbol{x}_\nu - \omega t_\nu)}, \tag{6.23}$$

we can write instead of (6.22)

$$\int\int \hat{Q}_{ij}(\boldsymbol{k}, \omega)\, X_i(\boldsymbol{k}, \omega)\, X_j^*(\boldsymbol{k}, \omega)\, \mathrm{d}\boldsymbol{k}\, \mathrm{d}\omega \geqq 0, \tag{6.24}$$

This inequality holds for arbitrary $c_{i\nu}$, $\boldsymbol{x}_\nu$, t_ν if and only if

$$\hat{Q}_{ij}(\boldsymbol{k}, \omega)\, X_i X_j^* \geqq 0, \tag{6.25}$$

i.e. if $\hat{Q}_{ij}(\boldsymbol{k}, \omega)$ is a positive semidefinite Hermitian tensor. This is a form of Bochner's theorem far more convenient than (6.2).

6.5. Isotropic turbulence

In (6.3) we already introduced the correlation tensor of the second rank of a homogeneous isotropic steady turbulence. Having in mind the determination of the Fourier transformed tensor we note the relations

$$\widehat{B\xi_i\xi_j} = -\frac{\partial^2 \hat{B}}{\partial k_i\, \partial k_j}, \quad \widehat{C\xi_i} = i\,\frac{\partial \hat{C}}{\partial k_i}, \tag{6.26}$$

which are easily derived from (6.7), (6.14) and (6.15) by regarding that

$$\left(\hat{F} * \frac{\partial \hat{G}}{\partial k_i}\right) = \frac{\partial}{\partial k_i}(\hat{F} * \hat{G}), \tag{6.27}$$

for arbitrary functions $\hat{F}$ and $\hat{G}$.

From (6.3) and (6.26) it follows for the Fourier transformed correlation tensor of the second rank of a homogeneous isotropic steady turbulence

$$\hat{Q}_{ij}(\boldsymbol{k}, \omega) = \hat{A}(k, \omega)\, \delta_{ij} - \frac{\partial^2 \hat{B}(k, \omega)}{\partial k_i\, \partial k_j} + i\varepsilon_{ijk} \frac{\partial \hat{C}(k, \omega)}{\partial k_k}. \tag{6.28}$$

The functions $\hat{A}$, $\hat{B}$, $\hat{C}$ depend only on the magnitude of $\boldsymbol{k}$. On carrying out the differentiations we therefore obtain

$$\hat{Q}_{ij}(\boldsymbol{k}, \omega) = \left(\hat{A} - \frac{1}{k}\frac{\partial \hat{B}}{\partial k}\right)\delta_{ij} - \left(\frac{\partial^2 \hat{B}}{\partial k^2} - \frac{1}{k}\frac{\partial \hat{B}}{\partial k}\right)\frac{k_i k_j}{k^2} + \frac{i}{k}\frac{\partial \hat{C}}{\partial k}\varepsilon_{ijk} k_k. \tag{6.29}$$

We now derive the conditions which Bochner's theorem imposes on the functions $\hat{A}$, $\hat{B}$, $\hat{C}$. For simplicity we write

$$\hat{Q}_{ij}(\boldsymbol{k}, \omega) = \hat{F}(k, \omega)\, \delta_{ij} + \hat{G}(k, \omega)\, k_i k_j + i\hat{H}(k, \omega)\, \varepsilon_{ijk} k_k, \tag{6.30}$$

where

$$\hat{F} = \hat{A} - \frac{1}{k}\frac{\partial \hat{B}}{\partial k}, \quad \hat{G} = -\frac{1}{k^2}\left(\frac{\partial^2 \hat{B}}{\partial k^2} - \frac{1}{k}\frac{\partial \hat{B}}{\partial k}\right), \quad \hat{H} = \frac{1}{k}\frac{\partial \hat{C}}{\partial k}. \tag{6.31}$$

$\hat{Q}_{ij}$ is positive semidefinite if and only if

(i) the trace of $\hat{Q}_{ij}$ is non-negative, i.e. if

$$3\hat{F} + k^2\hat{G} = 0; \tag{6.32}$$

(ii) the trace of the tensor of the algebraic complements, $\hat{q}_{ij}$,is non-negative, where $\hat{q}_{ij}$ is defined by

$$\hat{q}_{ij}(\boldsymbol{k}, \omega) = \varepsilon_{imn}\varepsilon_{jpq}\hat{Q}_{mp}\hat{Q}_{nq}. \tag{6.33}$$

Thus we have

$$\varepsilon_{imn}\varepsilon_{ipq}\hat{Q}_{mp}\hat{Q}_{nq} = 4\hat{F}(\hat{F} + k^2\hat{G}) + 2(\hat{F}^2 - k^2\hat{H}^2) \geqq 0; \tag{6.34}$$

(iii) the determinant of the tensor $\hat{Q}_{ij}$ is non-negative, i.e.

$$\varepsilon_{ijk}\varepsilon_{pqr}\hat{Q}_{ip}\hat{Q}_{jq}\hat{Q}_{kr} = 6(\hat{F} + k^2\hat{G})\,(\hat{F}^2 - k^2\hat{H}^2) \geqq 0. \tag{6.35}$$

(6.32), (6.34) and (6.35) can be replaced by the more convenient conditions

$$\hat{F} + k^2\hat{G} \geqq 0, \quad \hat{F} \geqq |k\hat{H}|. \tag{6.36}$$

(6.32), (6.34) and (6.35) are clearly a consequence of (6.36). In order to prove the converse let us assume (6.32), (6.34) and (6.35) are valid and one of the conditions (6.36) is violated. Because of (6.35) the other relation (6.36) must be violated too. Then (6.34) requires $\hat{F} < 0$, thus giving $2\hat{F} + (\hat{F} + k^2\hat{G}) < 0$, in contradiction to (6.32). Consequently, according to Bochner's theorem the tensor $\hat{Q}_{ij}$ given by (6.3) is the correlation tensor of the second rank of a homogeneous isotropic steady random field, if and only if

$$\hat{A} - \frac{\partial^2 \hat{B}}{\partial k^2} \geqq 0, \quad \hat{A} - \frac{1}{k}\frac{\partial \hat{B}}{\partial k} \geqq \left|\frac{\partial \hat{C}}{\partial k}\right|. \tag{6.37}$$

(Krause and Roberts [2]). This follows from (6.36) in combination with (6.31).

6.6. Two special cases: Incompressible turbulence and random sound waves

For incompressible turbulence we have

$$\frac{\partial u_i'(\boldsymbol{x}, t)}{\partial x_i} = 0, \tag{6.38}$$

and, therefore, for the correlation tensor

$$\frac{\partial Q_{ij}(\xi, \tau)}{\partial \xi_i} = 0, \quad \frac{\partial Q_{ij}(\xi, \tau)}{\partial \xi_j} = 0. \tag{6.39}$$

In Fourier space these conditions read

$$k_i \hat{u}_i(\boldsymbol{k}, \omega) = 0, \tag{6.40}$$

and for the correlation tensor

$$k_i \hat{Q}_{ij}(\boldsymbol{k}, \omega) = 0, \quad k_j \hat{Q}_{ij}(\boldsymbol{k}, \omega) = 0. \tag{6.41}$$

If, in addition, the turbulence is isotropic we find from (6.29)

$$\hat{A} - \frac{\partial^2 \hat{B}}{\partial k^2} = 0, \tag{6.42}$$

and the correlation tensor simplifies to

$$\hat{Q}_{ij}(\boldsymbol{k}, \omega) = \hat{Q}(k, \omega)\,(k^2\,\delta_{ij} - k_i k_j) + \frac{i}{k}\,\frac{\partial \hat{C}(k, \omega)}{\partial k}\,\varepsilon_{ijk} k_k, \tag{6.43}$$

where

$$k^2 \hat{Q}(k, \omega) = \hat{A}(k, \omega) - \frac{1}{k}\,\frac{\partial \hat{B}(k, \omega)}{\partial k}, \tag{6.44}$$

and, due to Bochner's theorem (6.37),

$$\hat{Q}(k, \omega) \geqq \left| \frac{1}{k^2}\,\frac{\partial \hat{C}(k, \omega)}{\partial k} \right|. \tag{6.45}$$

Hence, in particular, $\hat{Q}$ is a non-negative function.

We note here the incompressibility condition in ξ-space

$$\frac{1}{\xi}\,\frac{\partial A}{\partial \xi} + \xi\,\frac{\partial B}{\partial \xi} + 4B = 0, \tag{6.46}$$

which can easily be derived by inserting (6.3) into (6.39). In terms of the longitudinal correlation function f introduced in (5.61) this condition can be rewritten

$$A = f + \frac{\xi}{2}\,\frac{\partial f}{\partial \xi}, \quad B = -\frac{1}{2\xi}\,\frac{\partial f}{\partial \xi}. \tag{6.47}$$

A different case we have assuming the turbulence is given by random sound waves thus having a potential:

$$u_i'(\boldsymbol{x}, t) = -\frac{\partial \Phi(\boldsymbol{x}, t)}{\partial x_i}. \tag{6.48}$$

Φ is a homogeneous random function. For the correlation tensor we find

$$\begin{aligned}Q_{ij}(\xi,\tau) &= \overline{\frac{\partial\Phi(\boldsymbol{x},t)}{\partial x_i}\,\frac{\partial\Phi(\boldsymbol{x}+\xi,t+\tau)}{\partial\xi_j}}\\ &= \frac{\partial}{\partial x_i}\overline{\left[\Phi(\boldsymbol{x},t)\,\frac{\partial\Phi(\boldsymbol{x}+\xi,t+\tau)}{\partial\xi_j}\right]} - \overline{\Phi(\boldsymbol{x},t)\,\frac{\partial^2\Phi(\boldsymbol{x}+\xi,t+\tau)}{\partial\xi_i\,\partial\xi_j}}\\ &= -\frac{\partial^2 R(\xi.\tau)}{\partial\xi_i\,\partial\xi_j}\,,\end{aligned} \tag{6.49}$$

where R is the correlation function

$$R(\xi,\tau) = \overline{\Phi(\boldsymbol{x},t)\,\Phi(\boldsymbol{x}+\xi,t+\tau)}\,. \tag{6.50}$$

In Fourier space we have

$$\hat{Q}_{ij}(\boldsymbol{k},\omega) = k_i k_j \hat{R}(\boldsymbol{k},\omega)\,, \tag{6.51}$$

and Bochner's theorem (6.36) simply reads

$$\hat{R}(\boldsymbol{k},\omega) \geqq 0\,. \tag{6.52}$$

6.7. Fourier transform of the Green's function tensor. Evaluation of integrals in the limiting cases

As we said, this chapter shall be restricted to cases of vanishing mean flow. For these the Green's function tensor G_{jp} is known, given by (4.57) and (4.58). The special dependence on the arguments allows us to write

$$G_{jp}(\boldsymbol{x},\xi,t,\tau) = G_{jp}(\boldsymbol{x}-\xi,t-\tau) \tag{6.53}$$

and to introduce the Fourier transform by

$$G_{jp}(\boldsymbol{x}-\xi,t-\tau) = \int\!\!\int \hat{G}_{jp}(\boldsymbol{k},\omega)\,\mathrm{e}^{\mathrm{i}[\boldsymbol{k}(\boldsymbol{x}-\xi)-\omega(t-\tau)]}\,\mathrm{d}\boldsymbol{k}\,\mathrm{d}\omega\,, \tag{6.54}$$

where

$$\hat{G}_{jp}(\boldsymbol{k},\omega) = \delta_{jp}\hat{G}(\boldsymbol{k},\omega)\,. \tag{6.55}$$

We can easily derive the function $\hat{G}(\boldsymbol{k},\omega)$ from the Fourier transformed condition (iii) in section 4.5., which because of (6.4) reads

$$(-\mathrm{i}\omega + \eta k^2)\,\hat{G}_{jp} = \frac{\delta_{jp}}{(2\pi)^4}\,. \tag{6.56}$$

Hence we obtain

$$\hat{G}(\boldsymbol{k}, \omega) = \frac{1}{(2\pi)^4} \frac{1}{\eta k^2 - \mathrm{i}\omega}. \tag{6.57}$$

As was already seen in section 5.5. in our investigations there are certain integrals of interest in which the integrand is a product of the Green's function with another function of space and time. Let A be such a quantity. In virtue of Parseval's theorem (6.8) we can write

$$A = \iint G(\xi, \tau)\, F(\xi, \tau)\, \mathrm{d}\xi\, \mathrm{d}\tau = (2\pi)^4 \iint \hat{G}(\boldsymbol{k}, \omega)\, \hat{F}^*(\boldsymbol{k}, \omega)\, \mathrm{d}\boldsymbol{k}\, \mathrm{d}\omega, \tag{6.58}$$

or explicitily,

$$A = \int_0^\infty \!\! \int \left(\frac{\mu\sigma}{4\pi\tau}\right)^{3/2} \exp\left(-\frac{\mu\sigma\xi^2}{4\tau}\right) F(\xi, \tau)\, \mathrm{d}\xi\, \mathrm{d}\tau = \iint \frac{\hat{F}^*(\boldsymbol{k}, \omega)}{\eta k^2 - \mathrm{i}\omega}\, \mathrm{d}\boldsymbol{k}\, \mathrm{d}\omega. \tag{6.59}$$

Often we wish to know this quantity A in one of the limiting cases, the high-conductivity limit, i.e. $\tau_{\mathrm{cor}} \ll \mu\sigma\lambda_{\mathrm{cor}}^2$ or $\eta = \frac{1}{\mu\sigma} \to 0$, or the low-conductivity limit, i.e. $\tau_{\mathrm{cor}} \gg \mu\sigma\lambda_{\mathrm{cor}}^2$ or $\eta = \frac{1}{\mu\sigma} \to \infty$.

Inserting $\zeta = \sqrt{\mu\sigma}\,\xi$ into (6.59) we get

$$A = \int_0^\infty \!\! \int \frac{1}{(4\pi\tau)^{3/2}} \mathrm{e}^{-\zeta^2/4\tau} F\left(\frac{\zeta}{\sqrt{\mu\sigma}}, \tau\right) \mathrm{d}\zeta\, \mathrm{d}\tau$$

$$\to \int_0^\infty \!\! \int \frac{1}{(4\pi\tau)^{3/2}} \mathrm{e}^{-\zeta^2/4\tau} F(0, \tau)\, \mathrm{d}\zeta\, \mathrm{d}\tau = \int_0^\infty F(0, \tau)\, \mathrm{d}\tau, \text{ if } \sigma \to \infty. \tag{6.60}$$

Hence we obtain in the high-conductivity limit

$$A = \int_0^\infty F(0, \tau)\, \mathrm{d}\tau = \iint \frac{\hat{F}^*(\boldsymbol{k}, \omega)}{-\mathrm{i}\omega}\, \mathrm{d}\boldsymbol{k}\, \mathrm{d}\omega. \tag{6.61}$$

In case the integral in Fourier space does not exist, a special interpretation of relation (6.61) is needed: Let $\psi(t)$ be the integral of the δ-functional defined by

$$\psi(t) = \int_{-\infty}^{t} \delta(t')\, \mathrm{d}t'. \tag{6.62}$$

Then

$$\hat{\psi}(\omega) = \frac{1}{2\pi} \frac{1}{-\mathrm{i}\omega}. \tag{6.63}$$

Now we can understand the second integral in (6.61) as the value at $\hat{F}^*(\boldsymbol{k}, \omega)$ of the Fourier transform of the functional $(2\pi)^4 \psi(t)\, \delta(\boldsymbol{x})$. Now by the definition of Fourier transforms of functionals the first integral in (6.61) is equal to the second.

Substituting into (6.59) $\varrho = \dfrac{\mu\sigma}{4\tau}$, we find

$$A = \frac{\mu\sigma}{4\sqrt{\pi^3}} \int_0^\infty \int \frac{1}{\sqrt{\varrho}} \mathrm{e}^{-\varrho\xi^2} F\left(\xi, \frac{\mu\sigma}{4\varrho}\right) \mathrm{d}\xi\, \mathrm{d}\varrho \to \frac{\mu\sigma}{4\sqrt{\pi^3}} \int_0^\infty \int \frac{\mathrm{e}^{-\varrho\xi^2}}{\sqrt{\varrho}} F(\xi, 0)\, \mathrm{d}\xi\, \mathrm{d}\varrho$$

if $\sigma \to 0$. Carrying out the ϱ-integration we obtain in the low-conductivity limit

$$A = \frac{\mu\sigma}{4\pi} \int \frac{F(\xi, 0)}{\xi} \mathrm{d}\xi = \mu\sigma \iint \frac{\hat{F}^*(\boldsymbol{k}, \omega)}{k^2} \mathrm{d}\boldsymbol{k}\, \mathrm{d}\omega. \tag{6.64}$$

In this case the equality of the two integrals is obvious because a function A is the regular solution of the equation

$$\Delta A(\xi) = -\mu\sigma F(\xi, 0), \tag{6.65}$$

there is the well-known representation

$$A(0) = \frac{\mu\sigma}{4\pi} \int \frac{F(\xi, 0)}{\xi} \mathrm{d}\xi. \tag{6.66}$$

Let $A(\xi)$ be represented by the Fourier integral

$$A(\xi) = \int \tilde{A}(\boldsymbol{k})\, \mathrm{e}^{\mathrm{i}\boldsymbol{k}\xi}\, \mathrm{d}\boldsymbol{k}, \tag{6.67}$$

then from (6.65) follows

$$\tilde{A}(\boldsymbol{k}) = \frac{\mu\sigma}{k^2} \int \hat{F}(\boldsymbol{k}, \omega)\, \mathrm{d}\omega, \tag{6.68}$$

and therefore

$$A(0) = \int \tilde{A}(\boldsymbol{k})\, \mathrm{d}\boldsymbol{k} = \mu\sigma \iint \frac{\hat{F}(\boldsymbol{k}, \omega)}{k^2} \mathrm{d}\boldsymbol{k}\, \mathrm{d}\omega. \tag{6.69}$$

As $F(\xi, 0)$ is real, the equality of the integrals in (6.64) is evident.

CHAPTER 7

MEAN-FIELD ELECTRODYNAMICS FOR HOMOGENEOUS TURBULENCE IN THE CASE OF VANISHING MEAN FLOW

7.1. Determination of the tensor a_{ij}

In section 5.5. we already derived the representation of the tensor a_{ij} in the frame of the second order correlation approximation. Taking into account Parseval's theorem (6.8) and the symmetry relation (5.54) we have according to (5.51)

$$\begin{aligned} a_{ij} &= \varepsilon_{ilm}\varepsilon_{mnp}\varepsilon_{pqj}\iint \frac{\partial G(\xi,\tau)}{\partial\xi_n}\, Q_{ql}(\boldsymbol{\xi},\tau)\,\mathrm{d}\boldsymbol{\xi}\,\mathrm{d}\tau \\ &= -\varepsilon_{ilm}\varepsilon_{mnp}\varepsilon_{pqj}\iint G(\xi,\tau)\,\frac{\partial Q_{ql}(\boldsymbol{\xi},\tau)}{\partial\xi_n}\,\mathrm{d}\boldsymbol{\xi}\,\mathrm{d}\tau \\ &= +\mathrm{i}\varepsilon_{ilm}\varepsilon_{mnp}\varepsilon_{pqj}\iint \frac{k_n\hat{Q}_{lq}(\boldsymbol{k},\omega)}{\eta k^2-\mathrm{i}\omega}\,\mathrm{d}\boldsymbol{k}\,\mathrm{d}\omega\,. \end{aligned} \tag{7.1}$$

Of special interest is the quantity α which we define by

$$\alpha = \frac{1}{3}\,a_{ii}\,, \tag{7.2}$$

thus including non-isotropic conditions too. By contracting (7.1) we find

$$\begin{aligned} \alpha &= -\frac{1}{3}\,\varepsilon_{nlq}\iint G(\xi,\tau)\,\frac{\partial Q_{ql}(\boldsymbol{\xi},\tau)}{\partial\xi_n}\,\mathrm{d}\boldsymbol{\xi}\,\mathrm{d}\tau \\ &= -\frac{1}{3}\iint G\,(\xi,\tau)\,\overline{\boldsymbol{u}'(\boldsymbol{x},t)\cdot\operatorname{curl}\boldsymbol{u}'(\boldsymbol{x}+\boldsymbol{\xi},t+\tau)}\,\mathrm{d}\boldsymbol{\xi}\,\mathrm{d}\tau \\ &= +\frac{\mathrm{i}}{3}\,\varepsilon_{nlq}\iint \frac{k_n\hat{Q}_{lq}(\boldsymbol{k},\omega)}{\eta k^2-\mathrm{i}\omega}\,\mathrm{d}\boldsymbol{k}\,\mathrm{d}\omega\,. \end{aligned} \tag{7.3}$$

The first two lines show that the definition (7.2) of α leads back to the same formula as for the isotropic case (c.f. (5.55)), the last line is due to Parseval's theorem.

From the analysis in section 5.4. we can take that it is of interest to know whether the tensor a_{ij} is symmetric or not. For this reason we consider the vector $\gamma \boldsymbol{g}$ defined by

$$\gamma g_k = \frac{1}{2} \varepsilon_{ijk} a_{ij} . \tag{7.4}$$

In order to fix the value of γ let $\boldsymbol{g}$ be a unit vector. From (7.1) we obtain

$$\gamma g_k = -\frac{1}{2} \iint G(\xi, \tau) \left[\frac{\partial Q_{kl}(\xi, \tau)}{\partial \xi_l} + \frac{\partial Q_{lk}(\xi, \tau)}{\partial \xi_l}\right] \mathrm{d}\xi \, \mathrm{d}\tau . \tag{7.5}$$

Using the symmetry condition (5.54) and exchanging ξ for $-\xi$ in the second summand we can rewrite (7.5) in the form

$$\gamma g_k = -\frac{1}{2} \iint G(\xi, \tau) \left[\frac{\partial Q_{kl}(\xi, \tau)}{\partial \xi_l} - \frac{\partial Q_{kl}(\xi, -\tau)}{\partial \xi_l}\right] \mathrm{d}\xi \, \mathrm{d}\tau . \tag{7.6}$$

This relation enables us to conclude that a_{ij} is symmetric, i.e. $\gamma = 0$, for a number of interesting cases:

(i) The tensor a_{ij} is symmetric for an incompressible turbulence.

(ii) The tensor a_{ij} is symmetric for a turbulence where the correlation tensor is an even function of the relative time τ.

This is obvious from (6.75). An interesting example illustrating (ii) is isotropic turbulence. By taking into account (6.58) and (6.64) it can easily be confirmed that:

(iii) The tensor a_{ij} is symmetric in the low-conductivity limit.

Combining statements (i) and (iii) we confirm Moffatt's result [2] that the tensor a_{ij} is symmetric for an incompressible turbulence in the low-conductivity limit.

The equation of continuity,

$$\frac{\partial \varrho}{\partial t} + \operatorname{div} \varrho \boldsymbol{u} = 0 , \tag{7.7}$$

furnishes by way of second order correlation approximation the relation

$$\frac{\partial}{\partial \tau} \overline{u_k'(\boldsymbol{x}, t) \, \varrho'(\boldsymbol{x} + \xi, t + \tau)} + \bar{\varrho} \frac{\partial}{\partial \xi_l} Q_{kl}(\xi, \tau) = 0 , \tag{7.8}$$

if we put for the mass density $\varrho = \bar{\varrho} + \varrho'$. This enables us to rewrite (7.6) in the form

$$\gamma \boldsymbol{g} = \frac{1}{2\bar{\varrho}} \iint G(\xi, \tau) \frac{\partial}{\partial \tau} \overline{\boldsymbol{u}'(\boldsymbol{x}, t) \left[\varrho'(\boldsymbol{x} + \xi, t + \tau) + \varrho'(\boldsymbol{x} + \xi, t - \tau)\right]} \mathrm{d}\xi \, \mathrm{d}\tau , \tag{7.9}$$

from which, with the aid of (6.61), we obtain in the high-conductivity limit

$$\gamma \boldsymbol{g} = -\frac{1}{\bar{\varrho}} \overline{\boldsymbol{u}'(\boldsymbol{x}, t) \, \varrho'(\boldsymbol{x}, t)} = \overline{\boldsymbol{u}} = 0 , \tag{7.10}$$

since we assume, for physical reasons, that there is no mean mass transport, i.e. $\overline{\varrho \boldsymbol{u}} = \bar{\varrho}\bar{\boldsymbol{u}} + \overline{\varrho' \boldsymbol{u}'} = 0$.

Thus we can add a fourth statement:

(iv) The tensor a_{ij} is symmetric in the high-conductivity limit.

7.2. The pumping effect

If we take into account only the turbulent electromotive force $\mathfrak{E}$ provided by the antisymmetric part of the tensor a_{ij} then, by the definition (7.4) of $\boldsymbol{g}$, the behaviour of the mean magnetic field is governed by the equation

$$\frac{\partial \overline{\boldsymbol{B}}}{\partial t} + \operatorname{curl}\,(\gamma \boldsymbol{g} \times \overline{\boldsymbol{B}}) - \frac{1}{\mu\sigma} \Delta\, \overline{\boldsymbol{B}} = 0. \tag{7.11}$$

From this equation it is clear that the action of $\mathfrak{E}$ on the mean magnetic field is the same as that of a constant velocity field $\boldsymbol{u} = -\gamma \boldsymbol{g}$, i.e. the mean magnetic field can be transported through the turbulent medium with the velocity $-\gamma \boldsymbol{g}$, although there is no mean motion. Following DROBYSHEVSKIJ and YUFEREV [1] we call the action of such a turbulence "pumping effect".

DROBYSHEVSKIJ and YUFEREV proved the pumping effect to exist for an incompressible stationary cellular motion by numerical calculations. Since such a motion resembles a random motion in the low-conductivity limit one must suspect that statements (i) and (iii) derived in the foregoing paragraph are due to the approximation level only. This is, indeed, the case as shown by MOFFATT [6], who considered the electromotive force in a third order approximation. Let us, therefore, derive the vector $\gamma \boldsymbol{g}$ on the basis of the third order correlation approximation.

According to (4.56), (4.57) and (5.46) we have for a homogeneous steady turbulence

$$\begin{aligned} a_{ij} = &-\varepsilon_{ikl}\varepsilon_{lmn}\varepsilon_{npj} \iint G(\xi, \tau) \frac{\partial Q_{pk}(\xi, \tau)}{\partial \xi_m} \,\mathrm{d}\xi\, \mathrm{d}\tau \\ &+ \varepsilon_{ikl}\varepsilon_{lmn}\varepsilon_{npq}\varepsilon_{qrs}\varepsilon_{stj} \iiiint G(\xi, \tau)\, G(\xi', \tau') \\ &\quad \frac{\partial^2 Q_{kpt}(-\xi, -\xi', -\tau, -\tau')}{\partial \xi_m\, \partial \xi'_r} \,\mathrm{d}\xi\, \mathrm{d}\tau\, \mathrm{d}\xi'\, \mathrm{d}\tau', \end{aligned} \tag{7.12}$$

where the correlation tensor of the third rank, Q_{kpt}, is defined by (4.12). We clearly have the relation

$$Q_{kpt}(-\xi, -\xi', -\tau, -\tau') = Q_{tpk}(\xi', \xi, \tau', \tau). \tag{7.13}$$

Hence we obtain from (7.4) and (7.12), (7.13)

$$\gamma g_j = -\frac{1}{2}\int\int G(\xi,\tau)\left[\frac{\partial Q_{jl}(\xi,\tau)}{\partial \xi_l} - \frac{Q_{jl}(\xi,-\tau)}{\partial \xi_l}\right] d\xi\, d\tau$$
$$+ \frac{1}{2}\int\int\int\int G(\xi,\tau)\, G(\xi',\tau')\frac{\partial^2}{\partial \xi_k\, \partial \xi_l'}[Q_{ljk}(\xi,\xi',\tau,\tau') - Q_{kjl}(\xi,\xi',\tau,\tau')$$
$$- Q_{jlk}(\xi,\xi',\tau,\tau') - Q_{lkj}(\xi,\xi',\tau,\tau')]\, d\xi\, d\xi'\, d\tau\, d\tau'. \qquad (7.14)$$

For a homogeneous incompressible turbulence the correlation tensor of third rank fulfils the conditions

$$\frac{\partial Q_{pqr}(\xi,\xi',\tau,\tau')}{\partial \xi_p} = 0, \qquad (7.15)$$

$$\frac{\partial Q_{pqr}(\xi,\xi',\tau,\tau')}{\partial \xi_q} = \frac{\partial Q_{pqr}(\xi,\xi',\tau,\tau')}{\partial \xi_q'}, \qquad (7.16)$$

$$\frac{\partial Q_{pqr}(\xi,\xi',\tau,\tau')}{\partial \xi_r'} = 0, \qquad (7.17)$$

which are easily obtained from the definition (4.12) if div $\boldsymbol{u}' = 0$ is taken into account. Consequently we have for an incompressible turbulence

$$\gamma g_j = \frac{1}{2}\int\int\int\int G(\xi,\tau)\, G(\xi',\tau')\frac{\partial^2}{\partial \xi_k\, \partial \xi_l'}[Q_{ljk}(\xi,\xi',\tau,\tau')$$
$$- Q_{jlk}(\xi,\xi',\tau,\tau') - Q_{lkj}(\xi,\xi',\tau,\tau')]\, d\xi\, d\xi'\, d\tau\, d\tau'. \qquad (7.18)$$

The model studied by Drobyshevskij and Yuferev and by Moffatt is one example in which the value of γ given by (7.18) does not vanish.

7.3. Dynamo action of homogeneous turbulence

The symmetric part of the tensor a_{ij} describes qualitatively new features of the behaviour of the magnetic field: Dynamo action of the turbulent motion will overcome the Ohmic dissipation thus providing for growing or—in case of equilibrium—non-decaying magnetic fields.

We get insight into this situation most easily by considering homogeneous isotropic turbulence having helicity, i.e. the turbulent electromotive force $\mathfrak{E}$ is given by (5.37) with $\alpha \neq 0$ and the mean magnetic field is governed by the equation

$$\frac{\partial \overline{\boldsymbol{B}}}{\partial t} = \alpha \operatorname{curl} \overline{\boldsymbol{B}} + \eta_T \Delta \overline{\boldsymbol{B}}, \quad \operatorname{div} \overline{\boldsymbol{B}} = 0, \qquad (7.19)$$

where we introduced the total magnetic diffusivity,

$$\eta_T = \eta + \beta. \tag{7.20}$$

We have already demonstrated by physical arguments (chapter 3) that dynamo excitation may originate from a turbulence having helicity. Here we shall start from the ansatz

$$\boldsymbol{B} = \hat{\overline{\boldsymbol{B}}} e^{i(\boldsymbol{k}\cdot\boldsymbol{x} - \omega t)}, \quad \boldsymbol{k} \cdot \hat{\overline{\boldsymbol{B}}} = 0, \tag{7.21}$$

and look for non-decaying solutions of equation (7.19), i.e. for solutions with Re $(-i\omega) = 0$. Inserting (7.21) into (7.19) we obtain the algebraic system

$$(p\,\delta_{ij} - i\alpha\varepsilon_{ipj}k_p)\,\hat{\overline{B}}_j = 0, \quad p = -i\omega + \eta_T k^2. \tag{7.22}$$

The condition for having non-zero solutions leads us to the dispersion relation

$$\det(p\,\delta_{ij} - i\alpha\varepsilon_{ipj}k_p)$$

$$= \frac{1}{6}\varepsilon_{ijk}\varepsilon_{lmn}(p\,\delta_{il} - i\alpha\varepsilon_{ipl}k_p)(p\,\delta_{jm} - i\alpha\varepsilon_{jqm}k_q)(p\,\delta_{kn} - i\alpha\varepsilon_{krn}k_r)$$

$$= p^3 - \alpha^2k^2p = p(p + \alpha k)(p - \alpha k) = 0, \tag{7.23}$$

with the two solutions

$$-i\omega = -\eta_T k^2 + |\alpha|\,k, \quad -i\omega = -\eta_T k^2 - |\alpha|\,k. \tag{7.24}$$

The third root, $p = 0$, does not correspond to a solenoidal field. The first of the solutions (7.24) is clearly positive for sufficiently small k, hence we find indeed, growing fields. In figure 7.1 the two branches of the solutions of the dispersion relation are depicted.

In this way we just deduced a fundamental statement: A non-mirrorsymmetric homogeneous isotropic turbulence provides for dynamo action.

Let us now consider the case of a general homogeneous turbulence with the electromotive force $\mathfrak{E}$ given by (5.35). We split the tensor a_{ij} into its symmetric and its antisymmetric part by writing

$$a_{ij} = \alpha_{ij} + \gamma\varepsilon_{ijk}g_k. \tag{7.25}$$

The induction equation for the mean field then reads

$$\frac{\partial \overline{B}_i}{\partial t} = \varepsilon_{ijk}\frac{\partial}{\partial x_j}\left[(\alpha_{kl} + \gamma\varepsilon_{klm}g_m)\,\overline{B}_l + b_{klm}\frac{\partial \overline{B}_l}{\partial x_m}\right] + \eta\,\Delta\overline{B}_i, \tag{7.26}$$

and with (7.21) we find the algebraic system

$$(q\,\delta_{il} - i\varepsilon_{ijk}k_j\alpha_{kl} + \varepsilon_{ijk}k_jb_{klm}k_m)\,\hat{\overline{B}}_l = 0, \tag{7.27}$$

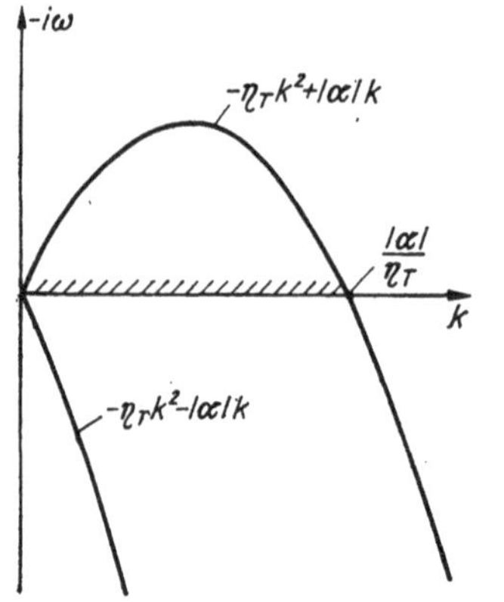

Fig. 7.1. The two branches of the solution of the dispersion relation for homogeneous isotropic non-mirrorsymmetric turbulence. Growing modes exist for wave vectors with a magnitude smaller than $\frac{|\alpha|}{\eta_T}$

where

$$q = p - \mathrm{i}(\gamma \boldsymbol{k} \cdot \boldsymbol{g}) = -\mathrm{i}\omega + \eta k^2 - \mathrm{i}(\gamma \boldsymbol{k} \cdot \boldsymbol{g}). \tag{7.28}$$

Investigating dynamo excitation provided by homogeneous turbulence we neglect the tensor b_{klm} since its contribution is of second order in $\boldsymbol{k}$. Therefore, if growing solutions are found, the understanding in the following will always be that there are growing solutions for sufficiently small wave vectors $\boldsymbol{k}$.

Neglecting the tensor b_{klm} in (7.27) we have to consider the system

$$(q\, \delta_{il} - \mathrm{i}k_j \varepsilon_{ijk} \alpha_{kl})\, \hat{\bar{B}}_l = 0, \tag{7.29}$$

where non-decaying solutions require Re $(q) > 0$. This problem was first treated by Moffatt [2], and later by Krause [6].

For the determinant of (7.29) we find

$$\det\,(q\, \delta_{il} - \mathrm{i}k_j \varepsilon_{ijk} \alpha_{kl}) = q(q^2 - A_{pq} k_p k_q), \tag{7.30}$$

where A_{pq} is the tensor of the algebraic complements of α_{kl}:

$$A_{pq} = \frac{1}{2} \varepsilon_{pkl} \varepsilon_{qmn} \alpha_{km} \alpha_{ln}. \tag{7.31}$$

The root $q = 0$, is of no interest here, since it corresponds to a decaying field, if it exists at all. Thus we have to consider the dispersion relation

$$q^2 - A_{pq} k_p k_q = 0. \tag{7.32}$$

From this we can see that for $A_{pq} k_p k_q > 0$ growing solutions, i.e. those with Re $(-\mathrm{i}\omega) > 0$, exist for sufficiently small magnitude of $\boldsymbol{k}$.

Now we can easily state some theorems concerning dynamo excitation:

(i) A necessary and sufficient condition for the existence of dynamo excitation for some wave vectors $\boldsymbol{k}$ is that the tensor A_{pq} is not negative semi-definite.

(i′) There is no dynamo excitation if, and only if, the tensor A_{pq} is negative semi-definite.

Since

$$\det (A_{pq}) = (\det (\alpha_{pq}))^2 , \tag{7.33}$$

the tensor A_{pq} cannot be negative semi-definite if α_{pq} is non-singular. Therefore we can state

(ii) Dynamo excitation exists for some wave vectors $\boldsymbol{k}$ in case the tensor α_{pq} is non-singular.

This statement clearly shows that dynamo excitation does not require $\alpha \neq 0$, although this condition is of some importance as will be revealed in the following.

(iii) $\alpha \neq 0$ is a necessary condition for having dynamo excitation for all wave vectors $\boldsymbol{k}$ of sufficiently small magnitude.

In order to prove this, we remark that dynamo excitation for all $\boldsymbol{k}$ of sufficiently small magnitude requires a positive definite quadratic form $A_{pq}k_pk_q$. This is the case if, and only if, α_{pq} is either positive or negative definite, consequently $\alpha \neq 0$.

We define the tensor $\tilde{\alpha}_{ij}$ by

$$\alpha_{ij} = \alpha\, \delta_{ij} + \tilde{\alpha}_{ji} , \quad \tilde{\alpha}_{ii} = 0 . \tag{7.34}$$

With this definition we can formulate a sufficient condition:

(iv) $\alpha^2 > \tilde{\alpha}_{kl}\tilde{\alpha}_{kl}$ is a sufficient condition for having dynamo excitation for all wave vectors $\boldsymbol{k}$ of sufficiently small magnitude.

In order to prove this statement we derive from (7.31) and (7.34)

$$A_{pq}k_pk_q = \frac{1}{2}\left[(2\alpha^2 - \tilde{\alpha}_{kl}\tilde{\alpha}_{kl})\, k^2 - 2\alpha\tilde{\alpha}_{kl}k_kk_l + 2\tilde{\alpha}_{jk}\tilde{\alpha}_{jl}k_kk_l\right], \tag{7.35}$$

an expression which can be rewritten as

$$A_{pq}k_pk_q = \frac{1}{2}\left[(\alpha^2 - \tilde{\alpha}_{kl}\tilde{\alpha}_{kl})\, k^2 + (\alpha\, \delta_{jk} - \tilde{\alpha}_{jk})\, (\alpha\, \delta_{jl} - \tilde{\alpha}_{jl})\, k_kk_l + \tilde{\alpha}_{jk}\tilde{\alpha}_{jl}k_kk_l\right]. \tag{7.36}$$

The second and the third summands are clearly non-negative and the first is positive according to our assumption in (iv), hence A_{pq} is positive definite.

We apply the statement (i′) to two-dimensional turbulence. For such turbulence the velocity field vectors lie in planes orthogonal to a given direction, say $\boldsymbol{e}$, and do not vary in the direction of $\boldsymbol{e}$. Accordingly, the correlation tensor in the Fourier space can easily be written down, namely

$$\hat{Q}_{jn}(\boldsymbol{k}, \omega) = \delta(\boldsymbol{k} \cdot \boldsymbol{e})\, \hat{Q}^{(2)}_{jn}(\tilde{\boldsymbol{k}}, \omega), \tag{7.37}$$

where

$$\tilde{\boldsymbol{k}} = \boldsymbol{k} - (\boldsymbol{e} \cdot \boldsymbol{k})\, \boldsymbol{e}, \tag{7.38}$$

and

$$e_j \tilde{Q}^{(2)}_{jn} = 0, \quad e_n \hat{Q}^{(2)}_{jn} = 0. \tag{7.39}$$

Inserting (7.37) into (7.1) we find

$$a_{ij} = \mathrm{i}(\varepsilon_{ilq}\, \delta_{nj} - \varepsilon_{ilj}\, \delta_{nq}) \iint \frac{\tilde{k}_n \hat{Q}^{(2)}_{lq}(\tilde{\boldsymbol{k}}, \omega)}{\eta \tilde{k}^2 - \mathrm{i}\omega}\, \mathrm{d}\tilde{\boldsymbol{k}}\, \mathrm{d}\omega. \tag{7.40}$$

Let us now assume that $\boldsymbol{e} = (0, 0, 1)$ and, consequently, $\tilde{\boldsymbol{k}} = (k_1, k_2, 0)$. Then it is easily seen that

$$a_{11} = a_{22} = a_{12} = a_{21} = a_{33} = 0.$$

Hence α_{ij} takes the form

$$\alpha_{ij} = \begin{pmatrix} 0 & 0 & a \\ 0 & 0 & b \\ a & b & 0 \end{pmatrix},$$

which implies

$$A_{pq} = \begin{pmatrix} -b^2 & ab & 0 \\ ab & -a^2 & 0 \\ 0 & 0 & 0 \end{pmatrix}.$$

It is clearly to be seen that A_{pq} is negative semi-definite. Hence we find within the frame of the second order correlation approximation the statement (KRAUSE [16]):

(v) Two-dimensional turbulence cannot provide for dynamo excitation.

This result is in agreement with a statement derived by ZEL'DOVICH [1] (1956) that a two-dimensional velocity field cannot provide for dynamo excitation.

In order to quote yet another interesting result we consider an anisotropic turbulence on a rotating system. If restricted to linear expressions with respect to the direction of anisotropy, $\boldsymbol{g}$, and the angular velocity, $\boldsymbol{\Omega}$, we have according to (5.43)

$$\alpha_{ij} = -\alpha_1(\boldsymbol{g} \cdot \boldsymbol{\Omega})\, \delta_{ij} - \alpha_2(g_i \Omega_j + g_j \Omega_i), \tag{7.41}$$

with certain scalars α_1, α_2. From (7.31) we easily obtain

$$A_{pq} = \alpha_1^2(\boldsymbol{g} \cdot \boldsymbol{\Omega})^2 \, \delta_{pq} + \alpha_1\alpha_2(\boldsymbol{g} \cdot \boldsymbol{\Omega}) \, [2(\boldsymbol{g} \cdot \boldsymbol{\Omega}) \, \delta_{pq} - (g_p\Omega_q + g_q\Omega_p)] - \alpha_2^2(\boldsymbol{g}\times\boldsymbol{\Omega})_p \, (\boldsymbol{g}\times\boldsymbol{\Omega})_q . \tag{7.42}$$

Now we can prove the statement:

(vi) $\alpha_1 \neq 0$ is a necessary and sufficient condition for dynamo excitation.

A_{pq} is clearly negative semi-definite if $\alpha_1 = 0$. Consequently, $\alpha_1 \neq 0$ is necessary for dynamo excitation according to (i′).

We further have $A_{pq}g_pg_q = \alpha_1^2(\boldsymbol{g} \cdot \boldsymbol{\Omega})^2 g^2$ and, therefore, A_{pq} is not negative semi-definite if $\alpha_1 \neq 0$. Consequently, this condition is sufficient for dynamo excitation according to (i).

7.4. Determination of the tensor b_{ijk}: The turbulent magnetic diffusivity

In section 5.5. we already derived the representation of the tensor b_{ijk} within the frame of the second order correlation approximation. Taking into account Parseval's theorem (6.8) and the symmetry relations (6.19), (6.20) and (6.21) we obtain from (5.52)

$$\begin{aligned} b_{ijk} &= -\varepsilon_{ilm}\varepsilon_{mnp}\varepsilon_{pqj} \iint \frac{\partial G(\xi, \tau)}{\partial \xi_n} \xi_k Q_{ql}(\xi, \tau) \, \mathrm{d}\xi \, \mathrm{d}\tau \\ &= \varepsilon_{ilm}\varepsilon_{mnp}\varepsilon_{pqj} \iint G(\xi, \tau) \frac{\partial}{\partial \xi_n} [\xi_k Q_{ql}(\xi, \tau)] \, \mathrm{d}\xi \, \mathrm{d}\tau \\ &= -\varepsilon_{ilm}\varepsilon_{mnp}\varepsilon_{pqj} \iint \frac{k_n}{\eta k^2 - \mathrm{i}\omega} \frac{\partial \hat{Q}_{lq}(\boldsymbol{k}, \omega)}{\partial k_k} \, \mathrm{d}\boldsymbol{k} \, \mathrm{d}\omega . \end{aligned} \tag{7.43}$$

Our main interest is directed to the quantity β, the turbulent magnetic diffusivity, which we define by

$$\beta = \frac{1}{6} \varepsilon_{ijk} b_{ijk} . \tag{7.44}$$

From (7.43) we obtain

$$\beta = -\frac{1}{3} \iint \frac{1}{\xi} \frac{\partial G(\xi, \tau)}{\partial \xi} \xi_k \xi_l Q_{kl}(\xi, \tau) \, \mathrm{d}\xi \, \mathrm{d}\tau , \tag{7.45}$$

an expression which is identical with that given in section 5.5. or, in Fourier space

$$\begin{aligned} \beta &= -\frac{1}{6} \iint \frac{k_n}{\eta k^2 - \mathrm{i}\omega} \left[\frac{\partial \hat{Q}_{nq}(\boldsymbol{k}, \omega)}{\partial k_q} + \frac{\partial \hat{Q}_{qn}(\boldsymbol{k}, \omega)}{\partial k_q}\right] \mathrm{d}\boldsymbol{k} \, \mathrm{d}\omega \\ &= \frac{1}{3} \iint \frac{1}{\eta k^2 - \mathrm{i}\omega} \left\{\hat{Q}_{qq}(\boldsymbol{k}, \omega) - \frac{1}{2} \frac{\partial}{\partial k_q} [k_n(\hat{Q}_{nq}(\boldsymbol{k}, \omega) + \hat{Q}_{qn}(\boldsymbol{k}, \omega))]\right\} \mathrm{d}\boldsymbol{k} \, \mathrm{d}\omega . \end{aligned} \tag{7.46}$$

This opens possibilities of gaining information about the sign of β. For incompressible turbulence, for example, we have

$$\beta = \frac{1}{3} \iint \frac{\hat{Q}_{qq}(\boldsymbol{k}, \omega)}{\eta k^2 - \mathrm{i}\omega} \mathrm{d}\boldsymbol{k} \, \mathrm{d}\omega$$
$$= \frac{1}{3} \iint \frac{\eta k^2 \hat{Q}_{qq}(\boldsymbol{k}, \omega)}{\eta^2 k^4 + \omega^2} \mathrm{d}\boldsymbol{k} \, \mathrm{d}\omega + \frac{1}{3} \iint \frac{\omega \hat{Q}_{qq}(\boldsymbol{k}, \omega)}{\eta^2 k^4 + \omega^2} \mathrm{d}\boldsymbol{k} \, \mathrm{d}\omega . \tag{7.47}$$

From the symmetry relations (6.19), (6.20) and (6.21) we can derive

$$\hat{Q}_{qq}(\boldsymbol{k}, \omega) = \hat{Q}^*_{qq}(\boldsymbol{k}, \omega) = \hat{Q}_{qq}(-\boldsymbol{k}, -\omega), \tag{7.48}$$

hence the trace of the Fourier-transformed correlation tensor is an even function of its arguments, and, therefore, the second integral in (7.47) vanishes. Consequently, for incompressible turbulence we have

$$\beta = \frac{\eta}{3} \iint \frac{k^2 \hat{Q}_{qq}(\boldsymbol{k}, \omega)}{\eta^2 k^4 + \omega^2} \mathrm{d}\boldsymbol{k} \, \mathrm{d}\omega \geqq 0 , \tag{7.49}$$

since the trace, $\hat{Q}_{qq}$, by Bochner's theorem is a non-negative function (Krause and Roberts [1, 2]).

As already mentioned, a different result is obtained, if the random velocity field has a potential. Inserting (6.51) into (7.46) we find

$$\beta = \frac{1}{3} \iint \frac{1}{\eta k^2 - \mathrm{i}\omega} \left[k^2 \hat{\Phi}(\boldsymbol{k}, \omega) - \frac{\partial}{\partial k_q} (k_q k^2 \hat{\Phi}(\boldsymbol{k}, \omega) \right] \mathrm{d}\boldsymbol{k} \, \mathrm{d}\omega$$
$$= -\frac{1}{3} \iint \frac{k^2}{\eta k^2 - \mathrm{i}\omega} \left[\hat{\Phi}(\boldsymbol{k}, \omega) + \frac{\partial}{\partial k_q} (k_q \hat{\Phi}(\boldsymbol{k}, \omega)) \right] \mathrm{d}\boldsymbol{k} \, \mathrm{d}\omega . \tag{7.50}$$

In the low-conductivity limit we easily derive with (6.64)

$$\beta = -\frac{1}{3\eta} \iint \hat{\Phi}(\boldsymbol{k}, \omega) \, \mathrm{d}\boldsymbol{k} \, \mathrm{d}\omega = -\frac{\overline{\varphi^2}}{3\eta}, \tag{7.51}$$

in agreement with (3.60).

For investigating the high-conductivity limit we start from relation (7.45), which we write in the form

$$\beta = \frac{1}{3} \iint G(\xi, \tau) \left[Q_{kk}(\xi, \tau) + \xi_l \frac{\partial Q_{kl}(\xi, \tau)}{\partial \xi_k} \right] \mathrm{d}\xi \, \mathrm{d}\tau . \tag{7.52}$$

In this limit we find with (6.61)

$$\beta = \frac{1}{3} \int_0^\infty Q_{kk}(0, \tau) \, \mathrm{d}\tau = \frac{1}{6} \int Q_{kk}(0, \tau) \, \mathrm{d}\tau , \tag{7.53}$$

where we also take into account that, because of (5.54), the trace $Q_{kk}(\xi, \tau)$ is an even function of its arguments. Representing now Q_{kk} by its Fourier transform we find

$$\beta = \frac{\pi}{3} \int \hat{Q}_{kk}(\boldsymbol{k}, 0) \, \mathrm{d}\boldsymbol{k} \geqq 0, \tag{7.54}$$

thus clearly showing that in virtue of Bochner's theorem (6.25) β is non-negative in the high-conductivity limit.

With the defnition (6.89) of the quantity β we can write

$$b_{ijk} = \beta \varepsilon_{ijk} + \beta_{ijk}, \tag{7.55}$$

where

$$\varepsilon_{ijk}\beta_{ijk} = 0. \tag{7.56}$$

If we consider now only the electromotive force $\mathfrak{E}$ due to the term $\beta\varepsilon_{ijk}$, the behaviour of the mean magnetic field is governed by the equation

$$\frac{\partial \overline{\boldsymbol{B}}}{\partial t} = (\eta + \beta) \, \Delta \overline{\boldsymbol{B}}; \tag{7.57}$$

thus β proves to be the turbulent magnetic diffusivity.

For physical reasons one expects β to be positive and therefore should be quite surprised by its negative sign for a potential flow (equ. (7.51)). However the total magnetic diffusivity, $\eta + \beta$, is positive, as the estimation in section 3.8 shows.

For investigating the possibility of a negative value of the total magnetic diffusivity we can restrict ourselves to a potential random field, since according to (4.49), the contribution of the solenoidal part of an arbitrary field is positive in any case.

From (7.50) we can take

$$\begin{aligned} \beta &= -\frac{1}{3\eta} \iint \frac{\eta k^2(\eta k^2 + \mathrm{i}\omega)}{(\eta k^2 - \mathrm{i}\omega)^2} \hat{\Phi}(\boldsymbol{k}, \omega) \, \mathrm{d}\boldsymbol{k} \, \mathrm{d}\omega \\ &= \frac{1}{3\eta} \iint \frac{\eta^2 k^4 (3\omega^2 - \eta^2 k^4)}{(\eta^2 k^4 + \omega^2)^2} \hat{\Phi}(\boldsymbol{k}, \omega) \, \mathrm{d}\boldsymbol{k} \, \mathrm{d}\omega. \end{aligned} \tag{7.58}$$

Since $\hat{\Phi} \geqq 0$ and

$$-1 \leqq \frac{\eta^2 k^4 (3\omega^2 - \eta^2 k^4)}{(\eta^2 k^4 + \omega^2)^2} \leqq \frac{9}{16}, \tag{7.59}$$

we can evaluate the integral of the right-hand side of (7.58) and obtain

$$\beta = \frac{1}{3\eta}\,\vartheta \iint \hat{\Phi}(\boldsymbol{k}, \omega)\,\mathrm{d}\boldsymbol{k}\,\mathrm{d}\omega = \frac{\vartheta}{3}\,\mathrm{Rm}^2\,\eta, \quad -1 \leqq \vartheta \leqq \frac{9}{16}. \tag{7.60}$$

Consequently, $\left|\frac{\vartheta}{3}\,\mathrm{Rm}^2\right| > 1$ is a necessary condition for having a negative value of the total magnetic diffusivity, i.e. $\mathrm{Rm}^2 > 3$. The condition for the validity of the second order correlation approximation, (4.30), then requires $\mathrm{S} \ll 1$, and we have all the more $\mathrm{S}/\mathrm{Rm} = \tau_{\mathrm{cor}}/\mu\sigma\lambda_{\mathrm{cor}}^2 \ll 1$. Hence we have the high-conductivity limit where $\beta > 0$, as we have just shown (cf. (7.54)).

In this way we have the result that the total magnetic diffusivity, $\eta + \beta$, within the frame of the second order correlation approximation is non-negative (Krause and Roberts [2]).

Finally we note that an evaluation of formulae (7.45) or (7.46) for β in the limiting cases leads to the results already given in (3.30) and (3.48).

7.5. Turbulence undergoing the influence of Coriolis forces

In section 7.2. we discussed the effect of an anisotropic turbulence on the turbulent electromotive force $\mathfrak{E}$ in the case that the anisotropy is due to a certain vector field $\boldsymbol{g}$. There is, furthermore, a situation of interest, where the anisotropy is due to a field represented by a pseudo-vector. A realization is simply given by a turbulence on a rotating system, where the only influence is that of the Coriolis forces. For simplicity we suppose this influence to be weak enough in order to neglect all quantities of higher than first order with regard to the angular velocity $\boldsymbol{\Omega}$. Since a_{ij} and b_{ijk} are pseudo-tensors we then have

$$a_{ij} = 0, \quad b_{ijk} = \beta\varepsilon_{ijk} - \beta_1\Omega_i\,\delta_{jk} - \beta_2\Omega_j\,\delta_{ki} - \beta_3\Omega_k\,\delta_{ij}, \tag{7.61}$$

or using the notation introduced in (7.55)

$$\beta_{ijk} = -\beta_1\Omega_i\,\delta_{jk} - \beta_2\Omega_j\,\delta_{ki} - \beta_3\Omega_k\,\delta_{ij}. \tag{7.62}$$

It is easily confirmed that condition (7.56) holds.

With the aid of (7.43) the constants $\beta_1, \beta_2, \beta_3$ can be related to the correlation tensor of the velocity field. For this purpose we take from (7.61) the relations

$$b_{ijj} = (-3\beta_1 - \beta_2 - \beta_3)\,\Omega_i, \tag{7.63}$$

$$b_{jij} = (-\beta_1 - 3\beta_2 - \beta_3)\,\Omega_i, \tag{7.64}$$

$$b_{jij} = (-\beta_1 - \beta_2 - 3\beta_3)\,\Omega_i. \tag{7.65}$$

For the sum of them we obtain

$$5\Omega_i(\beta_1 + \beta_2 + \beta_3) = -(b_{ijj} + b_{jij} + b_{jji}). \tag{7.66}$$

For β_3 we thus have

$$\beta_3\Omega_i = -\frac{1}{10}(4b_{jji} - b_{jij} - b_{ijj}), \tag{7.67}$$

and inserting (7.43) we get (Rädler [14])

$$\beta_3\Omega_i = -\frac{\varepsilon_{jkl}}{10}\iint \frac{1}{\xi}\frac{\partial G(\xi, \tau)}{\partial \xi}(3\xi_i\xi_j - \xi^2\,\delta_{ij})\,Q_{kl}(\xi, \tau)\,\mathrm{d}\xi\,\mathrm{d}\tau. \tag{7.68}$$

We do not give the corresponding expression for β_1 and β_2. These quantities are of less interest, because for the turbulent electromotive force $\mathfrak{E}$ with b_{ijk} given by (7.61) we have

$$\mathfrak{E} = -\beta\mu\bar{\boldsymbol{j}} - (\beta_2 + \beta_3)\,\mathrm{grad}\,(\boldsymbol{\Omega}\cdot\bar{\boldsymbol{B}}) + \mu\beta_3\boldsymbol{\Omega}\times\bar{\boldsymbol{j}}. \tag{7.69}$$

One notices that β_1 does not appear since the magnetic field is source-free, and β_2 is only involved in the summand which is a gradient. This part of the electromotive force is always compensated by space charges and does not influ- the magnetic field.

The most interesting feature of the result (7.69) is the occurrence of an electromotive force, $\mu\beta_3\boldsymbol{\Omega}\times\boldsymbol{j}$, often called "$\Omega\times j$-effect". It reminds us of the Hall effect. Just as the α-effect occurring with homogeneous isotropic non-mirrorsymmetric turbulence, the $\Omega\times j$-effect is also caused by helical motions, but it does not require a predominance of right- or left-handed helical motions. The anisotropy in combination with the spatial variation of the mean magnetic field produces a mean current despite the equipartition of both types of helical motions.

We shall now treat the interesting question whether dynamo excitation is possible for the turbulence considered here. From (7.27) we can see that we have to ask for roots of the equation

$$\det\,(p\,\delta_{il} + \varepsilon_{ijk}k_jk_m\beta_{klm}) = 0. \tag{7.70}$$

with $\mathrm{Re}\,(-\mathrm{i}\omega) > 0$, $p = -\mathrm{i}\omega + \eta_T k^2$.

Inserting (7.62) into (7.70) one readily finds

$$\det\,(p\,\delta_{il} + \varepsilon_{ijk}k_jk_m\beta_{klm}) = p(p^2 + k^2(\boldsymbol{\Omega}\cdot\boldsymbol{k})^2\,\beta_3^2) = 0, \tag{7.71}$$

and sees that no root giving a positive real part of $-\mathrm{i}\omega$ exists. Hence we can conclude that a turbulence of the type considered here cannot provide for dynamo excitation.

7.6. Two-dimensional turbulence

A type of turbulence which deserves some interest is two-dimensional turbulence. This turbulence is defined by the properties that (i) the velocity vectors lie completely in planes orthogonal to a given direction, $\boldsymbol{e}$, and (ii) do not vary along this direction, i.e.,

$$\boldsymbol{e} \cdot \boldsymbol{u}' = 0, \quad (\boldsymbol{e} \cdot \text{grad})\, \boldsymbol{u}' = 0, \tag{7.72}$$

or the equivalent in Fourier space

$$\boldsymbol{e} \cdot \hat{\boldsymbol{u}} = 0, \quad \hat{\boldsymbol{u}}(\boldsymbol{k}, \omega) = \delta(\boldsymbol{e} \cdot \boldsymbol{k})\, \hat{\boldsymbol{u}}^{(2)}(\tilde{\boldsymbol{k}}, \omega), \tag{7.73}$$

where

$$\tilde{\boldsymbol{k}} = \boldsymbol{k} - (\boldsymbol{e} \cdot \boldsymbol{k})\, \boldsymbol{e}. \tag{7.74}$$

For the correlation tensor we consequently have

$$Q_{ik}(\xi, \tau) = Q_{ik}^{(2)}(\tilde{\xi}, \tau), \quad e_i Q_{ik}^{(2)}(\tilde{\xi}, \tau) = 0, \quad e_k Q_{ik}^{(2)}(\tilde{\xi}, \tau) = 0,$$
$$\tilde{\xi} = \xi - (\boldsymbol{e} \cdot \xi)\, \boldsymbol{e}, \tag{7.75}$$

or in Fourier space

$$\hat{Q}_{ik}(\boldsymbol{k}, \tau) = \delta(\boldsymbol{e} \cdot \boldsymbol{k})\, \hat{Q}_{ik}^{(2)}(\tilde{\boldsymbol{k}}, \omega), \quad e_i \hat{Q}_{ik}^{(2)}(\tilde{\boldsymbol{k}}, \omega) = 0, \quad e_k Q_{ik}^{(2)}(\tilde{\boldsymbol{k}}, \omega) = 0. \tag{7.76}$$

We already found in 7.3. that no dynamo action will arise from two-dimensional turbulence. Here we shall concentrate our interest on the tensor b_{ijk} and the two-dimensional magnetic diffusivity. We start from (7.43) using the Fourier representation. Defining the differentiation within the planes orthogonal to $\boldsymbol{e}$ by

$$\frac{\partial}{\partial \tilde{k}_i} = (\delta_{ij} - e_i e_j) \frac{\partial}{\partial k_j}, \tag{7.77}$$

after carrying out a partial integration we can write

$$b_{ijk} = \varepsilon_{ilm} \varepsilon_{mnp} \varepsilon_{pqj} \iint \left[\frac{\partial}{\partial \tilde{k}_k} \left(\frac{k_n}{\eta k^2 - \mathrm{i}\omega} \right) + \frac{e_k e_n}{\eta k^2 - \mathrm{i}\omega} \right.$$
$$\left. - e_k k_n \frac{2\eta (\boldsymbol{e} \cdot \boldsymbol{k})}{(\eta k^2 - \mathrm{i}\omega^2)} \right] \hat{Q}_{lq}(\boldsymbol{k}, \omega)\, \mathrm{d}\boldsymbol{k}\, \mathrm{d}\omega\,. \tag{7.78}$$

Inserting now the specified tensor (7.76) we easily obtain

$$b_{ijk} = \varepsilon_{ilm} \varepsilon_{mnp} \varepsilon_{pqj} \iint \frac{\partial}{\partial \tilde{k}_k} \left(\frac{\tilde{k}_n}{\eta \tilde{k}^2 - \mathrm{i}\omega} \right) \hat{Q}_{lq}^{(2)}(\tilde{\boldsymbol{k}}, \omega)\, \mathrm{d}\tilde{\boldsymbol{k}}\, \mathrm{d}\omega$$
$$+ e_j e_k \varepsilon_{ilq} \iint \frac{\hat{Q}_{lq}^{(2)}(\tilde{\boldsymbol{k}}, \omega)}{\eta \tilde{k}^2 - \mathrm{i}\omega}\, \mathrm{d}\tilde{\boldsymbol{k}}\, \mathrm{d}\omega\,, \tag{7.79}$$

or, using Parseval's theorem (6.11),

$$b_{ijk} = -\varepsilon_{ilm}\varepsilon_{mnp}\varepsilon_{pqj}\iint \frac{1}{\tilde{\xi}}\,\frac{\partial G^{(2)}(\tilde{\xi},\tau)}{\partial\tilde{\xi}}\,\tilde{\xi}_k\tilde{\xi}_n Q^{(2)}_{ql}(\tilde{\xi},\tau)\,\mathrm{d}\tilde{\xi}\,\mathrm{d}\tau$$

$$-\, e_j e_k \varepsilon_{ilq}\iint G^{(2)}(\tilde{\xi},\tau)\,Q^{(2)}_{lq}(\tilde{\xi},\tau)\,\mathrm{d}\tilde{\xi}\,\mathrm{d}\tau. \tag{7.80}$$

$G^{(2)}(\tilde{\xi},\tau)$ denotes the two-dimensional Green's function given by

$$G_{(2)}(\tilde{\xi},\tau) = \frac{\mu\sigma}{4\pi\tau}\exp\left(-\frac{\mu\sigma\tilde{\xi}^2}{4\tau}\right). \tag{7.81}$$

The integrations in (7.79) and (7.80) are to be extended over planes orthogonal to $\boldsymbol{e}$, i.e. over a two-dimensional manifold.

For a more detailed discussion we restrict ourselves to the two-dimensional isotropic mirrorsymmetric case. Then the second integral in (7.79) or (7.80) clearly does not contribute, since it depends on $\boldsymbol{u}'(\boldsymbol{x},t)\cdot\operatorname{curl}\boldsymbol{u}'(\boldsymbol{x}+\xi,t+\tau)$, a quantity which is different from zero only in the case of an imbalance of clockwise and counter-clockwise motions. In addition, the tensor b_{ijk} can only be composed of the tensors e_i, $\delta_{ij}-e_ie_j$, $\varepsilon_{ijl}e_l$, and since it is skew we have the only possible ansatz

$$b_{ijk} = b_1 e_i\varepsilon_{jkl}e_l + b_2 e_j\varepsilon_{kil}e_l + b_3 e_k\varepsilon_{ijl}e_l, \tag{7.82}$$

with certain constants b_1, b_2, b_3. In the non-mirrorsymmetric case additional summands composed of the tensor $e_i(\delta_{jk}-e_je_k), \ldots, e_ie_je_k$ are possible.

Multiplying (7.82) and (7.80) by e_k one finds $b_3 = 0$. Multiplications by $\varepsilon_{jkr}e_r$ and $\varepsilon_{kir}e_r$ show that

$$b_1 = b_2 = \beta^{(2)} = -\frac{1}{2}\iint \tilde{\xi}\,\frac{\partial G^{(2)}(\tilde{\xi},\tau)}{\partial\tilde{\xi}}\,f^{(2)}(\tilde{\xi},\tau)\,\mathrm{d}\tilde{\xi}\,\mathrm{d}\tau, \tag{7.83}$$

where $f^{(2)}$ is the two-dimensional longitudinal correlation function defined by

$$\tilde{\xi}^2 f^{(2)}(\tilde{\xi},\tau) = \tilde{\xi}_k\tilde{\xi}_n Q^{(2)}_{kn}(\tilde{\xi},\tau), \tag{7.84}$$

in analogy to the three-dimensional case (Krause and Rüdiger [1]). Consequently, we find for the turbulent electromotive force

$$\mathfrak{E}_i = \beta^{(2)}(e_i\varepsilon_{jkl} + e_j\varepsilon_{kil})\,e_l\,\frac{\partial\overline{B}_j}{\partial x_k} = \beta^{(2)}(\delta_{kl}-e_ke_l)\,\varepsilon_{ijl}\,\frac{\partial\overline{B}_j}{\partial x_k}. \tag{7.85}$$

If we insert the latter expression given here into the induction equation for the mean field, i.e. into

$$\frac{\partial\overline{B}_i}{\partial t} - \eta\,\Delta\overline{B}_i = \varepsilon_{ijk}\frac{\partial\mathfrak{E}_k}{\partial x_j}, \tag{7.86}$$

we obtain the equation

$$\frac{\partial \overline{B}_i}{\partial t} - \eta \,\Delta \overline{B}_i = \beta^{(2)}(\delta_{jk} - e_j e_k) \frac{\partial^2 \overline{B}_i}{\partial x_j \, \partial x_k}. \tag{7.87}$$

In the general case this equation describes an anisotropic diffusion. There are, however, two configurations where the mean magnetic field itself has two-dimensional geometry. The first one is provided by a magnetic field parallel to $\boldsymbol{e}$, i.e.

$$\overline{\boldsymbol{B}} = (\boldsymbol{e} \cdot \overline{\boldsymbol{B}})\, \boldsymbol{e} = \overline{B} \boldsymbol{e}, \quad \boldsymbol{e} \cdot \operatorname{grad} \overline{B} = 0. \tag{7.88}$$

In this case the one component of the mean magnetic field, $\overline{B}$, satisfies the two-dimensional diffusion equation

$$\frac{\partial \overline{B}}{\partial t} - \eta_T \,\Delta^{(2)} \overline{B} = 0, \tag{7.89}$$

where η_T is the total magnetic diffusivity

$$\eta_T = \eta + \beta^{(2)} \tag{7.90}$$

analogously defined as in the three-dimensional case, and $\Delta^{(2)}$ the two-dimensional Δ-operator

$$\Delta^{(2)} = (\delta_{ij} - e_i e_j) \frac{\partial^2}{\partial x_i \, \partial x_j}. \tag{7.91}$$

The second case is given by a magnetic field having the structure of the turbulent motion, i.e.

$$\boldsymbol{e} \cdot \overline{\boldsymbol{B}} = 0, (\boldsymbol{e} \cdot \nabla)\, \overline{\boldsymbol{B}} = 0, \tag{7.92}$$

therefore, in particular,

$$\overline{B}_i = \overline{\overline{B}}_i = (\delta_{ij} - e_i e_j)\, \overline{B}_j.$$

Then, again, the mean magnetic field $\overline{\boldsymbol{B}}$ is governed by the two-dimensional equation

$$\frac{\partial \overline{\overline{B}}_i}{\partial t} - \eta_T \,\Delta^{(2)} \overline{\overline{B}}_i = 0. \tag{7.93}$$

Finally, we remark that there is no fundamental difference between the three-dimensional turbulent magnetic diffusivity, β, and the two-dimensional one, $\beta^{(2)}$. This is easily seen if (7.83) is compared with (5.62). In addition, evaluating (7.83) in the high-conductivity limit analogously to the three-dimensional case in section 7.4. we find

$$\beta^{(2)} = \frac{1}{2} \int_0^\infty Q_{kk}(0, \tau)\, \mathrm{d}\tau = \frac{1}{2} \overline{u'^2}\, \tau_{\mathrm{cor}}. \tag{7.94}$$

7.7. Higher order correlation approximation: Vainshtein's recurrence formula

We denote by $\tilde{\boldsymbol{u}}(\boldsymbol{k}, t)$ and $\tilde{\boldsymbol{B}}(\boldsymbol{k}, t)$ the Fourier transforms of the velocity field and the magnetic field with respect to the space coordinates only. As before, the mean velocity field should be zero. The induction equation then reads

$$\frac{\partial \tilde{B}_i}{\partial t} + \eta k_k \tilde{B}_i = i\, \varepsilon_{ijk}\varepsilon_{klm} k_j (\tilde{u}_l * \tilde{B}_m), \tag{7.95}$$

where the asterisk denotes the convolution operation introduced in (6.7).

We represent the magnetic field $\tilde{\boldsymbol{B}}$ by the series

$$\tilde{\boldsymbol{B}}(\boldsymbol{k}, t) = \sum_{n=0}^{\infty} \tilde{\boldsymbol{B}}^{(n)}(\boldsymbol{k}, t), \tag{7.96}$$

where

$$\tilde{\boldsymbol{B}}^{(0)}(\boldsymbol{k}, t) = \tilde{\boldsymbol{B}}(\boldsymbol{k}) \exp(-\eta k^2 t), \tag{7.97}$$

and

$$\frac{\partial \tilde{B}_i^{(n)}}{\partial t} + \eta k^2 \tilde{B}_i^{(n)} = i\varepsilon_{ijk}\varepsilon_{klm} k_j (\tilde{u}_l * \tilde{B}_m^{(n-1)}), \quad \tilde{B}_i^{(n)}(\boldsymbol{k}, 0) = 0, \quad n \geqq 1. \tag{7.98}$$

From (7.96), (7.97) and (7.98) it is clearly to be seen that the field $\tilde{\boldsymbol{B}}$ defined by (7.96) solves the induction equation (7.95) in case of convergence.

Equation (7.98) can be integrated by

$$\tilde{B}_i^{(n)} = i\varepsilon_{ijk}\varepsilon_{klm} k_j \int_0^t \mathrm{e}^{-\eta k^2 (t-t')} (\tilde{u}_l * \tilde{B}_m^{(n-1)})\, \mathrm{d}t', \quad n \geqq 1, \tag{7.99}$$

and, applying this formula twice, we obtain

$$\tilde{B}_i^{(n)}(\boldsymbol{k}, t) = -\varepsilon_{ijk}\varepsilon_{klm}\varepsilon_{mnp}\varepsilon_{pqr} k_j \int_0^t \int_0^{t'} \iint \tilde{u}_l(\boldsymbol{k} - \boldsymbol{k}', t')\, k'_n \times \tilde{u}_q(\boldsymbol{k}' - \boldsymbol{k}'', t'')\, \tilde{B}_r^{(n-2)}(\boldsymbol{k}'', t'')\, \mathrm{e}^{-\eta[k^2(t-t') + k'^2(t'-t'')]}\, \mathrm{d}\boldsymbol{k}'\, \mathrm{d}\boldsymbol{k}''\, \mathrm{d}t'\, \mathrm{d}t''. \tag{7.100}$$

We can successively substitute $\tilde{\boldsymbol{B}}^{(n-3)}$, $\tilde{\boldsymbol{B}}^{(n-4)}$, and so on, in this way finally arriving at a representation of $\tilde{\boldsymbol{B}}^{(n)}$ by $\tilde{\boldsymbol{B}}^{(0)}$.

We are interested in the mean value $\overline{\tilde{\boldsymbol{B}}^{(n)}}$. Restricting ourselves to the main features we find an expression

$$\overline{\tilde{B}_i^{(n)}} = \int\limits_0^t \int\limits_0^{t'} \cdots \int\limits_0^{t^{(n-1)}} \ldots \overline{\tilde{u}(t')\, \tilde{u}(t'') \ldots \tilde{u}(t^{(n)}} \ldots \tilde{B}^{(0)}(t^{(n)}) \ldots \mathrm{d}t'\, \mathrm{d}t'' \ldots \mathrm{d}t^{(n)}. \tag{7.101}$$

Following VAINSHTEIN [1] (c.f. also KAZANTSEV [1]) we now consider a Gaussian distribution for the velocity field, i.e. all correlation tensors of odd rank vanish and those of even rank are given by the sum of products of all possible pairs,

$$\overline{u_{i_1}(t')\, u_{i_2}(t'') \ldots u_{i_{2n}}(t^{(2n)})} = \sum \prod \overline{\tilde{u}_{i_\alpha}(t^{(\alpha)})\, \tilde{u}_{i_\beta}(t^{(\beta)})}. \tag{7.102}$$

As a consequence the mean values of the magnetic field constituents with an odd number vanish:

$$\overline{\tilde{\boldsymbol{B}}^{(2n+1)}} = 0. \tag{7.103}$$

For those with an even number we obtain from (7.101) and (7.102)

$$\overline{\tilde{B}_i^{(2n)}} = \int\limits_0^t \int\limits_0^{t'} \cdots \int\limits_0^{t^{(2n-1)}} \sum \prod \overline{\tilde{u}_{i_\alpha}(\boldsymbol{k}^{(\alpha)}, t^{(\alpha)})\, \tilde{u}_{i_\beta}(\boldsymbol{k}^{(\beta)}, t^{(\beta)})}\, \tilde{B}^{(0)}(\, \mathrm{d}t' \ldots, \tag{7.104}$$

where it is important to note that

$$t \geqq t' \geqq t'' \geqq \ldots \geqq t^{(2n-1)} = t^{(2n)}. \tag{7.105}$$

In addition to the requirement that the probability distribution of the velocity field is Gaussian, VAINSHTEIN assumes that the correlation time is very short as compared with all other characteristic time scales and takes for the correlation tensor of second rank

$$Q_{kl}(\xi, \tau) = 2\tau_{\mathrm{cor}}\, \delta(\tau)\, Q_{kl}(\xi), \tag{7.106}$$

where $Q_{kk}(0) = \overline{u'^2}$.

From (7.104) we now obtain

$$\overline{\tilde{B}_i^{(2n)}} = \int\limits_0^t \int\limits_0^{t} \cdots \int\limits_0^{t^{(2n-1)}} \sum \prod \tilde{Q}_{i_\alpha i_\beta}(\boldsymbol{k}^{(\alpha)} - \boldsymbol{k}^{(\beta)})\, \delta(t^{(\alpha)} - t^{(\beta)}) \ldots \tilde{B}^{(0)}\, \mathrm{d}t' \ldots, \tag{7.107}$$

where $\tilde{Q}_{kl}$ denotes the Fourier-transform of Q_{kl} introduced in (7.106) with respect to the space coordinates.

An evaluation of (7.107) can easily be carried out: There is one, and only one, summand in the integrand, where the arguments $t^{(\alpha)}$ have their natural order given in (7.105). In all the other summands there is at least one pair $t^{(\alpha)}$, $t^{(\beta)}$ where α and β are not neighbours. In this case we have

$$\int\limits_0^{t^{(\beta-1)}} \delta(t^{(\alpha)} - t^{(\beta)})\, \mathrm{d}t^{(\beta)} = \begin{cases} 0, & \text{if } t^{(\beta-1)} < t^{(\alpha)} \\ \dfrac{1}{2}, & \text{if } t^{(\beta-1)} = t^{(\alpha)} \end{cases}; \tag{7.108}$$

and this expression vanishes if the integration over $t^{(\beta-1)}$ is carrried out. Consequently, the sum under the integral reduces to one term only, thus leading to

$$\overline{B_i^{(2n)}} = \int\limits_0^t \int\limits_0^{t'} \cdots \int\limits_0^{t^{(2n-1)}} \cdots \tilde{Q}_{i_1 i_2}(\boldsymbol{k}^{(1)} - \boldsymbol{k}^{(2)}\, \delta(t' - t'')$$
$$\tilde{Q}_{i_3 i_4}(\boldsymbol{k}^{(3)} - \boldsymbol{k}^{(4)})\, \delta\,(t^{(3)} - t^{(4)}) \ldots \tilde{B}^{(0)} \mathrm{d}t' \ldots. \tag{7.109}$$

Moreover, it becomes clear that $\tilde{Q}_{i_1 i_2}$ is completely disengaged from all that follows, and all that follows is the mean of $\tilde{\boldsymbol{B}}^{(2n-2)}$. In this way we obtain the recurrence formula

$$\overline{\tilde{B}_i^{(2n)}(\boldsymbol{k}, t)} = -\varepsilon_{ijk}\varepsilon_{klm}\varepsilon_{mnp}\varepsilon_{pqr}k_j \int\limits_0^t \int\limits_0^{t'} \int\int \overline{k_n' \tilde{u}_l(\boldsymbol{k} - \boldsymbol{k}', t')\, \tilde{u}_q(\boldsymbol{k}' - \boldsymbol{k}'', t'')}$$
$$\overline{\tilde{B}_r^{(2n-2)}(\boldsymbol{k}'', t'')}\, \mathrm{e}^{-\eta[k^2(t-t') + k'^2(t-t'')]}\, \mathrm{d}\boldsymbol{k}'\, \mathrm{d}\boldsymbol{k}''\, \mathrm{d}t'\, \mathrm{d}t''. \tag{7.110}$$

Taking into account that according to (6.18) and (7.106) we have

$$\overline{\tilde{u}_l(\boldsymbol{k} - \boldsymbol{k}', t')\, \tilde{u}_q(\boldsymbol{k}' - \boldsymbol{k}'', t'')} = \delta(\boldsymbol{k} - \boldsymbol{k}'')\, \delta(t' - t'')\, \tilde{Q}_{lq}(\boldsymbol{k}' - \boldsymbol{k}'')\, 2\tau_{\text{cor}}, \tag{7.111}$$

and by carrying out the integrations,

$$\overline{\tilde{B}_i^{(2n+2)}(\boldsymbol{k}, t)} = -\int\limits_0^t A_{ir} \mathrm{e}^{-\eta k^2(t-t')}\, \overline{\tilde{B}_r^{(2n)}(\boldsymbol{k}, t')}\, \mathrm{d}t', \tag{7.112}$$

where

$$A_{ir} = \tau_{\text{cor}}\varepsilon_{ijk}\varepsilon_{klm}\varepsilon_{mnp}\varepsilon_{pqr}k_j \int k_n' \tilde{Q}_{lq}(\boldsymbol{k}' - \boldsymbol{k})\, \mathrm{d}\boldsymbol{k}'. \tag{7.113}$$

For isotropic conditions we have

$$\tau_{\text{cor}} \int k_n' Q_{lq}(\boldsymbol{k}' - \boldsymbol{k})\, \mathrm{d}\boldsymbol{k}' = \tau_{\text{cor}}[k_n \int \tilde{Q}_{lq}(\boldsymbol{k}')\, \mathrm{d}\boldsymbol{k}' + \int k_n' \tilde{Q}_{lq}(\boldsymbol{k}')\, \mathrm{d}\boldsymbol{k}']$$
$$= \beta k_n\, \delta_{lq} - \frac{\mathrm{i}}{2} \alpha \varepsilon_{nlq}. \tag{7.114}$$

Multiplying this equation successively by δ_{lq} and ε_{nlq} we easily obtain

$$\beta = \frac{\tau_{\text{cor}}}{3} \int \tilde{Q}_{qq}(\boldsymbol{k}')\,\mathrm{d}\boldsymbol{k}' = \frac{\tau_{\text{cor}}}{3} Q_{qq}(0) = \frac{1}{3}\,\overline{u'^2}\,\tau_{\text{cor}}, \tag{7.115}$$

and

$$\alpha = \tau_{\text{cor}} \frac{\mathrm{i}}{3} \int \varepsilon_{nlq} k_n' \tilde{Q}_{lq}(\boldsymbol{k}')\,\mathrm{d}\boldsymbol{k}' = \frac{\tau_{\text{cor}}}{6} \varepsilon_{nlq} \left.\frac{\partial Q_{lq}}{\partial \xi_n}\right|_{\xi=0}$$

$$= -\frac{\tau_{\text{cor}}}{3} \varepsilon_{lnq} \left.\overline{u_l'(\boldsymbol{x}, t) \frac{\partial\, u_q'(\boldsymbol{x} + \boldsymbol{\xi}, t)}{\partial \xi_n}}\right|_{\xi=0} = -\frac{1}{3}\,\overline{\boldsymbol{u}' \cdot \operatorname{curl} \boldsymbol{u}'}\,\tau_{\text{cor}}. \tag{7.116}$$

Inserting (7.114) into (7.113) we get

$$A_{ir} = -\mathrm{i}\alpha\varepsilon_{ijr} k_j + \beta(k^2\,\delta_{ir} - k_i k_r). \tag{7.117}$$

In order to obtain a final interpretation of our result we differentiate the recurrence formula (7.112) with respect to the time and find

$$\frac{\partial \overline{\tilde{B}_i^{(2n+2)}}}{\partial t} = -A_{ir} \overline{\tilde{B}_r^{(2n)}} - k^2 \overline{\tilde{B}_i^{(2n+2)}}. \tag{7.118}$$

Summing up these equations by taking into account that

$$\frac{\partial \tilde{\boldsymbol{B}}^{(0)}}{\partial t} = -\eta k^2 \tilde{\boldsymbol{B}}^{(0)}$$

we find for the mean magnetic field

$$\frac{\partial \overline{\tilde{B}}_i}{\partial t} = -A_{ir} \overline{\tilde{B}}_r - \eta k^2 \overline{\tilde{\boldsymbol{B}}}_i, \tag{7.119}$$

which, in the isotropic case, reduces to

$$\frac{\partial \overline{\tilde{\boldsymbol{B}}(\boldsymbol{k}, t)}}{\partial t} = -(\eta + \beta)\, k^2\, \overline{\tilde{\boldsymbol{B}}(\boldsymbol{k}, t)} + \mathrm{i}\alpha \boldsymbol{k} \times \overline{\tilde{\boldsymbol{B}}(\boldsymbol{k}, t)}, \tag{7.120}$$

or if written in the $(\boldsymbol{x}, t)$-space

$$\frac{\partial \overline{\boldsymbol{B}}(\boldsymbol{x}, t)}{\partial t} = \operatorname{curl} \alpha \overline{\boldsymbol{B}}(\boldsymbol{x}, t) + (\eta + \beta)\, \Delta \overline{\boldsymbol{B}}(\boldsymbol{x}, t). \tag{7.121}$$

This shows that the action of the turbulence is again that of an electromotive force $\mathfrak{E}$ given by (3.5), or (5.37), however, the main point is that the values of α and β are just the same as derived within the frame of the second order correlation approximation in the high-conductivity limit ((3.31), (3.32)).

7.8. The dispersion relation

As already mentioned in section 5.1., for applications of the mean-field theory it is appropriate to assume the turbulence to be two-scaled. Otherwise the use of the ergodic theorem is questionable. In addition, we saw that the two-scale property resulted in mathematical simplifications (possibility of expansion of the mean field), which allowed a more detailed discussion of the subject. In the case of homogeneous turbulence, however, there is a mathematical procedure, first proposed by Lerche [1, 6], which provides an alternative to the expansion technique.

Let us consider the integro-differential equation (4.50) deduced within the frame of the second order correlation approximation. For homogeneous turbulence and vanishing mean flow it reads

$$\left(\frac{\partial}{\partial t} - \eta\Delta\right)\overline{B}_i(\boldsymbol{x}, t) = \varepsilon_{ijk}\varepsilon_{klm}\varepsilon_{mnp}\varepsilon_{pqr}\frac{\partial}{\partial x_j}\iint\frac{\partial G(\xi, \tau)}{\partial \xi_n} Q_{ql}(\xi, \tau)\,\overline{B}_r(\boldsymbol{x} - \xi, t - \tau)\,\mathrm{d}\xi\,\mathrm{d}\tau . \tag{7.122}$$

Since the integral on the right is of convolution type the equation takes a particularly simple form in Fourier-transformed quantities, namely,

$$[p\,\delta_{ir} - A_{ir}(\boldsymbol{k}, \omega)]\,\hat{\overline{B}}_r(\boldsymbol{k}, \omega) = 0 , \tag{7.123}$$

where p is given by

$$p = -\mathrm{i}\omega + \eta k^2 \tag{7.124}$$

and

$$A_{ir}(\boldsymbol{k}, \omega) = \mathrm{i}\varepsilon_{ijk}\varepsilon_{klm}\varepsilon_{mnp}\varepsilon_{pqr}k_j\iint\frac{\partial G(\xi, \tau)}{\partial \xi_n} Q_{ql}(\xi, \tau)\,\mathrm{e}^{-\mathrm{i}(\boldsymbol{k}\cdot\xi - \omega\tau)}\,\mathrm{d}\xi\,\mathrm{d}\tau . \tag{7.125}$$

Non-trivial solutions $\hat{\overline{B}}_i$ of (7.123) only exist if

$$\det\,[p\,\delta_{ir} - A_{ir}(\boldsymbol{k}, \omega)] = 0 , \tag{7.126}$$

an equation which represents a dispersion relation for determining the frequencies ω for given $\boldsymbol{k}$.

At first we remark that for small $\boldsymbol{k}$ this dispersion relation is identical with that for two-scale turbulence discussed in sections 7.3. and 7.5. It is easily confirmed that in second order in $\boldsymbol{k}$

$$A_{ir} = \mathrm{i}\varepsilon_{ijk}a_{kr}k_j - \varepsilon_{ijk}k_jk_sb_{krs} , \tag{7.127}$$

where the tensors a_{kr} and b_{krs} are given by (7.1) and (7.43).

Secondly, we find by inspection of (7.125) that the integral is the Fourier transform of $\frac{\partial G}{\partial \xi_n} Q_{ql}$, up to a factor $(2\pi)^{-4}$. Therefore we can rewrite this formula using (6.7) and (6.57)

$$A_{ir}(\boldsymbol{k}, \omega) = -\varepsilon_{ijk}\varepsilon_{klm}\varepsilon_{mnp}\varepsilon_{pqr}k_j \iint \frac{(k_n - k_n') \, \hat{Q}_{ql}(\boldsymbol{k}', \omega')}{\eta(\boldsymbol{k} - \boldsymbol{k}')^2 - \mathrm{i}(\omega - \omega')} \, \mathrm{d}\boldsymbol{k}' \, \mathrm{d}\omega' . \tag{7.128}$$

This shows that $A_{ir} = \mathrm{O}(1)$ if $k \to \infty$, i.e. the dispersion relation (7.126) yields $p = 0$, or $-\mathrm{i}\omega = -\eta k^2$, if $k \to \infty$. This result is clear for physical reasons: The small-wavelength Fourier modes decay uninfluenced by the turbulent motion.

Statements for arbitrary $\boldsymbol{k}$ can hardly be gained in the general case. Therefore, we restrict ourselves to isotropic mirrorsymmetric turbulences. Since $k_i A_{ij} = 0$ we then have

$$A_{ij}(\boldsymbol{k}, \omega) = a(k, \omega) \left(\delta_{ij} - \frac{k_i k_j}{k^2} \right), \tag{7.129}$$

and the dispersion relation simply reads $p = a$, if the uninteresting solution $p = 0$ is excluded. Thus, contracting (7.125), we have

$$p = \mathrm{i}k_j \iint \frac{1}{\xi} \frac{\partial G(\xi, \tau)}{\partial \xi} \xi_k Q_{jk}(\boldsymbol{\xi}, \tau) \, \mathrm{e}^{-\mathrm{i}(\boldsymbol{k}\cdot\boldsymbol{\xi} - \omega\tau)} \, \mathrm{d}\boldsymbol{\xi} \, \mathrm{d}\tau , \tag{7.130}$$

or, if definition (5.61) of the longitudinal correlation function is taken into account,

$$\begin{aligned} p &= \mathrm{i} \iint \frac{(\boldsymbol{k} \cdot \boldsymbol{\xi})}{\xi} \frac{\partial G(\xi, \tau)}{\partial \xi} f(\xi, \tau) \, \mathrm{e}^{-\mathrm{i}(\boldsymbol{k}\cdot\boldsymbol{\xi} - \omega\tau)} \, \mathrm{d}\boldsymbol{\xi} \, \mathrm{d}\tau \\ &= -k \frac{\partial}{\partial k} \iint \frac{1}{\xi} \frac{\partial G(\xi, \tau)}{\partial \xi} f(\xi, \tau) \, \mathrm{e}^{-\mathrm{i}(\boldsymbol{k}\cdot\boldsymbol{\xi} - \omega\tau)} \, \mathrm{d}\boldsymbol{\xi} \, \mathrm{d}\tau . \end{aligned} \tag{7.131}$$

Equivalent representations of the dispersion relation are found if a is determined by contracting (7.128). We then obtain

$$\begin{aligned} p &= -\iint \frac{k_j(k_k - k_k') \, \hat{Q}_{jk}(\boldsymbol{k}', \omega')}{\eta(\boldsymbol{k} - \boldsymbol{k}')^2 - \mathrm{i}(\omega - \omega')} \, \mathrm{d}\boldsymbol{k}' \, \mathrm{d}\omega' \\ &= -\iint \frac{k_j(k_j - k_j')}{\eta(\boldsymbol{k} - \boldsymbol{k}')^2 - \mathrm{i}(\omega - \omega')} \hat{f}(k', \omega') \, \mathrm{d}\boldsymbol{k}' \, \mathrm{d}\omega' . \end{aligned} \tag{7.132}$$

The latter form of the dispersion relation is most useful for scrutinizing the interesting question whether growing solutions will exist, i.e. Re $(-\mathrm{i}\omega)$ positive or not. Let us write $\omega = \omega_r + \mathrm{i}\omega_i$, thus Re $(-\mathrm{i}\omega) = \omega_i$.

First, suppose the fluid is incompressible, so that equation (7.132) becomes

$$-\mathrm{i}\omega = -\eta k^2 - \iint \frac{k_j k_k \hat{Q}_{jk}(\boldsymbol{k}', \omega')}{\eta(\boldsymbol{k} - \boldsymbol{k}')^2 - \mathrm{i}(\omega - \omega')} \,\mathrm{d}\boldsymbol{k}' \,\mathrm{d}\omega'. \tag{7.133}$$

Suppose a root exists for which $\mathrm{Re}\,(-\mathrm{i}\omega) = \omega_i \geqq 0$. It is then permissible to take the ω'-contour in (7.133) to be the real axis. Take the real part of both sides of (7.133) to obtain

$$\mathrm{Re}\,(-\mathrm{i}\omega) = \omega_i = -\eta k^2 - \iint \frac{(\boldsymbol{k} - \boldsymbol{k}')^2 + \omega_i}{\eta^2(\boldsymbol{k} - \boldsymbol{k}')^4 + (\omega - \omega')^2} \, k_j k_k \hat{Q}_{jk}(\boldsymbol{k}', \omega') \,\mathrm{d}\boldsymbol{k}' \,\mathrm{d}\omega'. \tag{7.134}$$

In this connection it should be noted that in the mirrorsymmetric case, per definition, we have

$$\hat{Q}_{jk}(-\boldsymbol{k}, \omega) = \hat{Q}_{jk}(\boldsymbol{k}, \omega), \tag{7.135}$$

thus being able to derive from (6.19) and (6.20) that $\hat{Q}_{jk}$ is a real quantity.

The left-hand side of (7.134) is positive semi-definite by assumption, but the right-hand side is negative definite because of Bochner's theorem (6.25). This contradiction reduces the initial postulate $\mathrm{Re}\,(-\mathrm{i}\omega) = \omega_i \geqq 0$ to an absurdity (Krause and Roberts [1, 2]).

Considering the high-conductivity limit, $\mu\sigma\lambda_{\mathrm{cor}}^2 \gg \tau_{\mathrm{cor}}$, we realize that the summand $\eta(\boldsymbol{k} - \boldsymbol{k}')^2$ in the denominator remarkably contributes only if $k^2 > \mu\sigma/\tau_{\mathrm{cor}}$. Furthermore, since $\hat{Q}_{jk}(\boldsymbol{k}', \omega')$ is significantly different from zero only if $k'^2 \leqq 1/\lambda_{\mathrm{cor}}^2 \ll \mu\sigma/\tau_{\mathrm{cor}}$, we can simplify the dispersion relation (7.132) to

$$-\mathrm{i}\omega = -\eta k^2 - \iint \frac{k_j k_k \hat{Q}_{jk}(\boldsymbol{k}', \omega')}{\eta k^2 - \mathrm{i}(\omega - \omega')} \,\mathrm{d}\boldsymbol{k}' \,\mathrm{d}\omega'. \tag{7.136}$$

Now the same arguments will apply as did to (7.134): Assuming $\omega_i \geqq 0$ the real part of the left-hand side of (7.136) is positive semi-definite whereas the right-hand side is negative because of Bochner's theorem (Krause and Roberts [1, 2]).

The following estimations will show that no growing solutions can be found within the frame of the second order correlation approximation at all.

For any homogeneous isotropic mirrorsymmetric turbulence the Fourier-transformed correlation tensor can be written as

$$\hat{Q}_{ij}(\boldsymbol{k}, \omega) = \hat{Q}(k, \omega)\,(k^2 \delta_{ij} - k_i k_j) + \hat{Q}'(k, \omega)\, k_i k_j, \tag{7.137}$$

where

$$\hat{Q}(k, \omega) \geqq 0, \quad \hat{Q}'(k, \omega) \geqq 0, \tag{7.138}$$

because of Bochner's theorem (6.36). From the above investigations of incompressible turbulence it is clear that the contribution of the first summand in (7.137) on the right-hand side of the dispersion relation is always in the direction of negative ω_i. Therefore, the most favourable situation for having growing modes is provided by a potential random field, i.e. $\hat{Q} = 0$ and $\hat{Q}' = \hat{\Phi} \geqq 0$, with the denotation introduced in section 6.6. The dispersion relation (7.132) then simplifies to

$$p = \iint \frac{(\boldsymbol{k} \cdot \boldsymbol{k}')\,(k'^2 - (\boldsymbol{k} \cdot \boldsymbol{k}'))}{\eta(\boldsymbol{k} \cdot - \boldsymbol{k}')^2 - \mathrm{i}(\omega - \omega')} \hat{\Phi}(k', \omega')\,\mathrm{d}\boldsymbol{k}'\,\mathrm{d}\omega', \tag{7.139}$$

and assuming $\omega_i > 0$ we can write

$$\omega_i = \eta k^2 \Bigg[-1 + \frac{1}{\eta k^2} \iint \frac{(\boldsymbol{k} \cdot \boldsymbol{k}')\,(k'^2 - (\boldsymbol{k} \cdot \boldsymbol{k}'))\,(\eta(\boldsymbol{k} - \boldsymbol{k}')^2 + \omega_i)}{(\eta(\boldsymbol{k} - \boldsymbol{k}')^2 + \omega_i)^2 + (\omega_r - \omega')^2} \hat{\Phi}(k', \omega')\,\mathrm{d}\boldsymbol{k}'\,\mathrm{d}\omega' \Bigg], \tag{7.140}$$

where the ω'-contour is the real axis. Therefore $\omega_i > 0$ requires

$$\frac{1}{\eta k^2} \iint \frac{(\boldsymbol{k} \cdot \boldsymbol{k}')\,(k'^2 - (\boldsymbol{k} \cdot \boldsymbol{k}'))\,(\eta(\boldsymbol{k} - \boldsymbol{k}')^2 + \omega_i)}{(\eta(\boldsymbol{k} - \boldsymbol{k}')^2 + \omega_i)^2 + (\omega_r - \omega')^2} \hat{\Phi}(k', \omega')\,\mathrm{d}\boldsymbol{k}'\,\mathrm{d}\omega' > 1. \tag{7.141}$$

An inspection of the integrand shows that the region $|\boldsymbol{k}'| \ll |\boldsymbol{k}|$ always gives a negative contribution. The same holds for $|\boldsymbol{k}'| \approx |\boldsymbol{k}|$: The integrand is negative for $\boldsymbol{k}' \approx -\boldsymbol{k}$, positive for $\boldsymbol{k}' \approx \boldsymbol{k}$ but small, therefore altogether we have a negative contribution. Consequently, it is best to assume that $\Phi(\boldsymbol{k}', \omega') \approx 0$ for $|\boldsymbol{k}'| \lessapprox |\boldsymbol{k}|$, and $\Phi(\boldsymbol{k}', \omega') > 0$ for $|\boldsymbol{k}'| \gg |\boldsymbol{k}|$. The region where $\hat{\Phi} > 0$ is also characterized by the condition $|\boldsymbol{k}'| \approx 1/\lambda_{\text{cor}}$, thus we have the most favourable situation for having growing modes in case $1/\lambda_{\text{cor}} \gg |\boldsymbol{k}|$, i.e. for two-scale turbulence. However, in section 7.4. it was already shown that even for two-scale turbulence no growing modes exist. Consequently, we can state: Within the framework of the second order correlation approximation there is no evidence that homogeneous isotropic mirrorsymmetric turbulence can provide for dynamo excitation.

There are, however, suggestions that growing modes may exist in higher order approximations. Kasantzev [1] deduced a result of this kind using diagram techniques. The considerations of Gailitis [4] and of Kraichnan [5], however, give a much clearer idea by considering the helicity fluctuations in a homogeneous isotropic mirrorsymmetric turbulence to provide for dynamo excitation. The lowest level to prove this is the fourth order correlation approximation.

CHAPTER 8

THE TURBULENT ELECTROMOTIVE FORCE IN THE CASE OF NON-VANISHING MEAN FLOW

8.1. Introductory remarks

The considerations in the foregoing chapter already led to a number of important results and in this way quite an extensive insight in the subject was provided. However, just with regard to applications in cosmical physics neither homogeneity nor a non-vanishing mean flow can be assumed for those problems we intend to attack. The most obvious example in this respect is the convection in the upper layer of the Sun. In the convection zone of the Sun all physical quantities like pressure, temperature, mass density, etc., show a strong dependence on the radial coordinate. Therefore, the convection has to be looked upon as anisotropic and inhomogeneous, depending on the radial coordinate. Moreover, the turbulent convective motion undergoes the influence of the rotational motion, i.e. there is a non-vanishing mean motion. Consequently, an extension of the theory in two directions is desirable: Firstly, towards non-vanishing mean flow and, secondly, towards more general, especially inhomogeneous models of turbulence.

Our considerations in chapter 4 show that the first extension needs a determination of the Green's tensor for non-vanishing mean flow, a problem which can hardly be solved in a general way. However, for flows with constant rates of strain the Green's tensor can be represented in an almost explicit form (Krause [1, 2, 6, 9]). On the basis of this representation essential results can already be deduced, since, firstly, the rotational motion is a motion with constant rates of strain and, secondly, in the case of two-scale turbulence a motion of that kind can be considered to be a good approximation of a general motion.

As far as the extension to more general turbulence models is concerned we shall present here some examples of inhomogeneous turbulence undergoing the influence of Coriolis forces. It should be noted that we have arrived at a point that still lacks sufficient exploration. The results presented here, especially those of quantitative character, are therefore of limited applicability.

8.2. The Green's tensor for velocity fields with constant rates of strain

We represent the velocity field by

$$u_i = u_{ij}x_j + u_{0i}, \quad u_{ij}, u_{0i} \text{ constant}, \tag{8.1}$$

and introduce the tensor $\gamma_{ij}(t)$ by

$$\dot{\gamma}_{ij} = u_{ik}\gamma_{kj}, \quad \gamma_{ij}(0) = \delta_{ij}. \tag{8.2}$$

From the basic statements of the theory of ordinary differential equations it is clear that γ_{ij} exists and is uniquely defined. We have, e.g.,

$$\gamma_{ij}(t) = \begin{pmatrix} 1 & \omega^* t & 0 \\ 0 & 1 & 0 \\ 0 & 0 & 1 \end{pmatrix}, \tag{8.3}$$

if the shear flow

$$u_1 = \omega^* x_2, \quad u_2 = u_3 = 0, \tag{8.4}$$

is considered. For the rotational motion

$$\boldsymbol{u} = \boldsymbol{\Omega} \times \boldsymbol{x}, \quad \boldsymbol{\Omega} = \text{const}, \tag{8.5}$$

we obtain

$$\gamma_{ij}(t) = \frac{1}{\Omega^2}[\Omega_i\Omega_j + (\Omega^2\,\delta_{ij} - \Omega_i\Omega_j)\cos\Omega t] - \varepsilon_{ijp}\frac{\Omega_p}{\Omega}\sin\Omega t. \tag{8.6}$$

The first order result

$$\gamma_{ij}(t) = \delta_{ij} + u_{ij}t, \quad \text{if} \quad t \to 0, \tag{8.7}$$

holds for a general motion of type (8.1).

We note the following relations:

$$\gamma_{ij}(t_1 + t_2) = \gamma_{ik}(t_1)\,\gamma_{kj}(t_2), \tag{8.8}$$

$$\gamma_{ij}(-t) = \gamma_{ij}^{-1}(t), \tag{8.9}$$

$$u_{ij}\gamma_{jk}(t) = \gamma_{ij}(t)\,u_{jk}. \tag{8.10}$$

Relation (8.8) is clear since both the tensors, $\tilde{\gamma}_{ij}(t) = \gamma_{ij}(t + t_2)$ and $\tilde{\tilde{\gamma}}_{ij}(t) = \gamma_{ik}(t)\,\gamma_{kj}(t_2)$ solve equation (8.2) with the initial condition $\tilde{\gamma}_{ij}(0) = \tilde{\tilde{\gamma}}_{ij}(0) = \gamma_{ij}(t_2)$, hence both are identical. (8.9) follows immediately from (8.8) putting $t_1 = -t_2 = -t$. Differentiating the relation

$$\gamma_{ij}(t)\,\gamma_{jk}(-t) = \delta_{ik}$$

we obtain

$$\dot{\gamma}_{ij}(t)\,\gamma_{jk}(-t) - \gamma_{ij}(t)\,\dot{\gamma}_{jk}(-t) = 0$$

and with (8.2)

$$\gamma_{ik}(-t)\,[u_{il}\gamma_{lj}(t) - \gamma_{il}(t)\,u_{lj}] = 0\,.$$

From this follows relation (8.10).

For the determinant, $\gamma = \det\,(\gamma_{ij})$, we have $\dot{\gamma} = \dot{\gamma}_{ij}(t)\,\gamma_{ji}(-t)\,\gamma(t)$, if (8.9) is taken into account. (8.2) yields

$$\dot{\gamma}(t) = u_{ik}\gamma_{kj}(t)\,\gamma_{ji}(-t)\,\gamma(t) = u_{ii}\gamma(t)\,, \tag{8.11}$$

and we obtain finally

$$\gamma(t) = \mathrm{e}^{\operatorname{div} \boldsymbol{u}\cdot t}. \tag{8.12}$$

The equation of motion

$$\dot{\boldsymbol{x}} = \boldsymbol{u}\,, \tag{8.13}$$

with $\boldsymbol{u}$ given by (8.1) can now be integrated by

$$x_i(t) = \gamma_{ij}(t)\,x_{0j} + \int_0^t \gamma_{ij}(\tau)\,\mathrm{d}\tau\,u_{0j}\,. \tag{8.14}$$

With (8.2) and the inverse of (8.14) we find

$$\begin{aligned}\dot{x}_i &= \dot{\gamma}_{ij}x_{0j} + \gamma_{ij}u_{0j} = u_{ik}\left[x_k - \int_0^t \gamma_{kj}(\tau)\,\mathrm{d}\tau\,u_{0j}\right] + \gamma_{ij}u_{0j}\\ &= u_{ik}x_k + u_{0j}\left[\gamma_{ij} - \int_0^t \dot{\gamma}_{ij}(\tau)\,\mathrm{d}\tau\right] = u_{ik}x_k + u_{0i}\,,\end{aligned}$$

thus confirming the above statement.

(8.14) describes the path of a particle moving with the flow which was found at $\boldsymbol{x}_0$ for $t = 0$. This allows us to introduce co-moving coordinates $\boldsymbol{x}'$ by

$$x_i' = \gamma_{ij}(-t)\,x_j + \int_0^{-t} \gamma_{ij}(\tau)\,\mathrm{d}\tau\,u_{0j}\,, \tag{8.15}$$

and the equations for the magnetic field read

$$\frac{\partial B_i}{\partial t} = (-\operatorname{div} \boldsymbol{u}\,\delta_{ij} + u_{ij})\,B_j + \frac{1}{\mu\sigma}\gamma_{jr}(-t)\,\gamma_{kr}(-t)\,\frac{\partial^2 B_i}{\partial x_j'\partial x_k'}\,, \tag{8.16}$$

$$\operatorname{div} \boldsymbol{B} = \gamma_{ri}(-t)\,\frac{\partial B_i}{\partial x_r'} = 0\,. \tag{8.17}$$

Introducing Fourier transforms with respect to the space coordinates $\boldsymbol{x}'$ we obtain

$$\frac{\partial \tilde{B}_i(\boldsymbol{k},t)}{\partial t} = \left\{-\left[\operatorname{div} \boldsymbol{u} + \frac{1}{\mu\sigma}\gamma_{pr}(-t)\,\gamma_{qr}(-t)\,k_p k_q\right]\delta_{ij} + u_{ij}\right\}\tilde{B}_j(\boldsymbol{k},t), \tag{8.18}$$

$$\gamma_{ri}(-t)\,k_r \tilde{B}_i(\boldsymbol{k},t) = 0. \tag{8.19}$$

Using (8.2) and (8.12) we easily find the solution

$$\tilde{B}_i(\boldsymbol{k},t) = \frac{\gamma_{ij}(t)}{\gamma(t)}\exp\left[-\frac{t}{\mu\sigma}c_{pq}^{-1}(t)\,k_p k_q\right]\tilde{B}_{0j}(\boldsymbol{k}), \tag{8.20}$$

with

$$k_j \tilde{B}_{0j}(\boldsymbol{k}) = 0. \tag{8.21}$$

We introduced in (8.20) the symmetric positive definite tensor c_{pq}^{-1} defined by

$$c_{pq}^{-1}(t) = \frac{1}{t}\int_0^t \gamma_{pr}(-\tau)\,\gamma_{qr}(-\tau)\,\mathrm{d}\tau, \tag{8.22}$$

where the notation indicates that later on we shall use the inverse tensor c_{pq} defined by $c_{pq}c_{qr}^{-1} = \delta_{pr}$. The field $\tilde{\boldsymbol{B}}_0(\boldsymbol{k})$ introduced in (8.20) is clearly the Fourier transform of the initial field $B_i(\boldsymbol{x}, 0)$.

Let $\boldsymbol{x}_t$ denote the coordinates of a point that moves with the velocity $\boldsymbol{u}$ and at the time $t = 0$ was found at $\boldsymbol{x}$. Explicitly we have according to (8.14)

$$(\boldsymbol{x}_t)_i = \gamma_{ij}(t)\,x_j + \int_0^t \gamma_{ij}(\tau)\,\mathrm{d}\tau\, u_{0j}. \tag{8.23}$$

Then the coordinate $\boldsymbol{x}'$ introduced in (8.15) is clearly given by

$$\boldsymbol{x}' = \boldsymbol{x}_{-t}. \tag{8.24}$$

According to the above analysis we have

$$B_i(\boldsymbol{x},t) = \int \tilde{B}_i(\boldsymbol{k},t)\,\mathrm{e}^{\mathrm{i}\boldsymbol{k}\cdot\boldsymbol{x}_{-t}}\,\mathrm{d}\boldsymbol{k}, \quad B_i(\boldsymbol{x},0) = \int \tilde{B}_{0i}(\boldsymbol{k})\,\mathrm{e}^{\mathrm{i}\boldsymbol{k}\cdot\boldsymbol{x}}\,\mathrm{d}\boldsymbol{k}. \tag{8.25}$$

Now inserting (8.20) we obtain the representation of $B_i(\boldsymbol{x}, t)$ in the form

$$B_i(\boldsymbol{x},t) = \int G_{ij}(\boldsymbol{x},\xi,t,0)\,B_j(\xi,0)\,\mathrm{d}\xi, \tag{8.26}$$

where the tensor G_{ij} is given by

$$G_{ij}(\boldsymbol{x},\xi,t,\tau) = \gamma_{ij}(t-\tau)\,G'(\boldsymbol{x}_{-(t-\tau)} - \xi, t-\tau \mid \overline{\boldsymbol{u}}), \tag{8.27}$$

and

$$G'(\boldsymbol{x},t \mid \overline{\boldsymbol{u}}) = \begin{cases} \dfrac{1}{\gamma(t)}\dfrac{1}{(2\pi)^3}\displaystyle\int \exp\left\{-\frac{t}{\mu\sigma}c_{pq}^{-1}(t)k_p k_q + \mathrm{i}\boldsymbol{k}\boldsymbol{x}\right\}\mathrm{d}\boldsymbol{k}, & t \geqq 0, \\ 0\,, & t < 0. \end{cases} \tag{8.28}$$

(8.26) is the solution of the initial value problem of the induction equation for velocity fields with constant rates of strain. Consequently, the tensor G_{ij} introduced by (8.27) and (8.28) is, indeed, the Green's tensor as defined in section 4.5.

Let C_{kl} be a positive definite tensor. Then we have

$$\frac{1}{(2\pi)^3}\int \exp\left\{-C_{kl}k_k k_l + \mathrm{i}\boldsymbol{k}\cdot\xi\right\}\mathrm{d}\boldsymbol{k} = \frac{1}{\sqrt{4\pi^3}}\frac{1}{\sqrt{C}}\exp\left\{-\frac{1}{4}C_{pq}^{-1}\xi_p\xi_q\right\}, \quad (8.29)$$

a relation which is easily proved by using the principal-axis transformation of the tensor C_{kl}. This result enables us to evaluate the integral (8.28) and we find

$$G'(\boldsymbol{x},t\,|\,\boldsymbol{u}) = \begin{cases} \left(\dfrac{\mu\sigma}{4\pi t}\right)^{3/2}\dfrac{\sqrt{c}}{\gamma}\exp\left\{-\dfrac{\mu\sigma}{4t}c_{pq}x_p x_q\right\}, & \text{if } t \geqq 0, \\ 0\ , & \text{if } t < 0. \end{cases} \quad (8.30)$$

There is an alternative representation of the Green's tensor G_{ij}, which proves to be useful later on. The tensor d_{pq} shall be defined by

$$d_{pq}(t) = c_{rs}(t)\,\gamma_{rp}(-t)\,\gamma_{sq}(-t)\,. \quad (8.31)$$

Then we obtain from (8.27) and (8.30) the slightly different representation of the Green's tensor

$$G_{ij}(\boldsymbol{x},\xi,t,\tau) = \gamma_{ij}(t-\tau)\,G(\boldsymbol{x}-\xi_{t-\tau},t-\tau\,|\,\boldsymbol{u})\,, \quad (8.32)$$

with the function G given by

$$G(\boldsymbol{x},t\,|\,\boldsymbol{u}) = \begin{cases} \left(\dfrac{\mu\sigma}{4\pi t}\right)^{3/2}\sqrt{d}\exp\left\{-\dfrac{\mu\sigma}{4t}d_{pq}x_p x_q\right\}, & \text{if } t \geqq 0, \\ 0\ , & \text{if } t < 0. \end{cases} \quad (8.33)$$

We note the relation

$$d_{pq}^{-1}(t) = \frac{1}{t}\int_0^t \gamma_{pr}(\tau)\,\gamma_{qr}(\tau)\,\mathrm{d}\tau = c_{pq}^{-1}(-t)\,, \quad (8.34)$$

which follows from (8.8), (8.22) and (8.31). As a consequence we have

$$d_{pq}(t) = c_{pq}(-t)\,. \quad (8.35)$$

Some remarks shall conclude this section:

The tensors c_{pq} and d_{pq} are equal to the Kronecker tensor not only in the case $u_{ij} = 0$, but also for a rotational motion since $\gamma_{kr}(t)\,\gamma_{lr}(t) = \delta_{kl}$.

For the shear flow (8.3) we find from (8.34)

$$d^{-1}_{pq}(t) = c^{-1}_{pq}(-t) = \begin{pmatrix} 1 + \frac{1}{3}(\omega^* t)^2 & \frac{1}{2}\omega^* t & 0 \\ \frac{1}{2}\omega^* t & 1 & 0 \\ 0 & 0 & 1 \end{pmatrix}, \tag{8.36}$$

and

$$d_{pq}(t) = c_{pq}(-t) = \frac{1}{1 + \frac{1}{12}(\omega^* t)^2} \begin{pmatrix} 1 & -\frac{1}{2}\omega^* t & 0 \\ -\frac{1}{2}\omega^* t & 1 + \frac{1}{3}(\omega^* t)^2 & 0 \\ 0 & 0 & 1 \end{pmatrix}, \tag{8.37}$$

(Rädler [1], Krause [2]).

For a general flow of type (8.1) we note the first order result

$$d_{pq}(t) = c_{pq}(-t) = \delta_{pq} - \frac{1}{2}(u_{pq} + u_{qp})\, t, \tag{8.38}$$

which shows the tensors c_{pq} and d_{pq} to be closely connected with the deformations which a fluid element undergoes following the motion.

8.3. Representation of the turbulent electromotive force

We start from the representation of $\mathfrak{E}$ in the frame of second order correlation approximation

$$\mathfrak{E}_i(\boldsymbol{x}, t) = \varepsilon_{ijk}\varepsilon_{lmn}\varepsilon_{npq} \iint \frac{\partial G_{kl}(\boldsymbol{x}, \boldsymbol{x} - \boldsymbol{\xi}, t, t - \tau)}{\partial \xi_m} Q_{jp}(\boldsymbol{x}, -\boldsymbol{\xi}, t, -\tau)\, \overline{B}_q(\boldsymbol{x} - \boldsymbol{\xi}, t - \tau)\, \mathrm{d}\boldsymbol{\xi}\, \mathrm{d}\tau, \tag{8.39}$$

which we obtain from (4.54) and (4.55). Inserting (8.32) we find

$$\mathfrak{E}_i(\boldsymbol{x}, t) = \varepsilon_{ijk}\varepsilon_{lmn}\varepsilon_{npq} \iint \gamma_{kl}(\tau) \frac{\partial G(\boldsymbol{x} - (\boldsymbol{x} - \boldsymbol{\xi})_\tau, \tau \mid \overline{\boldsymbol{u}})}{\partial \xi_m} Q_{jp}(\boldsymbol{x}, -\boldsymbol{\xi}, t, -\tau)\, \overline{B}_q(\boldsymbol{x} - \boldsymbol{\xi}, t - \tau)\, \mathrm{d}\boldsymbol{\xi}\, \mathrm{d}\tau. \tag{8.40}$$

We now introduce the new variable $\boldsymbol{\xi}'$ by

$$\boldsymbol{x} - \boldsymbol{\xi}' = (\boldsymbol{x} - \boldsymbol{\xi})_\tau, \tag{8.41}$$

and can thus rewrite the integral by

$$\mathfrak{E}_i(\boldsymbol{x}, t) = \varepsilon_{ijk}\varepsilon_{lmn}\varepsilon_{npq} \iint \frac{\gamma_{kl}(\tau)\,\gamma_{rm}(\tau)}{\gamma(\tau)} \frac{\partial G(\boldsymbol{\xi}, \tau \mid \overline{\boldsymbol{u}})}{\partial \xi_r}$$

$$Q_{jp}(\boldsymbol{x}, (\boldsymbol{x} - \boldsymbol{\xi})_{-\tau} - \boldsymbol{x}, t, -\tau)\, \overline{B}_q((\boldsymbol{x} - \boldsymbol{\xi})_{-\tau}, t - \tau)\, \mathrm{d}\boldsymbol{\xi}\, \mathrm{d}\tau; \qquad (8.42)$$

deleting the dash at $\boldsymbol{\xi}$ when writing down this formula. If we insert the relations

$$\varepsilon_{lmn} = \gamma(\tau)\, \varepsilon_{stu}\gamma_{ls}(-\tau)\, \gamma_{mt}(-\tau)\, \gamma_{nu}(-\tau), \qquad (8.43)$$

$$\varepsilon_{npq} = \gamma(-\tau)\, \varepsilon_{vwx}\gamma_{vn}(\tau)\, \gamma_{wp}(\tau)\, \gamma_{xq}(\tau), \qquad (8.44)$$

(8.42) yields for a proper choice of the dummy indices

$$\mathfrak{E}_i(\boldsymbol{x}, t) = \varepsilon_{ijk}\varepsilon_{klm}\varepsilon_{mnp} \iint \frac{\partial G(\boldsymbol{\xi}, \tau \mid \overline{\boldsymbol{u}})}{\partial \xi_l} \gamma_{nq}(\tau)\, Q_{jq}(\boldsymbol{x}, (\boldsymbol{x} - \boldsymbol{\xi})_{-\tau} - \boldsymbol{x}, t, -\tau)$$

$$\frac{\gamma_{pr}(\tau)}{\gamma(\tau)}\, \overline{B}_r((\boldsymbol{x} - \boldsymbol{\xi})_{-\tau}, t - \tau)\, \mathrm{d}\boldsymbol{\xi}\, \mathrm{d}\tau. \qquad (8.45)$$

For an interpretation of this formula let us first introduce a coördinate system $\boldsymbol{y}$ co-moving with the mean flow $\overline{\boldsymbol{u}}$ by

$$x_k = \gamma_{kl}(t - t_0)\, y_l + \int_0^{t-t_0} \gamma_{kl}(\tau)\, \mathrm{d}\tau\, \overline{u}_{0l}; \qquad (8.46)$$

at the time t_0 both systems are identical. By taking the time derivative of (8.46) we obtain from (8.13), (8.14)

$$\frac{\mathrm{d}x_k}{\mathrm{d}t} = \overline{u}_{kl}x_l = \overline{u}_{0k} + \gamma_{kl}(t - t_0)\, \frac{\mathrm{d}y_l}{\mathrm{d}t}. \qquad (8.47)$$

The velocity with respect to the co-moving frame shall be denoted by $\boldsymbol{v}$, i.e.

$$\boldsymbol{v} = \frac{\mathrm{d}\boldsymbol{y}}{\mathrm{d}t}.$$

Taking into account that

$$\frac{\mathrm{d}\boldsymbol{x}}{\mathrm{d}t} = \boldsymbol{u} = \overline{\boldsymbol{u}} + \boldsymbol{u}', \qquad (8.48)$$

we have

$$v_k(\boldsymbol{y}, t) = \gamma_{kl}(t_0 - t)\, u_l'(\boldsymbol{x}, t), \qquad (8.49)$$

$$u_k'(\boldsymbol{x}, t) = \gamma_{kl}(t - t_0)\, v_l(\boldsymbol{y}, t), \qquad (8.50)$$

where the arguments are related by

$$\boldsymbol{x} = \boldsymbol{y}_{t-t_0}, \quad \boldsymbol{y} = \boldsymbol{x}_{t_0-t}. \qquad (8.51)$$

For our applications to the integral (8.45) we identify t_0 with t and t with $t - \tau$.

From (8.49), (8.50) and (8.51) we get

$$\mathfrak{E}_i(\boldsymbol{x}, t) = \varepsilon_{ijk}\varepsilon_{klm}\varepsilon_{mnp} \iint \frac{\partial G(\xi, \tau \mid \overline{\boldsymbol{u}})}{\partial \xi_l} Q_{jn}(\boldsymbol{x}, -\xi, t, -\tau \mid \overline{\boldsymbol{u}}) \frac{\gamma_{pr}(\tau)}{\gamma(\tau)} \overline{B}_r((\boldsymbol{x} - \xi)_{-\tau}, t - \tau) \, d\xi \, d\tau, \tag{8.52}$$

where we introduced the correlation tensor

$$Q_{jn}(\boldsymbol{x}, \xi, t, \tau \mid \overline{\boldsymbol{u}}) = \overline{v_j(\boldsymbol{x}, t) \, v_n(\boldsymbol{x} + \xi, t + \tau)}. \tag{8.53}$$

which is formed from the velocity components with respect to the frame co-moving with the mean motion.

Considering the latter part in the integrand of (8.52) we draw attention to the well-known representation of the solution of the induction equation in the case of an ideally conducting medium, which can be written in the form

$$\frac{\boldsymbol{B}(\boldsymbol{x}, t)}{\varrho(\boldsymbol{x}, t)} = \left(\frac{\boldsymbol{B}(\boldsymbol{x}_0, t_0)}{\varrho(\boldsymbol{x}_0, t_0)} \cdot \text{grad}_0\right) \boldsymbol{x}(\boldsymbol{x}_0, t_0), \tag{8.54}$$

where ϱ is the mass density and $\boldsymbol{x}(\boldsymbol{x}_0, t_0)$ the integral of the equation of motion $\dot{\boldsymbol{x}} = \boldsymbol{u}$. From the equation of continuity

$$\frac{\partial \varrho}{\partial t} + \text{div} \, \varrho \boldsymbol{u} = 0, \tag{8.55}$$

and the definition of γ in (8.12) we can take

$$\frac{\varrho(\boldsymbol{x}, t)}{\varrho(\boldsymbol{x}_0, t_0)} = \frac{1}{\gamma(t - t_0)}. \tag{8.56}$$

Consequently, we see from (8.14) that the field $\frac{\gamma_{pr}(\tau)}{\gamma(\tau)} \overline{B}_r((\boldsymbol{x} - \xi)_{-\tau}, t - \tau)$ would be identical with $\overline{B_p}(\boldsymbol{x} - \xi, t)$ when the mean magnetic field is frozen-in in the mean motion. Or, in other words, we have

$$\overline{B}_p(\boldsymbol{x}, t) = \frac{\gamma_{pr}(\tau)}{\gamma(\tau)} \overline{B}_r((\boldsymbol{x} - \xi)_{-\tau}, t - \tau) \tag{8.57}$$

as long as the mean magnetic field can be looked upon as frozen-in in the mean motion. Hence, relation (8.57) can be used for an evaluation of (8.52) when the mean magnetic field does not greatly diffuse over a time interval of length τ_{cor}, an assumption which is already familiar to us from the considerations of two-scale turbulence in section 5.4. Under this condition (8.52) takes the form

$$\mathfrak{E}_i(\boldsymbol{x}, t) = \varepsilon_{ijk}\varepsilon_{klm}\varepsilon_{mnp} \iint \frac{\partial G(\xi, \tau \mid \overline{\boldsymbol{u}})}{\partial \xi_l} Q_{jn}(\boldsymbol{x}, -\xi, -\tau \mid \overline{\boldsymbol{u}}) \overline{B}_p(\boldsymbol{x} - \xi, t) \, d\xi \, d\tau. \tag{8.58}$$

This representation of the electromotive force $\mathfrak{E}$ differs only slightly from that of the case $\overline{\boldsymbol{u}} = 0$.

Assuming that the mean magnetic field has the two-scale property also with respect to the space coordinates we obtain from (8.5) for the tensors a_{ip}, b_{ipq}

$$a_{ip} = \varepsilon_{ijk}\varepsilon_{klm}\varepsilon_{mnp} \iint \frac{\partial G(\xi, \tau \mid \overline{u})}{\partial \xi_l} Q_{jn}(x, -\xi, t, -\tau \mid \overline{u})\, d\xi\, d\tau, \tag{8.59}$$

$$b_{ipq} = -\varepsilon_{ijk}\varepsilon_{klm}\varepsilon_{mnp} \iint \frac{\partial G(\xi, \tau \mid \overline{u})}{\partial \xi_l} \xi_q Q_{jn}(x, -\xi, t, -\tau \mid \overline{u})\, d\xi\, d\tau. \tag{8.60}$$

8.4. On the influence of a mean motion on the correlation tensor

The results (8.58), (8.59) and (8.60) of the foregoing investigations show that we still have to determine the correlation tensor undergoing the influence of a mean motion. Attempting this we have to start from an ensemble of equations including Navier-Stokes equation, the equation of continuity, equations of state, etc. We see already that there is less hope of finding a sufficiently general model which can be treated. Therefore we restrict ourselves to the incompressible case, i.e. we consider the Navier-Stokes equation in the form

$$\frac{\partial \boldsymbol{u}}{\partial t} + (\boldsymbol{u} \cdot \nabla p)\, \boldsymbol{u} = -\frac{1}{\varrho} \nabla p + \boldsymbol{F} + \nu \Delta \boldsymbol{u}, \tag{8.61}$$

and the equation of continuity

$$\operatorname{div} \boldsymbol{u} = 0. \tag{8.62}$$

p denotes the pressure, $\boldsymbol{F}$ the forces and ν the viscosity. By taking the average we obtain the Reynolds equations

$$\frac{\partial \overline{u}_i}{\partial t} + \overline{u}_k \frac{\partial \overline{u}_i}{\partial x_k} - \nu \Delta \overline{u}_i = -\frac{1}{\varrho} \frac{\partial \overline{p}}{\partial x_i} + \overline{F}_i - \frac{\partial Q_{ik}(x, 0, t, 0)}{\partial x_k}, \tag{8.63}$$

$$\operatorname{div} \overline{\boldsymbol{u}} = 0. \tag{8.64}$$

The equation governing $\boldsymbol{u}'$ is obtained by subtracing (8.63) from (8.61). It is

$$\frac{\partial u_i'}{\partial t} - \nu \Delta u_i' = -\frac{1}{\varrho} \frac{\partial p'}{\partial x_i} - \frac{\partial}{\partial x_k} (\overline{u}_k u_i' + u_k' \overline{u}_i) + F_i' + \frac{\partial}{\partial x_k} (u_i' u_k' - Q_{ik}(x, 0, t, 0)). \tag{8.65}$$

We assume that the turbulent motion is due to the force $\boldsymbol{F}'$, i.e. $\boldsymbol{F}'$ excites $\boldsymbol{u}'$ in some way, which we do not discuss explicitly.

We now confine ourselves to the second order correlation approximation and therefore neglect in (8.65) the term which is of second order in the fluctuations. We then have to deal with the equations

$$\frac{\partial u_i'}{\partial t} - \nu \Delta u_i' = -\frac{1}{\varrho} \frac{\partial p'}{\partial x_i} - \frac{\partial}{\partial x_k} (\overline{u}_k u_i' + u_k' \overline{u}_i) + F_i', \tag{8.66}$$

$$\operatorname{div} \boldsymbol{u}' = \frac{\partial u_i'}{\partial x_i} = 0. \tag{8.67}$$

This procedure is permitted whenever

$$\min(\mathrm{Re}, \mathrm{S}) \ll 1, \tag{8.68}$$

where S was already defined by (3.14), and Re is the Reynolds number

$$\mathrm{Re} = \frac{u'\lambda_{\mathrm{cor}}}{\nu}. \tag{8.69}$$

Having in mind to determine the correlation tensor in the coordinate system co-moving with the mean motion, we restrict ourselves to those motions which have constant rates of strain, and use the coordinates introduced in (8.46). From (8.49) with (8.2) and (8.10) it is found that

$$\frac{\partial v_i}{\partial t} = \gamma_{ij}(t_0 - t)\left[\frac{\partial u_j'}{\partial t} + \bar{u}_l \frac{\partial u_j'}{\partial x_l} - u_l' \frac{\partial \bar{u}_j}{\partial x_l}\right], \tag{8.70}$$

thus leading to a representation of equations (8.66), (8.67) in a co-moving frame,

$$\frac{\partial v_i}{\partial t} + 2\bar{u}_{ij} v_j - \nu\gamma_{jr}(t_0 - t)\,\gamma_{kr}(t_0 - t)\frac{\partial^2 v_i}{\partial y_j \partial y_k} =$$
$$- \gamma_{ij}(t_0 - t)\,\gamma_{kj}(t_0 - t)\frac{\partial p'}{\partial y_k} + f_i', \tag{8.71}$$

$$\frac{\partial v_i}{\partial y_i} = 0. \tag{8.72}$$

f' denotes the force in the co-moving system,

$$f_i'(y, t) = \gamma_{ij}(t_0 - t)\, F_j'(x, t). \tag{8.73}$$

One realizes the generalized Coriolis forces as the second term on the left of equation (8.71).

Introduce now Fourier transforms with respect to the space coordinates. From (8.71), (8.72) follows

$$\frac{\partial \tilde{v}_i}{\partial t} + 2\bar{u}_{ij}\,\tilde{v}_j + \nu\gamma_{jr}(t_0 - t)\,\gamma_{kr}(t_0 - t)\,k_j k_k \tilde{v}_i$$
$$= - \gamma_{ij}(t_0 - t)\,\gamma_{kj}(t_0 - t)\, i k_k \tilde{p}' + \tilde{f}_i', \tag{8.74}$$

$$k_i \tilde{v}_i = 0. \tag{8.75}$$

Elimination of the pressure yields

$$\frac{\partial \tilde{v}_i}{\partial t} + 2\left[\delta_{ip} - \frac{\gamma_{ij}(t_0 - t)\,\gamma_{lj}(t_0 - t)\,k_l k_p}{\gamma_{mr}(t_0 - t)\,\gamma_{nr}(t_0 - t)\,k_m k_n}\right]\bar{u}_{pq}\tilde{v}_q \tag{8.76}$$
$$+ \nu\gamma_{jr}(t_0 - t)\,\gamma_{kr}(t_0 - t)\,k_j k_k \tilde{v}_i = \left[\delta_{ip} - \frac{\gamma_{ij}(t_0 - t)\,\gamma_{lj}(t_0 - t)\,k_l k_p}{\gamma_{mr}(t_0 - t)\,\gamma_{nr}(t_0 - t)\,k_m k_n}\right]\hat{f}_p'.$$

At least at this point we see that for the general case we cannot expect a result which is easy to comprehend. We, therefore, restrict ourselves to rotational motions in the following and rely for our representation of the deductions on a paper by RÜDIGER [5]. Another possibility of further treating equation (8.76) is the restriction to a first order theory in the mean motion (KRAUSE [2]).

8.5. On the influence of a rotational motion on the correlation tensor

For the rotational motion (8.5) equation (8.76) simply reads

$$\frac{\partial \tilde{v}_i}{\partial t} + \frac{2}{k^2}(k^2\,\delta_{ip} - k_ik_p)\,\bar{u}_{pq}\tilde{v}_q + \nu k^2\tilde{v}_i = (k^2\,\delta_{ip} - k_ik_p)\frac{\tilde{f}'_p}{k^2}. \tag{8.77}$$

Introduce the Fourier transforms $\hat{v}_i$, $\hat{f}_i$ with respect to space and time coordinates and write

$$\hat{v}_i^{(0)} = \frac{(k^2\,\delta_{ip} - k_ik_p)\,\hat{f}'_p}{(\nu k^2 - \mathrm{i}\omega)\,k^2}. \tag{8.78}$$

$\boldsymbol{v}^{(0)}$ is clearly that turbulence field which would be excited by the forces $\boldsymbol{f}'$ when there is no mean motion. The forces $\boldsymbol{f}'$ should not depend on the mean motion. In the following we assume that $\boldsymbol{v}^{(0)}$ has a simple structure, e.g. homogeneous isotropic, or inhomogeneous and anisotropic with respect to one preferred direction, and investigate the influence of the rotational motion on such turbulence.

As an equation for $\hat{v}_i$ (8.77) can be cast in the form

$$D_{ij}^{-1}\hat{v}_j = \hat{v}_i^{(0)}, \quad k_i\hat{v}_i = k_i\hat{v}_i^{(0)} = 0, \tag{8.79}$$

with

$$D_{ij}^{-1} = \delta_{ij} - \frac{1}{\nu k^2 - \mathrm{i}\omega}\frac{2\boldsymbol{\Omega}\cdot\boldsymbol{k}}{k^2}\varepsilon_{ijk}k_k. \tag{8.80}$$

The system (8.79) can be reversed by

$$\hat{v}_i = D_{ij}\hat{v}_j^{(0)},\ k_i\hat{v}_i = k_i\hat{v}_i^{(0)} = 0, \tag{8.81}$$

with

$$D_{ij} = \delta_{ij} + \frac{1}{\nu k^2 - \mathrm{i}\omega}\frac{2\boldsymbol{\Omega}\cdot\boldsymbol{k}}{k^2}\varepsilon_{ijk}k_k \tag{8.82}$$

in first order with respect to $\boldsymbol{\Omega}$. D_{ij} is an even function of $\boldsymbol{k}$. For later use we note the relations

$$D_{ik}D_{jk}^{*} = \delta_{ij} + \frac{4\mathrm{i}\omega\boldsymbol{\Omega}\cdot\boldsymbol{k}}{k^2(\nu^2k^4 + \omega^2)}\varepsilon_{ijk}k_k, \tag{8.83}$$

$$D_{ik}k_k = D_{ik}^{*}k_k = k_i. \tag{8.84}$$

From (8.53) follows

$$Q_{ij}(\boldsymbol{x}, \xi, t, \tau \mid \overline{\boldsymbol{u}}) = \iint \hat{Q}_{ij}(\boldsymbol{x}, \boldsymbol{k}, t, \tau \mid \overline{\boldsymbol{u}}) \, \mathrm{e}^{\mathrm{i}(\boldsymbol{k}\cdot\boldsymbol{\xi} - \omega\tau)} \, \mathrm{d}\boldsymbol{k} \, \mathrm{d}\omega \,, \tag{8.85}$$

with

$$\hat{Q}_{ij}(\boldsymbol{x}, \boldsymbol{k}, t, \omega \mid \overline{\boldsymbol{u}}) = \iint \overline{\hat{v}_i(\boldsymbol{k}', \omega') \, \hat{v}_j(\boldsymbol{k}, \omega)} \, \mathrm{e}^{\mathrm{i}((\boldsymbol{k}+\boldsymbol{k}')\boldsymbol{x} - (\omega+\omega')t)} \, \mathrm{d}\boldsymbol{k}' \, \mathrm{d}\omega' \,. \tag{8.86}$$

Let $\hat{Q}_{ij}^{(0)}(\boldsymbol{x}, \boldsymbol{k}, t, \omega)$ be accordingly defined as $\hat{Q}_{ij}$ in (8.86), then follows from (8.81)

$$\hat{Q}_{ij}(\boldsymbol{x}, \boldsymbol{k}, t, \omega \mid \overline{\boldsymbol{u}}) = \frac{1}{(2\pi)^4} \iint D_{ik}(\boldsymbol{k}', \omega') \, D_{jl}(\boldsymbol{k}, \omega)$$

$$\hat{Q}_{kl}^{(0)}(\boldsymbol{x} + \boldsymbol{x}', \boldsymbol{k}, t + t', \omega) \, \mathrm{e}^{-\mathrm{i}((\boldsymbol{k}+\boldsymbol{k}')\boldsymbol{x}' - (\omega+\omega')t')} \, \mathrm{d}\boldsymbol{k}' \, \mathrm{d}\omega' \, \mathrm{d}\boldsymbol{x}' \, \mathrm{d}t' \,. \tag{8.87}$$

In the case of homogeneous steady turbulence $\boldsymbol{v}^{(0)}$ we obtain

$$\hat{Q}_{ij}(\boldsymbol{k}, \omega \mid \overline{\boldsymbol{u}}) = D_{ik}^{*} D_{jl} \hat{Q}_{kl}^{(0)}(\boldsymbol{k}, \omega) \,. \tag{8.88}$$

Let $\hat{Q}_{kl}^{(0)}$ depend linearly on $\boldsymbol{x}$, thus we can write

$$\hat{Q}_{kl}^{(0)}(\boldsymbol{x} + \boldsymbol{x}', \boldsymbol{k}, \omega) = \hat{Q}_{kl}^{(0)}(\boldsymbol{x}, \boldsymbol{k}, \omega) + x_m' \, \frac{\partial \hat{Q}_{kl}^{(0)}(\boldsymbol{x}, \boldsymbol{k}, \omega)}{\partial x_m} \,. \tag{8.89}$$

Then from (8.87) follows

$$\hat{Q}_{ij}(\boldsymbol{x}, \boldsymbol{k}, \omega \mid \overline{\boldsymbol{u}}) = D_{ik}^{*}(\boldsymbol{k}, \omega) \, D_{jl}(\boldsymbol{k}, \omega) \, \hat{Q}_{kl}^{(0)}(\boldsymbol{x}, \boldsymbol{k}, \omega)$$

$$+ \mathrm{i} \, \frac{\partial D_{ik}^{*}(\boldsymbol{k}, \omega)}{\partial k_m} \, D_{jl}(\boldsymbol{k}, \omega) \, \frac{\partial \hat{Q}_{kl}^{(0)}(\boldsymbol{x}, \boldsymbol{k}, \omega)}{\partial x_m} \,. \tag{8.90}$$

Both the relations, (8.88) and (8.90), solve our problem, i.e. the determination of the influence of the mean motion on the correlation tensor, for the special turbulences considered here. It should be noted in particular that we now find more realistic turbulences with helicity. For, let $\hat{Q}_{kl}^{(0)} = \hat{Q}(k^2 \, \delta_{kl} - k_k k_l)$, so that

$$\hat{Q}_{ij}(\boldsymbol{x}, \boldsymbol{k}, \omega \mid \overline{\boldsymbol{u}}) = \hat{Q} \left[(k^2 \, \delta_{ij} - k_i k_j) + \frac{4\mathrm{i}\omega \boldsymbol{\Omega} \cdot \boldsymbol{k}}{\nu^2 k^4 + \omega^2} \varepsilon_{ijk} k_k \right] , \tag{8.91}$$

because of (8.88), (8.83), (8.84). The last term indicates, indeed, helicity, i.e. the imbalance of the two kinds of screw motions. However, in this case the integral helicity,

$$h = \mathrm{i} \, \varepsilon_{ijl} \iint k_l \hat{Q}_{ij}(\boldsymbol{x}, \boldsymbol{k}, \omega \mid \overline{\boldsymbol{u}}) \, \mathrm{d}\boldsymbol{k} \, \mathrm{d}\omega \,, \tag{8.92}$$

vanishes since $\hat{Q}$ is an even function of ω because of (6.20). If the turbulence $\boldsymbol{v}^{(0)}$ is still incompressible but anisotropic then $\hat{Q}$ has to be exchanged for $\hat{Q}(k, \omega) + \hat{Q}'(k, \omega) \, \boldsymbol{g} \cdot \boldsymbol{k}$, where $\hat{Q}'$ is an odd function of ω because of (6.20). Now we have a non-vanishing integral helicity (8.92).

CHAPTER 9

THE TURBULENT ELECTROMOTIVE FORCE IN THE CASE OF ROTATIONAL MEAN MOTION

9.1. Illustrating examples

We closed the foregoing chapter by showing that turbulences which have originally no helicity, do have helicity if they undergo the influence of a rotational motion. We could see this in both the cases of an originally isotropic and anisotropic turbulence. We assumed incompressibility, but that was for technical reasons only. A consideration of compressible turbulence would require more mathematical effort.

We shall present here physical arguments in order to show that it is quite natural for turbulences on a rotating body to have helicity. Figure 9.1 illustrates the situation in a compressible medium; it reflects the conditions in the convection zone of the Sun in the northern hemisphere. Rising matter will expand and rotate because of the action of Coriolis forces, thus providing for a left-handed helical motion. Sinking matter is compressed and is forced by the Coriolis forces to rotate in the opposite direction, again a left-handed helical motion. We realize that the convection in the northern hemisphere of the Sun shows a higher probability of left-handed helical motions than of right-handed ones. Obviously, in the southern hemisphere the right-handed helical motions will prevail.

Figure 9.2 illustrates the conditions for an incompressible fluid. A balance of left-handed and right-handed helical motions will exist in the medium layer

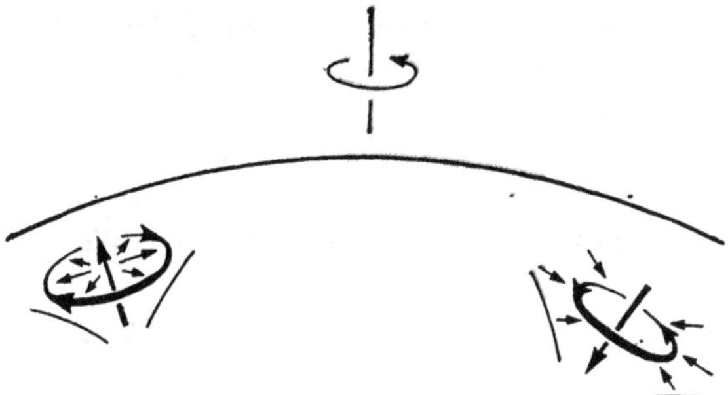

Fig. 9.1. Schematic drawing which explains that in the northern hemisphere of the Sun left-handed helical motions are more probable than right-handed ones

(the intersection of a and b) only if there is no gradient in the turbulence intensity, since one kind of helical motions comes from below (layer a) and the other from above (layer b). Consequently, a gradient in the turbulence intensity in a turbulent medium on a rotating body provides for helicity under the conditions of a flat geometry as considered in figure 9.2. For a spherical geometry this imbalance will occur for a special dependence of the turbulence intensity on the distance from the centre, generally a nonvanishing helicity has to be expected.

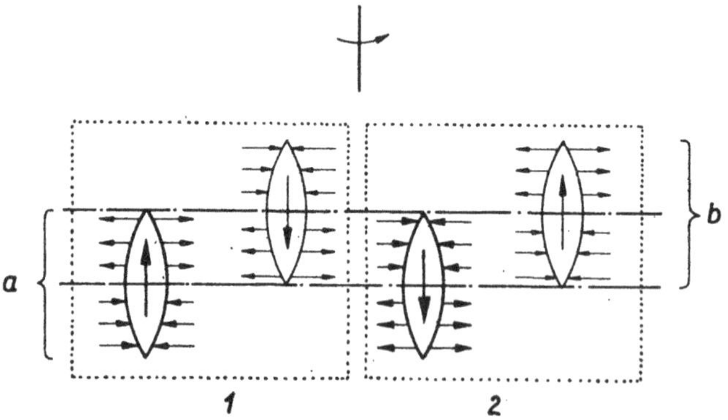

Fig. 9.2. In an incompressible medium the imbalance of right-handed and left-handed helical motions can be due to a gradient of the turbulence intensity $\overline{u'^2}$

9.2. The correlation tensor of an inhomogeneous turbulence

The investigations presented here are already restricted within the limits of two-scale turbulence. Therefore, considering inhomogeneous turbulence we assume a weak dependence of the mean values on the space coordinates, i.e. in our special concern we assume the correlation tensor $\hat{Q}_{ij}^{(0)}$ linearly dependent on $\boldsymbol{x}$ and not dependent on t. Moreover, we shall aim at a consideration of the convective layers of cosmical objects. There the radial direction is the direction of anisotropy and the only one in which the mean quantities vary. Therefore, we assume the correlation tensor $\hat{Q}_{ij}^{(0)}$ to be anisotropic with respect to a certain direction $\boldsymbol{g}$, to depend on $\boldsymbol{g} \cdot \boldsymbol{x}$, and to be linear in $\boldsymbol{g}$ and $\boldsymbol{x}$. We write

$$\hat{Q}_{ij}^{(0)}(\boldsymbol{x}, \boldsymbol{k}, \omega) = \hat{Q}_{ij}^{(00)}(\boldsymbol{k}, \omega) + \frac{i}{2} g_m \frac{\partial \hat{Q}_{ij}^{(01)}(\boldsymbol{k}, \omega)}{\partial k_m} + (\boldsymbol{g} \cdot \boldsymbol{x}) \hat{Q}_{ij}^{(01)}(\boldsymbol{k}, \omega), \tag{9.1}$$

where we shall immediately see the reasons for which we introduced the second summand on the right.

Because of the definition (4.3) of the correlation tensor we have the identity

$$Q_{ij}^{(0)}(\boldsymbol{x} - \boldsymbol{\xi}, \boldsymbol{\xi}, \tau) = Q_{ji}^{(0)}(\boldsymbol{x}, -\boldsymbol{\xi}, -\tau), \tag{9.2}$$

which furnishes the condition

$$\hat{Q}_{ij}^{(00)}(\boldsymbol{k}, \omega) + \frac{\mathrm{i}}{2} g_m \frac{\partial \hat{Q}_{ij}^{(01)}(\boldsymbol{k}, \omega)}{\partial k_m} + g_m x_m \hat{Q}_{ij}^{(01)}(\boldsymbol{k}, \omega) - \mathrm{i} g_m \frac{\partial \hat{Q}_{ij}^{(01)}(\boldsymbol{k}, \omega)}{\partial k_m}$$

$$= \hat{Q}_{ji}^{(00)}(-\boldsymbol{k}, -\omega) + \frac{\mathrm{i}}{2} g_m \left[\frac{\partial \hat{Q}_{ji}^{(01)}(\boldsymbol{k}, \omega)}{\partial k_m}\right]_{-\boldsymbol{k}, -\omega} + g_m x_m \hat{Q}_{ji}^{(01)}(-\boldsymbol{k}, -\omega), \tag{9.3}$$

if applied to the tensor given in (9.1).

First we obtain

$$\hat{Q}_{ij}^{(01)}(\boldsymbol{k}, \omega) = \hat{Q}_{ji}^{(01)}(-\boldsymbol{k}, -\omega), \tag{9.4}$$

and, as a consequence,

$$\left[\frac{\partial \hat{Q}_{ji}^{(01)}(\boldsymbol{k}, \omega)}{\partial k_m}\right]_{-\boldsymbol{k}, -\omega} = -\frac{\partial \hat{Q}_{ij}^{(01)}(\boldsymbol{k}, \omega)}{\partial k_m}. \tag{9.10}$$

From (9.3) thus follows

$$\hat{Q}_{ij}^{(00)}(\boldsymbol{k}, \omega) = \hat{Q}_{ji}^{(00)}(-\boldsymbol{k}, -\omega). \tag{9.11}$$

It should be noted that $\hat{Q}_{ij}^{(0)}$ has to fulfil a condition corresponding to Bochner's theorem, which can be deduced from (6.1). From this follows in particular that $\hat{Q}_{ij}^{(00)}$ has to be positive semi-definite, and that $\boldsymbol{x}$ is restricted to a bounded region.

Suppose the fluid is incompressible, so that

$$\frac{\partial \hat{Q}_{ij}^{(0)}(\boldsymbol{x}, \boldsymbol{k}, \omega)}{\partial x_i} = \mathrm{i} k_i \hat{Q}_{ij}^{(0)}(\boldsymbol{x}, \boldsymbol{k}, \omega), \quad \hat{k_j Q}_{ij}^{(0)}(\boldsymbol{x}, \boldsymbol{k}, \omega) = 0. \tag{9.12}$$

Inserting (9.1) we find the conditions

$$k_i \hat{Q}_{ij}^{(01)} = 0, \quad k_j \hat{Q}_{ij}^{(01)} = 0, \tag{9.13}$$

$$k_i \hat{Q}_{ij}^{(00)} = -\frac{\mathrm{i}}{2} g_i \hat{Q}_{ij}^{(01)}; \quad k_j Q_{ij}^{(00)} = \frac{\mathrm{i}}{2} g_j \hat{Q}_{ij}^{(01)}. \tag{9.14}$$

$Q_{ij}^{(01)}$ is isotropic because of the required linearity of $Q_{ij}^{(0)}$ with respect to $\boldsymbol{g}$, therefore

$$\hat{Q}_{ij}^{(01)}(\boldsymbol{k}, \omega) = \hat{Q}_1(k, \omega)\,(k^2\,\delta_{ij} - k_i k_j), \tag{9.15}$$

with

$$\hat{Q}_1(k, -\omega) = \hat{Q}_1(k, \omega). \tag{9.16}$$

Take for $Q_{ij}^{(00)}$ the general ansatz, i.e.

$$\hat{Q}_{ij}^{(00)}(\boldsymbol{k}, \omega) = \{A + (\boldsymbol{k} \cdot \boldsymbol{g})\, A'\}\, k^2\, \delta_{ij} + \{B + (\boldsymbol{k} \cdot \boldsymbol{g})\, B'\}\, k_i k_j + \mathrm{i} C k_i g_j + \mathrm{i} C' k_j g_i,$$

and find from (9.14)

$$B = -A = \hat{Q}(k, \omega), \quad A' = -B' = \hat{Q}'(k, \omega),$$

$$C = -C' = -\frac{1}{2}\hat{Q}_1(k, \omega), \tag{9.17}$$

where

$$\hat{Q}(k, \omega) = \hat{Q}(k, -\omega), \quad \hat{Q}'(k, \omega) = -\hat{Q}'(k, -\omega), \tag{9.18}$$

because of (9.11).

We finally obtain

$$\begin{aligned} \hat{Q}_{ij}^{(0)}(\boldsymbol{x}, \boldsymbol{k}, \omega) = {} & \{\hat{Q}(k, \omega) + (\boldsymbol{k} \cdot \boldsymbol{g})\, \hat{Q}'(k, \omega)\}\, (k^2\, \delta_{ij} - k_i k_j) \\ & + \frac{i}{2} (\boldsymbol{k} \cdot \boldsymbol{g}) \left\{ \frac{1}{k} \frac{\partial k^2 \hat{Q}_1(k, \omega)}{\partial k}\, \delta_{ij} - \frac{1}{k} \frac{\partial \hat{Q}_1(k, \omega)}{\partial k}\, k_i k_j \right\} \\ & - \mathrm{i} \hat{Q}_1(k, \omega)\, k_i g_j + (\boldsymbol{g} \cdot \boldsymbol{x})\, \hat{Q}_1(k, \omega)\, (k^2\, \delta_{ij} - k_i k_j), \end{aligned} \tag{9.19}$$

where the three functions $\hat{Q}(k, \omega)$, $\hat{Q}'(k, \omega)$ and $\hat{Q}_1(k, \omega)$ satisfy (9.16) and (9.18), and

$$\hat{Q}(k, \omega) + (\boldsymbol{k} \cdot \boldsymbol{g})\, \hat{Q}'(k, \omega) \geqq 0, \tag{9.20}$$

because of Bochner's theorem. There is no such relation concerning $\hat{Q}_1$, however, $\boldsymbol{x}$ must not be too large.

(9.17) is the most general representation of the correlation tensor of an incompressible turbulent flow which is a linear function of the vector $\boldsymbol{g}$ characterizing the direction of anisotropy as well as the direction of inhomogeneity.

The result (9.19) coincides with that derived by Rädler [2, 11] for a turbulence being inhomogeneous because of the gradient of the turbulence intensity in case $\hat{Q}_1$ is taken proportional to $\hat{Q}$.

Finally, we mention that the summands $\hat{Q}(k^2\, \delta_{ij} - k_i k_j)$ and $(\boldsymbol{g} \cdot \boldsymbol{x})\, \hat{Q}_1(k^2\, \delta_{ij} - k_i k_j)$ in (9.19) are even with respect to $\boldsymbol{k}$, the others are odd.

9.3. Determination of the tensor b_{ipq} for an inhomogeneous turbulence influenced by Coriolis forces

For our purposes (8.60) shall be recorded in convolution form

$$b_{ipq}(\boldsymbol{x}) = -\varepsilon_{ijk}\varepsilon_{klm}\varepsilon_{mnp} \iint \frac{k_l}{\eta k^2 - \mathrm{i}\omega} \frac{\partial \hat{Q}_{jn}(\boldsymbol{x}, \boldsymbol{k}, \omega \mid \overline{\boldsymbol{u}})}{\partial k_q} \, \mathrm{d}\boldsymbol{k} \, \mathrm{d}\omega$$

$$= \varepsilon_{ijk}\varepsilon_{klm}\varepsilon_{mnp} \iint \frac{\partial}{\partial k_q} \left(\frac{k_l}{\eta k^2 - \mathrm{i}\omega} \right) \hat{Q}_{jn}(\boldsymbol{x}, \boldsymbol{k}, \omega \mid \overline{\boldsymbol{u}}) \, \mathrm{d}\boldsymbol{k} \, \mathrm{d}\omega . \qquad (9.21)$$

Since the even part of Q_{jn} only contributes to the integral in (9.21) we obtain from (8.83), (8.84), (8.90) and (9.19)

$$b_{ipq}(\boldsymbol{x}) = \varepsilon_{ijk}\varepsilon_{klm}\varepsilon_{mnp} \iint \frac{\partial}{\partial k_q} \left(\frac{k_l}{\eta k^2 - \mathrm{i}\omega} \right) D^*_{jr}(\boldsymbol{k}, \omega) \, D_{ns}(\boldsymbol{k}, \omega)$$

$$\{\hat{Q}(k, \omega) + (\boldsymbol{g} \cdot \boldsymbol{x}) \, \hat{Q}_1(k, \omega)\} \, (k^2 \, \delta_{rs} - k_r k_s) \, \mathrm{d}\boldsymbol{k} \, \mathrm{d}\omega$$

$$= \varepsilon_{ijk}\varepsilon_{klm}\varepsilon_{mnp} \iint \frac{\partial}{\partial k_q} \left(\frac{k_l}{\eta k^2 - \mathrm{i}\omega} \right)$$

$$\{\hat{Q}(k, \omega) + (\boldsymbol{g} \cdot \boldsymbol{x}) \, \hat{Q}_1'(k, \omega)\} \, (k^2 \, \delta_{jn} - k_j k_n) \, \mathrm{d}\boldsymbol{k} \, \mathrm{d}\omega$$

$$- 4\mathrm{i}\varepsilon_{ijk}\varepsilon_{klm}\varepsilon_{mnp}\varepsilon_{jnr}\Omega_s \iint \frac{\partial}{\partial k_q} \left(\frac{k_l}{\eta k^2 - \mathrm{i}\omega} \right)$$

$$\omega \, \{\hat{Q}(k, \omega) + \hat{Q}_1(k, \omega) \, (\boldsymbol{g} \cdot \boldsymbol{x})\} \frac{k_r k_s}{\nu^2 k^4 + \omega^2} \, \mathrm{d}\boldsymbol{k} \, \mathrm{d}\omega . \qquad (9.22)$$

The first summand is clearly of the form $\beta\varepsilon_{ipq}$ and by multiplying it by ε_{ipq} we obtain

$$\beta = \frac{2}{3} \iint \frac{\hat{Q}(k, \omega) + (\boldsymbol{g} \cdot \boldsymbol{x}) \, \hat{Q}_1(k, \omega)}{\eta k^2 - \mathrm{i}\omega} \, k^2 \, \mathrm{d}\boldsymbol{k} \, \mathrm{d}\omega . \qquad (9.23)$$

This relation can be rewritten as

$$\beta = \frac{1}{3} \iint \frac{\hat{Q}_{jj}(\boldsymbol{x}, \boldsymbol{k}, \omega \mid \overline{\boldsymbol{u}})}{\eta k^2 - \mathrm{i}\omega} \, \mathrm{d}\boldsymbol{k} \, \mathrm{d}\omega , \qquad (9.24)$$

since $\hat{Q}_{jj} - 2k^2(\hat{Q} + (\boldsymbol{g} \cdot \boldsymbol{x}) \, \hat{Q}_1)$ is odd with respect to $\boldsymbol{k}$, because of (8.90) and (9.19).

With (9.24) we generalize the representation (7.47) of the turbulent diffusivity to an inhomogeneous incompressible turbulence influenced by a rotational motion.

For the second summand in (9.22), i.e. β_{ipq} with the notation (7.55), we find

$$\beta_{ipq} = -4\mathrm{i}\,(\delta_{il}\delta_{pr} + \delta_{ir}\delta_{pl})\,\Omega_s \iint \frac{(\eta k^2 - \mathrm{i}\omega)\,\delta_{lq} - 2\eta k_l k_q}{(\eta k^2 - \mathrm{i}\omega)^2\,(\nu^2 k^4 + \omega^2)} \times \omega k_r k_s\,\{\hat{Q}(k,\omega) + (\boldsymbol{g}\cdot\boldsymbol{x})\,\hat{Q}_1(k,\omega)\}\,\mathrm{d}\boldsymbol{k}\,\mathrm{d}\omega$$

$$= -\frac{2}{15}\Omega_s \iint \frac{(\delta_{iq}\delta_{ps} + \delta_{is}\delta_{pq})\,(3\eta^2k^4 - 5\omega^2) + 8\eta^2k^4\,\delta_{ip}\delta_{qs}}{(\eta^2k^4 + \omega^2)^2\,(\nu^2k^4 + \omega^2)} \omega^2\hat{Q}_{jj}(\boldsymbol{x},\boldsymbol{k},\omega\mid\overline{\boldsymbol{u}})\,\mathrm{d}\boldsymbol{k}\,\mathrm{d}\omega\,. \tag{9.25}$$

For the evaluation we used (5.27). This result was already predicted in section 7.5. For the scalars β_1, β_2, β_3 introduced there we find (Roberts and Soward [3]).

$$\beta_1 = \beta_2 = \frac{2}{15}\iint \frac{(3\eta^2k^4 - 5\omega^2)\,\omega^2}{(\eta^2k^4 + \omega^2)^2\,(\nu^2k^4 + \omega^2)}\,\hat{Q}_{jj}(\boldsymbol{x},\boldsymbol{k},\omega\mid\overline{\boldsymbol{u}})\,\mathrm{d}\boldsymbol{k}\,\mathrm{d}\omega\,, \tag{9.26}$$

$$\beta_3 = \frac{16}{15}\iint \frac{\eta^2k^4\omega^2\hat{Q}_{jj}(\boldsymbol{x},\boldsymbol{k},\omega\mid\overline{\boldsymbol{u}})}{(\eta^2k^4 + \omega^2)^2\,(\nu^2k^4 + \omega^2)}\,\mathrm{d}\boldsymbol{k}\,\mathrm{d}\omega\,. \tag{9.27}$$

First expressions for β_1, β_2, β_3 were derived by Rädler [6].

It is essential to note that the quantities β_1, β_2, and β_3 were non-zero already in the case where the undisturbed turbulence is homogeneous and sotropic, i.e. $\hat{Q}' = \hat{Q}_1 = 0$. We find that the inhomogeneity did not produce basically new features.

9.4. Determination of the tensor a_{ip} for an inhomogeneous turbulence influenced by Coriolis forces

We start from relation (8.59) again recorded in convolution form

$$a_{ip} = \mathrm{i}\varepsilon_{ijk}\varepsilon_{klm}\varepsilon_{mnp}\iint \frac{k_l}{\eta k^2 - \mathrm{i}\omega}\,\hat{Q}_{jn}(\boldsymbol{x},\boldsymbol{k},\omega\mid\overline{\boldsymbol{u}})\,\mathrm{d}\boldsymbol{k}\,\mathrm{d}\omega\,. \tag{9.28}$$

For the incompressible case considered here it reduces to

$$a_{ip} = \mathrm{i}\varepsilon_{ijk}\iint \frac{k_p\hat{Q}_{jk}(\boldsymbol{x},\boldsymbol{k},\omega\mid\overline{\boldsymbol{u}})}{\eta k^2 - \mathrm{i}\omega}\,\mathrm{d}\boldsymbol{k}\,\mathrm{d}\omega\,. \tag{9.29}$$

First, suppose the turbulence to be homogeneous so that $\hat{Q}_1 = 0$. (8.83), (8.84), (8.88) and (9.19) give rise to

$$a_{ip} = \mathrm{i}\varepsilon_{ijk}\iint \frac{k_p}{\eta k^2 - \mathrm{i}\omega}\,(D^*_{jl}D_{km}\hat{Q}^{(0)}_{lm})\,\mathrm{d}\boldsymbol{k}\,\mathrm{d}\omega$$

$$= -4\varepsilon_{ijk}\varepsilon_{jkl}g_m\Omega_n\iint \frac{\omega k_l k_m k_n k_p\hat{Q}'(k,\omega)}{(\eta k^2 - \mathrm{i}\omega)\,(\nu^2k^4 + \omega^2)}\,\mathrm{d}\boldsymbol{k}\,\mathrm{d}\omega \tag{9.30}$$

$$= -\frac{8\eta}{15}\iint \frac{\omega k^6\hat{Q}'(k,\omega)}{(\eta^2k^4 + \omega^2)\,(\nu^2k^4 + \omega^2)}\,\mathrm{d}\boldsymbol{k}\mathrm{d}\omega\,\{\delta_{ip}(\boldsymbol{g}\cdot\boldsymbol{\Omega}) + (\Omega_i g_p + \Omega_p g_i)\}\,.$$

Thus we find (Rüdiger [5]) for the quantity α introduced in (7.2)

$$\alpha = -\frac{8\eta}{9}\iint \frac{\omega k^6 \hat{Q}'(k,\omega)}{(\eta^2k^4+\omega^2)(\nu^2k^4+\omega^2)}\,\mathrm{d}\boldsymbol{k}\,\mathrm{d}\omega\,(\boldsymbol{g}\cdot\boldsymbol{\Omega}). \tag{9.31}$$

In order to appreciate this result it shall be noted that this is the first point where we find the quantity α to be non-zero for a real turbulence, in our case a homogeneous anisotropic turbulence influenced by a rotational motion. This has to be underlined because of the importance of α in connection with dynamo excitation as shown in section 7.3.

α proves to be proportional to the scalar product $\boldsymbol{g}\cdot\boldsymbol{\Omega}$, that is, if we consider a convective shell on a rotating body, α is antisymmetric with respect to the equatorial plane.

Finally we note that the tensor a_{ip} in (9.30) is symmetric, in accordance with our results in section 7.1.

The restriction to homogeneity will now be lifted, i.e. $\hat{Q}_1 \neq 0$ is assumed.

In order to investigate at first the antisymmetric part we introduce the vector $\gamma^*\boldsymbol{g}^*$ by

$$\gamma^* g_k^* = \frac{1}{2}\varepsilon_{ipk}a_{ip} = \frac{\mathrm{i}}{2}\iint \frac{k_j\hat{Q}_{jk}(\boldsymbol{x},\boldsymbol{k},\omega\mid\overline{\boldsymbol{u}})}{\eta k^2-\mathrm{i}\omega}\,\mathrm{d}\boldsymbol{k}\,\mathrm{d}\omega. \tag{9.32}$$

According to (8.84), (8.90) and (9.12) we have

$$k_j\hat{Q}_{jk} = -\,\mathrm{i}D_{nl}^*D_{km}\frac{\partial\hat{Q}_{lm}^{(0)}}{\partial x_n}, \tag{9.33}$$

and from (9.19) we thus find

$$\begin{aligned}\gamma^* g_k^* &= \frac{1}{2}g_n\iint\frac{k^2\delta_{kn}-k_kk_n}{\eta k^2-i\omega}\hat{Q}_1(k,\omega)\,\mathrm{d}\boldsymbol{k}\,\mathrm{d}\omega\\ &\quad + 2g_n\Omega_m\varepsilon_{knp}\iint\frac{\mathrm{i}\omega k_mk_p}{(\eta k^2-\mathrm{i}\omega)(\nu^2k^4+\omega^2)}\hat{Q}_1(k,\omega)\,\mathrm{d}\boldsymbol{k}\,\mathrm{d}\omega\\ &= \frac{1}{3}\iint\frac{\eta k^4}{\eta^2k^4+\eta\,\omega^2}\hat{Q}_1(k,\omega)\,\mathrm{d}\boldsymbol{k}\,\mathrm{d}\omega\,g_k\\ &\quad - \frac{2}{3}\iint\frac{\omega^2k\hat{Q}_1(k,\omega)}{(\eta^2k^4+\omega^2)(\nu^2k^4+\omega^2)}\,\mathrm{d}\boldsymbol{k}\,\mathrm{d}\omega\,\varepsilon_{klm}g_l\Omega_m.\end{aligned} \tag{9.34}$$

This result clearly shows that for an inhomogeneous turbulence the tensor a_{ip} is non-symmetric. Its antisymmetric part shall be recorded in the form

$$a_{ip}^{(a)} = \varepsilon_{ipk}(\gamma g_k + \gamma'\varepsilon_{klm}g_l\Omega_m), \tag{9.35}$$

with

$$\gamma = \frac{1}{3}\iint \frac{\eta k^4}{\eta^2 k^4 + \omega^2}\hat{Q}_1(k, \omega)\,\mathrm{d}\boldsymbol{k}\,\mathrm{d}\omega,$$

$$\gamma' = -\frac{2}{3}\iint \frac{\omega^2 k^2 \hat{Q}_1(k, \omega)}{(\eta^2 k^4 + \omega^2)(\nu^2 k^4 + \omega^2)}\,\mathrm{d}\boldsymbol{k}\,\mathrm{d}\omega. \tag{9.36}$$

In contrast to the cases considered in section 7.1., in the case of an inhomogeneous incompressible turbulence a pumping effect occurs, even if there is no mean motion. The mean motion only modifies the direction in which the mean magnetic field is transported.

In order to determine the symmetric part α_{ip} of the tensor α_{ip} we recall that the general form of this tensor is already known, given in (5.43). We thus can write

$$\alpha_{ip} = -\alpha_1(\boldsymbol{g}\cdot\boldsymbol{\Omega})\,\delta_{ip} - \alpha_2(\Omega_i g_p + \Omega_p g_i), \tag{9.37}$$

or

$$\alpha_{ip} = I_{ipqr} g_q \Omega_r, \tag{9.38}$$

with the isotropic tensor of rank four

$$I_{ipqr} = -\alpha_1\,\delta_{ip}\delta_{qr} - \alpha_2(\delta_{iq}\delta_{pr} + \delta_{ir}\delta_{pq}). \tag{9.39}$$

Let

$$D_{ij} = \delta_{ij} + D\Omega_l \varepsilon_{ijk} k_k k_l, \tag{9.40}$$

and

$$\hat{Q}_{ij}^{(0)} = \hat{q}_{ij} + g_k\,[\hat{q}_{ijk} + x_k \hat{Q}_1(k^2\,\delta_{ij} - k_i k_j)], \tag{9.41}$$

where

$$D = \frac{2}{k^2}\,\frac{1}{\nu k^2 - \mathrm{i}\omega}, \tag{9.42}$$

and

$$\hat{q}_{ijk} = \left(\hat{Q}' + \frac{\mathrm{i}}{2k}\frac{\partial \hat{Q}_1}{\partial k}\right)(k^2\,\delta_{ij} - k_j k_i)\,k_k + \mathrm{i}\hat{Q}_1(k_k\,\delta_{ij} - k_i\,\delta_{jk}), \tag{9.43}$$

because of (8.82) and (9.19).

From (8.90), (9.29), (9.40) and (9.41) we thus find

$$I_{ipqr} = \frac{\mathrm{i}}{2}\iint \frac{k_p \varepsilon_{ijk} + k_i \varepsilon_{pjk}}{\eta k^2 - \mathrm{i}\omega}\Big\{(D^* \varepsilon_{jls} k_s\,\delta_{km} + D\varepsilon_{kms} k_s\,\delta_{jl})\,k_r \hat{q}_{lmq}$$
$$+ \mathrm{i}\left[2\frac{\partial D^*}{\partial (k^2)} k_q \varepsilon_{jls} k_s k_r + D^* \varepsilon_{jlq} k_r + D^* \varepsilon_{jls} k_s \delta_{qr}\right]\hat{Q}_1(k^2\,\delta_{kl} - k_k k_l)\Big\}\,\mathrm{d}\boldsymbol{k}\,\mathrm{d}\omega. \tag{9.44}$$

Our problem is the determination of the scalars α_1 and α_2, or equivalent quantities. Those are, e.g., the scalars I_{iiqq} and I_{ipip} which can be derived from (9.44) by contraction. Since

$$k_q\hat{q}_{lmq} = \left[k^2\hat{Q}' + \frac{\mathrm{i}}{2}\left(k\frac{\partial\hat{Q}_1}{\partial k} + 2\hat{Q}_1\right)\right](k^2\,\delta_{lm} - k_lk_m), \tag{9.45}$$

$$\varepsilon_{ijm}\hat{q}_{lmi} = \left(k^2\hat{Q}' + \mathrm{i}\hat{Q}_1 + \frac{\mathrm{i}}{2}k\frac{\partial\hat{Q}_1}{\partial k}\right)\varepsilon_{ijl}k_i, \tag{9.46}$$

$$\varepsilon_{ilk}\hat{q}_{lmi} = \left(k^2\hat{Q}' + 2\mathrm{i}\hat{Q}_1 + \frac{\mathrm{i}}{2}k\frac{\partial\hat{Q}_1}{\partial k}\right)\varepsilon_{imk}k_i, \tag{9.47}$$

because of (9.43), we obtain from (9.44)

$$\begin{aligned} I_{iiqq} &= -\iint\frac{k^4}{\eta k^2 - \mathrm{i}\omega}\Big\{(D^* - D)\left(-2\mathrm{i}k^2\hat{Q}' + 2\hat{Q}_1 + k\frac{\partial\hat{Q}_1}{\partial k}\right) \\ &\quad + \left[4k^2\frac{\partial D^*}{\partial(k^2)} + 8D^*\right]\hat{Q}_1\Big\}\,\mathrm{d}\boldsymbol{k}\,\mathrm{d}\omega \\ &= -\iint\frac{k^4}{\eta k^2 - \mathrm{i}\omega}\Big\{(D^* - D)\left(-2\mathrm{i}k^2\hat{Q}' - 5\hat{Q}_1 + \frac{2\eta k^2}{\eta k^2 - \mathrm{i}\omega}\hat{Q}_1\right) \\ &\quad + \left[2k^2\frac{\partial}{\partial(k^2)}(D^* + D) + 8D^*\right]\hat{Q}_1\Big\}\,\mathrm{d}\boldsymbol{k}\,\mathrm{d}\omega, \end{aligned} \tag{9.48}$$

$$\begin{aligned} I_{ipip} &= -\iint\frac{k^4}{\eta k^2 - \mathrm{i}\omega}\Big\{(D^* - D)\left(-2\mathrm{i}k^2\hat{Q}' + 2\hat{Q}_1 + k\frac{\partial\hat{Q}_1}{\partial k}\right) \\ &\quad + \left[4k^2\frac{\partial D^*}{\partial(k^2)} - D + 5D^*\right]\hat{Q}_1\Big\}\mathrm{d}\boldsymbol{k}\,\mathrm{d}\omega \\ &= -\iint\frac{k^4}{\eta k^2 - \mathrm{i}\omega}\Big\{(D^* - D)\left(-2\mathrm{i}k^2\hat{Q}' - 5\hat{Q}_1 + \frac{2\eta k^2}{\eta k^2 - \mathrm{i}\omega}\hat{Q}_1\right) \\ &\quad + \left[2k^2\frac{\partial}{\partial(k^2)}(D^* + D) - D + 5D^*\right]\hat{Q}_1\Big\}\mathrm{d}\boldsymbol{k}\,\mathrm{d}\omega. \end{aligned} \tag{9.49}$$

Our main interest was always directed to the determination of the quantity α, one third of the trace of the tensor a_{ip}, for which we find from (9.37), (9.38) and (9.39)

$$\alpha = \frac{1}{3}I_{iiqr}g_q\Omega_r = -\alpha_0(\boldsymbol{g}\cdot\boldsymbol{\Omega}), \tag{9.50}$$

with

$$\alpha_0 = \alpha_1 + \frac{2}{3}\alpha_2 = -\frac{1}{9}I_{iiqq}. \tag{9.51}$$

Thus it becomes clear that we already determined α_0 in (9.48). Inserting the explicit expressions for D from (9.42) we obtain after some reductions (RÜDIGER [5])

$$\alpha_0 = -\frac{8\eta}{9}\iint \frac{\omega k^6 \hat{Q}'(k,\omega)\,\mathrm{d}\boldsymbol{k}\,\mathrm{d}\omega}{(\eta^2k^4+\omega^2)(\nu^2k^4+\omega^2)}$$
$$+\frac{4}{9}\iint \frac{k^2\hat{Q}_1(k,\omega)}{(\eta^2k^4+\omega^2)^2(\nu^2k^4+\omega^2)^2}\{\eta\nu(4\eta^2+3\eta\nu)\,\omega^2k^8 \tag{9.52}$$
$$+(3\eta^2+4\eta\nu-\nu^2)\,\omega^4k^4-\omega^6\}\,\mathrm{d}\boldsymbol{k}\,\mathrm{d}\omega\,.$$

The first summand is already known to us from (9.31). In order to derive a second equation for the scalars α_1 and α_2 we recall that in the case of homogeneous turbulence both are equal, therefore the difference can be expected to be a simple expression. From (9.39) follows that

$$\alpha_1-\alpha_2=\frac{1}{6}\,(I_{ipip}-I_{iiqq})\,. \tag{9.53}$$

On inserting (9.48) and (9.49), we find (RÜDIGER [5])

$$\alpha_1-\alpha_2=\frac{1}{6}\iint \frac{k^4}{\eta k^2-\mathrm{i}\omega}\,(D+3D^*)\,\hat{Q}_1(k,\omega)\,\mathrm{d}\boldsymbol{k}\,\mathrm{d}\omega \tag{9.54}$$
$$=\frac{2}{3}\iint \frac{k^2(2\eta\nu k^4+\omega^2)}{(\eta^2k^4+\omega^2)(\nu^2k^4+\omega^2)}\,\hat{Q}_1(k,\omega)\,\mathrm{d}\boldsymbol{k}\,\mathrm{d}\omega\,.$$

With this result we have a complete determination of the tensor a_{ip} for an incompressible inhomogeneous turbulent flow undergoing the influence of a rotational motion. We especially see that the inhomogeneity, in addition to the anisotropy, provides for a non-vanishing α-effect.

9.5. Discussion of the tensor a_{ip}

We have considered an inhomogeneous incompressible turbulence, where, by assumption, the inhomogeneity consists of a linear dependence of the mean quantities of the turbulent velocity field on $(\boldsymbol{g}\cdot\boldsymbol{x})$. Under those conditions we found the turbulent electromotive force to be

$$\mathfrak{E}=-\gamma\boldsymbol{g}\times\overline{\boldsymbol{B}}, \tag{9.55}$$

with γ given by (9.36).

For an interpretation of this result we conclude from (8.85) and (9.19) that

$$\overline{u'^2}=\iint 2\,[\hat{Q}(k,\omega)+(\boldsymbol{g}\cdot\boldsymbol{x})\,\hat{Q}_1(k,\omega)]\,k^2\,\mathrm{d}\boldsymbol{k}\,\mathrm{d}\omega\,, \tag{9.56}$$

and obtain

$$\nabla \overline{u'^2} = 2 \iint \hat{Q}_1(k, \omega)\, k^2\, \mathrm{d}\boldsymbol{k}\, \mathrm{d}\omega\, \boldsymbol{g}. \tag{9.57}$$

If $\iint \hat{Q}_1\, k^2\, \mathrm{d}\boldsymbol{k}\, \mathrm{d}\omega \neq 0$, we can rewrite (9.55) in the form

$$\mathfrak{E} = -\frac{\eta}{6} \frac{\displaystyle\iint \frac{k^4 \hat{Q}_1(k, \omega)}{\eta^2 k^4 + \omega^2}\, \mathrm{d}\boldsymbol{k}\, \mathrm{d}\omega}{\displaystyle\iint k^2 \hat{Q}_1(k,\omega)\, \mathrm{d}\boldsymbol{k}\, \mathrm{d}\omega} (\nabla\, \overline{u'^2} \times \overline{\boldsymbol{B}}). \tag{9.58}$$

We now see that the mean magnetic field is transported out of the region in which there is turbulence, provided both the integrals in (9.58) have the same sign. This behaviour of the mean magnetic field was called "turbulent diamagnetism" by Rädler [2, 4]. Rädler discussed the case where the inhomogeneity is due to the gradient of $\overline{u'^2}$ only and found $\hat{Q}_1$ to be proportional to $\hat{Q}$ and, consequently, $\hat{Q}_1$ to have always the same sign. Then the ratio of the integrals in (9.58) is positive. However, in our slightly more general case we have no condition concerning the sign of $\hat{Q}_1$. It is even possible that $\overline{u'^2} = \text{const}$ and still $\gamma \neq 0$.

Relation (9.35) shows that an additional transport of the mean magnetic field occurs in the direction $\boldsymbol{g} \times \boldsymbol{\Omega}$, which is due to the influence of the mean rotational motion. Since $\boldsymbol{g} \times \boldsymbol{\Omega}$ is parallel to $\overline{\boldsymbol{u}}$ this term can also be interpreted as that given by the scalar γ'' in (5.45). We thus see that the scalars α_2', α_3', γ'' in (5.45) do not describe independent effects.

In order to appreciate the derivation of the symmetric part of the tensor a_{ip} we would like to emphasize here that the essential result is to be seen in the fact that there is, indeed, a non-zero α-effect shown to exist for a real turbulence. It is left as a point of discussion whether these values α_0, α_1, α_2 can be used for a special investigation or whether an alternative derivation can be carried out.

For the purpose of an estimation of the order of magnitude we refer to relation (3.30) which was derived for the high-conductivity limit. We obtain

$$\alpha \approx \tau_{\mathrm{cor}} \left| \overline{\boldsymbol{u}' \cdot \operatorname{curl} \boldsymbol{u}'} \right|. \tag{9.59}$$

α proves to be proportional to the turbulence intensity, $\overline{u'^2}$, divided by a certain length scale, say λ_0. This length scale λ_0 can be derived from the gradient of $\overline{u'^2}$ or another mean quantity of the turbulent field; or from the gradient of the mass density or the pressure, e.g. the scale-height. We know, furthermore, that a non-vanishing helicity can be expected only if there is the influence of a mean rotational motion. Therefore an estimation of α must involve the product $\Omega\tau_{cor}$. All these arguments lead us to the relation

$$|\alpha| \approx \frac{\overline{u'^2}\tau_{cor}^2}{\lambda_0}\,\Omega. \tag{9.60}$$

In the case the Strouhal number S is assumed to be approximately unity, i.e. $\tau_{cor}u' \approx \lambda_{cor}$, we have the estimation

$$|\alpha| \approx \frac{\lambda_{cor}}{\lambda_0}\,u'\Omega\tau_{cor}. \tag{9.61}$$

9.6. Further results concerning the tensor a_{ip}

In our considerations up to now we have realized how important the tensor a_{ip} and, in particular the quantity α, is for the solution of the dynamo problem. This fact shall increasingly be brought out in the following chapters on the generation of the magnetic fields of cosmical bodies. On account of this close connection one should expect to find first results concerning a_{ip} or α in early works about dynamo theory. First of all one should mention the pioneering investigation by PARKER [2] (1955); see also PARKER [7, 8, 10]. Considering an axisymmetric geometry with respect to the mean fields Parker found that a mean poloidal magnetic field is produced from a toroidal one by means of the so-called "cyclonic turbulence", i.e. a motion in convective cells undergoing the influence of Coriolis forces. In terms of our notation this effect can be looked upon as being a special realisation of the α-effect.

Similar results, although based on a quite different approach, were arrived at by BRAGINSKIJ [1, 2, 3]. He considered mean fields, defined to be the averages over the azimuth, and derived the governing equations in the limit of high magnetic Reynolds numbers. A direct comparison between the approach presented here in this book and that of BRAGINSKIJ cannot readily be made. Both of them, however, lead to similar equations for the mean fields. Above all, an effect corresponding to the α-effect appears in BRAGINSKIJ's theory too. (See also TOUGH [1], TOUGH and GIBSON [2], SOWARD [1, 2]).

First determinations of the tensor a_{ip} and of α were actually carried out by STEENBECK, KRAUSE and RÄDLER [2] in the low-conductivity limit and for turbulent velocity fields $\boldsymbol{u}^{(0)}$ of the type

$$\boldsymbol{u}^{(0)} = e^{a\boldsymbol{g}\cdot\boldsymbol{x}}\,\mathrm{curl}\,\mathrm{curl}\,(\boldsymbol{A}(\boldsymbol{x}, t)\,e^{-(a+b)\boldsymbol{g}\cdot\boldsymbol{x}}),$$

where $\boldsymbol{A}$ is homogeneous and steady. $a\boldsymbol{g}$ is clearly the density gradient and $b\boldsymbol{g}$ the gradient of $\boldsymbol{u}^{(0)}$. There are some other restrictions within the deductions which are too complex to be described here. The result shows a non-zero α-effect due to the interaction of one of the gradients with the rotational motion. For the ratio $\alpha_2:\alpha_1$ the value $-\frac{1}{4}$ was found.

Without restrictions concerning the conductivity and with inclusion of a mean shear analoguous calculations were carried out by KRAUSE [1]. In addition to the confirmation of the above-mentioned results an electromotive force due to the rate of strain tensor $\frac{\partial u_i}{\partial x_j} + \frac{\partial u_j}{\partial x_i}$ was determined.

On the basis of a technique of double Fourier transformations ROBERTS and SOWARD [3] deduced a number of results concerning the pseudo-tensors a_{ij}, b_{ijk}. Some of their results are identical with those presented here, as mentioned above. They, too, found the value $-\frac{1}{4}$ for the ratio $\alpha_2:\alpha_1$.

A model largely identical with that presented here was treated in KRAUSE and RÄDLER [2], however, the calculations were carried out in the (x, t)-space thus requiring more mathematical effort.

MOFFATT [3] and subsequently SOWARD [5] determined the tensor a_{ip} for a random superposition of inertial waves in a rotating conducting fluid. MOFFATT's investigations are not restricted to small rotational rates and the same is true for RÜDIGER's [4]. It is interesting to note that for fast rotation the tensor a_{ip} becomes two-dimensional with respect to the axis of rotation, i.e. it takes the form

$$a_{ip} \approx a\left(\delta_{ip} - \frac{\Omega_i\Omega_p}{\Omega^2}\right), \quad \text{if} \quad \Omega \to \infty, \tag{9.62}$$

where $a = O(1)$.

HELMIS [1, 2, 3] carried out investigations on the basis of Ohm's law with the inclusion of a term due to the Hall effect. For a homogeneous isotropic non-mirrorsymmetric turbulence the parameters α and β are found to be decreasing functions of the Hall parameter, but the influence of the Hall effect is reduced by increasing electrical conductivity.

We would also like to refer to investigations in which these problems are not treated in a general way but rather on the basis of a concept of more specialized models. LEIGHTON [1, 2] described the turbulent diffusion of magnetic regions in the solar convection zone by a random walk process under the influence of the shear mechanism due to the differential rotation. In the investigations of YOSHIMURA [2, 3, 4] we find a rederivation of the basic equations for the mean fields.

CHAPTER 10

ON THE BACK-REACTION OF THE MAGNETIC FIELD ON THE MOTIONS

10.1. Introductory remarks

The considerations up to this point were based on the assumption that the motion exists uninfluenced by the magnetic field. The velocity was treated as a given quantity and we studied its influence on the magnetic field. This situation is characterized by the inequality

$$\frac{\overline{\boldsymbol{B}^2}}{2\mu} \ll \frac{\varrho}{2} \overline{\boldsymbol{u}^2}, \tag{10.1}$$

i.e. the mean magnetic energy is small compared with the kinetic energy.

It is the objective of this chapter to give some insight into situations, where the back-reaction of the magnetic field on the motion becomes noticeable. The relations then clearly take a nonlinear form, in particular, the turbulent electromotive force $\mathfrak{E}$ is no longer a linear functional of the mean magnetic field. The pseudo-tensors a_{ik}, b_{ikl}, for example, become functions of $\overline{\boldsymbol{B}}$.

It is generally expected that the turbulence is suppressed by the magnetic field, and that those characteristic parameters like α and β are decreasing functions of $\overline{B}$. But this is not correct in all cases. As we shall see in the following the turbulence intensity $\overline{\boldsymbol{u}'^2}$ can grow for small $\overline{B}$, although it tends to zero if $\overline{B} \to \infty$. Moreover, experiments with liquid sodium have shown that the turbulence is not simply suppressed by an applied magnetic field but is transformed to take a two-dimensional structure as described by Kit and Tsinober [1], where the motions take place within the planes orthogonal to the applied magnetic field and do not vary along the magnetic field. This result is rather obvious: Let

$$\boldsymbol{B} = (0, 0, B), B = \text{const},$$

and

$$\boldsymbol{u} = \left(\frac{\partial A}{\partial y}, -\frac{\partial A}{\partial x}, 0\right), A = A(x, y),$$

then

$$\boldsymbol{u}\times\boldsymbol{B} = \left(-B\frac{\partial A}{\partial x}, -B\frac{\partial A}{\partial y}, 0\right) = -\text{grad}\,(AB), \tag{10.2}$$

a relation showing that the electromotive force $\boldsymbol{u}\times\boldsymbol{B}$ is a gradient and thus will be compensated by space charges. Consequently, no interaction exists between a homogeneous magnetic field and a two-dimensional incompressible flow.

Investigations of turbulent conducting fluids undergoing the influence of a magnetic field were initiated by LEHNERT [1] (1955), further works were carried out by DEISSLER [1], NESTLERODE and LUMLEY [1], MOFFATT [1], MOREAU [1, 2], VAINSHTEIN [3], RÄDLER [12], RÜDIGER [2], ROBERTS and SOWARD [3]. The course we shall follow here is mainly that elaborated by RÜDIGER [2]. Our considerations are based on the second order correlation approximation thus implying that the fluctuating magnetic field here is small compared with the mean magnetic field, i.e.

$$\overline{B'^2} \ll \overline{B}^2. \tag{10.3}$$

From this and (7.150) we see that, in addition, to (3.12) we have to demand

$$\min\,(\text{Rm}, \text{Rm S}) \ll 1. \tag{10.4}$$

The restriction to the second order correlation approximation also exclude considerations of those situations which are mainly an interplay of the fluctuating magnetic field and the fluctuating velocity field. Therefore, we do not provide for any statement concerning the hypothesis by BATCHELOR [1],

$$\frac{\overline{\boldsymbol{B}'^2}}{2\mu} \approx \frac{\varrho}{2}\,\overline{\boldsymbol{u}'^2}, \tag{10.5}$$

which is often assumed to be valid. Such investigations need higher correlation approximations and a certain closure procedure, or have to be carried out by using other methods. We refer here to the papers of FRISCH, LÉORAT and POUQUET [1], and that of FYFE and MONTGOMERY [1].

10.2. The influence of a uniform magnetic field on the correlation tensor

We consider an incompressible turbulent flow undergoing the influence of a magnetic field, $\overline{\boldsymbol{B}}$ shall be constant and $\overline{\boldsymbol{u}} = 0$. The velocity field is governed by the Navier-Stokes equation (8.61) with $\boldsymbol{F}$ specified to be the sum of the Lorentz-force divided by the mass density and a force $\boldsymbol{F}_0$ producing the turbulent motion, i.e.

$$\boldsymbol{F} = \frac{1}{\mu\varrho}\,\text{curl}\,\boldsymbol{B}\times\boldsymbol{B} + \boldsymbol{F}_0. \tag{10.6}$$

Restriction to the second order correlation approximation gives (8.66). Assuming, in addition, (10.3) we obtain the equations

$$\frac{\partial u_i'}{\partial t} - \nu \Delta u_i' = -\frac{1}{\varrho}\frac{\partial p'}{\partial x_i} - \frac{1}{\mu\varrho}\frac{\partial \overline{B}_j B_j'}{\partial x_i} + \frac{1}{\mu\varrho}\overline{B}_j \frac{\partial B_i'}{\partial x_j}, \tag{10.7}$$

$$\operatorname{div} \boldsymbol{u}' = \frac{\partial u_i'}{\partial x_i} = 0. \tag{10.8}$$

Using Fourier-transformed quantities we have

$$(-\mathrm{i}\omega + \nu k^2)\, \hat{u}_i = -\mathrm{i}k_i \left(\frac{\hat{p}}{\varrho} - \frac{1}{\mu\varrho}\overline{B}_j \hat{B}_j\right) + \mathrm{i}(\boldsymbol{k}\cdot\overline{\boldsymbol{B}})\, \hat{B}_i + \hat{F}_{0i}, \tag{10.9}$$

$$k_i \hat{u}_i = 0, \tag{10.10}$$

and find

$$(-\mathrm{i}\omega + \nu k^2)\, \hat{u}_i = \frac{\mathrm{i}}{\mu\varrho}(\boldsymbol{k}\cdot\overline{\boldsymbol{B}})\, \hat{B}_i + \left(\delta_{ij} - \frac{k_i k_j}{k^2}\right)\hat{F}_{0j}, \tag{10.11}$$

if the pressure is eliminated.

For a vanishing mean magnetic field (10.11) reads

$$(-\mathrm{i}\omega + \nu k^2)\, \hat{u}_i^{(0)} = \left(\delta_{ij} - \frac{k_i k_j}{k^2}\right)\hat{F}_{0j}. \tag{10.12}$$

Assume now the force driving the turbulent motion is independent of the applied magnetic field. Then we can write (10.11) in the form

$$(-\mathrm{i}\omega + \nu k^2)\, (\hat{u}_i - \hat{u}_i^{(0)}) = \frac{\mathrm{i}}{\mu\varrho}(\boldsymbol{k}\cdot\overline{\boldsymbol{B}})\, \hat{B}_i, \tag{10.13}$$

and thus have an equation which describes the distortion of the turbulence $\boldsymbol{u}^{(0)}$ caused by the mean magnetic field.

The set of equations governing our system is completed by the induction equation which, in our case, reads

$$(-\mathrm{i}\omega + \eta k^2)\, \hat{B}_i = \mathrm{i}(\boldsymbol{k}\cdot\overline{\boldsymbol{B}})\, \hat{u}_i. \tag{10.14}$$

Combining (10.13) and (10.14) we obtain

$$\left\{1 + \frac{(\boldsymbol{k}\cdot\overline{\boldsymbol{B}})^2}{\mu\varrho}\frac{1}{(-\mathrm{i}\omega + \eta k^2)(-\mathrm{i}\omega + \nu k^2)}\right\}\hat{u}_i(\boldsymbol{k}, \omega) = \hat{u}_i^{(0)}(\boldsymbol{k}, \omega). \tag{10.15}$$

Writing down this equation once more with the index j and the arguments $\boldsymbol{k}', \omega'$ and multiplying both these equations we obtain from (6.18) after integrating over $\boldsymbol{k}$ and ω

$$\left\{1+\frac{(\boldsymbol{k}\cdot\overline{\boldsymbol{B}})^2}{\mu\varrho}\frac{1}{(-\mathrm{i}\omega+\eta k^2)(-\mathrm{i}\omega+\nu k^2)}\right\}$$
$$\times\left\{1+\frac{(\boldsymbol{k}\cdot\overline{\boldsymbol{B}})^2}{\mu\varrho}\frac{1}{(\mathrm{i}\omega+\eta k^2)(\mathrm{i}\omega+\nu k^2)}\right\}\hat{Q}_{ij}(\boldsymbol{k},\omega)=\hat{Q}_{ij}^{(0)}(\boldsymbol{k},\omega), \tag{10.16}$$

or, more explicitely (RÜDIGER [3]),

$$\hat{Q}_{ij}(\boldsymbol{k},\omega)=\frac{\hat{Q}_{ij}^{(0)}(\boldsymbol{k},\omega)}{1+\dfrac{(\boldsymbol{k}\cdot\overline{\boldsymbol{B}})^2}{\mu\varrho}\dfrac{2\eta\nu k^4-2\omega^2+(\boldsymbol{k}\cdot\overline{\boldsymbol{B}})^2/\mu\varrho}{(\eta^2k^4+\omega^2)(\nu^2k^4+\omega^2)}}. \tag{10.17}$$

Both tensors, $\hat{Q}_{ij}$, $\hat{Q}_{ij}^{(0)}$ are positive semi-definite when one of them is positive semi-definite, since the factor in (10.16) and (10.17) is clearly positive.

A very important although also quite obvious result is the fact that according to (10.17) the correlation tensor of a two-dimensional turbulence as given in (7.76) is not altered by the magnetic field in the case when $\boldsymbol{e}$ is parallel to $\overline{\boldsymbol{B}}$.

10.3. Discussion of the result

We first consider the case of a weak magnetic field where (10.17) yields

$$\hat{Q}_{ij}(\boldsymbol{k},\omega)=\hat{Q}_{ij}^{(0)}(\boldsymbol{k},\omega)\left\{1-\frac{(\boldsymbol{k}\cdot\overline{\boldsymbol{B}})^2}{\mu\varrho}\,2\,\frac{\eta\nu k^4-\omega^2}{(\eta^2k^4+\omega^2)(\nu^2k^4+\omega^2)}\right\}. \tag{10.18}$$

For the turbulence intensity we thus find

$$\overline{u'^2}=\overline{u_0'^2}-2\frac{\overline{B}_i\overline{B}_j}{\mu\varrho}\iint\frac{k_ik_j(\eta\nu k^4-\omega^2)}{(\eta^2k^4+\omega^2)(\nu^2k^4+\omega^2)}\hat{Q}_{kk}^{(0)}(\boldsymbol{k},\omega)\,\mathrm{d}\boldsymbol{k}\,\mathrm{d}\omega. \tag{10.19}$$

It is quite surprising to see that the turbulence is not necessarily damped, since the first factor in the integrand has no definite sign. (10.19) can be rewritten in the form

$$\overline{u'^2}=\overline{u_0'^2}+\frac{\overline{B}_p\overline{B}_q}{\mu\varrho}\iint k_pk_q\frac{\partial(\hat{Q}_{ii}^{(0)}(\boldsymbol{k},\omega)+\hat{Q}_{ii}^{(0)}(\boldsymbol{k},-\omega))}{\partial\omega}$$
$$\frac{\arctan\dfrac{(\eta-\nu)k^2}{\eta\nu k^4+\omega^2}}{(\eta-\nu)k^2}\,\mathrm{d}\boldsymbol{k}\,\mathrm{d}\omega, \tag{10.20}$$

which shows that the turbulence intensity is always diminished for turbulences where $\hat{Q}_{ii}^{(0)}(\boldsymbol{k}, \omega) + \hat{Q}_{ii}^{(0)}(\boldsymbol{k}, -\omega)$ is a decreasing function for positive ω. For an increase of $\overline{u'^2}$ a growth of this function is necessary in a sufficiently large ω-range.

The quantity α is found to be

$$\alpha = \alpha_0 - \frac{2\mathrm{i}}{3} \frac{B_l B_m}{\mu \varrho} \int\int \frac{k_l k_m (\eta \nu k^4 - \omega^2)}{(\eta^2 k^4 + \omega^2)(\nu^2 k^4 + \omega^2)} \frac{\varepsilon_{ijk} k_i \hat{Q}_{jk}^{(0)}(\boldsymbol{k}, \omega)}{\eta k^2 - \mathrm{i}\omega} \mathrm{d}\boldsymbol{k}\, \mathrm{d}\omega, \tag{10.21}$$

and we see, again, that α also is not necessarily reduced by the action of the magnetic field. In the low-conductivity limit, however, both quantities, $\overline{u'^2}$ as well as α, will be reduced, as is to be seen in (10.19) and (10.21) for $\eta \to \infty$. This result is, as far as $\overline{u'^2}$ is concerned, in agreement with experimental findings by Alemany, Moreau, Sulem and Frisch [1].

$\overline{B}$ shall now be large and the case of two-dimensional turbulence shall be excluded. We consider the mean square of the velocity fluctuations and from (10.17) we find

$$\overline{u'^2} = 2\pi \int_{-\infty}^{\infty}\int_0^{\infty}\int_0^{\pi} \frac{\hat{Q}_{ii}(k, \omega)\, k^2\, \mathrm{d}k \sin\vartheta\, \mathrm{d}\vartheta\, \mathrm{d}\omega}{(1 + A\overline{B}^2 \cos^2\vartheta)(1 + A^*\overline{B}^2 \cos^2\vartheta)}, \tag{10.22}$$

with

$$A = \frac{k^2}{\mu\varrho} \frac{1}{(\eta k^2 - \mathrm{i}\omega)(\nu k^2 - \mathrm{i}\omega)}. \tag{10.23}$$

Substituting $s = -\overline{B} \cos\vartheta$ we obtain

$$\overline{u'^2} = \frac{2\pi}{\overline{B}} \int_{-\infty}^{\infty}\int_0^{\infty}\int_{-\overline{B}}^{\overline{B}} \frac{\hat{Q}_{ii}(k, \omega)\, k^2\, \mathrm{d}k\, \mathrm{d}s\, \mathrm{d}\omega}{(1 + As^2)(1 + A^* s^2)}. \tag{10.24}$$

Considering now the limit $\overline{B} \to \infty$ we realize that the integral takes a finite value thus showing that

$$\overline{u'^2} = O\left(\frac{1}{\overline{B}}\right), \quad \text{if } \overline{B} \to \infty. \tag{10.25}$$

To a certain degree this is a surprising result since inspecting (10.22) one would expect at first glance a decrease of $\overline{u'^2}$ with $\overline{B}^{-4}$. Obviously, the much slower decay is due to the modes with $\boldsymbol{k} \cdot \overline{\boldsymbol{B}} \approx 0$.

On account of this slow decay we have to conclude that the turbulent electromotive force $\mathfrak{E}$ must not tend to zero if $\overline{B} \to \infty$, since it is connected with the product $\hat{Q}_{ij}\overline{B}_k$. However, considering dynamo excitation one expects the motion to stop being capable of further generating the magnetic field by which it is influenced.

Let us consider homogeneous isotropic turbulence with its correlation tensor given by (6.43). We saw in section 3.9. that the self-excitation is due to the α-effect, i.e. to the ability of the motion to create an electromotive force parallel to the magnetic field being excited. Let us, therefore, ask how the component of $\mathfrak{E}$ parallel to $\overline{\boldsymbol{B}}$ behaves if $\overline{B} \to \infty$. From (5.35) and (7.1) we find

$$\mathfrak{E}_{\parallel} = \frac{\overline{B}_i \mathfrak{E}_i}{\overline{B}} = \mathrm{i}\varepsilon_{ilq} \frac{\overline{B}_i \overline{B}_j}{\overline{B}} \iint \frac{k_j \hat{Q}_{lq}(\boldsymbol{k}, \omega)}{\eta k^2 - \mathrm{i}\omega} \,\mathrm{d}\boldsymbol{k}\,\mathrm{d}\omega\,. \tag{10.26}$$

We take $\hat{Q}_{ij}^{(0)}$ from (6.43) and with (10.17) we obtain

$$\mathfrak{E}_{\parallel} = -4\pi\overline{B} \int_{-\infty}^{\infty}\int_{0}^{\infty}\int_{0}^{\pi} \frac{k^3 \cos^2\vartheta \sin\vartheta}{(\eta k^2 - \mathrm{i}\omega)\,(1 + A\overline{B}^2\cos^2\vartheta)\,(1 + A^*\overline{B}^2\cos^2\vartheta)} \frac{\partial \hat{C}}{\partial k}\,\mathrm{d}k\,\mathrm{d}\vartheta\,\mathrm{d}\omega \tag{10.27}$$

$$= -\frac{4\pi}{\overline{B}^2} \int_{-\infty}^{\infty}\int_{0}^{\infty}\int_{-\overline{B}}^{+\overline{B}} \frac{k^3 u^2\,\mathrm{d}u}{(\eta k^2 - \mathrm{i}\omega)\,(1 + Au^2)\,(1 + A^*u^2)} \frac{\partial \hat{C}}{\partial k}\,\mathrm{d}k\,\mathrm{d}\omega\,.$$

Again, the u-integral converges to a finite value if $\overline{B} \to \infty$. Consequently, it becomes clear that

$$\mathfrak{E}_{\parallel} = O\left(\frac{1}{\overline{B}^2}\right), \text{ if } \overline{B} \to \infty, \tag{10.28}$$

i.e. the component of the turbulent electromotive force $\mathfrak{E}$, which is parallel to the mean magnetic field, tends to zero if the mean magnetic field tends to infinity. This result, indeed, indicates that the motion has no longer the ability of generating the magnetic field if the generated field becomes larger and larger.

10.4. Two-dimensional turbulence

We mentioned in section 10.1. that experiments with liquid sodium show turbulence taking a two-dimensional structure if subjected to the influence of a strong magnetic field. First results of this kind were published by KIT and TSINOBER [1], further work was done by KOLESNIKOV and TSINOBER [1, 2], VOTSISH and KOLESNIKOV [1, 2]. The transition of homogeneous turbulence from an initially isotropic three-dimensional state to a two-dimensional state was also demonstrated by a numerical simulation (SCHUMANN [1]).

In section 7.6. we derived the two-dimensional magnetic diffusivity. The result (7.94) shows that there is no difference in the order of magnitude if compared with the three-dimensional case. However, the derivation was carried out within the frame of mean-field electrodynamics, i.e. without taking into account the back-reaction of the magnetic field on the motion, and we do not know, therefore, whether this result can be applied to situations with strong magnetic fields.

In order to provide more insight in this subject we recall relation (10.2) which shows that no currents are induced by the interaction of a constant magnetic field with an incompressible two-dimensional flow. Let us now proceed to a more general model (KRAUSE and RÜDIGER [1]): The magnetic field shall be parallel to a certain direction which we identify with the z-direction of a cartesian coordinate system x, y, z; apart from this it can have an arbitrary dependence on the space coordinates and the time, i.e.

$$\boldsymbol{B} = (0, 0, B(x, y, t)) . \tag{10.29}$$

There is no dependence of B on z in virtue of div $\boldsymbol{B} = 0$. The two-dimensional flow, $\boldsymbol{u}$, shall always lie completely in the planes orthogonal to $\boldsymbol{B}$ and not vary along the direction of $\boldsymbol{B}$. Hence it can be represented by

$$\boldsymbol{u} = \operatorname{curl} \boldsymbol{A}, \quad \text{with} \quad \boldsymbol{A} = (0, 0, A(x, y, t)) . \tag{10.30}$$

First we shall note that the interaction of $\boldsymbol{u}$ and $\boldsymbol{B}$ provides for currents since

$$\operatorname{curl} (\boldsymbol{u} \times \boldsymbol{B}) = \operatorname{grad} A \times \operatorname{grad} B . \tag{10.31}$$

These currents lie completely in the planes orthogonal to the z-direction and do not vary with z. Consequently, the induced magnetic field is also of the type (10.29), i.e. it does not vary with z and is parallel to the z-direction.

Let us now consider the dependence on time. An electromotive force is induced according to Maxwell's first law,

$$\operatorname{curl} \boldsymbol{E} = -\dot{\boldsymbol{B}} . \tag{10.32}$$

The currents driven by this electromotive force lie, again, in the planes orthogonal to $\boldsymbol{B}$ and do not vary along $\boldsymbol{B}$. Thus, our analysis leads to the conclusion: A magnetic field of type (10.29) continues to be of this type if it interacts with a two-dimensional incompressible flow of the type (10.30).

The Lorentz-force

$$j \times B = \frac{1}{\mu} \operatorname{curl} B \times B = -\frac{1}{2\mu} \operatorname{grad} B^2 + \frac{1}{\mu} (B \cdot \operatorname{grad})\, B, \tag{10.33}$$

of the magnetic field (10.29) is not zero, but is a gradient since $(B \cdot \operatorname{grad})\, B = 0$. Consequently, the Lorentz force of the magnetic field considered is compensated by pressure and does not influence the motion.

Thus we find the remarkable result that a two-dimensional flow of the type (10.30) can influence and deform a magnetic field of the type (10.29) without being influenced by the magnetic field, even if this is very strong.

Let us apply these findings to the case where $u = u'$ is a two-dimensional isotropic random flow as considered in section 7.6. As before we split B into its mean and its fluctuating part,

$$B(x, y, t) = \overline{B}(x, y, t) + B'(x, y, t), \tag{10.34}$$

and assume the scales of the mean part to be large compared with those of the fluctuating part. Then according to the results deduced in section 7.6. the action of the turbulent motion on the mean magnetic field is a turbulent decay, with the two-dimensional turbulent magnetic diffusivity, $\beta^{(2)}$, given by (7.83) and (7.94). This result holds, in contrast to the decay caused by a three-dimensional isotropic tubulence, for a mean magnetic field of the type (10.29) of arbitrary field strength.

Thus we see that even a strong magnetic field cannot prevent its decay by suppressing the turbulence. It can only transform the turbulence to take a two-dimensional structure. However, these motions destroy the magnetic field without being influenced by it.

In view of applications to sunspots we note that the above results also hold for stratified media with $\varrho = \varrho(z)$, since the motions of the type (10.30) fulfil the equation of continuity $\operatorname{div} \varrho u = 0$ also in this case.

10.5. Applications to the decay of sunspots

According to the data given in section 3.7. for the solar convection zone we have

$$\eta = \frac{1}{\mu\sigma} \approx 10^3 \frac{\mathrm{m}^2}{\mathrm{s}}, \tag{10.35}$$

and for a sunspot with a diameter $\overline{\lambda} = 10^4$ km we find the decay time

$$\overline{\tau} = \frac{\overline{\lambda}^2}{\eta} \approx 3 \cdot 10^3 \text{ years}, \tag{10.36}$$

a result which clearly contradicts the observations. We should, however, interpret this phenomenon as a turbulent decay. The data in section 3.7. further give

$$\eta_T \approx \beta \approx 10^7 \frac{\mathrm{m}^2}{\mathrm{s}} \approx 10^4 \, \eta. \tag{10.37}$$

Deriving the decay time of a sunspot from

$$\bar{\tau} = \frac{\bar{\lambda}^2}{\eta} \approx 0.3 \text{ years} \approx 4 \text{ month}, \tag{10.38}$$

we find, indeed, the correct order of magnitude observed for long-lived, recurrent spots.

This analysis, however, suffers from an important gap, since the action of the strong magnetic field in the sunspot is not taken into account. Therefore, the deductions of the foregoing section are of importance here. Although the magnetic field influences the turbulence, forcing it to be two-dimensional, it cannot prevent its own decay, for the two-dimensional turbulence enhances the decay to the same order of magnitude provided the scales of the two-dimensional turbulence are of the same order of magnitude as those of the three-dimensional turbulence uninfluenced by the magnetic field. Thus the estimate (10.38) remains correct if η_T is replaced by $\eta_T^{(2)}$.

It is worth noting that the assumption of a suppressed convection provides an explanation of the darkness of sunspots but not for the rapid decay within some weeks or months. The assumption of two-dimensional turbulence in a sunspot explains both the rapid decay and the darkness, since a two-dimensional turbulence does not allow a convective transfer of energy along the magnetic field either.

A consideration of a simple model shows that the conception of a turbulent decay of the magnetic fields in sunspots can also be used for the explanation of further details found by observations (Meyer and Schmidt [1], Krause and Rüdiger [1], Meyer, Schmidt, Weiss and Wilson [1]).

For $B(x, y, t)$ in (10.29) we take

$$B(x, y, t) = \Phi_0 \frac{1}{4\eta_T^{(2)} t} \exp\left(-r^2/4\eta_T^{(2)} t\right), \quad r^2 = x^2 + y^2, \tag{10.39}$$

thus describing a decaying magnetic field in z-direction, where the flux, Φ_0, penetrating the (x, y)-plane is independent of time and concentrated at $r = 0$ for $t = 0$.

The umbra of the spot shall be represented by the circular region, where the magnetic field strength is larger than a critical value B_c. Let the area of this region be A_u and its radius r_u. A_u and r_u are functions of time. $\bar{\tau}$ denotes the lifetime of a spot. At $t = \bar{\tau}$ the maximum value of B is B_c, and A_u will vanish. Introducing B_c and $\bar{\tau}$ into (10.39) we obtain

$$B(x, y, t) = B_c \frac{\bar{\tau}}{t} \exp\left(-\frac{r^2}{4\eta_T^{(2)} t}\right), \tag{10.40}$$

and find the relation

$$1 = \frac{\bar{\tau}}{t} \exp\left(-\frac{r_u^2}{4\eta_T^{(2)} t}\right), \tag{10.41}$$

and, consequently, for the model umbra

$$A_u(t) = 4\pi\eta_T^{(2)} t\,(\log \bar{\tau} - \log t). \tag{10.42}$$

We see that $A_u(t)$ has a maximum at $t_{\max} = \frac{\bar{\tau}}{\mathrm{e}}$ which is

$$A_{u,\max} = \frac{4\pi}{\mathrm{e}} \eta_T^{(2)} \bar{\tau}, \tag{10.43}$$

and, furthermore, that at $t = \bar{\tau}$ the area $A_u(t)$ has the decay rate

$$\left(\frac{\mathrm{d}A_u}{\mathrm{d}t}\right)_{t=\bar{\tau}} = -4\pi\eta_T^{(2)}. \tag{10.44}$$

From the analysis of a large number of observations WALDMEIER derived the rule

$$\bar{\tau} = 0.1 A_{u,\max}, \tag{10.45}$$

where the lifetime is measured in days and the area in millionths of the visible hemisphere of the sun. Interpreting (10.43) as WALDMEIER's rule we obtain the estimate

$$\frac{4\pi}{\mathrm{e}} \eta_T^{(2)} = 10 \cdot 10^{-6} \frac{(\text{hemisphere})_{\text{sun}}}{\text{day}}, \tag{10.46}$$

i.e., the turbulent diffusivity is

$$\eta_T^{(2)} \approx 7 \cdot 10^7 \frac{\text{m}^2}{\text{s}}. \tag{10.47}$$

The agreement with (10.37) is fairly satisfactory. The fact that the value $\eta_T^{(2)}$ derived from WALDMEIER's rule is larger than that derived from convection will become more understandable by taking into account the more detailed investigations of BUMBA [1]. BUMBA presents the results of a statistical analysis of the time dependence of sunspot areas. He finds two categories of sunspot groups: (A) groups with rapid area decrease, (B) groups with a slow part in the curve of decrease. All groups show rapid growth and decrease in the first days, thus belonging to category (A). Some of them, the long-lived ones, especially the recurrent groups, become slow at the end of their lifetime, thus belonging to category (B).

BUMBA's analysis shows that the long-lived spots, category (B), decay at a constant rate towards the end of their lifetime independent of their size. This result is in agreement with relation (10.44). The decay rate found from the observations is

$$\left(\frac{\mathrm{d}A_u}{\mathrm{d}t}\right)_{t=\tau} = -4.2 \cdot 10^{-6} \, \frac{(\text{hemisphere})_{\text{Sun}}}{\text{day}}, \tag{10.48}$$

and from (10.44) it follows that

$$\eta_T^{(2)} \approx 10^7 \, \frac{\mathrm{m}^2}{\mathrm{s}}, \tag{10.49}$$

a result which is in striking agreement with the value (10.37) derived from the data of the observed convection.

Let us now compare the curves of our model (figure 10.1) with the curves derived from observations of the growth and the early decrease of sunspot group areas as described in category (A). Figure 10.1 gives two examples, where

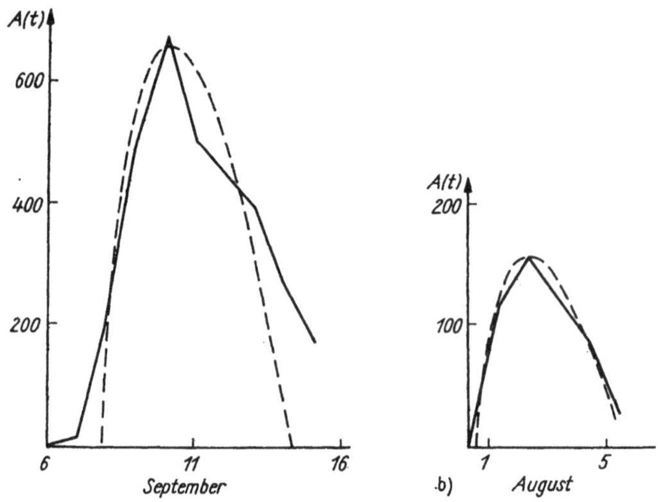

Fig. 10.1. Model curves (dashed lines) fitted to the time development curves of the spot group areas for the non-recurrent groups No. 18195, (a), and No. 18143, (b), according to Bumba. Growth and decay correspond to values of the turbulent diffusivity, $\eta_T^{(2)}$, which are larger than that of the convection in non-active regions by a factor 70 in case (a), and 20 in case (b)

models are fitted to two spot groups with quite different values for the maximum of the areas and for $\eta_T^{(2)}$ too. From the estimation of the area decay rate by Bumba for a large number of sunspot groups of category (A) follows that

$$(\eta_T^{(2)})_{(A)} = 25(\eta_T^{(2)})_{(B)}. \tag{10.50}$$

Now we can see why the value of $\eta_T^{(2)}$ derived from Waldmeier's rule, (10.45), (10.47), lies between the value of category (A) and that of (B): Waldmeier's rule is deduced by averaging over all sunspot groups.

Combining (7.94) and (10.50) we are led to the relation

$$(\overline{u'^2}\tau_{\text{cor}})_{(A)} \approx 25(\overline{u'^2}\tau_{\text{cor}})_{(B)}, \tag{10.51}$$

which suggests an explanation for the different behaviours of the spots of categories (A) and (B), which is based on different scales of the turbulence. Indeed, the emerging of a sunspot is a violent process, which provides for additional causes of turbulence. A turbulent velocity enhanced by a factor 5 would explain (10.51). Furthermore, the emerging of a large spot group is a more violent process than that of a small group. This might provide an explanation of the considerable difference between the values of $\eta_T^{(2)}$ for the two examples in figure 10.1.

CHAPTER 11

THE DYNAMO PROBLEM OF MAGNETOHYDRODYNAMICS

11.1. The question of the origin of cosmical magnetic fields

The dynamo theory to which the following chapters will be devoted has been motivated mainly by the desire to find an explanation of the origin and the behaviour of the magnetic fields of the Earth, the Sun and other cosmical objects.

Let us recall the basic knowledge of these fields in very general terms (for more detailed information see sections 17.1., 17.3., and 17.5.). The Earth shows a magnetic field which, at the surface and in outer space, has a dipole-like structure. This field is to some extent symmetric with respect to the axis of rotation. Over long time intervals it may be considered as steady. At the Sun a great number of magnetic phenomena has been observed. They are related to a general magnetic field, which mainly consists of two oppositely orientated belts under the surface, one in each hemisphere, and a dipole-like part, all with some symmetry with respect to the axis of rotation. This general field oscillates with the period of the solar acitivity cycle, i.e. 22 years. At several stars too magnetic fields have been observed. In many cases one has to assume that these fields show considerable deviations from symmetry with respect to the axis of rotation. For a co-rotating observer they may be steady.

In the following we want to analyse possible causes for such magnetic fields. As is well known, magnetic fields are either due to magnetization of matter originating from magnetic moments localized in atomic or molecular regions or due to electric currents caused by the motion of free charged particles.

A magnetization which is supposed to be the origin of a magnetic field must be of ferromagnetic nature. The existence of ferromagnetism, however, is subject to special conditions, e.g. with respect to the temperature, which are scarcely fulfilled in the cosmical bodies mentioned. In all probability the causes of the Earth's magnetic field are located in its core, the temperature of which is so high that any ferromagnetism has to be excluded. As for the Sun, an additional difficulty arises from the fact that an alternating field has to be explained. By these and other reasons, ferromagnetism can be ruled out as an origin for the magnetic fields of the objects considered.

The existence of electric currents requires both electrically conducting matter and an electric field or electromotive forces. The Earth's and the planetary interiors consist of matter with metallic properties, and in the Sun and in normal stars the matter is in the plasma state, i.e. in all these objects high electric conductivity may be assumed.

We first discuss the case in which an electric field has been created by some kind of cause and then exists in absence of electromotive forces. In any case this electric field, and thus also the electric currents and the magnetic field connected with it, are bound to decay. The energy stored in these fields is converted into heat. For the Earth the decay time has been estimated to be of the order of only 10^5 years (cf. section 11.3.). Therefore, the presence of the geomagnetic field, which proved to be constant over much longer intervals, cannot be understood without the assumption of suitable electromotive forces. For the Sun and stars of comparable dimensions the decay times may reach or exceed the order of 10^{10} years and, hence, the presumed ages of these objects (cf. section 11.3.). Yet, this does not provide for an explanation of the solar magnetic field, since it is periodic in time. Stellar magnetic fields not considerably varying in time could be thought of as relics from earlier stages of the stellar evolution, and may now exist without the assistance of any electromotive force. Of course, the early processes which led to the generation of these fields still remain to be discussed.

As far as the electromotive forces are concerned we shall distinguish between those of non-electromagnetic and those of electromagnetic nature depending on whether the force on the charged particles exists already without or only due to the presence of electromagnetic fields.

There is a series of electromotive forces of non-electromagnetic nature which may occur in cosmical bodies. The different masses of positively and negatively charged particles lead to different inertial behaviours when being accelerated, especially in the case of rotation. The result is an electromotive force analogous to that occurring with the Tolman effect observed in rigid conductors. Inhomogeneities in composition and in temperature of the matter may also cause electromotive forces which correspond to galvanic or thermoelectric effects. A detailed analysis shows that all electromotive forces of that kind are hardly suitable for an explanation of the magnetic fields of the cosmical bodies considered. In the case of the Earth the fields to be generated in this way differ from the observed one by many orders of magnitude. Likewise, the Sun's magnetic field can scarcely be understood on this basis simply because of its time dependence. For some stars the electromotive force due to different inertial behaviour of differently charged particles may lead to fields with flux densities of some 10^2 G but with geometrical structures not concurring with the observations. In any case we may state that also the electromotive forces of non-electromagnetic nature cannot provide a general explanation of magnetic fields of cosmical objects.

Let us now turn to electromotive forces of electromagnetic nature. The simplest of them is that which is crucial for all magnetohydrodynamics: the electromotive force which acts in matter moving in the presence of a magnetic field and which is described by the Lorentz term in Ohm's law, i.e. the $\boldsymbol{u} \times \boldsymbol{B}$ term in the last equation (2.2). As is well known, this electromotive force is also responsible for the action of dynamo machines used for the production of electric current. In the externally excited dynamo machine the magnetic field necessary for the appearance of the electromotive force in the moving anchor exists independently of this force and the currents produced by it. In a self-excited dynamo machine, as first proposed by von Siemens (1866), the magnetic field is generated with the help of those currents. Only at the first instant, when the machine shall commence to work, a magnetic field produced by some other source is necessary, but this seed field may be arbitrarily small. It only initiates a process in which the electromotive force, the electric currents, and the magnetic fields permanently grow due to their mutual influence. Then, of course, also the Lorentz forces grow, which act against the motion of the anchor. If the mechanical forces available are no longer able to maintain the motion, or if any other limiting effect occurs, the growth will be restricted. Depending on the special construction of the machines both direct and alternating currents and corresponding magnetic fields can be generated.

This leads us to the question whether the magnetic fields of cosmical bodies could be produced by a process which corresponds to that in a self-excited dynamo machine. This possibility was, with respect to the Sun, first proposed by Larmor [1] (1919). As we have seen before, seed fields are always available. Besides, in all cosmical bodies under consideration internal motions may be assumed. There is, however, a drastic difference between the situations in a dynamo machine and that of a cosmical body. A dynamo machine consists not only of conducting but also of insulating parts, especially conducting wires enveloped by insulating material; thus the conducting matter covers a region with a multiple connection. Special arrangements of the wires offer the possibilities to determine the current paths and therefore also shape and magnitude of the magnetic field in order to meet the requirements of the dynamo principle. In a cosmical body the conducting matter generally fills a certain region completely which is to be considered as simply-connected. If an initial magnetic field and the motion are given, the distribution of the electric current and the magnetic field generated by this motion is already fixed. It can by no means be taken for granted that initial fields and motions are to be found which enable processes like those in a self-excited dynamo machine. Only after considerable research it did become clear that magnetic fields can indeed be generated in this way. The dynamo principle has proved to be the most attractive and most convincing possibility of an all-embracing explanation of the origin of the magnetic fields observed at cosmical bodies.

11.2. General view of the dynamo problem

The considerations on the origin of cosmical magnetic fields given in the foregoing chapter lead to the dynamo problem of magnetohydrodynamics. In this context we speak of a "dynamo" if a magnetic field is generated or maintained due to motions inside an electrically conducting fluid medium which fills a simply-connected region. Sometimes it is also called "homogeneous dynamo" in order to emphasize that the medium does not contain any insulating part. Some general aspects of the dynamo problem will now be discussed briefly.

Let us consider a body of a fluid electrically conducting medium occupying a simply-connected region and surrounded by vacuum. We exclude any magnetization of this medium and any electromotive force except those described by the Lorentz term in Ohm's law. At a given instant a weak magnetic field shall be present. In absence of motions it is, of course, bound to decay. Its energy is, due to Ohmic dissipation, converted into heat. At first we have to ask the crucial question: Is it at all possible to find internal motions such that the magnetic field does not decay or that it even grows? Of course, this presupposes a permanent input of mechanical energy which is converted into magnetic energy and, finally, into heat. The question posed here can easily be reduced to: Is it possible to find a magnetic field and a motion such that this magnetic field, which may be stationary or oscillatory, can be maintained by this motion?

Let us now assume that the question is answered positively and that corresponding magnetic fields and motions are known. Then, of course, a further question arises: Under what conditions and by what kind of forces can such motions be generated?

A magnetic field which is growing at a given instant, inevitably continues to grow as long as the motions remain unchanged. In reality, however, the motions are influenced by the Lorentz forces which appear as a consequence of the magnetic field. As long as the magnetic field is sufficiently weak this influence may be neglected. If the field becomes stronger this influence will be of crucial importance. It prevents the incessant increase of the field and determines its magnitude in the final state. A complete treatment of the dynamo problem requires that this complicated interaction between magnetic field and motions is taken into account.

We shall speak of the kinematic dynamo problem, and of kinematic dynamo models, if the motion is fixed without regard to dynamic aspects. This means that any back-reaction of the magnetic field on the motions is ignored. A solution of the kinematic dynamo problem provides the excitation condition of a magnetic field but no information about its magnitude. The study of the kinematic problem has to be understood as a first step towards the solution of the full magnetohydrodynamic problem, with the dynamics of the motion being taken into account, i.e. where the motion is considered as a consequence of other factors, especially forces including those due to the magnetic field. Only by solving this full magnetohydrodynamic problem the magnitude of the magnetic field can be determined.

11.3. Mathematical formulation of the dynamo problem and simple consequences

The dynamo problem as discussed in the foregoing section is equivalent to a mathematical problem which shall be formulated now.

As before, a body of a fluid electrically conducting medium is considered which occupies a simply-connected bounded region. All space outside this body is assumed to show the electromagnetic properties of vacuum. We denote that region by V, its surface by S, and the space outside by V', furthermore the unit outward normal to S by $\boldsymbol{n}$, and a jump of any quantity, $\boldsymbol{F}$, across S by $[\boldsymbol{F}]$.

Again, the electrically conducting medium is assumed to show no magnetization and no other electromotive forces than those described by the Lorentz term in Ohm's law. Starting from the basic electromagnetic equations in the magnetohydrodynamic approximation, for the magnetic flux density, $\boldsymbol{B}$, we obtain the equations

$$\frac{1}{\mu}\,\mathrm{curl}\left(\frac{1}{\sigma}\,\mathrm{curl}\,\boldsymbol{B}\right) - \mathrm{curl}\,(\boldsymbol{u}\times\boldsymbol{B}) + \frac{\partial \boldsymbol{B}}{\partial t} = 0, \tag{11.1a}$$

$$\mathrm{div}\,\boldsymbol{B} = 0, \qquad \text{in } V. \tag{11.1b}$$

For the velocity field, $\boldsymbol{u}$, inside the medium no restrictions are made at first. Contrary to the permeability, μ, which is identical with that of vacuum, the electrical conductivity, σ, may depend on position. As for the space outside the body, in accordance with the magnetohydrodynamic approximation only quasi-steady electromagnetic processes are taken into account, so that

$$\mathrm{curl}\,\boldsymbol{B} = 0, \quad \mathrm{div}\,\boldsymbol{B} = 0, \text{ in } V'. \tag{11.2a, b}$$

Since there is no reason to include surface currents, we arrive at the condition

$$[\boldsymbol{B}] = 0, \quad \text{on } S. \tag{11.3a, b}$$

It implies that $\boldsymbol{n} \cdot \operatorname{curl} \boldsymbol{B} = 0$, on S. In order to ensure that the shape of the body is conserved we require

$$\boldsymbol{n} \cdot \boldsymbol{u} = 0, \text{ on } S. \tag{11.3c}$$

Finally, only magnetic fields due to self-excitation by processes inside the body shall be considered. In order to exclude external excitation by causes located at infinity, it is claimed that the magnetic field vanishes at infinity at least like a dipole field, i.e.

$$\boldsymbol{B} = O(r^{-3}), \text{ as } r \to \infty, \tag{11.4}$$

where r means a distance from a point inside the body.

The problem of constructing a kinematic dynamo model consists in a suitable specification of the $\boldsymbol{u}$-field. It has to be chosen in such a way that the equations and conditions formulated here allow a $\boldsymbol{B}$-feild which does not vanish as $t \to \infty$. If we restrict attention to a steady state it is sufficient to find a non-trivial $\boldsymbol{B}$-field.

It is useful to consider the energy balance too. Departing again from the basic equations for the electromagnetic fields in the magnetohydrodynamic approximation we obtain

$$\frac{\mathrm{d}}{\mathrm{d}t} \int\limits_{V+V'} \frac{\boldsymbol{B}^2}{2\mu} \mathrm{d}\boldsymbol{x} = - \int\limits_{V} \frac{\boldsymbol{j}^2}{\sigma} \mathrm{d}\boldsymbol{x} - \int\limits_{V} \boldsymbol{u} \cdot (\boldsymbol{j} \times \boldsymbol{B}) \, \mathrm{d}\boldsymbol{x}. \tag{11.5}$$

Here $\boldsymbol{B}^2/2\mu$ represents the magnetic energy density, $\boldsymbol{j}^2/\sigma$ the Ohmic heat production in a unit volume, and $\boldsymbol{u} \cdot (\boldsymbol{j} \times \boldsymbol{B})$ the work done by the Lorentz force in a unit volume during a time unit. It can easily be shown that

$$- \int\limits_{V} \boldsymbol{u} \cdot (\boldsymbol{j} \times \boldsymbol{B}) \, \mathrm{d}\boldsymbol{x}$$
$$= \frac{1}{\mu} \int\limits_{V} \left(e_{ij} - \frac{1}{2} \operatorname{div} \boldsymbol{u} \cdot \delta_{ij} \right) B_i B_j \, \mathrm{d}\boldsymbol{x} - \frac{1}{\mu} \int\limits_{S} (\boldsymbol{u} \cdot \boldsymbol{B}) \, (\boldsymbol{B} \cdot \mathrm{d}\boldsymbol{f}), \tag{11.6}$$

where e_{ij} is the rate of strain tensor defined by

$$e_{ij} = \frac{1}{2} \left(\frac{\partial u_i}{\partial x_j} + \frac{\partial u_j}{\partial x_i} \right), \tag{11.7}$$

and $\mathrm{d}\boldsymbol{f}$ the surface element parallel to the outward normal. The last term on the right-hand side of (11.6) is zero not only if $\boldsymbol{u}$ vanishes on S but also if it corresponds to a rigid rotation of S. As is to be seen from (11.5) and (11.6) a conversion of mechanical into magnetic energy, or vice versa, requires a deformation of the conducting medium, which is, of course, always connected with a deformation of the magnetic field lines. The magnetic energy grows in the case of stretching and decreases in the case of contraction of the field lines.

Let us at first consider the case of a medium at rest. Then the behaviour of the magnetic field is governed by Ohmic dissipation only. As can be seen from (11.5), any magnetic field is bound to decay. On the basis of the usual scaling laws the decay time, T, can be estimated from (11.1) or (11.5). Supposing that σ is constant we obtain

$$T = \mu\sigma L^2. \tag{11.8}$$

Here L represents a characteristic scale of the magnetic field the order of which, at least in simple cases, will coincide with a characteristic dimension of the conducting body. As we shall see in section 14.4., for a spherical body with the radius R we should put $L = R/\pi$. Then T coincides with the time in which the slowest decaying mode is weakened by a factor $1/e$.

At this point we are able to justify some data used in section 11.1. For the Earth's core we may accept $\mu = \mu_0 = 4\pi \cdot 10^{-7}\,\mathrm{VsA^{-1}\,m^{-1}}$, $\sigma = 3 \cdot 10^5\,\Omega^{-1}\,\mathrm{m^{-1}}$ and $L = R/\pi$ with $R = 3 \cdot 10^6$ m. Hence, $T \approx 1 \cdot 10^5$ a. With regard to the Sun we choose $\mu = \mu_0$, $\sigma = 10^7\,\Omega^{-1}\,\mathrm{m^{-1}}$, and $L = R/\pi$ with $R = 7 \cdot 10^8$ m, thus obtaining $T \approx 2 \cdot 10^{10}$ a.

A necessary condition for the existence of a dynamo is a sufficiently intense motion with a proper geometrical structure so that the induction effect of this motion balances or exceeds the dissipative effect considered before. As explained above, the motion must result in a deformation of the medium by which the magnetic field lines are essentially stretched.

We compare the magnitude of the induction term and the dissipative term in (11.1) or in (11.5). If σ is again assumed to be constant, its ratio can be estimated to be smaller than or of the order of the magnetic Reynolds number, Rm, defined by

$$\mathrm{Rm} = \mu\sigma U L\,, \tag{11.9}$$

where U is a characteristic value of the velocity and L has the same meaning as above. Only in the case of a proper geometrical structure of the velocity field, the ratio mentioned can indeed reach the order of Rm. In an estimation referring to (11.6), a modified magnetic Reynolds number, Rm^+, appears instead of the usual one, namely

$$\mathrm{Rm}^+ = \mu\sigma U^+ L^2\,, \tag{11.10}$$

with U^+ being a characteristic value of that part of the velocity gradient which corresponds to a deformation of the medium, and L again as above. It has to be expected that in the case of a dynamo both numbers, Rm and Rm^+, have to exceed certain bounds in the order of unity. As shall be seen in section 11.4., for a spherical body with the radius R it is reasonable to put again $L = R/\pi$ in both (11.9) and (11.10).

For cosmical bodies the values of Rm and Rm$^+$ can generally be assumed to be much higher than unity. This mainly appears as a consequence of the large dimensions of these objects. In order to illustrate this we again consider the Earth's core. Taking the same numerical values for σ and L as above we only need $U \approx 3 \cdot 10^{-6}$ ms^{-1} and $U^+R \approx 9 \cdot 10^{-6}$ ms^{-1} in order to get Rm ≈ 1 and Rm$^+ \approx 1$, respectively. There are, however, certainly internal motions with much higher values of U and U^+R so that also much higher values of Rm and Rm$^+$ appear. Likewise, for the Sun and similar objects values of Rm and Rm$^+$ have to be expected which exceed unity considerably.

It would be desirable that we could reproduce in the laboratory a dynamo process as assumed to take place at a cosmical body. A suitable medium for such experiments is liquid sodium for which $\mu = \mu_0$ and $\sigma = 6 \cdot 10^6\, \Omega^{-1}\, \mathrm{m}^{-1}$. We consider a spherical volume of sodium with a diameter of 1 m, putting $L = R/\pi$ with $R = 0.5$ m. Then we need already $U \approx 0.8$ ms^{-1} and $U^+R \approx 2.6$ ms^{-1} in order to get Rm ≈ 1 and Rm$^+ \approx 1$. We may conclude that the experimental realization of magnetic field generation due to the motion of a conducting fluid seems to be possible. It requires, however, enormous technical efforts. Up to now no experiment of this kind has been carried out.

In this context it should be mentioned that in special types of thermonuclear reactors, in particular fast breeders, the cooling is due to the circulation of liquid metals, e.g. liquid sodium. The possibility of operating trouble due to the excitation of magnetic fields must be taken into account as far as very large cooling systems are concerned involving very high velocities. We refer to investigations by Bevir [1] and Pearson [1].

So far we have only dealt with the kinematic aspects of the dynamo problem. When the full magnetohydrodynamic problem is treated, the equations given above have to be supplemented by equations governing the behaviour of the velocity field $\boldsymbol{u}$. We only mention the Navier-Stokes equation completed by the Lorentz force, and the continuity equation,

$$\varrho\left(\frac{\partial \boldsymbol{u}}{\partial t} + (\boldsymbol{u} \cdot \nabla)\, \boldsymbol{u}\right) = -\nabla p + \frac{1}{\mu} \operatorname{curl} \boldsymbol{B} \times \boldsymbol{B} + \varrho \boldsymbol{F}, \tag{11.11a}$$

$$\frac{\partial \varrho}{\partial t} + \operatorname{div}(\varrho \boldsymbol{u}) = 0, \qquad \text{in } V. \tag{11.11b}$$

Here ϱ is the mass density, p the hydrodynamic pressure, and $\boldsymbol{F}$ stands for several forces like those due to gravity, internal friction etc. In dependence on the special model considered, these equations have to be completed by other ones, e.g. the equations of state or of internal energy, and by suitable boundary conditions.

11.4. Some necessary conditions for dynamos

The difficulties in the construction of dynamo models result from the geometrical structure of both the magnetic and the velocity field rather than from the magnitude of the velocity field. Some theorems shall be introduced which contain necessary conditions especially for the geometrical structures of the fields.

A remarkable theorem of this kind has been proved by COWLING [1] (1934) and in several respects generalized by some other authors. According to this theorem a steady magnetic field being symmetric with respect to a given axis cannot be maintained by a steady velocity field which is symmetric with respect to the same axis. It can easily be shown that such a magnetic field cannot be maintained by any other velocity field either. In this way COWLING's theorem leads to the conclusion that a steady axisymmetric magnetic field can never be maintained by dynamo action.

For spherical models with constant electrical conductivity BRAGINSKIJ [1] (1964) has generalized this theorem by including non-steady magnetic fields. He has shown that any field which is symmetric with respect to a given axis is bound to decay if the velocity field is solenoidal and symmetric with respect to the same axis. We can add that this statement remains valid for all solenoidal velocity fields regardless of their symmetry properties.

While dynamos with steady axisymmetric magnetic fields turn out to be impossible, those with a steady axisymmetric velocity field cannot be excluded. GAILITIS [2] presented an example for the maintenance of a non-axisymmetric magnetic field by steady axisymmetric motions.

Besides COWLING's theorem, the essence of which can be understood as a condition for the magnetic field, there are other theorems which contain conditions for the motions. A theorem of this type traces back to ELSASSER [1] (1946) and BULLARD and GELLMAN [1] (1954) and has been reconsidered by MOFFATT [8]. It presupposes constant electrical conductivity. It states that a magnetic field cannot be maintained by solenoidal motions without radial components, i.e. by a solenoidal flow with streamlines which lie in concentric spherical surfaces. This implies that a magnetic field may exist due to motions of an incompressible medium only if these motions show radial components too. Furthermore, maintenance of a magnetic field turns out to be impossible even in the case of a compressible medium if, e.g., only rotational motions are present regardless of the dependence of the angular velocity on radius or latitude. A lower bound for the magnitude of the radial motion necessary for dynamo action has been given by BUSSE [4] (1975).

A theorem by BACKUS [2] (1958) concerns both the geometrical structure and the magnitude of the velocity field. It poses a condition for the rate of strain tensor e_{ij} defined by (11.7). Again a solenoidal motion, i.e. div $\boldsymbol{u} = 0$, is supposed so that the highest eigenvalue of this tensor is positive. Of course, like the tensor itself, also this highest eigenvalue varies in space. BACKUS' theorem requires that its maximum value occurring inside the body, say $U_{\max}^{+}$, cannot be smaller than the lowest decay rate of the magnetic field in absence of motion. This can be formulated as a condition for a modified magnetic Reynolds number like (11.10). We restrict ourselves to a spherical model with constant electric conductivity. Then this condition reads

$$\mu\sigma U_{\max}^{+} R^2/\pi^2 \geqq 1 \,, \tag{11.12}$$

where, as before, R denotes the radius of the conducting body.

Finally, we mention a theorem by CHILDRESS [1] (1969) concerning the magnitude of the velocity field. It makes more precise the observation that in the case of a dynamo a magnetic Reynolds number like (11.9) has to exceed a certain bound. For several models such bounds were estimated. In the case of a spherical model with constant electrical conductivity and solenoidal motions one obtains

$$\mu\sigma U_{\max} R/\pi \geqq 1 \,, \tag{11.13}$$

where $U_{\max}$ is the maximum relative velocity inside the body and R again its radius.

11.5. Successful attempts to construct kinematic dynamo models

There have been numerous attempts to construct kinematic dynamo models, i.e. to find solutions of the corresponding mathematical problem. Many of them failed because of the great difficulties arising for several reasons, especially as a consequence of the necessary conditions discussed above.

HERZENBERG [1] (1958) was the first to construct a kinematic dynamo model. His solution of the governing equations also played the role of an existence proof for dynamos. In this model the conducting medium occupies a sphere. Apart from two smaller separate spherical regions inside this sphere the medium is at rest. In each of the two regions it rotates like a rigid body. For special rates of rotation and a special arrangement of the axes of rotation self-excitation occurs. As GAILITIS [3] has shown not only steady but also oscillatory magnetic fields are possible. Similar models with three spherical rotors, the action of which is in some respect easier to comprehend, have been investigated by GIBSON [1, 2] and by KROPACHEV, GORSHKOV and SEREBRYANAYA [1, 2].

A modification of HERZENBERG'S dynamo model where the two spherical rotors are replaced by two cylindrical ones has been constructed in the laboratory and successfully put into action by LOWES and WILKINSON [1, 2]. Both the nonmoving and the moving parts were made from solid electrically conducting material, and the contact between these parts was provided by a mercury film.

Other examples of kinematic dynamos have been given by LORTZ [2, 3] (1968, 1972). His first model supposes a conducting medium of infinite spatial extent. He showed that special non-axisymmetric steady motions within a cylindrical region, the stream lines of which are helices, are able to maintain a steady magnetic field, which also shows some helical structure. In a second model the conducting medium only occupies a torus which is surrounded by vacuum. Also in this case special helical motions may maintain a magnetic field which passes as an axisymmetric field into the vacuum.

Ideas developed by TVERSKOJ [1] (1966) led to a further interesting kinematic dynamo model elaborated by GAILITIS [2] (1970). A modification of it has been investigated by GAILITIS and FREIBERG [1]. Again, the conducting medium is assumed to be of infinite spatial extent. The motion is restricted to a pair of thin vortex rings. It is symmetric with respect to a given axis, to a plane perpendicular to this axis and to all planes containing this axis. By this simple kind of motion magnetic fields can indeed be maintained. In agreement with COWLING's theorem these fields lack symmetry with respect to the axis mentioned.

Remarkable investigations on kinematic dynamo models were carried out by BULLARD and GELLMAN [1] (1954). In their models the conducting medium occupies a sphere which is embedded in vacuum. The authors established a mathematical method which allows to reduce the basic equations without any restriction on magnetic field or motion to an infinite system of differential equations for scalar functions; in the steady case ordinary differential equations for these functions appear. For a special model, i.e. a special pattern of motions, BULLARD and GELLMAN tried to solve this system of equations numerically. However, their conclusion that this model may act as a dynamo was rejected by GIBSON and ROBERTS [2] who pointed out that the numerical method applied does not converge. A modification of this model by LILLEY [1] was refuted by PEKERIS, ACCAD and SHKOLLER [1] who, in turn, proposed a model which indeed seems to work as a dynamo. In this model, which is adapted to the situation inside the Earth's core, the motions form spherical convective cells.

The hitherto mentioned dynamo models, apart from the last one, scarcely apply to situations as they occur at the Earth, at the Sun or at stars. There are, however, two approaches to the understanding of dynamo processes and to the construction of dynamo models which are of interest for these cosmical bodies. The basic features of both approaches are very similar. In both cases the magnetic field and the velocity field are each split up into a mean and a residual field. The mean fields are defined by a proper averaging procedure which ensures relatively simple geometrical structures and time dependencies, whereas the residual fields necessarily show a more complicated behaviour. Instead of the complete magnetic field only its mean part is considered, the behaviour of which under the influence of a given motion is determined by the mean velocity field and some averages taken over quantities which depend on the remaining velocity field.

The first of these two approaches mentioned consists in the theory of the "nearly symmetric dynamo" established by BRAGINSKI [1, 2, 3] (1964). In this case the mean fields are those parts of the original fields which are symmetric with respect to a given axis. In this frame spherical dynamo models have been considered in which the magnetic field occurs as a consequence of the simultaneous presence of a mean, i.e. axisymmetric motion consisting of differential rotation and meridional circulation and some special non-axisymmetric motions. Models of that kind provide for one of the possibilities to explain the existence and some fundamental properties of the magnetic field of the Earth.

The second approach is based on mean-field magnetohydrodynamics as introduced in the foregoing chapters, and it is often referred to as the theory of the "turbulent dynamo". In this case the mean fields are usually defined by statistical or space or time averages and they are not necessarily axisymmetric. As we have seen in the foregoing chapters a homogeneous isotropic non-mirror-symmetric turbulence, which leads to an α-effect, is able to maintain a mean magnetic field. Furthermore, it is also shown that turbulent motions in rotating bodies, i.e. under the influence of Coriolis forces, also give rise to an α-effect. Spherical dynamo models have been proved to be possible where the maintenance of the magnetic field is only due to the α-effect. Also such spherical dynamo models have been constructed where the magnetic field is a consequence of both mean motions, e.g. differential rotation, and the α-effect, or other effects caused by turbulent motions. A series of models of that kind have been investigated up to now, which also provide explanations of the origin and the behaviour of magnetic fields of some cosmical bodies, especially of the Earth and the Sun.

In the following chapters we shall deal with this special branch of dynamo theory, the theory of the turbulent dynamo, and with some of its applications with respect to cosmical bodies.

CHAPTER 12

FUNDAMENTALS OF THE THEORY OF THE TURBULENT DYNAMO

12.1. Basic concept

We shall now consider the dynamo problem as discussed in the foregoing chapter within the framework of mean-field magnetohydrodynamics. As we have seen, in the case of a dynamo generally both the magnetic field and the motion will have rather complicated geometrical structures. We now do not ask for all details of the magnetic field but only for a mean magnetic field with a more simple structure, defined by a proper averaging procedure. Of course, the behaviour of this mean magnetic field depends not only on the mean velocity field but also on the electromotive force caused by the residual part of the velocity field. In this way we arrive at a special approach to the dynamo problem. Since this approach also leads to dynamos with turbulent motions and hence turbulent magnetic fields, it has become known as the theory of the turbulent dynamo.

We point out the fact that the general concept of mean-field magnetohydrodynamics applies to all cases in which an averaging procedure is devised for electromagnetic and hydrodynamic fields, no matter whether or not these fields correspond to any definition of turbulence. Only the validity of the Reynolds relations (cf. section 2.4.) must be required. Likewise, the general considerations of this chapter do not only apply to cases with the presence of some kind of turbulence. We may also think of more or less regular flow patterns. Nevertheless, we shall use the terminology adapted to situations with turbulence.

Until further notice we assume that the mean fields are defined by a statistical average, for which the Reynolds relations are automatically fulfilled. In addition, we adopt all assumptions and notations introduced in the mathematical formulation of the dynamo problem given in section 12.2.

By virtue of the fact that only statistical averages will be used the basic electromagnetic equations for mean fields, (2.5) and (2.6), may be accepted for all space; of course, in vacuum the electric current vanishes. Starting from these equations, or taking the average of the relations (11.1)...(11.4), we may easily derive the basic equations for the turbulent dynamo. The equations governing the mean magnetic flux density, $\overline{\boldsymbol{B}}$, inside the conducting medium read

$$\frac{1}{\mu}\operatorname{curl}\left(\frac{1}{\sigma}\operatorname{curl}\overline{\boldsymbol{B}}\right) - \operatorname{curl}(\overline{\boldsymbol{u}}\times\overline{\boldsymbol{B}} + \mathfrak{E}) + \frac{\partial\overline{\boldsymbol{B}}}{\partial t} = 0, \tag{12.1a}$$

$$\operatorname{div}\overline{\boldsymbol{B}} = 0, \qquad \text{in } V, \tag{12.1b}$$

where $\mathfrak{E}$ is again the electromitive force caused by the fluctuating motions, i.e. is identical with $\overline{\boldsymbol{u}'\times\boldsymbol{B}'}$. For several purposes it is convenient to put (12.1) in the form

$$\frac{1}{\mu}\operatorname{curl}\left(\frac{1}{\sigma_T}\operatorname{curl}\overline{\boldsymbol{B}}\right) - \operatorname{curl}(\overline{\boldsymbol{u}}\times\overline{\boldsymbol{B}} + \mathfrak{E}^+) + \frac{\partial\overline{\boldsymbol{B}}}{\partial t} = 0, \tag{12.2a}$$

$$\operatorname{div}\overline{\boldsymbol{B}} = 0, \qquad \text{in } V, \tag{12.2b}$$

with the turbulent conductivity, σ_T, and a reduced electromotive force, $\mathfrak{E}^+$, defined by

$$\sigma_T = \sigma/(1 + \mu\sigma\beta), \quad \mathfrak{E}^+ = \mathfrak{E} + \beta\operatorname{curl}\overline{\boldsymbol{B}}, \tag{12.2c, d}$$

where β remains to be fixed suitably. In addition, we have the equations

$$\operatorname{curl}\overline{\boldsymbol{B}} = 0, \quad \operatorname{div}\overline{\boldsymbol{B}} = 0, \text{ in } V', \tag{12.3a, b}$$

and the conditions

$$[\overline{\boldsymbol{B}}] = 0, \quad \boldsymbol{n}\cdot\overline{\boldsymbol{u}} = 0, \text{ on } S, \tag{12.4a, b}$$

and

$$\overline{\boldsymbol{B}} = O(r^{-3}), \text{ as } r\to\infty. \tag{12.5}$$

As explained in section 2.3., the electromotive force may be comprehended as a functional of $\overline{\boldsymbol{u}}$, $\boldsymbol{u}'$, and $\overline{\boldsymbol{B}}$ which proves to be linear in $\overline{\boldsymbol{B}}$. Correspondingly the above equations have to be supplemented by a relation

$$\mathfrak{E} = \mathfrak{E}(\overline{\boldsymbol{B}}), \tag{12.6}$$

the form of which is determined by $\overline{\boldsymbol{u}}$ and $\boldsymbol{u}'$. For all cases considered in the following we shall assume that $\mathfrak{E}$ is zero if $\overline{\boldsymbol{B}}$ vanishes everywhere and that $\mathfrak{E}$ at a given point may be expressed by $\overline{\boldsymbol{B}}$ and its first spatial derivatives in this point. Then (12.6) takes the special form

$$\mathfrak{E}_i = a_{ij}\overline{B}_j + b_{ijk}\frac{\partial\overline{B}_j}{\partial x_k}, \tag{12.7}$$

with a_{ij} and b_{ijk} depending only on $\overline{\boldsymbol{u}}$ and $\boldsymbol{u}'$.

In order to construct a kinematic dynamo model in addition to the $\overline{\boldsymbol{u}}$-field those properties of the $\boldsymbol{u}'$-field relevant for the electromotive force $\mathfrak{E}$ have to be specified in such way that the equations formulated above allow $\overline{\boldsymbol{B}}$-fields which do not vanish as $t \to \infty$.

For many purposes it will be of interest to have an energy equation analogous to (11.5). The mean energy density $\overline{\boldsymbol{B}^2}/2\mu$ of the magnetic field can always be split in the two parts $\overline{\boldsymbol{B}}^2/2\mu$ and $\overline{\boldsymbol{B}'^2}/2\mu$ related to the mean and the fluctuating part of the magnetic field. We are only interested in the first part. Starting from the basic equations (2.5) and (2.6) for the mean fields we obtain

$$\frac{\mathrm{d}}{\mathrm{d}t} \int\limits_{V+V'} \frac{\overline{\boldsymbol{B}}^2}{2\mu} \mathrm{d}\boldsymbol{x} = - \int\limits_V \frac{\overline{\boldsymbol{j}}^2}{\sigma} \mathrm{d}\boldsymbol{x} - \int\limits_V \overline{\boldsymbol{u}} \cdot (\overline{\boldsymbol{j}} \times \overline{\boldsymbol{B}}) \, \mathrm{d}\boldsymbol{x} + \int\limits_V \overline{\boldsymbol{j}} \cdot \mathfrak{E} \, \mathrm{d}\boldsymbol{x}. \tag{12.8}$$

This relation retains its validity if σ and $\mathfrak{E}$ are replaced by σ_T and $\mathfrak{E}^+$.

If instead of a kinematic dynamo model, a true magnetohydrodynamic model is treated we have to take into account that both the mean and the fluctuating part of the motion are influenced by the magnetic field. In this way we are confronted with a rather complex problem. We at first may supplement the equations (12.1) for $\overline{\boldsymbol{B}}$ by corresponding equations for $\overline{\boldsymbol{u}}$. Departing from (11.11) and restricting ourselves to incompressible media, i.e. $\varrho = \mathrm{const}$, we obtain

$$\varrho \left(\frac{\partial \overline{\boldsymbol{u}}}{\partial t} + (\overline{\boldsymbol{u}} \cdot \nabla) \, \overline{\boldsymbol{u}} \right) = -\nabla \overline{p} + \frac{1}{\mu} \operatorname{curl} \overline{\boldsymbol{B}} \times \overline{\boldsymbol{B}} + \varrho (\overline{\boldsymbol{F}} + \mathfrak{F}), \tag{12.9a}$$

$$\operatorname{div} \overline{\boldsymbol{u}} = 0, \qquad \text{in } V, \tag{12.9b}$$

with

$$\mathfrak{F} = -\overline{(\boldsymbol{u}' \cdot \nabla) \, \boldsymbol{u}'} + \frac{1}{\mu\varrho} \overline{\operatorname{curl} \boldsymbol{B}' \times \boldsymbol{B}'}. \tag{12.9c}$$

Analogous to $\mathfrak{E}$ now a further quantity, $\mathfrak{F}$, occurs which is determined by the fluctuations $\boldsymbol{u}'$ and $\boldsymbol{B}'$. The equations for these fluctuations can be derived from (11.1) and (11.11), and also contain $\overline{\boldsymbol{u}}$ and $\overline{\boldsymbol{B}}$. We therefore may try to find relations connecting $\mathfrak{E}$ and $\mathfrak{F}$ with $\overline{\boldsymbol{u}}$, $\overline{\boldsymbol{B}}$, and, e.g., the forces which cause the turbulence. This presupposes that suitable solutions of the equations mentioned are available. If we are indeed successful in establishing relations of that kind for $\mathfrak{E}$ and $\mathfrak{F}$ we may insert them into equations (12.1) and (12.9). In this way we then arrive at a system of partial differential equations for $\overline{\boldsymbol{u}}$ and $\overline{\boldsymbol{B}}$, which remains to be integrated. Up to now the problem sketched here has been far from being completely solved.

12.2. Remarks concerning averaging procedures and the scales of mean and fluctuating quantities

When the concept explained above is applied to special problems, some points require special attention.

Up to now statistical averages have been used. In view of a comparison between theoretical and observational results it is desirable to admit also space or time averages. In doing so we have to put up with some restrictions concerning the scales of the mean and fluctuating fields. For the following considerations we denote the characteristic length and time scales of the mean fields by $\bar{\lambda}$ and $\bar{\tau}$, and those of the fluctuations by λ_{cor} and τ_{cor}.

Let us first deal with space averages defined by an integration over a certain three-dimensional range. The scale of the averaging range is denoted by λ_{av}. In order to ensure the validity of the Reynolds relations we have to require that the condition

$$\bar{\lambda} \gg \lambda_{\mathrm{av}} \gg \lambda_{\mathrm{cor}} \tag{12.10}$$

is fulfilled. Generally, $\bar{\lambda}$ cannot exceed the characteristic dimensions of the conducting body. Therefore λ_{cor} must be much smaller than these dimensions. In a model of the Earth's core, e.g., an irregular motion with a length scale which is not much smaller than the radius of the core can therefore never be treated as a fluctuation. At the Sun the same difficulty arises for the motions occurring with the giant cells of the convection zone.

We want to mention a further difficulty. In the case of space averages Ohm's law, i.e. the last equation (2.2), and therefore the induction equations (12.1 a) and (12.2 a) for mean fields, can only be justified if the spatial variations of the electrical conductivity, σ, are negligible within the averaging range. In general, there will be a jump in the electrical conductivity at the boundary. For points whose averaging range contains this jump the equations (12.1 a), (12.2 a), and also (12.3 a) are not exactly justified. Possible errors would then have to be estimated for each special situation.

There is, however, a special version of a space average which is defined by an integration over a single coordinate. For this type of average, at least under special suppositions, the restrictions discussed before do not hold. We refer to a cylindrical or a spherical coordinate system with the azimuthal coordinate φ. The average mentioned of a scalar function is defined as a suitably normalized integral of this function over all φ, and the average of a vector as the result of averaging its components related to one of these coordinate systems. Then, of course, all averaged fields are automatically symmetric with respect to the polar axis of the coordinate system. For this special average the Reynolds relations hold exactly. Let us also suppose the shape of the conducting body and the distribution of the electrical conductivity to be symmetric with respect to the polar axis. Then the basic equations for the mean fields, (2.1) and (2.2), and the relations (12.1)...(12.5) hold without any restriction.

The average explained is used throughout in the theory of the nearly symmetric dynamo, and may be used here too. In applying it, however, we must bear in mind that even in the case of a field with large-scale structures the corresponding mean field may vanish. This always happens if this field contains no part which is symmetric with respect to the axis mentioned. In so far the use of the average explained implies a restriction to special situations here. It should be mentioned that if this average is used some of the relations for averaged quantities given in the foregoing chapters have to be modified.

We now consider time averages which are defined by means of an integration over certain time intervals. The averaging time is denoted by τ_{av}. With respect to the Reynolds relations we have to require that

$$\bar{\tau} \gg \tau_{av} \gg \tau_{cor}. \tag{12.11}$$

In comparison with the space averages defined by integrations over a three-dimensional range, generally the time average seems to be more suited for models which are to be applied to cosmical objects. When dealing with a model for the Earth we may utilize the fact that the spectrum of the most important time scales of the relevant quantities shows a clear gap separating regions with large and small scales. The large scales are greater than or in the order of that belonging to the westward drift of the magnetic field, i.e. at least 10^3 years. All other important scales are smaller than 1 year. We then may choose an averaging interval of a few decades. In this way (12.11) is fairly satisfied. All quantities with the large scales mentioned appear as mean fields, and all with small scales as fluctuations, regardless of their spatial extent. In the case of the Sun the essential time scales are greater than or equal to the period of the solar cycle, i.e. 22 years, or they are comparable with or smaller than a rotational period, i.e. one month. An averaging interval of one or two years seems to be appropriate. Then the above considerations apply analogously.

In the case of a time average, provided the electrical conductivity does not vary in time, the basic equations for the mean fields (2.1) and (2.2) and the relations (12.1)...(12.5) can readily be justified.

We now turn to the assumptions under which the electromotive force $\mathfrak{E}$ takes the special form (12.7), which is supposed for all models considered in the following.

At first, the existence of any part of $\mathfrak{E}$ is ignored which is independent of $\bar{\boldsymbol{B}}$, i.e. which is non-zero if $\bar{\boldsymbol{B}}$ vanishes. As explained in section 2.4. a part of $\mathfrak{E}$

being independent of $\bar{\boldsymbol{B}}$ is to be expected only if fluctuating motions in certain small regions are already able to constitute a dynamo. We do not want to deal with this possibility but refer instead to a discussion given by RÄDLER [15].

Furthermore, $\mathfrak{E}$ at a given point generally depends on the $\bar{\boldsymbol{B}}$-field in a certain range around this point. The relation (12.7) presupposes a sufficiently weak variability of the $\bar{\boldsymbol{B}}$-field so that its behaviour within this range can be expressed by $\bar{\boldsymbol{B}}$ and its first spatial derivatives in the given point. Thus regardless of the conditions resulting from the averaging procedure, further conditions for the scales of mean and fluctuating quantities appear. Let us denote the length and time scales of $\bar{\boldsymbol{B}}$ again by $\bar{\lambda}$ and $\bar{\tau}$, those of the range mentioned by λ^+ and τ^+, and those of $\boldsymbol{u}'$ by λ_{cor} and τ_{cor}. Clearly, we have to require that

$$\bar{\lambda} \gg \lambda^+, \quad \bar{\tau} \gg \tau^+. \tag{12.12a, b}$$

According to our general considerations about $\mathfrak{E}$, the quantities λ^+ and τ^+ cannot exceed the orders of λ_{cor} and τ_{cor}, respectively. They may even be much smaller than λ_{cor} and τ_{cor}. From the considerations of sections 4.6. and 4.7. we may conclude that in the second order correlation approximation

$$\lambda^+ = \min\left(\lambda_{\text{cor}}, \sqrt{\tau_{\text{cor}}/\mu\sigma}\right), \tag{12.13a}$$

$$\tau^+ = \min\left(\tau_{\text{cor}}, \mu\sigma\lambda_{\text{cor}}^2\right). \tag{12.13b}$$

For higher approximations similar relations have to be expected.

Let us again consider the situation in the Earth. We use a time average for which (12.11) holds. Then (12.12b) is also fulfilled. Only (12.12a) remains to be discussed. It is reasonable to assume that $\bar{\lambda}$ is in the order of the radius of the core, i.e. $3 \cdot 10^6$ m. With respect to λ^+ we accept (12.13a) and conclude $\lambda^+ \leqq \sqrt{\tau_{\text{cor}}/\mu\sigma}$. If $\tau_{\text{cor}} < 1$ year and $\sigma = 3 \cdot 10^5\,\Omega^{-1}\,\text{m}^{-1}$ (cf. section 11.3.) we find $\lambda^+ < 1 \cdot 10^4$ m. Thus (12.12a) too may be considered as fulfilled. An analogous situation appears at the Sun. By reasons which will be explained later on (cf. section 17.4.) we may restrict our considerations to the solar convection zone. We assume $\bar{\lambda}$ in the order of the thickness of the convection zone, i.e. in the order of 10^8 m. We again use $\lambda^+ \leqq \sqrt{\tau_{\text{cor}}/\mu\sigma}$. With $\tau_{\text{cor}} < 1$ month and $\sigma = 3 \cdot 10^3\,\Omega^{-1}\,\text{m}^{-1}$ (cf. section 17.4.) we obtain $\lambda^+ < 3 \cdot 10^4$ m. Again, (12.12a) may be considered as fulfilled.

CHAPTER 13

TOROIDAL AND POLOIDAL VECTOR FIELDS

13.1. Preliminary remarks

For the treatment of spherical dynamo models it has proved to be advantageous to represent vector fields, like the magnetic flux density, as a sum of a toroidal and a poloidal field and to profit from the special properties of these fields. On this basis, e.g., Bullard and Gellman [1] reduced the relevant vector equations to a system of equations for scalar functions. In a similar way we may proceed in the theory of the turbulent dynamo too.

In this chapter we shall explain the definition and some properties of toroidal and poloidal vector fields. In doing so we shall follow the ideas of a paper by Rädler [10]. We also want to refer to other introductions to this topic, e.g. Roberts [1].

The subject of our following considerations is a vector field, $\boldsymbol{U}$, which is defined inside a certain simply-connected region of the Euclidean space, whose shape will be specified later on. As to the regularity of $\boldsymbol{U}$ we assume the existence of the spatial derivatives up to the second order.

We introduce a spherical polar coordinate system with the coordinates r, ϑ, and φ, the corresponding unit vectors $\boldsymbol{e}_r$, $\boldsymbol{e}_\vartheta$, and $\boldsymbol{e}_\varphi$, and the radius vector $\boldsymbol{r}$. For any scalar F we then have

$$\nabla F = \frac{\partial F}{\partial r}\boldsymbol{e}_r + \frac{1}{r}\frac{\partial F}{\partial \vartheta}\boldsymbol{e}_\vartheta + \frac{1}{r\sin\vartheta}\frac{\partial F}{\partial \varphi}\boldsymbol{e}_\varphi, \tag{13.1a}$$

$$\Delta F = \frac{1}{r^2}\left(\frac{\partial}{\partial r}\left(r^2\frac{\partial F}{\partial r}\right) + \Omega F\right), \tag{13.1b}$$

$$\Omega F = \frac{1}{\sin\vartheta}\frac{\partial}{\partial\vartheta}\left(\sin\vartheta\frac{\partial F}{\partial\vartheta}\right) + \frac{1}{\sin^2\vartheta}\frac{\partial^2 F}{\partial\varphi^2}, \tag{13.1c}$$

where $(1/r^2)\,\Omega$ is the Laplacean operator for a surface $r = \text{const}$. Concerning integrals over such surfaces we use the notation

$$\oint\!\!\oint F\,\mathrm{d}\tilde{\omega} = \int_{\vartheta=0}^{\pi}\int_{\varphi=0}^{2\pi} F\sin\vartheta\,\mathrm{d}\vartheta\,\mathrm{d}\varphi. \tag{13.2}$$

Denoting the components of $\boldsymbol{U}$ by U_r, U_ϑ, and U_φ we have

$$\operatorname{div} \boldsymbol{U} = \frac{1}{r^2} \frac{\partial}{\partial r} (r^2 U_r) + \frac{1}{r \sin\vartheta} \frac{\partial}{\partial \vartheta} (\sin\vartheta\, U_\vartheta) + \frac{1}{r \sin\vartheta} \frac{\partial U_\varphi}{\partial \varphi}, \tag{13.3a}$$

$$\begin{aligned} \operatorname{curl} \boldsymbol{U} = {} & \frac{1}{r \sin\vartheta} \left(\frac{\partial}{\partial \vartheta} (\sin\vartheta\, U_\varphi) - \frac{\partial U_\vartheta}{\partial \varphi} \right) \boldsymbol{e}_r \\ & + \frac{1}{r} \left(\frac{1}{\sin\vartheta} \frac{\partial U_r}{\partial \varphi} - \frac{\partial}{\partial r} (r U_\varphi) \right) \boldsymbol{e}_\vartheta \\ & + \frac{1}{r} \left(\frac{\partial}{\partial r} (r U_\vartheta) - \frac{\partial U_r}{\partial \vartheta} \right) \boldsymbol{e}_\varphi . \end{aligned} \tag{13.3b}$$

13.2. Toroidal and poloidal vector fields in the axisymmetric case

Let us at first assume that the vector field $\boldsymbol{U}$, and also the region of definition, are axisymmetric and the coordinate system fixed in such way that its polar axis coincides with the axis of symmetry. Then the components U_r, U_ϑ, and U_φ do not depend on φ.

We now consider the field $\boldsymbol{U}$ as a sum of a toroidal field, $\boldsymbol{U}_t$, and a poloidal field, $\boldsymbol{U}_p$, so that

$$\boldsymbol{U} = \boldsymbol{U}_t + \boldsymbol{U}_p \tag{13.4}$$

and define

$$\boldsymbol{U}_t = U_\varphi \boldsymbol{e}_\varphi, \quad \boldsymbol{U}_p = U_r \boldsymbol{e}_r + U_\vartheta \boldsymbol{e}_\vartheta . \tag{13.5a, b}$$

Hence, we can state:

(i) If, at a point, $\boldsymbol{U} = 0$ then also $\boldsymbol{U}_t = \boldsymbol{U}_p = 0$.

(ii) If a is any scalar, $a\boldsymbol{U}_t$ is toroidal and $a\boldsymbol{U}_p$ is poloidal.

(iii) If $\boldsymbol{U}^+$ is any axisymmetric vector field, at any fixed point $\boldsymbol{U}_t^+ \times \boldsymbol{U}_t$ is zero, $\boldsymbol{U}_t^+ \times \boldsymbol{U}_p$ and $\boldsymbol{U}_p^+ \times \boldsymbol{U}_t$ are poloidal, and $\boldsymbol{U}_p^+ \times \boldsymbol{U}_p$ is toroidal; especially $\boldsymbol{r} \times \boldsymbol{U}_t$ is poloidal and $\boldsymbol{r} \times \boldsymbol{U}_p$ is toroidal.

(iv) $\operatorname{div} \boldsymbol{U}_t = 0$.

(v) $\operatorname{curl} \boldsymbol{U}_t$ is poloidal, $\operatorname{curl} \boldsymbol{U}_p$ is toroidal.

(vi) If, throughout the whole region, $\operatorname{curl} \boldsymbol{U}_t = 0$ then $\boldsymbol{U}_t = 0$.

(vii) At any fixed point $\boldsymbol{U}_t$ and $\boldsymbol{U}_p$ are orthogonal, i.e. $\boldsymbol{U}_t \cdot \boldsymbol{U}_p = 0$.

Most of the foregoing statements are self-evident; we mention them with a view to generalizing them later. Statements (iv) and (v) become clear by considering the special representations of $\operatorname{div} \boldsymbol{U}_t$, $\operatorname{curl} \boldsymbol{U}_t$, and $\operatorname{curl} \boldsymbol{U}_p$ in spherical coordinates, where, of course, all derivatives with respect to φ vanish. As for (vi), the simple-connectedness of the region permits to conclude from curl $\boldsymbol{U}_t = 0$ that $\boldsymbol{U}_t$ is a gradient of a single-valued potential. Of course, this gradient must be axisymmetric. Such gradients, however, are always poloidal. Hence, on account of (i) we have $\boldsymbol{U}_t = 0$.

In connection with statements (iv) and (v) we should take a brief look at the quantity $\Delta \boldsymbol{U}$ which may be written as $\Delta \boldsymbol{U}_t + \Delta \boldsymbol{U}_p$. We have

$$\Delta \boldsymbol{U}_t = -\text{curl curl } \boldsymbol{U}_t, \tag{13.6a}$$

$$\Delta \boldsymbol{U}_p = -\text{curl curl } \boldsymbol{U}_p + \nabla \text{ div } \boldsymbol{U}_p. \tag{13.6b}$$

Clearly, $\Delta \boldsymbol{U}_t$ proves to be toroidal and $\Delta \boldsymbol{U}_p$ to be poloidal.

We now assume the axisymmetric field $\boldsymbol{U}$ to be solenoidal, i.e. satisfying

$$\text{div } \boldsymbol{U} = 0. \tag{13.7}$$

As $\boldsymbol{U}_t$ is solenoidal in any case, $\boldsymbol{U}_p$ must be solenoidal too. Hence, $\boldsymbol{U}_p$ can be replaced by curl $\hat{\boldsymbol{U}}$ with $\hat{\boldsymbol{U}}$ being a vector potential. Assuming that $\hat{\boldsymbol{U}}$ is also axisymmetric we may represent it by $\hat{\boldsymbol{U}}_t + \hat{\boldsymbol{U}}_p$. Yet only curl $\hat{\boldsymbol{U}}_t$ is poloidal; curl $\hat{\boldsymbol{U}}_p$ is toroidal and therefore has to vanish. Thus we may write

$$\boldsymbol{U}_p = \text{curl } \hat{\boldsymbol{U}}_t. \tag{13.8}$$

Like $\boldsymbol{U}_t$, also $\boldsymbol{U}_p$ can be expressed by one scalar quantity.

The assumption concerning $\hat{\boldsymbol{U}}$ does not imply a serious restriction. If a $\hat{\boldsymbol{U}}$ exists at all, the components of which are single-valued functions of φ, an averaging with respect to φ readily provides another one which is axisymmetric. As long as $\boldsymbol{U}_p$ is supposed to be continuous in all infinite space the existence of such $\hat{\boldsymbol{U}}$ can easily be proved. If, however, $\boldsymbol{U}_p$ shows this property only in a bounded region, there are exceptional cases where no such $\hat{\boldsymbol{U}}$ are to be found. For instance, $\boldsymbol{U}_p = \boldsymbol{r}/r^3$ is continuous in all regions not containing the origin $r = 0$, but it cannot be represented by a $\hat{\boldsymbol{U}}$ with the properties assumed above.

13.3. A special representation of a vector field

Let us now deal with an arbitrary field $\boldsymbol{U}$ defined inside a sphere or a spherical shell. The centre of the sphere or shell is taken as the origin of the spherical coordinate system. The sphere may also be extended to the infinite space.

We start from the fact that any continuously differentiable vector field $\boldsymbol{U}$ can be represented in the form

$$\boldsymbol{U} = \boldsymbol{r} \times \nabla U + \boldsymbol{r} V + \nabla W \tag{13.9}$$

by three single-valued scalar fields U, V, and W. In components this reads

$$U_r = rV + \frac{\partial W}{\partial r}, \tag{13.10a}$$

$$U_\vartheta = -\frac{1}{\sin\vartheta}\frac{\partial U}{\partial\varphi} + \frac{1}{r}\frac{\partial W}{\partial\vartheta}, \tag{13.10b}$$

$$U_\varphi = \frac{\partial U}{\partial\vartheta} + \frac{1}{r\sin\vartheta}\frac{\partial W}{\partial\varphi}. \tag{13.10c}$$

In order to justify this representation we consider at first the field $U_\vartheta \boldsymbol{e}_\vartheta + U_\varphi \boldsymbol{e}_\varphi$. As is well known, any such field can be represented at a spherical surface $r = \text{const}$ by means of a single-valued stream function, U, and a single-valued potential, W, in such a way that (13.10b) and (13.10c) hold. For a field $U_r \boldsymbol{e}_r$ we are always entitled to write (13.10a), with a further single-valued function, V. In this way, for the sum $U_r\boldsymbol{e}_r + U_\vartheta\boldsymbol{e}_\vartheta + U_\varphi\boldsymbol{e}_\varphi$ of these fields, we obtain (13.10).

We note that the determination of the functions U, V, and W generally requires the integration of a system of partial differential equations, namely of the system (13.10) where U_r, U_ϑ, and U_φ are to be understood as inhomogeneities. The main difficulty is the determination of U and W. From (13.10b) and (13.10c) we get

$$\Omega U = \frac{1}{\sin\vartheta}\left(\frac{\partial}{\partial\vartheta}(\sin\vartheta U_\varphi) - \frac{\partial U_\vartheta}{\partial\varphi}\right), \tag{13.11a}$$

$$\Omega W = \frac{r}{\sin\vartheta}\left(\frac{\partial}{\partial\vartheta}(\sin\vartheta U_\vartheta) + \frac{\partial U_\varphi}{\partial\varphi}\right). \tag{13.11b}$$

If W is known, (13.10a) immediately provides V.

The representation (13.9) for $\boldsymbol{U}$ implies the possibility of gauge transformations of U, V, and W. Obviously, $\boldsymbol{U}$ is invariant under replacement of U, V, and W by $\tilde{U}$, $\tilde{V}$, and $\tilde{W}$ provided that

$$U - \tilde{U} = g, \quad V - \tilde{V} = -\frac{1}{r}\frac{\mathrm{d}h}{\mathrm{d}r}, \quad W - \tilde{W} = h, \tag{13.12a, b, c}$$

where g and h may arbitrarily depend on r but never on ϑ and φ. The transformations given by (13.12) turn out to be the only possible ones. In order to see this we make sure that (13.10) with $U_r = U_\vartheta = U_\varphi = 0$ admits only $U = g$, $V = -\frac{1}{r}\frac{\mathrm{d}h}{\mathrm{d}r}$, and $W = h$ with g and h as above. From (13.10b, c) we obtain $\Omega U = 0$ and therefore $U = g$. Hence, (13.10b, c) immediately leads to $W = h$, and (13.10a) further to $V = -\frac{1}{r}\frac{\mathrm{d}h}{\mathrm{d}r}$.

It should be pointed out that not only $\boldsymbol{U}$ but also $\boldsymbol{r}\times\nabla U$ and $\boldsymbol{r}V+\nabla W$ remain unchanged under gauge transformations. Consequently, any field $\boldsymbol{U}$ can be split in a unique manner in two parts of the form $\boldsymbol{r}\times\nabla U$ and $\boldsymbol{r}V+\nabla W$.

For several purposes it is useful to remove the non-uniqueness of U, V, and W by a normalization condition. In that sense U, V, and W may be fixed by the requirement that, for all r,

$$\oint\!\!\oint U \,\mathrm{d}\tilde{\omega} = \oint\!\!\oint W \,\mathrm{d}\tilde{\omega} = 0 . \tag{13.13}$$

As is easily seen, this condition can always be fulfilled. If, instead of functions U, V, and W satisfying (13.13), other functions, $\tilde{U}$, $\tilde{V}$, and $\tilde{W}$, are given, we may put

$$\oint\!\!\oint \tilde{U} \,\mathrm{d}\tilde{\omega} = -4\pi g, \quad \oint\!\!\oint \tilde{W} \,\mathrm{d}\tilde{\omega} = -4\pi h . \tag{13.14a, b}$$

Then (13.12) provides U, V, and W in agreement with (13.13). Since (13.12) are the only possible gauge transformations, (13.13) indeed fixes U, V, and W uniquely.

If only U and V are to be fixed, conditions (13.13) may be replaced by

$$\oint\!\!\oint U \,\mathrm{d}\tilde{\omega} = \oint\!\!\oint V \,\mathrm{d}\tilde{\omega} = 0 . \tag{13.15}$$

These conditions, too, can always be fulfilled. Then U and V are really uniquely fixed, whereas W is determined only up to an additive constant.

When using the representation (13.9), we should also keep in mind some relations of the vector analysis. For any scalar F we have

$$\operatorname{curl}(\boldsymbol{r}F) = -\boldsymbol{r}\times\nabla F , \tag{13.16a}$$

$$\operatorname{curl}\operatorname{curl}(\boldsymbol{r}F) = -\operatorname{curl}(\boldsymbol{r}\times\nabla F) = -\boldsymbol{r}\,\Delta F + \nabla\frac{\partial}{\partial r}(rF) , \tag{13.16b}$$

$$\operatorname{curl}\operatorname{curl}\operatorname{curl}(\boldsymbol{r}F) = \Delta(\boldsymbol{r}\times\nabla F) = -\operatorname{curl}(\boldsymbol{r}\,\Delta F) = \boldsymbol{r}\times\nabla\,\Delta F , \tag{13.16c}$$

$$\boldsymbol{r}\times\operatorname{curl}(\boldsymbol{r}F) = -\boldsymbol{r}\times(\boldsymbol{r}\times\nabla F) = -\frac{\boldsymbol{r}}{r}\cdot\frac{\partial}{\partial r}(r^2F) + \nabla(r^2F) . \tag{13.16d}$$

In connection with the normalization conditions it may be of interest that, again for any F,

$$\oint\!\!\oint \Omega F \,\mathrm{d}\tilde{\omega} = 0 . \tag{13.17}$$

With the help of (13.1b) we conclude that

$$\oint\!\!\oint \Delta F \,\mathrm{d}\tilde{\omega} = 0, \text{ if } \oint\!\!\oint F \,\mathrm{d}\tilde{\omega} = 0 . \tag{13.18}$$

13.4. Toroidal and poloidal vector fields in the general case

We shall now consider an arbitrary vector field $\boldsymbol{U}$ defined in a sphere or a spherical shell. As we have done in the axisymmetric case, in this general case too, we understand the field $\boldsymbol{U}$ as a sum of a toroidal field, $\boldsymbol{U}_t$, and a poloidal field, $\boldsymbol{U}_p$, so that

$$\boldsymbol{U} = \boldsymbol{U}_t + \boldsymbol{U}_p. \tag{13.19}$$

We define $\boldsymbol{U}_t$ and $\boldsymbol{U}_p$ by requiring that they can be represented as

$$\boldsymbol{U}_t = \boldsymbol{r} \times \nabla U, \tag{13.20a}$$

$$\boldsymbol{U}_p = \boldsymbol{r} V + \nabla W, \tag{13.20b}$$

or, in component form,

$$\boldsymbol{U}_t = -\frac{1}{\sin\vartheta}\frac{\partial U}{\partial\varphi}\boldsymbol{e}_\vartheta + \frac{\partial U}{\partial\vartheta}\boldsymbol{e}_\varphi, \tag{13.21a}$$

$$\boldsymbol{U}_p = \left(rV + \frac{\partial W}{\partial r}\right)\boldsymbol{e}_r + \frac{1}{r}\frac{\partial W}{\partial\vartheta}\boldsymbol{e}_\vartheta + \frac{1}{r\sin\vartheta}\frac{\partial W}{\partial\varphi}\boldsymbol{e}_\varphi. \tag{13.21b}$$

According to the foregoing considerations any vector field $\boldsymbol{U}$ can indeed be represented in this manner, and $\boldsymbol{U}_t$ and $\boldsymbol{U}_p$ are uniquely fixed. Obviously, this definition of $\boldsymbol{U}_t$ and $\boldsymbol{U}_p$ implies that given in the axisymmetric case. Because in a suitably chosen coordinate system we have in this case $\partial U/\partial\varphi = \partial W/\partial\varphi = 0$ so that (13.5) and (13.21) are in agreement.

In the general case the splitting of a given field $\boldsymbol{U}$ into the parts $\boldsymbol{U}_t$ and $\boldsymbol{U}_p$ is more complicated than in the axisymmetric case. It requires the knowledge of U, V, and W, which, as explained above, generally have to be determined as solutions of a system of partial differential equations. This implies a further difference. In the axisymmetric case the splitting of the field at a given point does not require any information on the behaviour of this field in the neighbourhood of this point. In the general case, however, the splitting at a given point depends on the behaviour of the field at the surface $r = \text{const}$ containing this point.

If a field is given in the form of the right-hand side of (13.20a) or (13.20b) it is clearly toroidal or poloidal, respectively. In particular, any gradient of a single-valued function is poloidal.

Now statements similar to those given for the axisymmetric case are possible:

(i) If, at a surface $r = \text{const}$, $\boldsymbol{U} = 0$ then also $\boldsymbol{U}_t = \boldsymbol{U}_p = 0$.

(ii) If a is a scalar depending only on r, but not on ϑ and φ, then $a\boldsymbol{U}_t$ is toroidal and $a\boldsymbol{U}_p$ is poloidal.

(iii) $\boldsymbol{r}\times\boldsymbol{U}_\mathrm{t}$ is poloidal and $\boldsymbol{r}\times\boldsymbol{U}_\mathrm{p}$ is toroidal.
(iv) div $\boldsymbol{U}_\mathrm{t} = 0$.
(v) curl $\boldsymbol{U}_\mathrm{t}$ is poloidal, and curl $\boldsymbol{U}_\mathrm{p}$ is toroidal.
(vi) If, throughout the whole region, curl $\boldsymbol{U}_\mathrm{t} = 0$ then $\boldsymbol{U}_\mathrm{t} = 0$.
(vii) $\boldsymbol{U}_\mathrm{t}$ and $\boldsymbol{U}_\mathrm{p}$ are orthogonal to each other in the sense of $\oint\!\!\oint \boldsymbol{U}_\mathrm{t}\cdot\boldsymbol{U}_\mathrm{p}\,\mathrm{d}\tilde{\omega} = 0$.

Statement (i) can easily be proved with the help of the considerations of the foregoing section according to which $\boldsymbol{U} = 0$ results in $U = g$; this again leads to $\boldsymbol{U}_\mathrm{t} = 0$ and, hence, to $\boldsymbol{U}_\mathrm{p} = 0$. Statement (ii) is a simple consequence of definition (13.20). As for the statements (iii), (iv), and (v), the proof is given by the vector formulae (13.16) in connection with definition (13.20). In order to justify statement (vi), again referring to the simple-connectedness of the region, we at first conclude from curl $\boldsymbol{U}_\mathrm{t} = 0$ that $\boldsymbol{U}_\mathrm{t}$ is a gradient of a single-valued potential; because such gradients are always poloidal we then obtain $\boldsymbol{U}_\mathrm{t} = 0$. With respect to statement (vii) we note at first that

$$\oint\!\!\oint \boldsymbol{U}_\mathrm{t}\cdot\boldsymbol{U}_\mathrm{p}\,\mathrm{d}\tilde{\omega} = \frac{1}{r}\int\limits_{\vartheta=0}^{\pi}\int\limits_{\varphi=0}^{2\pi}\left(\frac{\partial U}{\partial\vartheta}\frac{\partial W}{\partial\varphi} - \frac{\partial U}{\partial\varphi}\frac{\partial W}{\partial\vartheta}\right)\mathrm{d}\vartheta\,\mathrm{d}\varphi$$

$$= \frac{1}{r}\left(\int\limits_0^{2\pi}\left[U\frac{\partial W}{\partial\varphi}\right]_{\vartheta=0}^{\vartheta=\pi}\mathrm{d}\varphi - \int\limits_0^{\pi}\left[U\frac{\partial W}{\partial\vartheta}\right]_{\varphi=0}^{\varphi=2\pi}\mathrm{d}\vartheta\right), \tag{13.22}$$

where the last line is the result of partial integrations. Since U is supposed to be non-singular everywhere, it follows that $\partial W/\partial\varphi = 0$ at $\vartheta = 0$ and $\vartheta = \pi$ and, therefore, the first integral of the last line vanishes. Due to the fact that U and W are single-valued the second integral of this line vanishes too.

The remarks on $\Delta\boldsymbol{U}$ given for the axisymmetric case remain valid, in particular formulae (13.6). Again, $\Delta\boldsymbol{U}_\mathrm{t}$ and $\Delta\boldsymbol{U}_\mathrm{p}$ turn out to be toroidal and poloidal, respectively.

Dealing with fields $\boldsymbol{U}$ which are solenoidal we may essentially repeat considerations given for the axisymmetric case. As far as $\boldsymbol{U}_\mathrm{p}$ can be represented by a vector potential $\hat{\boldsymbol{U}}$ which is single-valued we again arrive at (13.8). Concerning the existence of suitable $\hat{\boldsymbol{U}}$ we refer to the remarks under (13.8).

By contrast with the axisymmetric case, the general case considered here was started from the assumption that the field $\boldsymbol{U}$ is defined in a spherical region. Then for the definition of the toroidal and poloidal parts, $\boldsymbol{U}_\mathrm{t}$ and $\boldsymbol{U}_\mathrm{p}$, we made reference to a spherical coordinate system, especially of the spherical coordinate surface $r = \mathrm{const}$. The question arises whether it is possible to extend these considerations to other regions or other coordinate systems in a way so that statements similar to (i)...(vii) hold. It is not difficult to represent a field $\boldsymbol{U}$ as a sum of two parts which are defined like $\boldsymbol{U}_\mathrm{t}$ and $\boldsymbol{U}_\mathrm{p}$ but with respect to other surfaces. However, only in the case of planes or spherical surfaces statements like (iv) and (v) are to be expected; see RÄDLER [10]. Already in the case of ellipsoidal surfaces statements of this kind can no longer be justified.

13.5. Expansions in spherical harmonics

As we have pointed out, the determination of the toroidal and the poloidal parts of a given vector field $\boldsymbol{U}$ generally requires the solution of a system of partial differential equations for the functions U, V, and W. In many cases it is appropriate to expand these functions with respect to spherical harmonics. Thus, the integration of differential equations can be reduced to quadratures. In this section we shall present some relations relevant for such expansions with spherical harmonics.

Let each of the functions U, V, and W be expanded as

$$F = \sum_{n,m} F_n^m(r)\, Y_n^m(\vartheta, \varphi). \tag{13.23}$$

The functions F_n^m are complex quantities, and the spherical harmonics Y_n^m are defined by

$$Y_n^m = P_n^{|m|}(\cos\vartheta)\, \mathrm{e}^{\mathrm{i}m\varphi}, \tag{13.24}$$

with P_n^m being associated Legendre polynomials. The summation is over all n and m with $n \geqq 0$ and $|m| \leqq n$. Since F should be real we have to require that $F_n^{-m} = F_n^{m*}$.

We may, of course, understand the vector field $\boldsymbol{U}$ too as a sum of special fields which are related to the terms in the expansions of U, V, and W. These fields are ascribed to special multipoles. We designate all fields which correspond to terms of U, V, or W with $n = 1$ as dipole fields, if $n = 2$ as quadrupole fields, if $n = 3$ as octupole fields, etc.

As is well known the spherical harmonics Y_n^m satisfy the differential equation

$$\Omega Y_n^m + n(n+1)\, Y_n^m = 0 \tag{13.25}$$

and the orthogonality relation

$$\oint Y_n^m Y_\nu^{-\mu}\, \mathrm{d}\tilde{\omega} = \begin{cases} A_n^m \text{ if } n = \nu \text{ and } m = \mu \\ 0 \text{ otherwise.} \end{cases} \tag{13.26}$$

Adopting Ferrer's normalization of the P_n^m we have

$$A_n^m = \frac{4\pi(n + |m|)!}{(2n+1)\,(n - |m|)!}. \tag{13.27}$$

With the help of (13.16) from (13.19) and (13.20) we now conclude

$$\Omega U = \boldsymbol{r} \cdot \operatorname{curl} \boldsymbol{U}, \tag{13.28a}$$

$$\Omega V = -\boldsymbol{r} \cdot \operatorname{curl} \operatorname{curl} \boldsymbol{U}, \tag{13.28b}$$

$$\Omega W = \boldsymbol{r} \cdot \operatorname{curl} (\boldsymbol{r} \times \boldsymbol{U}), \tag{13.28c}$$

of which (13.28a) and (13.28c) are only repetitions of (13.11). Expressing U, V, and W by expansions like (13.23), and using (13.25) and (13.26) we then obtain

$$U_n^m = -(n(n+1)\, A_n^m)^{-1} \oiint (\boldsymbol{r} \cdot \operatorname{curl} \boldsymbol{U})\, Y_n^{-m}\, \mathrm{d}\tilde{\omega}, \tag{13.29a}$$

$$V_n^m = (n(n+1)\, A_n^m)^{-1} \oiint (\boldsymbol{r} \cdot \operatorname{curl} \operatorname{curl} \boldsymbol{U})\, Y_n^{-m}\, \mathrm{d}\tilde{\omega}, \tag{13.29b}$$

$$W_n^m = -(n(n+1)\, A_n^m)^{-1} \oiint (\boldsymbol{r} \cdot \operatorname{curl} (\boldsymbol{r} \times \boldsymbol{U}))\, Y_n^{-m}\, \mathrm{d}\tilde{\omega}, \text{ for } n \geqq 1. \tag{13.29c}$$

Analogously it results

$$r^2 V + r \frac{\partial W}{\partial r} = \boldsymbol{r} \cdot \boldsymbol{U} \tag{13.30}$$

and

$$V_n^m + \frac{1}{r} \frac{\partial W_n^m}{\partial r} = (r^2 A_n^m)^{-1} \oiint (\boldsymbol{r} \cdot \boldsymbol{U})\, Y_n^{-m}\, \mathrm{d}\tilde{\omega}, \text{ for } n \geqq 0. \tag{13.31}$$

Owing to the possibility of gauge transformations, U_0^0 is not fixed by these relations, and V_0^0 and W_0^0 are only obliged to satisfy (13.31).

If $\boldsymbol{U}$ is solenoidal, we may use (13.8) instead of (13.20b), and express $\hat{\boldsymbol{U}}_t$ according to (13.20a) by a function $\hat{U}$. Doing so we find

$$\Omega \hat{U} = \boldsymbol{r} \cdot \boldsymbol{U} \tag{13.32}$$

and

$$\hat{U}_n^m = -(n(n+1)\, A_n^m)^{-1} \oiint (\boldsymbol{r} \cdot \boldsymbol{U})\, Y_n^{-m}\, \mathrm{d}\tilde{\omega}, \text{ for } n \geqq 1. \tag{13.33}$$

In agreement with the possibility of gauge transformations, $\hat{U}_0^0$ may be chosen arbitrarily.

With regard to the relations occuring here we note that, for any $\boldsymbol{U}$ and $\boldsymbol{F}$,

$$\boldsymbol{r} \cdot \operatorname{curl} \boldsymbol{U} = -\operatorname{div} (\boldsymbol{r} \times \boldsymbol{U}) \tag{13.34}$$

and

$$\begin{aligned} \oiint (\boldsymbol{r} \cdot \operatorname{curl} \boldsymbol{U})\, \boldsymbol{F}\, \mathrm{d}\tilde{\omega} &= -\oiint \operatorname{div} (\boldsymbol{r} \times \boldsymbol{U})\, \boldsymbol{F}\, \mathrm{d}\tilde{\omega} \\ &= -\oiint \boldsymbol{U} \cdot (\boldsymbol{r} \times \nabla \boldsymbol{F})\, \mathrm{d}\tilde{\omega}. \end{aligned} \tag{13.35}$$

CHAPTER 14

A SIMPLE MODEL OF AN α-EFFECT DYNAMO

14.1. Description of the model

In this chapter we shall deal with an extremely simple spherical model of a turbulent dynamo. We consider a sphere of an electrically conducting medium which shows no mean motion but only a homogeneous isotropic non-mirror-symmetric steady turbulence. It is assumed that the influence of this turbulence on the electromagnetic fields is described correctly simply by the turbulent electrical conductivity and the α-effect. This presupposes, in particular, that the scales of the turbulence are sufficiently small compared with those of the mean magnetic field. All space outside the conducting medium is again assumed to be vacuum.

At first the model shall be considered from the kinematic point of view, i.e. no influence of the magnetic field on the motion is taken into account. Only at the end of this chapter we shall modify this model by admitting a back-reaction of the magnetic field on the turbulence and, therefore, on the α-effect.

Up to now the model envisaged has been treated only with regard to axisymmetric magnetic fields. Within this frame Krause and Steenbeck [2] (1967) dealt with the steady case, Voigtmann [1] (1968) also studied the non-steady case, and Rüdiger [1] (1973) made a first step towards including the back-reaction of the magnetic field on the turbulence. In the following we shall generalize these considerations by admitting arbitrary magnetic fields.

Of course, our model is rather unrealistic. It is hard to imagine a mechanism which would create and maintain a homogeneous isotropic non-mirrorsymmetric turbulence. Besides, even if such turbulence exists in some inner regions of the sphere, it must be accompanied by an inhomogeneous anisotropic turbulence near the boundary. In this way other influences on the electromagnetic fields will occur, which are, however, ignored here. Nevertheless it is very instructive to study this model. Since it allows an analytical treatment it is well suited to demonstrate some features of turbulent dynamos. Thus it provides some orientation for the investigation of more realistic models, which in all cases requires extensive numerical computations.

14.2. Basic equations and their reduction to equations for scalar functions

We now specify the basic equations (12.2)...(12.5) for models of turbulent dynamos to the special situations considered here. Again, a spherical coordinate system with the coordinates r, ϑ, and φ and the radius vector $\boldsymbol{r}$ is used. The origin of this system coincides with the centre of the sphere occupied by the conducting medium. The radius of the sphere is denoted by R. As far as the space inside the sphere is concerned we put $\overline{\boldsymbol{u}} = 0$ and $\mathfrak{E}^+ = \alpha\overline{\boldsymbol{B}}$, and we suppose σ_{T} and α to be constant. In this way we obtain the equations

$$\frac{1}{\mu\sigma_{\mathrm{T}}}\Delta\overline{\boldsymbol{B}} + \alpha \operatorname{curl} \overline{\boldsymbol{B}} - \frac{\partial\overline{\boldsymbol{B}}}{\partial t} = 0, \tag{14.1a}$$

$$\operatorname{div} \overline{\boldsymbol{B}} = 0, \qquad \text{for } r < R. \tag{14.1b}$$

We have to supplement them by the equations

$$\operatorname{curl} \overline{\boldsymbol{B}} = 0, \quad \operatorname{div} \overline{\boldsymbol{B}} = 0, \text{ for } r > R, \tag{14.2a, b}$$

and the conditions

$$[\overline{\boldsymbol{B}}] = 0, \quad \text{on } r = R, \tag{14.3a}$$

$$\overline{\boldsymbol{B}} = O(r^{-3}), \text{ as } r \to \infty. \tag{14.3b}$$

When solving these equations we want to recall the mathematical considerations of the foregoing chapter. We shall utilize the basic ideas of sections 13.3., 13.4., and 13.5., especially the statements (i)...(vii), without special reference. For simplicity, instead of $\overline{\boldsymbol{B}}$ we shall write $\boldsymbol{B}$ in the following.

At first we split $\boldsymbol{B}$ into a toroidal part, $\boldsymbol{B}_{\mathrm{t}}$, and a poloidal part, $\boldsymbol{B}_{\mathrm{p}}$, so that

$$\boldsymbol{B} = \boldsymbol{B}_{\mathrm{t}} + \boldsymbol{B}_{\mathrm{p}}. \tag{14.4}$$

By reason of (14.1b) and (14.2b) we then put

$$\boldsymbol{B}_{\mathrm{p}} = \operatorname{curl} \boldsymbol{A}_{\mathrm{t}}, \tag{14.5}$$

with $\boldsymbol{A}_{\mathrm{t}}$ being a vector potential which is purely toroidal.

We focus attention on equation (14.1a). Inserting (14.4) and separating the toroidal and the poloidal parts of this equation we obtain

$$\frac{1}{\mu\sigma_{\mathrm{T}}}\Delta\boldsymbol{B}_{\mathrm{t}} + \alpha \operatorname{curl} \boldsymbol{B}_{\mathrm{p}} - \frac{\partial\boldsymbol{B}_{\mathrm{t}}}{\partial t} = 0, \tag{14.6a}$$

$$\frac{1}{\mu\sigma_{\mathrm{T}}}\Delta\boldsymbol{B}_{\mathrm{p}} + \alpha \operatorname{curl} \boldsymbol{B}_{\mathrm{t}} - \frac{\partial\boldsymbol{B}_{\mathrm{p}}}{\partial t} = 0, \text{ for } r < R. \tag{14.6b}$$

By virtue of (14.5) the first equation may be rewritten as

$$\frac{1}{\mu\sigma_T}\Delta(\boldsymbol{B}_t - \mu\sigma_T\alpha\boldsymbol{A}_t) - \frac{\partial \boldsymbol{B}_t}{\partial t} = 0, \text{ for } r < R, \tag{14.7a}$$

and the second one allows an integration which results in

$$\frac{1}{\mu\sigma_T}\Delta\boldsymbol{A}_t + \alpha\boldsymbol{B}_t - \frac{\partial \boldsymbol{A}_t}{\partial t} = 0, \text{ for } r < R. \tag{14.7b}$$

Likewise, equation (14.2a) leads to

$$\boldsymbol{B}_t = 0, \quad \Delta\boldsymbol{A}_t = 0, \text{ for } r > R. \tag{14.8a, b}$$

The conditions (14.3) result in

$$\boldsymbol{B}_t = 0, \quad [\text{curl}\, \boldsymbol{A}_t] = 0, \text{ on } r = R, \tag{14.9a, b}$$

$$\boldsymbol{A}_t = O(r^{-2}), \text{ as } r \to \infty. \tag{14.9c}$$

Let us now represent $\boldsymbol{B}_t$ and $\boldsymbol{A}_t$ by

$$\boldsymbol{B}_t = -\boldsymbol{r}\times\nabla T, \tag{14.10a}$$

$$\boldsymbol{A}_t = -\boldsymbol{r}\times\nabla S, \tag{14.10b}$$

where T and S are single-valued scalar functions normalized by

$$\oint\!\!\oint T\, d\tilde{\omega} = \oint\!\!\oint S\, d\tilde{\omega} = 0. \tag{14.11}$$

It should be noted that by combining (14.4), (14.5), and (14.10) one obtains

$$\boldsymbol{B} = -\boldsymbol{r}\times\nabla T - \boldsymbol{r}\,\Delta S + \nabla\frac{\partial}{\partial r}(rS). \tag{14.12}$$

Again we turn to equations (14.7). Using (14.10) we are able to reduce them to

$$\boldsymbol{r}\times\nabla\left\{\frac{1}{\mu\sigma_T}\Delta(T - \mu\sigma_T\alpha S) - \frac{\partial T}{\partial t}\right\} = 0, \tag{14.13a}$$

$$\boldsymbol{r}\times\nabla\left\{\frac{1}{\mu\sigma_T}\Delta S + \alpha T - \frac{\partial S}{\partial t}\right\} = 0, \text{ for } r < R. \tag{14.13b}$$

From this we may at first conclude that the expressions $\{\cdots\}$ are functions of r and t alone. By reason of (13.18) and (14.11) these functions, however, turn out to be zero. Thus we have

$$\frac{1}{\mu\sigma_T}\Delta(T - \mu\sigma_T\alpha S) - \frac{\partial T}{\partial t} = 0, \tag{14.14a}$$

$$\frac{1}{\mu\sigma_T}\Delta S + \alpha T - \frac{\partial S}{\partial t} = 0, \text{ for } r < R. \tag{14.14b}$$

Analogously, from (14.8) we obtain

$$T = 0, \quad \Delta S = 0, \quad \text{for } r > R. \tag{14.15a, b}$$

Finally, (14.9) provides for

$$T = 0, \quad [S] = [\partial S/\partial r] = 0, \text{ on } r = R, \tag{14.16a, b}$$

$$S = O(r^{-2}), \text{ as } r \to \infty. \tag{14.16c}$$

We introduce dimensionless coordinates,

$$x = r/R, \quad \tau = t/\mu\sigma_{\mathrm{T}}R^2, \tag{14.17a, b}$$

and a dimensionless parameter,

$$C = \mu\sigma_{\mathrm{T}}\alpha R, \tag{14.18}$$

which represents a measure for the α-effect. In addition, we define an operator, D_n, by

$$D_n f = \frac{1}{x^2}\left(\frac{\partial}{\partial x}\left(x^2 \frac{\partial f}{\partial x}\right) - n(n+1) f\right), \tag{14.19}$$

with f being any function and n an integer.

Furthermore, we represent the functions T' and S by series of spherical harmonics,

$$T = \sum_{n,m} T_n^m(x, \tau)\, Y_n^m(\vartheta, \varphi), \tag{14.20a}$$

$$S = R \sum_{n,m} S_n^m(x, \tau)\, Y_n^m(\vartheta, \varphi). \tag{14.20b}$$

The factor R accomplishes the agreement of the dimensions of the T_n^m and S_n^m. As for the Y_n^m we refer to (13.24) ... (13.27). The summation is over all n and m with $n \geqq 1$ and $|m| \leqq n$; because of (14.11) $n = 0$ has to be excluded. Since T and S should be real quantities we require $T_n^{-m} = T_n^{m*}$ and $S_n^{-m} = S_n^{m*}$.

The equations (14.14) for T and S now reduce to

$$D_n(T_n^m - CS_n^m) - \partial T_n^m/\partial\tau = 0, \tag{14.21a}$$

$$D_n S_n^m + CT_n^m - \partial S_n^m/\partial\tau = 0, \qquad \text{for } 0 \leqq x \leqq 1. \tag{14.21b}$$

From (14.15) and (14.16c) follows

$$T_n^m = 0, \quad S_n^m = a_n^m x^{-(n+1)}, \text{ for } x \geqq 1, \tag{14.22a, b}$$

with a_n^m being independent of x. Then (14.16a) is equivalent to

$$T_n^m = 0, \text{ at } x = 1. \tag{14.23}$$

From (14.16 b) one gets

$$S_n^m = a_n^m, \quad \partial S/\partial x = -(n+1)\, a_n^m, \text{ at } x = 1, \tag{14.24a, b}$$

and, by eliminating a_n^m,

$$\partial S_n^m/\partial x + (n+1)\, S_n^m = 0, \text{ at } x = 1. \tag{14.25}$$

As a result of our deductions the problem of solving the system of partial differential equations (14.1) and (14.2) with the conditions (14.3) governing the vector field $\boldsymbol{B}$ for all space is now reduced to the problem of solving the differential equations (14.21) with the boundary conditions (14.23) and (14.25) determining the scalar functions T_n^m and S_n^m in $0 \leqq x \leqq 1$.

It is noteworthy that neither the equatons (14.21) nor the conditions (14.23) and (14.25) provide any coupling between pairs of T_n^m and S_n^m which differ in n or m. In addition to this, these equations and conditions do not depend on m.

Finally, we want to point out that the basic equations for $\boldsymbol{B}$ are only justified if the scales of $\boldsymbol{B}$ exceed certain bounds determined by the scales of turbulence. This requires a restriction to sufficiently small n and m. The physical sense of our considerations becomes questionable if n and m are too large.

14.3. The steady case

We ask at first for steady $\boldsymbol{B}$-fields. In this case the equations (14.20) reduce to

$$D_n(T_n^m - CS_n^m) = 0, \tag{14.26a}$$

$$D_n S_n^m + CT_n^m = 0, \qquad \text{for } 0 \leqq x \leqq 1. \tag{14.26b}$$

Again the conditions (14.23) and (14.25) have to be added. In this way an eigenvalue problem results, in which C is the eigenvalue parameter.

Until further notice we consider the T_n^m and S_n^m for an arbitrary but fixed pair of n and m. The case $C = 0$ shall at first be excluded.

From (14.26) we may derive an equation for T_n^m alone, namely

$$(D_n + C^2)\, T_n^m = 0, \text{ for } 0 \leqq x \leqq 1. \tag{14.27}$$

Its only solution without singularities in the interval considered reads

$$T_n^m = (c_n^m/\sqrt{x}) J_{n+1/2}(Cx), \tag{14.28}$$

where c_n^m is a constant and $J_{n+1/2}$ is the Bessel function of the order $n + 1/2$. Condition (14.23) requires $c_n^m = 0$ unless

$$J_{n+1/2}(C) = 0. \tag{14.29}$$

In the case $c_n^m = 0$ we may easily conclude from (14.22)...(14.26) that $T_n^m = S_n^m = 0$ for all x. We pay special attention to the case $c_n^m \neq 0$ which only occurs if equation (14.29) is satisfied. By this equation discrete values of C are defined which represent the eigenvalues of our problem. Until further notice we suppose that C is specified to be one of these eigenvalues. Using now equation (14.26a), and again excluding singularities, we obtain

$$S_n^m = \frac{c_n^m}{C\sqrt{x}} J_{n+1/2}(Cx) + d_n^m x^n, \text{ for } 0 \leqq x \leqq 1, \tag{14.30}$$

where d_n^m is a new constant. In order to satisfy condition (14.25) this constant must be properly fixed. In doing so and using general relations for Bessel functions we get

$$S_n^m = \frac{c_n^m}{C}\left(\frac{1}{\sqrt{x}} J_{n+1/2}(Cx) - \frac{C}{2n+1} J_{n-1/2}(C)\, x^n\right), \quad \text{for} \leqq x \leqq 1. \tag{14.31}$$

Referring to the relations (14.22) and (14.24a), we supplement (14.28), (14.29) and (14.31) with

$$T_n^m = 0, \tag{14.32a}$$

$$S_n^m = -\frac{c_n^m}{2n+1} J_{n-1/2}(C)\, x^{-(n+1)}, \text{ for } x \geqq 1. \tag{14.32b}$$

For the case $C = 0$, which is again included in the following considerations, we easily find that $T_n^m = S_n^m = 0$ for all x.

We return to the series for T and S given by (14.20) where, of course, again all n and m with $n \geqq 1$ and $|m| \geqq n$ are to be considered. As long as C does not coincide with one of the eigenvalues defined by (14.29), T and S vanish everywhere. Only if C equals one of these eigenvalues, T and S may differ from zero. According to the properties of the $J_{n+1/2}$ the eigenvalues for different n are always different from each other. Therefore, in the series for T and S the summation over n can be omitted; there are only contributions from one special n. Clearly, the eigenvalues for a given n but different m coincide, i.e. there is a degeneration with respect to m. Therefore, T and S may remain sums over terms with different m.

We see from these calculations that stationary $\boldsymbol{B}$-fields are only possible if the parameter C, which is a measure for the α-effect, takes special values, namely the eigenvalues mentioned. These $\boldsymbol{B}$-fields correspond to multipoles of a given order which depends on the special eigenvalue. The presence of a $\boldsymbol{B}$-mode of the order n excludes the occurrence of modes with other n. However, the coexistence of modes with the same n but different m is possible.

Discussing now some details, we restrict ourselves at first to the case $\alpha \geqq 0$ so that $C \geqq 0$. We again consider the eigenvalue equation (14.29). According to the properties of the $J_{n+1/2}$, for any given n we have an infinite sequence of eigenvalues which we denote by C_{nl} with $l = 1, 2, \ldots$ We arrange them such that the C_{nl} grow monotonically with l. Again referring to the properties of the $J_{n+1/2}$ we may then state that the C_{nl}, for any fixed l, also grow monotonically with n. Therefore, C_{11} turns out to be the smallest of all values C_{nl}.

Let us discuss the case $n = 1$. The related $\boldsymbol{B}$-modes are dipole fields, where those for $m = 0$ and for $m = \pm 1$ differ only by a rotation about an axis running through the origin of the coordinate system. From (14.29), which for $n = 1$ reduces to

$$(1/C_{1l}) \tan C_{1l} - 1 = 0, \quad C_{1l} > 0, \tag{14.33}$$

we get

$$C_{11} = 4.4934, \quad C_{12} = 7.7253, \tag{14.34a, b}$$

$$C_{13} = 10.9041, \quad C_{14} = 14.0662. \tag{14.34c, d}$$

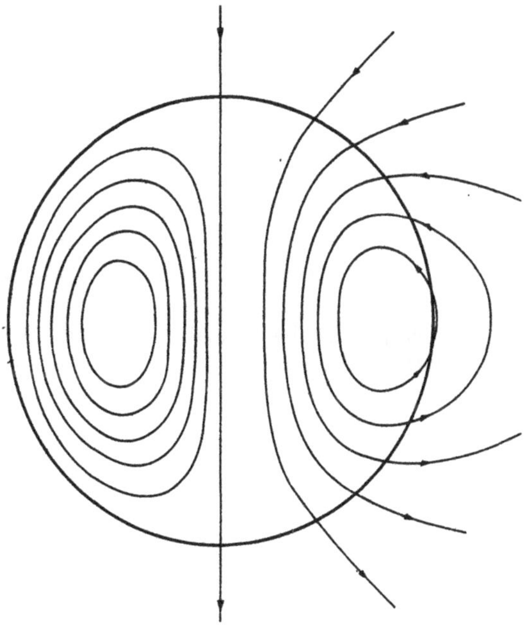

Fig. 14.1. The steady $\boldsymbol{B}$-field in the case $n = l = 1$. The left-hand side of the picture shows the lines of constant magnitude of the toroidal field, the right-hand side field lines of the poloidal field. (After KRAUSE and STEENBECK [2])

By means of (14.12), (14.17), (14.28), (14.31), and (14.32) the corresponding $\boldsymbol{B}$-fields can be calculated. For that belonging to $l = 1$ the field lines are given in figure 14.1. In the case of $l > 1$ the field patterns inside the sphere are more complicated.

We now consider the case of $n > 1$ and, therefore, $\boldsymbol{B}$-modes which correspond to quadrupole fields, octupole fields, etc. Such modes with $m = 0$, $m = \pm 1, \ldots$ possess quite different field structures which can become congruent after rotation only in special cases. In this respect it is remarkable that the eigenvalues are independent of m. On the basis of (14.29) it results

$$C_{21} = 5.7635, \quad C_{22} = 9.0950, \tag{14.35a, b}$$

$$C_{23} = 12.3229, \quad C_{24} = 15.5146. \tag{14.35c, d}$$

Obviously, the equations (14.26) and the corresponding boundary conditions remain valid if, at the same time, the signs of C and of either T or S are changed. Consequently, for each positive eigenvalue C_{nl} there exists a negative one, namely $-C_{nl}$. Starting from a $\boldsymbol{B}$-field belonging to C_{nl} we get a field belonging to $-C_{nl}$ by changing the sign of either $\boldsymbol{B}_\mathrm{t}$ or $\boldsymbol{B}_\mathrm{p}$.

14.4. The non-steady case

Now the initial value problem for the $\boldsymbol{B}$-field shall be considered. We suppose that $\boldsymbol{B}(\boldsymbol{x}, 0)$ is given and ask for $\boldsymbol{B}(\boldsymbol{x}, t)$ for $t > 0$. Due to the foregoing deductions this problem can also be formulated in terms of the T_n^m and S_n^m. We then suppose all $T_n^m(x, 0)$ and $S_n^m(x, 0)$ to be given and ask for $T_n^m(x, \tau)$ and $S_n^m(x, \tau)$ for $\tau > 0$.

In preparation of this, a simpler problem shall be solved. We look for $\boldsymbol{B}$-fields with a purely exponential dependence on time, i.e. for such of the form $\boldsymbol{B}(\boldsymbol{x}, 0)\, \mathrm{e}^{\lambda t}$ with some real constant λ. To this end we put, by way of trial,

$$T_n^m = T_{nl}^m(x) \exp\{\lambda_{nl}\tau\}, \tag{14.36a}$$

$$S_n^m = S_{nl}^m(x) \exp\{\lambda_{nl}\tau\}. \tag{14.36b}$$

This notation implies that, if such T_n^m and S_n^m are possible, the λ_{nl} may not depend on m. The index l will be specified later.

We now refer to the equations (14.21). Inserting (14.36) we obtain

$$D_n(T_{nl}^m - CS_{nl}^m) - \lambda_{nl}T_{nl}^m = 0, \tag{14.37a}$$

$$D_nS_{nl}^m + CT_{nl}^m - \lambda_{nl}S_{nl}^m = 0, \text{ for } 0 \leqq x \leqq 1. \tag{14.37b}$$

The general solution which is non-singular in the interval considered reads

$$T_{nl}^m = \frac{c_{nl}^{(1)m}}{\sqrt{x}} J_{n+1/2}(u_{nl}^{(1)}x) + \frac{c_{nl}^{(2)m}}{\sqrt{x}} J_{n+1/2}(u_{nl}^{(2)}x), \tag{14.38a}$$

$$S_{nl}^m = \frac{c_{nl}^{(1)m}}{u_{nl}^{(1)}\sqrt{x}} J_{n+1/2}(u_{nl}^{(1)}x) + \frac{c_{nl}^{(2)m}}{u_{nl}^{(2)}\sqrt{x}} J_{n+1/2}(u_{nl}^{(2)}x), \text{ for } 0 \leqq x \leqq 1, \tag{14.38b}$$

where $c_{nl}^{(1)m}$ and $c_{nl}^{(2)m}$ are arbitrary constants and

$$u_{nl}^{(1,2)} = \frac{1}{2}(C \pm \sqrt{C^2 - 4\lambda_{nl}}). \tag{14.39}$$

The conditions (14.23) and (14.25) together with special relations for Bessel functions result in

$$c_{nl}^{(1)m} J_{n+1/2}(u_{nl}^{(1)}) + c_{nl}^{(2)m} J_{n+1/2}(u_{nl}^{(2)}) = 0, \tag{14.40a}$$

$$c_{nl}^{(1)m} J_{n-1/2}(u_{nl}^{(1)}) + c_{nl}^{(2)m} J_{n-1/2}(u_{nl}^{(2)}) = 0. \tag{14.40b}$$

We only look for non-trivial T_{nl}^m and S_{nl}^m. More precisely, we require T_{nl}^m and S_{nl}^m, i.e. $c_{nl}^{(1)m}$ and $c_{nl}^{(2)m}$, not to vanish simultaneously for any fixed n and m. In this case, (14.40) implies

$$J_{n+1/2}(u_{nl}^{(1)})\, J_{n-1/2}(u_{nl}^{(2)}) - J_{n-1/2}(u_{nl}^{(1)})\, J_{n+1/2}(u_{nl}^{(2)}) = 0. \tag{14.41}$$

If supplemented by (14.39), this relation determines an infinite set of values λ_{nl} for each given n and each C. We now number the λ_{nl} and the corresponding T_{nl}^m and S_{nl}^m by $l = 1, 2, \ldots$ in such way that the λ_{nl} for any fixed n grow with l. In order to evaluate the λ_{nl} as functions of C it is useful at first to determine pairs $u_{nl}^{(1)}$ and $u_{nl}^{(2)}$. Then related values of λ_{nl} and C result from the formulae

$$\lambda_{nl} = u_{nl}^{(1)} u_{nl}^{(2)}, \tag{14.42a}$$

$$C = u_{nl}^{(1)} + u_{nl}^{(2)}, \tag{14.42b}$$

which are a consequence of (14.39).

On this basis we may specify the ***B***-modes with a purely exponential dependence on time.

In the special case $C = 0$ these modes coincide with the modes of free decay. For this case, referring to (14.42b), we put $u_{nl}^{(1)} = -u_{nl}^{(2)} = u_{nl}$, where $u_{nl} > 0$. Regarding the properties of $J_{n-1/2}$ and $J_{n+1/2}$ we then may replace (14.41) by

$$J_{n-1/2}(u_{nl})\, J_{n+1/2}(u_{nl}) = 0, \tag{14.43}$$

and (14.42a) by

$$\lambda_{nl} = -(u_{nl})^2 < 0. \tag{14.44}$$

For the dipole modes, i.e. $n = 1$, we obtain

$$\sin u_{1l}((1/u_{1l}) \tan u_{1l} - 1) = 0, \tag{14.45}$$

leading to

$$\lambda_{11} = -\pi^2, \qquad \lambda_{12} = -(4.4934)^2, \tag{14.46a, b}$$

$$\lambda_{13} = -(2\pi)^2, \qquad \lambda_{14} = -(7.7253)^2. \tag{14.46c, d}$$

Similarly, for the quadrupole modes, i.e. $n = 2$, we obtain

$$\lambda_{21} = -(4.4934)^2, \qquad \lambda_{22} = -(5.7635)^2, \tag{14.47a, b}$$

$$\lambda_{23} = -(7.7253)^2, \qquad \lambda_{24} = -(9.0950)^2. \tag{14.47c, d}$$

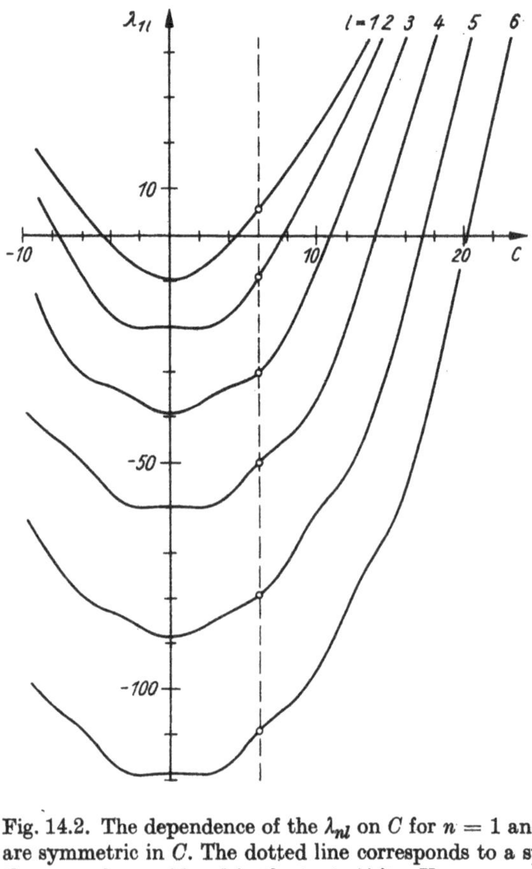

Fig. 14.2. The dependence of the λ_{nl} on C for $n = 1$ and $l = 1, 2, \ldots, 6$. The λ_{nl} are symmetric in C. The dotted line corresponds to a special value of C used in the example considered in the text. (After VOIGTMANN [1])

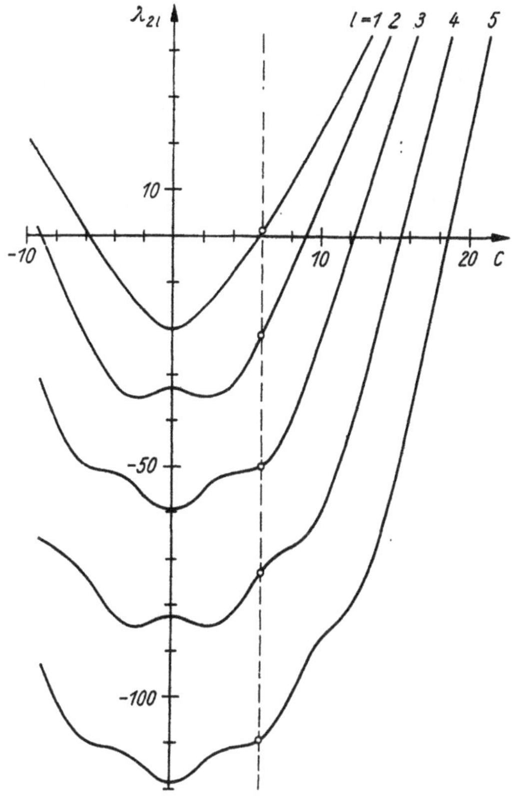

Fig. 14.3. The dependence of the λ_{nl} on C for $n = 2$ and $l = 1, 2, \ldots, 5$. The λ_{nl} are symmetric in C. The dotted line corresponds to a special value of C used in the example considered in the text. (After VOIGTMANN [1])

In the case $C \neq 0$ the $\boldsymbol{B}$-fields are influenced by the α-effect. Then the λ_{nl} are not necessarily negative. For sufficiently large $|C|$ positive λ_{nl} may also occur, and the corresponding modes will grow in time. As for the dipole and quadrupole modes, i.e. $n = 1$ and $n = 2$, the dependence of the λ_{nl} on C is shown in figures 14.2 and 14.3. Obviously, $\lambda_{nl} = 0$ corresponds to the steady modes, for which $C = C_{nl}$. Comparing the λ_{nl} at any fixed C for different modes we find that they are the larger the smaller the $|C_{nl}|$ related to these modes. Therefore a mode belonging to a given $|C_{nl}|$ will grow more slowly, or decay more rapidly, than one with a smaller $|C_{nl}|$.

For any fixed C the λ_{nl} increase if n or l grows. Therefore, the $\boldsymbol{B}$-modes with smaller n and l decay more slowly, or grow more rapidly, than those with higher

n and l. This becomes clear if the connection between n and l and the geometrical structure of the $\boldsymbol{B}$-fields is considered. Obviously, n is a measure for the variations with ϑ and φ. More precisely, for $m = 0$ there are only variations with ϑ, and if n is fixed but $|m|$ grows, those with ϑ become smaller and those with φ larger. Furthermore, l is a measure for the variations with r. If l grows, the dependence on r becomes more complex. The stronger the spatial variations of a $\boldsymbol{B}$-field the more effective is the Ohmic dissipation, i.e. the destructive influence on the field.

We now return to the initial value problem for the $\boldsymbol{B}$-field posed above. It can be shown that it has a unique solution. On grounds of the foregoing considerations all basic relations for $\boldsymbol{B}$, i.e. (14.1)...(14.3), are satisfied if we put

$$T_n^m = \sum_l T_{nl}^m(x) \exp\{\lambda_{nl}\tau\}, \tag{14.48a}$$

$$S_n^m = \sum_l S_{nl}^m(x) \exp\{\lambda_{nl}\tau\}, \text{ for } 0 \leqq x \leqq 1, \tag{14.48b}$$

and supplement them according to (14.20) and (14.22a) with suitable relations for $x > 1$. Obviously, (14.48) already constitutes the solution of the initial value problem provided that $T_n^m(x, 0)$ and $S_n^m(x, 0)$, which must be considered as given but, of course, satisfying (14.23) and (14.25), may be represented by

$$T_n^m(x, 0) = \sum_l T_{nl}^m(x), \tag{14.49a}$$

$$S_n^m(x, 0) = \sum_l S_{nl}^m(x), \text{ for } 0 \leqq x \leqq 1; \tag{14.49b}$$

the relations for $x > 1$ cause no difficulties. In the case $C = 0$ it can easily be seen that the representations (14.49) are always possible. For $C \neq 0$ a proof seems to be more complicated.

Without going into detail we assume that our solution of the initial value problem for the $\boldsymbol{B}$-field indeed applies to all initial fields. We envisage a special value of C so that, e.g., λ_{11} and λ_{21} are positive whereas all other λ_{nl} are negative; this situation corresponds to the dotted lines in figures 14.2 and 14.3. Let us also suppose that in the initial fields particularily those modes are present which belong to λ_{11} and λ_{21}, i.e. special dipole and quadrupole modes. Then only these modes will grow whereas the others will decay. Since $\lambda_{11} > \lambda_{21}$, the modes belonging to λ_{11}, i.e. the dipole modes, will grow more rapidly than those belonging to λ_{21}, i.e. the quadrupole modes. Independent of the inital ratio of the magnitudes, the dipole modes will dominate after a certain time. In other words, those modes will dominate which are related to the smallest value of $|C_{nl}|$.

This finding will be of interest for other models too. As long as it is true that the λ_{nl} for different modes are the larger the smaller the corresponding $|C_{nl}|$, the modes with the smallest $|C_{nl}|$ will generally dominate.

The treatment of the kinematic dynamo model considered so far may be understood as a stability problem. The possibility of growing magnetic fields corresponds to an instability. In terms of the stability theory we have stability if $\lambda_{11} < 0$, marginal stability if $\lambda_{11} = 0$, and instability if $\lambda_{11} > 0$. In this sense C_{11} shall be called the marginal value of C.

14.5. Considerations involving the back-reaction of the magnetic field on the motions

So far our model has been considered only from the kinematic point of view. In particular, the influence of the Lorentz force on the motion of the medium has been ignored. Since the Lorentz force is proportional to the square of the magnetic field it may be neglected as long as the field is sufficiently small, but it becomes very important if the field grows. The mean part of the Lorentz force will give rise to a mean motion so that $\overline{\boldsymbol{u}}$ may no longer be supposed to be zero. The fluctuating part will influence the turbulence and, therefore, the electromotive force $\mathfrak{E}$, which loses its linearity with respect to $\boldsymbol{B}$. Thus we are confronted with a rather complex situation.

In treating our model we do not intend to consider every effect of the magnetic field. In order to point out some special aspects drastic simplifications shall be introduced. As before, no mean motion is taken into account. As for the effects of turbulence we modify earlier assumptions only by admitting that α may depend on $\boldsymbol{B}$, whereas σ_T continues to be treated as a constant. Only the steady case is considered. Then, instead of equation (14.1a), we have

$$\frac{1}{\mu\sigma_{\mathrm{T}}}\Delta\boldsymbol{B} + \operatorname{curl}(\alpha\boldsymbol{B}) = 0, \text{ for } r < R. \tag{14.50}$$

Due to the dependence of α on $\boldsymbol{B}$ this equation is non-linear with respect to $\boldsymbol{B}$. The relations (14.1b)...(14.3b) remain unchanged. We assume that the $\boldsymbol{B}$-field is small, and write

$$\alpha = \alpha_0 - \alpha_B\boldsymbol{B}^2, \tag{14.51}$$

with α_0 and α_B being constants. Presupposing that $|\alpha|$ decreases with growing $|\boldsymbol{B}|$ we require that α_0 and α_B have the same signs; for simplicity we only consider $\alpha_0, \alpha_B > 0$. Furthermore, we only deal with the case where α_0 slightly exceeds α_{11} but no other α_{nl}, where the α_{nl} are defined by $\mu\sigma_{\mathrm{T}}\alpha_{nl}R = C_{nl}$.

Hence,

$$\alpha_0 = \alpha_{11} + \delta\alpha, \tag{14.52}$$

with $\delta\alpha$ being a small positive constant.

Clearly, $\boldsymbol{B}$ must tend to zero as $\delta\alpha$ vanishes. Therefore, it seems to be reasonable to put

$$\boldsymbol{B} = \left(\frac{\delta\alpha}{\alpha_B}\right)^{1/2} \boldsymbol{b} \tag{14.53}$$

and to assume that $\boldsymbol{b}$ can be represented as a power series of the form

$$\boldsymbol{b} = \boldsymbol{b}^{(0)} + \varepsilon \boldsymbol{b}^{(1)} + \varepsilon^2 \boldsymbol{b}^{(2)} + \dots, \tag{14.54}$$

where ε is a small parameter defined by

$$\varepsilon = \delta\alpha/\alpha_{11}. \tag{14.55}$$

In this way equation (14.50) leads to

$$\frac{1}{\mu\sigma_T} \Delta \boldsymbol{b}^{(0)} + \alpha_{11} \operatorname{curl} \boldsymbol{b}^{(0)} = 0, \tag{14.56a}$$

$$\frac{1}{\mu\sigma_T} \Delta \boldsymbol{b}^{(1)} + \alpha_{11} \operatorname{curl} \boldsymbol{b}^{(1)} = -\alpha_{11} \operatorname{curl} \left(\left(1 - \boldsymbol{b}^{(0)2}\right) \boldsymbol{b}^{(0)}\right), \tag{14.56b}$$

$$\frac{1}{\mu\sigma_T} \Delta \boldsymbol{b}^{(2)} + \alpha_{11} \operatorname{curl} \boldsymbol{b}^{(2)} = -\alpha_{11} \operatorname{curl} \left(\left(1 - \boldsymbol{b}^{(0)2}\right) \boldsymbol{b}^{(1)} - 2\left(\boldsymbol{b}^{(0)} \cdot \boldsymbol{b}^{(1)}\right) \boldsymbol{b}^{(0)}\right). \tag{14.56c}$$

These equations have to be supplemented by corresponding relations resulting from (14.1b)...(14.3c).

At first the equations for $\boldsymbol{b}^{(0)}$ are considered. They possess a non-trivial solution which can be extracted from section 14.3.; it is fixed apart from a constant factor. As for the equations for $\boldsymbol{b}^{(1)}$, which show an inhomogeneity containing $\boldsymbol{b}^{(0)}$, we point out that the corresponding homogeneous equations also possess a non-trivial solution. Therefore, the complete equations allow such solution only if the inhomogeneity satisfies a certain condition which results in a requirement for $\boldsymbol{b}^{(0)}$. In this way $\boldsymbol{b}^{(0)}$ is fixed. Of course, $\boldsymbol{b}^{(1)}$ again contains a free constant. The equations for $\boldsymbol{b}^{(2)}$, however, pose a condition by which $\boldsymbol{b}^{(1)}$ is fixed. In this way, the terms in the expansion (14.54) can be determined successively.

As far as the details of these calculations are concerned we refer to the paper by RÜDIGER [1]. Explaining his result we again rely on the representation of the $\boldsymbol{B}$-field given by (14.4), (14.5), (14.10), (14.11), and (14.17). We first consider the zero order approximation, where in the result for $\boldsymbol{B}$ the expansion (14.54) for $\boldsymbol{b}$ is reduced to the term $\boldsymbol{b}^{(0)}$; this corresponds to $\varepsilon = 0$. According to the above assumptions the expansions (14.20) for T and S can only have terms with $n = 1$, and we choose $m = 0$, which is possible here without any loss of generality. Clearly, the $\boldsymbol{B}$-field is a dipole field. Of course, T_1^0 and S_1^0 are again given by (14.28), (14.30), (14.31), and (14.32) with $C = C_{11}$, and the field pattern is identical with that given in figure 14.1. We can now add that

$$c_1^0 = z(\delta\alpha/\alpha_B)^{1/2}, \tag{14.57}$$

with z being a dimensionless constant. The numerical calculations have led to

$$z = 1.1525. \tag{14.58}$$

Let us now take the first order approximation where in the result for $\boldsymbol{B}$ not only the term $\boldsymbol{b}^{(0)}$ but also that with $\boldsymbol{b}^{(1)}$ is included, i.e. small positive ε are admitted. In this case T and S have not only terms with $n = 1$ but also such

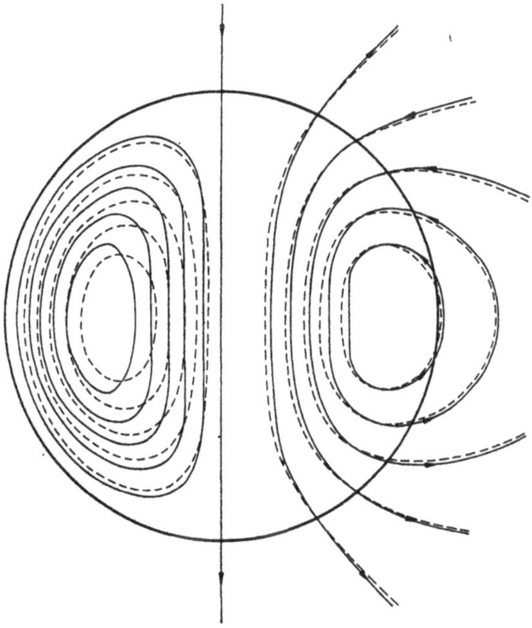

Fig. 14.4. The steady $\boldsymbol{B}$-field in a model with a dependence of α on $\boldsymbol{B}$ in the case $n = l = 1$. The left-hand side of the picture shows the lines of constant magnitude of the toroidal field, the right-hand side field lines of the poloidal field. The dotted lines correspond to $\varepsilon = 0$; they are identical with the full lines of figure 14.1. The full lines correspond to $\varepsilon = 1/C_{11}$. (After Rüdiger [1])

with $n = 3$, both of which with $m = 0$. Thus the $\boldsymbol{B}$-field is a sum of a dipole and an octupole part. The functions T_1^0, S_1^0, T_3^0, and S_3^0 are already rather complicated and shall not be given here. In figure 14.4 the field pattern for $\varepsilon = 1/C_{11}$, i.e. $\mu\sigma_T\,\delta\alpha R = 1$ is drawn. Compared with the case $\varepsilon = 0$, both the line of maximum toroidal field and the line of zero poloidal field are shifted outward.

The problem considered here, i.e. the case implying a non-linear equation for $\boldsymbol{B}$, has been tackled by other methods too. In a further paper by Rüdiger [3] the equations for $\boldsymbol{B}$ have been integrated numerically on the basis of a grid-point method.

CHAPTER 15

SPHERICAL MODELS OF TURBULENT DYNAMOS AS SUGGESTED BY COSMICAL BODIES. GENERAL ASPECTS

15.1. General description of the models

We shall now be concerned with spherical dynamo models reflecting essential features of the processes which are assumed to take place in cosmical objects. In all cases again a spherical body consisting of an electrically conducting medium is considered which rotates about a fixed axis running through its centre. Together with the axis of rotation also an equatorial plane is defined. The distribution of the electrical conductivity is supposed to be symmetric with respect to both the axis of rotation and the equatorial plane; later on we shall restrict attention to the case where the conductivity depends on radius only. As far as the mean motion is concerned, in the simplest case only a rigid body rotation is assumed. Yet we also admit a differential rotation with an angular velocity which may depend on radius or latitude, and a meridional circulation. In any case, however, we again require the mean motion to be symmetric with respect to both the axis of rotation and the equatorial plane and, in addition, to be steady. As well as the mean motion, fluctuating or turbulent motions are assumed which result in an electromotive force acting on the mean electromagnetic fields. The distribution of these motions is assumed to show the same symmetries and to be steady. More precisely, we require the invariance of all mean quantities depending on these motions under arbitrary virtual rotations of the fluctuating velocity field about the axis of rotation, under reflection of this field at the equatorial plane, and under time displacements. As for the mean electromotive force we restrict ourselves to such situations in which this quantity is non-zero only in the presence of a mean magnetic field and may be expressed at a given point by the mean magnetic flux density and its first spatial derivatives at this point. All space outside the conducting body is regarded as vacuum.

We shall only deal with kinematic models. The influence of the magnetic field on the motions is ignored. Within this frame we may study the occurrence of dynamos, the excitation conditions and the structures of the magnetic fields in the case of small field strengths. The question of what the behaviour of the dynamos will be at higher field strengths must remain unanswered here.

15.2. Basic equations and some of their symmetry properties

We again start from the general equations (12.1)...(12.5) for models of turbulent dynamos. As in the foregoing chapter a spherical polar coordinate system with the coordinates r, ϑ, and φ and the radius vector $\boldsymbol{r}$ is used. The origin of this system coincides with the centre of the sphere occupied by the conducting medium, and the polar axis with the axis of rotation. In the following, axisymmetry shall always be understood as symmetry with respect to the axis of rotation. The radius of this sphere is denoted by R.

As for the $\overline{\boldsymbol{B}}$-field inside the conducting medium we have the equations

$$\frac{1}{\mu}\operatorname{curl}\left(\frac{1}{\sigma}\operatorname{curl}\overline{\boldsymbol{B}}\right)-\operatorname{curl}\left(\overline{\boldsymbol{u}}\times\overline{\boldsymbol{B}}+\mathfrak{E}\right)+\frac{\partial\overline{\boldsymbol{B}}}{\partial t}=0, \tag{15.1a}$$

$$\operatorname{div}\overline{\boldsymbol{B}}=0,\ \text{for}\ r<R, \tag{15.1b}$$

where σ, $\overline{\boldsymbol{u}}$ and $\mathfrak{E}$ have to be specified according to the assumptions introduced above. Again, we may replace σ and $\mathfrak{E}$ by σ_{T} and $\mathfrak{E}^{+}$. Furthermore, we have the equations

$$\operatorname{curl}\overline{\boldsymbol{B}}=0,\quad \operatorname{div}\overline{\boldsymbol{B}}=0,\ \text{for}\ r>R, \tag{15.2a, b}$$

and the conditions

$$[\overline{\boldsymbol{B}}]=0,\quad \boldsymbol{r}\cdot\overline{\boldsymbol{u}}=0,\ \text{on}\ r=R, \tag{15.3a, b}$$

$$\overline{\boldsymbol{B}}=O(r^{-3}),\ \text{as}\ r\to\infty. \tag{15.3c}$$

The assumptions on the symmetries of the conductivity distribution and of the motions lead to special properties of the solutions of these equations. Let us at first consider the models dealt with here within the scope of equations (11.1)...(11.4). We pay attention to special rotations and a special reflection of the $\boldsymbol{u}$ and $\boldsymbol{B}$-field occuring there. More precisely, we consider rotations about the polar axis which transform $\boldsymbol{u}$ into $\boldsymbol{u}^{\mathrm{rot}}$, and $\boldsymbol{B}$ into $\boldsymbol{B}^{\mathrm{rot}}$, so that

$$u^{\mathrm{rot}}_{r,\vartheta,\varphi}(r,\vartheta,\varphi)=u_{r,\vartheta,\varphi}(r,\vartheta,\varphi-\varphi_0), \tag{15.4a}$$

$$B^{\mathrm{rot}}_{r,\vartheta,\varphi}(r,\vartheta,\varphi)=B_{r,\vartheta,\varphi}(r,\vartheta,\varphi-\varphi_0), \tag{15.4b}$$

with some angle φ_0, and the reflection at the equatorial plane transforming $\boldsymbol{u}$ into $\boldsymbol{u}^{\mathrm{ref}}$, and $\boldsymbol{B}$ into $\boldsymbol{B}^{\mathrm{ref}}$, so that

$$u^{\mathrm{ref}}_{r,\varphi}(r,\vartheta,\varphi)=u_{r,\varphi}(r,\pi-\vartheta,\varphi),\ u^{\mathrm{ref}}_{\vartheta}(r,\vartheta,\varphi)=-u_{\vartheta}(r,\pi-\vartheta,\varphi), \tag{15.5a, b}$$

$$B^{\mathrm{ref}}_{r,\varphi}(r,\vartheta,\varphi)=-B_{r,\varphi}(r,\pi-\vartheta,\varphi),\ B^{\mathrm{ref}}_{\vartheta}(r,\vartheta,\varphi)=B_{\vartheta}(r,\pi-\vartheta,\varphi). \tag{15.5c, d}$$

Provided that equations (11.1)...(11.4) hold with given $\boldsymbol{u}$ and $\boldsymbol{B}$ they continue to hold if these are replaced by $\boldsymbol{u}^{\text{rot}}$ and $\boldsymbol{B}^{\text{rot}}$ or by $\boldsymbol{u}^{\text{ref}}$ and $\boldsymbol{B}^{\text{ref}}$. Taking the average of (11.1)...(11.4) we get the mean field equations (12.1)...(12.5). Clearly, they must show the same features. According to our assumptions, however, the transition from $\boldsymbol{u}$ to $\boldsymbol{u}^{\text{rot}}$ or $\boldsymbol{u}^{\text{ref}}$ is without any influence on mean fields, in particular on $\overline{\boldsymbol{u}}$, $\mathfrak{E}$, and $\overline{\boldsymbol{B}}$. Consequently, the validity of (12.1)...(12.5) remains unaffected even if only $\boldsymbol{B}$ is replaced by $\boldsymbol{B}^{\text{rot}}$ or $\boldsymbol{B}^{\text{ref}}$. We may suppose that $\boldsymbol{B}$ occurs only in the form of $\overline{\boldsymbol{B}}$; for $\mathfrak{E}$ can be expressed by $\boldsymbol{u}$ and $\overline{\boldsymbol{B}}$. Thus we find that the validity of (12.1)...(12.5) is maintained if $\overline{\boldsymbol{B}}$ is replaced by $\overline{\boldsymbol{B}}^{\text{rot}}$ or $\overline{\boldsymbol{B}}^{\text{ref}}$. Since equations (12.1)...(12.5) essentially coincide with (15.1)...(15.3) we may state that any $\overline{\boldsymbol{B}}$-field which is a solution of equations (15.1)...(15.3) turns again into a solution of these if it is rotated or reflected according to (15.4b) or (15.5c, d).

By reason of the steadiness of the conductivity distribution and the restricted time dependence of the motions an analogous conclusion may be drawn with respect to time displacements.

15.3. Special magnetic field modes

We may decompose any $\overline{\boldsymbol{B}}$-field into special modes. At first we split it in two fields, $\overline{\boldsymbol{B}}_{\text{A}}$ and $\overline{\boldsymbol{B}}_{\text{S}}$, where $\overline{\boldsymbol{B}}_{\text{A}}$ is antisymmetric and $\overline{\boldsymbol{B}}_{\text{S}}$ symmetric with respect to the equatorial plane. Carrying out a harmonic analysis we further decompose each of these fields into modes showing the form of the real or imaginary part of $\boldsymbol{C}^m e^{im\varphi}$ where $\boldsymbol{C}^m$ is a complex axisymmetric vector field, and m is a non-negative integer. Obviously, $m = 0$ corresponds to axisymmetric, $m \neq 0$ to non-axisymmetric fields.

We now assume that the $\overline{\boldsymbol{B}}$-field satisfies the basic equations (15.1)...(15.3). If it is not already in the form of one of these $\overline{\boldsymbol{B}}$-modes it can be decomposed into such modes. Owing to the linearity of these equations and the mentioned properties of their solutions we may conclude that each individual mode represents a solution.

We denote a $\overline{\boldsymbol{B}}$-mode by A or S depending on whether it is antisymmetric or symmetric with respect to the equatorial plane, and we add the number m indicating the dependence on φ. Simple examples of $\overline{\boldsymbol{B}}$-modes of A0, S0, A1, and S1 types may be given by dipole and quadrupole fields. Corresponding field patterns are depicted in figure 15.1. In general, of course, we may not expect those $\overline{\boldsymbol{B}}$-modes which are solutions of (15.1)...(15.3) to be pure dipole or quadrupole fields. These fields will only play the role of leading terms in multipole expansions which also contain higher order terms with the same symmetry properties.

Let us now bear in mind that the $\overline{\boldsymbol{B}}$-field generally varies in time. Extending its decomposition in this respect we arrive at $\overline{\boldsymbol{B}}$-modes showing the form of the

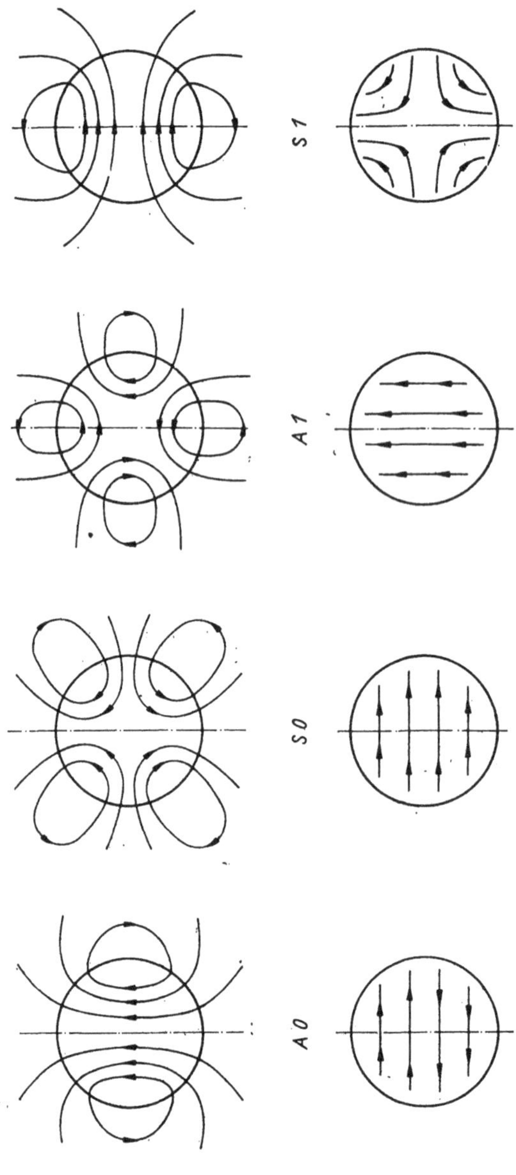

Fig. 15.1. Schematic representation of $\boldsymbol{B}$-fields of the A0, S0, A1, and S1 types. Above field lines of the poloidal parts in meridional planes are given. In the case of the A0 and S0-modes the patterns agree for all such planes, whereas in the case of the A1 and S1-modes the special planes have been chosen which are not crossed by field lines. Below projections of field lines of the toroidal parts on meridional planes are given

real or imaginary part of $C^m e^{im\varphi + pt}$ where C^m now is a complex axisymmetric vector field independent of t, and p is a complex constant.

If a $\overline{B}$-field which is a solution of the basic equations (15.1)...(15.3) does not possess the form of one of the $\overline{B}$-modes introduced here, it may be decomposed into such modes. We may again conclude that each of these modes is also a solution. Investigating dynamo models governed by equations (15.1)...(15.3) we may therefore restrict ourselves to these modes.

In order to study these $\overline{B}$-modes more precisely we put $p = \lambda - i\Omega$. Then their dependence on φ and t can be expressed by $\cos(m\varphi - \Omega t)\, e^{\lambda t}$ and $\sin(m\varphi - \Omega t)\, e^{\lambda t}$. The axisymmetric modes, for which $m = 0$, generally correspond to a growing or damped oscillation; in the case $\Omega = 0$ we have an aperiodic time dependence. Non-axisymmetric modes, for which $m \neq 0$, turn out to be waves migrating in azimuthal direction. In this case Ω depends, of course, on the frame of reference. For a given mode it is always possible to find a frame in which Ω vanishes so that a standing wave appears.

15.4. Specification of the mean velocity field and the turbulent electromotive force

We understand the mean velocity $\overline{\boldsymbol{u}}$ as a sum of two terms,

$$\overline{\boldsymbol{u}} = \overline{\boldsymbol{u}}_t + \overline{\boldsymbol{u}}_p, \tag{15.6}$$

where $\overline{\boldsymbol{u}}_t$ stands for the rotation, and $\overline{\boldsymbol{u}}_p$ for the meridional circulation. According to the assumptions introduced, both $\overline{\boldsymbol{u}}_t$ and $\overline{\boldsymbol{u}}_p$ show symmetry with respect to the axis of rotation and the equatorial plane, i.e. they are invariant under transformations like (15.4a) and (15.5a, b), and are steady. As indicated by our denotation, $\overline{\boldsymbol{u}}_t$ and $\overline{\boldsymbol{u}}_p$ are toroidal and poloidal, respectively.

In the following $\overline{\boldsymbol{u}}_t$ shall be represented in the form

$$\overline{\boldsymbol{u}}_t = \boldsymbol{\omega} \times \boldsymbol{r}, \quad \boldsymbol{\omega} = \omega \hat{\boldsymbol{\omega}}, \tag{15.7a, b}$$

with ω being an angular velocity and $\hat{\boldsymbol{\omega}}$ the unit vector parallel to the polar axis of the coordinate system. It should be mentioned that in the foregoing chapters the denotations $\boldsymbol{\Omega}$ and Ω have been used instead of $\boldsymbol{\omega}$ and ω. The components of $\overline{\boldsymbol{u}}_p$ are simply denoted by u_r and u_ϑ. According to (15.3c) we have to require that $u_r = 0$ at $r = R$.

As far as the electromotive force $\mathfrak{E}$ is concerned we may depart from relation (12.7) and specify the coefficients a_{ij} and b_{ijk} according to the special assumptions adopted here. Just as equations (11.1), from which this relation can be deduced, it must be compatible with the rotations and the reflection of the $\boldsymbol{u}$ and $\boldsymbol{B}$-fields as defined by (15.4) and (15.5). Under the rotations and reflection $\mathfrak{E}$ behaves like $\boldsymbol{u}\times\boldsymbol{B}$, and this in turn like $\boldsymbol{u}$; we therefore define $\mathfrak{E}^{\text{rot}}$ and $\mathfrak{E}^{\text{ref}}$ in the same way as $\boldsymbol{u}^{\text{rot}}$ and $\boldsymbol{u}^{\text{ref}}$, respectively. Provided (12.7) holds for given $\mathfrak{E}$, $\boldsymbol{u}$, and $\boldsymbol{B}$, it must continue to hold if they are replaced by $\mathfrak{E}^{\text{rot}}$, $\boldsymbol{u}^{\text{rot}}$, and $\boldsymbol{B}^{\text{rot}}$ or by $\mathfrak{E}^{\text{ref}}$, $\boldsymbol{u}^{\text{ref}}$, and $\boldsymbol{B}^{\text{ref}}$. According to our assumptions the coefficients a_{ij} and b_{ijk}, which depend on $\boldsymbol{u}$ only, cannot be influenced by replacing it by $\boldsymbol{u}^{\text{rot}}$ or $\boldsymbol{u}^{\text{ref}}$. Consequently, the validity of (12.7) must remain unaffected if only $\mathfrak{E}$ and $\overline{\boldsymbol{B}}$ are rotated or reflected. In this way requirements for the structure of the a_{ij} and b_{ijk} result. In addition to this the connection between $\mathfrak{E}$ and $\overline{\boldsymbol{B}}$ and therefore a_{ij} and b_{ijk} have to be independent of time. The most general expression for $\mathfrak{E}$ which satisfies these requirements turns out to be rather extensive. It shall be given at the end of this section.

Let us pay attention to a special case first. We recall the considerations given in section 5.3. and deal with a model in which the electrical conductivity is constant and the mean motion only consists of a rigid body rotation. We suppose an inhomogeneous turbulence the intensity of which only depends on the radius. In the turbulence field no other preferred direction should appear than those given by the intensity gradient and the axis of rotation, i.e. by the unit vectors $\hat{\boldsymbol{r}}$, defined by $\hat{\boldsymbol{r}} = \boldsymbol{r}/r$, and $\hat{\boldsymbol{\omega}}$. We furthermore restrict ourselves to the case where both the intensity gradient and the rotation rate are sufficiently small so that $\mathfrak{E}$ may be considered to be linear with respect to each of these quantities. Then we have

$$\begin{aligned}\mathfrak{E} = &-\beta \operatorname{curl} \overline{\boldsymbol{B}} \\ &- \gamma\hat{\boldsymbol{r}}\times\overline{\boldsymbol{B}} \\ &- \delta_1(\hat{\boldsymbol{\omega}}\cdot\nabla)\,\overline{\boldsymbol{B}} - (\delta_2-\delta_1)\,\nabla(\hat{\boldsymbol{\omega}}\cdot\overline{\boldsymbol{B}}) \\ &- \alpha_1(\hat{\boldsymbol{r}}\cdot\hat{\boldsymbol{\omega}})\,\overline{\boldsymbol{B}} - \alpha_2((\hat{\boldsymbol{r}}\cdot\overline{\boldsymbol{B}})\,\hat{\boldsymbol{\omega}} + (\hat{\boldsymbol{\omega}}\cdot\overline{\boldsymbol{B}})\,\hat{\boldsymbol{r}}) \\ &- \alpha_3((\hat{\boldsymbol{r}}\cdot\overline{\boldsymbol{B}})\,\hat{\boldsymbol{\omega}} - (\hat{\boldsymbol{\omega}}\cdot\overline{\boldsymbol{B}})\,\hat{\boldsymbol{r}}),\end{aligned} \tag{15.8}$$

where some terms may be rewritten according to

$$-\delta_1(\hat{\boldsymbol{\omega}}\cdot\nabla)\,\overline{\boldsymbol{B}} - (\delta_2-\delta_1)\,\nabla(\hat{\boldsymbol{\omega}}\cdot\overline{\boldsymbol{B}}) = \mu\,\delta_1\hat{\boldsymbol{\omega}}\times\overline{\boldsymbol{j}} - \delta_2\,\nabla(\hat{\boldsymbol{\omega}}\cdot\overline{\boldsymbol{B}}), \tag{15.9a}$$

$$-\alpha_3((\hat{\boldsymbol{r}}\cdot\overline{\boldsymbol{B}})\,\hat{\boldsymbol{\omega}} - (\hat{\boldsymbol{\omega}}\cdot\overline{\boldsymbol{B}})\,\hat{\boldsymbol{r}}) = \alpha_3(\hat{\boldsymbol{\omega}}\times\hat{\boldsymbol{r}})\times\overline{\boldsymbol{B}}. \tag{15.9b}$$

Provided the turbulence field is fixed the coefficients $\beta, \gamma, \ldots$ depend on r only. Compared with sections 5.4. and 9.3. the notation has been slightly changed by introducing $\delta_1 = \beta_3$ and $\delta_2 = \beta_2 + \beta_3$.

Despite the special suppositions we have referred to when establishing it, relation (15.8) for $\mathfrak{E}$ covers all effects which have been proved to be relevant in the basic turbulent dynamo mechanisms investigated up to now. We shall mainly rely on this relation in the following. As for the coefficients $\beta, \gamma, \ldots,$

however, a dependence on both r and ϑ is admitted; of course, symmetry with respect to the equatorial plane $\vartheta = \pi/2$ is required.

Let us briefly recall the meaning of the various contributions to $\mathfrak{E}$ which occur in (15.8). The term with β implies the possibility of introducing a turbulent electrical conductivity, and there are good reasons to assume that $1/\mu\sigma + \beta > 0$ (cf. sections 3.5... 9. and 7.4.). The term with γ describes a transport of magnetic flux similar to that due to a mean motion in radial direction and may also be comprehended by a turbulent magnetic permeability (cf. sections 5.4., 7.2., and 9.4.). The most important feature of the terms with δ_1 and δ_2 is that they cover the $\omega\times j$-effect, i.e. the occurrence of an electromotive force proportional to $\hat{\boldsymbol{\omega}}\times\bar{\boldsymbol{j}}$, which is indicated at the right-hand side of (15.9a). This effect is equivalent to the occurrence of a special anisotropic electrical conductivity (cf. sections 5.4. and 9.3.). Finally, the terms with α_1, α_2, and α_3 are connected with the α-effect. The most important of these terms is the one with α_1, which corresponds to the α-effect occurring in a homogeneous isotropic but not mirrorsymmetric turbulence (cf. sections 3.5 ... 10, 5.4., 7.3., and 9.4 ... 6.). In this context we shall speak of the "idealized α-effect" if only this term with α_1 is considered, and of the "real α-effect" if the others are included. The term with α_2 corresponds to an anisotropy of the α-effect. As can be seen from (15.9b) the term with α_3 describes a transport of magnetic flux like that by a rotational motion.

In the following the α-effect will prove to be very important. For many purposes it is useful to introduce the quantity α^+ defined by

$$\alpha^+ = -\alpha_1(\hat{\boldsymbol{r}} \cdot \hat{\boldsymbol{\omega}}) = -\alpha_1 \cos\vartheta. \tag{15.10}$$

Obviously, the role of α^+ is similar to that of the quantity α in the case of a homogeneous isotropic non-mirrorsymmetric turbulence. It should be emphasized, however, that α^+ does not agree with α as defined by (7.2), i.e. it is not identical with $(1/3)\, a_{ii}$. In the second order correlation approximation the dependence of α on the fluctuating motions may be expressed in the simple form (7.3). The dependence of α^+ is more complex; we refer to (9.51) ... (9.54).

Let us finally return to the most general expression for $\mathfrak{E}$ compatible with the symmetry conditions discussed above. As shown by Rädler [16] it may be written in the form

$$\begin{aligned}\mathfrak{E} = &- \boldsymbol{\alpha} \circ \overline{\boldsymbol{B}} - \boldsymbol{\gamma} \times \overline{\boldsymbol{B}} \\ &- \boldsymbol{\beta} \circ \operatorname{curl} \overline{\boldsymbol{B}} - \boldsymbol{\delta} \times \operatorname{curl} \overline{\boldsymbol{B}} \\ &- \boldsymbol{\beta}_r \circ (\hat{\boldsymbol{r}} \circ \nabla \overline{\boldsymbol{B}}) - \boldsymbol{\delta}_r \times (\hat{\boldsymbol{r}} \circ \nabla \overline{\boldsymbol{B}}) \\ &- \boldsymbol{\beta}_\omega \circ (\hat{\boldsymbol{\omega}} \circ \nabla \overline{\boldsymbol{B}}) - \boldsymbol{\delta}_\omega \times (\hat{\boldsymbol{\omega}} \circ \nabla \overline{\boldsymbol{B}}).\end{aligned} \tag{15.11}$$

This form corresponds to that which results from (15.8) after inserting (15.9). The quantities $\boldsymbol{\alpha}$, $\boldsymbol{\beta}$, $\boldsymbol{\beta}_r$, and $\boldsymbol{\beta}_\omega$ are symmetric tensors, and $\boldsymbol{\gamma}$, $\boldsymbol{\delta}$, $\boldsymbol{\delta}_r$, and $\boldsymbol{\delta}_\omega$

are vectors. Furthermore, $(\hat{\boldsymbol{r}} \circ \nabla \overline{\boldsymbol{B}})$ is a vector defined by $(\hat{\boldsymbol{r}} \circ \nabla \overline{\boldsymbol{B}})_i = \hat{r}_j\, \partial \overline{B}_j / \partial x_i$, and $(\hat{\boldsymbol{\omega}} \circ \nabla \overline{\boldsymbol{B}})$, which is defined analogously, is identical with $\nabla (\hat{\boldsymbol{\omega}} \cdot \overline{\boldsymbol{B}})$. We may represent $\boldsymbol{\alpha} \circ \overline{\boldsymbol{B}}$ and $\boldsymbol{\gamma}$ by

$$\begin{aligned}
\boldsymbol{\alpha} \circ \overline{\boldsymbol{B}} = \alpha^{(0)}(\hat{\boldsymbol{r}} \cdot \hat{\boldsymbol{\omega}})\, \overline{\boldsymbol{B}} \\
&+ \alpha^{(1)}(\hat{\boldsymbol{r}} \cdot \hat{\boldsymbol{\omega}})\, (\hat{\boldsymbol{r}} \cdot \overline{\boldsymbol{B}})\, \hat{\boldsymbol{r}} + \alpha^{(2)}(\hat{\boldsymbol{r}} \cdot \hat{\boldsymbol{\omega}})\, (\hat{\boldsymbol{\omega}} \cdot \overline{\boldsymbol{B}})\, \hat{\boldsymbol{\omega}} \\
&+ \alpha^{(3)}(\hat{\boldsymbol{r}} \cdot \hat{\boldsymbol{\omega}})\, (\boldsymbol{\lambda} \cdot \overline{\boldsymbol{B}})\, \boldsymbol{\lambda} \\
&+ \alpha^{(4)}((\hat{\boldsymbol{\omega}} \cdot \overline{\boldsymbol{B}})\, \hat{\boldsymbol{r}} + (\hat{\boldsymbol{r}} \cdot \overline{\boldsymbol{B}})\, \hat{\boldsymbol{\omega}}) \qquad (15.12\text{a}) \\
&+ \alpha^{(5)}(\hat{\boldsymbol{r}} \cdot \hat{\boldsymbol{\omega}})\, ((\boldsymbol{\lambda} \cdot \overline{\boldsymbol{B}})\, \hat{\boldsymbol{r}} + (\hat{\boldsymbol{r}} \cdot \overline{\boldsymbol{B}})\, \boldsymbol{\lambda}) \\
&+ \alpha^{(6)}((\boldsymbol{\lambda} \cdot \overline{\boldsymbol{B}})\, \hat{\boldsymbol{\omega}} + (\hat{\boldsymbol{\omega}} \cdot \overline{\boldsymbol{B}})\, \boldsymbol{\lambda}),
\end{aligned}$$

$$\boldsymbol{\gamma} = \gamma^{(1)}\hat{\boldsymbol{r}} + \gamma^{(2)}(\hat{\boldsymbol{r}} \cdot \hat{\boldsymbol{\omega}})\, \hat{\boldsymbol{\omega}} + \gamma^{(3)}\boldsymbol{\lambda}, \qquad (15.12\text{b})$$

and $\boldsymbol{\beta} \circ \operatorname{curl} \overline{\boldsymbol{B}}$ and $\boldsymbol{\delta}$ by

$$\begin{aligned}
\boldsymbol{\beta} \circ \operatorname{curl} \overline{\boldsymbol{B}} = \beta^{(0)} \operatorname{curl} \overline{\boldsymbol{B}} \\
&+ \beta^{(1)}(\hat{\boldsymbol{r}} \cdot \operatorname{curl} \overline{\boldsymbol{B}})\, \hat{\boldsymbol{r}} + \beta^{(2)}(\hat{\boldsymbol{\omega}} \cdot \operatorname{curl} \overline{\boldsymbol{B}})\, \hat{\boldsymbol{\omega}} \\
&+ \beta^{(3)}(\boldsymbol{\lambda} \cdot \operatorname{curl} \overline{\boldsymbol{B}})\, \boldsymbol{\lambda} \\
&+ \beta^{(4)}(\hat{\boldsymbol{r}} \cdot \hat{\boldsymbol{\omega}})\, ((\hat{\boldsymbol{\omega}} \cdot \operatorname{curl} \overline{\boldsymbol{B}})\, \hat{\boldsymbol{r}} + (\hat{\boldsymbol{r}} \cdot \operatorname{curl} \overline{\boldsymbol{B}})\, \hat{\boldsymbol{\omega}}) \qquad (15.13\text{a}) \\
&+ \beta^{(5)}((\boldsymbol{\lambda} \cdot \operatorname{curl} \overline{\boldsymbol{B}})\, \hat{\boldsymbol{r}} + (\hat{\boldsymbol{r}} \cdot \operatorname{curl} \overline{\boldsymbol{B}})\, \boldsymbol{\lambda}) \\
&+ \beta^{(6)}(\hat{\boldsymbol{r}} \cdot \hat{\boldsymbol{\omega}})\, ((\boldsymbol{\lambda} \cdot \operatorname{curl} \overline{\boldsymbol{B}})\, \hat{\boldsymbol{\omega}} + (\hat{\boldsymbol{\omega}} \cdot \operatorname{curl} \overline{\boldsymbol{B}})\, \boldsymbol{\lambda}),
\end{aligned}$$

$$\boldsymbol{\delta} = \delta^{(1)}(\hat{\boldsymbol{r}} \cdot \hat{\boldsymbol{\omega}})\, \hat{\boldsymbol{r}} + \delta^{(2)}\hat{\boldsymbol{\omega}} + \delta^{(3)}(\hat{\boldsymbol{r}} \cdot \hat{\boldsymbol{\omega}})\, \boldsymbol{\lambda}, \qquad (15.13\text{b})$$

where $\boldsymbol{\lambda}$ stands for $\hat{\boldsymbol{r}} \times \hat{\boldsymbol{\omega}}$. For $\boldsymbol{\beta}_r \circ (\hat{\boldsymbol{r}} \circ \nabla \overline{\boldsymbol{B}})$ and $\boldsymbol{\delta}_r$ we may write relations analogous to (15.12), with coefficients $\beta_r^{(0)}, \beta_r^{(1)}, \ldots \delta_r^{(3)}$, and for $\boldsymbol{\beta}_\omega \circ (\hat{\boldsymbol{\omega}} \circ \nabla \overline{\boldsymbol{B}})$ and $\boldsymbol{\delta}_\omega$ relations analogous to (15.13), with coefficients $\beta_\omega^{(0)}, \beta_\omega^{(1)}, \ldots \delta_\omega^{(3)}$. All coefficients $\alpha^{(0)}, \alpha^{(1)}, \ldots \delta_\omega^{(3)}$ may depend on r and ϑ but must be symmetric with respect to the equatorial plane $\vartheta = \pi/2$. It should be mentioned that, without any loss of generality, some of these coefficients may be fixed arbitrarily. We may choose, e.g.,

$$\alpha^{(3)} = \beta^{(3)} = \beta_r^{(3)} = \beta_\omega^{(3)} = \delta_r^{(3)} = \delta_\omega^{(3)} = 0, \qquad (15.14\text{a})$$

$$\beta^{(1)} + \beta^{(2)} + 2\beta^{(4)}(\hat{\boldsymbol{r}} \cdot \hat{\boldsymbol{\omega}})^2 - \delta_r^{(1)} - \delta_r^{(2)}(\hat{\boldsymbol{r}} \cdot \hat{\boldsymbol{\omega}})^2 - \delta_\omega^{(1)}(\hat{\boldsymbol{r}} \cdot \hat{\boldsymbol{\omega}})^2 - \delta_\omega^{(2)} = 0. \qquad (15.14\text{b})$$

Incidentally, (15.14b) ensures that $\beta^{(0)}$ coincides with $(1/6)\, \varepsilon_{ijk}\, b_{ijk}$ (cf. section 7.4.).

The general form of $\mathfrak{E}$ as defined by (15.11), (15.12), and (15.13) takes the special form given by (15.8) and (15.9) if we specify the coefficients $\alpha^{(0)}, \alpha^{(1)}, \ldots \delta_\omega^{(3)}$ so that

$$\alpha^{(0)} = \alpha_1, \quad \alpha^{(4)} = \alpha_2, \quad \gamma^{(1)} = \gamma, \quad \gamma^{(3)} = \alpha_3, \tag{15.15a...d}$$

$$\beta^{(0)} = \beta, \quad \delta^{(2)} = -\delta_1, \quad \beta_\omega^{(0)} = \delta_2 \tag{15.15e...g}$$

and all the others are zero.

Let us add some remarks on the meaning of the several contributions to $\mathfrak{E}$ occurring in (15.11). The contributions $\boldsymbol{\alpha} \circ \overline{\boldsymbol{B}}$ and $\boldsymbol{\gamma} \times \overline{\boldsymbol{B}}$ are generalizations of the α_1, α_2, α_3, and γ-terms in (15.8). Here $\boldsymbol{\alpha} \circ \overline{\boldsymbol{B}}$ describes an anisotropic α-effect, and $\boldsymbol{\gamma} \times \overline{\boldsymbol{B}}$ a transport of magnetic flux in $\boldsymbol{\gamma}$-direction. Likewise the contributions $\boldsymbol{\beta} \circ \operatorname{curl} \overline{\boldsymbol{B}}$ and $\boldsymbol{\delta} \times \operatorname{curl} \overline{\boldsymbol{B}}$ are generalizations of the β and δ_1-terms. The occurrence of $\boldsymbol{\beta} \circ \operatorname{curl} \overline{\boldsymbol{B}}$ is equivalent to that of an anisotropic turbulent conductivity with a symmetric conductivity tensor. As for $\boldsymbol{\delta} \times \operatorname{curl} \overline{\boldsymbol{B}}$ we may speak of a $\delta \times j$-effect analogous to the more special $\omega \times j$-effect. Of course, this $\delta \times j$-effect can also be comprehended by an anisotropic turbulent conductivity with a conductivity tensor no longer being symmetric. The remaining contributions to $\mathfrak{E}$ are more difficult to interpret; in a wider sense they are related to the δ_2-term.

The induction effects of the mean motions described by ω und $\overline{\boldsymbol{u}}_p$ are for short also referred to as ω-effect and $\boldsymbol{u}_p$-effect in the following, and the induction effects of the fluctuating motions covered by the single terms of $\mathfrak{E}$ as β-effect, γ-effect etc.

15.5. A further symmetry property of the basic equations

We want to point out a remarkable property of the basic equations (15.1)...(15.3) which shall be utilized in the following. For this purpose we at first consider our models again within the scope of equations (11.1)...(11.4). Whereas before we restricted ourselves to rotations of the $\boldsymbol{u}$ and $\boldsymbol{B}$-fields about the axis of rotation and to their reflections in the equatorial plane we now pay attention to reflections in meridional planes. With regard to the possibility of rotations it is sufficient to consider the reflection in the plane $\varphi = 0$, which transforms $\boldsymbol{u}$ into $\boldsymbol{u}^{\text{ref}}$, and $\boldsymbol{B}$ into $\boldsymbol{B}^{\text{ref}}$, so that

$$u_{r,\vartheta}^{\text{ref}}(r, \vartheta, \varphi) = u_{r,\vartheta}(r, \vartheta, -\varphi), \; u_\varphi^{\text{ref}}(r, \vartheta, \varphi) = -u_\varphi(r, \vartheta, -\varphi), \tag{15.16a, b}$$

$$B_{r,\vartheta}^{\text{ref}}(r, \vartheta, \varphi) = -B_{r,\varphi}(r, \vartheta, -\varphi), \; B_\varphi^{\text{ref}}(r, \vartheta, \varphi) = B_\varphi(r, \vartheta, -\varphi). \tag{15.16c, d}$$

Again, the validity of equations (11.1)...(11.4) remains unaffected if $\boldsymbol{u}$ and $\boldsymbol{B}$ are replaced by $\boldsymbol{u}^{\text{ref}}$ and $\boldsymbol{B}^{\text{ref}}$, and the same holds for the mean-field equations

(12.1)...(12.5) too. Contrary to the rotations and reflections considered before, the reflection of $\boldsymbol{u}$ in a meridional plane, i.e. the transition from $\boldsymbol{u}$ to $\boldsymbol{u}^{\mathrm{ref}}$, generally changes both $\overline{\boldsymbol{u}}$ and $\mathfrak{E}$. If according to (15.6) $\overline{\boldsymbol{u}}$ is split into $\overline{\boldsymbol{u}}_{\mathrm{t}}$ and $\overline{\boldsymbol{u}}_{\mathrm{p}}$, we have $\overline{\boldsymbol{u}}_{\mathrm{t}}^{\mathrm{ref}} = -\overline{\boldsymbol{u}}_{\mathrm{t}}$ and $\overline{\boldsymbol{u}}_{\mathrm{p}}^{\mathrm{ref}} = \overline{\boldsymbol{u}}_{\mathrm{p}}$. As far as $\mathfrak{E}$ is concerned, for simplicity we restrict ourselves to the special relation (15.8). By similar considerations as in the case of rotations and reflections considered before we find that the validity of this relation may not be disturbed if $\mathfrak{E}$ is replaced by $\mathfrak{E}^{\mathrm{ref}}$, again defined like $\boldsymbol{u}^{\mathrm{ref}}$, likewise $\overline{\boldsymbol{B}}$ by $\overline{\boldsymbol{B}}^{\mathrm{ref}}$, and if, according to the transition from $\boldsymbol{u}$ to $\boldsymbol{u}^{\mathrm{ref}}$, the coefficients $\beta, \gamma, \ldots$ are replaced by others, β^{ref}, γ^{ref}, ... From this requirement we may easily conclude that $\beta^{\mathrm{ref}} = \beta$, $\gamma^{\mathrm{ref}} = \gamma$, but $\beta_1^{\mathrm{ref}} = -\beta_1$, $\beta_2^{\mathrm{ref}} = -\beta_2$, $\alpha_1^{\mathrm{ref}} = -\alpha_1$, $\alpha_2^{\mathrm{ref}} = -\alpha_2$, and $\alpha_3^{\mathrm{ref}} = -\alpha_3$. Bearing in mind that transformation (15.16a, b) changes the $\boldsymbol{u}$-field in a way that right-handed helical motions turn into left-handed ones, and vice versa, the signs occurring here seem to be plausible.

This result allows an interesting conclusion. Let us suppose that a problem has been solved which is described by equations (15.1)...(15.3), (15.6), and (15.8) with some specification of $\overline{\boldsymbol{u}}_{\mathrm{t}}$, $\overline{\boldsymbol{u}}_{\mathrm{p}}$, β, γ, ... In other words we suppose that corresponding $\boldsymbol{B}$-fields are known. Then we are also able to treat another problem which is described by these equations after the transformation

$$\overline{\boldsymbol{u}}_{\mathrm{t}} \to -\overline{\boldsymbol{u}}_{\mathrm{t}}, \quad \overline{\boldsymbol{u}}_{\mathrm{p}} \to \overline{\boldsymbol{u}}_{\mathrm{p}}, \tag{15.17a, b}$$

$$\beta \to \beta, \ \gamma \to \gamma, \tag{15.17c, d}$$

$$\beta_1 \to -\beta_1, \ \beta_2 \to -\beta_2, \tag{15.17e, f}$$

$$\alpha_1 \to -\alpha_1, \ \alpha_2 \to -\alpha_2, \ \alpha_3 \to -\alpha_3. \tag{15.17g, h, i}$$

Its solution is given by the transformation

$$\overline{\boldsymbol{B}} \to \overline{\boldsymbol{B}}^{\mathrm{ref}}, \tag{15.18}$$

with $\overline{\boldsymbol{B}}^{\mathrm{ref}}$ defined in (15.16c, d).

15.6. Reduction of the basic equations

We now recall section 14.2. in which the equations (14.1)...(14.3) governing a very simple model of a turbulent dynamo have been reduced to equations for some scalar functions. Equations (15.1)...(15.3) shall be treated in a similar way. For simplicity, instead of $\overline{\boldsymbol{B}}$ and $\overline{\boldsymbol{u}}$ we write $\boldsymbol{B}$ and $\boldsymbol{u}$ in the following.

As before we split the $\boldsymbol{B}$-field into a toroidal part, $\boldsymbol{B}_{\mathrm{t}}$, and a poloidal one, $\boldsymbol{B}_{\mathrm{p}}$, so that

$$\boldsymbol{B} = \boldsymbol{B}_{\mathrm{t}} + \boldsymbol{B}_{\mathrm{p}}, \tag{15.19}$$

and by reason of (15.1 b) and (15.2 b) we put

$$\boldsymbol{B}_{\mathrm{p}} = \operatorname{curl} \boldsymbol{A}_{\mathrm{t}}, \tag{15.20}$$

with $\boldsymbol{A}_{\mathrm{t}}$ being a purely toroidal vector potential.

At first we restrict ourselves to the case of axisymmetric $\boldsymbol{B}$-fields. Equations (15.1 a) together with (15.19) lead to

$$\frac{1}{\mu} \operatorname{curl}\left(\frac{1}{\sigma} \operatorname{curl} \boldsymbol{B}_{\mathrm{t}}\right) - \operatorname{curl}\left((\boldsymbol{u}\times\boldsymbol{B})_{\mathrm{p}} + \mathfrak{E}_{\mathrm{p}}\right) + \frac{\partial \boldsymbol{B}_{\mathrm{t}}}{\partial t} = 0, \tag{15.21a}$$

$$\frac{1}{\mu} \operatorname{curl}\left(\frac{1}{\sigma} \operatorname{curl} \boldsymbol{B}_{\mathrm{p}}\right) - \operatorname{curl}\left((\boldsymbol{u}\times\boldsymbol{B})_{\mathrm{t}} + \mathfrak{E}_{\mathrm{t}}\right) + \frac{\partial \boldsymbol{B}_{\mathrm{p}}}{\partial t} = 0, \ \text{for } r < R. \tag{15.21b}$$

By virtue of (15.20) the last equation can be integrated to give

$$\frac{1}{\mu\sigma} \Delta \boldsymbol{A}_{\mathrm{t}} + (\boldsymbol{u}\times\boldsymbol{B})_{\mathrm{t}} + \mathfrak{E}_{\mathrm{t}} - \frac{\partial \boldsymbol{A}_{\mathrm{t}}}{\partial t} = 0, \quad \text{for} \quad r < R. \tag{15.22}$$

From equation (15.2a) we obtain

$$\boldsymbol{B}_{\mathrm{t}} = 0, \ \Delta \boldsymbol{A}_{\mathrm{t}} = 0, \ \text{for } r > R. \tag{15.23a, b}$$

The conditions (15.3) result in

$$\boldsymbol{B}_{\mathrm{t}} = 0, \ [\operatorname{curl} \boldsymbol{A}_{\mathrm{t}}] = 0, \ \text{on } r = R, \tag{15.24a, b}$$

$$\boldsymbol{A}_{\mathrm{t}} = O(r^{-2}), \ \text{as } r \to \infty. \tag{15.24c}$$

Let us now deal with the decomposition of $\boldsymbol{u}\times\boldsymbol{B}$ and $\mathfrak{E}$ into toroidal and poloidal parts. Splitting $\boldsymbol{u}$ according to (15.6) we obtain

$$(\boldsymbol{u}\times\boldsymbol{B})_{\mathrm{t}} = \boldsymbol{u}_{\mathrm{p}}\times\boldsymbol{B}_{\mathrm{p}}, \tag{15.25a}$$

$$(\boldsymbol{u}\times\boldsymbol{B})_{\mathrm{p}} = \boldsymbol{u}_{\mathrm{t}}\times\boldsymbol{B}_{\mathrm{p}} + \boldsymbol{u}_{\mathrm{p}}\times\boldsymbol{B}_{\mathrm{t}}. \tag{15.25b}$$

If $\mathfrak{E}$ is given by (15.8) we have

$$\mathfrak{E}_{\mathrm{t}} = -\beta \operatorname{curl} \boldsymbol{B}_{\mathrm{p}} - \gamma \hat{\boldsymbol{r}}\times\boldsymbol{B}_{\mathrm{p}} - \delta_1(\hat{\boldsymbol{\omega}}\cdot\nabla)\,\boldsymbol{B}_{\mathrm{t}} - \alpha_1(\hat{\boldsymbol{r}}\cdot\hat{\boldsymbol{\omega}})\,\boldsymbol{B}_{\mathrm{t}}, \tag{15.26a}$$

$$\begin{aligned} \mathfrak{E}_{\mathrm{p}} = {} & -\beta \operatorname{curl} \boldsymbol{B}_{\mathrm{t}} - \gamma \hat{\boldsymbol{r}}\times\boldsymbol{B}_{\mathrm{t}} - \delta_1(\hat{\boldsymbol{\omega}}\cdot\nabla)\,\boldsymbol{B}_{\mathrm{p}} - (\delta_2 - \delta_1)\,\nabla(\hat{\boldsymbol{\omega}}\cdot\boldsymbol{B}_{\mathrm{p}}) \\ & - \alpha_1(\hat{\boldsymbol{r}}\cdot\hat{\boldsymbol{\omega}})\,\boldsymbol{B}_{\mathrm{p}} - \alpha_2((\hat{\boldsymbol{r}}\cdot\boldsymbol{B}_{\mathrm{p}})\,\hat{\boldsymbol{\omega}} + (\hat{\boldsymbol{\omega}}\cdot\boldsymbol{B}_{\mathrm{p}})\,\hat{\boldsymbol{r}}) \\ & - \alpha_3((\hat{\boldsymbol{r}}\cdot\boldsymbol{B}_{\mathrm{p}})\,\hat{\boldsymbol{\omega}} - (\hat{\boldsymbol{\omega}}\cdot\boldsymbol{B}_{\mathrm{p}})\,\hat{\boldsymbol{r}}), \end{aligned} \tag{15.26b}$$

where $\boldsymbol{B}_{\mathrm{p}}$ can be replaced by $\operatorname{curl} \boldsymbol{A}_{\mathrm{t}}$. Analogously, also other expressions for $\mathfrak{E}$ can be treated.

We now put

$$\boldsymbol{B}_{\mathrm{t}} = B\boldsymbol{e}_{\varphi}, \quad \boldsymbol{A}_{\mathrm{t}} = A\boldsymbol{e}_{\varphi}, \tag{15.27a, b}$$

where B and A are scalar functions and $\boldsymbol{e}_\varphi$ is again the azimuthal unit vector. In this way we have

$$\boldsymbol{B} = B\boldsymbol{e}_\varphi + (1/r \sin\vartheta)\nabla(r \sin\vartheta A)\times\boldsymbol{e}_\varphi. \tag{15.28}$$

Analogous to (15.27) we introduce

$$(\boldsymbol{u}\times\boldsymbol{B})_t = C^{(uB)}\boldsymbol{e}_\varphi, \quad \text{curl}\,(\boldsymbol{u}\times\boldsymbol{B})_p = D^{(uB)}\boldsymbol{e}_\varphi, \tag{15.29a, b}$$

$$\mathfrak{E}_t = C^{(\mathfrak{E})}\boldsymbol{e}_\varphi, \quad \text{curl}\,\mathfrak{E}_p = D^{(\mathfrak{E})}\boldsymbol{e}_\varphi, \tag{15.29c, d}$$

with $C^{(uB)}$, $D^{(uB)}$, $C^{(\mathfrak{E})}$, and $D^{(\mathfrak{E})}$ being scalar functions.

In this context it is of interest that curl $(\boldsymbol{e}_\varphi/r \sin\vartheta) = 0$ and therefore, for any scalar F and any vector $\boldsymbol{U}$,

$$\text{curl}\,(F\boldsymbol{e}_\varphi/r \sin\vartheta) = \nabla F\times\boldsymbol{e}_\varphi/r \sin\vartheta, \tag{15.30a}$$

$$\text{div}\,(\boldsymbol{U}\times\boldsymbol{e}_\varphi/r \sin\vartheta) = \text{curl}\,\boldsymbol{U}\cdot\boldsymbol{e}_\varphi/r \sin\vartheta. \tag{15.30b}$$

If F is independent of φ we have

$$\Delta(F\boldsymbol{e}_\varphi) = (\Delta' F)\,\boldsymbol{e}_\varphi, \tag{15.31}$$

with an operator Δ' defined by

$$\Delta' F = (\Delta - 1/r^2 \sin^2\vartheta)\,F. \tag{15.32}$$

Equations (15.21a) and (15.22) for $\boldsymbol{B}_t$ and $\boldsymbol{A}_t$ can now be reduced to equations for B and A, namely

$$\frac{1}{\mu\sigma}\left(\Delta' B - \frac{1}{\sigma r \sin\vartheta}\nabla\sigma\cdot\nabla(r \sin\vartheta\, B)\right) + D^{(uB)} + D^{(\mathfrak{E})} - \frac{\partial B}{\partial t} = 0, \tag{15.33a}$$

$$\frac{1}{\mu\sigma}\Delta' A + C^{(uB)} + C^{(\mathfrak{E})} - \frac{\partial A}{\partial t} = 0, \quad \text{for} \quad r < R. \tag{15.33b}$$

From (15.23) and (15.24) results

$$B = 0, \; \Delta' A = 0, \; \text{for } r > R, \tag{15.34}$$

and

$$B = 0, \; [A] = [\partial A/\partial r] = 0, \; \text{on } r = R, \tag{15.35a, b}$$

$$A = O(r^{-2}), \; \text{as } r \to \infty. \tag{15.35c}$$

These equations have to be supplemented by relations connecting $C^{(uB)}$, $D^{(uB)}$, $C^{(\mathfrak{E})}$, and $D^{(\mathfrak{E})}$ with B and A. Relations of that kind can be derived by means of (15.25), (15.26), and (15.29). It should be noted, however, that the determination of $C^{(uB)}$, $D^{(uB)}$, $C^{(\mathfrak{E})}$, and $D^{(\mathfrak{E})}$ can be carried out even without the decomposition of $\boldsymbol{u}\times\boldsymbol{B}$ and $\mathfrak{E}$ as given by (15.25) and (15.26) because from (15.29) we may conclude

$$C^{(uB)} = (\boldsymbol{u}\times\boldsymbol{B})\cdot\boldsymbol{e}_\varphi, \tag{15.36a}$$

$$D^{(uB)} = \operatorname{curl}(\boldsymbol{u}\times\boldsymbol{B})\cdot\boldsymbol{e}_\varphi = r\sin\vartheta\operatorname{div}((\boldsymbol{u}\times\boldsymbol{B})\times\boldsymbol{e}_\varphi/r\sin\vartheta), \tag{15.36b}$$

$$C^{(\mathfrak{E})} = \mathfrak{E}\cdot\boldsymbol{e}_\varphi, \tag{15.36c}$$

$$D^{(\mathfrak{E})} = \operatorname{curl}\mathfrak{E}\cdot\boldsymbol{e}_\varphi = r\sin\vartheta\operatorname{div}(\mathfrak{E}\times\boldsymbol{e}_\varphi/r\sin\vartheta). \tag{15.36d}$$

Expressing $\boldsymbol{u}$ by ω and $\boldsymbol{u}_\mathrm{p}$, and $\boldsymbol{B}$ by B and A, we find

$$C^{(uB)} = -(1/r\sin\vartheta)\,\boldsymbol{u}_\mathrm{p}\cdot\nabla(r\sin\vartheta A), \tag{15.37a}$$

$$D^{(uB)} = -r\sin\vartheta\operatorname{div}(\boldsymbol{u}_\mathrm{p}B/r\sin\vartheta) + (\nabla\omega\times\nabla(r\sin\vartheta A))\cdot\boldsymbol{e}_\varphi. \tag{15.37b}$$

With $\mathfrak{E}$ as given by (15.8) we obtain

$$C^{(\mathfrak{E})} = \beta\Delta' A + \frac{\gamma}{r}\frac{\partial}{\partial r}(rA) - \delta_1\hat{\boldsymbol{\omega}}\cdot\nabla B - \alpha_1(\hat{\boldsymbol{r}}\cdot\hat{\boldsymbol{\omega}})\,B, \tag{15.38a}$$

$$\begin{aligned} D^{(\mathfrak{E})} &= r\sin\vartheta\operatorname{div}\left(\frac{\beta}{(r\sin\vartheta)^2}\nabla(r\sin\vartheta B)\right) + \frac{\hat{\boldsymbol{r}}}{r}\cdot\nabla(\gamma r B)\\ &\quad + r\sin\vartheta\,\hat{\boldsymbol{\omega}}\cdot\nabla\left(\frac{\delta_1}{r\sin\vartheta}\Delta' A\right) + \left(\nabla\delta_2\times\nabla\left(\frac{\hat{\boldsymbol{\omega}}\times\boldsymbol{e}_\varphi}{r\sin\vartheta}\cdot\nabla(r\sin\vartheta A)\right)\right)\cdot\boldsymbol{e}_\varphi\\ &\quad + r\sin\vartheta\operatorname{div}\left(\frac{\alpha_1(\hat{\boldsymbol{r}}\cdot\hat{\boldsymbol{\omega}})}{(r\sin\vartheta)^2}\nabla(r\sin\vartheta A)\right)\\ &\quad + (\hat{\boldsymbol{r}}\times\boldsymbol{e}_\varphi)\cdot\nabla\left(\frac{\alpha_2}{r\sin\vartheta}(\hat{\boldsymbol{\omega}}\times\boldsymbol{e}_\varphi)\cdot\nabla(r\sin\vartheta A)\right)\\ &\quad + (\hat{\boldsymbol{\omega}}\times\boldsymbol{e}_\varphi)\cdot\nabla\left(\frac{\alpha_2}{r\sin\vartheta}(\hat{\boldsymbol{r}}\times\boldsymbol{e}_\varphi)\cdot\nabla(r\sin\vartheta A)\right)\\ &\quad + \left(\nabla\left(\frac{\alpha_3}{r}\right)\times\nabla(r\sin\vartheta A)\right)\cdot\boldsymbol{e}_\varphi. \end{aligned} \tag{15.38b}$$

We may conclude from (15.37) that an axisymmetric $\boldsymbol{B}$-field cannot be influenced by a rigid body rotation, i.e. by a rotation with $\omega = \text{const}$. Likewise, (15.38) show that the δ_2 or the α_3-effect does not play any role if $\delta_2 = \text{const}$ or $\alpha_3/r = \text{const}$, respectively.

Let us now take the case of general, i.e. not necessarily axisymmetric $\boldsymbol{B}$-fields. For reasons of simplicity, in this case we assume that the conductivity σ only depends on r. Then equations (15.21)...(15.24) can again be justified. Relations (15.25) and (15.26) are, however, no longer valid.

We now put

$$\boldsymbol{B}_t = -\boldsymbol{r}\times\nabla T, \tag{15.39a}$$

$$\boldsymbol{A}_t = -\boldsymbol{r}\times\nabla S, \tag{15.39b}$$

furthermore

$$(\boldsymbol{u}\times\boldsymbol{B})_t = -\boldsymbol{r}\times\nabla U^{(uB)}, \tag{15.40a}$$

$$\text{curl}\,(\boldsymbol{u}\times\boldsymbol{B})_p = -\boldsymbol{r}\times\nabla V^{(uB)}, \tag{15.40b}$$

$$\mathfrak{E}_t = -\boldsymbol{r}\times\nabla U^{(\mathfrak{E})}, \tag{15.40c}$$

$$\text{curl}\,\mathfrak{E}_p = -\boldsymbol{r}\times\nabla V^{(\mathfrak{E})}, \tag{15.40d}$$

and we require

$$\oint\!\!\oint T\,\mathrm{d}\tilde{\omega} = \oint\!\!\oint S\,\mathrm{d}\tilde{\omega} = \ldots = \oint\!\!\oint V^{(\mathfrak{E})}\,\mathrm{d}\tilde{\omega} = 0. \tag{15.41}$$

On these grounds we may reduce equations (15.21a) and (15.22) to

$$\frac{1}{\mu\sigma}\left(\Delta T - \frac{1}{\sigma r}\frac{\mathrm{d}\sigma}{\mathrm{d}r}\frac{\partial}{\partial r}(rT)\right) + V^{(uB)} + V^{(\mathfrak{E})} - \frac{\partial T}{\partial t} = 0, \tag{15.42a}$$

$$\frac{1}{\mu\sigma}\Delta S + U^{(uB)} + U^{(\mathfrak{E})} - \frac{\partial S}{\partial t} = 0, \quad \text{for} \quad r < R, \tag{15.42)b}$$

equations (15.23) to

$$T = 0,\ \Delta S = 0, \quad \text{for} \quad r > R, \tag{15.43a, b}$$

and conditions (15.24) to

$$T = 0,\ [S] = [\partial S/\partial r] = 0,\ \text{on}\ r = R, \tag{15.44a, b}$$

$$S = O(r^{-2}),\ \text{as}\ r \to \infty. \tag{15.44c}$$

The problem remains to find relations connecting $U^{(uB)}$, $V^{(uB)}$, $U^{(\mathfrak{E})}$, and $V^{(\mathfrak{E})}$ with T and S. Taking the curls of equations (15.40) and multiplying the resulting equations by $\boldsymbol{r}$ we may conclude that

$$\Omega U^{(uB)} = -\boldsymbol{r}\cdot\text{curl}\,(\boldsymbol{u}\times\boldsymbol{B}), \tag{15.45a}$$

$$\Omega V^{(uB)} = -\boldsymbol{r}\cdot\text{curl}\,\text{curl}\,(\boldsymbol{u}\times\boldsymbol{B}), \tag{15.45b}$$

$$\Omega U^{(\mathfrak{E})} = -\boldsymbol{r}\cdot\text{curl}\,\mathfrak{E}, \tag{15.45c}$$

$$\Omega V^{(\mathfrak{E})} = -\boldsymbol{r}\cdot\text{curl}\,\text{curl}\,\mathfrak{E}, \tag{15.45d}$$

where the right-hand sides can also be rewritten by means of (13.34). Expressing $\boldsymbol{u}$ and $\boldsymbol{B}$ by ω, $\boldsymbol{u}_\mathrm{p}$, T, and S we get after some analysis

$$\Omega U^{(uB)} = -\boldsymbol{r}(\nabla(\boldsymbol{r}\cdot\boldsymbol{u}_\mathrm{p})\times\nabla T) - \omega\Omega\frac{\partial S}{\partial\varphi} - \operatorname{div}(\boldsymbol{u}_\mathrm{p}\,\Omega S) + \nabla(\boldsymbol{r}\cdot\boldsymbol{u}_\mathrm{p})\cdot\left(\boldsymbol{r}\,\Delta S - \nabla\frac{\partial}{\partial r}(rS)\right), \tag{15.46a}$$

$$\begin{aligned}\Omega V^{(uB)} = &-\Omega\left(\omega\frac{\partial T}{\partial\varphi} + \boldsymbol{u}_\mathrm{p}\cdot\nabla T\right) + \operatorname{div}(\boldsymbol{r}\times(\nabla(\boldsymbol{r}\cdot\boldsymbol{u}_\mathrm{p})\times\nabla T))\\ &-\Omega\left(\omega\hat{\boldsymbol{\omega}}\cdot\left(\boldsymbol{r}\,\Delta S - \nabla\frac{\partial}{\partial r}(rS)\right)\right) - \operatorname{div}(\boldsymbol{r}\times(\hat{\boldsymbol{\omega}}\times\nabla(\omega\,\Omega S)))\\ &+\operatorname{div}\left(\boldsymbol{r}\times\operatorname{curl}\left((\boldsymbol{r}\times\boldsymbol{u}_\mathrm{p})\,\Delta S + \boldsymbol{u}_\mathrm{p}\times\nabla\frac{\partial}{\partial r}(rS)\right)\right).\end{aligned} \tag{15.46b}$$

If we choose $\mathfrak{E}$ in the form (15.8) and again express $\boldsymbol{B}$ by T and S, we find

$$\begin{aligned}\Omega U^{(\mathfrak{E})} = &\ \boldsymbol{r}\cdot\left(\nabla\beta\times\nabla\frac{\partial}{\partial r}(rT)\right) - \operatorname{div}(\boldsymbol{r}\times(\boldsymbol{r}\times\beta\nabla\,\Delta S))\\ &+\boldsymbol{r}\cdot(\nabla(\gamma r)\times\nabla T) - \operatorname{div}\left(\boldsymbol{r}\times\left(\boldsymbol{r}\times(\gamma/r)\nabla\frac{\partial}{\partial r}(rS)\right)\right)\\ &-\hat{\boldsymbol{\omega}}\cdot\nabla(\delta_1\Omega T) + \nabla(\delta_1(\boldsymbol{r}\cdot\hat{\boldsymbol{\omega}}))\cdot\left(\boldsymbol{r}\,\Delta T - \nabla\frac{\partial}{\partial r}(rT)\right)\\ &+\boldsymbol{r}\cdot(\nabla(\delta_1(\boldsymbol{r}\cdot\hat{\boldsymbol{\omega}}))\times\nabla\,\Delta S)\\ &-\boldsymbol{r}\cdot\left(\nabla\delta_2\times\nabla\frac{\partial T}{\partial\varphi}\right) - \boldsymbol{r}\cdot\left(\nabla\delta_2\times\nabla\left(\hat{\boldsymbol{\omega}}\cdot\left(\boldsymbol{r}\,\Delta S - \nabla\frac{\partial}{\partial r}(rS)\right)\right)\right)\\ &+\operatorname{div}(\boldsymbol{r}\times(\boldsymbol{r}\times\alpha_1(\hat{\boldsymbol{r}}\cdot\hat{\boldsymbol{\omega}})\nabla T)) + \boldsymbol{r}\cdot\left(\nabla(\alpha_1(\hat{\boldsymbol{r}}\cdot\hat{\boldsymbol{\omega}}))\times\nabla\frac{\partial}{\partial r}(rS)\right)\\ &-\frac{\alpha_2+\alpha_3}{r}\Omega\frac{\partial S}{\partial\varphi},\end{aligned} \tag{15.47a}$$

$$\begin{aligned}\Omega V^{(\mathfrak{E})} = &-\operatorname{div}\left(\boldsymbol{r}\times\left(\boldsymbol{r}\times\nabla(\beta\,\Delta T) + \nabla\beta\times\nabla\frac{\partial}{\partial r}(rT)\right)\right)\\ &-\frac{1}{r}\frac{\partial}{\partial r}(r^2\boldsymbol{r}\cdot(\nabla\beta\times\nabla\,\Delta S))\\ &+\Omega\left(\gamma\frac{\partial T}{\partial r}\right) - \operatorname{div}(\boldsymbol{r}\times(\nabla(\gamma r)\times\nabla T))\\ &-\frac{1}{r}\frac{\partial}{\partial r}\left(r^2\boldsymbol{r}\cdot\left(\nabla(\gamma/r)\times\nabla\frac{\partial}{\partial r}(rS)\right)\right) -\end{aligned}$$

$$
\begin{aligned}
&-\left(\delta_1 - r\frac{\partial \delta_1}{\partial r}\right)\Delta\frac{\partial T}{\partial \varphi} - \nabla\,\delta_1\cdot\nabla\frac{\partial}{\partial r}\left(r\frac{\partial T}{\partial \varphi}\right)\\
&+\boldsymbol{r}\cdot\left((\hat{\boldsymbol{\omega}}\cdot\nabla)\left(\nabla\delta_1\times\nabla\frac{\partial}{\partial r}(rT)\right)\right)\\
&+\Omega(\delta_1\hat{\boldsymbol{\omega}}\cdot\nabla\,\Delta S) - \operatorname{div}(\boldsymbol{r}\times(\nabla(\delta_1(\boldsymbol{r}\cdot\hat{\boldsymbol{\omega}}))\times\nabla\,\Delta S)) \qquad (15.47\,\mathrm{b})\\
&+\operatorname{div}\left(\boldsymbol{r}\times\left(\nabla\delta_2\times\nabla\frac{\partial T}{\partial \varphi}\right)\right)\\
&+\operatorname{div}\left(\boldsymbol{r}\times\left(\nabla\delta_2\times\nabla\left(\hat{\boldsymbol{\omega}}\cdot\left(\boldsymbol{r}\,\Delta S - \nabla\frac{\partial}{\partial r}(rS)\right)\right)\right)\right)\\
&+\frac{1}{r}\frac{\partial}{\partial r}(r^2\boldsymbol{r}\cdot(\nabla(\alpha_1(\hat{\boldsymbol{r}}\cdot\hat{\boldsymbol{\omega}}))\times\nabla T))\\
&-\operatorname{div}(\boldsymbol{r}\times(\boldsymbol{r}\times\alpha_1(\hat{\boldsymbol{r}}\cdot\hat{\boldsymbol{\omega}})\,\nabla\,\Delta S))\\
&+\operatorname{div}\left(\boldsymbol{r}\times\left(\nabla(\alpha_1(\hat{\boldsymbol{r}}\cdot\hat{\boldsymbol{\omega}}))\times\left(\boldsymbol{r}\,\Delta S - \nabla\frac{\partial}{\partial r}(rS)\right)\right)\right)\\
&-\operatorname{div}\left(\boldsymbol{r}\times\left(\boldsymbol{\omega}\times\nabla\left(\frac{\alpha_2+\alpha_3}{r}\Omega S\right)\right)\right)\\
&+\Omega\left(\frac{\alpha_2-\alpha_3}{r}\frac{\partial T}{\partial \varphi}\right) + \Omega\left(\frac{\alpha_2-\alpha_3}{r}\hat{\boldsymbol{\omega}}\cdot\left(\boldsymbol{r}\,\Delta S - \nabla\frac{\partial}{\partial r}(rS)\right)\right).
\end{aligned}
$$

It may be of interest to note that, for any f and F,

$$\operatorname{div}(\boldsymbol{r}\times(\boldsymbol{r}\times f\,\nabla F)) = -\Omega(fF) - \operatorname{div}(\boldsymbol{r}\times(\boldsymbol{r}\times F\,\nabla f)). \qquad (15.48)$$

If $\partial f/\partial\varphi = 0$ we have

$$\boldsymbol{r}\cdot(\nabla f\times\nabla F) = \frac{1}{r\sin\vartheta}\frac{\partial f}{\partial \vartheta}\frac{\partial F}{\partial \varphi}. \qquad (15.49)$$

Unfortunately, equations (15.46) and (15.47) cannot readily be integrated. Nevertherless, they show that in contrast to an axisymmetric $\boldsymbol{B}$-field a non-axisymmetric one can be influenced by a mean rotation with $\omega = \text{const}$, and also by the α_3-effect with $\alpha_3/r = \text{const}$. As before, the δ_2-effect does not occur if $\delta_2 = \text{const}$.

Let us return once more to the statement formulated with transformations (15.17) and (15.18). For an axisymmetric $\boldsymbol{B}$-field the transformation (15.18) simply means $\boldsymbol{B}_t \to -\boldsymbol{B}_t$ and $\boldsymbol{B}_p \to \boldsymbol{B}_p$, and the statement mentioned can immediately be confirmed by means of equations (15.21)...(15.26). In the general case, including also non-axisymmetric $\boldsymbol{B}$-fields, the transformation

(15.18) is equivalent to $T(r, \vartheta, \varphi, t) \to -T(r, \vartheta, -\varphi, t)$ and $S(r, \vartheta, \varphi, t) \to S(r, \vartheta, -\varphi, t)$. The statement under consideration may also be derived from equations (15.42)...(15.44), (15.46) and (15.47), albeit in a troublesome manner.

15.7. Possibilities of dynamo mechanisms

In order to know what types of turbulent dynamo mechanisms are possible we shall investigate which parts of the mean motion and of the electromotive force caused by the fluctuating motions are able to generate or to maintain magnetic fields.

The mean velocity field $\boldsymbol{u}$ is, according to (15.6), again understood as a sum of two parts, $\boldsymbol{u}_t$ and $\boldsymbol{u}_p$, describing rotation and meridional circulation. As for the electromotive force $\mathfrak{E}$, until further notice only the terms given in (15.8) are taken into account, and $1/\mu\sigma + \beta$ is considered to be positive.

We consider the $\boldsymbol{B}$-field again as a sum of a toroidal and a poloidal part, $\boldsymbol{B}_t$ and $\boldsymbol{B}_p$. Discussing the possibilities of dynamo mechanisms we should distinguish between different kinds of coupling between $\boldsymbol{B}_t$ and $\boldsymbol{B}_p$.

First we deal with the case in which the $\boldsymbol{B}$-field, and therefore $\boldsymbol{B}_t$ and $\boldsymbol{B}_p$, are axisymmetric. By means of equations (15.21), (15.25), and (15.26) it can easily be followed up how the effects involved in $\boldsymbol{u}$ and $\mathfrak{E}$ influence $\boldsymbol{B}_t$ and $\boldsymbol{B}_p$. A scheme of these influences is given in figure 15.2. One should bear in mind that the mean rotation becomes effective, i.e. an ω-effect occurs, only if ω varies in space. Likewise, the δ_2-effect plays a role only if δ_2 is not constant.

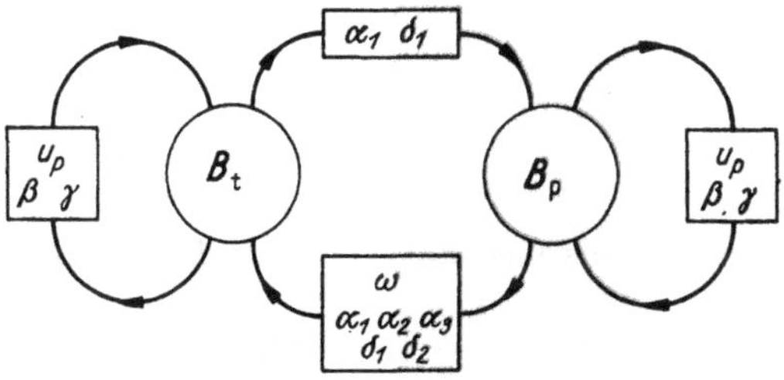

Fig. 15.2. The influences of the induction effects covered by $\boldsymbol{u}$ and $\mathfrak{E}$ on the toroidal and the poloidal parts, $\boldsymbol{B}_t$ and $\boldsymbol{B}_p$, of an axisymmetric $\boldsymbol{B}$-field

To begin with we ask for the possibility of dynamos without any coupling between the $\boldsymbol{B}_t$ and $\boldsymbol{B}_p$-fields. According to the scheme of figure 15.2 a dynamo of that kind could only exist due to the u_p, β, or γ-effect. In order to avoid any coupling between the $\boldsymbol{B}_t$ and $\boldsymbol{B}_p$-fields generally the ω, α_1, α_2, α_3, δ_1 and δ_2-effects have to be excluded. A dynamo as envisaged here would be able to generate a purely toroidal or a purely poloidal $\boldsymbol{B}$-field. We point out that a dynamo with a purely toroidal $\boldsymbol{B}$-field represents an "invisible dynamo" since a field of this kind is always confined in the conducting sphere, i.e. is zero at its surface and in outer space. Besides, in this case only the α_1 and δ_1-effects have to be excluded; the ω, α_2, α_3 and δ_2-effects are not involved anyway.

Since we consider only axisymmetric $\boldsymbol{B}$-fields here, it can be concluded from COWLING's theorem that there are no dynamos due to the u_p, β or γ-effect with steady fields. If $\boldsymbol{u}_d + \gamma\hat{\boldsymbol{r}}$ is solenoidal, and β is constant, due to BRAGINSKIJ's version of COWLING's theorem the same also holds for non-steady fields. Finally, if $\boldsymbol{u}_p = 0$ and $\gamma = 0$ any dynamo proves to be impossible by relation (12.8). In conclusion we may state that in the majority of cases the existence of dynamos without coupling between the $\boldsymbol{B}_t$ and $\boldsymbol{B}_p$-fields can be excluded. In all other cases it is at least not hinted.

Let us now assume that there is a coupling between $\boldsymbol{B}_t$ and $\boldsymbol{B}_p$ which consists, however, only in an influence of $\boldsymbol{B}_t$ on $\boldsymbol{B}_p$, or vice versa, but does not allow an interaction between $\boldsymbol{B}_t$ and $\boldsymbol{B}_p$. As long as dynamos without coupling between $\boldsymbol{B}_t$ and $\boldsymbol{B}_p$ are impossible, we may conclude that there cannot be any dynamo with this simple type of coupling.

In this way we arrive at the presumption that dynamos with axisymmetric $\boldsymbol{B}$-fields can only exist due to the simultaneous influences of both $\boldsymbol{B}_t$ on $\boldsymbol{B}_p$ and vice versa, i.e. an interaction of $\boldsymbol{B}_t$ and $\boldsymbol{B}_p$. As can be seen from figure 15.2 this interaction requires the α_1 or the δ_1-effect. Thus the presence of the α_1 or the δ_1-effect seems to be a necessary condition for the existence of dynamos with axisymmetric fields.

Dealing with the dynamo action of the α_1-effect, we begin with the case in which no turbulence effects other than the α_1-effect and no mean motion other than a rigid body rotation are taken into account. Even in this simple case a dynamo mechanism indeed turns out to be possible, which is able to maintain steady $\boldsymbol{B}$-fields (cf. section 16.3.). Since both the generation of $\boldsymbol{B}_t$ from $\boldsymbol{B}_p$ and that of $\boldsymbol{B}_p$ from $\boldsymbol{B}_t$ is due to the α_1-effect, we speak of an α^2-mechanism, or an α^2-process. A typical feature of this mechanism is that $\boldsymbol{B}_t$ and $\boldsymbol{B}_p$ are of the same order of magnitude.

Let us have a short look at the energy relation (12.8). In the case of a dynamo the right-hand side has to be non-negative. Since the first term gives a negative contribution and the second one is zero, the third one must provide for a sufficiently strong positive contribution. Hence, a necessary condition for an α^2-mechanism consists in the requirement that $\alpha_1(\hat{\boldsymbol{r}} \cdot \hat{\boldsymbol{\omega}})\,(\boldsymbol{j} \cdot \boldsymbol{B})$ is mainly negative so that the integral of this quantity taken over the volume of the conducting body is negative. This is equivalent to the requirement that $\alpha^+\boldsymbol{B} \cdot \operatorname{curl} \boldsymbol{B}$, with α^+ being defined according to (15.10), is mainly positive in the above sense.

We now modify the assumptions by replacing the α_1-effect by the δ_1-effect. In this case no dynamo has been found. The reasons for this can easily be seen from the relation (12.8). Like the second term of the right-hand side also the third term is always zero; for even the integrand vanishes everywhere. Hence, any $\boldsymbol{B}$-field is bound to decay.

We now consider the possibility of dynamos which act on the basis of a combination of the α_1 or the δ_1-effect with other induction effects.

If the α_1-effect is combined with other induction effects, certain modifications of the α^2-mechanism have to be expected. Only the combination of the α_1-effect with a non-uniform rotation, i.e. the ω-effect, shall be discussed here. As long as the ω-effect is small a dynamo may occur which mainly works on the basis of an α^2-mechanism. A sufficiently strong rotational shear, however, will be much more effective in generating $\boldsymbol{B}_t$ from $\boldsymbol{B}_p$ than the α_1-effect. Thus another dynamo mechanism turns out to be possible in which the generation of $\boldsymbol{B}_t$ from $\boldsymbol{B}_p$ is mainly by virtue of the rotational shear, i.e. the ω-effect, and the essential role of the α_1-effect is restricted to the generation of $\boldsymbol{B}_p$ from $\boldsymbol{B}_t$. By this mechanism both steady and oscillatory $\boldsymbol{B}$-fields can be maintained (cf. section 16.4.). We speak of an $\alpha\omega$-mechanism, or an $\alpha\omega$-process. It clearly implies that the order of $\boldsymbol{B}_t$ exceeds that of $\boldsymbol{B}_p$.

Again a look at relation (12.8) is of interest. As long as the non-uniform rotation supplies energy to the mean magnetic field the second term on the right-hand side will give a positive contribution to the expression on this side. With the $\alpha\omega$-mechanism it is essentially this second term which compensates the first one, and the third one is of minor importance.

Whereas the δ_1-effect alone is unable to provide for a dynamo, a combination of this effect with other induction effects may lead to dynamo action. Like the α_1-effect also the δ_1-effect together with a sufficiently strong rotational shear, i.e. the ω-effect, implies the possibility of a dynamo mechanism. Again, $\boldsymbol{B}_t$ is generated from $\boldsymbol{B}_p$ mainly by virtue of the ω-effect, but $\boldsymbol{B}_p$ from $\boldsymbol{B}_t$ due to the δ_1-effect. In this way again both steady and oscillatory $\boldsymbol{B}$-fields can be maintained (cf. section 16.5.). Analogous to the $\alpha\omega$-mechanism we then speak of a $\delta\omega$-mechanism or a $\delta\omega$-process. Here too, $\boldsymbol{B}_t$ will be much greater than $\boldsymbol{B}_p$.

Let us once more return to the relation (12.8). In the case of a $\delta\omega$-mechanism the third term of the right-hand side is zero. Only the non-uniform rotation supplies energy to the mean magnetic field, more precisely to its toroidal part. The δ_1-effect is unable to feed the mean magnetic field; it only provides for a transfer of energy from the toroidal to the poloidal part.

It remains to be scrutinized whether a combination of the δ_1-effect with the δ_2, α_2, or α_3-effect may lead to dynamo action. As far as we can see there are no rigorous arguments against dynamos working on this basis. On the other hand no example of a dynamo of this kind has been constructed up to now. Since the α_3-effect plays the same role as an ω-effect a combination of the δ_1-effect with a sufficiently strong α_3-effect must allow a dynamo process analogous to the $\delta\omega$-process. In this context, however, we have to bear in mind that together with the δ_1 and the α_3-effect generally other induction effects occur too, e.g. the α_1-effect, so that the mechanism envisaged here is in concurrence with other ones, e.g. the α^2-mechanism, and possibly never dominates.

An illustration of the generation of axisymmetric $\boldsymbol{B}$-fields of both A0 and S0 types by the α^2, $\alpha\omega$, and $\delta\omega$-mechanisms is given in figures 15.3 and 15.4. There we have sketched which $\boldsymbol{B}_p$-fields result from $\boldsymbol{B}_t$-fields, and vice versa, as a consequence of α_1-effect, δ_1-effect, or non-uniform rotation with radial shear, i.e. ω-effect. For the original fields simple dipole or quadrupole structures are assumed. We restrict ourselves to the cases where α_1, δ_1, and $d\omega/dr$ do not change their signs within the conducting sphere. With the resulting fields, again only the dipole and quadrupole parts are regarded; parts corresponding to higher multipoles have been ignored. By means of figures 15.3 and 15.4 we may follow up the different types of interaction between $\boldsymbol{B}_t$ and $\boldsymbol{B}_p$-fields, which correspond to the different types of dynamo mechanisms.

It can easily be seen in which way the interaction of $\boldsymbol{B}_t$ and $\boldsymbol{B}_p$ due to the α_1-effect may lead to a maintenance of steady $\boldsymbol{B}$-fields, i.e. in which way the α^2-mechanism works. Besides, no possibility is indicated of generating oscillatory fields by means of this mechanism.

Replacing the α_1-effect by the δ_1-effect we arrive at a different situation. The difference consists in the orientation of $\boldsymbol{B}_t$ and $\boldsymbol{B}_p$. In agreement with the above considerations according to which the δ_1-effect alone cannot lead to a dynamo, no mechanism becomes apparent which could maintain steady $\boldsymbol{B}$-fields. The fact that also oscillatory $\boldsymbol{B}$-fields have to be excluded is more difficult to explain.

Let us now turn to the combination of the α_1-effect with a strong rotational shear, i.e. a strong ω-effect, which results in an $\alpha\omega$-mechanism. As long as α^+ is positive in the northern hemisphere we see that steady $\boldsymbol{B}$-fields of the A0 or S0 type are to be expected if $d\omega/dr$ is positive or negative, respectively. Extending the considerations to both signs of α^+ we may conclude that steady fields of the A0 or S0 type will occur depending on whether the signs of α^+ and $d\omega/dr$ in the northern hemisphere coincide or differ. In addition, the possibility of oscillatory fields of S0 or A0 type is indicated for the other sign combinations.

Finally, we deal with the combination of the δ_1-effect and a rotational shear, i.e. a strong ω-effect, which allows a $\delta\omega$-mechanism. For both signs of δ_1 we find that steady $\boldsymbol{B}$-fields, of both the A0 and the S0 types, seem to be possible if the signs of δ_1 and $d\omega/dr$ differ, and oscillatory fields if these signs coincide.

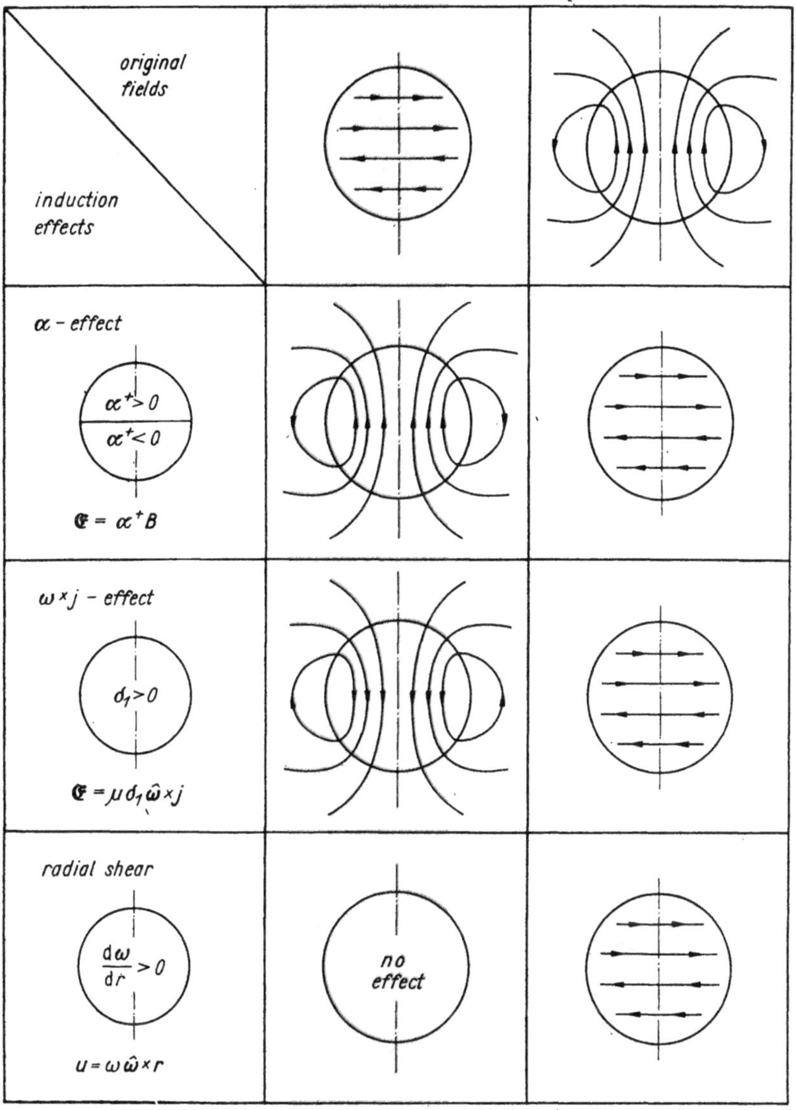

Fig. 15.3. $\boldsymbol{B}_t$-fields of A0 type generated from $\boldsymbol{B}_p$-fields of the same type, and vice versa, by the idealized α-effect, the $\omega \times j$ effect and the rotational shear. The representations of the fields correspond to those in figure 15.1. The signs of α^+ correspond to $\alpha_1 < 0$. If the signs of α^+, δ_1 or $\mathrm{d}\omega/\mathrm{d}r$ are inverted, the directions of the generated fields have to be inverted too

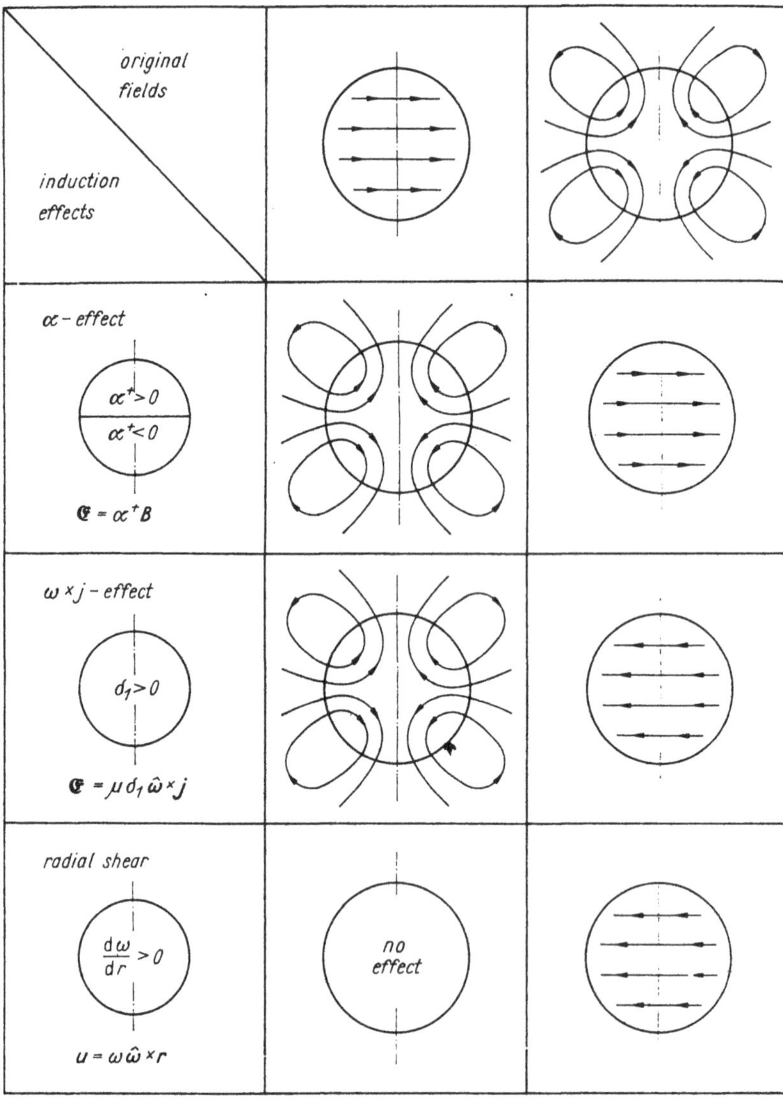

Fig. 15.4. $\boldsymbol{B}_t$-fields of S0 type generated from $\boldsymbol{B}_p$-fields of the same type, and vice versa, by the idealized α-effect, the $\omega\times j$ effect and the rotational shear. The explanations given with figure 15.3 apply here too

We want to emphasize that these considerations carried out by means of figures 15.3 and 15.4 hold, of course, only for the mentioned special assumptions on the signs of α_1, δ_1 and $d\omega/dr$. Furthermore, we have ignored all parts of the $\boldsymbol{B}$-fields which correspond to higher multipoles. It is already for this that our statements are just presumptions. They might give some orientation. Detailed investigations show, however, that some of these statements, especially those concerning the conditions for oscillatory fields, have to be modified.

We now remove the restriction to axisymmetric $\boldsymbol{B}$-fields, i.e. we admit again arbitrary $\boldsymbol{B}$-fields. Then the influences of $\boldsymbol{u}$ and $\mathfrak{E}$ on $\boldsymbol{B}_t$ and $\boldsymbol{B}_p$ can no longer be concluded from the equations (15.21), (15.25), and (15.26) but require a more complicated investigation on the basis of (15.42), (15.46), and (15.47). A scheme of these influences is given in figure 15.5.

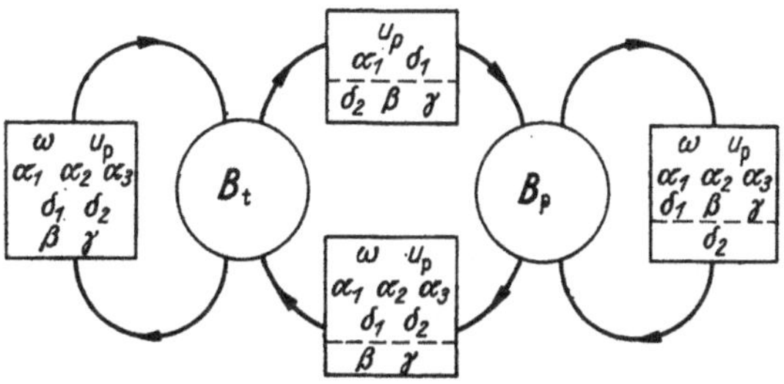

Fig. 15.5. The influences of the induction effects covered by $\boldsymbol{u}$ and $\mathfrak{E}$ on the toroidal and poloidal parts, $\boldsymbol{B}_t$ and $\boldsymbol{B}_p$, of an arbitrary, i.e. not necessarily axisymmetric $\boldsymbol{B}$-field. The effects given below the dotted lines only occur if the corresponding coefficients, i.e. β, γ, and δ_2, depend on latitude

Compared with the case of axisymmetric $\boldsymbol{B}$-fields, the situation looks more complex and more effort would have to be put into a detailed discussion of the possibilities of dynamo mechanisms. Therefore we shall only deal with some special points.

As above, we first ask for possibilities of dynamos without any coupling between $\boldsymbol{B}_t$ and $\boldsymbol{B}_p$, or with a coupling which, however, does not allow an interaction between $\boldsymbol{B}_t$ and $\boldsymbol{B}_p$. Again, the majority of these possibilities can be excluded. As for the remaining ones, there is no suggestion that dynamos exist.

Let us now take the case of interaction between $\boldsymbol{B}_t$ and $\boldsymbol{B}_p$. According to figure 15.5, this interaction occurs due to the u_p, α_1 or δ_1-effects or, if β, γ or δ_2 depend on latitude, also by the β, γ or δ_2-effects.

We have good reasons to assume that there are spherical dynamos operating due to a meridional circulation, i.e. the u_p-effect. Dynamos of this kind would be only a modification of that proposed by GAILITIS [2]. In this case fluctuating motions do not play any role. Of course, only $\boldsymbol{B}$-fields without any axisymmetric part may be generated.

Dynamos due to the α_1-effect, i.e. due to an α^2-mechanism have been discussed before. We now add that the α_1-effect is not only able to generate axisymmetric but also non-axisymmetric $\boldsymbol{B}$-fields (cf. section 16.3.). The arguments excluding dynamos due to the δ_1-effect also hold for non-axisymmetric $\boldsymbol{B}$-fields.

Again, combinations of the α_1 or δ_1-effect with non-uniform rotation, i.e. the ω-effect, should be considered, which lead to the $\alpha\omega$ or the $\delta\omega$-mechanism. We must, however, bear in mind that these mechanisms presuppose the generation of a sufficiently strong toroidal field from a poloidal field by means of the rotational shear. Whereas this is possible for axisymmetric fields, no comparable process is known for non-axisymmetric fields. This suggests the presumption that the $\alpha\omega$ and $\delta\omega$-mechanisms are not able to generate or maintain non-axisymmetric fields.

The possibility of dynamos due to the β-effect can, of course, again be excluded on grounds of relation (12.8). As for the γ and δ_2-effects, a dynamo process is at least not hinted.

The illustrations given for axisymmetric $\boldsymbol{B}$-fields in figures 15.3 and 15.4 shall now be extended to non-axisymmetric $\boldsymbol{B}$-fields of both A1 and S1 types in figures 15.6 and 15.7. The general explanations are the same as before; the rotational shear, however, is not considered. Again it can be seen that the interaction of $\boldsymbol{B}_t$ and $\boldsymbol{B}_p$ due to the α_1-effect may provide for the maintenance of $\boldsymbol{B}$-fields, and it is also demonstrated that a dynamo is impossible due to the δ_1-effect alone.

It should be mentioned that in these considerations one important point has been ignored. In the case of a non-axisymmetric $\boldsymbol{B}_p$-field the α-effect does not only result in a generation of a $\boldsymbol{B}_t$-field but also in a variation of the $\boldsymbol{B}_p$-field. This variation consists mainly in a rotation about the axis of rotation of the conducting body. Therefore the non-axisymmetric $\boldsymbol{B}$-fields maintained by an α^2-mechanism have the form of waves travelling round the equator.

Let us sum up the results of these considerations on the possibilities of dynamo mechanisms. It should be emphasized that in these considerations the general form (15.6) of the mean velocity field $\boldsymbol{u}$ was taken into account but only the special form (15.8) of the electromotive force $\mathfrak{E}$. Apart from a dynamo mechanism which is only due to meridional circulation, three others, the α^2, $\alpha\omega$, and $\delta\omega$-mechanisms, have been found which presuppose induction effects by fluctuating motions. Whereas the α^2-process is able to generate and maintain both axisymmetric and non-axisymmetric $\boldsymbol{B}$-fields, the $\alpha\omega$ and $\delta\omega$-processes preferably lead to axisymmetric fields. On the other hand only in the case

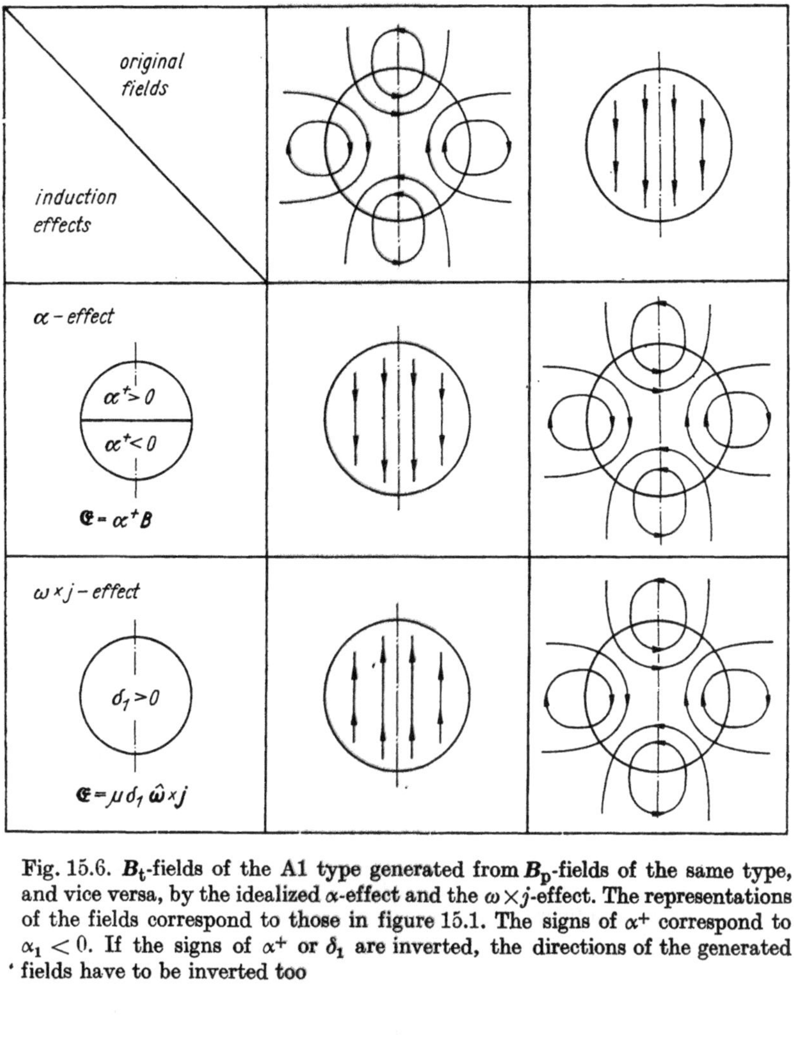

Fig. 15.6. **B_t-fields of the A1 type generated from B_p-fields of the same type, and vice versa, by the idealized α-effect and the $\omega \times j$-effect. The representations of the fields correspond to those in figure 15.1. The signs of α^+ correspond to $\alpha_1 < 0$. If the signs of α^+ or δ_1 are inverted, the directions of the generated fields have to be inverted too**

of the last two processes one has also to expect axisymmetric fields with an oscillatory time dependence.

If we replace the special form (15.8) of the electromotive force $\mathfrak{E}$ by the general form (15.11), a variety of further possibilities for dynamo mechanisms occur. Some of them turn out to be only modifications of the mechanisms mentioned before. Still to be thoroughly investigated remain processes resulting from, e.g., combinations of the $\beta^{(5)}$, $\beta^{(6)}$, or $\delta^{(1)}$-effects with the ω-effect.

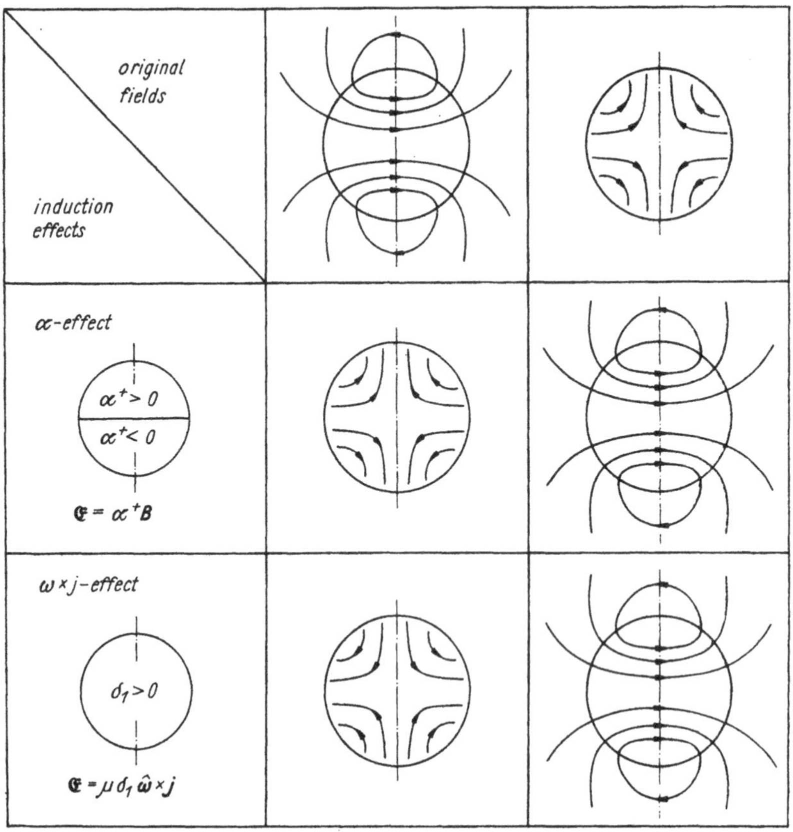

Fig. 15.7. $\boldsymbol{B}_t$-fields of the S1 type generated from $\boldsymbol{B}_p$-fields of the same type, and vice versa, by the idealized α-effect and the $\omega \times j$-effect. The explanations given with figure 15.6 apply here too

15.8. Further reductions of the basic equations

In the foregoing we have reduced the equations governing the $\boldsymbol{B}$-field to equations for certain scalar functions. When looking only for axisymmetric $\boldsymbol{B}$-fields we may restrict ourselves to equations (15.33)...(15.35), (15.37), and (15.38) for B and A. The occurrence of the operator Δ' suggests B and A be represented by series of associated Legendre polynomials $P_n^1(\cos\vartheta)$. On this basis the first investigations of spherical models of turbulent dynamos have been carried out, cf. e.g. Steenbeck and Krause [6, 7]. In the general case, where also non-axisymmetric $\boldsymbol{B}$-fields are included, we have to deal with the equations (15.42)...(15.44), (15.46), and (15.47) for T and S. It proves useful to develop T and S in series of spherical harmonics $Y_n^m(\vartheta, \varphi)$. We shall derive those relations most relevant for the treatment of dynamo models in this way.

At first some dimensionless quantities are introduced. For the conductivity we write

$$\sigma = \sigma_0 \tilde{\sigma}, \tag{15.50}$$

where σ_0 is a constant and $\tilde{\sigma}$ a dimensionless function; if σ is constant we put $\sigma = \sigma_0$, i.e. $\tilde{\sigma} = 1$. Furthermore, we define dimensionless coordinates by

$$x = r/R, \quad \tau = t/\mu\sigma_0 R^2, \tag{15.51a, b}$$

and an operator, D_n, by

$$D_n f = \frac{1}{x^2}\left(\frac{\mathrm{d}}{\mathrm{d}x}\left(x^2\,\frac{\mathrm{d}f}{\mathrm{d}x}\right) - n(n+1)\,f\right), \tag{15.52}$$

where f is any function and n an integer.

As explained in section 15.3. we may decompose any $\boldsymbol{B}$-field which is a solution of the basic equations into $\boldsymbol{B}$-modes of the Am and Sm types, which are again solutions of them. We ask only for these special modes. For clarity we speak of Al and Sl modes at this stage, i.e. denote the parameter m introduced above by l.

For each of these $\boldsymbol{B}$-modes the functions T and S, and also $U^{(uB)}$, $V^{(uB)}$, $U^{(\mathfrak{E})}$, and $V^{(\mathfrak{E})}$ are represented by series of spherical harmonics. We write

$$T = T^+, \quad S = RS^+, \tag{15.53a, b}$$

$$U^{(uB,\mathfrak{E})} = (\mu\sigma_0 R)^{-1} U^{(uB,\mathfrak{E})+}, \quad V^{(uB,\mathfrak{E})} = (\mu\sigma_0 R^2)^{-1} V^{(aB,\mathfrak{E})}, \tag{15.53c, d}$$

where T^+, S^+, $U^{(uB,\mathfrak{E})+}$, and $V^{(uB,\mathfrak{E})+}$ are defined as

$$F^+ = \Big(\sum_{n,m} F_n^m(x)\; Y_n^m(\vartheta, \varphi)\Big) \exp\{(\lambda - \mathrm{i}\Omega)\,\tau\}. \tag{15.54}$$

The factors R, $(\mu\sigma_0 R)^{-1}$, and $(\mu\sigma_0 R^2)^{-1}$ ensure that T_n^m, S_n^m, $U_n^{(uB,\mathfrak{E})m}$, and $V_n^{(uB,\mathfrak{E})m}$ have the same dimensions. As for the Y_n^m we refer to (13.24)...(13.27). Both λ and Ω are real quantities independent of n and m. The summation is at first over all n and m with $n \geqq 0$ and $|m| \leqq n$. Because of (15.41), however, the terms with $n = 0$ have to be omitted. Furthermore, for an Al mode the T_n^m and $V_n^{(uB,\mathfrak{E})m}$ are non-zero only if $n = l + 2k$ and $m = \pm l$, the S_n^m and $U_n^{(uB,\mathfrak{E})m}$ only if $n = l + 2k + 1$ and $m = \pm l$ where k is a non-negative integer. For an Sl mode we have the same situation; we then have only to exchange the two relations for n with each other.

We are now able to reduce equations (15.42) for T and S to

$$D_n T_n^m - \frac{1}{x}\frac{\mathrm{d}\ln\tilde{\sigma}}{\mathrm{d}x}\frac{\mathrm{d}}{\mathrm{d}x}(xT_n^m) + V_n^{(uB)m} + V_n^{(\mathfrak{E})m} - (\lambda - \mathrm{i}\Omega)\, T_n^m = 0, \quad (15.55\text{a})$$

$$D_n S_n^m + U_n^{(uB)m} + U_n^{(\mathfrak{E})m} - (\lambda - \mathrm{i}\Omega)\, S_n^m = 0, \quad \text{for} \quad 0 \leqq x \leqq 1. \quad (15.55\text{b})$$

From (15.43) and (15.44c) follows

$$T_n^m = 0, \quad S_n^m = a_n^m x^{-(n+1)}, \quad \text{for} \quad x \geqq 1, \quad (15.56\text{a, b})$$

where the a_n^m are constants. Finally, (15.44a, b) result in

$$T_n^m = 0, \quad \mathrm{d}S_n^m/\mathrm{d}x + (n+1)\, S_n^m = 0, \quad \text{at} \quad x = 1. \quad (15.57\text{a, b})$$

From the relations (15.45) for $U_n^{(uB)m}$, $V_n^{(uB)m}$, $U_n^{(\mathfrak{E})m}$, and $V_n^{(\mathfrak{E})m}$ we conclude

$$U_n^{(uB)m} = \mu\sigma_0 R B_n^m \oiint (\boldsymbol{r} \cdot \operatorname{curl}(\boldsymbol{u}\times\boldsymbol{B}))\, Y_n^{-m}\, \mathrm{d}\tilde{\omega}, \quad (15.58\text{a})$$

$$V_n^{(uB)m} = \mu\sigma_0 R^2 B_n^m \oiint (\boldsymbol{r} \cdot \operatorname{curl}\operatorname{curl}(\boldsymbol{u}\times\boldsymbol{B}))\, Y_n^{-m}\, \mathrm{d}\tilde{\omega}, \quad (15.58\text{b})$$

$$U_n^{(\mathfrak{E})m} = \mu\sigma_0 R B_n^m \oiint (\boldsymbol{r} \cdot \operatorname{curl}\mathfrak{E})\, Y_n^{-m}\, \mathrm{d}\tilde{\omega}, \quad (15.58\text{c})$$

$$V_n^{(\mathfrak{E})m} = \mu\sigma_0 R^2 B_n^m \oiint (\boldsymbol{r} \cdot \operatorname{curl}\operatorname{curl}\mathfrak{E})\, Y_n^{-m}\, \mathrm{d}\tilde{\omega}, \quad (15.58\text{d})$$

with

$$B_n^m = (n(n+1)\, A_n^m)^{-1}. \quad (15.59)$$

The integrals are defined as in (13.2), and A_n^m is given by (13.27). Incidentally, the integrals can be rewritten according to (13.35). In $\boldsymbol{u}\times\boldsymbol{B}$, and $\mathfrak{E}$ as well, $\boldsymbol{B}$ can be expressed by T and S. If this is done the integrands differ from the right-hand sides of relations (15.46) and (15.47) only by the factor Y_n^{-m}. For T and S in turn the series mentioned above should be inserted. Then the $U_n^{(uB)m}$, $V_n^{(uB)m}$, $U_n^{(\mathfrak{E})m}$, and $V_n^{(\mathfrak{E})m}$ can be calculated as functions of T_n^m, S_n^m, and their derivatives. For special forms of $\boldsymbol{u}$ and $\mathfrak{E}$ explicit but lengthy expressions for $U_n^{(uB,\mathfrak{E})m}$ and $V_n^{(uB,\mathfrak{E})m}$ have been given in a paper by Rädler [9].

We may interpret the investigations of the kinematic dynamo models considered in this chapter again in terms of stability theory. Then $\lambda = 0$ corresponds to marginal stability. In this sense we shall speak of marginal values of the parameters determining λ, of marginal $\boldsymbol{B}$-modes etc. in the following.

CHAPTER 16

SPHERICAL MODELS OF TURBULENT DYNAMOS AS SUGGESTED BY COSMICAL BODIES. RESULTS OF COMPUTATIONS

16.1. General definitions

In the foregoing chapter we dealt with some general considerations of those spherical models of turbulent dynamos which are of interest for cosmical bodies. Quite a number of numerical investigations have been carried out for models working on the basis of α^2, $\alpha\omega$, and $\delta\omega$-mechanisms. Here we shall give a survey of the essential features of the results obtained.

We shall adhere to the assumptions introduced in the foregoing chapter. Unless defined otherwise the conductivity σ shall be constant. As for the electromotive force $\mathfrak{E}$ only the contributions given by the expression (15.8) are taken into account. For the coefficients appearing there we put

$$\alpha_1 = \alpha_0\tilde{\alpha}_1, \quad \alpha_2 = \alpha_0\tilde{\alpha}_2, \quad \alpha_3 = \alpha_0\tilde{\alpha}_3, \tag{16.1a, b c}$$

$$\delta_1 = \delta_0\,\tilde{\delta}_1, \quad \delta_2 = \delta_0\,\tilde{\delta}_2, \tag{16.1d, e}$$

$$\beta = \beta_0\tilde{\beta}, \qquad \gamma = \gamma_0\tilde{\gamma}, \tag{16.1f, g}$$

where α_0, δ_0, β_0, and γ_0 are constants and $\tilde{\alpha}_1$, $\tilde{\alpha}_2$, ... are dimensionless quantities which may generally depend on x and ϑ. As for the mean motion given by $\boldsymbol{u}$ we recall (15.6) and (15.7) and add

$$\omega = \omega_0 + \Delta\omega\, w, \tag{16.2a}$$

$$u_r = u_0 v_r, \quad u_\vartheta = u_0 v_\vartheta, \tag{16.2b, c}$$

with ω_0, $\Delta\omega$, and u_0 being constants, and w, v_r, and v_ϑ dimensionless functions of x and ϑ.

We furthermore define the parameters

$$C_\alpha = \mu\sigma_0\alpha_0 R, \qquad C_\delta = \mu\sigma_0\,\delta_0, \tag{16.3a, b}$$

$$s = \mu\sigma_0\beta_0, \qquad g = \mu\sigma_0\gamma_0 R, \tag{16.3c, d}$$

$$C_\omega = \mu\sigma_0\,\Delta\omega\, R^2, \quad C_u = \mu\sigma_0 u_0 R, \tag{16.3e, f}$$

which are also dimensionless. They are normalized measures for induction effects involved in $\mathfrak{E}$ and $\boldsymbol{u}$.

In relation (15.54) we have already introduced the dimensionless frequency, Ω, of a $\boldsymbol{B}$ mode. For an axisymmetric mode we choose $\Omega \geqq 0$ in the following. In the case of a non-axisymmetric mode we relate Ω to a frame of reference in which the equator is at rest, and we fix the sign such that $\Omega > 0$ or $\Omega < 0$ corresponds to eastward or westward migration, respectively.

When describing results of numerical investigations we refrain from giving information on the numerical methods applied and refer to the papers cited.

16.2. Definitions for special types of models

In the following, various models shall be considered which are determined by various specifications of the electromotive force $\mathfrak{E}$ and the mean velocity $\boldsymbol{u}$, i.e. of the functions $\alpha_1, \alpha_2, \ldots, \omega$, u_r, and u_ϑ. On several occasions special examples are taken from investigations by RÄDLER [16, 17]. The corresponding special choice of these functions shall be explained first.

In order to motivate the specification of $\mathfrak{E}$, we recall the corresponding results obtained in the second order correlation approximation (cf. sections 9.3., 9.4., and 9.5.) and assume that the dependence of $\alpha_1, \alpha_2, \ldots$ on the correlation tensor of the turbulent velocity field $\boldsymbol{u}'$ may simply be reduced to a dependence on $\overline{\boldsymbol{u}'^2}$, λ_{cor}, and τ_{cor}. Furthermore, $\overline{\boldsymbol{u}'^2}$ may depend on radius but λ_{cor} and τ_{cor} are considered as constant. We then put

$$\tilde{\alpha}_1 = \mathrm{d}\chi/\mathrm{d}x, \quad \tilde{\alpha}_2 = \zeta_\alpha/\tilde{\alpha}_1, \quad \tilde{\alpha}_3 = 0, \tag{16.4a, b, c}$$

$$\tilde{\delta}_1 = \chi, \quad \tilde{\delta}_2 = \zeta_\delta\, \tilde{\delta}_1, \tag{16.4d, e}$$

$$\tilde{\beta} = \chi, \quad \tilde{\gamma} = \mathrm{d}\chi/\mathrm{d}x, \tag{16.4f, g}$$

and, in addition,

$$\overline{\boldsymbol{u}'^2} = u_0'^2 \chi. \tag{16.5}$$

The function χ, which may depend on x only, represents a normalized distribution of the turbulence intensity; u_0' means a characteristic value of the turbulent velocity. The parameters ζ_α and ζ_δ are supposed to be independent of x. As explained above, the α_3-effect is equivalent to a special non-uniform rotation and so the assumption $\tilde{\alpha}_3 = 0$ is no serious restriction.

The function χ is specified to be

$$\chi = \begin{cases} 0 & \text{for} \quad x \leqq x_{\chi 1} - d_{\chi 1} \\ \frac{1}{16}(8 + 15\xi - 10\xi^3 + 3\xi^5) & \xi = (x - x_{\chi 1})/d_{\chi 1} \\ & \text{for} \quad x_{\chi 1} - d_{\chi 1} \leqq x \leqq x_{\chi 1} + d_{\chi 1} \\ 1 & \text{for} \quad x_{\chi 1} + d_{\chi 1} \leqq x \leqq x_{\chi 2} - d_{\chi 2} \\ \frac{1}{16}(8 - 15\xi + 10\xi^3 - 3\xi^5) & \xi = (x - x_{\chi 2})/d_{\chi 2} \\ & \text{for} \quad x_{\chi 2} - d_{\chi 2} \leqq x \leqq x_{\chi 2} + d_{\chi 2} \\ 0 & \text{for} \quad x_{\chi 2} + d_{\chi 2} \leqq x . \end{cases} \tag{16.6}$$

In the following we distinguish between two different cases, *a* and *b*, characterized by $\chi(0) \neq 0$ and $\chi(0) = 0$, respectively. In the case *a* the turbulence also covers the centre of the sphere, in the case *b* it is restricted to some outer layers of the sphere. The corresponding χ-profiles are depicted in figure 16.1. In view of later considerations, in figure 16.2 the distribution of the sign of α^+, defined by (15.10), for different types of χ-profiles is given.

We may, of course, digress from the above motivation given for relations (16.4) and use them without interpreting χ according to (16.5), i.e. as normalized turbulence intensity. Thus the results of computations for which (16.4) and (16.6) have been used allow applications to a wide range of suppositions on $\mathfrak{C}$.

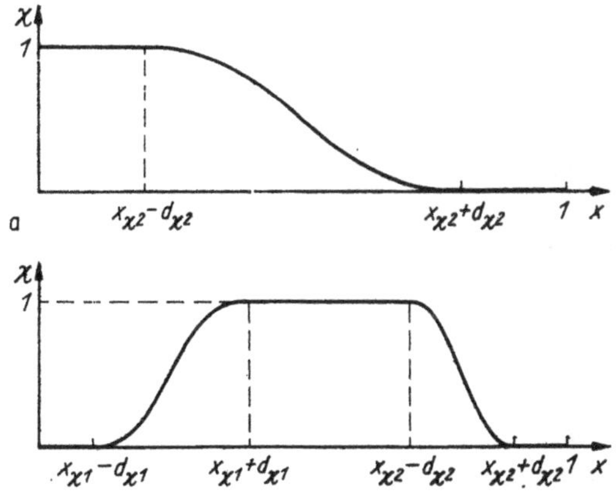

Fig. 16.1. The profiles of the normalized turbulence intensity χ, defined by (16.6).
Case a: The turbulence covers the centre of the sphere. Case b: The turbulence is restricted to some outer layers of the sphere

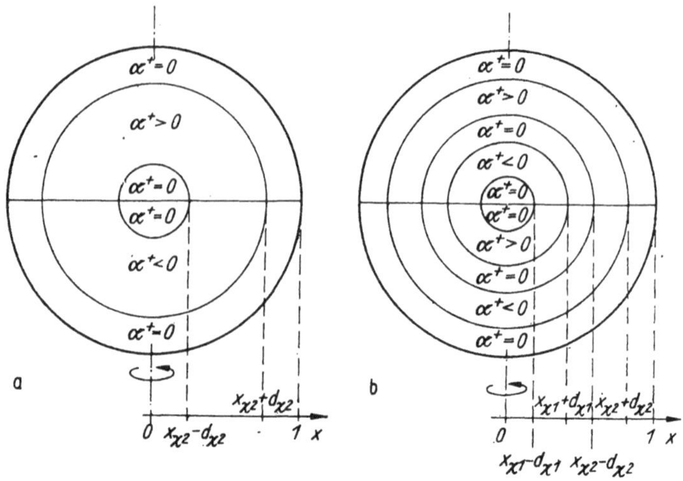

Fig. 16.2. The distribution of the signs of the quantity α^+, defined by (15.10), for the profiles of the turbulence intensity of types *a* and *b* as depicted in figure 16.1. The signs given here correspond to $\alpha_0 > 0$, i.e. $C_\alpha > 0$, and have to be inverted if $\alpha_0 < 0$, i.e. $C_\alpha < 0$

Let us now turn to the mean velocity $\boldsymbol{u}$. We assume that the angular velocity ω of the rotation depends on radius only and put

$$w = \begin{cases} 0 & \text{for} \quad x \leqq x_w - d_w \\ \dfrac{1}{4}(2 + 3\xi - \xi^3) & \xi = (x - x_w)/d_w \\ & \text{for} \quad x_w - d_w \leqq x \leqq x_w + d_w \\ 1 & \text{for} \quad x_w + d_w \leqq x. \end{cases} \tag{16.7}$$

As for the meridional circulation we suppose $\boldsymbol{u}_p$ to be solenoidal so that

$$v_r = \frac{1}{x \sin\vartheta} \frac{\partial}{\partial\vartheta} (\sin\vartheta\psi), \quad v_\vartheta = -\frac{1}{x} \frac{\partial}{\partial x} (x\psi), \tag{16.8a. b}$$

with ψ being a stream function specified to be

$$\psi = -f \sin\vartheta \cos\vartheta, \tag{16.9a}$$

$$f = \begin{cases} 0 & \text{for} \quad x \leqq x_u \\ \xi^3 & \xi = 4(x - x_u)(1 - x)/(1 - x_u)^2 \\ & \text{for} \quad x_u \leqq x \leqq 1. \end{cases} \tag{16.9b}$$

Profiles of ω and streamlines $\psi = \text{const}$ are given in figures 16.3 and 16.4.

According to these specifications we have $C_\omega > 0$ for a differential rotation with $d\omega/dr > 0$, and $C_\omega < 0$ for $d\omega/dr < 0$. If $C_u > 0$ the meridional circulation runs in the outer layers from the equator to the poles, and if $C_u < 0$ from the poles to the equator. $C_\omega = \pm 2\pi$ means that the outer parts carry out one revolution more, or one less, than the inner ones within the time $\mu\sigma_0 R^2$. Analogously, $C_u = \pm 1$ corresponds to about one revolution in maximum velocity region within that time $\mu\sigma_0 R^2$.

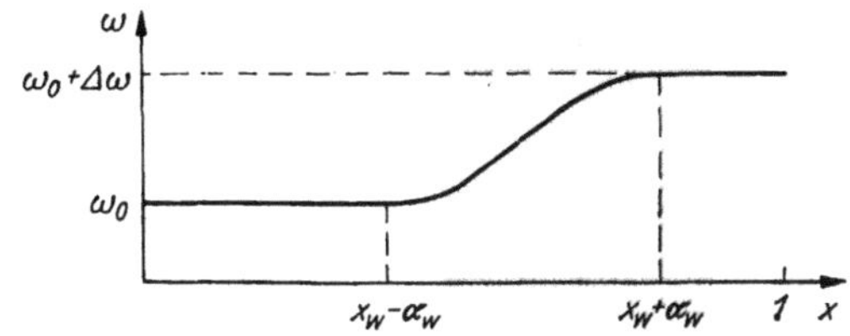

Fig. 16.3. The profile of the angular velocity ω of the non-uniform rotation, defined by (16.2 a) and (16.7). This ascending curve corresponds to $\Delta\omega > 0$, i.e. $C_\omega > 0$, a descending one occurs if $\Delta\omega < 0$, i.e. $C_\omega < 0$

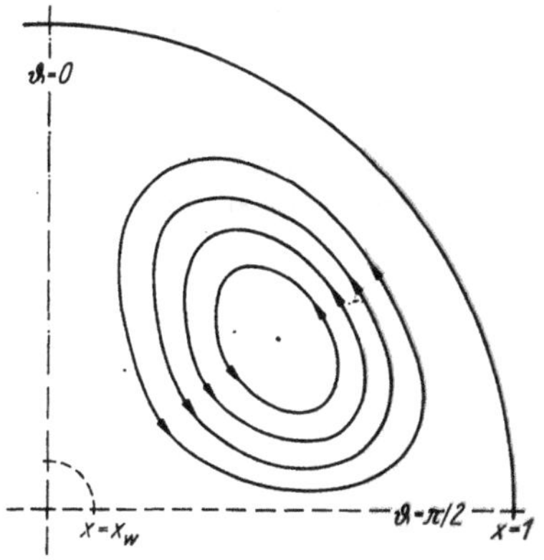

Fig. 16.4. The streamlines $\psi = \text{const}$ of the meridional circulation, defined by (16.2b, c), (16.8) and (16.9). The arrows correspond to $u_0 > 0$, i.e. $C_u > 0$, and have to be inverted if $u_0 < 0$, i.e. $C_u < 0$

16.3. Models with α^2-mechanism

We direct our attention to models in which the magnetic field is generated by means of the α^2-mechanism. As explained above, in this case the generation of the toroidal from the poloidal field, and vice versa, is due to the α-effect. This presupposes that C_α is non-zero. We may restrict our discussion to the case $C_\alpha > 0$. Starting from results for $C_\alpha > 0$ we easily arrive at corresponding results for $C_\alpha < 0$ by virtue of the statement formulated with (15.17) and (15.18).

In the most simple case apart from the idealized α-effect no other induction effects are included. As long as this holds we speak of a pure α^2-mechanism.

The first models with magnetic field regeneration due to an α^2-mechanism have been proposed and computed by Steenbeck and Krause [3, 7] (1966, 1969). These models have been constructed with the intention to explain the origin of the Earth's magnetic field. Only a pure α^2-mechanism was taken into account. For the main part of the investigation referred to here, the coefficient $\tilde{\alpha}_1$ was specified according to

$$\tilde{\alpha}_1 = \mathrm{d}\chi/\mathrm{d}x, \quad \chi = \begin{cases} 0 & \text{for} \quad x \leqq x_\alpha \\ \dfrac{27}{4} \dfrac{(x - x_\alpha)^2 (1 - x)}{(1 - x_\alpha)^3} & \\ & \text{for} \quad x_\alpha \leqq x \leqq 1, \end{cases} \tag{16.10a, b}$$

with various values of x_α. Only axisymmetric $\boldsymbol{B}$-fields, i.e. A0 and S0-modes were considered, and these turned out to be steady. Marginal values of C_α in dependence on x_α are given in table 16.1. Field patterns for a special case are depicted in figures 16.5 and 16.6.

Table 16.1. Model with a pure α^2-mechanism; $\tilde{\alpha}_1$ given by (16.10). Marginal values of C_α for the A0 and S0-modes in dependence on x_α. These modes are steady, i.e. $\Omega = 0$

x_α	A0	S0
0.0	3.734	3.732
0.1	3.656	3.654
0.3	3.467	3.471
0.5	3.164	3.174
0.7	2.712	2.726
0.8	2.629	2.638

The results obtained by Steenbeck and Krause have been confirmed and supplemented by calculations by Roberts [4], which are also based on the assumption of a pure α^2-mechanism and are also restricted to axisymmetric fields. Roberts and Stix [2] studied models with an α^2-mechanism modified by the presence of a differential rotation. They also included the case of non-axisymmetric fields. Finally, in investigations by Rädler [17] in addition to the idealized α-effect other induction effects have also been taken into account, and again the cases of both axisymmetric and non-axisymmetric modes have been studied.

Let us explain and illustrate the essential findings of models with α^2-mechanisms on the basis of special results gathered from the investigations by RÄDLER [17]. For these investigations the specifications of section 16.2. hold.

At first we again consider a pure α^2-mechanism and suppose that $\tilde{\alpha}_1$ is given by (16.4a) and (16.6). In addition to the axisymmetric also non-axisymmetric $\boldsymbol{B}$-modes turn out to be possible. For special χ-profiles of types a and b marginal values of C_α and corresponding values of Ω are presented in tables 16.2 and 16.3 and in figure 16.7.

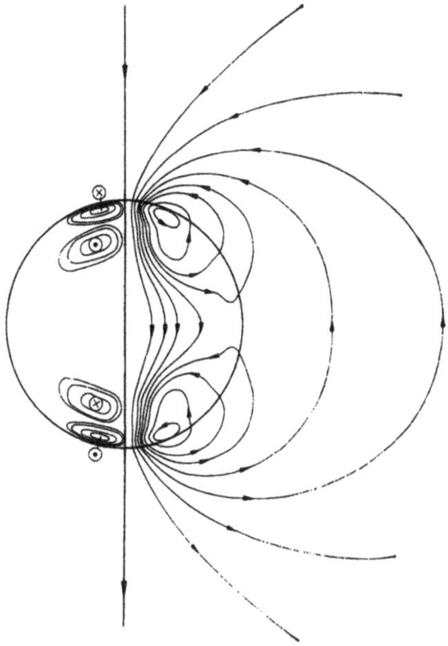

Fig. 16.5. Model with a pure α^2-mechanism; $\tilde{\alpha}_1$ given by (16.10), $x_\alpha = 0.5$. Field pattern for the A0-mode belonging to $C_\alpha = 3.164$. The left-hand side shows lines of constant magnitude of the toroidal field, the right-hand side field lines of the poloidal field

Table 16.2. Model with a pure α^2-mechanism; $\tilde{\alpha}_1$ given by (16.4a) and (16.6); χ-profile of type a, $x_{\chi 1} + d_{\chi 1} \leqq 0$, $x_{\chi 2} = 0.5$, $d_{\chi 2} = 0.4$. Marginal values of C_α and corresponding values of Ω

	A0	S0	A1	S1	A2	S2
C_α	4.66	4.75	4.86	4.75	6.31	6.27
Ω	0	0	−0.20	1.95	−0.16	0.81

Table 16.3. Model with a pure α^2-mechanism; $\tilde{\alpha}_1$ given by (16.4a) and (16.6); χ-profile of type *b*, $x_{\chi 1} = 0.5$, $x_{\chi 2} = 0.9$, $d_{\chi 1} = d_{\chi 2} = 0.1$. Marginal values of C_α and corresponding values of Ω

	A0	S0	A1	S1	A2	S2
C_α	2.68	2.70	2.78	2.77	3.12	3.12
Ω	0	0	−1.39	−2.65	−0.24	−0.85

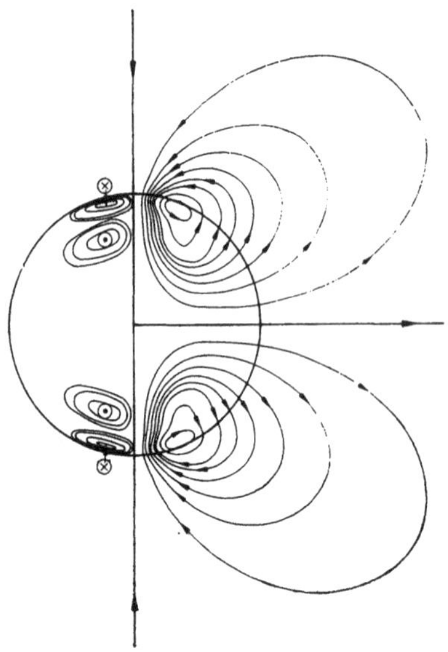

Fig. 16.6. Model with a pure α^2-mechanism; $\tilde{\alpha}_1$ given by (16.10), $x_\alpha = 0.5$. Field pattern of the S0-mode belonging to $C_\alpha = 3.174$. As for the representation of field lines the explanations given with figure 16.5 apply

In all investigated cases the A0, S0, A1, and S1-modes show marginal values of C_α which are rather close together. Mostly the A0-mode has the smallest of these marginal values. Therefore all these modes can be excited with almost equal ease; generally the A0-mode is slightly preferred. The A2 and S2-modes have higher marginal values of C_α and are less easily excited. These different properties of different modes may be understood as a consequence of the

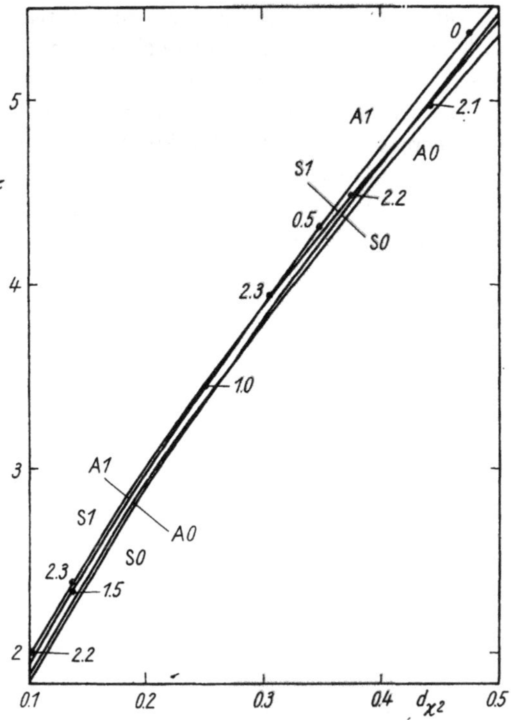

Fig. 16.7. Model with a pure α^2-mechanism; $\tilde{\alpha}_1$ given by (16.4a) and (16.6); χ-profile of type a, $x_{\chi 1} + d_{\chi 1} \leqq 0$, $x_{\chi 2} = 0.5$. Marginal values of C_α in dependence on $d_{\chi 2}$. For the A0 and S0-modes holds $\Omega = 0$, for the A1 and S1-modes Ω is given by the figures at the curves

fact that fields with less complicated geometrical structures show less dissipative effects than those with more complicated structures.

In the case of χ-profiles of type a with non-axisymmetric modes the eastward migration dominates. This result becomes plausible if we consider the distribution of the electromotive force due to the α-effect for simple field structures. It can easily be followed up that these structures indeed should change in time in the sense of an eastward migration. For χ-profiles of type b, however, a westward migration appears. Since such profiles lead to more complex distributions of the electromotive force this result is more difficult to explain.

Now in addition to the idealized α-effect other induction effects are taken into account too. More precisely, in each case only one of the other effects is included.

Studying at first the transition from the idealized to the real α-effect we allow ζ_α to be non-zero. There are some reasons to believe that ζ_α is generally negative; in special cases $\zeta_\alpha = -1/4$ has been found (cf. section 9.6.). For all hitherto investigated cases, with χ-profiles of types a and b, the marginal values of C_α increase if ζ_α decreases. Again, the A0, S0, A1, and S1-modes were observed to have marginal values of C_α lying closely together. A typical example is given in figure 16.8. In this case for sufficiently small ζ_α it is no longer the A0-mode but the S1-mode which has the smallest marginal value of C_α, i.e. which is excited most easily.

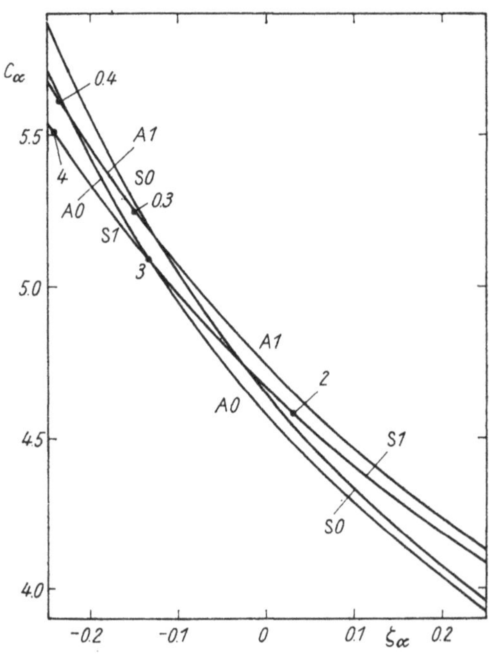

Fig. 16.8. Model including α_1 and α_2-effect; $\tilde{\alpha}_1$ given by (16.4a) and (16.6); χ-profile of type a, $x_{\chi 1} + d_{\chi 1} \leqq 0$, $x_{\chi 2} = 0.5$, $d_{\chi 2} = 0.4$. Marginal values of C_α in dependence on ζ_α. As for Ω the explanations given with figure 16.7 apply

Let us now replace the original by the turbulent electrical conductivity, i.e. include the β-effect so that the parameter s is no longer zero. Contrary to the original conductivity the turbulent conductivity generally depends on radius. Assuming that the turbulent conductivity is always smaller than the original one we have $s \geqq 0$. It is to be expected that the marginal values of C_α grow with s. Indeed in all investigations so far, again involving χ-profiles of types a and b, the marginal values of C_α show such dependence on s. A typical example is given in figure 16.9.

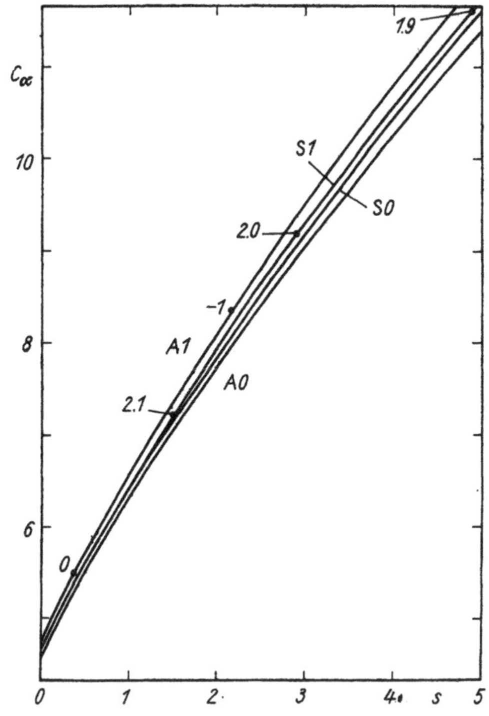

Fig. 16.9. Model including α_1 and β-effect; $\tilde{\alpha}_1$ and $\tilde{\beta}$ given by (16.4) and (16.6); χ-profile of type a, $x_{\chi 1} + d_{\chi 1} \leqq 0$, $x_{\chi 2} = 0.5$, $d_{\chi 2} = 0.4$. Marginal values of C_α in dependence on s. As for Ω the explanations given with figure 16.7 apply

Now the transport of magnetic flux due to the γ-effect is considered, which is connected with the parameter g. As long as the γ-effect is due to a gradient of turbulence intensity we have $g \geqq 0$. Then this transport of magnetic flux can also be described in terms of an enhanced magnetic permeability. This fact suggests that the marginal values of C_α grow with g. Again all investigations prove that this is indeed the case. An example is given in figure 16.10.

As far as the influence of the δ_1 and δ_2-effects is concerned, unfortunately only rather incomplete results are available.

We now consider the influence of a differential rotation, i.e. allow C_ω to be non-zero. The marginal values of C_α for different modes turn out to depend on C_ω in a different way. In all investigated cases for sufficiently high values of $|C_\omega|$ always one of the axisymmetric modes is clearly favoured from all other modes. With χ-profiles of type *a* the A0-mode is favoured for $C_\omega > 0$, and

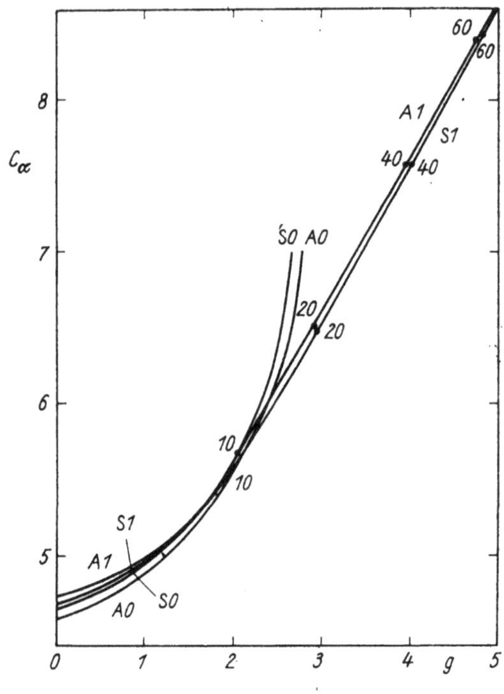

Fig. 16.10. Model including α_1 and γ-effect; $\tilde{\alpha}_1$ and $\tilde{\gamma}$ given by (16.4) and (16.6); χ-profile of type *a*, $x_{\chi 1} + d_{\chi 1} \leqq 0$, $x_{\chi 2} = 0.5$, $d_{\chi 2} = 0.4$. Marginal values of C_α in dependence on g. As for Ω the explanations given with figure 16.7 apply

the S0-mode for $C_\omega < 0$. An example is given in figure 16.11. The different behaviour of the A0 and S0-modes is plausible. As can easily be followed up in figures 15.3 and 15.4, in the case of an A0-mode a differential rotation with $C_\omega > 0$ is able to assist the α-effect in generating the toroidal from the poloidal field, and the same holds for an S0 mode and $C_\omega < 0$. In the region of small values of $|C_\omega|$ we have a rather complex situation. The results strongly depend on the χ and ω-profiles. It should be noted that Roberts and Stix [2] observed a preferrence for the S1 mode for special values of $|C_\omega|$.

Finally, a meridional circulation is taken into account, i.e. C_u is allowed to be non-zero. There are striking similarities between the dependencies of the marginal values of C_α on C_ω and on C_u. In all investigated cases for sufficiently high values of $|C_u|$ the axisymmetric modes are favoured compared with the non-axisymmetric ones. Among the axisymmetric modes again the A0 or S0-mode is more easily to be excited for $C_u < 0$ or $C_u > 0$, respectively.

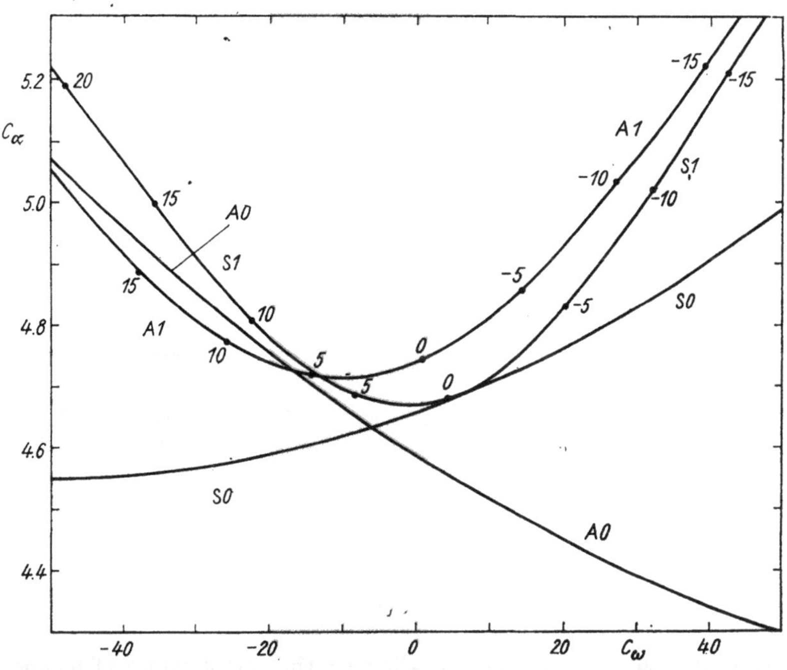

Fig. 16.11. Model including α_1 and ω-effect; $\tilde{\alpha}_1$ given by (16.4a) and (16.6); χ-profile of type a, $x_{\chi 1} + d_{\chi 1} \leqq 0$, $x_{\chi 2} = 0.5$, $d_{\chi 2} = 0.4$; w given by (16.7), $x_w = 0.5$, $d_w = 0.4$. Marginal values of C_α in dependence on C_ω. As for Ω the explanations given with figure 16.7 apply

An example is shown in figure 16.12. Contrary to the differential rotation, in the case of axisymmetric modes the meridional circulation does not provide for any coupling between the toroidal and poloidal fields. However, it is, obviously, able to influence axisymmetric field structures in a way that the interaction due to the α-effect is enhanced.

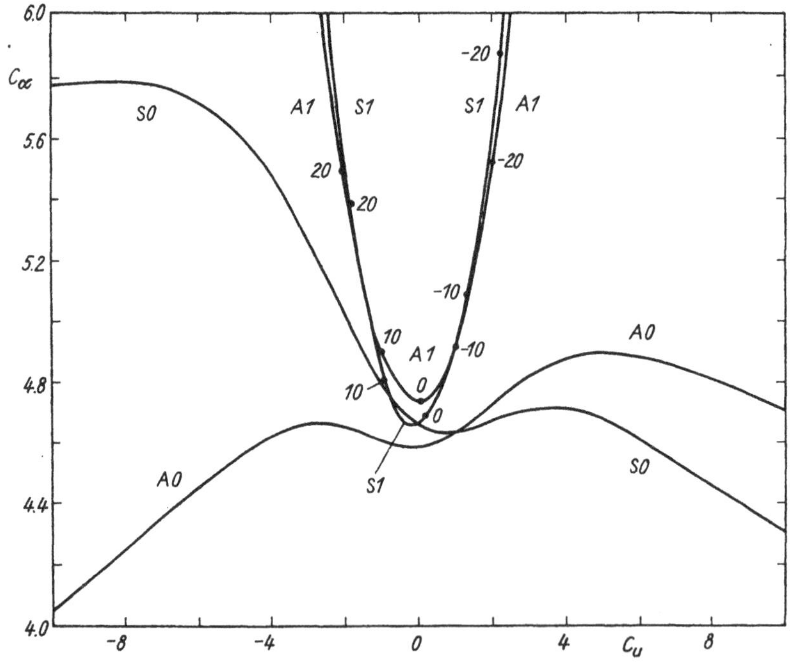

Fig. 16.12. Model including α_1 and u_p-effect; $\tilde{\alpha}_1$ given by (16.4a) and (16.6); χ-profile of type a, $x_{\chi 1} + d_{\chi 1} \leqq 0$, $x_{\chi 2} = 0.5$, $d_{\chi 2} = 0.4$; v_r and v_ϑ given by (16.8) and (16.9), $x_u = 0.1$. Marginal values of C_α in dependence on C_u. As for Ω the explanations given with figure 16.7 apply

16.4. Models with $\alpha\omega$-mechanism

We shall now deal with models allowing the maintenance of magnetic fields on the basis of an $\alpha\omega$-mechanism. In this case the generation of the poloidal from the toroidal field is due to the α-effect, more precisely the α_1-effect, and for the generation of the toroidal from the poloidal field the main role is played by the rotational shear, i.e. the ω-effect. Therefore, both C_α and C_ω have to be non-zero. Again, we shall largely restrict our considerations to $C_\alpha > 0$. They can easily be extended to $C_\alpha < 0$ by the help of the statement formulated with (15.17) and (15.18).

Let us at first assume that beside the idealized α-effect and the ω-effect no other induction effects are present, and that the generation of the toroidal field is exclusively due to the ω-effect, i.e. without any assistance of the α-effect. As long as these assumptions are fulfilled we speak of a pure $\alpha\omega$-mechanism.

The conditions for the generation of axisymmetric $\boldsymbol{B}$-fields by a pure $\alpha\omega$-mechanism show a remarkably simple dependence on C_α and C_ω, that is one on $C_\alpha C_\omega$ only. In order to see this it is useful to specify equations (15.21 a) and (15.22) for $\boldsymbol{B}_t$ and $\boldsymbol{A}_t$ according to the above suppositions and to rewrite them, after introducing C_α and C_ω, into equations for $\boldsymbol{B}_t$ and $\boldsymbol{A}_t^+$ where $\boldsymbol{A}_t^+ = C_\alpha^{-1}\boldsymbol{A}_t$. Since in (15.21 a) the term with α_1 is to be omitted the resulting equations contain C_α and C_ω only in the form $C_\alpha C_\omega$. Contrary to the conditions for the generation of axisymmetric $\boldsymbol{B}$-fields their structures do vary with C_α or C_ω even if $C_\alpha C_\omega$ remains unchanged. As can be seen from the foregoing considerations the ratio of $\boldsymbol{B}_t$ to $\boldsymbol{B}_p$ behaves like $(C_\omega/C_\alpha)^{1/2}$ if $C_\alpha C_\omega$ is fixed. It should be emphasized that these statements do not apply to non-axisymmetric $\boldsymbol{B}$-fields.

The first models in which magnetic fields are produced by an $\alpha\omega$-mechanism have been elaborated by Steenbeck and Krause [3, 6] (1966, 1969). These models are intended to reflect the situation at the Sun. Only a pure $\alpha\omega$-mechanism is taken into account. Calculations have been carried out with, e.g.,

$$\tilde{\alpha}_1 = -\frac{1}{2}\left(1 + \Phi((x - x_\alpha)/d_\alpha)\right), \tag{16.11a}$$

$$w = \frac{1}{2}\left(1 - \Phi((x - x_w)/d_w)\right), \tag{16.11b}$$

where Φ denotes the error function, for various x_α, d_α, x_w, and d_w. The authors looked only for axisymmetric $\boldsymbol{B}$-modes. They found such modes with an oscillatory time dependence. As an example we take the special case determined by $x_\alpha = 0.9$, $x_w = 0.7$, and $d_\alpha = d_\omega = 0.075$. In this case there is an oscillatory A0-mode with the marginal value $C_\alpha C_w = 2.07 \cdot 10^4$, and $\Omega = 31.8$. The oscillatory S0-mode is less easy to excite. As for the A0-mode a sequence of field patterns of different phases of the oscillation is depicted in figure 16.13.

The results by Steenbeck and Krause have been supported by an investigation by Deinzer and Stix [1]. Their model also acts on the basis of a pure $\alpha\omega$-mechanism but $\tilde{\alpha}_1$ is essentially reduced to a delta function and w to a step function. Again only axisymmetric $\boldsymbol{B}$-modes were considered. The authors found such modes with an oscillatory dependence on time. Stix [1] modified this model so that the α-effect takes part in the generation of the toroidal field too, and studied also non-axisymmetric $\boldsymbol{B}$-modes. Further investigation of models with an $\alpha\omega$-mechanism allowing oscillatory $\boldsymbol{B}$-modes has been carried out by Roberts and Stix [2], Roberts [4], Köhler [1], Stix [4, 6], Deinzer, v. Kusserow and Stix [1], Jepps [1], Ivanova and Ruzmaikin [1, 2, 3]. In some of these investigations in addition to the α-effect also other turbulent induction effects have been included, and in addition to the differential rotation also a meridional circulation.

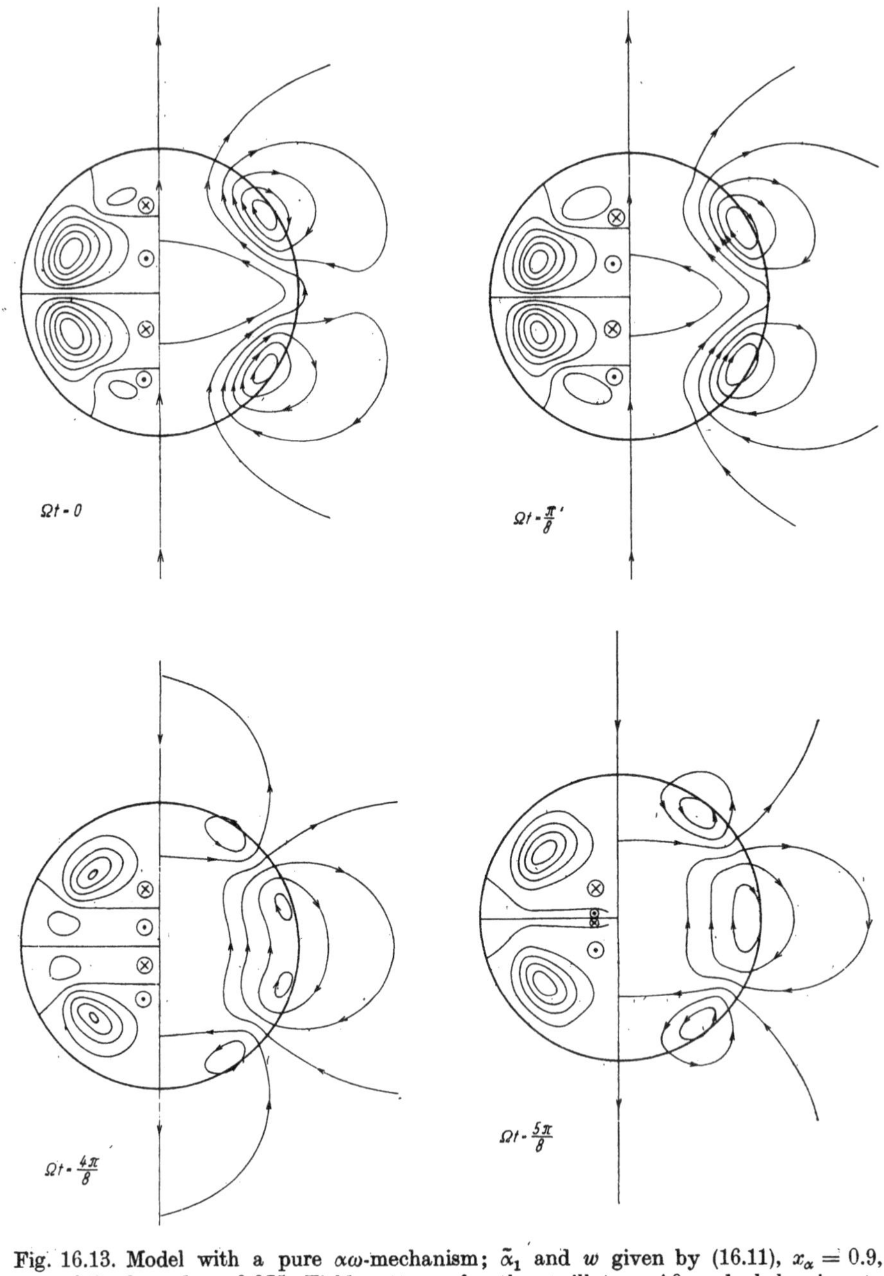

Fig. 16.13. Model with a pure $\alpha\omega$-mechanism; $\tilde{\alpha}_1$ and w given by (16.11), $x_\alpha = 0.9$, $x_w = 0.7$, $d_\alpha = d_w = 0.075$. Field patterns for the oscillatory A0-mode belonging to

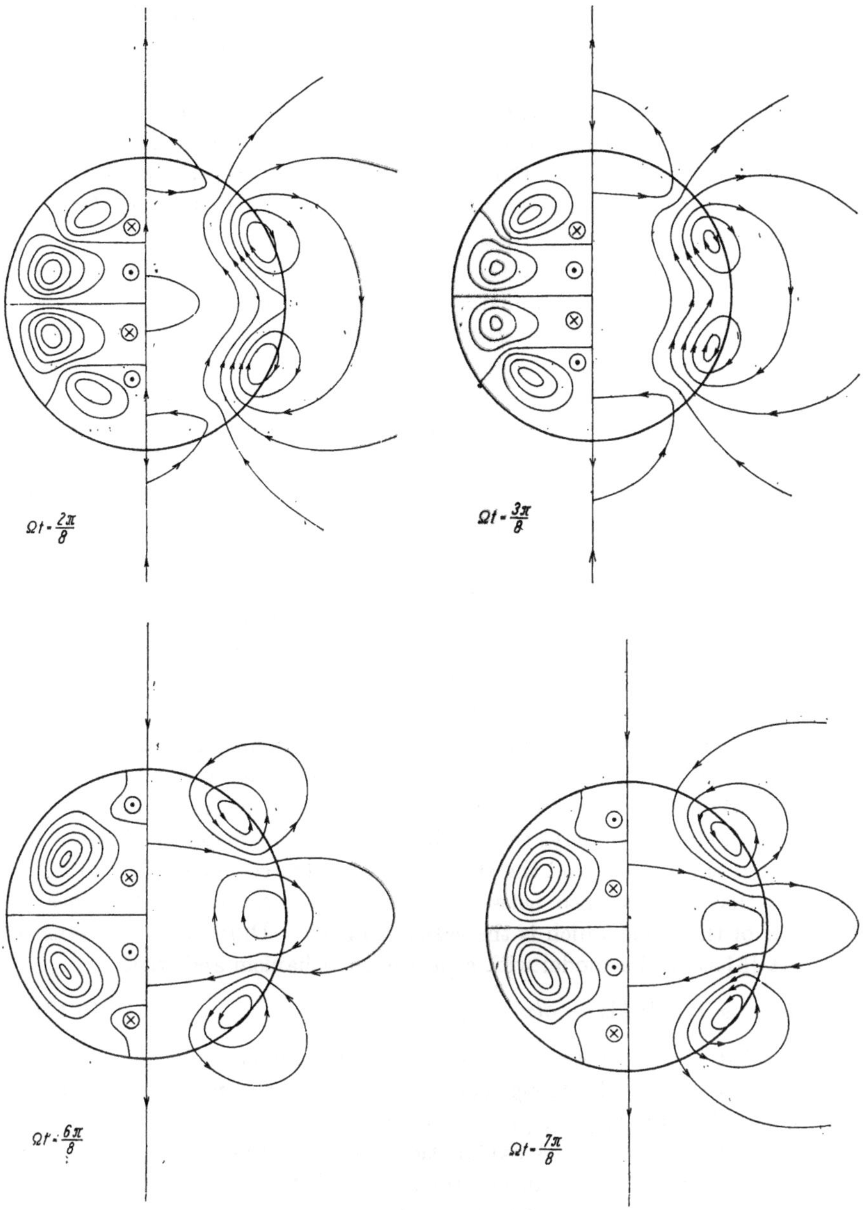

$C_\alpha C_w = 2.07 \cdot 10^4$ and $\Omega = 31.8$ for 8 phases. The left hand sides of the pictures show lines of constant magnitude of the toroidal field, the right hand sides field lines of the poloidal field

Up to now we have paid attention only to oscillatory $\boldsymbol{B}$-fields. Following BRAGINSKIJ [3] it was proved by ROBERTS [4] that an $\alpha\omega$-mechanism in the presence of a meridional circulation admits the existence of axisymmetric steady modes too. The investigations by LEVY [1] have shown also a pure $\alpha\omega$-mechanism is able to generate axisymmetric steady $\boldsymbol{B}$-modes. This result has been confirmed by STIX [4]. Further investigation on $\alpha\omega$-mechanisms which can generate axisymmetric steady $\boldsymbol{B}$-modes has been carried out by DEINZER, v. KUSSEROW and STIX [1, 2, 3] and by RÄDLER [17].

The fact that models with $\alpha\omega$-mechanism allow a variety of $\boldsymbol{B}$-modes raises the question which modes dominate under given conditions.

Let us first deal with the steady axisymmetric modes only. We restrict ourselves to cases in which α^+ does not change its sign inside the northern or southern hemisphere and, furthermore, ω depends only on r, and $\mathrm{d}\omega/\mathrm{d}r$ does not change its sign. As is to be expected from the considerations with figures 15.3 and 15.4 in all investigated cases among the steady modes, the A0-mode is clearly favoured compared with the S0-mode if in the northern hemisphere the signs of α^+ and $\mathrm{d}\omega/\mathrm{d}r$ coincide, and the S0-mode is favoured compared with the A0-mode, if these signs differ.

The situation with the oscillatory axisymmetric modes is more complex. The maintenance of an oscillatory mode presupposes rather complicated processes. In particular, special phase relations for the regeneration of the toroidal and the poloidal field have to be fulfilled. Even with the above simple assumptions on α^+ and $\mathrm{d}\omega/\mathrm{d}r$ it is not always the S0-mode among the oscillatory modes which is easiest to excite if in the northern hemisphere the signs of α^+ and $\mathrm{d}\omega/\mathrm{d}r$ coincide, and not always the A0-mode if these signs differ.

One would like to know at least whether it is one of the steady or one of the oscillatory modes which plays the dominant role. In the majority of the models investigated the α-effect and the shear are concentrated in certain thin layers. It seems that the distance between these layers essentially determines the character of the mode which is the easiest to excite. DEINZER, v. KUSSEROW, and STIX [3] studied a model with a pure $\alpha\omega$-mechanism and with

$$\tilde{\alpha}_1 = \delta(x - x_\alpha), \quad \mathrm{d}w/\mathrm{d}x = \delta(x - x_w), \tag{16.12 a,b}$$

where x_α and x_w are constants. Only axisymmetric modes were considered. In this model for sufficiently strong spatial separation of the induction effects, i.e. for sufficiently large $| x_\alpha - x_w |$ always one of the steady modes dominantes. In agreement with the above explanation it is the A0-mode if $C_\alpha C_\omega > 0$, and the S0-mode if $C_\alpha C_w < 0$. For certain small values of $|x_\alpha - x_\omega|$ one of the oscillatory modes is the easiest to be excited.

A remark should be added on the axisymmetric oscillatory $\boldsymbol{B}$-modes caused by the $\alpha\omega$-mechanism. As can be seen from the example given in figure 16.13

not only the magnitude of the field but also its geometrical structure varies in time. A typical feature of these modes is a migration of the toroidal field belts. This migration, which plays an important role for solar models, may be interpreted in terms of the dynamo waves discovered by PARKER [7].

As explained in section 15.7. the $\alpha\omega$-mechanism is presumably not able to generate or maintain non-axisymmetric $\boldsymbol{B}$-fields. Indeed, at least in all cases of models with a pure $\alpha\omega$-mechanism, the existence of non-axisymmetric $\boldsymbol{B}$-modes has not yet been proved. At first sight a model by KRAUSE [4], which corresponds to the suppositions of a pure $\alpha\omega$-mechanism, seems to allow of non-axisymmetric $\boldsymbol{B}$-modes. The suppositions used there, however, cannot be justified for these modes.

In order to illustrate some of the foregoing statements let us explain some special results of investigations by RÄDLER [17], for which again the specifications of section 16.2. hold.

We consider models which involve the α-effect, more precisely the α_1-effect, and a rotational shear, i.e. the ω-effect. As long as only C_α is non-zero but C_ω vanishes we will have an α^2-mechanism, and if C_ω grows we may arrive at an

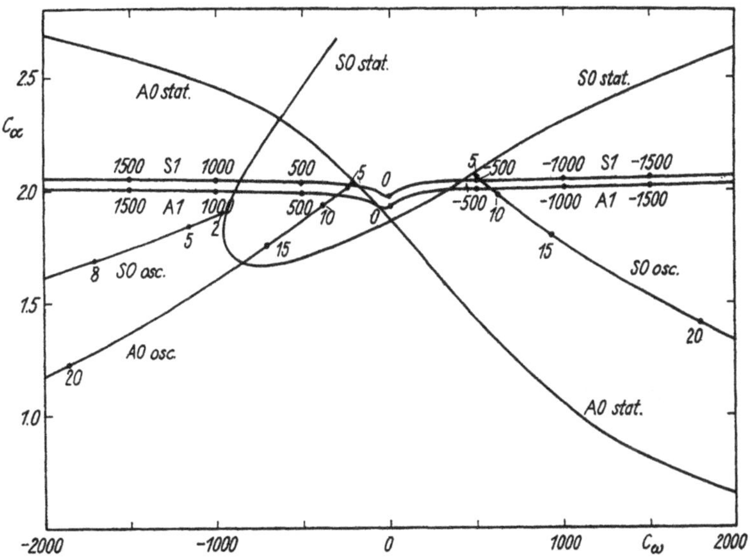

Fig. 16.14. Model including the α_1 and ω-effect; $\tilde{\alpha}_1$ given by (16.4a) and (16.6); χ-profile of type a, $x_{\chi1} + d_{\chi1} \leqq 0$, $x_{\chi2} = 0.5$, $d_{\chi2} = 0.1$; w given by (16.7), $x_w = 0.8$, $d_w = 0.1$. Marginal values of C_α in dependence on C_ω. For the steady modes holds $\Omega = 0$, for all other modes Ω is given by the figures at the curves

$\alpha\omega$-mechanism. It is instructive to study the transition from the $\boldsymbol{B}$-modes generated by an α^2-mechanism to those due to an $\alpha\omega$-mechanism.

We pay attention to a special model in which the α_1 and the ω-effect are restricted to rather thin separate spherical layers; the α-effect is concentrated in the inner, the ω-effect in the outer layer. In figure 16.14 marginal values of C_α and corresponding values of Ω are given for various $\boldsymbol{B}$-modes.

Let us focus on the case $C_\omega > 0$. Then, apart from very small C_ω, the steady A0-mode is the one to be excited most easily. For small C_ω it is due to an α^2-mechanism. For large C_ω, however, it must be ascribed to an $\alpha\omega$-mechanism. In this case the marginal value of $C_\alpha C_\omega$ may not be influenced by a further increase of C_ω. As can be seen from figure 16.15 this requires at least $C_\omega \gtrapprox 1000$. Only then the steady A0-mode is generated by a more or less pure $\alpha\omega$-process, i.e. the α-effect is by far less effective in the generation of the poloidal field than the ω-effect.

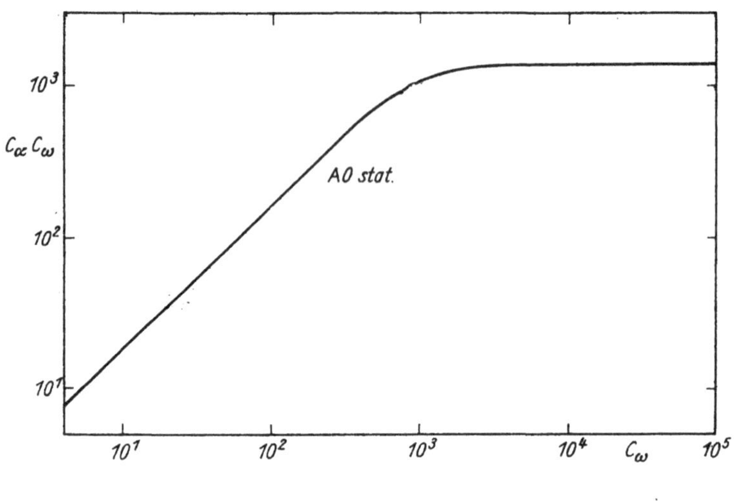

Fig. 16.15. Model including α_1 and ω-effect; $\tilde{\alpha}_1$ given by (16.4a) and (16.6); χ-profile of type a, $x_{\chi 1} + d_{\chi 1} \leqq 0$, $x_{\chi 2} = 0.5$, $d_{\chi 2} = 0.1$; w given by (16.7), $x_w = 0.8$, $d_w = 0.1$. Marginal values of $C_\alpha C_\omega$ in dependence on C_ω for the steady A0-mode

The steady S0-mode, however, shows quite different features for $C_\omega > 0$. It must be interpreted as a consequence of an α^2-mechanism which is to some extent modified by the presence of the ω-effect, but there is no indication of an $\alpha\omega$-mechanism. Likewise, the A1 and S1-modes can scarely be related to an $\alpha\omega$-mechanism.

Contrary to the hitherto discussed modes which exist for both small and large C_ω, the oscillatory A0 and S0-modes have been found for sufficiently large C_ω only. They must be understood as a consequence of an $\alpha\omega$-mechanism. The marginal values of $C_\alpha C_\omega$ tend to a constant as C_ω grows.

The dependence of the marginal values of $C_\alpha C_\omega$ on the distance between the layer with α-effect and that with ω-effect has been studied for the steady A0-mode and the oscillatory S0-mode. Figure 16.16 shows, for $C_\omega = 2000$, that these values decrease if the distance is diminished. Moreover, the difference of these values for the two modes becomes smaller.

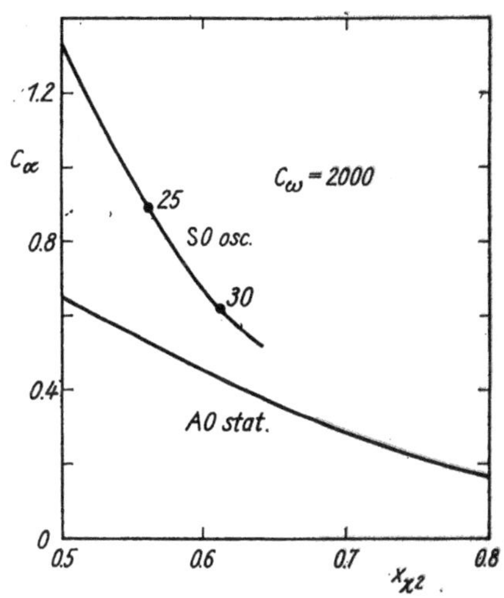

Fig. 16.16. Model including α_1 and ω-effect; $\tilde{\alpha}_1$ given by (16.4a) and (16.6); χ-profile of type a, $x_{\chi 1} + d_{\chi 1} \leqq 0$, $d_{\chi 2} = 0.1$; w given by (16.7), $x_w = 0.8$, $d_w = 0.1$. Marginal values of C_α, at $C_\omega = 2000$, in dependence on $x_{\chi 2}$ for the steady A0-mode and the oscillatory S0-mode. As for Ω the explanations given with figure 16.14 apply

For $C_\omega < 0$ a more complex situation occurs, which should not be discussed in detail. We point out that only the oscillatory A0 and S0-modes result from an $\alpha\omega$-mechanism.

For a model of this kind in which the α-effect is concentrated in the outer layer, and the ω-effect in the inner one, very similar results have been obtained.

Still to be discussed is the way in which the $\alpha\omega$-mechanism will be influenced if in addition to the α_1-effect and the ω-effect other induction effects occur.

The transition from the idealized to the real α-effect is of less importance. Provided that only axisymmetric fields are considered, this transition can only affect the contribution of the α-effect to the generation of the toroidal from the poloidal field, and this contribution is small anyway, or even negligible, compared with that of the rotational shear.

As far as the modification of electrical conductivity due to the β-effect and the turbulent transport of magnetic flux due to the γ-effect are concerned we have a similar situation as in the case of an α^2-mechanism. It is to be expected that the marginal values of C_α and also the corresponding values of Ω will grow with s and g. This is confirmed by results by KÖHLER [1] and by IVANOVA and RUZMAIKIN [1].

Studying the influence of the $\omega \times j$-effect we must bear in mind that this effect, even without any assistance of the α-effect, together with a rotational shear may give rise to a dynamo mechanism, that is the $\delta\omega$-mechanism. If in addition to the α_1-effect the δ_1-effect is also present, a combination of an $\alpha\omega$ and a $\delta\omega$-mechanism will occur. The two mechanisms can act in the same or the opposite sense. We again assume that α^+ does not change its sign inside the northern or the southern hemisphere, and that δ_1 does not change its sign at all. Let us first consider the case where both signs in the northern hemisphere coincide. As we may conclude from figures 15.3 and 15.4 the action of the $\alpha\omega$-mechanism for the A0-modes is weakened by the presence of the $\delta\omega$-mechanism,

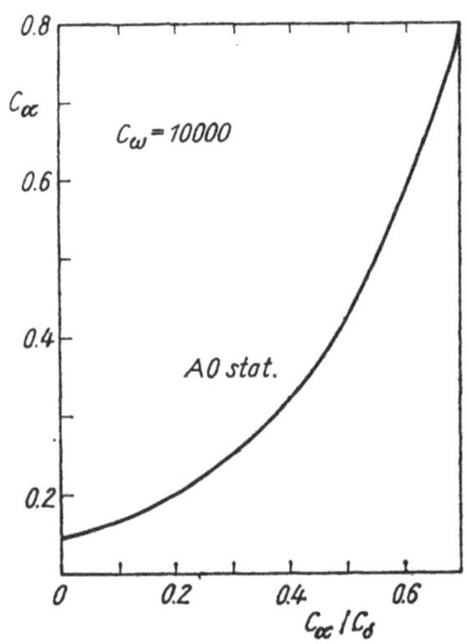

Fig. 16.17. Model including α_1, δ_1, and ω-effect; $\tilde{\alpha}_1$ and $\tilde{\delta}_1$ given by (16.4a), (16.4d) and (16.6); χ-profile of type a, $x_{\chi 1} + d_{\chi 1} \leq 0$, $x_{\chi 2} = 0.5$, $d_{\chi 2} = 0.1$; w given by (16.7), $x_w = 0.8$, $d_w = 0.2$. Marginal values of C_α, at $C_\omega = 10000$, in dependence on C_δ / C_α for the steady A0-mode

and supported for the S0-modes. If the signs of α^+ and δ_1 in the northern hemisphere differ, the A0-modes are favoured, and the S0-modes are restrained. A special result supporting these statements is shown in figure 16.17.

The influence of meridional circulations is more complex. As can be seen from investigations by Roberts and Stix [2] and Roberts [4], meridional circulations are able to favour the steady axisymmetric $\boldsymbol{B}$-modes over the oscillatory ones.

Models with $\alpha\omega$-mechanism in which the back-reaction of the magnetic field on the α-effect is taken into account have been studied by Jepps [1] and by Ivanova and Ruzmaikin [3].

16.5. Models with $\delta\omega$-mechanism

After having discussed the maintenance of magnetic fields by virtue of an $\alpha\omega$-mechanism we finally turn to the $\delta\omega$-mechanism. In this case the generation of the poloidal from the toroidal field is no longer a consequence of the α-effect but of the $\omega\times j$-effect whereas the generation of the toroidal from the poloidal field is again due to rotational shear. Hence C_δ and C_ω have to be non-zero. We restrict ourselves to $C_\delta > 0$; with respect to $C_\delta < 0$ we again refer to the statement formulated with (15.17) and (15.18).

There is some analogy between the $\alpha\omega$ and the $\delta\omega$-mechanisms. If besides the $\omega\times j$-effect, i.e. the δ_1-effect, and the rotational shear, i.e. the ω-effect, no other induction effects are included and, furthermore, the generation of the toroidal field is exclusively due to ω-effect we speak of a pure $\delta\omega$-mechanism. The conditions for the generation of axisymmetric $\boldsymbol{B}$-fields by a pure $\delta\omega$-mechanism, which depend on C_δ and C_ω, may be formulated as a requirement for $C_\delta C_\omega$ only.

The first model in which a $\delta\omega$-mechanism is responsible for the generation of a magnetic field has been proposed and calculated by Rädler [7, 8] (1969, 1970). A pure $\delta\omega$-mechanism with

$$\tilde{\delta}_1 = 1, \quad w = x \tag{16.13a,b}$$

was taken into account, and only axisymmetric steady modes were considered. For the S0-mode, which turned out to be most readily excited, a marginal value $C_\delta C_\omega = -166.5$ was found. The field pattern of this mode is given in figure 16.18. The essential results of this investigation have been confirmed and supplemented by Roberts [4]. Further results have been given by Rädler [17].

As Rädler [15, 17] has shown, a pure $\delta\omega$-mechanism is also able to generate oscillatory axisymmetric fields. This finding has been confirmed by Stix [6].

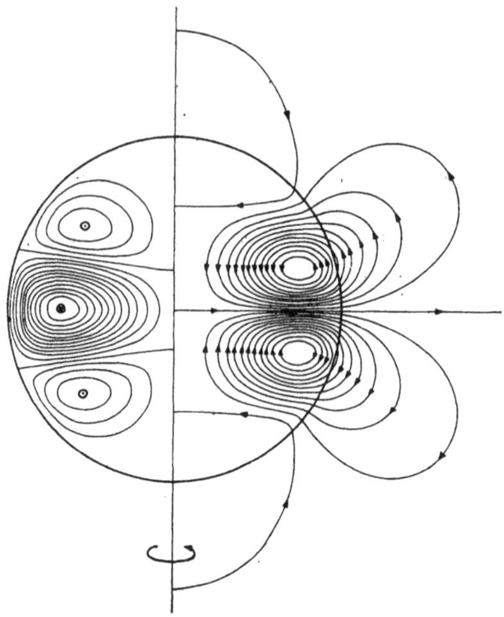

Fig. 16.18. Model with a pure $\delta\omega$-mechanism; $\tilde{\delta}_1$ and w given by (16.13). Field pattern of the S0-mode belonging to $C_\delta C_\omega = -166.5$. The left-hand side shows lines of constant magnitude of the toroidal field, the right-hand side field lines of the poloidal field

As explained in section 15.7. a pure $\delta\omega$-mechanism is probably unable to maintain non-axisymmetric $\boldsymbol{B}$-modes.

Again we are confronted with the question which modes dominate under given conditions. Unfortunately no satisfying answer can be given at present. We restrict ourselves to a pure $\delta\omega$-process with ω depending only on r and suppose that δ_1 and $\mathrm{d}\omega/\mathrm{d}r$ do not change their signs. From the considerations on the basis of figures 15.3 and 15.4 we may conjecture that steady modes only occur if the signs of δ_1 and $\mathrm{d}\omega/\mathrm{d}r$ differ. In all hitherto investigated cases this could be confirmed. Depending on the special δ_1 and ω-profiles in some cases the steady A0-mode, in other cases the steady S0-mode, proves to be dominant. Oscillatory modes, however, have been found for all combinations of the signs of δ_1 and $\mathrm{d}\omega/\mathrm{d}r$.

Let us illustrate the foregoing explanations by some results for special models with pure $\delta\omega$-mechanism by Rädler [17]. Again, the specifications of section 16.2. apply. Only axisymmetric $\boldsymbol{B}$-modes have been investigated.

There is a number of models with different specifications of δ_1 and ω for which steady A0 and S0-modes have been found. For various cases marginal

Table 16.4. Model with a pure $\delta\omega$-mechanism; $\tilde{\delta}_1$ given by (16.4d) and (16.6); w given by (16.7). Marginal values of $C_\delta C_\omega$ for steady A0 and S0-modes for various δ_1 and ω-profiles

δ_1-profile	ω-profile	A0	S0
$x_{\chi 1} + d_{\chi 1} \leqq 0$ $x_{\chi 2} - d_{\chi 2} \geqq 1$	$x_w = 0.5$ $d_w = 0.5$	-115.4	-110.6
$x_{\chi 1} = 0.75 \quad d_{\chi 1} = 0.25$ $x_{\chi 2} - d_{\chi 2} \geqq 1$	$x_w = 0.75$ $d_w = 0.25$	-166.4	-185.6
$x_{\chi 1} + d_{\chi 1} \leqq 0$ $x_{\chi 2} = 0.5 \quad d_{\chi 2} = 0.4$	$x_w = 0.5$ $d_w = 0.4$	-250.2	-291.5

values of $C_\delta C_\omega$ are listed in table 16.4. Depending on the special δ_1 and ω-profiles either the A0 or S0-mode may dominate.

Results for a model allowing oscillatory A0 and S0-modes are given in table 16.5. In this case the S0 or the A0-mode is preferred if $C_\delta C_\omega > 0$ or $C_\delta C_\omega < 0$, respectively. No steady modes have been found which could be excited more easily than the oscillatory modes.

Table 16.5. Model with a pure $\delta\omega$-mechanism; $\tilde{\delta}_1$ given by (16.4d) and (16.6); χ-profile of type b, $x_{\chi 1} = 0.8$, $d_{\chi 1} = 0.2$, $x_{\chi 2} - d_{\chi 2} \geqq 1$; w given by (16.7), $x_w = 0.5$, $d_w = 0.2$. Marginal values of $C_\delta C_\omega$ and corresponding values of Ω for oscillatory A0 and S0-modes

	A0	A0	S0	S0
$C_\delta C_\omega$	-2349	19268	-2217	4914
Ω	16.6	73.4	6.5	35.4

It remains to be discussed in which way the $\delta\omega$-mechanism is modified if in addition to the δ_1-effect and the ω-effect further induction effects are included.

The δ_1-effect is generally accompanied by the δ_2-effect. As explained above the δ_2-effect can influence a dynamo process only if δ_2 is not constant. But even in this case it is of less importance for a $\delta\omega$-mechanism. As long as δ_2 depends only on r the δ_2-effect influences only the generation of the toroidal field, the main contribution to which is provided by the ω-effect.

As for the turbulent electrical conductivity and the turbulent transport of magnetic flux the situation is presumably similar to that in the case of an α^2-mechanism. There are, however, no special investigations relating to this.

If the α-effect is included, we have again a combination of an $\alpha\omega$ and a $\delta\omega$-mechanism. In this respect we refer to the corresponding considerations of the foregoing section.

The influence of a meridional circulation on a $\delta\omega$-mechanism has not been investigated up to now.

CHAPTER 17

APPLICATIONS TO COSMICAL OBJECTS

17.1. Observational facts on the magnetic fields of the Earth, the Moon and the planets

Best and longest known among the cosmical magnetic fields is that of the Earth, the geomagnetic field. Contrary to the fields of other cosmical objects it is, at least at the surface of the Earth, accessible to direct measurements. Information on this field in outer space has been obtained from spacecraft studies.

Roughly speaking, the magnetic field in the closer regions around the Earth shows the structure of a dipole field with some symmetry with respect to the axis of rotation. The flux density at the equator is about $3 \cdot 10^{-1}$ G. A more detailed analysis reveals that the field cannot be completely described by a dipole located in the centre. The dipole plays only the role of the leading term in a multipole expansion. At the surface the dipole part exceeds the remaining part by a factor in the order of 10. The most striking deviation of the field from the symmetry with respect to the axis of rotation consists in an inclination of the dipole axis by an angle of 11°. Also the non-dipole part is not completely symmetric.

At first sight, the magnetic field of the Earth may be assumed to be steady yet there are some remarkable variations in time. We shall refrain here from the spectrum of the weak local or regional variations with time scales from minutes up to years; the causes of these variations are located outside the Earth's body. We refer, however, to the secular variations. The dipole axis shows a westward precession in the order of 0.05° per year, and the non-axisymmetric field structures related to higher multipoles a westward drift of about 0.2° per year. This corresponds to one revolution in $7 \cdot 10^3$ or $2 \cdot 10^3$ years, respectively. Paleomagnetic studies provided some information on the geomagnetic field in earlier epochs. Most of the time a dipole-like field of today's order of magnitude has existed. A remarkable phenomenon is that reversals of the field occur, i.e. sudden changes of its polarity. The length of the intervals with constant polarity varies from 10^5 to more than 10^7 years and seems to be statistically distributed; a reversal ranges over less than 10^5 years.

Quite unexpected, the Moon too showed to possess some magnetism, which was detected by spacecraft missions. The flux densities observed at the surface are, however, only in the order of 10^{-4} or 10^{-3} G. A striking feature of the field is its rather irregular structure. If a dipole component exists at all it is very small compared with the other components.

Some planets too have magnetic fields. As for Jupiter, the existence of a field has already been concluded from its radio emission. Details of this field and some information about fields of other planets are known due to spacecraft missions.

Jupiter's field is stronger than that of the Earth. It also possesses a dominant dipole component. The flux density at the equator is about 4 G, and the dipole axis is inclined against the rotational axis by an angle of about 10°.

On Mercury too a field with a dominant dipole component has been found. The flux density at the equator is about $4 \cdot 10^{-3}$ G, and the dipole axis is probably inclined by about 7°.

It should be noted that Mars possesses a magnetic field, the flux density of which at the surface is, however, only in the order of 10^{-3} G.

As far as Venus is concerned, no magnetic field with flux densities greater than $5 \cdot 10^{-5}$ G has been detected. The other planets could not yet be successfully investigated with respect to the presence of magnetic fields.

17.2. Dynamo theory of the Earth's magnetic field

A first step towards a theory of the Earth's magnetic field consists in the understanding of a mechanism which is able to maintain a steady dipole-like field. It is generally believed that the Earth's magnetic field is a consequence of a dynamo process which essentially takes place inside the core. The core shows an electrical conductivity like that of normal metals, and in all probability at least some parts of the core show internal motions. The mantle and the outer space, which show much smaller electrical conductivities, are of less importance for the process mentioned.

Treating the Earth's magnetic field as steady we refer to the time intervals between reversals, which are generally longer, sometimes much longer than 10^5 years, i.e. than the free decay time (cf. section 11.3.). The reversals require a special explanation.

An interesting and important step towards the understanding of the origin and the behaviour of the Earth's magnetic field is the theory of the nearly symmetric dynamo established by Braginskij [1, 2, 3] (1964) (cf. section 11.5.). As explained above, this theory deals with mean fields which are defined to be the axisymmetric parts of the original fields (cf. section 12.2.). It has been shown within this frame that a steady dipole-like field may exist as a consequence of non-uniform rotation, meridional circulation and some special non-axisymmetric motions. The mechanism of field generation is similar to the $\alpha\omega$-mechanism in the theory of the turbulent dynamo. The toroidal field is produced from the poloidal field by non-uniform rotation and the poloidal field in turn from the toroidal one due to non-axisymmetric motions. The toroidal field is much stronger than the poloidal field. Of course, the theory of the nearly symmetric dynamo can only give an explanation for the axisymmetric part of the geomagnetic field. As for the non-axisymmetric parts and their westward drift BRAGINSKIJ [6] proposed an interpretation in terms of the so-called MAC waves, i.e. special magnetohyrodynamic waves in presence of buoyancy and Coriolis forces (M stands for magnetic, A for Archimedean, and C for Coriolis forces).

Further promising suggestions for an explanation of the origin and some essential features of the Earth's magnetic field have arisen from the theory of the turbulent dynamo. First models were proposed by STEENBECK and KRAUSE [3, 7] (1966, 1969). We shall discuss some of these suggestions in the following.

We consider spherical dynamo models as described in section 15.1. and adopt all assumptions mentioned there. For reasons discussed in section 12.2. we define the mean fields on the basis of a time average with an averaging interval of some decades. We identify the spherical electrically conducting body with the Earth's core and suppose the conductivity to be constant. In agreement with the generally accepted data for the Earth's core, which were already used in section 11.3., we put $R = 3 \cdot 10^6$ m, $\mu = \mu_0 = 4\pi \cdot 10^{-7}$ VsA^{-1} m^{-1}, and $\sigma = \sigma_0 = 3 \cdot 10^5\, \Omega^{-1}$ m^{-1}. The Earth's mantle, and all outer space as well, is then treated as electrically insulating.

As far as the mean motion is concerned, the rotation of the core has to be taken into account. The rotation of the core essentially coincides with that of the mantle, i.e. we have one revolution per day, or $\omega_0 = 7.3 \cdot 10^{-5}$ s^{-1}. Opinions differ on whether or not a small relative motion of core and mantle is present. If it does not exist we put $\Delta\omega = 0$ so that $C_\omega = 0$. There are, however, some reasons to assume that the rotation rate of the main parts of the core slightly differs from that of the mantle. Then the outer layer of the core inevitably show a shear. Some concepts proceed from the assumption that, e.g., the dipole part of the magnetic field participates in the motion of the inner core, and that the westward drift immediately indicates the rotation of the inner core against the mantle. This would mean that $\Delta\omega = 3.10^{-11}$ s^{-1} and $C_\omega \approx 100$. There are hardly reasons to assume a meridional circulation inside the core. Therefore we at first put $u_0 = 0$ and, consequently, $C_u = 0$.

Let us now deal with the fluctuating motions. There are good reasons to assume that the inner core, the radius of which is about half the radius of the whole core, is in a solid state. Consequently, motions of that kind only occur in the remaining part of the core, the outer core. They may be a consequence of an unstable stratification of the core, of the precessional motion of the Earth or of other causes. Unfortunately, only little information is available on the structure, the magnitude and the length and time scales of these motions.

Let us give a rough estimate of the parameters C_α, C_δ, s, and g on the basis of the results of the second order correlation approximation. We first consider the quantity $\mu\sigma_0\lambda_{\text{cor}}^2/\tau_{\text{cor}}$. It seems reasonable to assume that $\lambda_{\text{cor}} > 5 \cdot 10^3$ m and $\tau_{\text{cor}} < 1$ d. In doing so we find that $\mu\sigma_0\lambda_{\text{cor}}^2/\tau_{\text{cor}}$ exceeds 10^2 and, therefore, the relations for the high conductivity limit may be used.

As for C_α we then rely on (16.3a), replace α_0 by $|\alpha|$ given by (9.60) and furthermore $\overline{\boldsymbol{u}'^2}$ by $u_0'^2$, Ω by ω_0, and λ_0 by R. Thus we see that $|C_\alpha|$ is of the order of $\mu\sigma_0 u_0'^2 \omega_0 \tau_{\text{cor}}^2$. If we put, e.g., $u_0' = 10^{-2}$ ms^{-1} and $\tau_{\text{cor}} = 5 \cdot 10^4$ s this expression takes the value of 20. Of course, the data used have a high degree of uncertainty. Nevertheless it can be seen that values of $|C_\alpha|$ exceeding unity may be possible.

A similar estimate can be carried out for C_δ. It shows that $|C_\delta/C_\alpha|$ is of the order of $(\mu\sigma\lambda_{\text{cor}}^2/\tau_{\text{cor}})^{-1}$. According to the above results this expression is smaller than 10^{-2}. Thus $|C_\delta|$ may be assumed to be much smaller than $|C_\alpha|$.

Finally, s and g prove to be of the same order of magnitude, which is given by $\mu\sigma_0 u_0'^2 \tau_{\text{cor}}$. With the data used above this expression takes the value of 2. Hence, s and g may be assumed to have the order of unity.

Let us now deal with some general features of models of turbulent dynamos suitable for an explanation of the origin and some of the basic properties of the Earth's magnetic field.

We first consider the case in which the mean motion consists simply in a rigid body rotation so that $C_\omega = C_u = 0$. Then only an α^2-mechanism will be at work. We discuss this possibility, which was first proposed by Steenbeck and Krause [6] (1969), on the basis of the special results presented in section 16.3.

In the simplest models of that kind apart from the idealized α-effect no other turbulence effect is included, i.e. a pure α^2-mechanism is taken into account. Comparing marginal values of C_α for the above examples with the estimate for C_α given before we see that there are good reasons to believe that the condition for the generation of magnetic fields is fulfilled. The improvement of these models by adding other turbulence effects generally increases the marginal values of $|C_\alpha|$, i.e. makes this condition more difficult to fulfil. But there is at least no strong argument which excludes the generation of magnetic fields.

In almost all investigated cases the marginal values of $|C_\alpha|$ for the A0-mode are slightly smaller than those for the other modes. Therefore a magnetic field is to be expected which to a large extent coincides with the A0-mode, so that the leading multipole of the poloidal part is a dipole parallel to the axis of rotation.

The marginal values of C_α for the A0, S0, A1, and S1-modes are, however, always close together. It seems reasonable to speculate that the magnetic field consists not only of a part similar to the A0-mode but also contains smaller parts similar to the S0, A1, and S1-modes. The coexistence of parts belonging to the A0 and S1-modes corresponds to an inclined dipole.

The non-axisymmetric modes, in particular the A1 and S1-modes are not steady but migrate round the equator. Therefore the non-axisymmetric parts of the magnetic field inevitably show drifts of that kind. In the special cases considered above the direction of migration depends on the turbulence distribution. Since the inner core is presumed to be solid, the distributions of type *a* seem to be less realistic than those of type *b*. For distributions of type *a* we have eastward drifts, for those of type *b*, however, westward drifts. The revolution times are given by $2\pi\mu\sigma_0 R^2/\Omega$. With the data used above we have $(9.2/\Omega) \cdot 10^5$ years. They are rather high compared with those of the drifts observed. We should bear in mind, however, that Ω considerably decreases if parameters like s and g grow.

As we see from these considerations, models of turbulent dynamos working on the basis of an α^2-mechanism offer an interesting possibility to explain not only the existence of the Earth's magnetic field and of its dipole-like structure but also the occurrence of non-axisymmetric parts of this field and its westward drift.

Up to now the mean motion has been considered as a rigid body rotation. The presence of a non-uniform rotation or a meridional circulation provides a completely different situation. Even for rather small values of $|C_\omega|$ and $|C_u|$ the marginal values of C_α for the A0, S0, A1, and S1-modes are no longer close together. Then the above explanation of the occurrence of non-axisymmetric parts of the magnetic field and of its westward drift can not be sustained anymore.

Let us now proceed on the assumption that the Earth's core shows a non-uniform rotation for which $|C_\omega|$ exceeds the order of unity. In this case $\alpha\omega$ or $\delta\omega$-mechanisms have to be envisaged.

We first discuss models which allow an $\alpha\omega$-mechanism. Compared with the case $C_\omega = 0$, in which only an α^2-mechanism is possible, in the region of such values of C_ω which are sufficient for an $\alpha\omega$-mechanism the marginal values of $|C_\alpha|$ for the dominant mode are generally smaller. Thus we may suppose that the conditions for the generation of magnetic fields are fulfilled. In view of the above estimation for C_ω we add that for $C_\omega = 100$ by no means a pure $\alpha\omega$-mechanism is to be expected. On the contrary, the α-effect may still play a considerable role in the generation of the toroidal field.

With respect to the Earth such models have to be selected in which under realistic conditions the smallest of the marginal values of $|C_\alpha|$ belongs to the steady A0-mode, so that this mode is the one to be excited most easily. As long as conditions of this kind can be justified we again find an explanation of the Earth's magnetic field, more precisely of its axisymmetric part.

A remarkable difference of the α^2 and the $\alpha\omega$-mechanism consists in the ratio of the magnitudes of the toroidal and the poloidal field. Whereas in the case of an α^2-mechanism the orders of both magnitudes agree, in the case of an $\alpha\omega$-mechanism the magnitude of the toroidal field exceeds that of the poloidal one considerably. This difference is, of course, of interest with respect to the dynamics of the Earth's core.

Contrary to the situation with the α^2-mechanism in the case of an $\alpha\omega$-mechanism the marginal values of C_α for different modes are generally quite different. Therefore the above straightforward interpretation of the deviations of the Earth's magnetic field from the axisymmetry and of its drift does not apply here.

As explained above there is some analogy between the nearly symmetric dynamo models by Braginskij and the turbulent dynamo models with an $\alpha\omega$-mechanism. In both cases we get at first only an explanation of the axisymmetric part of the Earth's magnetic field, although this restriction is due to different causes. Departing from the conception of a strong toroidal part of the field Braginskij [6] proposed an interpretation of the occurrence and the behaviour of the non-axisymmetric part in terms of MAC waves. We want to point out that this interpretation also applies in connection with models with an $\alpha\omega$-mechanism.

Finally, the possibility of a $\delta\omega$-mechanism remains to be discussed. According to the above estimation $|C_\delta|$ is much smaller than $|C_\alpha|$. Therefore the $\delta\omega$-mechanism will presumably never assert itself against the $\alpha\omega$-mechanism.

In conclusion we may state that the theory of the turbulent dynamo offers a promising basis for an explanation of the origin and of some fundamental features of the Earth's magnetic field. The main obstacle in the detailed elaboration of suitable models consists in the lack of information on the motions inside the core. As soon as more precise conceptions on these motions are available, more precise models appear to be possible which will reflect more special properties of the Earth's magnetic field.

17.3. Observational facts on magnetic fields at the Sun

The Sun shows a great number of magnetic phenomena. Our knowledge on the magnetic fields originates from the Zeeman displacement of spectral lines.

For a long time it has been well known that the phenomena of solar activity like sunspots, flares, and protuberances are accompanied by local magnetic fields with flux densities of up to a few 10^3 G. There are good reasons to interpret the local magnetic fields as consequences of a general field under the solar surface which has the same order of magnitude and varies in time with the period of the solar cycle, i.e. 22 years.

Sunspots commonly occur in pairs roughly aligned along a line of constant latitude. The spots of a pair have different magnetic polarities. Thinking of the rotation of the solar body we speak of a preceeding and a following spot of a pair. During a half-period of the solar cycle the preceeding spots in one hemisphere have the same polarity, and those of the other hemisphere the opposite polarity. In the next half-period all polarities are reversed. The distribution of sunspots in latitude varies with the phase of the cycle. At the beginning of a half-period the spots preferably occur at moderate latitudes but later on at latitudes near the equator. This behaviour may be represented by MAUNDER's butterfly diagram as reproduced in figure 17.1.

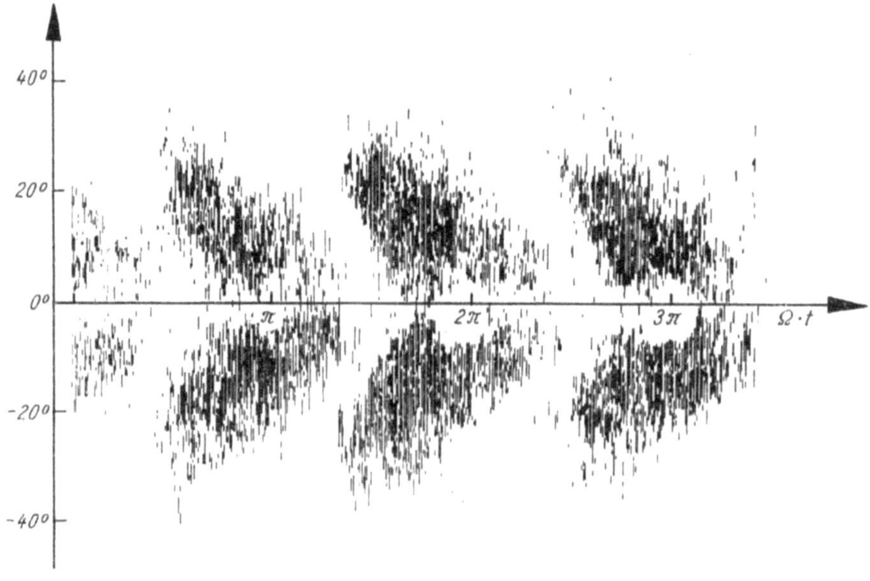

Fig. 17.1. MAUNDER's butterfly diagram according to observations from 1874 to 1913 showing the incidence of sunspots in dependence on the heliographic latitude and the phase of the solar cycle, $\Omega\tau$.

From the observational material about sunspots some conclusions may be drawn on the structure and the behaviour of the general magnetic field mentioned. It must be assumed to be a toroidal field symmetric with respect to the axis of rotation and antisymmetric with respect to the equatorial plane. It mainly consists of two oppositely orientated belts, one in each hemisphere. At the beginning of each half-period these belts occur at moderate latitudes. While the field grows and again diminishes, these belts migrate towards the equator. In the next half-period this is repeated with opposite field directions. The extrema and zeros of this field correspond to the maxima and minima of solar activity.

Observations of the corona show that in addition to this toroidal field a poloidal field of dipole-type exists with some symmetry with respect to the axis of rotation. Its flux densities at the surface are, however, only of the order of 1 G. It proves to be also an alternating field with the period of the solar cycle. It reaches its extrema roughly at the minimum phases and disappears at the maximum phases of solar activity.

It must be emphasized that we have drawn a somewhat simplified picture of the solar magnetic field. It should be noted that also some sectorial structures of the fields, i.e. deviations from the axisymmetry, have been observed, and that the oscillations are not purely harmonic.

17.4. Dynamo theory of the solar cycle

The key to an understanding of the magnetic phenomena observed at the Sun seems to be the understanding of the origin of a magnetic field with the structure and the time behaviour as described before. It is hardly conceivable that an oscillatory field with a period of 22 years also covers the deep interior of the Sun. Because of the skin effect it may only be present in some outer layers. It is widely believed that the general magnetic field of the Sun is a consequence of a dynamo process which is essentially restricted to the convection zone the thickness of which is about 15% of the solar radius.

Pioneering work in the theory of the solar dynamo has been done by Parker [2] (1955) even before the concept of mean-field magnetohydrodynamics was available. Following an idea of Babcock [1] he assumed that the toroidal field is generated from the poloidal field by virtue of differential rotation. He showed that the poloidal field in turn can be created from the toroidal field by the action of a cyclonic turbulence. In mean-field magnetohydrodynamics this process is described by the α-effect.

It was the theory of the turbulent dynamo which was most successful in explaining the origin and the behaviour of the Sun's general magnetic field and, therefore, in understanding the solar cycle. Within this frame first models were given in investigations by STEENBECK and KRAUSE [3, 6] (1966, 1969). We shall discuss here some general features of turbulent dynamo models for the Sun.

We consider spherical dynamo models with some symmetric structure as described in section 15.1. For reasons discussed in section 12.2. we suppose a definition of the mean quantities on the basis of a time average with an averaging interval of one or two years. We identify the radius R of the models with the solar radius, i.e. $R = 7 \cdot 10^8$ m, and for the magnetic permeability we put again $\mu = \mu_0 = 4\pi \cdot 10^{-7}\,\mathrm{VsA^{-1}\,m^{-1}}$. As for the electrical conductivity σ at least a radial dependence should be admitted. The conductivity of the convection zone is in the order of $3 \cdot 10^3\,\Omega^{-1}\,\mathrm{m}^{-1}$. As explained in section 3.8. the turbulent conductivity σ_T of the convection zone is smaller by a factor of about 10^{-4}. In the following we refer to that version of the relevant equations where σ is replaced by σ_T, i.e. we do not use (12.1) but (12.2). In this sense we choose $\sigma_0 = 3 \cdot 10^{-1}\,\Omega^{-1}\,\mathrm{m}^{-1}$.

The skin depth, d, for an alternating electromagnetic field with a period T is given by $d = (T/\mu\sigma)^{1/2}$. Using $T = 22$ a, $\mu = \mu_0$, and identifying σ with σ_0, we obtain $d = 4 \cdot 10^7$ m, i.e. $d = 0.06R$. Thus the assumption that the dynamo process essentially takes place in the convection zone seems to be justified.

As far as the mean motion is concerned the rotation of the Sun has to be taken into account. As is well known, the Sun shows a differential rotation. The angular velocity at the surface, which can be immediately derived from the observations, depends on latitude, i.e. $\partial\omega/\partial\vartheta \neq 0$. The revolution time for the equatorial regions is about 25 days. Accordingly we put $\omega_0 = 2.9 \cdot 10^{-6}\,\mathrm{s}^{-1}$. The time for the polar regions, however, is about 27 days, which corresponds to $\Delta\omega = 2.2 \cdot 10^{-7}\,\mathrm{s}^{-1}$. With respect to the dynamo theory it is very important to know in what way the angular velocity depends on depth. Unfortunately this dependence is inaccessible to observations. The opinions differ not only with respect to the magnitude but also with respect to the sign of $\partial\omega/\partial r$. It seems reasonable to assume that the variations of ω with r are not smaller than those with ϑ. With the data given here we may therefore conclude that $|C_\omega| > 4 \cdot 10^4$. There is no observational evidence for a meridional circulation within the convection zone. We therefore put $u_0 = 0$ and, consequently, $C_u = 0$.

Turning now to the fluctuating motions we have to deal essentially with those motions of the convection zone which are connected with the granules and supergranules. These motions can be characterized by typical velocities, u_0', typical lengths, λ_{cor}, and typical times, τ_{cor}. For the granules we put $u_0' = 2 \cdot 10^3\,\mathrm{ms}^{-1}$, $\lambda_{cor} = 2 \cdot 10^6$ m, and $\tau_{cor} = 3 \cdot 10^2$ s, and for the supergranules

$u_0' = 4 \cdot 10^2\ \mathrm{ms}^{-1}$, $\lambda_{\mathrm{cor}} = 3 \cdot 10^7$ m, and $\tau_{\mathrm{cor}} = 5 \cdot 10^4$ s. Not only the typical lengths mentioned but the scale height, h, of the mass density will be of interest. We may put $h = 10^5$ m.

With regard to the parameters C_α, C_δ, s, and g we at first calculate the quantity $\mu\sigma\lambda_{\mathrm{cor}}^2/\tau_{\mathrm{cor}}$. With the above data we get for both granules and supergranules $\mu\sigma\lambda_{\mathrm{cor}}^2/\tau_{\mathrm{cor}} > 10^7$. Consequently, relations developed for the high conductivity limit may be used.

For a very rough estimate of C_α we again rely on (16.3a) and replace α_0 by $|\alpha|$ given in (9.60), $\overline{u'^2}$ by $u_0'^2$, Ω by ω_0, and λ_0 by h. Thus we find that $|C_\alpha|$ should be of the order of $\mu\sigma_0 u_0'^2 \omega_0 \tau_{\mathrm{cor}}^2 R/h$. Depending on whether the data for granules or supergranules are used the last expression takes the values 10 or 10^2, respectively. Thus we have good reasons to assume that $|C_\alpha|$ at least exceeds the order of unity.

From a similar estimate for C_δ it may be concluded that $|C_\delta/C_\alpha|$ is of the order of $(\mu\sigma\lambda_{\mathrm{cor}}^2/\tau_{\mathrm{cor}})^{-1}\, h/R$. With the above data this expression is definitely smaller than 10^{-10}. Hence, $|C_\delta|$ is much smaller than $|C_\alpha|$.

Finally, s and g prove to be of the same order of magnitude. Since σ_0 was chosen to be of the order of σ_{T}, we may conclude that s, and therefore g too, must be in the order of unity.

We have to ask now which type of dynamo mechanism is responsible for the solar magnetic field. The α^2-mechanism can be ruled out. There is no hint that it is able to maintain axisymmetric fields with an oscillatory dependence on time. Thus the $\alpha\omega$ and $\delta\omega$-mechanisms have to be considered.

In all models elaborated up to now an $\alpha\omega$-mechanism has been supposed. Comparing the results given in section 16.4. with the above estimates of C_α and C_ω we see that this mechanism is able to maintain magnetic fields which show the wanted symmetries with respect to the axis of rotation and the equatorial plane and also an oscillatory dependence on time. We recall the example originating from Steenbeck and Krause [6] illustrated by figure 16.13. The period of oscillation is given by $2\pi\mu\sigma_0 R^2/\Omega$, i.e., with the above data, $(4.8 \cdot 10^4/\Omega)$ years, and so for this example we find a period of 80 years, which is at least of the required order of magnitude.

We are now faced with the question whether models of this kind also reflect the equatorward migration of the toroidal field belts during each half-cycle as indicated by Maunder's butterfly diagram. For special models such diagrams have been calculated on the basis of the assumption that sunspots only occur in those regions where the magnitude of the toroidal field in a certain depth exceeds a critical value. For the model illustrated in figure 16.13 the calculated butterfly diagram is given in figure 17.2. It shows an impressive similarity with that derived from observations.

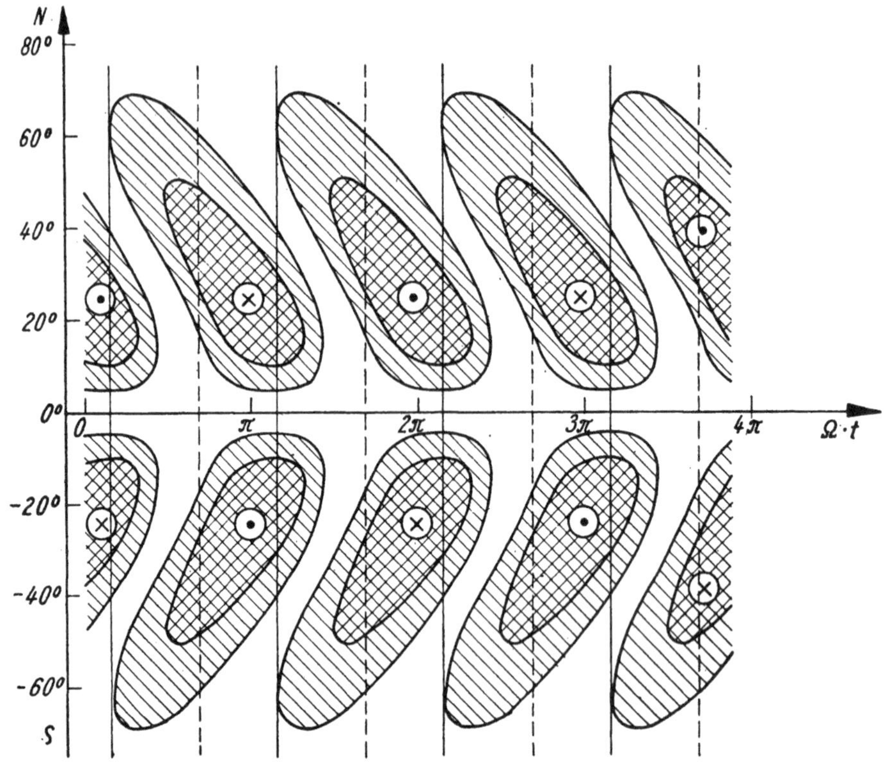

Fig. 17.2. Butterfly diagram calculated for a model with a pure $\alpha\omega$-mechanism mentioned in section 16.4. and illustrated by figure 16.13. The hatched area corresponds to $B_t > \frac{1}{3} B_{t\,max}$, the cross-hatched area to $B_t > \frac{2}{3} B_{t\,max}$, where B_t is the magnitude of the toroidal field and $B_{t\,max}$ its maximum value for all space and time

Many efforts have been made in order to find models which reflect as many features of the observational material as possible. We again refer to the investigations by Roberts and Stix [2], Roberts [4], Yoshimura [2, 4, 5], Köhler [1], Stix [4, 6], Deinzer, v. Kusserow and Stix [1], Jepps [1], and Ivanova and Ruzmaikin [1, 2, 3]. A survey of the essential findings concerning solar dynamo models has been given by Stix [7].

Only one of these findings shall be explained here. It is apparently a general rule that the requirement of an equatorward migration of the toroidal field belts is only fulfilled if the signs of α^+ and $\partial\omega/\partial r$ in the northern hemisphere coincide; in this context $\partial\omega/\partial\vartheta$ plays a minor role.

According to the considerations of section 9.1., illustrated by figure 9.1, there are preferably left-handed helical motions in the northern hemisphere. This suggests that α^+ in this hemisphere is positive. Besides, the same conclusion may be drawn from the requirement that the phase relation between the toroidal and the poloidal field agrees with the observations; see Stix [7].

In this way we arrive at the requirement that $\partial\omega/\partial r$ is mainly positive. We remark that this result of the dynamo theory is in conflict with some of the theoretical investigations on the differential rotation of the convection zone according to which $\partial\omega/\partial r$ is mainly negative.

Like the $\alpha\omega$-mechanism also the $\delta\omega$-mechanism is able to maintain oscillatory magnetic fields. According to the above considerations, however, $|C_\alpha|$ is much greater than $|C_\delta|$. For this reason it is not very likely that the $\delta\omega$-mechanism is responsible for the solar magnetic field. Besides, according to an investigation by Stix [6] this mechanism hardly provides an equatorward migration of the toroidal field belts.

17.5. Observational facts on magnetic fields of stellar objects

At several stars too magnetic fields have been observed. In almost all cases the existence of these fields has been concluded from the Zeeman displacement of the spectral lines. Compared with the situation at the Sun, the corresponding investigations of stars are more difficult. Of course, only a relatively weak radiation flux can be received. In addition to this, the radiation flux always represents an integral over the radiation originating from different places of the stellar surface with different magnetic flux densities, motions and other properties so that the influence of the Zeeman effect on the spectral lines is rather complicated and can be obscured by the Doppler and other effects. That is why even under the best conditions only global fields of the order of 10^2 G can be detetced. If the Sun were so far away that it appeared like a star, there would be almost no chance of finding any magnetic field. The existence of very strong magnetic fields of stars with flux densities of more than 10^7 G can also be concluded from the polarization in the continuous spectrum.

Most of the stars on which magnetic fields were detected are, according to their spectral type, to be classified as Ap-stars. There are about one hundred such stars for which magnetic fields could be measured. The flux densities are of the orders of 10^3 or 10^4 G. But by no means all stars of this spectral type show discernable magnetic fields. The majority of the fields detected vary periodically in time with periods of the order of some days. The most probable explanation of this variation consists in the concept of a non-axisymmetric rotator. It is assumed that the magnetic field considerably deviates from the symmetry with respect to the axis of rotation; in a very simple example the field may correspond to a dipole which lies in the equatorial plane. Then, due to the rotation of the star, a non-corotating observer would register periodic variations of the field. A remarkable property of these stars with magnetic fields is the fact that some elements occur in anomalous abundances, especially rare earths. In some cases the abundances vary in time, then always having the same period as the magnetic field. It is probably the magnetic field that somehow causes a non-uniform distribution of those elements at the surface. Due to the rotation and this non-uniform distribution variations of abundances occur.

Among the white dwarfs too some objects with strong magnetic fields have been found. The flux densities are of the order of some 10^6 up to 10^8 G. As for the geometrical structure and the time dependence of these fields, no reliable information has been available up to now.

It should be added that for pulsars very strong magnetic fields are assumed because otherwise some observed phenomena like deceleration and the synchrotron radiation could not be explained. Flux densities of up to 10^{12} or 10^{13} G and field structures which correspond to an oblique rotator have been envisaged.

17.6. Remarks on dynamo mechanisms on magnetic stars

As explained in section 11.1. magnetic fields as observed on magnetic stars may exist for several reasons. The assumption that they are maintained by dynamo mechanisms is by no means imperative. As long as no observational evidence is given for time variations other than those due to rotation, the magnetic fields of Ap-stars can be considered to be primordial. Nevertheless, we shall deal here only with the possibility of magnetic fields generated by internal motions.

It seems reasonable to assume that the gravitational energy of magnetic stars is large compared with their magnetic and rotational energies, of which the latter is large compared with the first. As a consequence we consider a magnetic star to be a spherical body and assume that internal motions exist which show some symmetry with respect to the axis of rotation and the equatorial plane. More precisely, models as described in section 15.1. are envisaged. We have to look for dynamo mechanisms which are able to maintain non-axisymmetric magnetic fields.

Let us first consider the case where the motions show no fluctuating part. Then a dynamo might only be possible by virtue of meridional circulations; of course, it may be modified by the presence of differential rotation. As can be concluded from Cowling's theorem the magnetic field generated by a dynamo of that kind cannot contain any axisymmetric part. In particular, if in the multipole expansion a dipole occurs it must lie in the equatorial plane.

If fluctuating motions are present, turbulent dynamo mechanisms are to be envisaged, i.e. the α^2, $\alpha\omega$, and $\delta\omega$-mechanisms. According to the results presented in the foregoing, however, non-axisymmetric fields are only to be expected in the case of α^2-mechanisms. Thus we have to require that the rotational shear is not too strong. More precisely, $|C_\omega|$ may by no means exceed the order of 10^3. We recall that for the solar differential rotation $|C_\omega|$ is hardly smaller than $5 \cdot 10^4$. Therefore the turbulent dynamo mechanisms under consideration can only provide non-axisymmetric fields in the case of rather small deviations from a non-uniform rotation.

Since the magnetic fields on Ap-stars are rather strong, their influence on the motions may play an important role. Like these fields the internal motions too will then considerably deviate from symmetry with respect to the axis of rotation. However it cannot be expected that the symmetry with respect to the equatorial plane is broken too. Apart from the special case in which the excitation conditions for different magnetic field modes coincide, fields showing symmetry with respect to the equatorial plane will be generated. This symmetry will not be destroyed by the interaction of magnetic fields and motions.

These considerations suggest that observational data of magnetic stars should be interpreted in terms of field configurations which show symmetry with respect to the equatorial plane; cf. Krause [4] and Krause and Oetken [1]. Thus the 'symmetric rotator' constitutes an alternative to the 'oblique rotator', which has been preferred until now. The incompleteness of accessible observational data is the reason that for the time being neither model can be made solely compulsory. A detailed analysis of the most thoroughly investigated Ap-stars was carried out by Oetken [1, 2] relying on the assumption of equatorial symmetry as well for the magnetic fields as for the element inhomogeneities. In this way a close connection between the geometrical structures of both these quantities becomes visible which promises an access to a better understanding of the mechanisms producing the anomalous structures of these cosmical objects.

BIBLIOGRAPHY

For the papers denoted by an asterisk, which were written in German, a translation into English has been given by ROBERTS *and* STIX [1].

ACUNA, M. H., and N. F. NESS:
[1] The main magnetic field of Jupiter. J. Geophys. Res **81** (1976) 2917—2922
ALEMANY, A., R. MOREAU, P. L. SULEM and U. FRISCH:
[1] Influence of an external magnetic field on homogeneous mhd turbulence. J. Mécanique **18** (1979) 277—313
ANDRÉ, J. D., and M. LESIEUR:
[1] Evolution of high Reynolds number isotropic three-dimensional turbulence; influence of helicity. J. Fluid Mech. **81** (1977) 187—208
ANGEL, J. R. P.:
[1] Strong magnetic fields in White Dwarfs. Ann. New York Acad. Sci. **257** (1975) 80—81
BABCOCK, H. D.:
[1] The Sun's polar magnetic field. Astrophys. J. **130** (1959) 364—380
BABCOCK, H. W.:
[1] Zeeman effect in stellar spectra. Astrophys. J. **105** (1947) 105—119
[2] The topology of the Sun's magnetic field and the 22-year cycle. Astrophys. J. **133** (1961) 572—587
BABCOCK, H. W., and H. D. BABCOCK:
[1] Mapping the magnetic fields of the Sun. In "The Sun", ed. G. R. KUIPER, Univ. of Chicago Press 1953, 70—710
[2] The Sun's magnetic field 1952—1954. Astrophys. J. **121** (1955) 349—366
BACKUS, G. E.:
[1] The axisymmetric self-excited fluid dynamo. Astrophys. J. **125** (1957) 500—524
[2] A class of self-sustaining dissipative spherical dynamos. Ann. Phys. **4** (1958) 372—447
BACKUS, G. E., and S. CHANDRASEKHAR:
[1] On Cowling's theorem on the impossibility of self-maintained axisymmetric homogeneous dynamos. Proc. Nat. Acad. Sci. **42** (1956) 105—109
BATCHELOR, G. K.:
[1] On the spontaneous magnetic field in a conducting liquid in turbulent motion. Proc. Roy. Soc. **A 201** (1950) 405—416
[2] The theory of homogeneous turbulence. Cambridge Univ. Press 1953
BEVIR, M. K.:
[1] Possibility of electromagnetic self-excitation in liquid metal flows in fast reactors. J. Brit. Nuclear Soc. **4** (1973) 455—458

BIERMANN, L.:
[1] Bemerkungen über das Rotationsgesetz in irdischen und stellaren Instabilitätszonen. Z. Astrophys. **28** (1951) 304—309

BOCHNER, S.:
[1] Monotone Funktionen, Stieltjessche Integrale und harmonische Analyse. Math. Ann. **108** (1933) 378—410

BRAGINSKIJ, S. I.: (БРАГИНСКИЙ, С. И.):
[1] О самовозбуждении магнитного поля при движении хорошо проводящей жидкости. ЖЭТФ **47** (1964) 1084—1098 (Self excitation of a magnetic field during the motion of a highly conducting fluid. Sov. Phys.-JETP **20** (1964) 726—735)
[2] К теории гидромагнитного динамо. ЖЭТФ **47** (1964) 2178—2193 (Theory of the hydromagnetic dynamo. Sov. Phys.-JETP **20** (1964) 1462—1471)
[3] Кинематические модели гидромагнитного динамо земли. Геомагн. и Аэрономия **4** (1964) 732—747 (Kinematic models of the Earth's hydromagnetic dynamo. Geomagn. Aeron. **4** (1964) 572—583)
[4] Магнитогидродинамика земного ядра. Геомагн. и Аэрономия **4** (1964) 898—916 (Magnetohydrodynamics of the Earth's core. Geomagn. Aeron. **4** (1964) 698—711)
[5] Об основах теории гидромагнитного динамо земли. Геомагн. и Аэрономия **7** (1967) 401—410 (Principles of the theory of the Earth's hydromagnetic dynamo. Geomagn. Aeron. **7** (1967) 323—329)
[6] Магнитные вольны в ядре земли. Геомагн. и Аэрономия **7** (1967) 1050—1060 (Magnetic waves in the Earth's core. Geomagn. Aeron. **7** (1967) 851—859)
[7] Магнитогидродинамические крутильные колебания в земном ядре и вариации длины суток. Геомагн. и Аэрономия **10** (1970) 1—12 (Torsional magnetohydrodynamic vibrations in the Earth's core and variations in day length. Geomagn. Aeron. **10** (1970) 1—8)
[8] О спектре колебаний гидромагнитного динамо земли. Геомагн. и Аэрономия **10** (1970) 221—233 (Oscillation spectrum of the hydromagnetic dynamo of the Earth. Geomagn. Aeron. **10** (1970) 172—181)
[9] Почти аксиально-симметричная модель гидромагнитного динамо земли. 1. Геомагн. и Аэрономия **15** (1975) 149—156
[10] On the nearly axially-symmetrical model of the hydromagnetic dynamo of the Earth. Phys. Earth and Plan. Int. **11** (1976) 191—199

BRÄUER, H. J.:
[1] Some properties of the Green's tensor of the induction equation. ZAMM **53** (1973) 719—722
[2] The non-linear dynamo problem: Small oscillatory solutions in a strongly simplified model. Astron, Nachr. **300** (1979) 43-49

BRÄUER, H. J., and F. KRAUSE:
[1] Remark on the mean energy of the fluctuating magnetic field in mean-field magnetohydrodynamics. Astron. Nachr. **294** (1973) 179—182
[2] The mean energy of a decaying magnetic field in mhd-turbulence. Astron. Nachr. **295** (1974) 223—228

BRISSAUD, A., U. FRISCH, J. LEORAT, M. LESIEUR and A. MAZURE:
[1] Helicity cascades in fully developed isotropic turbulence. Phys. Fluids **16** (1973) 1366—1367

BULLARD, E. C., and H. GELLMAN:
[1] Homogeneous dynamos and terrestrial magnetism. Phil. Trans. Roy. Soc. **A 247** (1954) 213–278

BULLARD, E. C., and D. GUBBINS:
[1] Generation of magnetic fields by fluid motions of global scale. Geophys. Fluid Dyn. **8** (1977) 43–56

BUMBA, V.:
[1] Development of spot group areas in dependence on the local magnetic field. Bull. Astron. Inst. Czech. **14** (1963) 91–97

BUSSE, F. H.:
[1] Steady fluid flow in a precessing spheroidal shell. J. Fluid Mech. **33** (1968) 739–751
[2] Thermal instabilities in rapidly rotating systems. J. Fluid Mech. **44** (1970) 441–460
[3] Generation of magnetic fields by convection. J. Fluid Mech. **57** (1973) 529–544
[4] A necessary condition for the geodynamo. J. Geophys. Res. **80** (1975) 278–280
[5] A model of the geodynamo. Geophys. J. Roy. Astr. Soc. **42** (1975) 437–459
[6] Generation of planetary magnetism by convection. Phys. Earth Planet. Int. **12** (1976) 350–358
[7] Mathematical problems of dynamo theory. In "Applications of bifurcation theory", Academic Press Inc. New York-San Francisco-London 1977, 175–202
[8] An example of non-linear dynamo action. J. Geophys. **43** (1977) 441–452

CHILDRESS, S.:
[1] Théorie magnétohydrodynamique de l'effet dynamo. Report from Département Méchanique de la Faculté des Sciences Paris 1969

COWLING, T. G.:
[1] The magnetic fields of sunspots. Mon. Not. Roy. Astr. Soc. **94** (1934) 39–48
[2] On the Sun's general magnetic field. Mon. Not. Roy. Astr. Soc. **105** (1945) 166–174
[3] Solar electrodynamics. In "The Sun", ed. G. P. KUIPER, Univ. Chicago Press 1953, 532–591
[4] The axisymmetric dynamo. Mon. Not. Roy. Astr. Soc. **140** (1968) 547–548
[5] Sunspots and the solar cycle. Nature **255** (1975) 189–190

CRAMER, H.:
[1] On the theory of stationary random processes. Annals of Mathematics **41** (1940) 215–230

CSADA, I. K.:
[1] On the magnetic effect of turbulence in ionized gases. Acta Phys. Hung. **1** (1951) 235–246

DEINZER, W.:
[1] Zur Theorie des solaren Magnetfeldes. Mitt. Astron. Gesellsch. **30** (1971) 67–74

DEINZER, W., and M. STIX:
[1] On the eigenvalues of Krause-Steenbeck's solar dynamo. Astron. & Astrophys. **12** (1971) 111–119

DEINZER, W., H. U. VON KUSSEROW and M. STIX:
[1] Gibt es auch stationäre $\alpha\omega$-Dynamos? Mitt. Astron. Gesellsch. **34** (1973) 155–158
[2] Steady and oscillatory $\alpha\omega$-dynamos. Astron. & Astrophys. **36** (1974) 69–78

DEISSLER, R. G.:
[1] Magneto-fluid dynamic turbulence with a uniform imposed magnetic field. Phys. Fluids **6** (1963) 1250—1259

DOLGINOV, A. Z. (Долгинов, А. З.):
[1] Приливные течения в компонентах двойных звёзд с осью вращения наклонной к орбите и генерация магнитного поля. Астрон. Ж. **51** (1974) 388—394
[2] Генерация магнитного поля и ускорение заряженных частиц в двойных звёздных системах. Изв. АН. Серия Физическая **39** (1975) 354—358
[3] Генерация магнитного поля в двойных звёздах и звёздах, окруженных оболочкой. Магнитные Ар-Звёзды, Издательство ,,Элм", Baku 1975, 147—150

DOLGINOV, SH. SH. (Долгинов, Ш. Ш.):
[1] Магнетизм планет и проблема механизма динамо. Препринт № 15, ИЗМИРАН, Moscow 1976 (Planetary magnetism and dynamo mechanism problem. Preprint Nr. 15a, IZMIRAN Moscow 1976)

DROBYSHEVSKIJ, E. M., and V. S. YUFEREV:
[1] Topological pumping of magnetic flux by three-dimensional convection. J. Fluid Mech. **65** (1974) 33—44

ELSASSER, W. M.:
[1] Induction effects in terrestrial magnetism. Phys. Rev. **69** (1946) 106—116
[2] Hydromagnetic dynamo theory. Rev. Mod. Phys. **28** (1956) 135—163
[3] The terrestrial dynamo. Proc. Nat. Acad. Sci. **43** (1957) 14—24

FRAZER, M. C.:
[1] The dynamo problem and the geomagnetic field. Contemp. Phys. **14** (1973) 213—228

FRENKEL, YA. I. (Френкель, Я. И.):
[1] О происхождении земного магнетизма. ДАН **49** (1945) 98—101

FRISCH, U., J. LÉORAT, A. MAZURE and A. POUQUET:
[1] Possibility of an inverse cascade of magnetic helicity in magnetohydrodynamic turbulence. J. Fluid Mech. **68** (1975) 769—778

FYFE, D., and D. MONTGOMERY:
[1] High-beta turbulence in two-dimensional magnetohydrodynamics. J. Plasma Physics **16** (1976) 181—191

GAILITIS, A.: (Гаилитис, А.):
[1] Условия самовозбуждения лабораторной модели геомагнитного динамо. Магнитная Гидродинамика **1967**, **3**, 45—54
[2] Самовозбуждение магнитного поля парой кольцевых вихрей. Магнитная Гидродинамика **1970**, **1**, 19—22 (Self-excitation of a magnetic field by a pair of annular vortices. Magnetohydrodynamics **6** (1970) 14—17)
[3] К теории динамо Герценберга. Магнитная Гидродинамика **1973**, **4**, 12—16
[4] О генерации магнитного поля зеркало-симметричной турбулентностью. Магнитная Гидродинамика **1974**, **2**, 31—35

GAILITIS, A., and YA. FREIBERG (Гаилитис, А., и Я. Фрейберг):
[1] Самовозбуждение магнитного поля парой колбцевих вихрей. Магнитная Гидродинамика **1974**, **1**, 37—42

[2] К теории винтого МГД-линамо. Магнитная Гидродинамика **1976, 2,** 3–6

[3] Расчёт динамо-неустойчивости винтого потока. АН ЛатвССР Инст. Физ. Рига, ,,Зинатне'' (1977) 1–48

GAILITIS, A., and O. LIELAUSIS (ГАИЛИТИС, А., и О. ЛИЕЛАУСИС):

[1] Теория МГД-динамо и лабораторный эксперимент. In: ,,Магнитные Ар-Звёзды'', Издателбство ,,Элм'', Baku 1975, 140–146

GAILITIS, A., O. LIELAUSIS and YA. FREIBERG: (ГАИЛИТИС, А., О. ЛИЕЛАУСИС и Я. ФРЕЙБЕРГ):

[1] О путах наблюдения генерации магнитного поля в потоках жидкого натрия. Препринт № 1 (1977), АН ЛатвССР Инст. Физ. Рига, 1–35

GIBSON, R. D.:

[1] The Herzenberg dynamo. I. Q. J. Mech. Appl. Math. **21** (1968) 243–255

[2] The Herzenberg dynamo. II. Q. J. Mech. Appl. Math. **21** (1968) 257–287

GIBSON, R. D., and P. H. ROBERTS:

[1] Some comments on the theory of homogeneous dynamos. In: Magnetism and the Cosmos, eds. W. R. HINDMARSH, F. J. LOWES, P. H. ROBERTS and S. K. RUNCORN, Oliver & Boyd Ltd., Edinburgh 1967, 108–120

[2] The Bullard-Gellman dynamo. In: The Application of Modern Physics to the Earth and Planetary Interiors, ed. S. K. RUNCORN, Wiley Interscience 1969, 577–601

GILLILAND, J. M.:

[1] Mean-field electrodynamics and dynamo theories of planetary magnetic fields. Thesis, University of Alberta (Edmonton, Canada) 1973

GOLITSYN, G. S. (Голицин, Г. С.):

[1] Флуктуации магнитного поля и плотности тока в турбулентном потоке слабо проводящей жидкости. ДАН **132** (1960) 315–318 (Fluctuations of the magnetic field and current density in a turbulent flow of a weakly conducting fluid. Sov. Phys. Dokl. **5** (1960), 536–539)

GREENSPAN, H.:

[1] On α-dynamos. Studies in Appl. Math. **13** (1974) 35–43

GUBBINS, D.:

[1] Kinematic dynamos and geomagnetism. Nature Phys. Sci. **238** (1972) 119-122

[2] Numerical solutions of the kinematic dynamo problem. Phil. Trans. Roy. Soc. **A 274** (1973) 493–521

[3] Theories of the geomagnetic and the solar dynamo. Revs. Geophys. Space Phys. **12** (1974) 137–154

[4] Dynamo action of isotropically driven motions of a rotating fluid. Studies in Appl. Math. 8 (1974) 157-164

[5] Observational constraints on the generation process of the Earth's magnetic field. Geophys. J. Roy. Astr. Soc. **47** (1976) 19-39

GUREVICH, L. S., and A. I. LEBEDINSKIJ (ГУРЕВИЧ, Л. Э., и А. И. ЛЕБЕДИНСКИЙ):

[1] Магнитное поле солнечных пятен. ДАН **49** (1945) 92–94

HELMIS, G.:

[1] Untersuchungen zur Elektrodynamik turbulent bewegter leitender Medien unter Berücksichtigung des Halleffektes. Mon.ber. dtsch. Akad. Wiss. Berlin **10** (1968) 280–291

[2] Zur Elektroydnamik turbulent bewegter leitender Medien unter Berücksichtigung des Halleffektes. Cosmic Electrodynamics **2** (1971) 197–210

[3] Zum Halleffekt in der Elektrodynamik turbulent bewegter leitender Medien Beitr. Plasma Physik **11** (1971) 417—430

HERZENBERG, A.:

[1] Geomagnetic dynamos. Phil. Trans. Roy. Soc. **A 250** (1958) 543—583

IVANOVA, T. S. (ИВАНОВА, Т. С.):

[1] Метод решения задачи магнитогидродинамического динамо. Ж. Вычисл. Матем. Физ. **16** (1976) 958—968

IVANOVA, T. S., and A. A. RUZMAIKIN (ИВАНОВА, Т. С., и А. А. РУЗМАЙКИН):

[1] Магнитогидродинамическая динамо-модель солнечного цикла. Астрон. Ж. **53** (1976) 398—410

[2] Нелинейная стабилизация колебаний в мгд-динамо солнца. Препринт Ин-та прикл. Математики АН СССР, № 47, 1976

[3] Нелинейная магнитогидродинамическая модель динамо солнца. Астрон. Ж. **54** (1977) 846—858

JEPPS, S. A.:

[1] Numerical models of hydromagnetic dynamos. J. Fluid Mech. **67** (1975) 629—646

KAZANTSEV, A. P. (КАЗАНЦЕВ, А. П.):

[1] Об усленнии магнитного поля проводящей жидкостью. ЖЭТФ **53** (1967) 1806—1813 (Enhancement of a magnetic field by a conducting fluid. Sov. Phys.-JETP **26** (1968) 1031—1034)

KIPPENHAHN, R., and C. MÖLLENHOFF:

[1] Elementare Plasmaphysik. Bibliographisches Institut Mannheim - Wien - Zürich 1975

KIT, L. G., and A. B. TSINOBER (КИТ, Л. Г., и А. Б. ЦИНОБЕР):

[1] О возможности создания и исследования двумерной турбулентности в сильном магнитном поле. Магнитная Гидродинамика **1971, 3,** 27—34

KÖHLER, H.:

[1] The solar dynamo and estimates of the magnetic diffusivity and the α-effect. Astron. & Astrophys. **25** (1973) 467—476

KOLESNIKOV, YU. B. (КОЛЕСНИКОВ, Ю. Б.):

[1] Двумерное турбулентное течение в канале с неоднородной электропроводностью стенок. Магнитная Гидродинамика **1972, 3,** 32—36

KOLESNIKOV, YU. B., and A. B. TSINOBER (КОЛЕСНИКОВ, Ю. Б., и А. Б. ЦИНОБЕР):

[1] Двумерное турбулентное течение за круглым цилиндром. Магнитная Гидродинамика **1972, 3,** 23—31

[2] Экспериментальное исследование двумерной турбулентности за решеткой. Изв. АН СССР, Механика жидкости и газа **1974, 4,** 146—150

KRAICHNAN, R. H.:

[1] Inertial-range spectrum of hydrodmagnetic turbulence. Phys. Fluids **8** (1965) 1385—1387

[2] Helical turbulence and absolute equilibrium. J. Fluid Mech. **59** (1973) 745—752

[3] Diffusion of weak magnetic fields by isotropic turbulence. J. Fluid Mech. **75** (1976) 657—676

[4] Diffusion of passive-scalar and magnetic fields by helical turbulence. J. Fluid Mech. **77** (1976) 753—768

KRAICHNAN, R. H., and S. NAGARAJAN:

[1] Growth of turbulent magnetic fields. Phys. Fluids **10** (1967) 859—870

KRAUSE, F.:

[1]* Eine Lösung des Dynamoproblems auf der Grundlage einer linearen Theorie der magnetohydrodynamischen Turbulenz. Habilitationsschrift, Univ. Jena 1967

[2] Zum Anfangswertproblem der magnetohydrodynamischen Induktionsgleichung. ZAMM **48** (1968) 333–343

[3] Explanation of stellar and planetary magnetic fields by dynamo action of turbulent motions. Acta Univ. Wratislaviensis **77** (1969) 157–170

[4] Zur Dynamotheorie magnetischer Sterne: Der „symmetrische Rotator" als Alternative zum „schiefen Rotator". Astron. Nachr. **293** (1971) 187–193

[5] Heat flow and magnetic field diffusion in turbulent fluids. Astron. Nachr. **294** (1972) 83–87

[6] The turbulent emf $\overline{\boldsymbol{u}' \times \boldsymbol{B}'}$ in the case of non-vanishing mean flow. ZAMM **53** (1973) 479–481

[7] The present status of mean-field magnetohydrodynamics and the turbulent dynamo problem. Ann. New York Acad. Sc. **257** (1975) 156–172

[8] Динамотеория. In: Магнитные Ар-Звёзды, Издательство „Элм", Baku 1975, 129–138

[9] Annotation on the paper "The turbulent emf $\overline{\boldsymbol{u}' \times \boldsymbol{B}'}$ in the case of non-vanishing mean flow". ZAMM **56** (1976) 172–173

[10] Mean-field magnetohydrodynamics of the solar convection zone. In: Basic Mechanism of Solar Activity, eds. V. Bumba and J. Kleczek, D. Reidel Publishing Company, Dordrecht-Holland 1976, 309–321

[11] Mean-field electrodynamics and dynamo theory of the Earth's magnetic field. Journ. Geophys. **43** (1977) 421–440

Krause, F., and H. Hiller:

[1] Zur Dynamotheorie stellarer und planetarer Magnetfelder. III. Über die Lösung des Eigenwertproblemes und die Berechnung der Feldgrößen. Astron. Nachr. **291** (1969) 271–286

Krause, F., and L. Oetken:

[1] On equatorially-symmetric models for magnetic stars as suggested by dynamo theory. In: Physics of Ap-stars, IAU-Colloqu. Nr. 32, eds. W. W. Weiss, H. Jenkner and H. J. Wood, Vienna 1976, 29–36

Krause, F., and K.-H. Rädler:

[1] Dynamo theory of the Sun's general magnetic field on the basis of a mean-field magnetohydrodynamics. In: Solar Magnetic Fields, ed. R. Howard, Reidel Publishing Company, Dordrecht-Holland 1971, 770–779

[2] Elektrodynamik der mittleren Felder in turbulenten leitenden Medien und Dynamotheorie. In: Ergebnisse der Plasmaphysik und der Gaselektronik. Bd. II, eds. R. Rompe and M. Steenbeck, Akademie-Verlag Berlin 1971, 1–154

Krause, F., K.-H. Rädler and G. Rüdiger:

[1] Über die Bedeutung des Nichols-Tolman-Effektes für das Zustandekommen kosmischer Magnetfelder. Gerlands Beitr. Geophys. **85** (1976) 26–34

Krause, F., and P. H. Roberts:

[1] Some problems of mean-field electrodynamics. Astrophys. J. **191** (1973) 977–992

[2] Bochner's theorem and mean-field electrodynamics. Mathematika **20** (1973) 24–33

[3] Comments on the paper "On the application of Cramer's theorem to axisymmetric incompressible turbulence" by I. Lerche. Astrophys. Space Sc. **22** (1973) 193–195

[4] The high-conductivity limit in mean-field electrodynamics. J. Math. Phys. **17** (1976) 1808–1809

KRAUSE, F., and G. RÜDIGER:
[1] On the turbulent decay of strong magnetic fields and the development of sunspots areas. Solar Physics **42** (1975) 107—119

KRAUSE, F., and M. STEENBECK:
[1] Models of magnetohydrodynamic dynamos for alternating fields. Czech. Slov. Acad. Sc. Astron. Inst. Publ. **51** (1964) 36—38
[2]* Untersuchung der Dynamowirkung einer nichtspiegelsymmetrischen Turbulenz an einfachen Modellen. Z. f. Naturf. **22a** (1960) 671—675

KROPATSHEV, E. P., S. N. GORSHKOV and P. M. SEREBRYANAYA (КРОПАЧЕВ. Э. П., С.Н. ГОРШКОВ и П. М. СЕРЕБРЯНАЯ):
[1] Модель кинематического динамо трёх сферических вихрей. I. Геомагн. и Аэрономия **17** (1977) 507—511
[2] Модель кинематического динамо трёх сферических вихрей. II. Геомагн. и Аэрономия **17** (1977) 927—929

KUMAR, S., and P. H. ROBERTS:
[1] A three-dimensional kinematic dynamo. Proc. Roy. Soc. **A 344** (1975) 239—258

LANDSTREET, J. D., and J. R. P. ANGEL:
[1] The polarisation spectrum and magnetic field strength of the White Dwarf Grw + 70° 8247. Astrophys. J. **196** (1974) 819—825

LARMOR, J.:
[1] How-could a rotating body such as the Sun become a magnet? Rep. Brit. Assoc. Adv. Sc. 1919, 159—160

LEHNERT, B.:
[1] The decay of magnetoturbulence in the presence of a magnetic field and Coriolis force. Qu. J. Appl. Math. **12** (1955) 321—341

LEIGHTON, R. B.:
[1] Transport of magnetic fields on the Sun. Astrophys. J. **140** (1964) 1547—1562
[2] A magneto-kinematic model of the solar cycle. Astrophys. J. **156** (1969) 1—26

LÉORAT, J.:
[1] La turbulence magnétohydrodynamique hélicitaire et la géneration des champs magnétique a grande échelle. Thése doctoral, Univ. de Paris VII, 1975

LÉORAT, J., U. FRISCH and A. POUQUET:
[1] Helical magnetohydrodynamic turbulence and the non-linear dynamo problem. Ann. New York Acad. Sc. **257** (1975) 173—176

LERCHE, I.:
[1] Kinematic dynamo theory. Astrophys. J. **166** (1971) 627—638
[2] Kinematic dynamo theory. II. Dynamo action in infinite media with isotropic turbulence. Astrophys. J. **166** (1971) 639—649
[3] Kinematic dynamo theory. III. The effect of turbulent diffusivity in the dynamo equations. Astrophys. J. **168** (1971) 115—121
[4] Kinematic dynamo theory. IV. Dynamo action in non-rotating spheres with isotropic turbulence. Astrophys. J. **168** (1971) 123—129
[5] On the applications of Cramer's theorem to axi-symmetric, incompressible turbulence. Astrophys. Space Sc. **19** (1972) 189—193
[6] Kinematic dynamo theory. V. Comments on diverse matters including historical development, isotropic turbulence, and expansion techniques. Astrophys. J. **181** (1973) 993—1002
[7] Reply to foregoing comments. Astrophys. Space Sc. **22** (1973) 197

LERCHE, I., and B.-C. LOW:
[1] Kinematic dynamo action under incompressible, isotropic velocity turbulence. Astrophys. J. **168** (1971) 503—508
LERCHE, I., and E. N. PARKER
[1] The generation of magnetic fields in astrophysical bodies. VII. The internal small scale field. Astrophys. J. **168** (1971) 231—237
LEVY, E. H.:
[1] Effectiveness of cyclonic convection for producing the geomagnetic field. Astrophys. J. **171** (1972) 621—633
[2] Kinematic reversal schemes for the geomagnetic dipole. Astrophys. J. **171** (1972) 635—642
LIELAUSIS, O., A. KLYAVINYA and L. TIMANIS (Лиелаусис, О., А. Клявиня и Л. Тиманис):
[1] О возможности специфических мгд-явлений при жидкометаллическом охлаждении мощных энергетических установок. Аннотация, АН ЛатвССР Инст. Физ. Рига, 1974
LILLEY, F. E. M.:
[1] On kinematic dynamos. Proc. Roy. Soc. **A 316** (1970) 153—167
LORTZ, D.:
[1] Impossibility of steady dynamos with certain symmetries. Phys. Fluids **11** (1968) 913—915
[2] Exact solutions of the hydromagnetic dynamo problem. Plasma Phys. **10** (1968) 967—972
[3] A simple stationary dynamo model. Z. Naturforsch. **27a** (1972) 1350—1354
LOW, B.-C.:
[1] Root mean square fluctuations of a weak magnetic field in an infinite medium of homogeneous stationary turbulence. Astrophys. J. **173** (1972) 549—555
[2] Errata. Astrophys. J. **178** (1972) 277
LOWES, F. J., and I. WILKINSON:
[1] Geomagnetic dynamo: a laboratory model. Nature **198** (1963) 1158—1160
[2] Geomagnetic dynamo: an improved laboratory model. Nature **219** (1968) 717—718
MALKUS, W. V. R., and M. R. E. PROCTOR:
[1] The macrodynamics of α-effect dynamos in rotating fluids. J. Fluid Mech. **67** (1975) 417—444
MEYER, F., and H. U. SCHMIDT:
[1] On the decay of sunspots. Mitt. Astron. Gesellsch. **32** (1973) 174—175
MEYER, F., H. U. SCHMIDT, N. O. WEISS and P. R. WILSON:
[1] The growth and decay of sunspots. Mon. Not. Roy. Astron. Soc. **169** (1974) 35—57
MOFFATT, H. K.:
[1] On the suppression of turbulence by a uniform magnetic field. J. Fluid Mech. **28** (1967) 571—592
[2] Turbulent dynamo action at low magnetic Reynolds number. J. Fluid Mech. **41** (1970) 435—452
[3] Dynamo action associated with random inertial waves in a rotating conducting fluid. J. Fluid Mech. **44** (1970) 705—719
[4] An approach to a dynamic theory of dynamo action in a rotating fluid. J. Fluid Mech. **53** (1972) 385—399
[5] The mean electromotive force generated by turbulence in the limit of perfect conductivity. J. Fluid Mech. **65** (1974) 1—10

[6] Appendix to the paper of Drobyshevski and Yuferev. "Topological pumping of magnetic flux by three-dimensional convection". J. Fluid Mech. **65** (1974) 41—44

[7] Generation of magnetic fields by fluid motion. Adv. Appl. Mech. **16** (1976) 119—181

[8] Magnetic field generation in electrically conducting fluids. Cambridge University Press. Cambridge - London - New York - Melbourne 1978

MOREAU, R.:

[1] Homogeneous turbulence in the presence of a uniform magnetic field when the magnetic Reynolds' number is small. C. R. Acad. Sci. **A 263** (1966) 586—587

[2] Une solution simple pour le déclin de la turbulence homogene en présence d'un champ magnétique uniforme lorsque le nombre de Reynolds magnétique est petit. C. R. Acad. Sci. **A 264** (1967) 75—78

[3] On magnetohydrodynamic turbulence. Proc. Symp. on turbulence of fluids and plasmas, Brooklyn 1968, 359—372

MOSS, D. L.:

[1] A numerical model of hydromagnetic turbulence. Mon. Not. R. astr. Soc. **148** (1970) 173—191

NESTLERODE, I. A., and I. L. LUMLEY:

[1] Initial response of the spectrum of isotropic turbulence to the sudden application of a strong magnetic field. Phys. Fluids **6** (1963) 1260—1262

OETKEN, L.:

[1] An equatorially-symmetric rotator model for magnetic stars. Astron. Nachr. **298** (1977) 197—207

[2] An equatorially-symmetric rotator model for magnetic stars. II. Inhomogeneous element distributions. Astron. Nachr. **300** (1979) 000—000

PARKER, E. N.:

[1] The formation of sunspots from the solar toroidal field. Astrophys. J. **121** (1955) 491—507

[2] Hydromagnetic dynamo models. Astrophys. J. **122** (1955) 293—314

[3] The solar hydromagnetic dynamo. Proc. Nat. Acad. Sci. **43** (1957) 8—13

[4] The dynamical state of the interstellar gas and field. Astrophys. J. **145** (1966) 811—833

[5] The occasional reversal of the geomagnetic field. Astrophys. J. **158** (1969) 815—827

[6] The origin of magnetic fields. Astrophys. J. **160** (1970) 383—404

[7] The generation of magnetic fields in astrophysical bodies. I. The dynamo equation. Astrophys. J. **162** (1970) 665—673

[8] The generation of magnetic fields in astrophysical bodies. II. The galactic field. Astrophys. J. **163** (1971) 255—278

[9] The generation of magnetic fields in astrophysical bodies. III. Turbulent diffusion of fields and efficient dynamos. Astrophys. J. **163** (1971) 279—285

[10] The generation of magnetic fields in astrophysical bodies. IV. The solar and terrestrial dynamos. Astrophys. J. **164** (1971) 491—509

[11] The generation of magnetic fields in astrophysical bodies .V. Behaviour at large dynamo numbers. Astrophys. J. **165** (1971) 139—146

[12] The generation of magnetic fields in astrophysical bodies. VI. Periodic modes of the galactic field. Astrophys. J. **166** (1971) 295—300

[13] The generation of magnetic fields in astrophysical bodies. VIII. Dynamical considerations. Astrophys. J. **168** (1971) 239—249

[14] The generation and dissipation of solar and galactic magnetic fields. Astrophys. Sp. Sci. **22** (1973) 279—291

[15] The dynamo mechanism for the generation of large-scale magnetic fields. Ann. New York Acad. Sc. **257** (1975) 141—155

PEKERIS, C. L., Y. ACCAD and B. SHKOLLER:

[1] Kinematic dynamos and the Earth's magnetic field. Phil. Trans. Roy. Soc. **A 275** (1973) 425—461

PIERSON, E. S.:

[1] Electromagnetic self-excitation in the liquid-metal fast breeder reactor. Nucl. Sc. Engineering **57** (1975) 155—163

PICHAKCHI, L. D. (Пичахчи, Л. Д.):

[1] К теории гидромагнитного динамо. ЖЭТФ **50** (1966) 818—820

PONOMARENKO, YU. B. (Пономаренко, Ю. Б.):

[1] К теории гидромагнитного динамо. ПМТФ **1973, 6,** 47—51

POUQUET, A., U. FRISCH and J. LÉORAT:

[1] Strong mhd turbulence and the nonlinear dynamo effect. J. Fluid Mech. **77** (1976) 321—354

POUQUET, A., and G. S. PATTERSON:

[1] Numerical simulation of helical magnetohydrodynamic turbulence. J. Fluid Mech. **85** (1978) 305—323

PROCTOR, M. R. E.:

[1] Numerical solutions of the nonlinear α-effect dynamo equations. J. Fluid Mech. **80** (1977) 769—784

[2] On the eigenvalues of kinematic α-effect dynamos. Astron. Nachr. **298** (1977) 19—25

RÄDLER, K.-H.:

[1] Analogiebetrachtungen zu ebenen Problemen der Magnetohydrodynamik. Beitr. Plasmaphys. **2** (1964) 21—31

[2] Zur Elektrodynamik turbulent bewegter leitender Medien. Thesis, Univ. Jena 1966

[3]* Zur Elektrodynamik turbulent bewegter leitender Medien. I. Grundzüge der Elektrodynamik der mittleren Felder. Z. f. Naturforsch. **23a** (1968) 1841—1851

[4]* Zur Elektrodynamik turbulent bewegter leitender Medien. II. Turbulenzbedingte Leitfähigkeits- und Permeabilitätsänderungen. Z. f. Naturforsch. **23a** (1968) 1851—1860

[5] On some electromagnetic phenomena in electrically conducting turbulently moving matter, especially in the presence of Coriolis forces. Geod. Geoph. Veröff. Reihe II, H. 13 (1969) 131—135

[6]* Zur Elektrodynamik in turbulenten, Coriolis-Kräften unterworfenen leitenden Medien. Mber. dtsch. Akad. Wiss. Berlin **11** (1969) 194—201

[7]* Über eine neue Möglichkeit eines Dynamomechanismus in turbulenten leitenden Medien. Mber. dtsch. Akad. Wiss. Berlin **11** (1969) 272—279

[8]* Untersuchung eines Dynamomechanismus in turbulenten leitenden Medien. Mber. dtsch. Akad. Wiss. Berlin **12** (1970) 468—472

[9] Zur Dynamotheorie kosmischer Magnetfelder. I. Gleichungen für sphärische Dynamomodelle. Astron. Nachr. **294** (1973) 213—223

[10] Zur Dynamotheorie kosmischer Magnetfelder. II. Darstellung von Vektorfeldern als Summe aus einem poloidalen und einem toroidalen Anteil. Astron. Nachr. **295** (1974) 73—84

[11] Über den Korrelationstensor zweiter Stufe für ein inhomogenes turbulentes Geschwindigkeitsfeld. Astron. Nachr. **295** (1974) 85—92

[12] On the influence of a large-scale magnetic field on turbulent motions in an electrically conducting medium. Astron. Nachr. **295** (1974) 265—273
[13] Some new results on the generation of magnetic fields by dynamic action. Mem. Soc. Roy. Sc. Liege **VIII** (1975) 109—116
[14] Замечания о генерировании неосесимметричных магнитных полей при помощи динамомеханизма. In: Магнитные Ар-Звёзды, Издательство ,,Элм'', Baku 1975, 139—140
[15] Mean-field magnetohydrodynamics as a basis of solar dynamo theory. In: Basic Mechanism of Solar Activity, eds. V. Bumba and J. Kleczek, D. Reidel Publishing Company, Dordrecht-Holland 1976, 323—344
[16] Mean-field approach to spherical dynamo models. Astron. Nachr. **301** (1980), in print
[17] Investigations of spherical mean-field dynamo models. Astron. Nachr. **301** (1980), in print

Roberts, G. O.:
[1] Spatially periodic dynamos. Phil. Trans. Roy. Soc. **A 266** (1970) 535—558
[2] Dynamo action of fluid motions with two-dimensional periodicity. Phil. Trans. Roy. Soc. **A 271** (1972) 411—454

Roberts, P. H.:
[1] An introduction to magnetohydrodynamics. Longmans, Green and Co. Ltd, London, 1967
[2] The dynamo problem. Woods Hole Oceanographic Inst. Rep. 67—54 (1967) 51—165
[3] Dynamo theory. In: Lectures on Applied Mathematics, ed. W. H. Reid, Amer. Mathematics Soc., Providence, R. I. **14** (1971) 129—206
[4] Kinematic dynamo models. Phil. Trans. Roy. Soc. **A 272** (1972) 663—703

Roberts, P. H., and A. M. Soward:
[1] Magnetohydrodynamics of the Earth's core. Ann. Rev. Fluid Mech. **4** (1972) 117—154
[2] On first order smoothing theory. J. Math. Phys. **16** (1975) 609—615
[3] A unified approach to mean-field electrodynamics. Astron. Nachr. **269** (1975) 49—64

Roberts, P. H., and M. Stix:
[1] The turbulent dynamo. A translation of a series of papers by F. Krause, K.-H. Rädler and M. Steenbeck. Techn. Note **60** (1971) NCRA Boulder, Colorado
[2] α-effect dynamos by the Bullard-Gellman formalism. Astron. & Astrophys. **18** (1972) 453—466
[3] On Vainshtein's simplest dynamo instability. Phys. Earth Plan. Int. **12** (1976) P19—P21

Rochester, M. G., J. A. Jacobs, D. E. Smylie and K. F. Chong:
[1] Can precession power the geomagnetic dynamo? Geophys. J. Roy. Astron. Soc. **43** (1975) 661—678

Rüdiger, G.:
[1] Behandlung eines einfachen hydromagnetischen Dynamos mittels Linearisierung. Astron. Nachr. **294** (1973) 183—186
[2] The influence of a uniform magnetic field of arbitrary strength on turbulence. Astron. Nachr. **295** (1974) 275—283
[3] Behandlung eines einfachen hydromagnetischen Dynamos mit Hilfe der Gitterpunktmethode. Publ. Astrophys. Obs. Potsdam **32** (1974) 25—29

[4] Die Wechselwirkung zwischen homogener Turbulenz und inhomogenem magnetischen Feld in der Umgebung neutraler Flächen. Astron. Nachr. **296** (1975) 133—141

[5] On α-effect for slow and fast rotation. Astron. Nachr. **299** (1978) 217—222

Schlüter, A., and L. Biermann:

[1] Interstellare Magnetfelder. Z. Naturforsch. **5a** (1950) 237—251

Schumann, U.:

[1] Numerical simulation of the transition from three- to two-dimensional turbulence under a uniform magnetic field. J. Fluid Mech. **74** (1976) 31—58

Soward, A. M.:

[1] Nearly symmetric kinematic and hydromagnetic dynamos. J. Math. Phys. **12** (1971) 1900—1906

[2] Nearly symmetric advection. J. Math. Phys. **12** (1971) 2052—2062

[3] A kinematic theory of large magnetic Reynolds number dynamos. Phil. Trans. Roy. Soc. **A 272** (1972) 431—462

[4] A convection-driven dynamo. I. The weak field case. Phil. Trans. Roy. Soc. **A 275** (1974) 611—651

[5] Random waves and dynamo action. J. Fluid Mech. **69** (1975) 145—177

[6] A thin disc model of the galactic dynamo. Astron. Nachr. **299** (1978) 25—33

Soward, A.M., and P. H. Roberts (Соуорд, А. М., и П. Х. Робертс):

[1] Современое состояние теории мгд-динамо. Магнитная Гидродинамика **1976, 1,** 3—51

Steenbeck, M.:

[1] Probleme und Ergebnisse der Elektro- und Magnetohydrodynamik. Dtsch. Akad. Wiss. Berlin, Vorträge und Schriften Heft 73, Akademie-Verlag Berlin 1961

[2] Elementare magnetohydrodynamische Behandlung chaotisch turbulenter Bewegungen. Mber. dtsch. Akad. Wiss. Berlin **5** (1963) 625—629

[3] Warum hat die Erde ein Magnetfeld? Phys. Bl. **26** (1970) 158—168

Steenbeck, M., and G. Helmis:

[1] Zur Deutung der Neigung und der Westdrift des erdmagnetischen Hauptfeldes. Mber. dtsch. Akad. Wiss. Berlin **11** (1969) 723—734

[2] Rotation of the Earth's solid core as a possible cause of declination, drift and reversals of the Earth's magnetic field. Geophys. J. Roy. Astron. Soc. **41** (1975) 237—244

Steenbeck, M., I. M. Kirko, A. Gailitis, A. P. Klawina, F. Krause, I. J. Laumanis and O. A. Lielausis:

[1]* Der experimentelle Nachweis einer elektromotorischen Kraft längs eines äußeren Magnetfeldes, induziert durch eine Strömung flüssigen Metalls (α-Effekt). Mber. dtsch. Akad. Wiss. Berlin **9** (1967) 714—719

[2] (Штеенбек, М., И. М. Кирко, А. Гаилитис, А. П. Клявиня, Ф. Краузе, И. Я. Лауманис и О. А. Лиелаусис): Экспериментальное обнаружение электродвижущей силы вдоль внешнего магнитного поля, индуцированной течением жидкого металла (α-эффект). ДАН **180** (1968) 326—329 (Experimental discovery of the electromotive force along the external magnetic field induced by a flow of liquid metal (α-effect). Sov. Phys.-Dokl. **13** (1968) 443—445)

Steenbeck, M., and F. Krause:

[1] Elektromagnetische Rückkopplung durch Turbulenz unter der Einwirkung von Coriolis-Kräften. Mitt. Astron. Gesellsch. **19** (1965) 95

[2] Elektromagnetische Rückkopplung durch Turbulenz unter der Einwirkung von Coriolis-Kräften. Mber. dtsch. Akad. Wiss. Berlin **7** (1965) 900—906

[3]* Erklärung stellarer und planetarer Magnetfelder durch einen turbulenzbedingten Dynamomechanismus. Z. Naturforsch. **21a** (1966) 1285—1296

[4] Die Entstehung stellarer und planetarer Magnetfelder als Folge turbulenter Materiebewegungen. Gustav-Hertz-Festschrift, Akademie-Verlag Berlin 1967

[5] Возниковение магнитных полей звёзд и планет в результате турбулентного движения их вещества. Магнитная Гидродинамика **1967, 3,** 19—44

[6]* Zur Dynamotheorie stellarer und planetarer Magnetfelder. I. Berechnung sonnenähnlicher Wechselfeldgeneratoren. Astron. Nachr. **291** (1969) 49—84

[7]* Zur Dynamotheorie stellarer und planetarer Magnetfelder. II. Berechnung planetenähnlicher Gleichfeldgeneratoren. Astron. Nachr. **291** (1969) 271—286

Steenbeck, M., F. Krause and K.-H. Rädler:

[1] Elektrodynamische Eigenschaften turbulenter Plasmen. Sitz.ber. dtsch. Akad. Wiss. Berlin, Klasse für Mathematik, Physik und Technik Nr. 1, Akademie-Verlag Berlin 1963

[2]* Berechnung der mittleren Lorentz-Feldstärke $\overline{\boldsymbol{v}\times\boldsymbol{B}}$ für ein elektrisch leitendes Medium in turbulenter, durch Coriolis-Kräfte beeinflußter Bewegung. Z. Naturforsch. **21a** (1966) 369—376

Stix, M.:

[1] A non-axisymmetric α-effect dynamo. Astron. & Astrophys. **13** (1971) 203—208

[2] Vergleich der Sonnenzyklen von Leighton und Steenbeck-Krause. preprint 1971

[3] Non-linear dynamo waves. Astron. & Astrophys. **20** (1972) 9—12

[4] Spherical $\alpha\omega$-dynamos, by a variational method. Astron. & Astrophys. **24** (1973) 275—281

[5] The galactic dynamo. Astron. & Astrophys. **42** (1975) 85—90

[6] Differential rotation and the solar dynamo. Astron. & Astrophys. **47** (1976) 243—254

[7] Dynamo theory and the solar cycle. In: Basic Mechanism of Solar Activity, eds. V. Bumba and J. Kleczek, D. Reidel Publishing Company. Dordrecht-Holland 1976, 367—388

Sweet, P. A.:

[1] The effect of turbulence on a magnetic field. Mon. Not. Roy. Astron. Soc. **110** (1950) 69—83

Tough, J. G.:

[1] Nearly symmetric dynamos. Geophys. J. Roy. Astron. Soc. **13** (1967) 393—406

[2] Corrigendum. Geophys. J. Roy. Astron. Soc. **15** (1900) 343

Tough, J. G., and R. D. Gibson:

[1] The Braginskij dynamo. In: The application of Modern Physics to the Earth and Planetary Interiors, ed. S. K. Runcorn, Wiley-interscience London - New York 1969, 55 —569

Tough, J. G., and P. H. Roberts:

[1] Nearly symmetric hydromagnetic dynamos. Phys. Earth Planet. Int. **1** (1968) 288—296

Tsinober, A. B. (Цинобер, А. Б.):

[1] Магнитогидродинамическая турбулентность. Магнитная Гидродинамика **1975, 1,** 7—22

TVERSKOJ, B. A. (ТВЕРСКОЙ, Б. А.):
[1] К теории гидродинамического самовозбуждения регулярных магнитных полей. Геомагн. и Аэрономия **6** (1966) 11—18 (Theory of hydrodynamical self-excitation of regular magnetic fields. Geomagn. i Aeron. **7** (1966) 7—12)

VAINSHTEIN, S. I. (ВАЙНШТЕЙН, С. И.):
[1] О генерации крупномасштабного магнитного поля турбулентной жидкостью. ЖЕТФ **58** (1970) 153—159 (Generation of a large scale magnetic field by a turbulent liquid. Sov. Phys.-JETP **31** (1970) 87)
[2] Задача о генерации магнитного поля при наличии акустической турбулентности. ДАН **195** (1970) 793—796
[3] Задача о магнитном поле в неоднородном турбулентном потоке. ПМТФ, № **1** (1971) 12—18
[4] О нелинейной задаче турбулентного динамо. ЖЕТФ **61** (1971) 612—620 (Non-linear problem of the turbulent dynamo. Sov. Phys.-JETP **34** (1972) 327—331)
[5] Функциональный подход в теории турбулентного динамо. ЖЕТФ **62** (1972) 1376—1385 (Functional approach to the turbulent dynamo. Sov. Phys.-JETP **35** (1972) 725)
[6] „Антидинамо" — возможный механизм явлений происходящих нейтральних слоях магнитного поля. ЖЕТФ **65** (1973) 550—561 ("Antidynamo"—a possible mechanism of phenomena occurring in neutral layers of a magnetic field. Sov. Phys.-JETP **38** (1973) 270—275)
[7] Перестройка магнитного поля плазменными механизмами. УФН **120** (1976) 613—645 (Modification of a magnetic field by plasma mechanism. Sov. Phys.-Usp. **19** (1976) 987—1006)
[8] Возбуждение магнитного поля ленгмюровскими колебаниями и ионным звуком (α-эффект в плазме). Gerlands Beitr. Geophys., Leipzig **85** (1976) 93—102
[9] Простейшая динамо-неустойчивость. ЖЭТФ **68** (1975) 997—1004 (Simplest dynamo-instability. Sov. Phys.-JETP **41** (1975) 494—000)

VAINSHTEIN, S. I., and YA. B. ZEL'DOVICH (ВАЙНШТЕЙН, С. И., и Я. Б. ЗЕЛЬДОВИЧ):
[1] О происхождении магнитних полей в астрофизике. УФН **106** (1972) 431—457 (Origin of magnetic fields in astrophys. Sov. Phys.-Usp. **15** (1972) 159—172)

VOIGTMANN, L.:
[1] Über das zeitliche Verhalten zylindersymmetrischer globaler Magnetfelder unter dem Einfluß einer nicht spiegelsymmetrischen homogenen isotropen Turbulenz. Diplomarbeit, Univ. Jena 1968

VOTSISH, A. D., and YU. B. KOLESNIKOV (Воциш, А., Ди Ю. Б. Колесников):
[1] Пространственная и завихренность в двумерной однородной турбулентности. Магнитная Гидродинамика **1976**, **3**, 25—28
[2] Аномальный перенос импулса в сдвиговом мгд-течении с двумерной структурной турбулентности. Магнитная Гидродинамика **1976**, **4**, 47—52

WEISS, N. O.:
[1] The dynamo problem. Q. J. Roy. Astron. Soc. **12** (1971) 432—446

YOSHIMURA, H.:
[1] Complexes of activity of the solar cycle and very large scale convection. Solar Physics **18** (1971) 417—433

[2] On the dynamo action of the global convection in the solar convection zone. Astrophys. J. **3** (1972) 863–886
[3] Solar-Cycle dynamo wave propagation. Astrophys. J. **201** (1975) 740–748
[4] A model of the solar cycle driven by the dynamo action of the global convection in the solar convection zone. Astrophys, J. Suppl. Series **294** (1975) 467–494
[5] Phase relation between the poloidal and toroidal solar-cycle general magnetic fields and location of the origin of the surface magnetic fields. Solar Physics **50** (1976) 3–23

Zel'dovich, Ya. B. (Зельдович, Я. Б.):
[1] Магнитное поле в проводящей турбулентной жидкости при двумерном движении. ЖЭТФ **31** (1956) 154–155 (The magnetic field in the two-dimensional motion of a conducting turbulent fluid. Sov. Phys.-JETP **4** (1957) 460–462)

INDEX

Bei Fragen zur Produktsicherheit wenden Sie sich bitte an:
If you have any questions regarding product safety,
please contact:

Walter de Gruyter GmbH
Genthiner Straße 13
10785 Berlin
productsafety@degruyterbrill.com